Research Methods for Public Administrators

Fifth Edition

Elizabethann O'Sullivan
North Carolina State University

Gary R. Rassel
University of North Carolina at Charlotte

Maureen Berner
University of North Carolina at Chapel Hill

PEARSON
Longman

New York San Francisco Boston
London Toronto Sydney Tokyo Singapore Madrid
Mexico City Munich Paris Cape Town Hong Kong Montreal

For Doug, Merry, and Andy—with much love

Editor-in-Chief:	Eric Stano
Executive Marketing Manager:	Ann Stypuloski
Production Manager:	Donna DeBenedictis
Project Coordination and Text Design:	Elm Street Publishing Services, Inc.
Electronic Page Makeup:	Integra Software Services, Pvt. Ltd.
Cover Designer/Manager:	John Callahan
Cover Image:	Courtesy of Getty Images
Manufacturing Buyer:	Roy Pickering

Library of Congress Cataloging-in-Publication Data

O'Sullivan, Elizabethann.
   Research methods for public administrators / Elizabethann O'Sullivan, Gary R. Rassel,
Maureen Berner.—5th ed.
      p. cm.
   Includes index.
   ISBN 978-0-321-43137-0 (hardcover)
   1. Public administration—Research—Methodology.   I. Rassel, Gary Raymond, 1944–
II. Berner, Maureen.   III. Title.
   JF1338.A2 O78 2008
   351'.07'2—dc22

                                                                          2007008573

Please visit us at www.ablongman.com

ISBN-13: 978-0-321-43137-0
ISBN-10:   0-321-43137-5

Contents

Preface   x

Chapter 1   Beginning a Research Project: The Preliminary Steps   1

Starting a Research Project: Defining the Research Question   2
Organizing the Research Study: The Use of Models   3
Identifying the Elements to Study: Model Building   7
Presenting the Model: Types of Models   11
Limitations of Models and Model Building for Specific Users   13
The Components of Models: An Introduction to the
    Terminology   14
Selecting a Research Question   19
Summary   20
    Notes   *21*
    Terms for Review   *21*
    Questions for Review   *22*
    Problems for Homework and Discussion   *22*
    Disk Work   *24*
    Recommended for Further Reading   *24*

Chapter 2   Designs for Description   25

Designs to Find Relationships and Show Trends   27
Qualitative Research and Designs to Fill in the Details   38
Meta-Analysis   45
Summary   48
    Notes   *49*
    Terms for Review   *51*
    Questions for Review   *51*

Problems for Homework and Discussion   *52*
Disk Work   *54*
Recommended for Further Reading   *54*

Chapter 3   Designs for Explanation   56

Internal and External Validity   58
Experimental Designs   68
Quasi-Experimental Designs   77
Nonexperimental Designs   88
Determining Causality with Cross-Sectional Studies   91
Summary   93
Notes   *95*
Terms for Review   *96*
Questions for Review   *96*
Problems for Homework and Discussion   *97*
Disk Work   *99*
Recommended for Further Reading   *100*

Chapter 4   Measuring Variables   101

Measurement and Measurement Scales   105
Reliability   109
Operational Validity   118
Sensitivity   125
Summary   126
Notes   *128*
Terms for Review   *129*
Questions for Review   *129*
Problems for Homework and Discussion   *130*
Disk Work   *131*
Recommended for Further Reading   *132*

Chapter 5   Sampling   133

Sampling Terminology   134
Probability Sampling Designs   137

Nonprobability Sampling Designs   146
Sample Size   150
Summary   162
  Notes   163
  Terms for Review   164
  Questions for Review   164
  Problems for Homework and Discussion   165
  Disk Work   166
  Recommended for Further Reading   167
  Appendix 5.1 *Calculation of the Standard Error   168*
  Appendix 5.2 *Calculation of Sample Size for Means   170*
  Appendix 5.3 *Sample Size for Small Populations   171*

Chapter 6   Contacting and Talking to Subjects   172

Contacting Subjects   173
Planning for a Survey   175
Mailed Questionnaires   176
Internet Surveys   182
Telephone Surveys   184
In-Person Interviewing   191
Selecting a Method of Data Collection   200
Summary   203
  Notes   206
  Terms for Review   208
  Questions for Review   208
  Problems for Homework and Discussion   209
  A Class Project   210
  Recommended for Further Reading   210

Chapter 7   Data Collection: Questions and Questionnaires   212

Questionnaire and Question Content   213
Questionnaire Structure   216
Question and Response Wording   224
Question Sequencing and Questionnaire Design   232
Summary   242

Notes   243

Terms for Review   244

Questions for Review   244

Problems for Homework and Discussion   245

Disk Work   247

Recommended for Further Reading   247

Chapter 8   Protection of Human Research Subjects and Other Ethical Issues   248

Illustrative Cases   249

Principles of Ethical Treatment of Human Subjects   252

Protecting Privacy and Confidentiality   257

Federal Policy on Protection of Human Subjects and Institutional Review Boards   260

Beyond Informed Consent and Confidentiality: Issues of Interest to Administrators   262

Summary   264

Notes   266

Terms for Review   268

Questions for Review   268

Problems for Homework and Discussion   268

Recommended for Further Reading   269

Chapter 9   Secondary Data Analysis: Finding and Analyzing Existing Data   270

Working with Secondary Data   271

U.S. Census Data   280

Using Census Data   289

Vital Statistics   292

Summary   294

Notes   295

Terms for Review   296

Questions for Review   296

Problems for Homework and Discussion   297

Disk Work   297

Recommended for Further Reading   298

Chapter 10   **Combining Indicators: Index Construction**   **299**

Defining the Concept   301
Selecting the Items   301
Combining the Items in an Index   303
Weighting the Separate Items   303
Creating Standardized Indicators for Indices   305
Examples of Creating Indices   308
Factor Analysis   312
Index Numbers   315
Summary   316
  Notes   *317*
  Terms for Review   *318*
  Questions for Review   *318*
  Problems for Homework and Discussion   *319*
  Disk Work   *319*
  Recommended for Further Reading   *320*
  Appendix 10.1 *Using z-Scores to Standardize Measures*
    for Indices   *321*
  Appendix 10.2 *Calculating Factor Scale Scores*   *322*

Chapter 11   **Univariate Analysis**   **323**

Computer Software for Data Management and Analysis   324
Analyzing and Presenting the Data   327
Visual Presentation of Data   331
Quantitative Measures   337
Characteristics of a Distribution   342
Exploratory Data Analysis   354
Summary   356
  Notes   *357*
  Terms for Review   *359*
  Questions for Review   *359*
  Problems for Homework and Discussion   *359*
  Disk Work   *362*
  Recommended for Further Reading   *363*
  Appendix 11.1 *Statistical Calculations*   *364*
  Appendix 11.2 *Data Preparation*   *366*

Chapter 12   Examining Relationships among Variables: Tests of Statistical Significance   368

Stating the Null Hypothesis   370
Selecting an Alpha Level   373
Selecting and Computing a Test Statistic   376
Making a Decision   381
Reporting Tests of Statistical Significance   383
Modifications and Alternatives to Tests of Statistical
    Significance   385
Summary   387
   Notes   *388*
   Terms for Review   *389*
   Questions for Review   *389*
   Problems for Homework and Discussion   *389*
   Disk Work   *392*
   Recommended for Further Reading   *392*
   Appendix 12.1 *Calculating Chi-Square and Two-Sample*
   t-Tests   *393*

Chapter 13   Examining Relationships among Variables: Contingency Tables with Measures of Association, Analysis of Variance   396

Constructing and Interpreting Contingency Tables   397
Selecting and Using Measures of Association   401
Measures of Association with Control Variables   408
Tests of Statistical Significance and Measures of
    Association   413
Comparison of Means and Analysis of Variance   413
Summary   418
   Notes   *419*
   Terms for Review   *420*
   Questions for Review   *420*
   Problems for Homework and Discussion   *423*
   Disk Work   *425*

Recommended for Further Reading   426

Appendix 13.1 Some Measures of Association for Nominal and Ordinal Data   427

Chapter 14   Regression Analysis and Correlation   430

Analyzing Two-Interval Variables   431

Regression Analysis: The Multivariate Case   439

Multicollinearity   446

Regression and Non-Interval Variables   449

Regression Models to Analyze Time-Series Data   451

Regression and Causality   454

Summary   455

Notes   456

Terms for Review   457

Questions for Review   458

Problems for Homework and Discussion   459

Disk Work   463

Recommended for Further Reading   464

Appendix 14.1 Calculating Regression Statistics for Bivariate Relationships   465

Chapter 15   Communicating Findings and Completing the Project   467

Variations in Audiences and Their Needs   468

Components of the Quantitative Report   469

Ethical Issues   478

Summary   483

Notes   484

Terms for Review   485

Questions for Review   485

Problems for Homework and Discussion   485

Recommended for Further Reading   486

Glossary   487

Index   497

Preface

WHY A NEW EDITION?

This fifth edition continues in the tradition of previous editions in that it is designed for advanced undergraduate and introductory graduate courses in research methods. The intended audiences are those who are or soon will be administrators and those who teach them. We are gratified with the response to the first four editions of this text and pleased that teachers and students have found them to be useful. However, we are also amazed at how dynamic research methods and statistical analysis can be. As administrative duties, committee work, and other responsibilities take more of the authors' time, it has been a treat to find so much new information to fill and make a new edition necessary.

While the fifth edition continues to emphasize methods, analysis, and application like previous editions, we have made many changes. We have updated information and exercises, making changes in current material where we thought it would be useful. We also rethought several issues in light of new technologies and public demands. The discussion of measurement concepts in Chapter 4 was revised in line with the current Standards for Educational and Psychological Testing. Chapter 6 presents up-to-date information on Internet surveys and the impact of cell phones on data collection. We discuss recent changes in the decennial U.S. Census in Chapter 9 and continue to incorporate material from the 2000 Census. The changes include the end of the long form and the use of the American Community Survey. Readers will recognize these changes as the Census Bureau prepares for the 2010 Census.

Perhaps the biggest and most influential technological change related to research methods involves the Internet. It has greatly expanded the access to data sources and made using data from them much more convenient than ever before. The Internet continues to increase the ability of researchers to find and use scholarly literature, secondary data, and government statistics. We have kept pace with this change by increasing the number of Internet references in this edition and have included more material on using the Internet for research. Internet examples and useful Internet addresses are included in the material in several chapters. Homework problems using the Internet are included as well.

The graphical user interface (GUI) or Windows environment is now universal, or so it seems, making software packages easier to use. New statistical software packages have been developed, more statistical analysis can be done with spreadsheets, and the capability of Geographic Information System (GIS) software to combine geographic analysis with statistical applications has grown extensively. We have expanded the coverage of all of these in this edition of the text.

We have revised many of the problems at the ends of the chapters and included new ones. A revised *Instructor's Manual* with solutions to the end-of-chapter problems has also been prepared for this edition. An innovation with the third edition of the text was the inclusion of a data disk and homework problems keyed to data files on the disk. The homework problems at the ends of the chapters include computer problems using the disk data file to illustrate concepts and techniques discussed in the chapters. A completely new set of data is available for the fifth edition and is on a disk included with the text. The new data set includes 43 variables on 100 counties allowing for a variety of exercises, statistical applications, and investigations of relevant administrative and policy issues. The disk includes data saved in spreadsheet format, information about the data, and instructions for using the data. A completely new set of problems has been developed for the new data set.

This edition of *Research Methods for Public Administrators* is the second to involve three authors. The relationship has worked well and any additional coordinating difficulties have been more than offset by the benefit of a new set of eyes and experiences. Maureen Berner's work with MPA students and practitioners has added new perspectives to the topics discussed in the text. The end-of-chapter review questions are more relevant to current administrative issues. Her careful reading of the manuscript uncovered several new ways to word material and introduced other improvements. Maureen prepared the new dataset and problems for the disk work assigned at the ends of the chapters.

PRESENTATION AND AUDIENCE

Although this text includes basic as well as more advanced material, we have attempted to present information in a way that is useful to administrators with a wide range of experiences. We intend for instructors to be able to select from the material, adapt it to their needs, and have more than enough for a one-semester course. Chapters can be omitted or used in different order depending on the instructor's needs and approach.

In writing and revising this book, we hope to help administrators collaborate more effectively with researchers. We observe administrators regularly asking for specific pieces of research from subordinates, colleagues, and consultants. They frequently question investigators about studies to decide whether a particular finding justifies further administrative action. They often read research reports to decide whether the findings can be used in their professions. We hope that administrators and students will find this book to be useful as a reference when they want to find out more about a topic or technique.

We intended to write a text for applied research that administrators would find useful and that related to the work they do. In doing so, we wanted to present a systematic approach to empirical investigation and to discuss the logic of research design and scientific method so that administrators could use this information when they read research reports, do research, or have research done for them. Research is a problem-solving process, and we wanted to present it as such. As authors, we have drawn on our experience and that of students, teachers, colleagues, researchers, and administrators. The process of translating teaching materials, ideas, lecture notes, examples, and exercises into a textbook has been difficult and time-consuming but very rewarding. As a field of study, research methods can be surprisingly dynamic. Keeping up with changes and new applications is interesting and challenging. Presenting them effectively to an audience of instructors and students is no less so.

ACKNOWLEDGMENTS

The fifth edition has also benefited from the suggestions, reactions, and encouragement of many people. Colleagues and faculty at various universities who have used or read the earlier editions have been especially helpful with comments and suggestions. Some have helped us to correct errors in the text or *Instructor's Manual*. Others have suggested material to add, delete, or revise. Student suggestions and questions are always useful and often humbling. They go to the heart of what we do as teachers, and we are glad to have them.

Many reviewers over the years have provided useful comments. Their suggestions have led to many changes and improvements, for which we are grateful. We hope that our response has had the intended effect and improved the book. We appreciate hearing from all who read or use the book.

We are very grateful to our publisher for supporting a fifth edition. The editorial staff of Longman has provided much critical help and support. Our association with Longman has been lengthy and has provided us the opportunity to work with many individuals. Eric Stano and his assistant Donna Garnier have been the editorial contacts for the fifth edition. We thank them for all their work, advice, and help. The manuscript copy editor, JoAnn Learman, has done an excellent job of reading the manuscript and catching errors.

We acknowledge the support and encouragement of our respective universities, North Carolina State University, the University of North Carolina at Charlotte, and the University of North Carolina at Chapel Hill. The index and glossary, originally prepared by Robin Goodpasture for the second edition, were updated for the third edition by Dina Smith, who also prepared the index for the fourth edition, while Jennifer Snow made changes in the glossary. Rodney Harris at the University of North Carolina at Charlotte prepared the index for the fifth edition. Robin, Dina, Jennifer, and Rodney are to be commended for their fine work. Many others read, commented, copied, retrieved books from the library, and listened during the process of revision. Among those are David Folz, University of Tennessee; Gabriel Kaplan, University of Colorado; Christopher Leu, California State University, Northridge; Will Miller, University of Arkansas; Kenneth Nichols, University of Maine; John Ostrowski, California State University, Long Beach; and Bruce Rogers, Tennessee State University. We are grateful to all.

And finally, we recognize the participation and support of our families, Doug Hale, Merry Chambers, Brendan and Colin O'Sullivan-Hale, Andy, Will, and Yvette Berner, in this endeavor. Families and family members have grown, changed, and matured during the years the authors have spent on manuscripts. We appreciate their encouragement and their understanding of the time devoted to revising the textbook.

ELIZABETHANN O'SULLIVAN
GARY R. RASSEL
MAUREEN BERNER

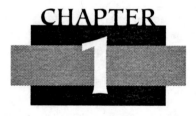

CHAPTER 1

Beginning a Research Project: The Preliminary Steps

In this chapter you will learn

1. Why knowledge of research methods is valuable for public administrators.
2. When, why, and how to go about building a model, the framework of social science research.
3. Strategies for presenting models.
4. Definitions of some common research terms, including *variables* and *hypotheses*.
5. What to consider in selecting a research question.

Public administrators often ask questions that begin "how many," "how much," "how efficient," "how effective," "how adequate," and "why." They may want to learn something about a group of people, how much a program will cost, or what it can accomplish for each dollar spent. They need to decide how serious a problem is, whether a policy solved a problem, what distinguishes more effective programs from less effective ones, and whether clients are satisfied with program performance. They are accountable to politicians, parents, citizens, program clients, and the courts for public services.

Administrators rely on data to make better decisions, to monitor them, and to examine their effects. *Data* is just another word for information. Understanding research methods is key to gathering, using, and evaluating information. And as a current or future public administrator, you know that adequate information is key to making effective decisions.

As an administrator you may need to collect and summarize data and act on your findings or supervise others who do so. You may conduct studies to answer questions about programs under your jurisdiction, or you may contract with others to perform studies for you. You may receive regular reports to monitor the performance of your organization and employees. You may read research and get ideas you wish to implement. Even if you never initiate a study, your knowledge of the research process should leave you better able to determine the adequacy of data, interpret reports, question investigators, and judge the value of published research.[1]

This book will provide you with the ability to produce and interpret valuable information using a variety of research tools. More importantly, we hope it will provide you with better judgment as you *use* information to make decisions. Our goal is to help you make better decisions, and in doing so, make you a better administrator.

STARTING A RESEARCH PROJECT: DEFINING THE RESEARCH QUESTION

Research should begin with careful planning. Even though determining the purposes of a study and whether or not it will produce the desired information is tedious, experience has convinced us that administrators who take the time to define clearly the purpose of a study and critique carefully the research plan spend their time well. They will have a better understanding of the problem being studied and be able to reduce the incidence of poorly conceived research strategies and useless data collection. In this chapter we present guidelines for better research planning. No matter who is actually carrying out a study, administrators who spend time defining the problem, planning the study, debating it with others, and reviewing related research markedly improve the work and experience fewer disappointments and wasted efforts.

An excellent starting point for any administrator involved with research is to understand if a decision needs to be made, when it needs to be made, the nature of that decision, and what information would be helpful to the decision makers. Focusing on the decision can help identify the true purpose of a study. In terms of timing, if it is not possible to influence the decision, then one must consider if the study will really be of value. In terms of the nature of the decision, what level of importance does the decision warrant? Trying to measure the impact of a multi-million-dollar program affecting thousands of citizens may be more important than evaluating an internal office recycling program. Are lives, jobs, public opinion at stake? Last, what information is needed by the decision makers to make the decision is key and provides a starting point for developing research questions.

Establishing a study's purpose goes beyond stating exactly why it is being done. An investigator must know who wants the study done, how she plans to use its findings, when she plans to use them, what resources she has to invest in the study, and what has been done before. After an investigator answers these questions, she can list the research questions and decide what evidence will provide adequate answers. Thus she avoids "shooting ants with an elephant gun." She also avoids planning a study that exceeds the available resources or yields information after it is needed. A study's purpose evolves; it becomes more focused and better understood as investigators and decision makers begin their work together.

Once you understand what a study can provide you—and what it cannot—the researcher should begin by stating the research question. A research question is a question with more than one possible answer. Otherwise, why spend the time and money needed to produce the answer? The research question requires empirical (observable) information in order to be answered. By definition, research involves the study of observable information, so without observable information no research can take place. This text stresses numerical or quantitative information; however, qualitative information also is empirical and may appropriately be used to answer a research question.

Let's consider the research question: "Does using a shared computer network improve the performance of office staff?" Note that the question has more than one answer. Furthermore, the answer requires empirical information. Still, this simple question masks the amount of work that lies ahead. What is meant by "a shared network"? How would you define "performance" and measure its quality? Which office staff? All staff members, or just people holding certain positions? Staff in all offices, or just particular types of offices? What type and how much impact is expected? To help limit the study's focus, the administrator indicates the purpose of a study. A study to determine whether to install a new computer system will be different from a study evaluating an existing system.

ORGANIZING THE RESEARCH STUDY: THE USE OF MODELS

After the research question and study's purpose are stated, a preliminary research model should be built. A model could be thought of as a simple explanation of relationships. A model includes selected elements, e.g., characteristics or events, and links them to each other. The elements included in any model depend on its purpose. Investigators use models to simplify reality by eliminating irrelevant details.

Models consist of *elements* and *relationships*. A single element does not constitute a model until the element is linked with another. Elements that have no relationship with at least one other element should be eliminated from a model. Elements that have only weak links also may be eliminated. Explicit models are the words, schematics, or equations that represent the variables and their relationships. The strength of explicit models is that they give others access to the model and allow them to critique, replicate, or improve it.

How does an investigator know which elements to include and how to link them? Even if the purpose of the study is to identify relevant elements and their linkages, she has to have a way to decide what to include. She draws on her own ideas and experiences and the ideas and experiences of colleagues. She may review previous research, manipulate existing datasets, and conduct a preliminary study. To find out how the elements are linked, an examination of previous research studies and exploratory data analysis is particularly helpful.

One can think about a model visually by sketching out the elements and the relationships. For example, in Figure 1.1, a person may want to look at the elements of automatic seat belts in cars and vehicle accident deaths and try to

FIGURE   1.1

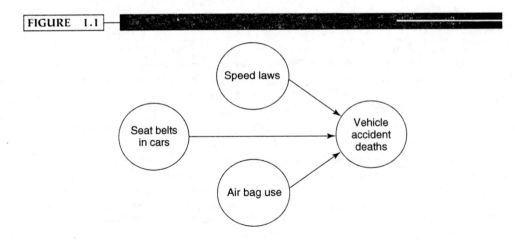

understand the relationship between them. Through her own experience and the advice of others, she may also want to consider the elements of speed laws and air bag use.

Before we study *model building* in depth, let's look at a preliminary model designed to guide a research project. Example 1.1 presents a model developed as part of a study to identify how to slow down the rate of increase in Medicare costs. Investigators identified the elements representing the general strategies available to reduce costs. The central element was the rate of increase of Medicare costs. The other elements were the number of beneficiaries, the number of services covered, and the payment for each service; these elements were linked to Medicare costs. If the number of beneficiaries, the number of covered services, or the amount paid for each service were reduced, the rate of increase in Medicare costs would decrease.

In Figure 1.1 and in Example 1.1 the models are presented as schematics or diagrams. The arrows link the elements and show which variables are thought to act on other variables. A model also may be presented as a statement. The sentence, "If the number of beneficiaries, the number of covered services, or the amount paid for each service were reduced, the rate of increase in Medicare costs would decrease," is another way to present the model. A model also may be presented as an equation.

The investigators assumed that reducing the number of beneficiaries, the number of covered services, or the amount paid for each service would reduce the rate of increase in Medicare costs. The major relationships are between reducing the rate of increase and the other elements; however, relations may exist among the other elements. For example, reducing the number of services covered probably will reduce the number of beneficiaries.

A model requires its creators to organize their thoughts and helps the creators and the users to communicate more effectively. The model in Example 1.1 should center policy makers' attention on possible solutions and facilitate their communications with each other and others concerned with Medicare costs. With the preliminary model, investigators can define what they mean by each

EXAMPLE 1.1

Applying a Model

Research question: How may the rapid increase in Medicare costs (Medicare: federally funded health care for the elderly) be reduced?

Purpose: To recommend change(s) in Medicare coverage that will contain the costs of the Medicare program.

Procedure: An initial model is sketched out with the major elements representing general strategies to reduce costs. Its purpose is to identify the basic types of strategies available.

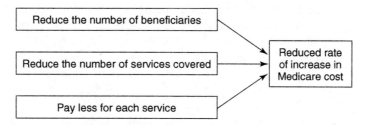

Discussion: The sketch places each element in a separate "box." The strategies, which also may be identified as "inputs," are placed on the left. Lines indicate the links between elements and arrows indicate the direction of the links. Here, each strategy was linked to the outcome of reducing the rate of increased costs. The arrows suggest that each strategy should reduce the rate of increase in Medicare costs. A sketch keeps track of the model's elements and relationships, helps communicate the model to others, and facilitates discussion about the model and the research plan.

With the elements identified, the investigators may:

1. Identify feasible strategies associated with each element. Should the number of beneficiaries be reduced by changing income requirements or age limits? What services should be reduced? How might less be paid for services?

2. Incorporate the specific strategies into the model.

3. Develop a research plan: What elements and relations will be studied first? Exactly how will they be studied?

element. They may include other elements and explore the linkages among elements. They can decide which linkages to investigate further and set priorities for examining them.

A model may be altered and refined often during the early stages of designing a study. Many elements may be listed and linked or only the essential components may be included. A common question among public administration students is how detailed a model must be. The answer is, "It depends." Investigators may brainstorm to identify all possible elements, and they may build a very detailed model. To confirm points of agreement, they may develop a simplified version with just a few elements included. The model in Example 1.1 was limited to the basic components of a study. Other models may elaborate on the basic model. For example, a model can spell out how specific strategies for reducing the number of beneficiaries would affect Medicare rates. Another model can focus on ways of reducing services and the effects of alternate strategies on Medicare rates. Regardless of the purpose or level of detail, a research model should be based on theory. That is, there should be reasonable theoretical linkages between the elements. We should have good reasons to expect linkages between the elements and be able to explain them.

In addition, one should think about the assumptions underlying the theory. For example, when thinking of the relationship between automatic seat belts in cars and vehicle accident deaths, theory would suggest that the greater the percentage of cars having automatic seat belts, the lower the number of vehicle accident deaths. However, that assumes the automatic seat belts are actually used and not disabled or turned off.

Maps provide a simple illustration of how models vary according to their purpose. For a mountain hike, you need a topographical map with details about the terrain. Such a detailed map, if you could find one and fit it into a car, would be virtually useless on a drive from New York to California. On the other hand, imagine using an ordinary road map to hike through the Grand Canyon! Elements important for one purpose may be useless for another purpose. And just as developing a research model is based on good theory, choosing a map is based on understanding where you want to go and how you think you might get there.

By the time they are ready to collect data, the investigators should be satisfied that they have included the relevant elements in the model. The included elements and their relationships become important components of decisions about which data to collect and how to analyze them. The model should be considered preliminary. It may change during the course of a study. However, even though models rarely stay the same throughout a study, a researcher should not begin working without an explicit model.

Model building starts the researcher on an iterative process to collect, analyze, and present data consistent with the study's purpose. Starting with a model is especially important for quantitative studies. Without a proper road map, researchers can wander in the wilderness of data—gathering numbers and facts without a clear direction. Models allow us to go beyond simply looking at data. They help identify why relationships are expected. Precise-looking data can be wrong and apparent relationships among elements may be due to statistical errors. By the end of a study, models enable users to organize their information and reach reasonable conclusions about the importance of elements and their relationships to one another.

Try to avoid "falling in love" with your model. This happens when a person has labored over a research plan and then becomes trapped by his own inflexibility. Instead of considering the model as preliminary and rejecting it or adjusting it as appropriate, the researcher goes through all sorts of data manipulations to demonstrate the preliminary model is correct. The model should not be the focus of your work. Having the best information for the right people in time for them to make an informed, considered decision should be the focus.

IDENTIFYING THE ELEMENTS TO STUDY: MODEL BUILDING

To identify the elements, defend their relevance, and postulate the nature of their relationships, investigators integrate their ideas, the observations of others, the research literature, and their own research. The process is seldom as systematic and logical as research reports or public presentations make it appear. Nor does each investigator follow the same strategy for identifying elements and their relationships. Designing a study requires creativity and insight. Furthermore, understanding the problem at hand is a prerequisite to good model-building skills.

The order associated with research presentations springs from a desire to communicate effectively. An audience can more easily follow a presentation that proceeds from a statement of the problem to a description of the model, its elements, and their relation to each other. Normally, a researcher does not dwell on false starts, mistakes, and backtracking.

Ideas

Ideas refer to the knowledge, beliefs, or impressions one has about a research question. We rarely approach a situation with no knowledge or insight. Most of us retain a wealth of information to help us solve problems. Do not downplay the value or importance of this information. If you do not make use of your experience, knowledge, or opinions when faced with problems, you will be an inefficient administrator.

Building a model requires you to make your ideas explicit. Through words, drawings, or equations, you identify the elements you consider important and how you believe they are related to each other. Thus you clarify fuzzy ideas and expose them to critical examination. You will find that some of your beliefs will not make sense. Some of your ideas suddenly may seem naive or incomplete. Some will be based on assumptions with which others do not agree. Nevertheless, unless you are willing to take the risk of having your ideas challenged, you may miss elements and relationships critical to problem solving.

Peer Interaction

Peer interaction refers to the discussions and debates among colleagues about the research question and possible answers. To understand model building, we recommend that you read about how scientists go about their work.[2] This should dispel the myth of the isolated scientist working alone. Research is much more dynamic than you might imagine. Administrators can learn much from scientists. A major lesson is the value of criticism and debate. Without it errors may go uncorrected and oversights may abound. However, few people find criticism easy to accept or arguments easy to verbalize.

Another notable aspect of peer interaction is the influence of our backgrounds. For example, our disciplines shape the questions we ask, the data we use, and how we use them. Imagine, as a city administrator, you are interested in studying ways to address homelessness in your city. As a first step, you want to gather data on the causes of homelessness in your area. One analyst with an economics background may want to focus on quantitative data from city employment and support programs. Another analyst with a background in social work may turn first to interviews with clients of local shelters. An analyst with a public safety background may wish to test a possible relationship between homelessness and parolees from the new federal prison in the area. If they had to work together, we suspect they might experience frustration and tension. Yet, ideally, the conflict of ideas and the resulting compromises should yield a research plan superior to that developed by any one of the individuals working alone. The concept of drawing from other disciplines has been called "borrowing strength."

Review of Existing Knowledge

Research often is an iterative process in which investigators build on the work of others. Shortly after identifying the purpose of a study, investigators search for information on similar studies. Some people assume that quantitative researchers have little need to do this. Applied researchers may not see their studies as part of a larger body of knowledge. Nevertheless, a few hours reviewing journals and reference documents should convince you of the value of published materials.

Too often researchers studying an unfamiliar problem may start by "reinventing the wheel." In other words, they may begin to build a model that has already been developed and refined many times. The objective of library research is not to ensure the originality of ideas. Rather, it provides a wealth of information and ideas that we may incorporate into our research. As we conduct a *literature review*, we think about the planned study and better understand its purpose and what we can expect to accomplish. An examination of existing research identifies

elements included in studies with a similar purpose.

definitions currently used for the elements.

techniques for measuring the elements.

sources of data.

strategies for collecting data.

methods of linking the elements.

the strength of the relationships between elements.

suggestions for further research.

With this information, investigators avoid wasting time. They may find that their research question has already been answered. They may learn that others failed to confirm relationships that at first seemed important or obvious. The investigators may find appropriate models, definitions, data, and the analytic techniques of others to incorporate into a study. Of course, the source of the ideas, data, or method must be acknowledged properly by the current researcher.

"State-of-the-art" articles that summarize the nature of existing research are especially helpful. They cite the major research work in the field and the major research themes. You will find such articles quickly bring you up to date. They should have covered the relevant literature, easing your burden. They may help you avoid the temptation to go too far afield in your investigation.

You will find a reference librarian is an invaluable resource in uncovering appropriate literature. This is especially true given the rapid changes taking place in information technology. A reference librarian can direct you to abstracts and indices that describe research articles and their findings. He can introduce you to useful online resources and suggest efficient search strategies for locating relevant research.

Conducting online research can be both valuable and frustrating. Search engines can uncover a wealth of information or a pile of useless, or worse yet, erroneous information. A reference librarian can help tailor your search so your time is spent productively, not scanning article after article to see if it is relevant.

Example 1.2 suggests how an investigator brings together ideas, peer interaction, and the existing literature to build a model. The example applies model building to the process of conducting citizen surveys. Surveys often start with a sample

---

 EXAMPLE 1.2

Building a Model

Research questions: What do residents think about their town? Are they satisfied with available services? What changes do they want?

Purpose: To consider citizen perceptions in preparing the town's comprehensive plan.

Procedure: The planning director planned to survey residents to learn how they judge the town and its services.

To identify variables of interest she

1. solicited existing surveys from local planners (peer interaction).

2. examined handbooks published by the American Planning Association and the International City/County Management Association to find sample surveys (literature review).

3. drew on what she learned during her professional training, from her career experience (ideas), and from shop talk (peer interaction).

Several variables seem linked to perceptions of public services. She selected the following variables as relevant:

1. where residents live; if they are homeowners or renters (based on the town council's interest)

2. the gender and age of residents; whether they work in town or in the nearest city (based on the planning staff's interest)

Continued

EXAMPLE 1.2   *Continued*

She met with the Planning Advisory Board to consider what services to include. They discussed the value of linking the demographic variables to satisfaction with services.

Summary of model: The survey will gather data on citizen satisfaction with public services, including trash collection, medical facilities, and housing. To see if the town government meets the needs of all residents, the planning staff will examine whether residents with different characteristics (gender, age, location of home or job, whether they rent or own) rate services differently.

To organize her presentations, she sketched the model:

Discussion: To develop the survey, the director had to decide which variables were relevant for the town's planning. To do this she used her own ideas, peer interaction, and the literature. She met with her staff, the manager's staff, an advisory board, and the town council to review and refine the survey's content. The director read the literature to identify possible survey questions and to get ideas on how to construct the sample, how to achieve a higher response rate, and how to analyze the data. Next, she will scrutinize the specific questions, pretest the questionnaire, and pilot the study. As she conducts these steps, she may make some modifications to the preliminary model.

questionnaire that investigators plan to adapt. The survey may be designed and conducted with no thought of explicit model building. Yet model building helps ensure the survey includes needed information. The study planners may find an existing questionnaire focuses their discussion on the information they want and whether it will be gathered in the survey. Nevertheless, one should not assume a questionnaire or questions developed for one study are appropriate for another.

Examining a Dataset

Investigators who have access to datasets, including data from a pilot test, may examine and manipulate the data as they focus and develop their ideas. In this way investigators may get a better idea of the importance of elements and the strength of their relationships.[3] If a dataset does not contain the specific elements desired, the investigator may study similar elements. The similar elements may be considered as stand-ins or proxies. For example, a neighborhood or postal ZIP code may act as a proxy measure for racial or ethnic groups, social class, or even family composition.

Investigators manipulating a dataset may simultaneously rethink the study's purpose and the model's adequacy. Through the process they may gain greater insight into the study and revise their original ideas.

Pilot Testing the Model

Before collecting data on a large scale, the research plan should be piloted or rehearsed. A small study, called a *pilot study*, is launched to test the adequacy of the proposed data-collection strategy. During the pilot study, investigators discover the feasibility of their research plans and how much time and effort will be needed to collect, compile, and analyze the data. Investigators should carry out the entire plan, including the data analysis and interpretation. Often investigators fail to analyze and interpret the pilot test data, which is unfortunate. From these data the investigators can infer the model's appropriateness. They may identify elements left out of the original model and find other elements are unneeded.

Collecting data without a preliminary model is not a sound research practice. Too often research projects begin prematurely. After identifying the research question, some investigators begin collecting data eagerly. They cut off further planning with comments such as, "Let's see what the data show," or, "I'll decide after I look at the data." Questionnaires are constructed, subjects are questioned, and data are analyzed with too little attention given to the investigators' objectives. Unfortunately, the investigators may not recognize problems until the end of the research project.

PRESENTING THE MODEL: TYPES OF MODELS

How do investigators present a model's elements and relationships? While many possibilities exist, ranging from physical models, such as mock-ups of buildings, to highly abstract verbal presentations, administrative researchers usually work with two types of models: schematic models and symbolic models. *Schematic models* refer to models that use pictures, lines, points, and similar paper-and-pencil products to designate the elements and illustrate their relationship to each other. The sketches in Figure 1.1 and Examples 1.1 and 1.2 present the model as a schematic, as do blueprints, flowcharts, and maps. *Symbolic models* refer to models that use words or equations to represent the elements and describe their relationships.

The type of model chosen depends on the model's purpose, the audience, and the investigator. More than one type of model may be used to present a set of elements and relationships. Consider getting directions to a person's house. Some people distribute maps—a schematic model. Others give verbal directions, listing roads, landmarks, and distances—a symbolic model. Others may give both a map and verbal directions. The choice depends largely on a host's preferences and perceptions of what will be easiest for his guests.

Many investigators build both a symbolic and a schematic model, as is done in Example 1.2. The example's symbolic model summarizes the planning director's actual verbal model, which establishes the importance of linking each specific demographic characteristic to the residents' perception of community services. The schematic model sacrifices the detail of the symbolic model, but it effectively identifies the model's essential features.

Schematic models work well in summarizing a model and drawing attention to its major features. Schematic models with a few elements can be understood quickly and focus people's attention. Consequently, schematics help an investigator think through the model and explain it to others. A schematic also may serve as an elaborate checklist. For example, an investigator can write down when the data are gathered on an element or when a relationship has been examined. Schematic models are less effective if they include too much detail. Only so much information can be included about an element and its relationship to other elements before a schematic becomes cluttered and confusing.

Symbolic models include verbal and mathematical models. Verbal models use words to describe the elements and define their relations to each other. Verbal models are often found in the introductory or theoretical sections of research articles. A newspaper account of a research study and its findings also may be considered a verbal model.

This type of model has distinct strengths. The investigators have all the potential offered by language to describe the model, allowing a full and detailed explanation of complex relationships. The researchers are not constrained by requirements to reduce the model to equations. A fuller range of users can understand and interpret a verbal model than can work with mathematical models. Verbal and mathematical models can complement each other in describing relationships. The verbal model provides the rich details, and the mathematical model looks at the precise nature of the relationships.

Mathematical models can condense a great deal of information by using equations to specify relationships. The mathematical models indicate whether relationships exist, indicate what direction they take, and measure their strength. Mathematical models allow administrators to predict needs, to estimate the impact of policy decisions, and to allocate resources more efficiently. In some areas of interest to administrators, such as operations research or management science, mathematical models guide the model-building process.

Particularly complicated mathematical models often are handled best with computers. In such instances a program can quickly manipulate the elements and depict their relationships. Unlike an analyst, the computer can keep track of a large number of elements and the relationships among them successfully and produce "error-free" results. A computer model differs from other models primarily in the amount of information it can manipulate, its speed, and its accuracy. As with other models, the accuracy of a computer model is a function of human judgment that creates the rules for selecting and manipulating elements. No matter how many elements are included, the model still represents a simplification of reality.

LIMITATIONS OF MODELS AND MODEL BUILDING FOR SPECIFIC USERS

Models simplify reality. They represent one view of which elements are relevant to the problem at hand and which elements can be ignored. Differing views may be entertained. The investigators who build a model and the people who critique it are subject to the full range of human weaknesses. Model builders contend with limited time, money, and knowledge. Their viewpoint may be colored by biases, which lead them to ignore others' comments and criticisms.

Users may be seduced by a model's clarity and its apparent usefulness. They may assume erroneously that it is accurate and adequate. Users who read a study or sit in an audience tend to focus on the details of the verbal description, a diagram, or an equation. Users may want to step back and reflect on what the model leaves out.

In initiating a research study, investigators have a similar concern. They do not want to force the administrator or policy maker who requested the study to conform to their way of approaching a problem. For analysts, models serve as a logical mechanism to organize their thoughts and studies, but this is not necessarily the case for their "clients." If a client must adapt to the investigator's methods, the study may be logical and well organized, but it may be ill suited to the client's needs.

Thus, in conducting research for specific users, the investigator works hard to understand why the study is being done and what the users want to do with the findings. Conversations between administrators and the investigators may seem far removed from identifying the model's components and relationships. Nevertheless, clients have valuable perspectives on potential models. A researcher also has to deal with the reality of trying to satisfy client demands or the clients' individual situation. For example, to evaluate strategies to have toddlers vaccinated, the analyst may ask the client to speculate on which factors motivate parents to do so, and which factors lead them to reject or to delay vaccinations. The analyst will then organize the information into a symbolic or schematic model.

The researcher may leave many of the research details in the background. A client may receive a list of research questions with a strategy for answering them or a description of an experiment. A user might review dummy graphs and tables similar to those planned for the final report. This strategy mirrors the model-building process. Beginning with the clients' perspective avoids the mistake of ignoring the observations and concerns of users who cannot articulate their ideas within the context of an explicit model. Focusing on the clients' concerns and needs ensures that a study will be planned to address a specific problem. Otherwise analysts may unconsciously plan a study around their own analytical preferences. Building the model with the client's involvement may help the client identify the true purpose of the study.

In conducting research to answer theoretical questions, such as the nature of organizational leadership, investigators pursue model building as described earlier. They include peer interaction, a literature review, and pilot-test information in building and refining their models. If they report their findings in a scholarly journal, they will use the shorthand afforded by research jargon. In theoretical research, a study evolves from the research that precedes it. Theoretical studies develop a discipline's body of knowledge and set the stage for further empirical research. Consequently, the researchers must provide a detailed discussion of their methodology and conduct extensive statistical analysis of their data.

Applied studies generally are done with intended users in mind. In these, the literature review may be less systematic and more narrowly focused. Specific users combine research findings with other information to guide their thinking about a problem or to make a decision. Investigators avoid research jargon in communicating with most administrators and policy makers. The jargon serves as a checklist for the researcher, so he does not overlook the numerous details that can weaken a study, but he avoids using jargon otherwise. If the terms are unfamiliar to audiences, their attention may shift to understanding the words, and they may ignore the important points that the investigator wants to emphasize. This point is valuable as you read this chapter's next section and Chapters 2 through 5. We introduce a wealth of terminology, but if you read a report you may never see these specific terms. Nevertheless, in any report, you still should find ample evidence that the researchers built models and applied standard research procedures in designing their study.

THE COMPONENTS OF MODELS: AN INTRODUCTION TO THE TERMINOLOGY

The elements in models are termed *variables* and *constants*. Variables are observable characteristics that can have more than one value, that is to say, characteristics that vary. Some examples of variables and their values include:

Variable	Values
Gender	Male, Female
Job satisfaction	Very satisfied, Satisfied Dissatisfied, Very dissatisfied
Salary	Actual dollar amount of salary

If the characteristic has only one value, it does not vary. Elements that do not vary are called *constants*.

To test a model, researchers examine the relationship between variables linked in the model. The investigators express the relationship between two variables in a simple model called a *hypothesis*. A hypothesis is a statement that specifies or describes the relationship between two variables in such a way that the relationship can be tested empirically. Hypotheses form the foundation of a research effort. A clearly written hypothesis helps researchers to decide what data to collect and how to analyze them. Consider the following three examples of hypotheses:

H_1:   Suicides in jail are more likely to occur during the first 24 hours of incarceration than at other times.

H_2:   The lower the turnover in inventoried items, the greater the amount of waste caused by spoilage, obsolescence, or loss.

H_3:   Training programs improve the quality of life of the chronically unemployed.

Can you identify the variables in each hypothesis? Frequently, the hypothesis contains only a *value of the variable*, and you must infer the actual variable. In the first hypothesis, the variables are the occurrence of suicides in jail and the length of incarceration. The variables in the second hypothesis are the turnover rate in inventoried items and the amount of waste. Note that these hypotheses are reasonably specific. We have a good idea of what data to collect to measure jailhouse suicides, length of incarceration, turnover in inventory, and the amount of waste.

Now look at the third hypothesis. Imagine the frustration of the researcher trying to test it. And yet it is not an unreasonable beginning point for a research project. It is just not a useful hypothesis since it is not easily testable as stated here. To what type of training program does the hypothesis refer, and what does its author mean by "quality of life"? We may even debate who qualifies as chronically unemployed. The vagueness of the hypothesis leads us to suspect that its author has a poorly developed model.

The decision on how specific a hypothesis should be is relative. Some elements, such as quality of life and who is chronically unemployed, can be defined, as the researcher decides how to measure a variable and from whom to collect data. Even apparently specific elements may need further definition. Consider jailhouse suicides. What types of penal institutions should the data represent? One could collect data from county jails, state penitentiaries, or detention centers.

A hypothesis typically implies that a change in one variable is caused by a change in another variable. The *independent variable* is used to explain the variation in the characteristic or event of interest. It is sometimes referred to as an "input" or "cause." The *dependent variable* represents or measures the characteristic or event being explained. It also is referred to as an "outcome" or an "effect." One may identify visually the independent and dependent variable with a schematic model; the arrow leads from the independent variable to the dependent variable. Another way to think about dependent and independent variables is to ask, "Which variable depends on the other?"

Some people find it helpful to rephrase a hypothesis as an "if-then" statement. For example, "If the age for Medicare eligibility is raised, then the rate of increase in Medicare costs will be slowed." The "if" statement contains the independent variable, that is, age for Medicare eligibility. The "then" statement contains the dependent variable, that is, rate of increase in Medicare costs. In our example hypotheses, the independent variables were length of incarceration, turnover rate in inventoried stock, and training programs. The respective dependent variables were the incidence of jailhouse suicides, the amount of waste in inventory, and quality of life.

We have defined hypotheses as consisting of an independent and a dependent variable. Consider a hypothesis with two independent variables. For example, women and older adults use public libraries more often than men and younger adults. Is it necessary that both women and older adults use public libraries more for the hypothesis to be supported? What if women and younger adults more often use public libraries? Or does the independent variable have four values: older women, younger women, older men, and younger men? If this is the case, the hypothesis should make the values explicit. Otherwise, to avoid the ambiguity of having one part of a hypothesis supported and the other part unsupported, it is conventional to have a hypothesis for each independent variable. In our example, the hypotheses would be: Women use public libraries more often than men; older adults use public libraries more often than younger adults.

The Nature of Relationships

An important characteristic of a hypothesis is the pattern of the relationships it postulates. *Covariation* refers to the patterned relationship between an independent and a dependent variable. Commonly, covariation between two variables takes one of three forms: *direct, inverse,* or *nonlinear.*

To describe the patterns of covariation, let's consider the relationship between the amount of job training received and salary on the first job after training. The relationship may be direct; that is, as the number of training hours received increases, the amount of salary increases. The relationship may be inverse; that is, as the number of training hours increases, the amount of salary decreases.

The relationship may be nonlinear, in that a distinctive but nonlinear pattern occurs. By way of example, two such patterns might emerge from a study of the relationship between training and salary levels. In the first, salary increases as the number of training hours increases, but only to a point, beyond which it begins to decrease or level off as training increases further. In the second, as the amount of training increases, salary increases to a point, after which the amount of salary received stays constant.

If the independent variable has no discernible effect on the dependent variable, we say that the two variables do not vary together. If two variables do not vary together, their relationship may be described as *random* or *null.*

In stating and testing a hypothesis, we may wonder about the effects of other variables on a hypothesized relationship. A *control variable* is believed to be related to the independent and dependent variables. It is a third variable that is added to the analysis to see how it alters the relationship between the independent and dependent variables. A control variable may show that the original relationship was in error, e.g., the relationship was false or spurious.

We have two examples that illustrate spurious relationships. First, consider the hypothesis that "arrests for assaults increase with ice cream sales." If subsequent research shows a statistical relationship, should you conclude that ice cream causes physical violence? Of course not; average daily temperatures (a control variable) may reveal that hot weather, not ice cream sales (the independent variable), is associated with more assault arrests (the dependent variable).

Similarly, hospital administrators challenge reports that their hospital has a higher than expected death rate. They contend that their hospital treats sicker patients. Thus they argue that patient prognosis at admission (a control variable), not the hospital itself (the independent variable), causes the higher death rate (the dependent variable).

In addition to helping identify a spurious relationship, control variables may alter the hypothesized relationship radically. Consider how noise affects productivity. If a task requires concentration, noise tends to diminish productivity, whereas if a task is monotonous, noise tends to increase productivity because it jolts workers out of their daydreams. In Example 1.3 we show how a control variable is used to interpret the effectiveness of three job-training programs. When the relationship between the training program and student employment is considered, one program appears to be markedly more successful than the other two. When the educational level of trainees is considered, the difference becomes less striking. For students without a high school diploma or with education after high school, two training programs have nearly identical success in placing trainees.

In the example of the relationship between noise and productivity, the relationship does not have the same direction for each value of the control variable. In the example of the relationship between job training programs and student employment, the relationship is notably stronger for one value of the control variable than for the others. The introduction of a control variable can show that: (1) the hypothesis is spurious, or (2) the relationship between the independent and dependent variables is stronger for some values of the control variable than for other values, does not have the same direction for each value of the control variable, or is supported for some values of the control variable and unsupported for other values, or (3) the control variable has little or no impact on the relationship.

If you study human behavior or attitudes, common control variables are age, sex, income, education, and race. If you study agencies, common control variables include agency size, stability, mission or purpose, budget, and region of the country or state. As you read the literature about a particular policy or program, you may locate other control variables that are used regularly to understand the relationship between the independent and dependent variables.

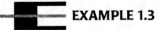 **EXAMPLE 1.3**

Illustrating Variables and Hypotheses

Problem: Identify successful job training programs for hard-to-place individuals.

Hypothesis: On-the-job training programs will be more successful than other training programs in placing participants in permanent positions.

Independent variable: Type of training program.

Dependent variable: Placement in a permanent position.

Control variable: Educational level.

Findings: The data reported in the list below supported the hypothesis that on-the-job training programs had the highest placement success. These data also showed that work-skills training had the lowest placement success.

Placement Success by Job Training Program

Vocational education program (attendance in a school-based training program): 31 percent of participants placed.

On-the-job training: 41 percent of participants placed.

Work-skills training (program to teach basic reading and mathematical skills, attitudes, and behavior needed for permanent, skilled employment): 23 percent of participants placed.

Placement Success by Program, Controlling for Years of Schooling (H.S. = high school)

Education	Vocational Training	On-the-Job Training	Work-Skills Training
< 12 years	33%	35%	23%
H.S. graduate	28%	43%	25%
> 12 years	38%	39%	25%

Discussion: The examination of the relationship between the independent and dependent variables for all participants shows that on-the-job training is markedly more successful in placing trainees. If education level is controlled and held constant, vocational education and on-the-job training do about equally well in placing participants who did not graduate from high school and those who continued beyond high school. Based on these findings, a counselor would refer trainees who only completed high school to on-the-job training. Other participants may do equally well in either on-the-job training or vocational education. If you funded these programs, what decisions would you make? Would you want to look at other control variables? Which ones? Why?

Before you leave this example, make sure you can interpret the figures in the table with the control data. For example, 33 percent means that 33 percent of the people in vocational education who had not completed high school had been placed. Researchers have different ways of presenting control data, so expect to take time to determine exactly what the reported data mean.

SELECTING A RESEARCH QUESTION

Students may be overwhelmed by seemingly limitless possibilities of topics from which to choose. Analysts face a similar situation as they decide what policies to study and how to study them. Administrators have to motivate themselves to do research; it often is not required in their jobs. Whether one is a student, analyst, or administrator, one wants to study relevant issues, that is, issues that engage public, professional, or agency attention. Recent relevant topics include welfare reform, privatization of public services, the implications of changing demographics, immigration, and the consequences of global warming. Other relevant issues can be gleaned from professional journals, professional meetings, and the national media. Once a topic is selected, the research question can be framed by using the questions we listed at the beginning of the chapter—questions that begin "how many," "how much," "how efficient," "how effective," "how adequate," and "why."

Students have the most freedom in selecting a topic. A required paper serves as an opportunity to study an unfamiliar topic or to develop new skills. Public administration students may seek projects that introduce them to agency officials or add to their resumés. In selecting a topic and framing the research question, students should (1) be interested in the topic, (2) have, or be able to develop, the required knowledge and skills to conduct the study, and (3) have sufficient time and resources. A student may be encouraged to select a topic simply because it is "hot." Unfortunately, a relevant topic has little value if the student cannot produce a credible study. Students may be hindered by a lack of interest in the topic or insufficient knowledge. For example, a review of the environmental policy literature may require knowledge of economics, statistics, or the physical or biological sciences—expertise that students rarely can develop within a semester. Students may underestimate the time and cost involved in empirical research—data collection and analysis take resources. It is hard not to overemphasize that a small, well-designed study is better than a large study that falls apart because of insufficient time or money.

Analysts' choice of research topics is more limited; topics must be relevant to the decision at hand. Similar to students, they should have requisite knowledge, sufficient time, and adequate resources; however, co-workers or contractors can supplement an analyst's knowledge or skills. In selecting a topic, analysts consider its relevance to the agency and their career. A relevant topic is important to the agency's mission, consumes substantial resources or affects the public's quality of life, and is amenable to change. Studies on inconsequential topics or on policy areas resistant to change are likely to be ignored. A record of producing unused studies is unlikely to lead to individual career or organizational success.[4]

Administrators rely on research findings to identify problems, evaluate solutions, and make decisions. Administrators use research findings to justify additional resources, to keep existing resources, to monitor programs, and to improve employee performance. An effective strategy for administrators in university towns or with strong alumni ties is to keep a list of research questions. The list is ready whenever a faculty member calls looking for a class project. The students get to work on a relevant project, and the agency benefits from a low-cost study. Even the most modest study teaches administrators more about a particular policy and its implementation.

Administrators may often rely on the knowledge and research skills of others. Nevertheless, as we stressed earlier, they should be sufficiently engaged to oversee the project and to question the research strategy and the findings. In our experience, working with researchers to define a research question, build a model, and critique the method and the findings contributes to administrators' knowledge of their agency and their programs. In the end, the topic should matter to someone. Otherwise, there is no point in doing the research.

SUMMARY

Effective quantitative research requires that investigators articulate the purpose of a study. With the purpose in mind, the investigators can select the elements or variables of interest and postulate their relationship to each other. These elements and relationships constitute a model. Investigators may find a model aids them in three ways. First, it helps them to explain their ideas to others and to solicit reactions and criticisms. Second, it helps investigators to understand their ideas better. Third, it provides a useful guide to the research. It is particularly valuable in ensuring that all specified elements are measured and analyzed.

In building a model, investigators consider their own ideas and the ideas of colleagues and review existing research. Models may also emerge as investigators work with existing data or examine the results of a pilot test. The specific way investigators use these information sources varies from person to person and requires some creativity. Nevertheless, one can expect to rethink his or her ideas several times as information from different sources is brought to bear.

In our opinion, the review of the literature is the most important source of information. A thorough review of the literature greatly reduces the likelihood of wasting resources, such as time and effort. It provides valuable information that can be used in the later stages of research planning. Frequently, it helps investigators to identify strategies they can copy or adapt. Investigators will want to make use of the resources of reference and documents libraries, particularly abstracts, statistical indices, and citation indices.

The preliminary model may be modified several times during the course of planning a study. Once a plan is developed, investigators should conduct a pilot test. It should include the analysis and interpretation of the findings. Pilot-test information can be reviewed by investigators and major study users to ensure that the final study fulfills its purpose.

Administrative researchers primarily use schematic and symbolic models. Schematic models help investigators to illustrate their model and explain it to others, but much of the detail that is needed to understand and test the model may be missing from the schematic. Symbolic models use words or equations to represent the elements and their relationships. Verbal and mathematical models often are complementary. The verbal model presents the model in all its detail;

the mathematical model gives precise descriptions of the relationships between elements.

Most elements in models are variables, that is, characteristics that vary. Others may be constants, or characteristics that do not vary. A hypothesis is a simple model that states a testable relationship between an independent and a dependent variable. Frequently, an investigator will add additional variables, called *control variables*, to see whether they alter the hypothesized relationship. Common control variables in studies of human behavior include race, gender, and age. In studies of organizations, size, stability, and mission often are used as control variables.

Once the preliminary model is outlined, the investigators decide when and how often to collect data, how much control to exert over the study, what data to collect, and from whom to collect the data. Chapters 2 and 3 discuss the purpose of a study, how it affects the timing and frequency of data collected, and the investigators' degree of control. Chapter 2 introduces the two most common sources of research information used by administrators—the cross-sectional study and time-series analysis. We also will discuss case studies, which produce in-depth descriptions of events or programs. Chapter 4 considers how to measure variables and evaluate the measures, and Chapter 5 deals with ways to select research subjects.

NOTES

1. See G. King, R. Keohane, and S. Verba, "The Importance of Research Design," in *Rethinking Social Inquiry: Diverse Tools, Shared Standards*, ed. E. Brady and D. Collier (Lanham, MD: Rowman and Littlefield, 2004), 181–192.

2. There is a multitude of electronic resources on the scientific method. For an interesting look at science as a culture, see *Science In Action: How to Follow Scientists and Engineers Through Society*, by Bruno Latour (Cambridge, MA: Harvard University Press, 1987). Another valuable text in this area is *How Does Social Science Work? Reflections on Practice* by Paul Diesing (Pittsburgh, PA: University of Pittsburgh Press, 1992). A continually evolving example of scientific method and practice is the research on DNA.

3. For a discussion on empirical analysis as part of model building, see J. W. Tukey and M. B. Wilk, "Data Analysis and Statistics: Techniques and Applications," in *The Quantitative Analysis of Social Problems*, ed. E. R. Tufte (Reading, MA: Addison-Wesley Publishing, 1970), 370–390. While an older reference, this article is still valuable. The authors warn against exploring data with no model in mind and advocate that researchers not take their models too seriously or be unwilling to change them.

4. See A. J. Meltsner's "Problem Selection," in *Policy Analysis in the Bureaucracy* (Berkeley: University of California Press, 1976), 81–113, for a provocative discussion on problem selection.

TERMS FOR REVIEW

models	constants	inverse relationship
model building	hypothesis	nonlinear relationship
literature review	values of a variable	random or null relationship
pilot study	independent variable	spurious relationship
schematic model	dependent variable	control variable
symbolic model	covariation	
variables	direct relationship	

QUESTIONS FOR REVIEW

The following questions should indicate whether you have a basic competency in this chapter's material.

1. Why should an investigator state a purpose for a model before building it?
2. Why should an investigator build an explicit, preliminary model before beginning a quantitative study?
3. Identify the steps involved in model building, and comment on their importance. Consider the effect on the model if any one step were eliminated.
4. In general, would models built by one person be superior to a model developed by a group? Justify your position.
5. In the following hypotheses, identify the independent and dependent variables, two or three possible values for each variable, and the direction of the relationship. Then identify at least two control variables for each:
   a. Death rates in automobile accidents are higher in less densely populated areas.
   b. The higher the average driving speed on a highway, the higher the automobile death rate on that highway.
   c. Defendants with records of alcohol abuse are more likely to miss scheduled court appearances.
   d. Parents of elementary and high school students are more satisfied with their children's schools than are parents of junior high students.

6. Develop three hypotheses, each with an independent, dependent, and control variable, on a topic of interest to you. Create a schematic and symbolic model for each.
7. Consider safety violations as an independent variable, and write three hypotheses. Indicate the direction of each hypothesis.
8. Evaluate the following proposed "hypotheses":

   H_1:   School boards should not be appointed.

   H_2:   There are more African Americans than Hispanics on U.S. school boards.

   H_3:   Appointed school boards are more likely to have African American members than elected school boards.

   H_4:   African American school board representation is measured by the percent of school board members who are African American.

9. Identify the independent variables and their values in the hypotheses:

   H_1:   Older mothers with a college education are most likely to participate in parks and recreation programs; younger mothers with only a high school education are least likely to participate.

   H_2:   Older mothers and more educated mothers are most likely to participate in parks and recreation programs.

   What, if any, changes would you make to H_1 or H_2?

PROBLEMS FOR HOMEWORK AND DISCUSSION

1. Process models or flowcharts are often developed to describe and guide a process. One may use a process model to describe ways to build a model. Use a schematic to illustrate what you consider a "good" way to build a model. Show all linkages and their direction. You should have described either a systematic step-by-step process or a dynamic process in which the steps are repeated and the model is revised several times. Defend the process you described.
2. Link the purposes of a literature review with the stages of model building. At what stage(s) of the model would you conduct a review, and what would be the purpose of the review at each stage?

3. Find a newspaper article that presents a verbal model.
   a. State the apparent purpose of the model.
   b. Draw a schematic to illustrate the model.
   c. State a hypothesis included in or implied by the model.
   d. Name and identify the independent and dependent variables in your hypothesis.

4. Because of your model-building skills you have been asked to head a committee studying the job training needs of a town's labor force. The committee's purpose is to identify ways to improve the quality of the town's labor force to meet the needs of existing employers and to attract new employers to the area.

   The committee's first meeting is next week. A committee member who has no particular political power wants to survey citizens and community leaders; she has offered to prepare a survey for the meeting.
   a. Would you encourage her to bring a draft survey? Justify your decision.
   b. Outline your agenda for the meeting.

5. Consider the problem of productivity in the United States. Identify recent publications that address the problem. Look at three of these publications. Find a definition for *productivity*. Note the elements the authors use to study productivity. Create a tentative model to study productivity. Then, state the purpose of your model. Sketch a schematic model that incorporates the elements you think are most important.

   In class, work with three to five classmates. Compare your models, and jointly develop and sketch a model that you think should be tested.

6. Many communities must take water conservation measures in the summer. List strategies to get citizens to decrease their water usage. Develop a water conservation model that includes water conservation strategies and strategies for getting citizen compliance.

   In class, work with three to five classmates. Compare your models, and jointly develop and sketch a model that you think should be tested.

7. Consider automobile accidents in the United States. Identify and read a recent publication that studies the problem.
   a. Indicate the elements linked to automobile injuries or fatalities.
   b. Create a preliminary model to arrive at a policy to reduce injuries and fatalities resulting from automobile accidents. State the research question and a purpose for the model. Sketch a schematic model that incorporates the elements that you consider most important.
   c. Prepare a presentation explaining and justifying your model.

   In class, work with three to five classmates. Compare your models, then jointly develop and sketch a model that you think should be tested.

8. Select one of the following topics or a topic assigned by your instructor:
   Teenage pregnancy (incidence, policies, or programs)
   Juvenile crime (incidence, policies, or programs)
   Quality of drinking water
   Welfare reform (policies, effectiveness)
   Municipal finance (innovations)
   Lobbying by nonprofit organizations (policies, activities)
   a. Use a web search engine to locate and explore a relevant site. What information did you find at the site that could help you design or carry out a study?
   b. Go to your university's library or another research library and do a keyword search of the catalogue. How many entries did you receive? How many seem worth consulting? Do the same with a web search engine. Compare your findings.
   c. Go to your university's library or another research library and do a keyword search of an electronic index or database (it should contain entries of research articles). How many entries did you receive? How many seem worth consulting?
   d. With a group of classmates develop a guide to effective online searching.

DISK WORK

The disk includes an Excel spreadsheet, ORB Research Methods.xls, consisting of a variety of information for all 100 counties in a state. The 2004 data were collected from a central data set of North Carolina data maintained by the state government. They come from a variety of sources, outlined in the accompanying word file. While it is tempting to jump into a dataset, before analyzing data, researchers would want to know what questions they are trying to answer.

a. Go to the disk and review the list of variables. State three questions a county administrator could answer by analyzing the data.
b. Go to the disk and review the list of variables. Select two variables and state (1) one hypothesis with a direct relationship and (2) one with an inverse relationship.

RECOMMENDED FOR FURTHER READING

Information technology is changing rapidly. Many texts exist to help Internet users with research, but most become quickly outdated. Reference librarians are the best source for learning about new technologies and how to use them effectively. See Karen Hartman and Ernest Ackermann, *Searching and Researching on the Internet and the World Wide Web*, 4th ed. (Wilsonville, OR: Franklin, Beedle, 2004).

2

Designs for Description

1. Criteria for selecting a cross-sectional, time-series, longitudinal, or case study design.
2. The major strengths and weaknesses of cross-sectional, time-series, longitudinal, and case study designs.
3. Ways to interpret findings from cross-sectional and time-series designs.
4. The value of case studies and how to judge their quality.
5. Methods of using focus groups as study designs.

After formulating a tentative model, investigators need a research plan. They outline how they intend to collect data on each variable and how they plan to analyze the relationships among the variables. When you study tables, graphs, or other quantitative presentations, you may never think of the decisions and actions required to gather and organize the data. Yet these decisions and actions determine the value of the research, and each step should be conducted carefully. Data collection and analysis include the following steps:

Deciding when and how often to collect data

Developing or selecting measures for each variable

Identifying a sample or test population

Choosing a strategy for contacting subjects

Planning the data analysis

Presenting the findings

These steps constitute *research methodology*. The quality of a set of data is determined by the research methodology, even though little discussion of the methodology is included in a final report. For this reason it is altogether too easy for readers or listeners to underestimate the importance of research techniques and to take for granted the accuracy of reported findings.

Research designs are plans that guide decisions about when and how often to collect data, what data to gather, from whom and how to collect data, and how to analyze data. The term *research design* has a general and a specific meaning. The general meaning of research design refers to the plan for the study's methodology. The design should indicate the purpose of the study, and demonstrate that the plan will answer the research question(s) and is consistent with the study's purpose. Frequently, research designs are described as blueprints for the final research product.

The specific meaning of research design refers to the type of study. Common types of studies are cross-sectional studies, time-series studies, case studies, and experiments. These types of studies or designs dictate when and how often to collect the data and how much control an investigator will exert over the research environment.

Cross-sectional studies, time-series studies, and case studies place researchers in an environment where they have little, if any, control over the events. Experimental studies allow the researcher to control the research environment. The experimental setting and subjects are selected carefully, and the investigator decides who will be exposed to a treatment or intervention, at what intensity, and for how long. We have labeled experimental designs as designs for explanation and discuss them in the next chapter.

We have labeled and categorized cross-sectional studies, time-series studies, and case studies as designs for description. These three designs for description may be used separately or they may be combined. Cross-sectional studies are often combined with time-series studies, and case studies may incorporate features of cross-sectional studies or time-series studies.

Descriptive designs provide a wealth of information that is easy to understand and interpret. They may identify problems and suggest solutions. The studies can be undertaken to answer the questions that we posed in Chapter 1— how many? how much? how efficient? how effective? how adequate? The designs are used frequently to produce the data needed for planning, monitoring, and evaluating.

The administrator who wants to know what caused a particular event or outcome may find the descriptive designs somewhat limited. Nevertheless, all three designs can eliminate untenable explanations and furnish valuable leads. If the designs are planned and analyzed carefully, they may produce reasonable estimates of a treatment's effect on a dependent variable.[1] Thus descriptive designs may suggest causality.

Administrators combine findings from descriptive studies with other information and decide what, if any, action to take. From the administrator's perspective, simply describing variables may be sufficient. Consider once again the problem of prison suicides. With stricter enforcement of drunk-driving laws, reports of prison suicides increased.[2] These reports led investigators to collect data on how many prison suicides were occurring and who committed suicide.

For each reported suicide, investigators noted whether the prisoner was incarcerated for a violent or nonviolent crime, intoxicated, or held in isolation. Upon analysis investigators found that suicides tended to occur among males incarcerated for drunkenness or kept in isolation.

The analysis did not tell prison officials why one male prisoner chose to commit suicide and another did not. But the data did tell them how widespread the problem of prison suicide was and what characterized the inmates who were more likely to commit suicide.

What could prison officials do with the information? They could identify how many inmates in their institution were at risk of committing suicide. In other words, how many males did they have incarcerated for drunkenness or placed in isolation each day? Was the number of such incarcerations steadily increasing? Did the number go up on weekends or during certain times of the year?

Officials could propose and evaluate solutions to prevent those prisoners at risk of committing suicide from doing so and determine the feasibility of implementing these solutions. If a solution involves separate facilities or increased staffing, how large a facility is needed to take care of anticipated peak needs? What changes, if any, need to be made in the current staff work schedules? If a solution is tried, its effectiveness can be monitored. Did the rate of suicides drop? If a suicide occurred, had the inmate been identified as being at risk? If identified, had he received the available treatment for a potential suicide?

The number of possible questions goes on. Data are needed to answer them. Other examples would lead to different questions requiring different data. Administrators need data to carry out their tasks. Administrators who understand how data were collected, whether they were involved or not, will be better prepared to use them effectively and efficiently.

DESIGNS TO FIND RELATIONSHIPS AND SHOW TRENDS

Cross-sectional Designs

A cross-sectional design collects data on all relevant variables at one time. The data may be collected from surveys, forms, or a database. A researcher may collect data from various sources and create a unique database. For example, to study factors associated with traffic fatalities, a researcher can collect data from several sources for each state on the number of fatalities, road conditions, traffic density, arrests and penalties for various traffic offenses, and so on.

Two analogies are often used to describe cross-sectional designs. In one analogy, the design is viewed as a physical "cross section" of the population of interest. In the other analogy, the design is seen as a "snapshot." Both analogies underscore the static, time-bound nature of the design. The design depicts what exists at one point in time. Clearly, events may change markedly at a later time, even in the next time interval.

Cross-sectional designs should be used to:

Answer questions of how many? how much? who? how efficient? how effective? how adequate?

Gather information on people's knowledge, attitudes, and behavior

Stimulate exploratory research and identify hypotheses for further research

Cross-sectional designs are particularly suited for studies that involve collecting data:

On many variables

From a large group of subjects

From subjects who are dispersed geographically

We normally think of cross-sectional studies in conjunction with surveys, where an individual or a representative of an organization answers a questionnaire or fills out a form. Analysts then compile the data and analyze the variables. Imagine a survey to answer the research question, "How do the careers of public and nonprofit executives compare?" The model may have included variables such as sex, age, and professional education. The data can be analyzed to compare the ages, gender, education, and professional experience of nonprofit and public executives. An advantage of well-designed, well-documented, and carefully implemented cross-sectional designs is that researchers with different interests and models often can work with data from a single cross-sectional study. The above survey data could be analyzed by other researchers whose primary interest is how gender, age, or academic preparation is related to career outcomes. The use of data by researchers who did not participate in their collection is called *secondary data analysis*, and is discussed in detail in Chapter 9.

The media often sponsor surveys on current issues. Interviewers ask respondents about their knowledge, opinions, or behavior. Then the magazine, newspaper, television network, or other media outlet reports the percent of respondents in the various categories: how many are familiar with an issue; how many agree or disagree with a stated opinion; how many act in a particular fashion. The reports may indicate how responses vary according to demographic characteristics: Do women feel differently from men? Do people who live on the East and West coast behave differently from other Americans? And so on. Undoubtedly, as you read this, you also will begin to note the many studies conducted and reported so that we can understand ourselves and our society better.

Some surveys are conducted on a regular basis. Over 100 U.S. federal agencies use cross-sectional designs to regularly collect data. The U.S. Census Bureau, which is a major source of demographic and economic data, regularly surveys individuals, governments, and businesses. These data, which constitute official statistics, may provide a snapshot of the state of the nation as they report the status of its people and of the natural and economic environments. The data guide the decisions of public agencies, nonprofit organizations, and businesses. For example, data on age distribution help estimate demands for services. With knowledge of how many young children are in a community, planners can predict how many children will enter school each year. Child care providers can develop business plans based on the number of eligible children, where they live, and their characteristics. Nonprofits may use the data to support the need for a proposed service.

Working from records a researcher can create a cross-sectional database. We already suggested how data from different sources can be combined to create a database. Another strategy is to collect data from records. Employee files, volunteer applications, budgets, and grant applications are all potential data sources. Employee files can yield detailed information on employee characteristics, which can be linked to performance evaluations, patterns of absenteeism, or turnover data. Applications for volunteer positions provide similar information. In both cases the information may suggest gaps in employee skills or volunteer interests that can help in designing training or recruiting strategies. The possibilities are endless and depend on the needs of an organization and the imagination of a researcher.

Cross-sectional studies may provide data on just one variable, e.g., the educational level of the population, but their greatest value is in describing the relationships among several variables. When the data are analyzed, cases are divided into different groups based on values of the independent variables. Basing a cross-sectional study on a carefully developed model helps to ensure that appropriate information is collected and provides a guide for data analysis. Although cross-sectional studies based on carefully developed models can provide useful information and be effective in testing hypotheses, they may suffer from less-than-careful research techniques.

In earlier editions we noted that surveys were often poorly implemented; an investigator may attempt to obtain information from too many people, be unable to make return calls or follow-up mailings, and be plagued with a low response rate. Questionnaires may be constructed without sufficient care to purpose and design. Investigators may fail to pilot test the survey instruments, and relevant variables may be ignored. We suspect that these problems have become worse with the ease of constructing online surveys. Respondents, especially those contacted by persons wanting data on public and nonprofit agencies and their administrators, may suffer from "respondent fatigue." A 20-minute survey, which may seem short to its designer, may seem burdensome to an administrator who receives several such requests, has limited interest in the topic, and has to take additional time to think about an answer or gather data. The result may be a low response rate. The surveyor may have no way of contacting nonrespondents or insufficient resources for follow-up mailings or phone calls.

The survey may produce the wrong data or have little or no usable data. It may have excluded critical variables. We know of a survey that received responses from 33,000 state employees and took 550 hours of staff time to process. All that could be done with the data was to report the answers to each question. The survey included only one independent variable, and that variable turned out to be unusable. The question asking respondents to indicate where they worked was phrased in such a way that the analysts couldn't tell if a person who answered "Personnel" was referring to the state office of personnel or another agency's personnel office. Such problems are preventable. Administrators should not begin to collect data without critically evaluating the survey items and data collection process to see if they will answer the research questions. An important safeguard is to conduct a pilot test, which is discussed in Chapter 7.

The data produced from cross-sectional designs can be analyzed in any number of ways using a variety of statistical tools. In this chapter we will use only frequencies and percents to illustrate how cross-sectional data can be analyzed. An example in the previous chapter was drawn from a cross-sectional design implemented to learn the placement record of state-funded job training programs.[3] Prior to the study, administrators had no data on the success of training programs in placing participants. The data on job training program participants were collected from state government files. The dependent variable was employment status at the end of the training program. The independent variables were type of training program, sex, race, age, and educational attainment.

For each type of training program, analysts examined placement outcomes by age, sex, race, and educational attainment. They found that participants in on-the-job training programs were most likely to be employed. Males were more likely to be employed than females; employment status did not vary with age, race, or educational attainment. Tables similar to Table 2.1 were produced. Administrators could study the detailed tables to learn whom the programs served and how well a program did in placing its various client groups.

Example 2.1 comes from a cross-sectional study conducted for the U.S. Internal Revenue Service to (1) determine satisfaction with online filing as well as ideas for product improvement, (2) identify reasons for not filing online, (3) compare perceptions of online filers and other taxpayers, and (4) determine ease of communicating with the IRS. The study, typical of cross-sectional studies, gathered data on many variables. Our example is from one part of the analysis. We chose an example that illustrates how cross-sectional designs can guide marketing decisions. We assume that the research team generated ideas (variables) to explain why some taxpayers choose to use e-file and others don't. We included the table, which considered both how users varied in their perception of e-file and what attributes were important to them.

We also chose this example to demonstrate the flexibility one has in analyzing and interpreting a dataset. What recommendations would you make to the IRS based on Table 2.2? The analysts focused on the differences between

TABLE 2.1	AGE AND EMPLOYMENT STATUS OF PARTICIPANTS IN ON-THE-JOB TRAINING PROGRAMS
Age	Employed after Training
16–21 years	40 (51%)
22–24 years	37 (74%)
25–54 years	84 (70%)
> 54 years	3 (75%)

An Application of a Cross-sectional Design

Problem: The Internal Revenue Service (IRS), the U.S. tax collection agency, compares taxpayer satisfaction with its products and services. One study compares online filers (users of e-file), lapsed users (those who discontinued using e-file), and nonusers. Comparison variables include demographic characteristics, ease of communicating with IRS, perceptions of e-file features, and perceptions of the IRS. Are attitudes about e-file attributes associated with product use?

Design: A telephone survey of 1,000 randomly sampled employed taxpayers between the ages of 18 and 74.

Findings:

TABLE 2.2

	Type of User		
Agreed that	Current Users (599)	Lapsed Users (106)	Nonusers (272)
Having accurate return			
is really important	95%	92%	91%
is true of e-file	69	53	39
Being assured return is private/secure			
is really important	92	92	87
is true of e-file	55	34	26
Easy to use/little hassle			
is really important	78	75	73
is true of e-file	65	30	32
Being inexpensive			
is really important	71	70	60
is true of e-file	53	45	40
Getting return to IRS			
is really important	71	58	46
is true of e-file	82	67	61
Getting refund faster			
is really important	61	44	42
is true of e-file	78	62	54
e-file is a better way to file your federal income taxes	63	26	27

Conclusions: The analysts concluded that attitudes affected usage. They noted that while accuracy, security, and ease are important to all taxpayers, nonusers, and lapsed users "have NOT gotten the message of e-file's benefits in three areas they actually care a lot about—Accuracy, Privacy/Security, and Ease of Use." (Capitals in original text)

SOURCE: Adapted from "Findings from the 2005 Taxpayer Statisfaction Study," U.S. Department of Treasury, Internal Revenue Service, July 2005. Publication 4241, Catalog. 373003 Q. Available at http://www.irs.gov/pub/irs-pdf/p4241. pdf importance and perceptions of e-file. They recommended that the IRS strive to make taxpayers aware that e-file is accurate, secure, and easy to use. Do the analysis yourself and see if you agree with them. Note that you can organize the data to determine the percentage of persons who want to get their return faster who use e-file. Of the 977 respondents, 526 reported that getting their return faster was important to them; 69 percent of them used e-file, while 22 percent had not.

Cross-sectional studies generally are inappropriate if investigators want to learn why something happened. They cannot demonstrate that a treatment, intervention, or other independent variable caused a given outcome. Investigators cannot exert the needed amount of control over the intervention or over the environment surrounding the study. Investigators may be unable to rule out alternative explanations as to why something happened. Nevertheless, a major use of cross-sectional designs is to uncover relationships that can be studied further in experimental studies.

Studies on the effects of estrogen show the progress from cross-sectional research to experimental studies. In 1985 a noted medical journal published two cross-sectional studies on estrogen.[4] One study examined data on 1,234 postmenopausal women living in a Boston suburb. The researchers found that in this sample, estrogen users were twice as likely as nonusers to experience heart disease. In another study researchers surveyed 121,964 postmenopausal nurses and found that estrogen users were one-third as likely to experience heart disease. Design features may have led to the different findings. The studies had different sample populations. One study used a mailed questionnaire to collect data; the other relied on personal interviews and physical examinations. One study collected data over a four-year period; the other collected them over an eight-year period. The results of both studies were plausible theoretically.[5]

Statistical association may be insufficient evidence that a treatment or program causes an observed outcome. Experiments are designed to produce evidence of causality and the effect that a treatment has on a dependent variable. To see if hormones were actually beneficial, the Women's Health Initiative recruited and randomly assigned 27,347 women to take either hormones or a placebo. The pills looked the same and the participants did not learn if they received hormones until the end of the study. It was discontinued after 11 years when women taking hormones were found to be at greater risk for heart disease.

Statisticians and methodologists have created techniques designed to obtain evidence of causality from cross-sectional data. We discuss these techniques briefly in Chapters 13 and 14.

Time Series

Time-series studies collect and present data on a single unit or set of subjects. The data are collected on the same variable(s) at frequent, closely spaced regular intervals over a relatively long period. The data can depict both short-term changes and long-term trends in a variable. Most of us are familiar with time series that regularly report indicators of some aspect of the nation's economic or social climate. Such time series include consumer price indices, the unemployment rate, and crime rates.

Time series are suited for situations where an administrator wants to:

Establish a baseline data measure

Describe changes over time

Keep track of trends

Forecast future trends

Evaluate the impact of a program or policy

Time-series data are neither hard to gather nor hard to arrange for analysis. The data may be gathered by investigators or taken from existing databases. The data come from one or more units, such as a state, county, or office. The data may be collected on the first workday of every month, the fourth Thursday of every November, or any other interval appropriate to the study. An accompanying account of events should be kept and consulted to help explain unexpected patterns: for example, a drop in swimming pool usage may be associated with an unusually cold or rainy summer.

Administrators find time-series data presented in graphs or tables easy to interpret and to combine with other information. They use time series to monitor programs and activities under their jurisdiction. For example, administrators in a social services department may decide to reallocate resources within a department based on the number of clients served, the number of services offered, and length of service time.

A time series may or may not include an explicit independent variable. Time, however, is an implied independent variable. The data are frequently presented in a graph with time along the horizontal axis and the dependent variable along the vertical axis. The reader's attention focuses on the dependent variable and its changes or variations over time. Figure 2.1 shows two time-series lines—one examines the unemployment rate and the other the property crime rate. Property crimes are burglary, larceny-theft, motor vehicle theft, and arson. The data will help us illustrate several features of times series. The data also show how you can examine the relationship between two time series.[6]

Note that our example reports U.S. data for the entire country; the employment data are collected from a sample of U.S. households, and the property crime statistics are from individual law enforcement agencies. You could have done the same analysis on a single state, county, or city.

Now, what do you look for in this time series? Your eye should scan each line to identify the overall patterns and noticeable dips and rises in the line. You look for four types of variations within a time series that reports yearly or monthly data[7]:

Long-term trends: general movement of a variable, either upward or downward over a number of years.

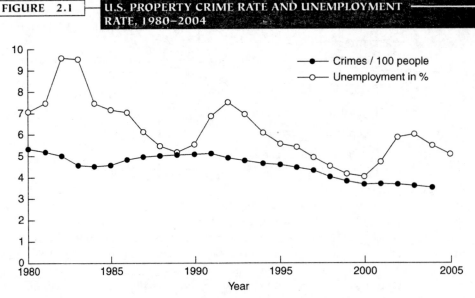

FIGURE   2.1 — U.S. PROPERTY CRIME RATE AND UNEMPLOYMENT RATE, 1980–2004

SOURCE: Crime and Justice Data-OnLine, U.S. Department of Justice, Bureau of Justice Statistics
http://bjsdata.ojp.usdoj.gov/dataonline/Search/Crime/State/TrendsInOneVar.cfm, Accessed December 6,
2006; Labor Force Statistics from the Current Population Survey, U.S. Department of Labor, Bureau
of Labor Statistics http://www.bls.gov/cps/prev_yrs.htm Accessed December 6, 2006

Cyclical variations: changes in a variable that occur within a long-term trend; cycles recur in one- to five-year intervals.

Seasonal variations: fluctuations traceable to seasonally related phenomena, e.g., holidays, weather.

Irregular (or random) fluctuations: changes that cannot be attributed to long-term trends, cyclical variations, or seasonal variations.

Since our example demonstrates long-term trends, cyclical variations, and irregular fluctuations, we will discuss these first and then consider seasonal variations. Look first at the changes in the property crime rate:

1980–1984: Property crime rate decreases.

1985–1991: Property crime rate increases.

1992–2000: Property crime rate decreases.

2001: Property crime rate increases.

2002–2004: Property crime rate decreases.

Variables neither increase nor decrease indefinitely. Changes in social, economic, and environmental conditions may lead to a change in direction. Since 1991 the U.S. crime rate, including property crimes, has steadily dropped; explanations for the decline included the state of the U.S. economy, the aging U.S. population, and changes in the criminal justice environment, e.g., more police and more people in prison.[8] The time series for the property crime rate from 1984 through 2004 shows two distinct long-term trends. From 1985 through 1991 the property crime rate increased. Since 1991 it has decreased. The only deviation was a 1 percent increase in 2001. Without 2002 data, the observer cannot tell if the 2001 increase signified a change in the trend's direction or an irregular fluctuation. The 2002 data indicate that the increase was an irregular fluctuation.

Cyclical variations are regularly occurring fluctuations within a long-term trend that last for more than a year; frequently, cyclical patterns recur in one- to five-year intervals. In some cases cycles may be very regular. For example, the percentage of Americans voting reaches a peak every four years during presidential elections. A complete cycle is from "peak to peak" or "valley to valley." The unemployment data from 1980 to 2004 have two cycles of approximately 10 years each. The data show long stretches when the unemployment rate kept decreasing. Between 1980 and 2004 periods of increasing unemployment rarely lasted more than three years. We can assume that political interventions brought about the change in direction. The variations as illustrated by the unemployment rate are more common than regular cycles. That is, there are up-and-down movements that take place throughout a time series but not in a regular pattern.

Seasonal variations describe changes that occur within the course of a year. Data must represent time intervals that recur within a year, such as days, weeks, months, or quarters. Seasonal variations include fluctuations traceable to weather, holidays, or similar seasonally related phenomena. The observed fluctuations occur within a single year and recur year after year. If we had included monthly data in Figure 2.1, you would have seen several fluctuations in any given year. Such fluctuations are considered seasonal variations only if a similar pattern is seen year after year. An administrator may use seasonal information to decide how to staff public facilities—for example, how many staff to hire for city parks and for how long to hire them (for 10, 12, or 14 weeks). A jail administrator finding that the number of people in jail is highest on Monday mornings can plan ahead for the increased demand. Ignorance of seasonal demands may result in erroneous conclusions. Imagine the disastrous consequences if a merchant assumed that his December sales of toys marked a business upswing that would carry through to January and February. Think of the problems of the jail administrator who orders food based on the number of inmates on Monday morning.

Irregular fluctuations are variations not associated with long-term trends, cyclical variations, or seasonal variations. The irregular fluctuations may be the result of nonrandom or random movements. A *nonrandom movement* is brought about by a condition or set of conditions that can be identified and explain the variation. The conditions may be inferred from records of concurrent events. For example, negative publicity about how police handle crime reports may explain a drop in reported crimes, or a community may be struck by a natural disaster, which impacts employment. If such factors are found, we might assume that the variation was nonrandom. Otherwise, we may assume the variation is random. *Random movements* are unexplained variations that most often are relatively minor.

The 1 percent increase in the property crime rate in 2001 was an irregular fluctuation that seems relatively inconsequential and random. A Google search suggested that the increase was largely ignored. Yet we found one item that suggested the hazards of prematurely assuming that a one-year shift marks the beginning of a longer trend. A research firm summarized the 2001 crime statistics and concluded that they confirmed its prediction that beginning in 2000 the crime rate would increase. In fairness to the firm, it looked at more than the one data source. The researchers assumed that a weakening U.S. economy, increased spending on terrorism, and the anticipated release of inmates reaching the end of their sentences would cause an increase in crime.[9]

For most administrative purposes, one simply needs to know the types of fluctuations and to recognize evidence of their occurrence in a table or a graph. Otherwise, you may misinterpret the ups and downs in a graphed time series and erroneously attribute changes in a time series to a specific event or administrative action.

It is important to draw a graph of the time series and analyze it visually. We will often see graphs with more than one variable, as is the case with Figure 2.1. However, for administrative purposes the clarity of time series diminishes if several variables are being examined together. In Figure 2.1 the graph included two variables: property crime rate and unemployment rate. You could scan the graph visually and note where the two varied together and where they went in different directions. Between 1980 and 1988, the two rates seemed to diverge. After 1992, they both appear to be declining. If more variables were placed on the graph, it would become increasingly difficult to follow and interpret.

Time-series data are used frequently in forecasting or in evaluating the effectiveness of a policy. In both cases statistical techniques take into account the fluctuations of a variable. For the most part, these techniques are beyond the scope of this book. Nevertheless, we can make some comments about forecasting that you may find useful. First, quantitative methods of forecasting that depend on time-series data work best for short-term forecasts, e.g., forecasting for up to two years. A parks director or jail administrator may use quantitative techniques to forecast park usage or jail occupancy. This information may help in making staffing decisions or ordering supplies. But forecasts made for longer periods are less likely to be accurate. A major problem is forecasting a change in direction of the long-term trend correctly.

Second, assuming that existing long-term trends may continue unchanged can work reasonably well, but the forecaster must be aware that rates of change eventually will vary and long-term trends will change direction. For example, a town whose population has grown by 10 percent each decade will at some time experience slower growth. An unanticipated slowdown has serious implications if public facilities are planned around the assumption of a much larger population.

Third, identifying long-term trends, cycles, and any seasonal variation is important in assessing the impact of a program or policy. Without knowing how the variable has been changing over time one may mistakenly conclude that a change in a time series is the result of the program or policy. The use of time-series data to evaluate programs and policies is discussed in more detail in Chapter 3.

Fourth, qualitative techniques are important for long-range forecasting. An administrator who wants to identify the types of demands that her agency will face in 10 years may wish to use focus groups or interviews to obtain opinions from citizens and experts. These techniques are discussed later in this chapter and in Chapter 6.

Longitudinal Designs

Longitudinal designs collect information on the same cases or comparable cases for two or more distinct time periods. *Panel designs* refer to longitudinal designs that gather data on the same individuals each time.[10] Typically the cases are individuals, but cases can consist of families, organizations, or some other unit of analysis. The design combines some characteristics of the cross-sectional design and the time-series design. The studies can reveal which individual cases change between data collections. This allows the researcher to determine the changes that take place within the group and establish a time order for variables. For example, a training director can organize unemployment data as a time series and note changes in the unemployment rate. However, unless a panel design is used, she cannot tell how individuals in this population changed. That is, some people employed at one time may be unemployed at a later time; some unemployed at the earlier time may be employed later. Since a panel design follows the same individual cases over time, shifts from one condition (employed) to another (unemployed) by individuals can be measured.

Until the late 1960s, poverty was considered to be a relatively permanent characteristic of individuals. Repeated cross-sectional surveys showed the same proportion of Americans living in poverty, and it was assumed that the same people were in poverty each time. These studies showed almost no change from one year to the next in the distribution of income. However, a study of American families, the Panel Survey of Income Dynamics, found that roughly one-third of those who were poor one year were not poor the next and were not poor the year before. The number of poor was stable because the number coming into poverty and the number leaving just about equaled each other.[11]

The way that information about the number of elderly receiving institutional care was obtained provides another example of the importance of panel studies. Federal, state, and local administrators have faced an increasing burden of providing care for elderly Americans. Cross-sectional samples of older persons taken at various times had shown consistently that about 5 percent of people aged 65 and older were in a nursing home, hospital, or other long-term care facility. This often was interpreted to mean that any person 65 and older has only a 5 percent chance of being institutionalized. But researchers tracked a panel of individuals over several years and found that many people enter and leave long-term care facilities several times in their later years. At any moment, only 5 percent may be in long-term care facilities, hospitals, or nursing homes, but over a period of years at least 20 percent of the elderly will spend some time in one or more of these places.[12]

Another example of a large-scale panel study is the Framingham, Massachusetts, Heart Study.[13] In this study 5,209 residents of the town of Framingham between the ages of 30 and 62 were recruited to submit to a detailed medical examination and lab tests every two years. The information from this study is being used to issue advice about diet, exercise, and other factors related to health conditions. In 1971, 5,124 children and spouses of the original participants were recruited for the offspring study. In 2001 researchers began the Third Generations study, consisting of 3,900 of the original participants' grandchildren. These follow-up studies have allowed further investigations of risk factors for health problems and identification of genes that contribute to various diseases.

A major problem of panel studies is in obtaining an initial representative sample of respondents willing to be interviewed at set intervals over an extended period of time. Panel members also may drop out of the study for one reason or another. This is called *subject attrition* or *experimental mortality*, a concept we discuss in Chapter 3. Another difficulty is that when people are the cases, the repeated interviews and observations may influence their behavior. When interviewed repeatedly over a period of months or years, people may change the way they answer questions in order to be consistent from one time to the next.[14]

When we follow groups of cases, we often refer to them as *cohorts*. A cohort consists of cases having experienced the same significant event at a specific time period. They may be individuals, organizations, or some other unit of analysis.[15] The term *cohort* may refer to birth cohort: those cases born in a specific year or period. Cohorts may also be defined by the year they entered the study or the occurrence of or exposure to a particular event such as the year having graduated from college or fought in a particular war. In a panel study, investigators obtain information on the same individuals each time. But a study using cohorts may be conducted in any number of ways. Note that not all studies involving cohorts are longitudinal studies. A different sample may be taken from the cohort group each time data are gathered, or a researcher may survey members of a cohort, such as residents of New Orleans, and compare the responses of those who relocated after two hurricanes, with those who returned.[16]

QUALITATIVE RESEARCH AND DESIGNS TO FILL IN THE DETAILS

Quantitative studies typically involve many cases and many variables that are measured in a predetermined and specific way. The data are numeric and can be summarized numerically. Since an important goal of quantitative studies is to compare cases on different variables, factors unique to individual cases are not included and information about context is often ignored. For example, the designs described above are used to obtain information on a standard set of items for a large number of cases, as with cross-sectional studies, or information on as few as a single case for many time periods, as with time series.

While quantitative research designs are important, these designs are not useful for obtaining detailed information about the context in which events or behaviors occur, nor do they allow flexibility in the type of data obtained from case to case in the same study. To obtain this type of information more qualitative and less quantitative approaches are used. Qualitative research methods have long been important in basic disciplines as well as in applied areas such as administration. Studies using a qualitative research approach typically obtain more in-depth, detailed information on fewer cases than do studies using more quantitative designs. Two important qualitative designs, described below, are the case study and the focus group.

Qualitative Research

Qualitative research methods have received more attention in recent years from both practitioners and researchers.[17] Qualitative research produces information, or data, difficult or impossible to convert to numbers. The qualitative study is defined by its extensive use of such information, its preference for developing full information on relatively few cases, and its consideration of the unique features of each case. Researchers may draw on both quantitative and qualitative methods in conducting any one study.

Qualitative studies may include information on the unique features and the environment of each case. Qualitative studies describe specific features of each individual, organization, jurisdiction, or program. Qualitative studies may involve extensive fieldwork; the researcher goes to where the cases are located and obtains information on them in their natural setting.[18] In this way the researcher does not attempt to manipulate any aspect of the situation being studied but takes it as it is. Nevertheless, the qualitative researcher's background and personality influence data collection and interpretation. Qualitative studies are often conducted by researchers who are participants in or close observers of the phenomena studied. Such researchers are more likely to have the knowledge and interest to design and conduct a sound qualitative study. The researchers use their experiences and insights to design a study and to interpret the findings. A researcher's interactions with subjects affect what he is told and what information he is given.

In qualitative studies the researcher usually works with a flexible design. Although the studies may have a clearly defined methodology and plan of action, the researcher usually has great flexibility. He may alter the design as the research progresses. Typically, he uses several sources of information. Multiple sources give a fuller picture of a case and its setting and help to verify other information.

Researchers using qualitative techniques need different skills than those using quantitative designs. An interviewer in a quantitative study receives a list of questions that she asks every respondent. All other interviewers would use the same set of questions and ask them in the same way. In a qualitative study, the interviewer may have a suggested set of questions but asks them as the situation dictates. Based on the response to one question, the interviewer asks another question; the researcher needs to ask the question, listen, interpret, and phrase a proper follow-up question.[19]

The researcher using qualitative methods must be able to record information accurately, write clearly, divide trivial from important details, and draw appropriate conclusions from the information. Since data from qualitative studies tend to be descriptions, observations, and responses to interview questions, a great deal of information is obtained. To make sense out of it may be difficult. Rather than doing statistical analysis of numerical data as in quantitative studies, the researcher looks for themes and concepts in the analysis of qualitative data.

Case Studies

Case studies are studies that examine in some depth persons, decisions, programs, or other entities that have a unique characteristic of interest. For example, a case study may be designed to study women in nontraditional jobs, a new approach to budgeting, or a high school health clinic.

Except for studies that involve a single case within an administrator's jurisdiction, administrators seldom initiate or participate in the design of case studies. Even the single case study may be a by-product of someone else's research needs. For example, some state and local administrators seek out university students to conduct case studies. The studies give the students a "real-world" experience, and the administrators learn more about their agency and its programs.

Case studies are the preferred research strategy if one wants to learn the details about how something happened and why it may have happened. Administrators may want a case study to investigate:

A program or a policy that has had remarkable success

Programs or policies that have unique or ambiguous outcomes

Situations where actors' behavior is discretionary

The case must be contemporary and the investigator must have direct access to the people involved. Analysts implementing cross-sectional or time-series designs may never contact program administrators, employees, or clients. An investigator conducting a case study cannot be so detached.

One of the hallmarks of a case study is the combination of several different sources of information. The sources of information used in case studies include documents, archival information, interviews, direct observation, participant observation, and physical artifacts.

The inclusion of information from multiple sources is a major strength of case studies. First, each data-collection strategy affects the types of questions a researcher can answer. For example, from direct observation an investigator learns how people behave. From interviews he hears their explanations of their behavior. The two sources of information give a more complete picture than either piece alone.

Second, the investigator can corroborate information gained from one source with information gathered from another source. For example, staff in a crisis intervention center may report a high level of community support. The claim will have greater credibility if an independent review of agency records confirms extensive community support.

Requiring information from multiple sources also is a drawback of case studies. Typically, different information sources are studied using different research techniques. For example, interviewing skills are needed for face-to-face meetings with subjects, questionnaire design skills are needed to conduct a mail or electronic survey, content analysis skills are needed for archival research. Most of us are skilled in only one or two research techniques. Thus a case study may require a research team or suffer from unevenness. We suspect that administrators find that they and their staff lack both the training and time needed to do effective case studies.

Each research technique and data collection strategy takes time to design, pretest, and carry out. Incorporating multiple data sources, employing different techniques and possibly multiple researchers, demands time, expertise, and energy. Consequently, researchers who conduct case studies often find that studying multiple cases is impractical because of the effort and resources required.

The case study may focus on the case as a whole (all of its components) or just on certain components. For example, to study a pretrial release program, the investigator may look at the program as a whole: why it was developed, how it was initially organized, what changes it has made, why those changes were made, how defendants are chosen for pretrial release, and how much discretion staff and judges have in making pretrial-release recommendations. Alternatively, the investigator may focus on released defendants: their ages, ties to the community, criminal records, and their compliance with the terms of pretrial release. In the first instance, the program is the case. In the second, each defendant could be a separate case.

Most administrative case studies seem to focus on components. In program evaluations the broad research question of how effective the program is may be displaced by the more immediate need to know what was accomplished. For example, in a study of a pretrial release program, "successful" defendants, who showed up for scheduled court appearances, were compared with "unsuccessful" defendants, who failed to appear. The study did not look for broader evidence of effectiveness, such as whether released defendants stayed at work or school or whether they pursued criminal activities. Nor did the study try to link the information on released defendants with characteristics of the program as a whole. This is a limited case study. Limiting a case study to an analysis of individual components doesn't take advantage of the strength of case studies—the value of bringing together diverse pieces of information to explain why and how things happened across a whole program.

Case studies may be conducted on a single case or on a set of similar cases. Each approach (using a single case study of a program, or comparing two or more programs through case studies of each) would be valuable in determining the effectiveness of the program. An individual case study of a phenomenon can provide research depth. Multiple cases of a phenomenon provide research breadth. Ideally, one would have both—depth and breadth. In reality, limited resources mean researchers often have to choose between the two, striking a balance that is appropriate for the task at hand. In some cases, this means sacrificing some contextual information to include more cases, or sacrificing having some more examples in order to explore just one or two in much greater detail.

Because of the potential value of case studies, you may want more information about them. They provide rich details. If you read a case study, you may gain greater insight into how to approach or solve a problem. Practically speaking, administrators' direct experience with case studies may be limited to their professional reading. Case studies may alert you to new management techniques, programs to solve chronic problems, or strategies to improve the quality of agency or community life. If the case study is well done, you should have a good idea of whether you could implement a similar solution. Even if the case study documents a failure or otherwise doesn't apply, it may spur you to think more about your work environment and responsibilities. A creative administrator may read a case study, contact the researcher or program administrator to learn more details, and implement a new program or strategy.

One author, Robert Yin, carefully distinguishes between the case study as a type of design on the one hand and the data collection typically conducted in a case study on the other.[20] He also implies that most people incorrectly assume that any qualitative study is a case study. Although case studies tend to be qualitative, Yin recommends an approach for case studies that follows the scientific method. This approach has the researcher stating a problem; formulating a research question, objective, or hypothesis; identifying the case to be studied; planning the data collection; collecting the data; analyzing the data; and writing a report.

You may wonder if a particular case study is any more than a good story.[21] Sometimes it may not be. The study is as good as the objectivity and training of the investigators. In some disciplines, particularly anthropology, researchers are trained extensively in case-study and qualitative methods. The researcher learns to state the research question and to formulate hypotheses. Without initial hypotheses he may become entangled in the idiosyncrasies of the case. The investigator conducting an exploratory study will have a research question, but appropriately may decide to forgo formulating initial hypotheses. Instead, he will develop hypotheses from the case study once it is completed and draw generalizations from later studies. The exploratory case study serves as the basis for establishing new research questions, new hypotheses, and a continuing research agenda.

Case-study researchers need to be particularly careful to follow sound research practice. They must decide what kind of and how much data would support a hypothesis before collecting the data. Otherwise, the natural wish of researchers to have the data support their hypotheses may bias the collection and interpretation of the evidence.

One should also be careful in terms of who conducts the case study. The researcher with limited knowledge of the organization and limited resources may not contribute much new information or insight. The researcher who works within the organization may reflect the organization's biases.

As part of the design, the researcher must decide what constitutes a case. Doing so may not be easy.[22] Deciding on what is the case to be studied, for example, may be a problem if the case involves a program. Consider an agency program to aid abused children. The agency may have a program for abused children specifically, but it may also have services for abused mothers and for families with a potential for abuse. Should these services be included? The program may have evolved from an earlier program. At what point should the case start? Should the case study include the board of directors, clients, or others in the community? The investigator must answer these questions in order to limit, or set boundaries around, the case study. An ill-defined case can be as distorting as a case without predetermined criteria for judging whether a hypothesis is supported. An ill-defined case can also allow the researcher to wander from her original research question.

As an administrator, you may want to determine the quality of the design so you can convince yourself you are reading more than just a good story. First, you should look for evidence the investigator had a specific, answerable research question. Second, did she have a model before starting the study? Third, you want to know that the investigator decided exactly what were the boundaries of the case. Fourth, the case study's procedures from design through implementation should be documented thoroughly, including any potential biases on behalf of the researcher.

Case studies may involve the investigator intensely in the case and usually require interpretation of qualitative information. Consequently, they are hard to replicate, and great care must be taken to document what was done, how, and why. Transparency of a case study is important, as in any form of research. It demonstrates the strengths and limitations of the work.

Focus Groups

Focus-group methods use group interviews to obtain qualitative data. Researchers have long used group interviews to save time and money by getting a number of people together to provide information.[23] Focus-group procedures have evolved in recent years and include a set of characteristics that distinguish them from other group techniques. Although focus-group research is qualitative, often it is used in conjunction with more quantitative procedures. Survey researchers use focus groups to generate and test the items to be used on a questionnaire or survey instrument. Focus groups also are used to elaborate on data collected in surveys.

Focus groups are semi-structured discussions by small groups of participants about a common topic or experience.[24] They are useful in obtaining information that is difficult to obtain with other methods. A focus-group interview is used to get in-depth information and reactions to a relatively small number of topics or questions, rather than to get answers to a large number of questions. Typically focus-group interviews include fewer than ten questions and often around five or six.

A study using focus groups usually includes several group interviews. Each group is relatively homogeneous with respect to background characteristics of the participants. The homogeneity helps to ensure that individuals will not be afraid to express their feelings about the issue at hand.[25] Homogeneity also helps guarantee the group has had a common experience to discuss, whether it is opinions about marketing material or crime victims' perceptions of police response. What distinguishes focus groups is the presence of group interaction in response to researchers' questions.

The focus-group discussion is led by a moderator who should be an experienced interviewer and who is skilled at group facilitation. The moderator also needs to be familiar with the questions and the purpose of the study. The moderator asks the questions and guides the discussion to ensure that all members of the group participate. The hallmark of focus groups is the explicit use of group interaction to produce data and insights that would be less accessible otherwise.

Focus groups constitute an accepted research method.[26] Not every group using discussion techniques is a focus group, however. Focus groups have specific defining characteristics; they are created by research teams for well-defined purposes. Focus groups rely on the strengths of qualitative methods, including exploration and discovery; understanding things in depth and in context; and interpreting why things are the way they are and how they got that way. To serve these purposes, focus groups, like other qualitative methods, require a great deal of openness and flexibility.[27]

Although the overall process of focus-group research usually is highly structured, the interviewing must be flexible. The information obtained is qualitative and usually voluminous. The researcher must identify themes, find answers to questions, and summarize the discussion of the group members. Having well-designed questions based on a clearly defined purpose will facilitate the analysis and use of the data. Careful planning should be done prior to assembling the group or groups and the interviewing. Clarifying the purpose of the study and discussing it with colleagues are important. The researcher should be clear about what information is needed, how it will be gathered (audiotapes or videotapes, notes, transcription) why, who will use it, and how, and its confidentiality or anonymity status. A written plan for the entire project, including a schedule and budget, should be developed in advance.

Focus groups are used in the public sector in many ways. A manager may find focus groups useful for needs assessments—to identify the services clients need, where they are best delivered, and which are not appropriate, and to develop a better understanding of concerns as perceived by relevant participants. A public organization might use focus groups to address such questions as: What are the most important problems of the jurisdiction as perceived by various citizen groups? Why?[28]

Focus groups aid in program design and planning where the objective is to develop ways to deal with a problem or situation. What are the possibilities for dealing with a problem? What options are feasible? How would they be received by the client group? Focus groups can be used to evaluate existing programs and to answer such questions as: How well is a program working? Are clients dissatisfied? Why? What changes will be acceptable? How well do clients think that they would respond to a change if one were instituted? As these situations suggest, the manager would probably want to get more explanation and discussion concerning responses to questions than generally would be possible in a large-scale survey.

The focus-group technique can be used as exploratory research in a new topic area, in generating hypotheses to guide the development of structured questionnaires or other research methods, in discovering perspectives and feelings of various groups, in understanding reasons for behaviors or attitudes, and in interpreting previously obtained quantitative results. Focus groups have been used with citizens to assess the quality of city services and to identify priorities for future activities; with groups of clients of rehabilitation programs to assess current services and explore the types of programs that are most effective; with top-level city administrators to obtain input to a planned survey of citizens; with employees to find out about and improve their working environment.[29] Although focus groups often are used in exploratory studies and as adjuncts to other forms of research, they can be used as the major procedure without being supplemented by quantitative methods.[30]

A health needs assessment in a rural county of North Carolina is one example of how focus groups can be used. Administrators and researchers chose focus groups as a nonthreatening way to obtain perceptions of health, health-related behaviors, and service delivery in the county. The researchers were advised specifically not to use surveys: "These people have been surveyed to death. They're tired of being asked if they are poor."[31]

The county was fragmented by its geography, numerous neighborhoods, and variety of agencies and schools. Researchers conducted 40 focus groups ranging in size from 3 to 37 individuals, greatly exceeding the optimal size of 8 usually recommended.[32] The sessions were not recorded. A two-person team of facilitators conducted the sessions, with one team member moderating and the other taking notes. The focus groups provided important data, involved residents in the project, and helped legitimize the research and its resulting interventions. Members of the groups were asked six questions addressing health problems and potential solutions. Participants were also given a copy of the questions to provide an opportunity for a written, private response. This proved to be useful. The focus-group data were combined with statistics on disease rates; mortality; causes of death and injuries; and with demographic, economic, and social data supplied by state and federal agencies to plan new services and to improve existing services and facilities. Cultural differences among residents and differences in values between the more traditional, longtime residents and the younger health care professionals were identified in the process.

META-ANALYSIS

Meta-analysis is a systematic technique to locate, retrieve, review, summarize, and analyze a set of existing quantitative studies.[33] Researchers conduct meta-analysis to draw general conclusions from several empirical studies on a given program or policy; develop support for hypotheses that merit further testing; and identify characteristics of a program, its environment, or its clients that are associated with effectiveness.

Imagine you want to learn if early childhood education programs for disadvantaged children, such as Head Start, are successful. You probably will begin by reviewing the literature. Assume you find 10 recent research articles examining the effectiveness of different programs. You identify similar and dissimilar findings among these studies. As you classify the findings, you may compare program clients, note how cases were chosen for analysis, note how program success is defined and measured, and record any unique features in the program or the research. If the findings are dissimilar, you may look for an explanation as to why they differ. Differences in program features or in the conduct of research may account for dissimilar findings. If the findings are similar, you may ask whether the program would seem as effective if the research methodology were different. Or you may question whether the program would be as effective with other groups or in other locations.

Proponents of meta-analysis argue simple reviews of literature such as described above are ineffective for arriving at conclusions about research results such as the effectiveness of Head Start. A researcher cannot summarize a large number of studies effectively, much less understand and interpret how they are integrated. If a subset of studies is selected for closer analysis, the reviewer's selection of studies may be colored by his own biases. In reviewing even 10 studies, the researcher may be unable to avoid inconsistent judgments. He may focus on sampling problems in one study and errors in data analysis in another.[34]

Meta-analysis, on the other hand, enables investigators to review a large body of literature and to integrate its findings. Meta-analysis requires the researcher to focus on the same specific components of every study analyzed. If you read a description of a meta-analysis, you should be able to repeat the researchers' steps and to come to the same conclusions. Unlike literature reviews, meta-analysis uses quantitative procedures in synthesizing the results of several studies.[35]

In conducting a meta-analysis, investigators record the same information from each study. Their goal is to identify hypotheses that are supported in study after study. In doing this they have to eliminate alternative explanations, such as chance, which may account for the observed relationships. The analysts record the statistical information reported on the dependent variables of interest and the statistical relationships between independent and dependent variables. They also record information on the study itself, such as the dates of data collection and of publication; who the research subjects were; how they were selected; the research design; evidence that research involved sound measures; and the type of publication, for example, a book, an academic journal, or an unpublished paper.

Once the data are collected, the investigators integrate the findings to create one database. To clarify the meaning of "integrating the findings," we consider two examples. In one meta-analysis, analysts examined 261 citizen surveys. They identified survey questions that asked people to rate specific urban services such as trash collection, and they categorized the questions by the type of service being rated. Neither the question wording nor the possible responses were identical. The analysts ignored variations in question wording and created a common scale so that responses to similar questions from different cities could be combined. After the data were combined, the investigators observed that citizens in cities throughout the United States gave the highest ratings to arts programs and public safety and the lowest ratings to planning.[36]

Integrating study findings goes beyond quantifying specific dependent variables. Analysts also identify relevant independent variables and incorporate them into a common database The second meta-analysis examined studies on survey response rates. Analysts identified 115 studies to evaluate strategies to improve the response rate for mail surveys published between 1940 and 1987, with response rate as the dependent variable. Across the studies, the analysts identified 17 different independent variables. Each of these variables had been tested in at least three studies. After detailed analysis, the investigators identified two factors that increased response rate to mail surveys, including a cover letter with an appeal to respond and keeping a questionnaire short (under five pages).[37]

Meta-analysis allows one to "see" a body of research rather than focus on the quality of individual studies. A researcher may be skeptical if a hypothesis is supported only in poor-quality studies. On the other hand, findings may have even greater credibility if a hypothesis is supported no matter what the quality of a study's methodology. Information on the dates of data gathering and publication help identify trends and changes in them. For example, the investigators in the response-rate study found that beginning in the mid-1970s, preliminary notification of subjects improved response rate.

A major problem in meta-analysis is locating a set of studies. At a minimum the topic must have been of interest long enough for a research history to develop. Little or no research may exist on a current, "hot" research topic. The researcher conducting a meta-analysis wants to include all appropriate studies or a representative sample of such studies in his analysis. Consequently, he must do a relatively exhaustive literature search. If he selects articles from a few journals or from a short time period, he runs the risk of working with a biased sample.

Each article selected does not have to include exactly the same dependent variables nor study the same relationships. Of the 261 cities whose citizen surveys were analyzed, 70 percent rated their police. Fewer than 25 percent rated animal control or street lighting. The independent variables used in the response-rate study varied from study to study.

Critics of meta-analysis point to the problems introduced by biased article selection. Let's go back to our early childhood education example, where 10 publications were studied. First, we mentioned the problem of bias, introduced if the studies analyzed do not represent the larger body of studies conducted on early childhood education. A critic may raise the related question of the "file drawer." The argument goes as follows. If many studies of a subject are done, chance alone will cause some hypotheses to be supported and the research reporting them to be published. Analysts who include only published studies may have a biased sample because many other unpublished studies on the same topic may be stashed in researchers' file drawers. Researchers put studies aside when preliminary data fail to support the hypotheses, and the study seems to be going nowhere. A statistical solution to this problem requires the analyst to calculate how many unpublished papers have to exist for the findings to be contradicted.[38]

Another criticism of meta-analysis has been termed the "apples and oranges" problem. The critics argue against combining dissimilar studies. Consider the citizen-survey data in which findings based on different question wording and different response patterns were grouped together to create a variable. G. V. Glass, a major proponent of meta-analysis, argues that these critics want replication of research, not comparison of similar findings. Meta-analysis is intended to mine information from related, but not identical, studies. Furthermore, he argues that combining different studies is not much different from combining responses from different subjects.[39]

Meta-analysis may seem deceptively simple. Yet it is time consuming to identify the appropriate studies and to conduct the data analysis. Understanding the quantitative procedures used to synthesize results requires statistical knowledge. Readers who wish to try their hand at meta-analysis should be familiar with the statistics discussed in this text, particularly in Chapters 12, 13, and 14. Then they should review one or more of the books included at the end of the reference section for this chapter. They should read several meta-analysis studies for examples. Given the amount of research literature available and the difficulty and expense of researching some topics, a good meta-analysis may be a very efficient alternative to large-scale original research.

SUMMARY

In this chapter we have discussed designs that guide studies describing the occurrence of a variable or the relationship between variables. These designs help a researcher to decide when to make observations and how many observations to make. The design selected may depend on the nature of the dataset or the problem-solving skills of the administrator.

Time-series and cross-sectional designs are particularly effective and efficient designs. Either singly or in combination with each other, they provide valuable information to administrators, legislators, and the public. The data derived from both designs may be organized to communicate information quickly through graphs or tables. Cross-sectional designs show relationships among variables of interest at one point in time. Cross-sectional designs often call for the collection of many pieces of data. Innumerable investigators may access, manipulate, and analyze the resulting database according to their individual interests.

Time-series designs demonstrate long-term, cyclical, and seasonal trends and identify irregular fluctuations in the occurrence of a variable. A time-series design requires an investigator to collect data on a measure at regular intervals. To distinguish between random and nonrandom irregular fluctuations, a historical record of events that can affect the occurrence of the variable is needed. Time-series designs help a researcher to describe a variable over time. They may forecast changes in a variable and assist in making operational decisions. For example, knowing the seasonal variations in arrests allows a court administrator to make staffing assignments.

With longitudinal designs investigators follow individual cases and obtain information on them for several time periods. This design allows investigators to measure the changes taking place within a group as well as to measure the change in a group characteristic over time.

Several qualitative approaches provide useful information for administrators. Case studies provide detail that shows how something happened and why it happened. Case studies usually include information on the natural surroundings of events. One of the strengths of case studies is that they can involve multiple sources of data. Because of the requirement for multiple data sources, we suspect that most administrators and their staff have neither the time nor resources to conduct case studies.

Nevertheless, administrators may be interested in case-study findings and how to use them if a particular case study turns out to be more than just a good story. To determine the quality of a case study, the administrator looks for evidence the investigator had a research question and model before collecting data, the case was clearly defined—which can at times be difficult—and case-study procedures were documented thoroughly.

Focus-group interviewing is used to obtain detailed information from a small group of individuals. A moderator asks a well-developed set of questions and leads the discussion in the focus group. The responses of the participants to the questions and to each other's comments provide data difficult to obtain with other methods. Focus groups often are used to supplement more quantitative studies, such as those using cross-sectional designs, and have many uses in the public sector.

Meta-analysis allows researchers to assemble a set of similar studies, use their data to form a single dataset, and determine what, if any, general hypotheses have been supported consistently. The major difficulty in performing meta-analysis is to identify a representative set of studies. It behooves the researcher to search through many sources to identify appropriate published and unpublished research. The conclusions reached through meta-analysis require thorough statistical analysis in order to provide evidence either supporting a hypothesis or arguing that it could have occurred by chance.

NOTES

1. The issue of causality in cross-sectional and time-series designs is discussed briefly in Chapters 3 and 14, and further references are cited. Robert K. Yin discusses using case studies to infer causality in *Applications of Case Study Research* (Newbury Park, CA: Sage, 1993) and in *Case Study Research: Design and Methods*, 2d ed. (Thousand Oaks, CA: Sage, 1994).

2. M. Specter, "Suicide Rate of Jail Inmates Rising Sharply," *Washington Post*, February 18, 1985, A–1, 18. For recent data see Bureau of Justice Statistics at www. ojp. usdoj. gov/ bjs/.

3. B. Braddy et al., "An Evaluation of CETA Adult Training Programs in North Carolina Division of Employment and Training" (Raleigh: Department of Political Science and Public Administration, May 1983). Unpublished manuscript.

4. See J. C. Bailar III, "When Research Results are in Conflict," *New England Journal of Medicine*, October 24, 1985, pp. 1080–1081. Summary of research results reported in "Studies Reach Opposite Conclusions About How Estrogen Pills Affect Heart," *Raleigh News and Observer*, October 24, 1985, 1A.

5. Biochemical chemical research suggested that the estrogen improves cholesterol levels, decreasing the probability of heart disease. Biochemical research also suggested that estrogen increases blood clotting, increasing the probability of heart disease.

6. A similar graph for the years 1960 through 1980 accompanied N. D. Kristol's article, "Scholars Disagree on Connection between Crime and the Jobless," *Washington Post*, August 7, 1982, which discusses further the relationship between the two variables.

7. Time-series analysis may involve much smaller intervals, e.g., hours and days. These intervals will show analogous patterns. For the sake of clarity we have focused on longer time intervals; we assume that readers who

are dealing with other intervals will be able to interpret their data.

8. Steven D. Levitt, "Understanding Why Crime Fell in the 1990s: Four Factors That Explain the Decline Plus Six That Do Not," *Journal of Economic Perspectives* 18 (Winter 2004): 163–190.

9. R. J. Erickson and K. M. Balzar, *Summary and Interpretation of Crime in the United States, 2001 Uniform Crime Report, Federal Bureau of Investigation, Released October 28, 2002* (San Diego: Athena Research Corp., 2003).

10. Scott Menard, *Longitudinal Research*, 2d ed. (Thousand Oaks, CA: Sage, 2002), 2. In practice panel designs may be referred to as "longitudinal" designs. Someone using the data will want to check the documentation.

11. Julian Simon and Paul Burstein, *Basic Research Methods in Social Science*, 3d ed. (New York: Random House, 1985), 161–162.

12. Morton Hunt, *Profiles of Social Research* (New York: Russell Sage Foundation, 1985), 209.

13. Up-to-date information on the study and its design is at http://www.clinicaltrials.gov/ct/show/NCT00005121. To locate articles reporting analysis of the Framingham data, consult the Science Citation Index and the Social Science Index.

14. Robert F. Boruch and Robert W. Pearson discuss in detail the advantages and disadvantages of panel designs. See "Assessing the Quality of Longitudinal Surveys," *Evaluation Review* 12 (1988): 3–18. Menard's chapter 4 also covers the issues in panel designs.

15. Norvelle Glenn, *Cohort Analysis*, 2d ed. (Thousand Oaks, CA: Sage, 2005).

16. See Glenn, *Cohort Analysis*, for information on analyzing panel data.

17. For example, see M. Patton, *How To Use Qualitative Methods in Evaluation* (Newbury Park, CA: Sage, 1987); and P. Haas and J. Springer, *Case Studies in Applied Policy Research* (New York: Garland Publishing, 1996).

18. J. Creswell, *Research Design: Qualitative and Quantitative Approaches* (Thousand Oaks, CA: Sage, 1994), 145.

19. S. Caudle, "Using Qualitative Approaches," in J. Wholey, H. Hatry, and K. Newcomer, eds., *Handbook of Practical Program Evaluation* (San Francisco: Jossey-Bass, 1994), 69–95. Also see H. Rubin and I. Rubin, *Qualitative Interviewing: The Art of Hearing Data* (Thousand Oaks, CA: Sage, 1995).

20. Robert K. Yin, *Applications of Case Study Research*, 3d ed. (Thousand Oaks, CA: Sage, 2003), 12–15.

21. For a view of how managers obtain knowledge through the use of stories, see Ralph P. Hummel, "Stories Managers Tell: Why They Are as Valid as Science," *Public Administration Review* 51 (January/February 1991), 31–41.

22. See Charles C. Ragin and Howard S. Becker, *What Is a Case? Exploring the Foundations of Social Inquiry* (Cambridge, England: Cambridge University Press, 1992).

23. Robert K. Merton, "The Focused Interview and Focus Groups," *Public Opinion Quarterly* 51 (1987), 550–566; R. K. Merton, M. Fiske, and P. Kendall, *The Focused Interview*, 2d ed. (Glencoe, IL: The Free Press, 1990); Richard A. Kreuger, *Focus Groups: A Practical Guide for Applied Research*, 2d ed. (Thousand Oaks, CA: Sage, 1994), 7–15.

24. Ralph Hambrick, Jr., and James McMillan, "Using Focus Groups in the Public Sector," *Journal of Management Science and Policy Analysis* 6 (Summer 1989), 44.

25. Ibid., 48.

26. David Morgan, *The Focus Group Guidebook* (Thousand Oaks, CA: Sage, 1997), 29.

27. Ibid., 31.

28. Hambrick and McMillan, "Using Focus Groups in the Public Sector," 44–45.

29. These and other examples are cited in Hambrick and McMillan, "Using Focus Groups in the Public Sector," 46–47. Also see Christopher McKenna, "Using Focus Groups to Study Library Utilization," *Journal of Management Science and Policy Analysis* 7 (Summer 1990), 316–329.

30. David Morgan and Richard Krueger, "When to Use Focus Groups and Why," in Morgan, ed., *Successful Focus Groups: Advancing the State of the Art* (Newbury Park, CA: Sage, 1993), 3–19. Also see Debra L. Dean, "How To Use Focus Groups," in J. S. Wholey, H. Hatry, and K. Newcomer, eds., *Handbook of Practical Program Evaluation* (San Francisco: Jossey-Bass, 1994), 341.

31. T. Plaut, S. Landis, and J. Trevor, "Focus Groups and Community Mobilization: A Case Study from Rural North Carolina," in Morgan, *Successful Focus Groups: Advancing the State of the Art* (Newbury Park, CA: Sage, 1993), 205.

32. Ibid., 206.

33. D. Cordray and R. Fischer, "Synthesizing Evaluation Findings," in Wholey, Hatry, and Newcomer, *Handbook of Practical Program Evaluation*, 202.

34. For more details on the limitations of traditional reviews of the literature, see F. M. Wolf, *Meta-Analysis: Quantitative Methods for Research Synthesis* (Beverly Hills: Sage Publications, *Quantitative Applications in the Social Sciences*, no. 59, 1986), 10–11, and J. E. Hunter, F. L. Schmidt, and G. B. Jackson, *Meta-Analysis: Cumulating Research Findings Across Studies* (Beverly Hills: Sage Publications; *Studying Organizations: Innovations in Methodology Series*, no. 4, 1981), 129–130.

35. D. Cordray and R. Fischer, "Synthesizing Evaluation Findings," in Wholey, Hatry, and Newcomer, *Handbook of Practical Program Evaluation*, 200–206.

36. T. I. Miller and M. A. Miller, "Standards of Excellence: U.S. Residents' Evaluations of Local Government Services," *Public Administration Review* (November/December 1991), 503–514.

37. F. J. Yammarino, S. J. Skinner, and T. L. Childers, "A Meta-Analysis of Mail Surveys," *Public Opinion Quarterly* (Winter 1991), 613–639.

38. R. Rosenthal, *Judgment Studies: Design, Analysis, and Meta-Analysis* (New York: Cambridge University Press, 1987), 223–225.

39. G. V. Glass, B. McGaw, and M. L. Smith, *Meta-Analysis in Social Research* (Beverly Hills: Sage, 1981), 220.

TERMS FOR REVIEW

research methodology
research designs
cross-sectional design
longitudinal design
time-series designs
long-term trends

cyclical variations
seasonal variations
random variations
nonrandom variations
quantitative studies
qualitative studies

panel design
cohort
case study
focus group
meta-analysis

QUESTIONS FOR REVIEW

The following questions should indicate whether you have a basic competency in this chapter's material.

1. What is the value of a research design?
2. a. List the advantages and disadvantages of cross-sectional, time series, longitudinal studies, and case studies.
   b. When should an investigator use a panel design instead of a time-series design?
   c. Under what conditions would a focus group be the best method to use?
3. Select one of the following topics: automobile accidents, water quality, drug abuse, homeless persons, single-parent families, management information systems, personnel training, strategic management, or outsourcing. For the selected topic, describe a research question appropriate to a cross-sectional design, a panel design, a time-series design, a case study, a focus group. If you like, also describe a setting or situation in which the research question would be investigated.
4. Update the data in Figure 2.1 using the *Statistical Abstract of the United States* or an online data source. Draw a graph to show the time series as in Figure 2.1.
5. Data have been collected annually on air quality in Smokey for the past 15 years.

Explain why the data can be analyzed using a time-series design. What types of trends or variations should a researcher look for? How might a researcher distinguish random variations from nonrandom variations?

6. The Metro Hospital collected data on nurses every three years from 1985 to 1996. Beginning with 1996, the data were collected every year. What limitations would an analyst encounter in studying nursing trends from 1975 to the present?
7. Explain why public agencies are unlikely to conduct case studies.
8. Distinguish between units and components in conducting a case study.
9. For one of the topics in Question 3, generate a list of questions that might be asked of members of a focus group.
10. Why might government agencies use focus groups more now than in the past? What objections might managers have to the use of focus groups?
11. Compare literature reviews to meta-analyses, and discuss why researchers would invest time in conducting a meta-analysis instead of original research.

PROBLEMS FOR HOMEWORK AND DISCUSSION

1. For each of the following studies, identify the variables; state the implied hypothesis(es); identify the research design, and briefly evaluate its appropriateness. (Note: A study may modify a common design or combine features from more than one design.)

   a. A random audit of Unemployment Insurance (UI) sampled eight UI payments per week. If a payment error was found, auditors determined the dollar amount and classified the error by type, source, and cause. Errors were categorized as overpayment with fraud, overpayment without fraud, or underpayment. Sources of errors were the claimant, employer, or agency. Causes were identified by law or regulation violation.

   b. To evaluate the effectiveness of Head Start, an early education program, children who had been in Head Start and who were in the first through third grades were given cognitive tests.

   c. Before the adoption of the Magnuson-Moss Warranty Act, the Federal Trade Commission collected data from 4,300 respondents who had purchased a major durable good the previous year. Each respondent rated the performance and servicing of products purchased during the year. The 4,300 members of the sample were randomly selected from a national consumer mail panel. To evaluate the act, the Commission later asked 8,000 respondents drawn from the same national consumer mail panel the same questions.

   d. To develop a statistical base on private foundations, data were gathered from tax records on selected foundations' resources and expenses in 1987, 1994, 1998, and annually beginning in 2001.

   e. To assess training needs and how the government could work best with a private agency to meet them, the private agency invited two groups of its clients to participate in discussions led by a moderator from the nearby university.

2. The following figures report the percent of high school seniors who have smoked in the previous 30 days.

Year	Percent of High School Seniors Who Have Smoked
1976	38.8
1977	38.4
1978	36.7
1979	34.4
1980	30.5
1981	29.4
1982	30.0
1983	30.3
1984	29.3
1985	30.1
1986	29.6
1987	29.4
1988	28.7
1989	28.6
1990	29.4
1991	28.3
1992	27.8
1993	29.9
1994	31.2
1995	33.5
1996	34.0
1997	36.5
1998	35.1
1999	29.5
2000	26.7
2001	24.4
2002	34.6
2003	31.4
2004	25.0
2005	23.2

Draw a graph to illustrate this trend over time. Comment on the variations found in this dataset. What policy recommendations can be made based on these data? (Data from Institute for Social Research, University of Michigan, Monitoring the Future Project.)

| TABLE 2.3 | UNEMPLOYMENT RATE |

	Oct.	Nov.	Dec.	Jan.	Feb.	Mar.	Apr.	May	Jun.	Jul.	Aug.	Sep.
Year 1	6.8%	5.5%	5.0%	6.4%	6.3%	6.4%	5.4%	6.7%	6.4%	6.5%	6.7%	8.1%
Year 2	7.9	7.5	7.3	7.7	7.1	8.6	7.9	7.3	7.7	7.5	7.8	8.2
Year 3	9.2	9.5	9.5	10.4	9.5	8.9	8.4	8.7	8.8	8.2	8.2	8.1
Year 4	8.6	8.1	7.5	7.4	6.1	5.4	5.7	6.1	6.6	6.8	6.2	6.2

3. An administrator for a state employment commission wants to study seasonal variations in the unemployment rate so she can schedule staff vacations and conferences at times when the demand for services (as measured by the unemployment rate) is lowest. The data are shown in Table 2.3.
   a. Graph the data.
   b. Comment on any trends you notice in these data.
   c. What times of year would you prefer for staff vacations and conferences?

4. For each of the following problems, suggest a research design and justify your choice:
   a. Identify revenues generated by a county sales tax first adopted in 1980 and increased periodically since then.
   b. Learn whether change in state penalties for drunk driving was associated with fewer drinking-related traffic fatalities.
   c. Identify what computer hardware and software are used by local governments and how the governments use them.
   d. See whether consolidating purchasing by Middletown decreased costs of buying supplies.
   e. See whether agency managers who attended a decision-making seminar used the skills taught.
   f. Determine whether police personnel involved in a wellness program took fewer sick days and had fewer claims against the department's health insurance plan after enrolling in the wellness program.

5. A state has 10 high school health clinics. These clinics have been opened within the last four years to serve the physical and mental health needs of high school students. Some of the clinics are located within a high school, and others are within a block of the school. The state Department of Education has decided to do a case study of these clinics to evaluate their performance and to see whether similar clinics should be established throughout the state. (In answering the following questions you may make your own assumptions to fill in specific details about the clinics.)
   a. Identify the units and components that could be the subjects of the case study. What information would you want on the units? on the components?
   b. List possible data sources you would use. Indicate the type of information you would want from each data source.
   c. Write a memorandum discussing why a case study would be a valuable research strategy.

6. Look at Example 1.3 in Chapter 1. Assume that you are a management analyst in the department administering the job-training program. Write a memorandum to the program manager outlining what actions you would recommend based on these data. Remember that conducting further research can be a recommended action.

7. Locate a study or article that you would classify as a meta-analysis, and attempt to answer the following questions concerning it. What was the topic? How many studies were reviewed? Was a specific hypothesis investigated in the meta-analysis? What did the authors of the meta-analysis conclude from the study?

DISK WORK

1. Load the ORB Research Methods dataset from the data disk. Analyze the data to see how income, population density, and the number of active primary care physicians varies by region of the state. Report your findings in a table. To simplifying your task you may want to create three groups for each different variable. Write a paragraph summarizing your findings.

2. Cross-sectional data can be reported in tables showing differences in percents or means. Go to the disk and load the ORB Research Methods dataset. From the income variable, create three categories of counties, for example, high income, medium income, and low income.

   a. For each county income category, calculate the mean values for the number of child abuse and neglect cases, number of individuals served in drug and alcohol facilities, and the crime index variables. Do the data show that these items vary across low, medium, and high income counties? What evidence supports your observations? Write a paragraph reporting your findings.

   b. Categorize the variables number of child abuse and neglect cases, number of individuals served in drug and alcohol facilities, and the crime index into two groups, a high and a low category. For each of the three income categories, what percent of the observations fall into the various high categories for each variable? What percent fall into the low categories? In this analysis, do the data show that the items vary by income? Do these findings support the findings you had in 2(a)? Write a paragraph reporting your findings.

   c. Of the two options, that used in 2(a), comparing the means, and the one used in 2(b), comparing percents, which way of presenting this information would you recommend using in a report on this issue? Justify your choice.

3. Go to the disk and load the OSB Research Methods dataset to test the hypotheses that you formulated as part of the Chapter 1 exercise. Do the data support your hypotheses? Cite evidence to support your answer.

4. Go to the disk and load the OSB Research Methods dataset. Sort the data according to crime index, from lowest to highest. Plot this as a series. In a short paragraph, describe the pattern you see in the data. Do the same with population. Compare the pattern to the one for crime index. What can you conclude?

RECOMMENDED FOR FURTHER READING

See the references listed at the end of Chapter 7 for information on cross-sectional designs.

A good place to find information on time series, especially as a forecasting tool, is in management science texts. One widely available text is D. R. Anderson, D. J. Sweeney, and T. A. Williams, *Quantitative Methods for Business*, 10th ed. (Mason, OH: Thomson South-Western, 2006), chap. 6. Also, D. W. Williams, "Forecasting Methods for Serial Data," *Handbook of Research Methods in Public Administration*, eds. G. L. Miller and M. L. Whicker (New York: Marcel Dekker, 1999), pp. 301–352.

For a discussion of various types of longitudinal designs, see Scott Menard, *Longitudinal Research*, 2d ed. (Thousand Oaks, CA: Sage, 2002).

Robert K. Yin, *Case Study Research: Design and Methods*, 3d ed. (Thousand Oaks, CA: Sage, 2003) is an excellent starting point for information on case studies. This chapter's section on case studies made extensive use of Yin's book. *Applications of Case Study Research* (Newbury Park, CA: Sage, 2003) by the same author provides detailed examples of case studies.

For more information on focus groups, see the references listed at the end of Chapter 7, especially Richard Krueger and Mary Anne Casey, *Focus Groups: A Practical Guide for Applied Research*, 3d ed. (Thousand Oaks, CA: Sage, 2000). For a more advanced and analytical presentation, see Edward E. Fern, *Advanced Focus Group Research* (Thousand Oaks, CA: Sage, 2001).

The reader interested in meta-analysis should review G. V. Glass, B. McGaw, and M. L. Smith, *Meta-Analysis in Social Research* (Beverly Hills: Sage, 1981). T. D. Cook, et al., eds., *Meta-analysis for Explanation: A Casebook* (New York: Russell Sage Foundation, 1992) has four chapters on the method and four studies. Also highly recommended is Morton Hunt, *How Science Takes Stock: The Story of Meta-Analysis* (New York: Russell Sage Foundation, 1997). Hunt discusses how agencies of the American national government are using meta-analysis more frequently, especially in areas of medical research.

CHAPTER 3

Designs for Explanation

In this chapter you will learn

1. The evidence necessary to establish that two variables are causally related.

2. The questions to ask to evaluate empirical evidence that a program or treatment caused an outcome.

3. The questions to ask to determine whether findings can be generalized to cases other than the research subjects.

4. The common experimental and quasi-experimental designs to infer causality.

5. The characteristics about nonexperimental designs and their value.

If an administrator wants to go beyond describing the values of a dependent variable and explain why it changes or differs from case to case, he needs to show that an independent variable is causally related to the dependent variable. Often the administrator wants to show that some independent variable, such as a program activity, affected a dependent variable, such as nutrition, health care, level of absenteeism, and so forth. For example, the manager of the Women, Infants and Children (WIC) program may want to determine if this program improved infant nutrition. Simply demonstrating a decrease in the percent of malnourished infants is insufficient evidence that the WIC program is responsible. Instead, the manager needs a research design that unambiguously links the WIC program to the outcome of decreased malnutrition.

The administrator may be able to demonstrate with descriptive designs that two variables are linked to each other. That is, he may be able to show that they are associated. However, the administrator may want to go further and demonstrate that one variable caused another. When we say that X has caused a change in Y, we mean that a change in the value of the dependent variable, Y, comes about as a result of a change in the independent variable, X, and not as a result of something else.[1] If one variable causes another, an investigator expects to find a statistical relationship between them. For example, the manager of a city's rapid transit program may want to demonstrate that reducing fares increased ridership. Simply demonstrating that the number of riders per day increases following a fare reduction is insufficient evidence that the fare reduction was responsible. He would also need to show that the number of riders would have been less or stayed the same without the fare decrease.

To establish a causal relationship requires more than just a relationship between two variables. One of the real difficulties in determining whether public programs have had their intended impact is to separate the changes that may be due to other factors from changes that are due to the program. For example, an increase in the price of gasoline or construction on a major highway may encourage more people to use public transit. Or, to return to the earlier example of the WIC program, if the number of undernourished infants decreased after the WIC program started, the reduction may have been due to something else, perhaps a general improvement in the state's economy and more jobs in the community. To say that it reduced infant malnutrition, an investigator would need to demonstrate that without WIC, infant malnutrition would have been greater than it was with the program.

To claim *causality*, that one variable causes another, requires the following:

1. A statistical association of the two variables: The variables covary with each other or a change in one variable is accompanied by a change in the other.
2. The sequential order of the variables: The independent variable—the presumed cause—must have occurred before the dependent variable—the presumed result or effect.
3. The elimination of rival independent variables as causes of the dependent variable: Variables other than the independent variable of interest must be ruled out as causes of the dependent variable.
4. A theoretical link between the independent and dependent variable: The analyst should have some logical argument for assuming that two variables covary.

Descriptive designs begin the process of translating administrative concerns and program dynamics into quantitative information. They yield findings that alone or in combination with other information support action or prevent unnecessary further study. Cross-sectional, time-series, and case-study designs produce data that identify variables worth further study. Cross-sectional and time-series designs identify relationships among variables and describe changes in variables over time. They may incorporate sophisticated statistical analysis to build complex mathematical models that provide strong evidence of causal links between variables. Still, policy makers and administrators may want more conclusive evidence that an independent variable causes a value of a dependent variable, especially if they need to determine whether a program has achieved its intended objectives. To gain such evidence, they prefer to have a design that incorporates as many components of an experimental design as possible.

An *experimental design* is one in which the researcher can assign subjects to different research groups and control who is exposed to the independent variable, when they are exposed to it, and the conditions under which the experiment takes place. Since this kind of control seldom is possible in administrative work, administrative studies rely on *quasi-experimental designs*. These designs lack some of the characteristics of experiments and some of the control afforded with them. The researcher may need to rely on a naturally occurring independent variable or base her comparisons on naturally occurring groups over which she has no control. Both quasi-experimental and nonexperimental designs limit the researcher's ability to judge the impact of an independent variable. Researchers often distinguish between true experiments and other experimental designs.[2] A true experiment is one with the characteristics noted above.

We can never prove conclusively that one variable causes another. Nevertheless, having a model and showing that the variables are related statistically, that the independent variable occurs before the dependent variable, and that rival independent variables have been ruled out make a convincing case for a causal relationship. Experimental designs provide a means of obtaining this evidence. When a researcher cannot implement an experimental design, a quasi-experimental design may be used. In this chapter we present two experimental and three quasi-experimental designs useful in administration and policy research.

INTERNAL AND EXTERNAL VALIDITY

In evaluating the results of a program, a manager looks for a relationship between the program implementation, the independent variable, and some hoped-for results—the dependent variable. Typically, the manager wants to know if the program caused a change in some condition. As we have already suggested, a change in the target condition or population accompanied by a program change does not mean that the program change was the cause. Thus additional evidence is necessary to determine whether lower fares by the transit system or the efforts of WIC, respectively, contributed to an increase in the number of riders over a given time period and to less infant malnutrition.

Internal validity refers to the evidence that a specific independent variable, such as a program, policy, or action, caused a change in an observed dependent variable. If an investigator is confident that the independent variable of interest and not something else caused the observed outcomes, the investigator can say that the study was internally valid.

An evaluation of a national 55-mile-per-hour speed-limit law adopted by Congress in 1973 found that a reduction in speed was accompanied by a reduction in the number of traffic deaths. The conclusion that the change in speed limit caused a change in fatalities is internally valid only if the investigators were able to show that no other plausible factor caused the reduction in traffic deaths. Other factors alone or in combination with the lower speed limit could have caused the reduction. For example, an increase in the price of gasoline may have caused people to drive less.

External validity of a study speaks to the issue of generalizing the findings of a study beyond the specific cases involved. Typically, not all people involved in or affected by a program are studied. Only a portion are included in a study, and the investigator wants to know about the entire group. Let us say that we had established for a sample of WIC program participants that the program had reduced undernourishment in children. Would this be true of all WIC participants? Would programs similar but not identical to WIC have the same results? Assume that we determine from a study conducted in North Dakota that the 55-mile-per-hour speed limit reduced fatal traffic accidents. Would these results be true of other states or of the nation as a whole? These examples and questions all concern external validity.

In considering external validity researchers are usually concerned about generalizing in one or more of three different ways. These are (1) generalizing from a sample to a larger population, (2) generalizing from one research situation or study to another, and (3) generalizing from a research study to a real-world situation.[3] This last case is often the one when the programs of government or a non-profit agency are adopted by other organizations. A specific program in a specific location is evaluated to find out if it works. However, administrators may want to know that it would work in other locations or under different conditions.

Investigators also are concerned with validity when measuring variables. We refer to this type of validity as *operational validity* and discuss it in Chapter 4. As a general concept, validity has to do with whether or not we are making correct assumptions about the data and the observed relationships. Operational validity asks if variables have been appropriately and accurately measured. Internal validity asks whether our study procedures allow us to claim that we have identified the cause of a change in a dependent variable. External validity asks whether the results of a study apply to cases not in the study. Any component of a research study that raises doubts about the quality of the research process or the accuracy of the results is a threat to validity.

Threats To Internal Validity

One cannot conclude that a change in one variable is responsible for changes in another unless one has ruled out the possibility that the observed change in the dependent variable was caused by some factor other than the independent variable. These other factors are known as *threats to internal validity*.[4] Each threat identifies a plausible alternative explanation for the observed relationship between the independent and dependent variables. They may be categorized and defined as follows:

History: Events other than the independent variable that could have affected the dependent variable.

Selection: The way that cases are selected for groups or conditions for a program or a study could affect the way they react to the independent variable.

If the cases in the group receiving the intervention are different from those in other groups, then any difference in the dependent variable may be due to differences in the cases and not to the intervention.

Maturation: Natural changes taking place in the units being studied.

Statistical regression: If cases for study or action are picked because of an extreme position, such as a low performance score, the instability of extreme scores may cause the observed change. This is a special case of selection.

Experimental mortality: Cases, particularly people, who begin a study or program may drop out before the study or the program is completed. If they are systematically different from those who remain, the results will not be internally valid.

Testing effects: A situation in which the initial measure or test influences the subjects, which then affects the outcome of the posttest. Employees who score low on a pretest may change their behavior because of this and not because of some program.

Instrumentation: If the measuring instrument used to collect data changes between the beginning of a study and its conclusion, the results may not be valid.

Design contamination: A condition occurring when participants know that they are in a study and act differently because of it or if subjects being compared interact. If study subjects have an incentive to behave in a specific way to make the program succeed or fail, the design has been contaminated.

Threats may occur because the environments of groups being compared are different, either to start with or over time, or because the cases in the groups are systematically different. For example, if younger people, ages 18 to 22 years old, are compared to those who are 25 to 30, any difference between these groups could be due to differences in ages and not due to the intervention.

The threat to internal validity known as *history* arises when events or policies other than the independent variable cannot be ruled out as a source of the changes in the dependent variable. Usually such events are those occurring during the same time as the independent variable. In 1973 an oil embargo brought about a gasoline shortage; gasoline prices soared, long lines were found at gas stations, and Americans drove less. To reduce gas consumption, a national 55-mile-per-hour speed limit was established. Auto fatalities decreased and the national 55-mile-per-hour speed limit continued for more than 20 years. It is entirely possible that the observed reduction in highway fatalities was the result, not of reduced speed, but of less driving. It is also possible that improvements in automobile manufacturing increased the safety of automobiles.

Following the terrorist attacks of September 11, 2001, commentators compared changes in unemployment, consumer confidence, and confidence in government before and after September 11, 2001. Prior to the attacks Americans were receiving tax rebate checks intended to stimulate spending. Policy observers debated if the recipients would spend the rebate money or save it. In the latter case the economy would continue to weaken. Nevertheless, the debate became moot and the effects of the attacks could not be separated from other factors affecting the economy.

Selection is a problem when the basis on which cases are chosen for a study or program condition is nonrandom. In such instances the group of cases in the independent variable condition may be systematically different from the cases to which they are compared. If so, the difference between the groups rather than the influence of the independent variable may account for any observed change in the dependent variable. For example, imagine a study in which eighth grade students are allowed to volunteer for a class using a new method of teaching math. At the end of the semester the math skills of these students are compared to those of eighth graders in the more traditional classes to assess improvement in math skills. The differences in improvement could be due to the differences between those who volunteered and those who did not rather than to the difference in teaching methods. The volunteers may have been more highly motivated to study math.

Also consider the recruitment strategy used by some job-training programs when program survival depended on placement rate. The training staff enrolled highly motivated trainees who already possessed good job skills or high aptitudes. Women on maternity leave from typing jobs were recruited into secretarial training programs and placed successfully, sometimes in jobs they had left. Thus the apparent success of the program resulted from recruiting trainees who were eminently employable. As a result, the apparent success of the program was due to the way the recruits were selected, not to the effect of the training program itself.

Sometimes changes that occur in dependent variables during the course of the study are due to natural processes. The resulting threat to internal validity is called *maturation*. People, groups, and other units of observation change over time. These changes occur naturally, rather than as the result of specific, identifiable events or interventions. One may assume erroneously that an independent variable caused a change in a dependent variable when the change involved would have occurred with the passage of time, regardless of whether the independent variable was present. Most juvenile delinquents, for example, decrease their antisocial behavior as they grow older. Thus the apparent success of delinquency programs may result from the aging of the clientele rather than program activities. If one records the behavior of one group of children in the morning and another group in the afternoon, differences between the groups may not be due to a particular independent variable but to the changes in children's behavior during the course of a day.

A fourth threat is *statistical regression*. Consider an experience most of us have had during school. Early in our academic career, most of us learn that, on the average over time, we receive roughly the same grade in courses or on exams. But on occasion we may be pleasantly surprised by our score on a test. And we may find that on the next test, our score is noticeably lower than on the first. Or we may have a classmate who scores very low, much lower than expected on an exam. On the second exam, she is likely to do better than on the first. Over time, these students' test scores will approach their average performance. In short, any time that we observe a test score that is exceptionally high or exceptionally low for a given student, we usually can predict that that student's next score will be closer to her average.

Social problems show analogous patterns. If a program is created in reaction to an extreme situation, then any subsequent change in the desired direction may occur because of statistical regression. A city with an unusually high number of traffic deaths one month may experience a significant improvement the next. So, a program installed in response to a rash of fatal accidents may appear to have been effective, when in actuality the number of traffic deaths had simply regressed toward the average. The result may have been due to statistical regression, not the program. Statistical regression is a particular threat whenever cases for treatment or study are chosen because of an extreme value on some measure. If the variable is measured again, the cases will be less extreme; they will have regressed toward the average. When cases for a study are chosen because of their extreme values on the dependent variable, statistical regression represents a special case of the threat of selection.

The threat of *experimental mortality* arises when people begin a program and later drop out before the study is completed. The difficulty with this is that dropouts may be different from those who complete the program, and the difference may affect the outcome. If the results are taken as evidence of the success of the program, they may not be valid. It may be that those who are successful stay with the program and those who are not leave. Consider the example of a successful delinquency program whose goal was to keep participants in school. Despite the program's apparent success, it may have been that the youths who dropped out of the program were those who had little motivation to remain in school. Those who continued in school might have done so even if the program had not existed.

Testing effects as a threat to internal validity occur when an initial measurement changes the values of the dependent variable. In some studies an observation is taken before and after the introduction of an independent variable. The observation taken before exposure to the independent variable is called a *pretest*. The observation taken after exposure is the *posttest*. The risk in such a procedure is that the pretest and not the independent variable may have caused an observed change in the dependent variable. For example, a person exposed to a training program to increase knowledge may show increased knowledge from the pretest to the posttest because the pretest stimulated his interest and he looked up the answers. The pretest, not the program, caused this increased knowledge. Oftentimes people do less well with an unfamiliar task; a pretest serves as practice and may improve later performances on the same or similar test. We observed this when the GREs were first given on computers. Students who had not practiced and took the GRE more than once improved their scores between the first and second testing; most likely their familiarity with the new format led to the improved performance. The effect of testing also is known as the *reactivity of measurement*; people react to the measuring process and change their behavior because of it.

Instrumentation is a threat to internal validity when the method of measurement changes between the pretest and the posttest. The instrument used may have changed, or the definition of the variable may have changed. Suppose that the legal definition of a particular crime changed between two measurements of the crime rate. The change in definition alone may make it appear that the crime rate had changed. If a program to reduce the crime rate were initiated during the period between the two observations, we could not be sure whether any recorded change in the crime rate was due to the way crime was measured, to the program, or to both. Investigators using agency records need to be alert as to how variables are defined and records are kept. Changes in these, if unrecognized, can cause problems of instrumentation. Instrumentation is also cited as a threat when different methods are used to measure the dependent variable in the groups being compared.

The final threat to internal validity is known as *design contamination*. Several types of contamination are possible. Subjects exposed to a treatment may talk to those not exposed, and eventually both groups experience the same program or treatment. Consider the director of human resources (HR) who wishes to evaluate a program designed to prepare people for retirement. The program has been offered to some employees on an experimental basis. The HR director wants to know whether employees who participated in the program have fewer economic problems after they retire than those who did not participate. However, if participants had shared the information obtained from the program with their colleagues, both groups might have made similar economic plans, effectively eliminating any difference between participants and nonparticipants. As a result the program would appear to have been unsuccessful. As this example illustrates, one can sometimes falsely assume that an independent and a dependent variable are not related because of a threat to internal validity.

A second type of design contamination occurs when participants guess the purpose of the research and alter their behavior so as to achieve an outcome in their best interests. Suppose a researcher wants to learn whether reducing the size of work crews on sanitation trucks from four persons to two persons will increase productivity. Fearing the breakup of their work units and increased job pressures, the workers might alter their behavior, with the smaller crews slowing down their work rate and the larger crews increasing theirs.

Yet another type of contamination occurs if a group receiving no treatment changes its behavior in the hypothesized direction because of anger or low morale. Imagine a study to determine if assigning mentors to new employees improves their productivity. Employees not selected to participate may become aware of the program and wonder why they were not included. They may assume they are less valued employees and react by decreasing their own productivity. The researcher mistakenly could assume that the mentoring program explains the difference in productivity, whereas the difference actually was caused by the poor morale of the control group.

Whenever you, as an administrator, examine empirical research, you will want to raise questions to identify any potential weaknesses in the study design and, more specifically, threats to the internal validity of the findings. A list of such questions follows. The purpose of these questions is to help you decide whether you should take action based on such findings. If a study concludes that a causal relationship exists between two variables, then you must be reasonably confident that none of the threats to internal validity account for the apparent relationship. Plausibility should be the key word in determining how much weight to put on the failure of a research design to control for any one threat to internal validity.[5] You should ask whether it is plausible that no factor other than the independent variable is the cause. You also should ask whether it is plausible that some factor other than the independent variable was the cause of the dependent variable.

Questions to Ask to Help Evaluate Possible Threats to Internal Validity When Examining Research Reporting a Causal Relationship between Two Variables

1. Based on history: Could an event other than the independent variable have caused this relationship?

2. Based on selection: Were the people exposed to the independent variable systematically different from those not exposed? If subjects were volunteers who could choose which group to be in, could this have affected the findings?

3. Based on maturation: Would a similar change in the dependent variable have taken place with the same passage of time without the occurrence of the independent variable? Could the changes found in the subjects have resulted from natural changes such as maturity, aging, or tiring?

4. Based on statistical regression: Were subjects chosen for the study because of a high or low value of the dependent variable?

5. Based on experimental mortality: Were some people initially exposed to the treatment later assigned to the nontreatment group? Did some people who started the study drop out before finishing?

6. Based on testing: Was a pretest administered that could have affected responses to the posttest? Did the pretest provide practice at performing certain tasks and thus affect the posttest scores?

7. Based on instrumentation: Did the instrument to collect data change between the pretest and the posttest?

8. Based on design contamination: Did the program participants mingle with nonparticipants? Did program participants, nonparticipants, or both have an incentive to change their behavior and make the program succeed or fail?

External Validity

External validity refers to the appropriateness of extending or generalizing research findings to a group beyond that involved in the study. Only the findings of a study that has external validity may be generalized to other cases. Sampling strategy affects the external validity of a design. If research subjects are randomly drawn from a defined group, then the findings should be generalizable to that group, but this by itself is not enough to ensure external validity. External validity also refers to the ability to generalize the results of a study to other places, times, and programs.

An investigator may do a formal study of a program to determine whether the program has had a beneficial or a harmful effect. He first wants to know if the program works. That is the question of internal validity. But he also wants to know if the program will work for others. That is the problem of external validity. The study may be very informal; a manager may simply observe that his program works as he thinks it should. If he or others wish to conclude that the program will work for other groups or in other locations, they must be aware of several external validity problems. Threats to external validity come about because the conditions of the study are not duplicated for cases not in the study. Unique features of the study subjects, the study setting or conditions, and the implementation of the study program itself, as well as the fact that people may know that they are being studied, contribute to problems with external validity.

Threats to external validity include the following:

unique program features

effects of selection

effects of setting

effects of history

effects of testing

reactive effects of experimental arrangements[6]

Sometimes in constructing an experimental study, an entire program is treated as a single independent variable. However, programs typically consist of clusters of several variables. Thus any program may have *unique features* that affect its results. The program may be unsuccessful in the absence of one or more of the unique features. Creators of experimental programs in a controlled environment may be unable to duplicate the results in a natural, nonexperimental setting where they would be most needed. Consider a demonstration project to enable elderly persons to live independently. The project may have staff who are younger, less experienced, more energetic, and in other ways different from staff usually found in ongoing programs housed in social services agencies. The results of the demonstration project may be atypical and not apply to other programs.

Program managers and investigators need to be aware that programs that appear to be similar may be different enough in the way they are implemented to affect how they work. A program for reducing drug use among adolescents may appear to work. A program analyst may then infer that all such programs will work. But external validity must be considered. If the programs were only similar, not exactly the same, the analyst may not be able to generalize from one to the rest. Differences in staff, client interactions, activities, or community dynamics may affect program outcomes.

The *effects of selection* arise as a threat to external validity when the subjects in the study are not representative of others to which we want to apply the results. The group being studied may have responded differently to the program treatment than others who would be likely to participate. The resulting findings are therefore not representative beyond the group being studied. As an example, consider a training program for teachers that is tested on a group of senior career teachers. Even if the results of this experiment are favorable, the program may not work with teachers who are much younger and less experienced.

The project's *location or setting* can threaten external validity. A project based in a hospital may not work as well as one located in a senior citizens' club, simply because the hospital setting may increase feelings of dependency and work against program goals. Or, a program in a New England community may have more success than one in a Southwestern city where community support systems may be weaker.

History can affect external validity in a number of ways. History as a threat to external validity is somewhat different from history as a threat to internal validity. An evaluation of a particular program may be undertaken at a time when clients and the community are unusually receptive to its services. A local scandal about conditions in nursing homes may motivate aged persons and their families to seek alternatives to institutional care. A recent fire in a community may motivate homeowners to respond favorably to an education program presented by the fire department. Other communities whose historical circumstances differ may not respond in the same way. An event that happened prior to the study or during the study may make the community in which the study takes place unique. If that is the case, the ability to generalize the findings to other communities will be limited. You may think of other conditions that make a program work at one time or in one place but not at other times or in other places.

If a pretest given for study purposes affects the subject's receptivity to the program, *testing* poses a threat to external validity. Consider a parent education program. Giving the parents a pretest that asks how to handle a child's behavior may motivate the parents to become involved in the program and achieve its objectives. The pretest may then be a unique feature, and the program will not work in its absence. If a pretest affects the behavior of the study subjects, the results will not necessarily apply to clients who were not pretested. Testing here differs from the threat it poses to internal validity in that, as a threat to external validity, studied subjects are pretested and other likely participants are not. Testing is a threat to internal validity if studied subjects change their behavior as a result of the pretest, not as a result of the program.

Reactive effects of experimental arrangements refers to the fact that study situations often are necessarily artificial, and thus the study setting itself may affect the outcome. If participants know that they are being studied, they may alter their behavior accordingly. The results of such a study could not be transferred to others who were not being studied. Consider a group of community residents recruited to test participation in a voluntary recycling program. Since they know that they are in a study, they may be especially cooperative and work hard to make the program work. (They may also guess that if the voluntary program does not work, recycling may become mandatory.) If the program were to be implemented, the results might not apply to other households.

The reader should note that these problems of external validity can occur in combination with each other. A problem of unrepresentative selection also may involve a problem of setting. If an investigator tested a new program by selecting a specialized group, such as Native American children, and conducted the demonstration program in a town in Tennessee, she would have both of these problems. If the program was meant to apply to all minorities, the selection of only Native Americans may bias the results. The geographical setting also may introduce a bias. Something about the particular town may contribute to the success or failure of the program. When an intervention is successful but only in the presence of one or more of the factors discussed, we refer to the interaction of the intervention with the other factor. The absence of the other factor may severely limit the extent to which results can be generalized to other cases and settings.

External validity can be increased by replicating a program in different settings with different personnel. If a demonstration program seems to have worked in one small town in the state, and a state administrator wants to make sure that it will work throughout the state, his best strategy is to try the same program in other locations and with different-sized towns. If the program is successful in dissimilar towns, the administrator should feel more confident that it will work statewide.

A program conducted initially with a representative sample of the program's target group should increase external validity. However, replicating a program with a number of smaller, haphazardly chosen samples may offer more external validity than conducting a single study with a carefully drawn sample.[7] This argument rests on the likelihood that some program participants will quit; thus, a study starting with a representative sample may not end up with one. Experimental mortality could render the outcome of a single study externally invalid.

One approach is to select subjects who are markedly different, and infer that if the program works for a wide number of different types of test subjects, then it should work for everybody. This strategy, *deliberately sampling for heterogeneity*, could result in demonstration projects targeted at the elderly in an Eastern city, a rural Southern town, and an urban Native American community. In any one study, problems with internal and external validity are unavoidable. Replication of findings under varying experimental conditions offers reasonably sound evidence of a program's transferability.

Descriptive designs such as sample surveys often have high external validity. Experimental designs, on the other hand, have high internal validity but often low external validity. Administrators want to be sure that a program or policy achieves its desired ends, a matter of internal validity, before identifying the various conditions under which it will work, a matter of external validity. As with internal validity, a series of questions should be asked to help evaluate the external validity of a study. A list of such questions follows.

Evaluating External Validity: Questions to Ask to Determine Whether a Relationship between Two Variables Can Be Generalized beyond the Research Subjects

1. What group did the research subjects represent? Were they selected in a way to make them representative of that group? (As we will see in later sections, the best way to guarantee accurate representation is to randomly select the research subjects from the larger group they are to represent.)

2. Did the program or treatment involve demands that may have affected the representativeness of the subjects, such as excessive commitments of time?

3. Has the program been replicated among different types of subjects, in different settings and locations?

4. Exactly what was the program or treatment? Were unplanned or unexamined features, such as personnel or setting, critical to program success?

5. Was the program as offered to the research group different from what will be offered to others?

EXPERIMENTAL DESIGNS

Experimental designs provide the best means of obtaining the evidence necessary to infer the existence of a causal relationship between two well-defined variables. In an experimental design, the researcher can assign subjects to different groups, manipulate the independent variable, and control most environmental influences. The researcher assigns some subjects to the group that is exposed to the independent variable and other subjects to groups that are not. Using random assignment, subjects are assigned so that there is no systematic difference between the groups. If subjects are randomly assigned to groups, any change in the dependent variable should not be due to differences between the study groups. In evaluating studies claiming to have used an experimental design, you should see whether this random assignment was used to help control threats to internal validity. If subjects were randomly selected from a larger population, threats to external validity may have also been controlled.

We discuss two experimental designs in this section, the classical experimental design and the randomized posttest-only design. If you understand them, you should have little trouble understanding more complicated variations. The designs we discuss involve one or two treatment groups. A treatment group is a set of research subjects who are exposed to the independent variable and are then compared on the dependent variable to another group, the control group, whose members have not been exposed to the independent variable.

The *classical experimental design* has long served as the model for experimental research. It allows us to control the time order of exposure to the variables under study, to determine which subjects are exposed to the independent variable, to identify statistical association among variables, and to control for other possible causal factors. Properly utilized, it can provide the strongest evidence of a causal relationship. It is also an excellent model for demonstrating the logic of explanatory designs. Its characteristics include the following:

1. Subjects are randomly assigned to an *experimental* or a *control group* so that no systematic difference exists between the two groups. Random assignment provides that each subject has the same chance as any other subject of being in either the experimental group or the control group.

2. A pretest, measuring the dependent variable, is administered to both groups.

3. The experimental group is exposed to the treatment; the control group is not. Both groups should experience the same conditions, except for exposure to the independent variable. The researcher controls exposure to the independent variable, determining who receives it and who does not.

4. A posttest, which again measures the dependent variable, is administered to both groups following exposure to the independent variable.

5. The amount of change in the dependent variable between the pretest and posttest is determined for each group. The difference between the two groups is attributed to the independent variable.

Note that this design yields the three types of evidence needed to demonstrate that one variable causes another. Like other designs it can provide evidence of a statistical relationship between variables. It allows us to determine whether any changes in the values of the dependent variable take place after exposure to the independent variable; with this information and by controlling exposure to the independent variable, the investigator can rule out the possibility that the values of the dependent variable changed before the independent variable occurred. Random assignment of subjects to experimental or control groups eliminates most rival independent variables, although problems associated with experimental mortality and design contamination may persist. This design has very high internal validity. It may not, however, have high external validity.

The classical experimental design is represented symbolically as follows:

$$RO_1 \ X \ O_2 \ \text{(experimental group)}$$
$$RO_1 \ \ \ \ \ O_2 \ \text{(control group)}$$

where:

R = randomly assigned subjects

O = observation or measurement of dependent variable

X = independent variable occurs

With experimental designs it is important to establish equivalent experimental and control groups and maintain their similarities throughout the experiment. The preferred method of creating equivalent groups is to randomly assign half of a pool of subjects to the experimental group and half to the control group. The theory underlying random assignment is that if enough subjects are used, differences among groups of subjects tend to disappear as long as no bias enters in the way that subjects are assigned to one group or the other. With random assignment, each subject has the same probability of being in either group. Random assignment allows researchers to begin their study by controlling for the threats to validity associated with nonequivalent research groups. Specifically, random assignment controls for selection bias, maturation, testing effects, and statistical regression; however, it only ensures comparability at the initial stage of the research.

An alternative method of assigning subjects is to *match* each individual or unit in the experimental group with an individual or unit in the control group. The researcher identifies characteristics that may affect the dependent variable, gathers data on them in the sample pool, and pairs units with similar characteristics. Subjects that cannot be paired are eliminated from the study. The researcher then randomly assigns one member of the pair to the experimental group and the other to the control group. For example, if she believes that education, sex, and age affect program outcomes, she identifies each subject's education, sex, and age. She then pairs the available subjects; that is, two young (18–29) females who attended college could be a pair, two older males (30–45) with high school degrees could be another pair, and so on. The assignment of the members of the pair to experimental or control groups is random.

Researchers, particularly in the field of medicine, may use matching retrospectively to create comparison groups. For example, researchers match subjects who have a disease with similar persons who do not have the disease. The researchers then try to determine why one group developed the disease and the other did not.

Matching can reduce the number of subjects required because it reduces the variation within the treatment and control groups. Nevertheless, methodologists usually prefer random assignment and seldom recommend matching.[8] With more than four relevant characteristics, matching becomes difficult. It also increases the potential for bias, even if efforts are made to avoid it. Matching may reduce internal validity if it focuses on variables actually unrelated to the dependent variable and ignores variables related to it. Matching assumes that the researcher knows which other variables are related to the dependent variable and, hence, knows which to match. The difficulties that stem from this last assumption are virtually eliminated by random assignment, which assumes that the two groups are equivalent in all respects except for exposure to the independent variable.

Experimental designs generally control for other threats to internal validity. To illustrate this characteristic, let's consider history as a threat to internal validity. Outside events (history) occurring between the pretest and the posttest may not affect internal validity if both experimental and control groups experience the same event. The event is assumed to have a similar effect on each group. If both groups experience the same conditions and events, other than exposure to the independent variable, the independent variable and other factors associated with the threats to internal validity, such as history or maturation, may cause changes in the dependent variable for the experimental group. Changes in the control group dependent variable may be attributed to a threat such as history, maturation, or another threat. The posttest differences between the experimental and control groups may then be attributed to the independent variable.

Example 3.1 summarizes an experiment structured along the lines of a classical experimental design to determine whether a training program increased the empathy of first-year medical students. Students assigned to the control group received the same small-group training immediately after the experiment was

---

 EXAMPLE 3.1

Using a Classical Experiment Design in the Field

Problem: Determine if small-group discussions increase medical students' ability to respond to the emotional concerns of patients.

Subjects: 134 first-year medical students registered for Medical Interviewing and History Taking. Students were randomly assigned to a small group (65 students) or a control group (69 students).

Independent variable (treatment): Small groups of approximately 16 students and a professional staff member met four times for a total of 12 hours. The students interviewed simulated patients; the groups discussed the interviews and interviewing techniques.

Dependent variable: Number out of three written scenarios where a student used an emotional term to describe a patient's concern.

Design diagram:

$$RO_1 \; X \; O_2$$
$$RO_1 \quad\;\; O_2$$

Pretest was given at the first class meeting of Medical Interviewing and History Taking. Experimental-group posttest was given at the last small-group session; control-group posttest was given at beginning of the first small-group session (after the experiment was over).

Threats to internal validity: None noted in research report. Random assignment allows us to rule out selection and statistical regression. Use of the same paper-and-pencil test for pretest and posttest allows us to rule out instrumentation and testing. Most likely the threat to internal validity was design contamination, especially if experimental-group members shared information with control-group members. Sharing should decrease differences between the experimental and control groups.

Threats to external validity: None noted; however, possible threats can be assumed easily. For example, the professional staff who facilitated the groups may have been enthusiastic and committed because of their involvement in implementing a new program. Also, a medical school may have its own unique culture, which affects its students' receptivity to classes and other training activities. Best evidence of external validity would be replication of this training in other medical schools.

Continued

EXAMPLE 3.1   *Continued*

Analysis and findings: The average numbers of scenarios where subjects used an emotional word in the response are shown below.

	Pretest	Posttest
Experimental Group	0.68	2.02
Control Group	0.89	1.13

Random assignment does not necessarily result in two identical groups; statistics help researchers decide if differences between groups could have occurred by chance. In the classical experimental design, researchers focus on the change between the pretest and posttest. The researchers compare the change in the experimental group with the change in the control group. Here, the experimental group showed an increase of 1.34; that is, it more than doubled its average use of emotional responses; the control group showed an increase of only 0.24.

SOURCE: Based on F. M. Wolf et al., "A Controlled Experiment in Teaching Students to Respond to Patients' Emotional Concerns," *Journal of Medical Education* 62 (1987): 25–34.

over. The strategy of randomly assigning subjects to a group that either receives the treatment first (experimental group) or second (control group) helps resolve the political and ethical problems of deciding whether or not a person receives treatment solely on the basis of random assignment.

In Example 3.1 medical students in both the experimental and control groups showed more empathy on the posttest. Some of the change may have been caused by the lecture on patient interviewing (history), which both groups attended after taking the pretest. Since both groups heard the lecture, it is not a threat to internal validity. History would not be controlled as a threat if only the experimental group heard the lecture, since either the experiment or the lecture may have caused the change. To determine if an experiment controls for history, maturation, or another threat to internal validity requires detailed knowledge of how the experiment was conducted.

Typically, to determine the amount of change researchers use the same procedure to measure the dependent variable at both pretest and posttest. This is not necessary to ensure internal validity. An experiment may still be internally valid even if the pretest and posttest measuring procedures are not the same, or if the pretest causes a change in the dependent variable. The equivalence of the control and experimental groups neutralizes instrumentation and testing as threats to internal validity. Both groups should respond in the same way to the pretest. Nevertheless, the pretest may sensitize the experimental group to the independent variable and affect the external validity of the design, in which case the pretest becomes part of the treatment or program. We would say that the pretest interacted with the independent variable to affect the dependent variable.

Experimental designs assume the control of the laboratory experiment, a situation that rarely applies to administrative and policy research. Field researchers, that is, researchers who work outside the confines of the laboratory, have markedly less control over subjects and events.[9] Still, researchers conduct field experiments frequently and draw reasonable conclusions from them.

Example 3.2 illustrates an adaptation of the classical experimental design. In this experiment a university housing office created a contest among college residences with cash incentives to try to decrease natural-gas consumption. The independent variable, cash awards, was introduced several times. In a sense, this amounted to doing the experiment six times with the same groups of subjects. We selected this example because it also shows how researchers combine techniques. The researchers' cost-benefit analysis found that the cash awards alone cost more than the fuel savings.

The *randomized posttest design* avoids the possible sensitizing effect of a pretest by eliminating it, which results in a design identical to that of the classical experiment except for the absence of a pretest. The underlying assumption is that a pretest is expendable because random assignment will result in equivalent

 EXAMPLE 3.2

An Adaptation of the Classical Experimental Design

Problem: Determine effective ways to reduce energy consumption by residents in master-meter housing, where individual residents do not pay utility bills.

Subjects: Five university-owned apartment complexes. Analysts paired one set of complexes of comparable size, family mix, and energy source. One complex was randomly assigned to the experimental group, the other to the control group. The remaining three complexes could not be paired.

Independent variable (treatment): Contest with cash awards held six times two weeks apart.

Dependent variable: Savings in natural-gas consumption = Cost × (predicted consumption − actual consumption).

Design diagram:

$$RO_1 \ X \ O_2 \ X \ O_3 \ X \ O_4 \ X \ O_5 \ X \ O_6 \ X \ O_7$$
$$RO_1 \quad O_2 \quad O_3 \quad O_4 \quad O_5 \quad O_6 \quad O_7$$

Threats to internal validity:

History: possible problem because experimental complex also received a 15-page saving guide.

Maturation, statistical regression, selection, testing instrumentation, controlled by the design.

Experimental mortality: none.

Contamination: unlikely; control group members expressed little interest in contest.

Continued

EXAMPLE 3.2   *Continued*

Threats to external validity:
Nothing indicated to suggest findings could not be generalized to other university-owned complexes.

Contest Number	Savings in Experimental Group
1	$137.85
2	$ 79.31
3	$ 98.35
4	$ 67.19
5	$ 66.41
6	$ 39.19

Conclusion: The contest reduced natural-gas consumption, but not enough to offset contest costs. Questions of history and contamination as threats to internal validity were moot. Findings replicated those found in a study of an apartment complex; the approach worked better in a university that had contests among dormitories.

SOURCE: Adapted from L. McClelland and S. W. Cook, "Promoting Energy Conservation in Master-Metered Apartments through Group Financial Incentives," *Journal of Applied Social Psychology* 10 (1980): 20–31.

experimental and control groups. This assumption is most likely to be valid for large study populations. The design is diagrammed as:

$$R \ X \ O_1$$
$$R \quad O_1$$

The randomized posttest design has a number of advantages. Eliminating the pretest reduces costs. The administration of a pretest is often difficult or even impossible. It may not be necessary. The randomized posttest design relieves the researcher of identifying a reasonable pretest. Consider a prison work-release program tested to determine whether it reduced the recidivism rate of prisoners. Qualified prisoners were randomly assigned either to a work-release program or to serve out their full terms. Upon release, all prisoners were followed to determine whether they were arrested for additional crimes. Recidivism rates for the work-release program subjects and full-term subjects were compared.[10] Consider what might happen if the researchers had to obtain pretest data. The data may not exist; the prison may not have reliable records on whether an inmate had been in prison before, how many times, or for how long. Even if sound data exist, confidentiality requirements may prohibit researchers from having access to them. We may reasonably assume that inmates with a history of recidivism would not be among the "qualified" prisoners eligible for work release.

If experimental groups are large enough for the investigator to be confident that they are similar, the randomized posttest design is efficient and effective. If a study has relatively few subjects, a researcher needs pretest data to ensure the comparability of the experimental and control groups. Pretest data also are necessary if an investigator needs to determine the extent of change attributable to the independent variable.

Example 3.3 illustrates the application of a randomized posttest design to determine whether coaching improves performance in leaderless groups. In this study, measuring performance in leaderless groups prior to introducing the independent variable would have increased the study's costs. Furthermore, the

---

 EXAMPLE 3.3

An Application of the Randomized Posttest Design

Problem: A university placement office wants to learn whether coaching improves performance in assigned-role leaderless groups (a technique used by major employers to select professional employees).

Subjects: Thirty-six female students from introductory psychology classes randomly assigned to one of three groups.

Independent variable: Type of preparation for leaderless group. Two treatments were used, so two experimental groups were set up:

X_1 = Subjects attended two coaching sessions and received feedback on their performance in practice leaderless groups.
X_2 = Subjects saw a short tape of someone giving a biased account about her experience in a leaderless group.

Control group: Subjects did not attend coaching sessions, did not view tape, or have any other preparation.

Dependent variable: Overall performance in an assigned-role leaderless group. Scores on leadership, behavioral flexibility, oral presentation, initiative, and persuasion were averaged for each subject.

Design diagram:

$$R \quad X_1 \quad O_1$$
$$R \quad X_2 \quad O_1$$
$$R \qquad\;\; O_1$$

Threats to internal validity:

History: controlled by design and carefully implemented procedures for conducting the experiment.
Maturation, statistical regression, selection: controlled by the design.
Testing, instrumentation: not applicable with this design.
Experimental mortality: none.
Contamination: none documented.

Threats to external validity:

Possible interaction of selection and treatment: These were all college women who might respond to the coaching program differently from the general population of professionals seeking employment.

Continued

EXAMPLE 3.3   *Continued*

Possible interaction of setting and treatment: These students had no immediate prospects of using the skills to obtain a job. Thus the experimental setting did not duplicate the natural setting where subjects would be competing for a position.

Findings:

	Group		
	Coached	**Viewed Tape**	**Control**
Average performance*	5.08	2.83	2.58

*Individual mean scores on separate performance indicators. The higher the score, the better the performance.

Conclusion: Hypothesis that coaching can improve performance in an assigned-role leaderless group was supported. Tape was meant to duplicate "grapevine" advice; it may not have represented the effect of informal advice. Researchers did not determine whether coaching only makes participants test-wise or whether they later apply learned behaviors to work settings. Also not known was whether coaching would work as well with persons who had management experience.

SOURCE: P. M. Kurecka et al., "Full and Errant Coaching Effects on Assigned Role Leaderless Group Discussion Performance," *Personnel Psychology* (1982): 805–812.

additional time required may have led to greater problems with experimental mortality and increased the opportunities for design contamination, particularly if members of the experimental and control groups had contact with each other.

Administrators are likely to see experimental designs in conjunction with program evaluation, although they are used in other areas as well. A major purpose of program evaluation is to determine whether a planned intervention or program has produced its intended effects. Experimental designs are useful research strategies for determining the effect of the policy or program on a given population. As we mentioned earlier, a major problem encountered when attempting to use experimental designs for program evaluation is the loss of researcher control. This lack of control makes experimental designs impractical for evaluating established programs. Such programs are sufficiently complex, with well-established procedures, and researchers cannot expect to spell out who will receive services, exactly what services they will receive, and exactly how the services will be delivered.

Thomas Cook and Donald Campbell have identified other situations in which experimental designs will not work.[11] True experimental research in administrative settings rarely can be done quickly, so an alternative design should be chosen if a decision must be made quickly. Sometimes, important variables such as age, race, or the occurrence of a disaster cannot be manipulated or randomly assigned. The decision to evaluate most programs is made independently of the decision to implement the program and often after the program has begun, making true experimentation impossible because it is too late to manipulate the intervention (the independent variable) or to assign subjects to groups. True experimental designs also are expensive to conduct in realistic social settings. Preliminary studies should be conducted to avoid premature experimentation.

Experimental designs seem most relevant to the study of new or controversial programs at a time of scarce resources.[12] Programs that are specific, clearly described, and implemented all at once rather than phased in gradually lend themselves to experimental evaluation. The effects of modest treatments, such as changing office accounting procedures, may be more easily and reasonably studied experimentally than ambitious programs to achieve broad social goals. A researcher may have difficulty ensuring that the latter programs are carried out as designed or intended; pressures to participate in the program may make random assignment nearly impossible, and subject attrition and design contamination may be inevitable. One objection to the use of experimental designs in the study of social programs has revolved around the question of whether the control group can be offered a treatment. Although traditional experimental design calls for identifying what would happen without "treatment," the resulting practical and ethical problems have made offering alternative treatment to the control group an acceptable practice.[13] Such problems have been particularly prominent in medical research, where there has been much debate over the morality of withholding a new medical treatment from a group so that its effects can be verified experimentally.

QUASI-EXPERIMENTAL DESIGNS

The classic experimental design relies on the researcher's ability to control the research setting. The researcher exercises control from the initiation of the experiment to its conclusion, selecting and assigning subjects and exposing the experimental group to the independent variable. As much as possible, she ensures that groups equivalent at the beginning undergo the same conditions during the study, except for exposure to the independent variable. The tradition of referring to the independent variable as a "treatment" emphasizes the objective of manipulating and controlling exposure to the independent variable.

In research conducted outside a laboratory setting, the amount of control required by the classical experimental model may be unattainable. True experiments require (1) the manipulation of at least one intervention (independent variable), (2) the random assignment of subjects to groups, (3) the random assignment of the independent variable to groups, and (4) the exposure of the experimental group or groups to the treatment in isolation from other factors. If one of these conditions cannot be met, the appropriate research design is a *quasi-experimental* one. Donald Campbell and Julian Stanley refer to "many natural settings in which the [researcher] can introduce something like experimental design into his scheduling of data collection procedures even though he lacks the full control over the scheduling of experimental stimuli which makes a true experiment possible."[14] In other words, the researcher makes use of as many features of the classical experimental design as possible and adopts other measures to control threats to internal validity. Unlike the groups in true experimental designs, members of the treatment group and the control group in quasi-experimental designs are not randomly assigned; therefore, the analyst cannot assume that the groups are equivalent at the beginning.

We discuss three of the more commonly used quasi-experimental designs: the comparison group pretest/posttest design, the interrupted time-series design, and the interrupted time-series design with comparison group.

On the surface, the *comparison group pretest/posttest design* may look like the classic experimental design. However, its subjects are not selected by random assignment but by identifying a group of subjects that seems comparable to the group involved in the test. This is a useful strategy because frequently programs or policies develop in a way that precludes random assignment. Suppose a police department wanted to study the effect of a compressed workweek of four 10-hour days. The study may have problems if officers object to being randomly assigned to the experimental schedule. Hence, researchers may prefer to limit the testing of the schedule to units where everyone agrees to participate. The resulting research design would require finding platoons willing to submit to the new schedule, and then designating a comparison group from among the other platoons. One way of constructing a comparison group is to match each platoon in the experimental group on the basis of selected characteristics.[15] Note, however, that unlike true experimental designs, members of the groups here are not randomly assigned, so the analyst cannot assume that the groups are equivalent. Nor is the "experimental" treatment randomly assigned to one of the groups.

Comparison groups also are constructed for contrast with intact experimental groups. This provided a useful strategy for one group of researchers who wanted to study how organic farming affected crop production. Since the researchers were not in a position to convince farmers to switch to organic farming, they identified known organic farms and matched each with a farm of similar size and soil composition. Similarly, in a study of the effects of day care on children, kindergarten students who had been in day care for five years formed the experimental group. Kindergarten children in the same school system who had not been in day care, and whose parents agreed to their participation, formed the comparison group. After the comparison group was selected, researchers studied the characteristics of both groups to identify systematic differences between them.

The comparison group pretest/posttest design is diagrammed as:

$$O_1 \; X \; O_2$$
$$O_1 \qquad O_2$$

Sometimes the comparison group design is called "the nonequivalent control-group design," but we prefer to restrict the term "control group" to groups whose members are randomly assigned. The major limitation of the comparison group design is the inability to control for biases introduced by selection. The greater the similarity between the experimental and comparison groups, the more confidence a researcher may have in making inferences from his findings. The design can control for history, maturation, pretesting, and instrumentation, but this must be confirmed. Unless a researcher can keep conditions between the experimental and comparison group the same from pretest to posttest, one group may have an experience that affects its posttest data. For example, if the comparison and experimental groups consisted of police precincts, and if the precincts used different criteria for data collection, then instrumentation would be a possible threat to validity as the measure of the dependent variable would be different for the two groups. Experimental mortality could be checked by examining records. The analysts could determine whether any platoons discontinued the experimental schedule prematurely, essentially dropping out of the study prior to its conclusion.

Statistical regression constitutes a threat to validity in this design. This threat is of particular concern if the experimental group and the comparison group differ systematically on some dimension. Imagine that the pretest turnover rates were higher than usual in the experimental platoons and lower than usual in the comparison platoons. If each group regressed toward its average, a posttest might show a lower turnover rate for the experimental group and a higher rate for the comparison group—both due to a statistical effect, not the difference in scheduling. This is not an unlikely scenario. You would expect administrators to pick the platoon with the highest turnover rate for an experimental program.

The comparison group pretest/posttest design may have high external validity if it replicates a program's effect in a variety of settings. Thus if the change in scheduling reduced turnover in all platoons where it was tried, and the platoons included ones with high morale and low morale, ones in good neighborhoods and ones in tough neighborhoods, ones with easygoing leadership and ones with authoritarian leadership, the administrators would feel confident that shifting the entire police force to compressed scheduling would prove successful. Another application of a comparison group pretest/posttest design is illustrated in Example 3.4.

The comparison group design controls for the threats to internal and external validity in the following fashion:

History, maturation: may be controlled by design. Note a possible threat of local history, that is, the event affects one group and not another. Similarly, selection and maturation may interact, that is, independent of the experiment, one group may change faster than another.

Experimental mortality: not well controlled by design, but can be detected.

Selection, statistical regression, contamination: not controlled by design.

Testing effects: controlled by design.

External validity: may be reduced since neither experimental nor control group is randomly assigned. However, external validity may be improved greatly by replication in different settings.

In the comparison group pretest/posttest design illustrated in Example 3.4, the experimental group consisted of people who first signed up to have their homes weatherized. The comparison group consisted of people who signed up

EXAMPLE 3.4

An Application of a Comparison Group Pretest/Posttest Design

Problem: Determine whether a home weatherization program for low-income families reduced energy consumption.

Subjects: 59 weatherized homes and 37 homes waiting for weatherization in Minnesota.

Independent variable: Participation in the weatherization program that provided as needed: insulation, weatherstripping, storm doors and windows, glass replacement, repairs.

Dependent variables:
Percentage British Thermal Units (BTUs) saved.
BTUs saved per degree day per square foot of living space. $(O_2 - O_1)$
Dollars saved per degree day. $(O_2 - O_1)$

Design diagram:

$$O_1 \ X \ O_2$$
$$O_1 \quad O_2$$

Threats to internal validity:

History: no apparent threat noted.

Maturation: controlled by design.

Selection, statistical regression: no apparent bias although comparison group had applied later than experimental group for weatherization; both groups had similar amount of floor space, number of occupants, percent owner occupied.

Experimental mortality: various subjects eliminated because of moves, being away from home, or inability to get accurate fuel records.

Testing, instrumentation: controlled by design.

Contamination: none noted.

Threats to external validity: Interaction between history and treatment; interaction between setting and treatment possible. Study took place in Minnesota in the late 1970s, a period of high energy costs.

Findings:

	Weatherized Home (Average)	Nonweatherized Home (Average)
Percent BTUs saved	10.95	− 2.48
BTUs saved per degree day per square foot	1.68	− 0.295
Dollars saved per degree day	.006	.001

Discussion: On the average, weatherized homes saved 13 percent in fuel consumption; the cost of weatherization was paid back in 3.5 years. Data and design support benefits of weatherization; more evidence needed to support generalizability of findings.

SOURCE: E. Hirst and R. Talwar, "Reducing Energy Consumption in Low-Income Homes," *Evaluation Review* (October 1981): 671–685. (Copyright © 1981 by Sage Publications. Reprinted by permission of Sage Publications.)

later and were on a waiting list. The researchers gathered data to make certain that the two groups were similar in respect to the size of their homes, the number of occupants, and the ratio of home owners to renters. Other unexamined differences between the groups may have existed. The initial group may be more motivated to save energy and may have used other methods in combination with the weatherizing improvements. To decide whether the evidence suggests that a weatherization program is effective, decision makers must use their own judgment and experience to decide whether plausible uncontrolled threats to internal validity may have changed the findings.

The *interrupted time-series design* incorporates an independent variable other than time into the time-series design. The design improves greatly upon the one-group before/after design. As contrasted to the simple time series, the interrupted time-series design introduces an independent variable and can be used to trace the effects of that variable upon other variables. The simple time-series design, on the other hand, is used to describe the values of one variable over time and not to explain changes in those values.

The interrupted time-series design calls for several observations before the introduction of the independent variable. These observations help to demonstrate that exposure to the independent variable resulted in a change in the dependent variable that cannot be attributed to long-term trends, cycles, or seasonal events. A series of observations made after the introduction of the independent variable provides evidence specifying the effect of an independent variable. The independent variable may have resulted in (1) an abrupt permanent change in the dependent variable, (2) an abrupt temporary change, which lessens and eventually returns to the baseline level, and (3) a gradual permanent change in which the initial change gradually increases or decreases to a point where it starts to level off.[16] Figure 3.1 illustrates this.

The energy-savings contest described in Example 3.2 seems to illustrate the second situation. Although the data were incomplete, one could imagine that as the weeks passed, the students would revert to their previous energy-consumption habits.[17]

In such designs, the independent variable may be introduced by the researcher. However, it is more likely that the independent variable is something that occurs naturally or is introduced by someone else. In many cases exposure to the independent variable has already occurred when the analyst is in a position to study its possible effects.

The design may be represented as follows:

$$O_1\ O_2\ O_3\ O_4\ X\ O_5\ O_6\ O_7\ O_8$$

The number of Os and their placement in relation to X depend on the number of observations made before and after the independent variable was introduced. The design controls best for maturation as a threat to internal validity because the observations capture how the dependent variable changes with the passage of time. The design also rules out the effects of statistical regression. Other threats to internal validity may be eliminated after a researcher checks into the probability that each occurred. Other events, for example, may have occurred at the same

FIGURE   3.1 ┤━━━POSSIBLE IMPACTS OF INTERRUPTED TIME SERIES ━━━━━━━

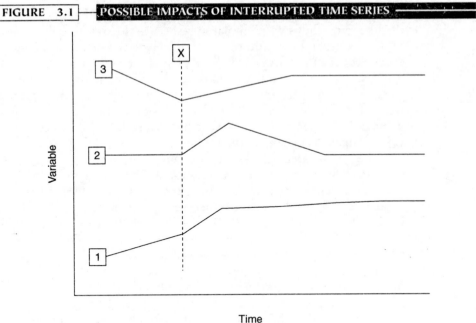

time as the independent variable. A careful investigation of current circumstances can identify these. Fluctuations in a time series may be due to long-term trends, cyclical variations, seasonal trends, and random fluctuations. If enough time is considered before and after the intervention, trend patterns can be identified. The interrupted time-series design can eliminate these alternative explanations of the changes occurring after an intervention.

A researcher should be especially alert for an interaction between selection and treatment, that is, he should be confident that the preintervention data represent a population similar to the postintervention data.[18] For example, to evaluate the effectiveness of a year-round school requires a researcher to determine if the school's student body changed after the year-round school program began. Students who disliked school and dreaded the prospect of losing their long summer vacation may have transferred to other schools and more competitive students may have transferred into the year-round school. Changes in student performance may then be due to changes in the student body and not to the longer school year. A review of the records may suggest other events that could have caused the dependent variable. A researcher should examine program records to determine the extent of experimental mortality. He should make sure that the way student performance was measured did not change during the time that the observations were made. For example, if a survey was used, were the questions reworded or different ones used? Was a different measure used, such as changing from the ACT (American College Testing) test to the SAT (Scholastic Aptitude Test)?

The list below summarizes how the interrupted time-series design protects against threats to internal and external validity.

Threats to Validity with Interrupted Time-Series Design

A. *To internal validity:*

> History, instrumentation: not protected against by the design. Researcher should review records to determine whether other events occurred at the same time as the intervention or whether any change in measurement procedure occurred.

> Maturation, statistical regression, testing: protected against by the design. Changes associated with long-term trends, cycles, seasonal variations, and random fluctuations can be ruled out if the design has a sufficient number of data points (at least 50 data points are recommended for statistical analysis).

> Selection: not ruled out by design. Researcher needs to make sure that intervention does not coincide with a major change in the population being measured.

> Experimental mortality: not ruled out by design. Researcher should check records to determine whether subjects dropped out after the occurrence of the independent variable.

B. *To external validity:* The design does not control against threats to external validity. Interaction between selection and treatment in particular is a potential problem.

The interrupted time-series design works best if the independent variable is expected to have a marked and immediate effect. Otherwise, its effect mistakenly may be attributed to long-term trends, cycles, or seasonal effects unless these are removed through statistical procedures or otherwise evaluated. Statistical procedures can help a researcher confirm his impressions that an effect is markedly greater than expected fluctuations.[19] This design also works best if the independent variable can be introduced all at once at a clearly identified time. If it is phased in gradually, its effects may be more difficult to identify. The researcher should also attempt to understand when the effect is likely to occur, that is, whether it will be almost immediate or will take a long time.

The interrupted time-series design provides journalists, politicians, and researchers a convenient, easily implemented way to track the impact of a public policy. In 1994, the police chief of New York City, newly appointed by then-Mayor Rudy Giuliani, instituted reforms that emphasized community policing targeted at crime "hot spots." The mayor's biography cites the program's success: "Under Mayor Giuliani's leadership, New York City has experienced an unprecedented 38 percent reduction in overall crime and 48 percent reduction in murder since 1993."[20] Figure 3.2 supports the mayor's boast. Although the city's crime rate began dropping in 1989, the crime rates in 1994 and 1995 were the lowest since 1980. The crime rate decreased 11 percent in 1994 and 16 percent in 1995, the greatest drops over the 15-year period. Although it appears that Mayor Giuliani's program was successful, researchers would want to inquire about the various threats to internal validity and how they could be assessed. We continue

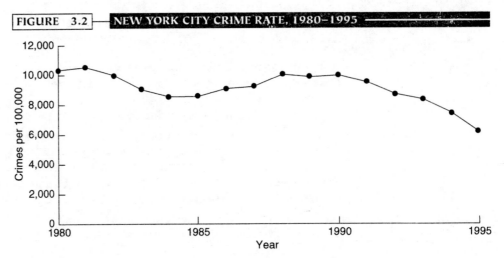

FIGURE 3.2 — NEW YORK CITY CRIME RATE, 1980–1995

SOURCE: "Criminal Justice Indicators New York City: 1980–1995," New York State Division of Criminal Justice Services February 13, 1997 (http://criminaljustice.state.nyu.us/crimnet/ojsa/areastate/areastat.cgi").

the example later with a discussion of these issues. As tracking and reporting statistical data become a common way to monitor and reward performance, a serious type of design contamination may occur. That is, data collectors, administrators, or analysts will be tempted to manipulate the data to their advantage. For example, one can imagine a police department reconsidering how it classifies some deaths in order to avoid showing an increased homicide rate.

Time-series data eliminate maturation or statistical regression as threats. Yet, they do not confirm the success of community policing or Giuliani's leadership. Other cities also experienced lower crime during the same time period. Other reasons cited for the drop included improvements in the economy, less use of crack cocaine, and relatively fewer teenagers in the population. Furthermore, the reported crime rate does not measure the incidence of crime. Cynical citizens may not call the police; busy police officers may not file crime reports. To demonstrate the effectiveness of police strategies requires more analysis. Investigators should confirm that reporting patterns were consistent. They should see if changes in the economy, in drug use, or in the population's age distribution coincide with changes in the crime rate. They should compare other cities' data with New York City's data.

To illustrate an interrupted time-series design with more complete analysis, we examined a study on the effect of the Illinois rape shield law. A common legal reform enacted by legislatures in the 1970s and 1980s, rape shield laws restricted the ability of defense attorneys to introduce evidence about the victim's past sexual history into a rape trial. Advocates of rape shield laws argued that a change in existing laws would encourage women to report rapes, press charges, and increase conviction rates. Illinois implemented a rape shield law in April 1978. Figure 3.3, based on data drawn from a more detailed study,[21] shows the yearly data on the conviction rates for rape or rape-related charges in Chicago.

The conviction rate went up in 1978, but in subsequent years the conviction rates dropped and did not look markedly different from those of the years before

FIGURE 3.3 — **PERCENTAGE OF DEFENDANTS CONVICTED ON RAPE OR RAPE-RELATED CHARGES, CHICAGO, 1970–1984**

SOURCE: Data from C. Spohn and J. Horney, "A Case of Unrealistic Expectations: The Impact of the Rape Reform Legislation in Illinois," *Criminal Justice Policy Research* 4 (1990): 11.

the reform. Recall that to implement a time-series design, a researcher should also collect qualitative information. The qualitative information allows the researcher to identify other factors that could have caused an observed change. In this study the researchers interviewed judges, state attorneys, and public defenders. From the interviews and extensive statistical evidence, the researchers concluded that the law "had no impact on the indictment rate, the conviction rate, or incarceration time." The researchers learned that prior to 1978, case law had started to restrict the use of sexual history as evidence; thus, the reform had been more gradual than it appeared. The researchers also observed that the law could have affected only cases a jury heard and in which a claim of consent was part of the defense. Since fewer than 10 percent of rape cases were heard by a jury, the potential of the law to affect overall conviction rates was less than its advocates expected.

This example suggests the complexity of interpreting an interrupted time-series design. The graphical information is helpful and easily understood. Often, the graphs are only a first step; they are usually followed by detailed statistical analysis.[22] Tracking a variable and viewing its changes raises interesting questions about what actually caused the shift. One strategy is to enrich the time-series design by collecting similar information from one or more untreated comparison groups.

An addition of a comparison time series of an untreated group is seen occasionally with the interrupted time-series design. This design is called *interrupted time series with comparison group* and allows the researcher to compare the dependent variable time series of the treatment group with the same series for a nonequivalent, nontreatment group.

In such a design, a time series, interrupted by the occurrence of the independent variable, is developed for the treatment group. In addition, a time series is developed concurrently for another group not exposed to the independent variable. If the groups are equivalent in important aspects, the addition of the comparison group can provide a check on some threats to internal validity.[23] To check the effectiveness of New York City's community policing, one might choose another major American city (Chicago, Philadelphia, or Boston) where community policing was not implemented. To control for selection as a threat to internal validity, the comparison city should have similar populations, e.g., similar variations in age, ethnic background, income, and drug use. One also looks for "local history," that is, events that occurred in one city and not in the other, which could have caused the changes in crime rate.

The interrupted time series with comparison group design is diagrammed as follows:

$$O_1\ O_2\ O_3\ O_4\ O_5\ X\ O_6\ O_7\ O_8\ O_9\ O_{10}$$
$$O_1\ O_2\ O_3\ O_4\ O_5\quad O_6\ O_7\ O_8\ O_9\ O_{10}$$

Example 3.5 summarizes an interrupted time series with a comparison group design.[24] The researchers were evaluating the impact of community development

---

EXAMPLE 3.5

An Application of an Interrupted Time-Series Design

Problem: A nonprofit organization sponsored the redevelopment of a commercial area in a declining neighborhood, called Belmont, in Portland, Oregon. Sponsors asked if efforts to revitalize distressed, inner-city neighborhoods made any difference. Research was conducted to provide an answer to this question.

Subjects: Belmont neighborhood, other low-income neighborhoods in Portland, City of Portland.

Independent variable: Commercial redevelopment in 1996 and 1997.

Dependent variable: Sales price of single-family housing units

Design: Yearly data were collected from 1988 through 1999.

Belmont: $\quad O_1\ldots O_4\ldots O_8\quad X\quad O_9\ldots O_{10}\ldots O_{11}\ldots O_{12}$

Other low-income
neighborhoods $O_1\ldots O_4\ldots O_8\qquad O_9\ldots O_{10}\ldots O_{11}\ldots O_{12}$

All of Portland: $\quad O_1\ldots O_4\ldots O_8\qquad O_9\ldots O_{10}\ldots O_{11}\ldots O_{12}$

EXAMPLE 3.5 *Continued*

Possible threats to internal validity:

History: Data from other low-income neighborhoods and the rest of Portland controlled for a general increase in housing values and the effects of other events and factors.

Instrumentation: the measurement of housing values did not change throughout the data collection period.

Selection: a possible threat. Belmont may have had characteristics making it a particularly good candidate for revitalization.

Maturation, statistical regression: controlled by the design.

Other threats were assumed not to apply.

Possible threats to external validity: Belmont had been a well-to-do neighborhood and the redevelopment was based on commercial concerns. A number of old homes surrounded the commercial district.

Findings: Figure 3.4 reports the median value of single-family housing for each year between 1988 and 1999. The redevelopment activities began in 1996 and were completed by the end of 1997. As the graph shows, the values of housing in the neighborhood began to increase before revitalization was completed.

Discussion: The researchers inspected the graphed raw data and conducted detailed statistical analysis. They concluded that the graphical data demonstrated that median value of housing in the Belmont neighborhood had increased during and just after revitalization by more than had the value of housing in other low-income neighborhoods and in the City of Portland as a whole. Statistical analysis verified the conclusions based on the visual data. However, the increase was in the base value of housing. The increase after revitalization in Belmont did not continue at a higher rate than in other low-income neighborhoods or in Portland as a whole. Researchers concluded that revitalization efforts had had a positive impact.

FIGURE 3.4 | **MEDIAN SALES PRICE OF SINGLE-FAMILY HOMES BY YEAR**

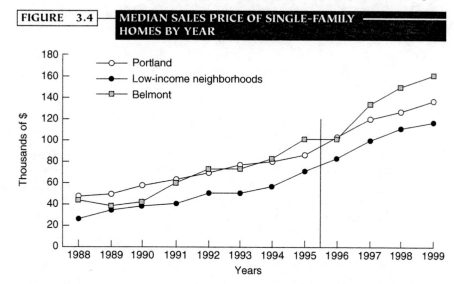

SOURCE: Adapted from George Galster, Kenneth Tempkin, Chris Walker, and Noah Sawyer, "Measuring Impacts of Community Development Initiatives. A New Application of the Adjusted Interrupted Time-Series Method," *Evaluation Review* 28 (2004): 502–538.

initiatives on housing values. They looked at the intervention of a redevelopment effort in a declining neighborhood in Portland, Oregon. To control for other changes, including trends such as the general increase in housing values, they collected data on housing values in other low-income neighborhoods and on average housing values in all of Portland. Thus they had two control groups.[25]

NONEXPERIMENTAL DESIGNS

Nonexperimental designs do not control for threats to internal validity. If an intervention is implemented on randomly selected subjects, which occurs occasionally, the designs have some external validity. The value of nonexperimental designs may be overlooked because of the obvious limitation of drawing conclusions when threats to validity, including history, maturation, statistical regression, and selection, are uncontrolled. The three nonexperimental designs are:

Single group posttest:		X	O_1
Single group pretest/posttest:	O_1	X	O_2
Nonequivalent groups posttest only:		X	O_1
			O_1

To illustrate the value and limitation of a single group posttest, we selected research descriptions from two news stories. The design of each study can be inferred from the following quotes:

About 400 people showed up yesterday to enroll for a special [farecard] available to senior citizens at half price after the Transit Authority sent a news release to three Chinese-language newspapers.[26]

In a single year [South Carolina's welfare-to-work program] has put 442 welfare recipients on its payroll without creating any new jobs or displacing any state workers.[27]

Although single group posttest studies do not control for any threats to internal validity, only plausible threats need to be considered. In the Chinese-language news release "experiment," history and maturation, the most plausible threats, can be eliminated. The press release announced that a mobile unit would come to New York City's Chinatown to take farecard applications. The mobile unit had been traveling throughout the city for six months; however, prior to the press release relatively few people had used it to apply for farecards. Thus the press release seems to have been a success.

The success of the welfare-to-work program is less certain. People who work in low-paying, low-skilled jobs rely on welfare during periods of unemployment. The 442 jobs were concentrated in food service, maintenance, and personal services. Maturation or history cannot be eliminated as threats. The 442 jobs normally may be held by people who move on and off welfare, depending on their employment status. The state did not know how many welfare recipients it had hired in previous years; 442 may have been a relatively large number, but perhaps it was not. Economic growth may have shrunk the pool of job applicants and forced the state to develop new employee sources. The state may have hired welfare recipients because of its inability to find other employees. A good economy, rather than the welfare-to-work program, may have contributed to hiring former welfare recipients.

Even if plausible threats to internal validity cannot be eliminated, the single group posttest provides useful information. First, the design indicates whether an intervention worked as well as expected. The Transit Authority expected 50 people to visit its mobile unit in Chinatown. Its expectations were greatly exceeded. If hardly any people had shown up, the Transit Authority might have concluded that press releases in foreign-language newspapers were not helpful. If South Carolina investigators found that the state had hired few welfare recipients, they would question the effectiveness of the welfare-to-work program. Second, researchers can collect other valuable, detailed information. In South Carolina, investigators studied the jobs welfare recipients had—the type of work, whether the jobs were temporary or permanent, whether they had benefits. Such information can identify additional issues that help in understanding the relationship between welfare-to-work programs and employment. The single group pretest/posttest design does no better at controlling for threats to internal validity, but it does add one useful piece of information. It indicates if something changed between the pretest and the posttest. A pretest/posttest design establishes if program participants changed. Participants are "tested" at a program's beginning and end. The change in their performance may be attributed to the program, but are there alternative explanations? Consider a 10-week course to train new staff how to answer taxpayer inquiries. Participants are tested on their knowledge of the tax code. At the beginning of the course, 30 percent had a score of 85 or better, and at the end, 80 percent had a score of 85 or better. What factors, other than the program, might have brought about the improvement? We can think of four:

> If participants work as they attend the training course, the posttest scores may reflect what they learned on the job about the tax code.

> People with low pretest scores may have dropped out of the course, leaving those who are doing well as a larger proportion of the whole class.

> The pretest may have motivated people to study the tax code on their own and their "homework," rather than the training, improved their posttest scores.

> An unfamiliar format may have lowered the performance on the pretest. Some posttest improvement may be attributed to familiarity with the test format.

Problems of design contamination may arise in studies of programs intended to change attitudes or behaviors. At the time of the posttest, participants may give answers or act in a way that suggests that they have adopted the expected attitudes or behaviors. Nevertheless, their attitudes may have stayed the same, and they may have not really altered their behavior.

The single group pretest/posttest has strengths similar to those of the single group posttest. First, investigators can decide if a policy or program appears to meet their expectations. Second, they can gather data to answer specific questions about a program. Third, they can combine their knowledge of the program with other information and make a plausible case that it is effective. Fourth, they can identify what questions they may want to investigate further.

Whether an investigator examines a policy's impact with a single group posttest, a single group pretest/posttest, or interrupted time-series design may depend on the availability of data. As policy agendas change, so do data requirements. For example, South Carolina apparently never saw a need to track how many former welfare recipients worked for the state. The single group posttest or single group pretest/posttest may be the best one can do.

The last nonexperimental design, nonequivalent groups posttest only, compares two groups: a group that experienced an intervention and a group that did not. The design has the same limitations as the other nonexperimental designs. One cannot tell if differences between groups existed prior to the intervention, nor can one tell what, if any, changes took place in each group. Yet, similar to the other nonexperimental designs, the nonequivalent group's posttest provides useful information.

Example 3.6 describes a nonequivalent groups posttest design to evaluate the effectiveness of parent training. The information identified the parts of the

---

 EXAMPLE 3.6

An Application of Nonequivalent Groups Posttest Design

Problem: A program conducts a parent education course for parents charged with child abuse. Program staff want to know how well the program is working.

Subjects: Data gathered from 22 people who had completed the parent training program and 20 people on a waiting list to attend the next training program. Only 20 people were on waiting list; 35 people have completed the course, but only 22 could be reached.

Intervention (Independent variable): Parent education course
Dependent variable: Knowledge of effective parenting strategies
Design:

$$XO_1$$
$$O_1$$

Findings:
Strategies for handling a child's temper tantrum:

68 percent course participants suggested a positive strategy
40 percent waiting list members suggested a positive strategy

EXAMPLE 3.6   *Continued*

Strategies for handling a child who doesn't want to go to school:

59 percent course participants suggested a positive strategy
60 percent waiting list members suggested a positive strategy

Threats to internal validity:

Selection: Waiting list members assumed similar to attendees, but criteria for referring to program or putting on waiting list may have changed over time.

Experimental mortality: Problems in reaching course participants; may have reached only more stable (and more successful) participants.

History: Not controlled.

Instrumentation: Controlled; investigators were randomly assigned course participants and waiting list members (which controlled for different interviewing styles).

Maturation, statistical regression, testing: Not applicable.

Discussion: The staff used information from the study to assess program components. They identified which concepts needed more emphasis and which needed less. Participants did not seem to give socially acceptable responses. When asked how they handled stress, some parents indicated that they used alcohol or overindulged in their favorite foods. Similarly, parents said they did not agree that they should negotiate with children, even though this was taught in the course.

SOURCE: Adapted from W. Combs et al., "The Evaluation of the Nurturing Program," unpublished evaluation, Department of Political Science and Public Administration, North Carolina State University (Raleigh, NC, 1996).

program that were working and the parts that needed improvement. The particular study had a problem often encountered in collecting data from social service clients, e.g., the inability to keep in contact with former clients. Contact information such as addresses, telephone numbers, and telephone service change often.

DETERMINING CAUSALITY WITH CROSS-SECTIONAL STUDIES

Administrators analyzing a cross-sectional study may want to infer causal relationships from the data. For example, administrators may survey graduates of employment training programs to determine the effectiveness of training. Imagine a survey finds that persons who received on-the-job training earn more than people who received only classroom training. Can one conclude that on-the-job training caused the higher incomes? The finding of greater earnings for on-the-job participants shows a statistical association between type of training and earnings. We can establish quickly if the training (the independent variable) occurred before reported earnings (the dependent variable). Nevertheless, the concluding piece of evidence, the ability to eliminate alternative hypotheses, is elusive.

When analyzing data from experiments and quasi-experiments, the analyst contends with a limited number of threats to internal validity. In cross-sectional studies a seemingly unlimited number of possible, uncontrolled threats can be identified. The major uncontrolled threat is the inability to control subject selection or assignment, as the researcher cannot control who enrolls in on-the-job training and who does not. The greater earnings of on-the-job training participants may be due to their greater job readiness at the beginning of training or their higher degree of motivation and ambition. If you had more information on the dataset, you could identify other problems with internal validity. For example, if the training programs were conducted in different locations, the on-the-job training participants may be merely benefiting from a more robust economy. Investigators may suggest other plausible third variables, any one of which may demonstrate that the relationship is spurious.

When designing studies to establish causality, researchers prefer experimental and quasi-experimental designs. The deliberate introduction and manipulation of an independent variable provides much stronger evidence of causality than can a cross-sectional study. Nevertheless, if an experimental or quasi-experimental design cannot be implemented, or if the analyst has to rely on existing cross-sectional data, she may employ sophisticated analytical techniques to make plausible inferences about causal relationships. The adequacy of her analysis depends on her ability to select and use tools accurately to represent complex interactions among variables.[28]

Drawing upon theoretical knowledge and empirical experience, she should build a model, such as the schematic shown in Figure 3.5 which specifies the sequence and direction of relationships. Such a schematic representation places variables in time order from left to right. The most distant event is placed on the left-hand side; the most recent event is placed on the right. Arrows are drawn to identify and give the direction of possible causal relationships. The model will guide her statistical analysis.

The model helps users and critics to analyze a problem better. They can debate whether the model includes the relevant variables and if the effect of included variables has been identified correctly. Whether the model offers a basis

FIGURE   3.5   MODEL TO INFER TRAINING EFFECT ON EARNINGS

for inferring causal relationships depends on its theoretical strength. That is, the analysts should have a coherent, logical explanation justifying the linkages between variables. Statistical tools allow the researcher to control for some variables statistically. This assumes, however, that these variables have been measured and are included in the dataset.

SUMMARY

Experimental and quasi-experimental designs provide us with useful models of how to conduct research to establish causal links between independent and dependent variables. Rather than just describing the changes in the values of dependent variables, the analyst uses these designs to help explain those changes. In an experimental design, the researcher has control over the assignment of subjects to groups, the introduction of the independent variable, and the research conditions. Quasi-experimental designs lack one or more of these controls.

With the constraints and resources of a given situation, each experimental or quasi-experimental design must be constructed to minimize possible threats to internal and external validity. An internally valid design is one that eliminates factors other than the independent variable as possible explanations of variation in the dependent variable. The common threats to internal validity are history, selection, maturation, statistical regression, testing effects, instrumentation, experimental mortality, and design contamination. Experimental designs eliminate most threats to internal validity at the onset of a research study through random assignment of subjects or a combination of matching and random assignment. Nevertheless, simply implementing an experimental design does not protect against subject attrition, nor can it prevent design contamination. If subjects drop out of a study, a researcher should document their attrition and attempt to document whether dropouts are systematically different from continuers. Contamination may be unavoidable in some studies. If participants are markedly affected by the outcome of a study, they can be expected to behave in such a way as to enhance their own interests.

An externally valid design yields findings that can be generalized beyond the test population. Unique features of a program can unintentionally become part of the treatment. A characteristic of the participants, the setting, or the time may interact with the treatment to make the program succeed or fail. Cook and Campbell have postulated that replication of program findings among different populations and settings provides acceptable evidence of external validity even if these studies have poorly designed samples.

An understanding of internal and external validity and the possible threats to each helps an administrator evaluate the quality of a design and decide whether she is justified in having confidence in a study's findings. An administrator must, therefore, seek to determine whether plausible threats to validity, which could radically change the findings and her decision, have been eliminated. The experimental and quasi-experimental designs discussed here are used widely to minimize threats to validity. Nevertheless, an administrator will want to go beyond identifying the type of design and determine if serious threats were considered and controlled.

Experimental designs depend on random assignment of subjects to a treatment or a control group. The two-group design may be modified to include several treatment groups and to eliminate a no-treatment control group. This modification frequently is necessary to avoid ethical problems of withholding treatment. Researchers will often prefer the ease and efficiency of the randomized posttest design to the classical experiment. In addition to checking for experimental mortality and design contamination, the researcher should make sure that, save for exposure to the independent variable, the experimental and control groups experience similar conditions from the beginning of the experiment to its end. If program personnel conduct the study, the researcher should ensure that subjects are randomly assigned to groups and that the study is implemented as designed.

Experimentation requires researchers to control the research environment. Frequently, they cannot exert such control and must, as a result, use a quasi-experimental design. In designing a quasi-experiment they try to control as many threats to internal and external validity as possible. The major difference between experimental and quasi-experimental designs is that the latter do not have randomly assigned subjects. Often researchers use comparison groups, but they cannot eliminate the possibility of a selection bias.

Nonexperimental designs lack internal validity. Nevertheless, they can demonstrate if an intervention met expectations. Information gathered using these limited designs may be useful in developing appropriate evaluations. Existing information may act to eliminate plausible threats to internal validity. A researcher may be able only to implement a nonexperimental design because no pretest data were gathered.

In deciding what type of design to use, administrators should define clearly what they want to find out and how they plan to use the information. If they want data on variables that have received little attention, they may want a limited study before authorizing a more extensive experimental study. Whether the design should be quasi-experimental or descriptive depends on the question to be investigated and the availability of data. Occasionally, the inability to control the implementation of a program or the selection of participants requires an analyst to settle for a cross-sectional design. If a cross-sectional design is utilized, analysts must understand fully the relationships among variables and collect data on relevant variables. With a carefully specified model, analysts may use sophisticated statistical tools to infer causality by controlling for some variables representing threats to validity.

Chapters 2 and 3 have discussed research designs—the planning of a study in such a way that the behavior of a variable can be described or explained. The next chapters take up the topics of measuring variables and the procedures for collecting data. Chapter 4 introduces another type of validity—operational validity. This is important for evaluating the measures of variables. The chapter also discusses various levels of measurement for variables. These are especially important in considering the appropriate statistical tests to use in order to analyze the data.

NOTES

1. See T. D. Cook and D. T. Campbell, *Quasi-Experimentation: Design and Analysis Issues for Field Settings* (Boston: Houghton Mifflin, 1979), 9–36, for a discussion of the concept of causality.

2. F. J. Graveter and L. B. Forzano, *Research Methods for the Behavioral Sciences*, 2d ed. (Belmont, CA: Wadsworth/Thomson Learning, 2006).

3. Graveter and Forzano.

4. D. T. Campbell and J. C. Stanley, *Experimental and Quasi-Experimental Designs for Research* (Chicago: Rand McNally, 1966), and Cook and Campbell, *Quasi-Experimentation*.

5. Cook and Campbell, *Quasi-Experimentation*, 55–56.

6. Any of these factors may act in combination with the treatment to produce the particular outcome of the study. Although the treatment may be present for other cases, the particular values of these factors may not be present. Hence, external validity would be affected and the results could not be generalized. Methodologists refer to the combination of these factors with the treatment as *interaction*.

7. Cook and Campbell, *Quasi-Experimentation*, 73, 75–76.

8. This material on matching is from L. S. Meyers and N. E. Grossen, *Behavioral Research* (San Francisco: W. H. Freeman, 1974), 126–127. For a more detailed, statistical discussion of matching, see D. G. Killeinbaum et al., *Epidemiological Research* (Belmont, CA: Wadsworth, Lifetime Learning Publications, 1982), chap. 18, or S. Anderson et al. in *Statistical Methods for Comparative Studies* (New York: Wiley-Interscience, 1980). S. Isaac, in *Handbook in Research and Evaluation* (San Diego: EDITS Publishers, 1971), 72, recommends A. L. Edwards, *Experimental Designs in Psychological Research*, 3d ed. (New York: Holt, Rinehart & Winston, 1968), chap. 9, for arguments in favor of matching.

9. See M. L. Dennis, "Assessing the Validity of Randomized Field Experiments: An Example from Drug Abuse Treatment Research," *Evaluation Review* 14 (1990): 347–373, for a bibliography on the use of randomized field experiments.

10. G. P. Waldo and T. G. Chiricos, "Work Release and Recidivism," *Evaluation Quarterly* (February 1977): 87–107.

11. Cook and Campbell, *Quasi-Experimentation*, 344–382, discuss the limitations of field experiments as well as situations when they are appropriate. P. H. Rossi, M.W. Lipsey, and H. E. Freeman discuss the limitations of randomized field experiments in *Evaluation: A Systemic Approach*, 7th ed. (Thousand Oaks, CA: Sage, 2004) 252–262.

12. E. J. Posavac and R. G. Carey, *Program Evaluation: Methods and Case Studies, Studies*, 4th ed. (Englewood Cliffs, NJ: Prentice-Hall, 1992), 184–186.

13. Cook and Campbell, *Quasi-Experimentation*, 367–369.

14. Campbell and Stanley, *Experimental and Quasi-Experimental Designs*, 34.

15. Posavac and Carey, *Program Evaluation*, 167–170 discuss the problems associated with selecting comparison groups and give examples.

16. G. Glaster, K. Tempkin, C. Walker, and Noah Sawyer, "Measuring Impacts of Community Development Initiatives: A New Application of the Adjusted Interrupted Time-Series Method," *Evaluation Review* (2004) 28 (6): 502–538. R. McCleary and R. A. Hay, Jr., *Applied Time Series Analysis for the Social Sciences* (Beverly Hills: Sage, 1980), chap. 3, present the statistical analysis procedures for confirming these patterns. Cook and Campbell, *Quasi-Experimentation*, chap. 5, discuss the types of effects, various time-series designs, and how to handle gradual implementation or delayed causation.

17. A dramatic example of this is a time series showing the number of monthly calls to directory assistance in Cincinnati and how they changed after the telephone company began charging for them. The number dropped immediately, and substantially, only to begin increasing again after a few months. See A.J. McSweeney, "The Effects of Response Cost on the Behavior of a Million Persons: Charging for Directory Assistance in Cincinnati," *Journal of Applied Behavioral Analysis* 11 (1978): 47–51.

18. S. G. West and J. W. Reich, "An Evaluation of Arizona's July 1982 Drunk Driving Law," *Journal of Applied Social Psychology*, 19(1989): 1213–1237.

19. Cook and Campbell, *Quasi-Experimentation*, 225–232 and chap. 6.

20. "Biography of Mayor Rudolph W. Giuliani," NYC Link, New York City's Official Web Site (http://www. ci. nyc. ny. us), February 13, 1997.

21. C. Spohn and J. Horney, "A Case of Unrealistic Expectations: The Impact of Rape Reform Legislation in Illinois," *Criminal Justice Policy Research* 4 (1990): 1–18.

22. McCleary and Hay, *Applied Time Series Analysis*, present statistical procedures to statistically analyze time-series data. Alternatively, the reader can consult L. J. McCain and R. McCleary, "The Statistical Analysis of Simple Interrupted Time-Series Quasi-Experiment," chap. 6, in Cook and Campbell, *Quasi-Experimentation*. Michael Lewis-Beck provides visual examples and discusses statistical tools for evaluating changes in interrupted time series. See Michal S. Lewis-Beck (1986), "Interrupted Time Series," chapter 9, 209–240 in William D. Berry and Michael S. Lewis-Beck (eds), *New Tools for Social Scientists: Advances and Applications*

(Beverly Hills, CA: Sage Publications). Meier, Brudney, and Bohte discuss using regression analysis to analyze statistically the effect of an intervention on a time series. See Kenneth Meier, Jeffrey Brudney, and John Bohte, *Applied Statistics for Public and Nonprofit Administration*, 6th ed. (Belmont, CA: Thomson/Wadsworth, 2006).

23. Shadish, Cook, and Campbell refer to this method as "interrupted time series with non-equivalent, no treatment control group time series." (Shadish, Cook, and Campbell, 2002, *Experimental and Quasi-Experimental Designs for Generalizing Causal Inference*.)

24. George Galster, Kenneth Tempkin, Chris Walker, and Noah Sawyer, "Measuring Impacts of Community Development Initiatives. A New Application of the Adjusted Interrupted Time Series Method," *Evaluation Review* 28 (2004): 502–538.

25. Galster, et al., 515–525.

26. G. Pierre-Pierre, "Chinatown Crowd Reveals Unexploited Market for Fare Cards," *New York Times*, May 16, 1997, A16.

27. J. Havemann, "Welfare-to-Work Program: A South Carolina Success Story," *Washington Post*, April 21, 1997, A7.

28. For information on making causal inferences from cross-sectional designs, see H. B. Asher, *Causal Modeling* (Beverly Hills: Sage, Series on Quantitative Applications in the Social Sciences, #3, 1976); O. Hellevik, *Introduction to Causal Analysis: Exploring Survey Data by Crosstabulation* (London: Allen & Unwin, Contemporary Social Research Series, #9, 1984), and Cook and Campbell, *Quasi-Experimentation*, chap. 7. All these works include extensive discussions on statistical techniques. For a discussion that focuses on the validity issues, see L. B. Mohr, *Impact Analysis for Program Evaluation* (Pacific Grove, CA: Brooks/Cole, 1988), chap. 10.

TERMS FOR REVIEW

experimental design
quasi-experimental design
internal validity
external validity
threats to internal validity

threats to external validity
reactive effects of experimental
   arrangements
random assignment
experimental group

control group
comparison group design
interrupted time-series design
nonexperimental designs

QUESTIONS FOR REVIEW

The following questions should indicate whether you have a basic competency in this chapter's material.

1. a. What types of evidence are necessary to support a claim that one variable is the cause of a change in another?
   b. Why is each of these types of evidence necessary?

2. Which of the threats to internal validity is likely to be the most common? Why?

3. Which of the threats to internal validity is likely to cause the most trouble or harm? Why?

4. Contrast history with maturation as threats to internal validity.

5. "Internal validity takes precedence over external validity." Evaluate this statement.

6. Discuss three ways to improve external validity. Compare history as a threat to internal validity with history as a threat to external validity.

7. Consider a study on the effects of noise. Fifty subjects will enter data on a computer spreadsheet. The researchers will introduce random noise in the room where the experimental group is working. Data will be gathered on the number of forms each subject processes correctly in an hour.
   a. The experiment will be held in two rooms (a "quiet" room and a "noisy" room) with 25 workstations. Subjects will not know which room is which. Should the subjects decide which room they want to work in, or should they be assigned to one of the rooms? Justify your answer.
   b. The study will begin at 9 a.m. A randomly selected experimental group will work for an hour without intermittent noise, and

the first hour's data will be collected. From 10 to 11 a.m., the researchers will introduce noise into the room and collect the second hour's data. The control group will work from 1 to 3 p.m. The data will be collected twice, but no intermittent noise will be introduced. Critique the internal validity of this design.

c. The study will begin at 9 a.m. The experimental and control groups will work in separate buildings from 9 to 11 a.m. In one of the buildings, a fire alarm (not part of the experiment) goes off and everyone leaves for 20 minutes. The group returns to the room and works until 11:20 a.m. How would the fire alarm affect the experiment?

8. Does the classical experimental design guarantee that the threats to internal validity are controlled? Explain your answer.

9. What conditions should be met for a posttest-only design to work well?

10. A researcher wants to see if question wording affects how much people say they are willing to pay for a program to prevent the deaths of birds from oil spills. He asks 200 people who come into a San Francisco science museum to volunteer to answer a questionnaire. The volunteers are randomly assigned to receive one of four versions of a questionnaire.

Version 1: How much a respondent is willing to donate for the program

Version 2: How much a respondent is willing to be taxed for the program

Version 3: How much a respondent is willing to donate for the program (with a reminder that other people will also be donating)

Version 4: How much a respondent is willing to be taxed for the program (with a reminder that other people will also be taxed)

a. Use the $R \ X \ O$ notation to summarize the study design.

b. Briefly assess if the author's use of a nonrandom (convenience) sample will affect the internal validity and external validity of the study.

11. Discuss the strengths and weaknesses of the comparison group pretest/posttest design.

12. Why is the interrupted time-series design used so often in administrative and policy research?

13. Summarize the advantages and disadvantages of nonexperimental designs.

14. A newspaper observes that after an "experiment" in cutting the cost of Internet access, half the residents of Blacksburg, Virginia, were "regular users of the global computer network."

Blacksburg, with a population of 37,000, is home to Virginia Tech, a university with a strong engineering program. Infer the study's design. What threats to internal validity seem plausible?

PROBLEMS FOR HOMEWORK AND DISCUSSION

1. To determine if halfway houses improve the transition from prison, 50 inmates who will be released in a month are randomly assigned to one of two groups. One group is sent to a halfway house to participate in a program called "ReEntry." The other group stays in prison until the time of release. Two months after release, data measuring "success in job placement" are gathered on the subjects in both groups.

a. Use the $R, \ X, \ O$ notation to sketch the research design.

b. Someone says that the design does not control for statistical regression since the subjects are inmates and thus represent an "extreme in their social behavior." Do you agree that the design has problems with statistical regression? Explain.

c. Define the terms *internal validity* and *external validity* in the context of this study.

2. Three hundred persons working in 40 state offices process X120 forms.

a. To evaluate a proposed change in the X120 form, would you randomly assign offices or individuals? That is, if offices are assigned, 15 offices would use the form with the proposed change, and 15 offices would continue to use the existing form. If individuals are assigned, roughly 50 percent of the individuals in the office would use the form with the proposed change, and 50 percent would continue with the existing form.

b. Would you allow subjects to volunteer to test the new X120 form? Justify your answer.

c. Would you test the new X120 form in the three slowest offices and evaluate the change in productivity? Justify your answer.

3. Rye County Hospital's Wellness Center is testing two programs to get smokers to quit. STOP is offered on Tuesday nights and QUIT is offered on Thursday nights. Ninety smokers volunteered to be subjects. They will be randomly assigned to STOP, QUIT, or No Treatment (neither group).

a. What two threats to internal validity are controlled by random assignment?

b. About the time the smoking study started, cigarette taxes increased sharply. Would this affect the internal validity of the study? Justify your answer.

c. Several subjects assigned to QUIT had a schedule conflict with their aerobics class. Before the program began, a secretary let them trade places with subjects assigned to STOP. Comment on how the secretary's action probably affected the study's internal validity.

d. STOP and QUIT begin and end in the same week. At the last session of the STOP program, data on the subjects' smoking behavior were gathered. The analysts forgot to gather the same data from the QUIT subjects. Three weeks later the oversight was discovered, and the data were collected. Comment on how the oversight may have affected the study's internal validity.

e. What is the value of having a No Treatment group?

4. A school system conducts a workshop on child abuse and neglect. Attendance is voluntary; 30 percent of school employees indicate that they will attend. To decide whether the workshops should be continued and attendance made mandatory, the staff selects a comparison group from among employees who did not preregister. Before the workshop, both groups are given a questionnaire on the signs of child abuse and neglect, attitudes about violence, and knowledge of reporting requirements. A similar questionnaire is given to members of both groups after the workshop is over.

a. Name this type of design. Use the R, X, O notation and diagram the design in symbols.

b. Consider each threat to validity, and explain whether it is a problem in this design.

c. Evaluate the external validity of this study.

d. Suggest a design that would provide better evidence for the decision. Would the staff find this alternative design practical to implement? Explain.

5. To reduce crime, a police force tries team policing, which has two officers walk a beat together. If trouble arises, the team calls a patrol car for backup reinforcement.

a. Suggest two different designs to determine the effectiveness of team policing.

b. Indicate how well each design handles the threats to internal validity.

c. Assess the external validity of these designs.

6. A state housing agency director wants to see if changing procedures in the emergency housing assistance program will speed the processing of claims. He selects a sample of 10 counties, then randomly selects 5 counties to adopt the new procedures and 5 to continue with current procedures. He measures the length of time required to process claims before and after the changes are adopted.

a. Name and diagram this design in the R, X, O symbols.

b. Revise the design, making it a randomized posttest design. Explain how the study would be conducted; diagram the new design. Would this design have any advantages over the original design?

c. Revise the design, making it an interrupted time-series design with comparison group.

Assume a time period of six years with data recorded every three months and the new procedures adopted at the end of year four. Draw a graph illustrating the time series if the new procedure was successful.

7. To study organic farming, researchers matched each organic farm with a nonorganic farm of the same size and soil composition. Some agricultural researchers criticized the study design, which they said should have compared small adjacent plots—one exposed to chemical fertilizers and insecticides and the other not exposed. Assess the benefits of the matched study over the classical experimental study to determine the effectiveness of organic farming.

8. A school system will conduct research prior to deciding to require Ninth graders to take Algebra I. (Currently, only 30 percent of Ninth graders take Algebra I. Very few students entering Ninth grade have completed Algebra; any Ninth grader who has passed Algebra I will not be required to take it again.) Three proposed research plans are outlined here:

Plan A: Select a random sample of files of students who complete Ninth grade in June. Compare the math achievement scores of students who took Algebra I with those of students who have not taken Algebra I.

Plan B: Require all Ninth graders in a "typical" high school to take Algebra I in this school year. Compare students' math achievement scores at the beginning of the year with their end-of-year scores.

Plan C: Select two similar high schools. Randomly assign one of the schools to require all Ninth graders to take Algebra I in this school year. In the other school, students may choose whether to take Algebra I. Compare the two schools' math achievement scores at the beginning of the year with their end-of-year scores.

a. Evaluate the three plans, and recommend which plan the school system should implement.

b. Assume the school system requires all Ninth graders to take Algebra I. The school system wants to conduct an interrupted time series to assess the requirement's effectiveness. What features should the time series include to yield useful information?

9. Design an experimental study to see whether administrators make better use of information from graphs or from tables. Your design should indicate, specifically, subject selection and assignment and how you will control exposure to the independent variable. Unless you plan to carry out the experiment, you do not need to select specific pretest or posttest measures, nor do you have to prepare specific tables and graphs. Generally describe the measures, tables, and graphs you would use.

DISK WORK

1. Since the beginning of the decade, 21 counties in North Carolina agreed to use experimental policies for county welfare programs. As a result, they hoped to reduce county spending. The rest of the counties stayed with their old policies, similar to each other and following a state model.

a. Separate the data into two groups—those with the experimental policies and those without. How do the variables Human Services Expenditures and Medicaid expenditures vary across the counties that participated in the experimental programs and those that did not? Are there differences? If you find differences, do you think participating in the program led to the differences? What else might account for the differences? If there are not differences, are you surprised? What might explain the lack of differences?

b. Can a researcher generalize from these findings to other states considering similar experiments? Who or why not?

2. What type of study might you recommend for another state interested in reducing its Human Services or Medicaid expenditures by experimenting with welfare reform at the county level?

3. Model how the original experiment might work, with counties with experimental policies hoping to have less human services expenditures. Make your model similar to the schematic in Figure 3.4. Make another model according to the study you designed in question 2.

RECOMMENDED FOR FURTHER READING

T. D. Cook and D. T. Campbell, *Quasi-Experimentation* (Boston: Houghton Mifflin, 1979) is a valuable resource for understanding fully experimental and quasi-experimental designs in field settings. The authors discuss and extend the ideas presented in D. T. Campbell and J. T. Stanley, *Experimental and Quasi-Experimental Design for Research* (Chicago: Rand McNally, 1966).

The recommended text on the statistical analysis of time-series data is R. McCleary and R. A. Hay, Jr., *Applied Time Series Analysis for the Social Sciences* (Beverly Hills: Sage, 1980).

Michael Lewis-Beck discusses interrupted time series designs and statistical tools used to analyze data from them. One of the tools is regression analysis, which most master's-level students have studied. See "Interrupted Time Series," Chapter 9 in William Berry and Michael Lewis-Beck (eds.), *New Tools for Social Scientists: Advances and Applications in Research Methods* (Beverly Hills, CA: Sage Publications, 1986).

Texts in program evaluation discuss these designs and give cases illustrating their use. See E. J. Posavac and R. G. Carey, *Program Evaluation: Methods and Case Studies,* 5th ed. (Englewood Cliffs, NJ: Prentice-Hall, 1997). P. H. Rossi, M.W. Lipsey, and H. E. Freeman, *Evaluation: A Systematic Approach,* 7th ed. (Thousand Oaks, CA: Sage Publications, 2004); *Handbook of Practical Program Evaluation,* ed. J. S. Wholey et al. (San Francisco: Jossey-Bass Publishers, 2004); and J. Valadez and M. Baberger, *Monitoring and Evaluating Social Programs in Developing Countries* (Washington, DC: World Bank, 1994) present 10 quasi-experimental designs with examples of their use.

Measuring Variables

In this chapter you will learn

1. Terms associated with quantifying or measuring variables: *conceptual* and *operational definition, measurement, measurement scales, reliability, operational validity, sensitivity.*

2. Why policy makers and administrators need to review a measure's operational definition and assess its quality.

3. Categories used to describe measurement scales and their role in developing measures.

4. Strategies for developing reliable, operationally valid, and sensitive measures.

5. Strategies for assessing the reliability, operational validity, and sensitivity of measures.

Researchers, reporters, administrators, and citizens should understand measurement, i.e., how numbers are assigned to phenomena. This is true whether data represent environmental conditions, the state of the economy, student achievement, public opinion, or something else. Data can influence policy decisions, demonstrate accountability, and classify people. Consequently, researchers must take care in designing measures, and data users must understand measurement concepts.

Measurement starts as investigators clarify the meaning of each variable of interest. We can label the variable under consideration as a concept and its meaning as a conceptual definition. A *concept* is an abstraction representing an idea. A *conceptual definition* indicates what one means by a concept. Conceptual definitions range from brief descriptions to thorough, detailed statements.[1] Their content depends on the intended use of the measure. Consider the concept of alcohol abuse. Its definition could include physical or physiological symptoms due to drinking; inability to meet work, social, or family obligations due to drinking; binge drinking; or self-identification of a drinking problem. The appropriate conceptual definition depends on a study's purpose. A university, wanting to identify the extent of alcohol abuse, may define it as involving binge drinking. An employer, wanting to identify sources of workplace problems, may define it as drinking that affects work performance. A physician making diagnoses may define it as involving verifiable symptoms.

Next, guided by the conceptual definition, the investigator finds a way to measure it. An *operational definition* is formulated from the conceptual definition. It details exactly how values will be assigned to a variable. Survey items and their responses provide examples of operational definitions. If the conceptual definition of alcohol abuse was whether or not a person indulged in binge drinking, the accompanying operational definition of alcohol abuse might be: "Alcohol abusers are persons who answered 'yes' to the question, 'Did you drink five or more drinks of wine, beer, or hard liquor at one time during the past month?'"

For another example, let us consider the concept of employee empowerment. First, you may want to consider what the concept means to you. One conceptual definition states that empowered employees have four characteristics. They believe that (1) their work is meaningful, (2) they are competent do their job, (3) they have autonomy in performing their work, and (4) their work has an impact on the organization.[2] This conceptual definition implies that the operational definition should measure meaning, competency, autonomy, and impact. Example 4.1 suggests items that could constitute the operational definition of empowerment. Each item is linked to one of the components of the conceptual definition. Respondents would read the statements describing their work and check the appropriate response to each statement. The investigator assigns each response a numerical value, adds up the responses, and, depending on the planned analysis, the responses may be grouped together. The survey including these items would also have items measuring other variables of interest.

Example 4.2 draws upon an incident in which an engineer convinced a budget director to approve a more productive strategy for resurfacing city highways. We assume that the budget director and the engineer never met to discuss either their conceptual definitions of productivity improvement or how the engineer operationally defined it. The engineer formulated an operational definition of productivity based on his conceptual definition of decreasing the cost per lane-mile paved. Using his operational definition, he analyzed alternative highway resurfacing programs. The budget director, who apparently equated productivity with paving more streets without increasing costs, approved the program that cost $2,500 less for each lane-mile paved. Unfortunately, he had also approved a resurfacing program that cost $187,500 over budget.

The misunderstanding in Example 4.2 should convince you of the importance of conceptual and operational definitions. Studies of the same phenomenon can arrive at different, even conflicting, conclusions if they used different conceptual or operational definitions. Administrators who ignore the details of defining variables may waste time and money. Studies based on faulty measures may generate misleading, incorrect, or useless data. A sound conceptual definition is consistent with the intended use of the data. An operational definition

EXAMPLE 4.1

An Operational Definition of Employee Empowerment

Survey Items and Responses:
Please indicate your level of agreement with each of the following statements.

1. The work I do is meaningful to me.
   _____ Strongly Agree
   _____ Agree
   _____ Neither Agree nor Disagree
   _____ Disagree
   _____ Strongly Disagree

2. I know what is expected of me on my job.
   _____ Strongly Agree
   _____ Agree
   _____ Neither Agree nor Disagree
   _____ Disagree
   _____ Strongly Disagree

3. In the past two years I have been given more flexibility to do my job.
   _____ Strongly Agree
   _____ Agree
   _____ Neither Agree nor Disagree
   _____ Disagree
   _____ Strongly Disagree

4. The work I perform contributes to the organization's mission.
   _____ Strongly Agree
   _____ Agree
   _____ Neither Agree nor Disagree
   _____ Disagree
   _____ Strongly Disagree

Step 1:   Assign values to each response, that is:
Assign 5 to every "Strongly Agree" response.
Assign 4 to every "Agree" response.
Assign 3 to every "Neither Agree nor Disagree" response.
Assign 2 to every "Disagree" response.
Assign 1 to every "Strongly Disagree" response.

Step 2:   Total the responses to statements 1–4 to determine a respondent's perceived degree of empowerment. Note: If all items are answered, values can range from 4 (least empowered) to 20 (most empowered).

Step 3:   Decide whether to group values, for example:
Not empowered: scores 4–10
Limited empowerment: scores 11–15
Most empowered: scores 16–20
Alternatively, the mean of responses may be calculated and grouped.

SOURCE: Adapted from items in *Merit Protection Survey 2000,* U.S. Merit Protection Board. In practice researchers would create several items to measure the separate components indicated in the conceptual definition.

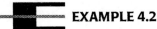 **EXAMPLE 4.2**

Concepts and Operational Definitions

Problem: Increase the productivity of New York City's highway resurfacing program.

Budget director's conceptual definition of productivity: Ability to produce more services with less resources.

Engineer's conceptual definition of productivity: "Efficiency value," i.e., the difference in cost between a more efficient and a less efficient method.

Operational definition of productivity (based on engineer's conceptual definition): Efficiency value = Reduction in cost per lane-mile × number of miles resurfaced.

Analysis: Compared two alternate policies: (1) paving 75 lane-miles; (2) paving 100 lane-miles.

1. Costs
   a. Labor: $10,000 per lane-mile to pave 75 lane-miles
      Labor: $ 7,500 per lane-mile to pave 100 lane-miles
   b. Asphalt: $7,500 per lane-mile
2. Efficiency value calculations
   a. Reduction in cost per lane-mile
      (1) cost per lane-mile for 75 lane-miles = $10,000 + $7,500 = $17,500
      (2) cost per lane-mile for 100 lane-miles = $7,500 + $7,500 = $15,000
      (3) reduction in cost per lane-mile for 100 lane-miles = $17,500 − $15,000 = $2,500
   b. Efficiency value = $2,500 × 100 lane-miles = $25,000

Action: Budget director accepted the 100 lane-mile proposal assuming a $25,000 cost saving. Note the actual costs for paving 75- and 100-lane-miles.

$$\text{Cost} = (\text{labor/lane-mile} + \text{asphalt/lane-mile}) \times \text{lane-miles}$$
$$\text{For 75 lane-miles} = (\$10,000 + \$7,500) \times 75 = \$1,312,500$$
$$\text{For 100 lane-miles} = (\$7,500 + \$7,500) \times 100 = \$1,500,000$$

Result: Cost was $187,500 over budget.

Discussion: The budget director's conceptual definition of productivity was that the city could produce more services (100 lane-miles resurfaced) with the same resources used to resurface 75 lane-miles. His conceptual definition required a different operational definition: a definition that linked annual program costs with the number of miles resurfaced.

SOURCE: P. D. Epstein, "The Value of Measuring and Improving Performance," *Public Productivity Review* 6 (September 1982): 157–166.

may be faulty because it is based on an inappropriate or inadequate conceptual definition or there are technical flaws in the operational definition. At a minimum, administrators should carefully review a proposed conceptual definition and how it is operationally defined. (This chapter and Chapter 7 focus on the technical issues that affect the quality of an operational definition.)

MEASUREMENT AND MEASUREMENT SCALES

The terms *operational definition* and *measurement* are similar. *Measurement* applies rules to assign numbers to the values of a variable. *Operational definitions* indicate exactly how a specific variable is being measured. For example, consider the variable "number of bedrooms." The U.S. Census Bureau defines a bedroom as a room "used mainly for sleeping." The number of bedrooms in a studio apartment or other one-room unit is zero. A guest room is counted if it is reserved primarily for sleeping, even if it is used infrequently. A living room with a sofa bed is not counted even if it is used for sleeping all the time. Not all operational definitions are as simple. For example, to measure the level of air pollution, the operational definition includes precise instructions on how to select an air sample, how many samples to take, requirements for calibrating instruments, and laboratory personnel competencies.[3]

Exactly what value should you assign to an object or event? To determine this, you need to understand *measurement scales* or *levels of measurement*. Most writers on measurement discuss four scales: nominal scales, ordinal scales, interval scales, and ratio scales. Each scale involves categorization. Each object or event observed should be described by one and only one value or category of a scale. In other words, the values or categories should be exhaustive and mutually exclusive. As we discuss in Chapters 11 through 14, a variable's level of measurement affects the statistics you choose and how you interpret them.

Nominal Scales

Nominal scales measure characteristics by identifying and labeling categories. Nominal scales do not rank categories. You cannot place the different values of a characteristic measured by a nominal scale along a continuum. Individual cases cannot be ordered according to their values on a nominal scale. Even though numbers are sometimes assigned to nominal categories, these numbers have no particular importance beyond allowing one to classify and count the number of cases in each category. One might, for example, classify town employees by department. You could devise the following nominal scale:

1 = Planning

2 = Human Resources

3 = Finance

4 = Budgeting

5 = Public Works

6 = Public Safety

Note that if other numbers were assigned to the various categories, the information would remain the same. The numbers are a device to identify categories; letters of the alphabet or other symbols could replace the numbers and the scale would be unchanged. Remember, too, that values of nominal scales are not ranked. In other words, the numbering system does not imply that Finance is more or less important than Budgeting. Typical examples of characteristics measured by a nominal scale are gender, region, and occupation.

Ordinal Scales

Ordinal scales identify and categorize values of a variable and put them in rank order according to those values. They do so, however, without regard to the distance between values. Ordinal scales measure characteristics by determining that one case has more or less of the characteristic than does another case. If you can rank values but not determine how far apart they are, you have an ordinal scale. The numbers assigned to the values must be in the same order as the ranking implied by the scale. For example, the value represented by 3 is greater than the value represented by 2, and the value represented by 2 is greater than the value represented by 1. However, the numbers do not imply an amount of the characteristic measured, only an order of more or less. Let's look at how you could assign numbers to ordinal scale items:

> 5 = Strongly Agree
>
> 4 = Agree
>
> 3 = Neither Agree nor Disagree
>
> 2 = Disagree
>
> 1 = Strongly Disagree

You can try other numbering schemes as long as the numbers preserve the rank order of the categories. For example, you could reverse the order and number "Strongly Agree" as "1" and "Strongly Disagree" as "5." Alternatively, you could skip numbers and number the categories 10, 8, 6, 4, and 2. Because you cannot determine the distance between values, you cannot argue that an employee who answers "Strongly Agree" to all items is five times happier than an employee who answers "Strongly Disagree" to all items.

Rankings commonly result in an ordinal scale. A supervisor may rank 10 employees and give the best employee a "10" and the worst a "1." The persons rated "10" and "9" may be exceptionally good, and the supervisor may have a hard time deciding which one is better. The employee rated with "8" may be good, but not nearly as good as the top two. Hence, the difference between employee "10" and employee "9" may be very small and much less than the difference between employee "9" and employee "8."

Interval and Ratio Scales

Interval and ratio scales measure characteristics by ranking their values on a scale and determining the numerical differences between them. The distance between objects whose characteristics have been measured can be determined by using standard intervals. The difference between 10 and 20, for example, measures the same amount of the characteristic as does the difference between 30 and 40. A *ratio scale* has a fixed or absolute zero; an *interval scale* does not. A fixed zero permits one to use ratios to describe relationships between scaled objects. You can add or subtract objects measured by interval and ratio scales. You can multiply and divide the values of the characteristics measured by a ratio scale. Temperature scales are the most common examples of an interval scale. You can state that 50°F is 25 degrees warmer than 25°F, but you cannot state that 50°F is twice as warm as 25°F.

In administrative research, investigators commonly work with ratio scales. Frequently used ratio measures include amount of a total budget or its components, program costs, the population size, or the number of program participants. Few characteristics in social and administrative research are measured by interval scales that are not also ratio scales. In this text we use a common social science convention and ignore the distinction between interval and ratio scales. We will usually refer to them both as "interval scales."

The numbers assigned to interval scales correspond to the magnitude of the phenomenon being measured. Thus the numbers assigned could be the actual number of persons working in an agency, the number of homeless persons in a given year, or the amount of per capita income in a city. If the county has 100 employees and one of its municipalities has 50, we can say that the county has 50 more employees than the town. We can also note that the county has twice as many employees as the town.

In practice, the boundary between ordinal and interval scales may be blurred, especially if the ordinal scale has a large number of values. Some ordinal scales have been created to approximate an interval measure, that is, to estimate the points along an underlying interval scale. For example, ordinal scales, such as IQ scores, suggest the magnitude of differences along the scale, have many categories, and appear to be interval. One can argue that such scales do not have equal-distance intervals; for example, one cannot state with certainty that the difference between an IQ of 100 and an IQ of 110 is the same as the difference between an IQ of 120 and one of 130. Analysts frequently treat summated scales, such as the employee empowerment scale in Example 4.1, as interval scales.

Students often mistakenly assume that groups or categories containing interval or ratio data form an interval scale. They do not. Rather, the new scale is ordinal. For example, although age is an interval scale, the following categories constitute an ordinal scale: under 21 years old, 21 to 30 years old, 31 to 40 years old, and so forth. The exact distance—that is, the age difference between any two people—cannot be determined. While we know a person who checks off 21 to 30 years old is younger than a person who checks off 31 to 40 years old, the age difference between them could be a few days or nearly 10 years.[4]

Alternative Terminologies

Not all statisticians classify measurement scales or variables as nominal, ordinal, interval, and ratio. Nominal and ordinal variables may be called *categorical variables*, while interval and ratio variables may be called *numerical variables*. The values of categorical variables have labels; the values of numerical variables are numbers that indicate quantities. Categorical variables may be divided further into *ordered categorical variables*, another term for ordinal scales, and *unordered categorical variables*, another term for nominal scales.

Variables also may be described as discrete or continuous. Discrete variables have a limited number of values; continuous variables can take on an unlimited number of values, depending on the precision of the measuring instrument. For example, the number of divisions in an organization is a discrete variable. An agency may have 10 or 11 divisions; it cannot have 10.3 divisions. The amount of time an employee spends on a task forms a continuous variable. An employee may be said to spend 5 hours on a task, 5.4 hours, 5.46 hours, and so on.

The nominal, ordinal, interval, and ratio classification system is widespread and adequate for our purposes. Nevertheless, you may come across the terms "categorical," "discrete," and "continuous" from time to time. Table 4.1 illustrates the relationships among these three classification schemes.

The Role of Measurement Scales

Before data are collected, someone needs to ensure that variables are measured at a level appropriate to the planned analysis. Some people may try to collect data at the interval or ratio level, because a greater number of statistical tools can be applied to interval data. Nevertheless, this is not always advisable. First, a shift in measurement level may require a change in the variable. In a study of office automation, for example, you might want to learn what types of computer hardware various agencies use, a nominal measure. By asking how many different types of hardware they own or how much the computer hardware costs, you could generate interval level data. In the process, however, you would have changed the definition of the variable radically. Equipment cost is not equivalent to types of equipment.

A second reason for not attempting to create an interval scale is that this sometimes leads to a request for information that respondents are unwilling to provide. For example, respondents may feel that requests for information on their exact age may be combined with other information on an anonymous survey to uncover their identity. Alternatively, a request for precise information that cannot be given without checking records may irritate a respondent. For some studies, such irritation may result in a lower response rate or made-up information. An investigator must then decide whether less-precise grouped data are consistent with a study's purpose. Annual income is an example. Although individuals may

TABLE 4.1	COMPARABLE TERMS FOR LEVELS OF MEASUREMENT CLASSIFICATION SCHEMES	
Scheme 1	Scheme 2	Scheme 3
Nominal	Categorical; Unordered Categorical	Discrete; Dichotomous; Unordered Categorical
Ordinal	Categorical; Ordered Categorical	Discrete; Ordered Categorical
Interval and Ratio	Numerical	Discrete; Integer Valued Continuous

know their approximate annual income, few have exact figures at hand. If asked, they may have to check tax records or may give a rough estimate. Questions that ask about income within ranges, such as $10,000 to $19,999; $20,000 to $29,999; and $30,000 to $39,999 often provide more data. Furthermore, the groupings may reduce the reluctance of Americans to reveal their incomes and increase the number who provide income information.

RELIABILITY

The critical factors in selecting a measure and a measurement scale are reliability, operational validity, and sensitivity. When you ask, "Is the measured difference between subjects a real difference?" or "Is a difference over time a real difference?" you are questioning the reliability of the measurement. When you ask, "Does this measure actually produce data on the concept or variable of interest?" you are questioning its operational validity. When you ask, "Is this measure sufficiently precise?" you are questioning its sensitivity.

Reliability evaluates the consistency of a measure. Differences over time or between subjects may be due to measurement errors. *Measurement errors* are random errors that result from the measurement process. No measurement is error free. Errors occur because of respondent characteristics, the measure itself, or the process of assigning values. Uninterested or distracted respondents introduce errors when they answer questions rapidly. Items with ambiguous terms or inappropriate responses lead to errors. Raters may be inconsistent in how they assign scores.

For a familiar example of an unreliable measure, consider a scale. If you weigh yourself and find that you have gained five pounds, you may react immediately by reweighing yourself. Suppose the second time the scale shows you lost three pounds, an eight-pound difference within seconds. You would consider the scale inconsistent or unreliable. While random error cannot be eliminated completely, the error rate should be kept at a tolerable level. A measure that yields a lot of random error should be judged unreliable and discarded.

Dimensions of Reliability

Reliability has three dimensions: stability, equivalence, and internal consistency. *Stability* refers to the ability of a measure to yield the same results time after time, if and only if what is being measured has not changed. The scale that indicates a different weight for an object each time it is weighed lacks stability. We ask about stability when we ask if an investigator assigns the same number to the same phenomenon each time. If a school counselor examines student files to identify children with learning difficulties, how consistent are her choices? Do her criteria, which constitute her measure of learning difficulties, change with mood changes, fatigue, degree of attention, or other uncontrolled factors? She should check a sample of her work to make sure each case was identified and recorded consistently. Did she identify the same students both times? If she finds relatively few inconsistencies in the sample, she can assume that her measure is reliable.

Equivalence considers (1) whether two or more investigators using a measure assign the same value to the same phenomenon, or (2) whether different versions of a measure assign the same value to a phenomenon. For example, different inspectors rating the quality of housing should give the same houses the same scores. To check the reliability of a rating system, each inspector rates all the houses in a sample of houses. The sample should represent the range of housing types and conditions apt to be encountered in an actual survey of housing. If the rating system is reliable, the inspectors' ratings for each house should be identical. Nevertheless, some random error must be anticipated, and a decision must be made as to how much error a reliable instrument may contain.

Occasionally, different versions of a measure must be used. This occurs most commonly in testing. Different versions of a test may be created to avoid cheating. Consider written driving tests. If each applicant took the same test, cheating would be a problem, so numerous versions are needed. Equivalence requires that any test taker receives the same score no matter which test version he takes.

Internal consistency applies to measures with multiple items. It considers whether all the items are related to the same phenomenon. For example, employee surveys may include questions measuring (a) job satisfaction, (b) empowerment, (c) fair treatment, and (d) training. To be internally consistent the measures for each concept should be homogeneous. In general, a measure's reliability increases as the number of questions increases. The importance of using more than one item to measure a variable depends on the underlying concept. A single item is sufficient to measure variables such as a person's age, sex, or similar demographic characteristic. However, measuring individual achievements, attitudes, and opinions usually requires multiple items. For example, in Example 4.1 we used four items to measure empowerment.

The following list summarizes the dimensions of reliability.

Dimensions of Reliability

Stability: measure gives same result when applied to the same phenomenon more than one time; that is, different results should occur only if the phenomenon being measured changes.

Equivalence: measure gives same result when applied to the same phenomenon by more than one investigator; different versions of a test give same result when applied to the same phenomenon.

Internal consistency: all items constituting a measure are homogeneous; they all are related to the same concept.

Establishing a Measure's Reliability

You cannot expect a measure to be completely free from random error. Mood, test conditions, and other factors can affect performance on any given day. Consequently, we must determine how much error to tolerate with respect to any given measure.

For example, to schedule advisors during the week when high school students can change their class schedules, a supervisor checks school files to identify patterns of schedule changes. She divides the files into four categories: no schedule changes, minor schedule changes, major schedule changes, and complicated schedule changes. She may feel that an error rate as high as 15 percent is tolerable. If so, to consider her data reliable, she needs to place at least 85 out of every 100 files rechecked in the same category as she did the first time. On the other hand, if she were reviewing files to identify students who were going to be assessed for learning disabilities, an error rate of 15 percent would be too high. A far lower error rate would be required to reduce the number of cases incorrectly referred for assessment. The counselor would want to reduce the following two errors. The first error is missing children in need of assessment. The second error is incorrectly referring children for assessment.

To establish a criterion for reliability, an administrator or policy analyst should consider the practical consequences of random error. Minimizing random error may seem desirable, but many measures cannot be refined to meet high standards of accuracy. Estimating and reducing the level of error may be costly. Procedures to estimate the degree of reliability have their own assumptions and limitations, further reducing our ability to establish with certainty a measure's reliability.

To estimate reliability or to apply a measure with known reliability, you should remember that reliability is not only a property of a measure. Reliability also is a function of the conditions under which it is applied. For example, most bathroom scales are unreliable at the extremes of body weight; that is, they do not give consistent weights for infants or very heavy people. Similarly, other measures are designed to work in certain settings. The school counselor may ably select cases from among her caseload. She may be unable to choose cases accurately from the caseload of a counselor with different training or working in another school system. A driver's test may not be reliable for persons with limited knowledge of English or poor reading skills. A form to rate housing quality may not work equally well in a city and in a rural area.

Investigators use qualitative and quantitative methods to estimate reliability. The qualitative methods cannot estimate a measure's degree of random error precisely; hence, their importance and value may be underestimated. In practice, the qualitative methods can pick up serious problems that will thoroughly discredit a measure. The *qualitative methods* require that the investigators make sure that persons responsible for data collection, assigning values, and entering data are sufficiently trained and supervised, and that the investigators review a measure to decide whether

terms are defined precisely.

ambiguous items or terms have been eliminated.

information is accessible to respondents.

multiple-choice responses cover all probable responses.

directions are clear and easy to follow.

Let us start with the characteristics of the measures to see how the problems of imprecise items, ambiguous items, inaccessible information, poor response choices, and unclear directions affect reliability. Remember that an unreliable measure is one in which observed differences between subjects or in the same subject over time are due to the instrument or data collection procedures rather than to actual differences. Any of the five listed problems can result in similar subjects giving dissimilar responses or dissimilar subjects giving similar responses.

To see the reliability problems associated with imprecise terms, consider trying to measure the number of deaths caused by fires. If you asked city clerks how many people in their towns died in fires during the past calendar year, you may assume incorrectly that each town counts fire deaths the same way. Yet, some jurisdictions may include only deaths that occur within a certain time period, such as within 72 hours of a fire. Other jurisdictions may include only deaths caused by burns or smoke inhalation. Thus a person who died from a heart attack while escaping a fire might not count as a fire death in Town A but will count as a fire death in Town B.

Similar to the problem of imprecise terms is the problem of ambiguity. For one reason or another, an item that seems perfectly clear to the investigators may confuse respondents. The reliability problem caused by ambiguous items may be seen easily by considering the following question and responses:

What is your marital status?

_____ Single

_____ Married

_____ Separated

_____ Divorced

_____ Widowed

As you know, many adults lead complicated lives, and if the word "current" does not appear in the question, a person can accurately check more than one response. Similarly, because many formerly married people consider themselves to be single, the single category should be "single, never married." If just "single" is used, some currently divorced people may check just "single," others "divorced," and others both "single" and "divorced."

If the requested information is not available to respondents, they may guess or use different rules to estimate the correct response. Consider the example of fire deaths. If towns place all fire deaths in one category and keep no records on specific causes, how will they answer a request to indicate how many deaths are caused by smoke inhalation?

If multiple-choice items do not include probable responses, respondents left to their own devices may guess the item's intent. Recall your classroom experiences with multiple-choice tests. What did you do if none of the listed answers seemed remotely related to your answer? Chances are you guessed. So too will some respondents when faced with choices that they find inappropriate. Unclear or complicated directions may cause unreliable data because respondents misinterpret the directions or answer more or less at random because of frustration, anger, or boredom.

Persons involved in data collection must be trained and supervised to reduce problems of reliability, that is, to minimize the number of individual and inconsistent decisions. Thus if investigators are sent to fire departments to collect data, each investigator should define fire deaths the same way and use the same procedures for resolving problems of inaccessible or ambiguous information. Similarly, raters may be uncertain how to score questionnaires on which respondents changed the response categories by combining responses, by embellishing a response category with their own comments, or by adding an alternative response. If individual raters decide on a case-by-case basis how to handle ambiguous responses, the decisions may be inconsistent and the data more unreliable.

Reliability may be estimated with mathematical procedures.[5] Specific tests estimate the measurement error associated with each dimension of reliability. We will limit our discussion to the most common tests that establish homogeneity, equivalence, and stability. Administrators who construct or work extensively with job tests, achievement tests, or personality tests will want to become familiar with other methods for mathematically estimating reliability.

Tests of internal consistency establish the homogeneity of the items in a measure. When a measure includes several items, an analyst should establish its internal consistency. A *test of internal consistency*, easily performed with statistical software, demonstrates if a measure has extensive random errors due to unreliable or heterogeneous items.[6] Example 4.3 applies a test of internal consistency to a measure of police professionalism. The items included citizen ratings of police officers' attitude, competence, performance, and courtesy, and an item about police visibility. The key statistic is alpha, a reliability coefficient. The closer alpha is to 1.0, the more reliable the measure. If alpha is close to 0.0, the measure has too few items or the items are unrelated to one another. (A negative alpha indicates that the items violate the assumption of homogeneity.) In the example, alpha = .7795; deleting the visibility item will increase alpha to .8787.

As is true with many statistics, there are no set criteria for an acceptable alpha. A major benefit of the test is that it identifies items that diminish the measure's internal consistency and should be excluded from the measure. An investigator who reports the results of a test of internal consistency has verified that she performed this reliability test. She has provided information that the reader can use to decide whether the evidence of the measure's internal consistency is weak, strong, or somewhere in between.

Inter-rater reliability establishes the equivalence or consistency of the measures reported by two or more observers. Inter-rater reliability applies to a wide range of administrative data collection projects when more than one person applies a measure. If two or more staff members review and rate job applicants, they should agree on who are the best applicants. Inter-rater reliability is established by having observers apply a measure to the same phenomena and independently record the scores. The scores are then compared using one of several procedures to determine whether the level of agreement is appropriate.

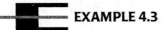 **EXAMPLE 4.3**

Establishing Internal Consistency

Problem: Establish the reliability of a measure of police professionalism.
   Procedure:

1. Create a measure of police professionalism by adding respondents' answers to the following items:
   In my most recent contact with a city police officer:
      The officer was courteous (Courteous)
      (1) Agree   (2) Strongly Agree   (3) Disagree   (4) Strongly Disagree

      The officer was competent (Competent)
      (1) Agree   (2) Strongly Agree   (3) Disagree   (4) Strongly Disagree

      The officer displayed a professional attitude (Attitude)
      (1) Agree   (2) Strongly Agree   (3) Disagree   (4) Strongly Disagree

      The officer's overall performance was good (Performance)
      (1) Agree   (2) Strongly Agree   (3) Disagree   (4) Strongly Disagree

      As I move around the city, city police are
      (1) Often visible   (2) Sometimes visible   (3) Rarely visible   (4) Never visible

2. Examine the correlation matrix. The closer a correlation coefficient is to 1.00, the stronger the relationship.

	Attitude	Courteous	Competent	Performance	Visible
Attitude	1.0000				
Courteous	.6121	1.0000			
Competent	.6403	.6652	1.0000		
Performance	.6311	.6505	.6675	1.0000	
Visible	.0580	.0298	.0827	.0233	1.0000

   Note that the variable "Visible" has virtually no relationship with any of the other items, i.e., how an individual rates the attitude, courtesy, competence, or performance of the police is unrelated to his perception of police visibility.

3. Note the value of alpha. For these 5 items alpha = .7795.

4. Note if alpha can be improved by deleting any one of the items.

Item	Alpha if Item Deleted
Attitude	.6940
Courteous	.6923
Competent	.6749
Performance	.6884
Visible	.8787

EXAMPLE 4.3   *Continued*

5. Decide to eliminate "Visible" from the scale. Eliminating "Visible" clearly improves the reliability of the scale, e.g., its homogeneity. The low correlation coefficients for "Visible" confirm that it is unrelated to the other scale items. Removing any other items would weaken the homogeneity of the scale.

6. Report the reliability test by simply noting the value of alpha. "Police performance was measured by summing respondents' perceptions of police officers' attitudes, courtesy, competence, and performance (alpha = .8787)."

Example 4.4 outlines the steps researchers took to ensure surveyors collecting data on racial profiling agreed on each driver's race. A similar procedure could be used to see if staff gave similar ratings to job applicants. The actual study on racial profiling found about 88 percent agreement in identifying an individual's race. As when using alpha values to test internal consistency, before

EXAMPLE 4.4

Establishing Inter-rater Reliability

Problem: To determine if police officers engage in racial profiling.
  Key variables:

  Police stops; all stops (either traffic or pedestrian) made by a police officer which do not result in a ticket
  Racial composition of transient population: Asian, Black, White, Middle Eastern, Other, Unknown

  Procedure for measuring racial composition of transient population: Two surveyors are posted at various intersections. Each identifies the race of the drivers driving in one lane of traffic.
  Establish reliability of measure of racial composition:

$$Reliability = \frac{A}{A + D} \times 100\%$$

where:

A = number of agreements (surveyors assign same race to an individual)
D = number of disagreements (surveyors record different race for an individual)

  Notes: (1) This measure indicates how surveyors perceived a person's race—it does not measure the person's actual race; (2) the findings on the racial composition of the transient population are then compared with the racial composition of the population subjected to a police stop.

SOURCE: Adapted from John C. Lamberth, "Ann Arbor: Police Department Traffic Stop Data Collection: Methods and Analysis Study" (Chadds Ford, PA: Lamberth Consulting, 2004).

adopting the measure, the researcher has to decide if 88 percent agreement is sufficient and what the consequences are of not requiring a higher percentage of agreement.

The equivalence of two or more versions of a measure can be established by the *alternative forms technique*. Two or more versions of a measure are prepared. Subjects are asked to answer both versions. The scores on both versions of the measure are compared. If the measures yield similar scores, the versions are considered to be reliable. Creating comparable versions of a test is difficult. Consequently establishing reliability with alternative forms occurs primarily in situations where tests will be given to large numbers of people over a period of time, such as tests for driver's licenses.[7]

The *test-retest* technique establishes the stability of a measure. Test-retest requires that an instrument or test be administered to a subject at two points in time. If the results are dissimilar, the measure may be assumed to be unreliable. This procedure seems direct and reasonable, but if you think about it, you may recognize its limitations. First, the initial testing may affect the responses to the retest. Suppose you asked people to rate the adequacy of police protection in their community. Responding to this question could focus their attention on policing in their community and eventually lead to a change in their perceptions. Their retest responses would change. Such a change would not mean the measure involved was unreliable. Conversely, they may remember their first response and repeat it. In such a case, the lack of change between Time 1 and Time 2 does not verify the measure's reliability. Second, with practice, respondents' performance may change. They may benefit from familiarity with previously unfamiliar question formats or tasks. Third, an actual change, independent of the first testing, may take place between the two administrations, or tests, of the measure. The more time that passes the more likely an actual change has occurred.

The test-retest procedure is adequate, and useful, if the attribute being measured is unlikely to be influenced by the first test or to change between tests. The review of a sample of files to determine the consistency of measurement is a form of test-retest. If an investigator checks her work by using the test-retest procedure, she should wait long enough to forget how she originally measured specific cases. Obviously, in establishing reliability she would ignore new data placed in the file after the first test.

The reliability of most measures of interest to administration cannot be established through test-retest. As you read management, policy analysis, or social science articles, notice how rarely the authors indicated that they used test-retest to establish their measures' reliability. The major problem is the influence of the first test. It may cause a change, or respondents may remember and reproduce the first set of answers. Just as the person asked to rate police service may pay more attention to her neighborhood's policing and change her rating, other measures have a similar effect on how respondents observe and evaluate their environment. Alternatively, respondents may mull over the answers and decide another answer would have been more appropriate.

From our teaching experience, we have learned that students (1) underestimate the problems of using test-retest to estimate reliability and (2) confuse test-retest with the pretest-posttest of experiments. All research designs, including experiments, should use reliable measures. The data collected for an experiment will use measures only after an investigator has established their reliability.

Administrators, depending on how much they work with data and in what capacity, vary in their concern with reliability. At a minimum they want to affirm that data are free of gross errors. If they know a measure's operational definition, they can apply the qualitative method and identify the most serious threats to reliability. In some situations administrators need quantitative information to estimate precisely a measure's error rate. In these cases, more attention is given to a measure's reliability. A standard rule of thumb is to understand how reliable a measure needs to be for the task at hand. Below we summarize the major features of reliability.

Reliability: A Summary for Administrators

Reliability: evidence that a measure distinguishes accurately between subjects or over time. If a measure is reliable, one can assume that differences between subjects or over time are real differences.

Evidence of a measure's reliability:

Qualitative method: used to evaluate the reliability of any measure.

Internal consistency: used to demonstrate empirically that several items of a single measure are homogeneous.

Inter-rater reliability: used if more than one investigator collects data on a measure. Inter-rater reliability produces empirical evidence demonstrating the equivalence of scores assigned by different raters.

Alternative forms: used to demonstrate empirically that two different versions of a measure are equivalent in assigning scores to subjects. Administrative researchers, other than those who construct tests, rarely use this method.

Test-retest: used to demonstrate empirically the stability of a measure. Test-retest will not produce useful evidence of reliability if the first testing is likely to affect retest responses or performance, or the phenomenon being measured is likely to have changed between the test and the retest.

When to determine reliability: reliability should be determined prior to testing a hypothesis, collecting data, or introducing an intervention. Internal consistency may be determined after collecting data but prior to data analysis. Nevertheless, specific problems, such as ambiguous terms, may have been accidentally overlooked during initial reviews of a measure and identified only after the data have been collected or analyzed.

Relative nature of reliability: the degree of accuracy required depends on the purpose of the measure. A measure may be reliable for one purpose and not another.

By definition, an unreliable measure contains an unacceptable amount of random error. Data produced by an unreliable measure should be discarded. Depending on degree and source of the unreliability, the measure itself may be discarded or simply revised. Demonstrating a measure's reliability is only one step in determining its value.

OPERATIONAL VALIDITY

In addition to knowing that a measure is reliable, we also want to know whether it has been named correctly and that it measures what we intend to measure. Measures that measure what they are devised to measure are said to be *operationally valid*. Operational validity commonly is referred to simply as *validity*. We have found that students commonly confuse the validity of measures with the internal and external validity of experimental and quasi-experimental research. Thus, for the purposes of clarity, we prefer to use the term *operational validity* when discussing the validity of measures.

Accepting a measure as operationally valid is a matter of judgment. Consider measures intended to compare and rank the quality of life in American cities. The measures are meant to determine how desirable people consider a community as a place to live. If one investigator were to choose items that focused on cultural and recreational resources, while another selected items that focused on the social climate, such as the crime rate, unemployment rate, and the number of strikes, the results surely would differ. The first investigator would probably conclude that major cities were the best places to live. The second would probably assign higher rankings to smaller, more homogeneous cities. The operational validity of either measure could be challenged by arguing that it does not really measure quality of life.

Measuring the incidence of crime may seem to be a simpler assignment. At first glance one might assume that the number of crimes reported to police would be a clear-cut measure of the crime rate. However, not all crimes are reported. As a result, officials in cities with a high number of reported crimes can argue that reported crime actually measures the vigilance of police officers rather than the actual crime rate. Officials may suggest that in cities with lower crime rates police discourage victims from reporting crimes or that these cities do not have procedures to ensure accurate recording of crimes. Five events must occur for an actual crime to become part of the crime report:[8]

1. The crime must be known or perceived by someone other than the offender; for example, you must know your home was burglarized.
2. The person perceiving the act or its consequence must define it as a crime; for example, acts of domestic violence may not be defined as a crime by the victim.
3. Someone must report the crime to the police.
4. The police must define the reported act as a crime.
5. The police must record the crime in the appropriate category.

The requirements that a reported crime must be perceived, recognized as a crime, reported to the police, defined by the police as a crime, and recorded correctly do not imply that the crime report constitutes an operationally valid measure of crime rate. Rather, each of the first four requirements presents an opportunity to miss a crime and undercount the crime rate. The fifth requirement means that one type of crime might be undercounted and other overcounted.

Policy makers and program administrators should carefully consider a measure's proposed use and pay attention to its operational definition. This is true whether they are developing a measure or interpreting its findings. They start with a clear idea of what information they need. Consider the measures of poverty.[9] The information may track how the poverty rate changes over time, determine who should receive financial assistance, or describe the consequences of poverty for individuals and their community. The U.S. Census counts a family as poor if its pretax income falls below the "poverty threshold." The measure was developed in the 1960s. To determine the poverty threshold the estimated cost of feeding different-size families a minimally adequate diet was multiplied by three. The multiplier was based on a 1955 finding that a typical family spent one-third of its income on food.

The poverty threshold has provided a consistent measure of the poverty rate for nearly half a century. Yet, questions about the measure arise when it is used to determine who needs financial assistance. How do 1955 circumstances apply in the 21st century? For example, the average American household spends less than 15 percent of its income on food.[10] Should nonincome benefits be considered? What constitutes income today? The Census Bureau collects data on 15 definitions of income. Should regional variations in cost of living be considered? Does relative poverty, which considers social inequality, provide more insights into the effects of poverty?

The way in which a measure is labeled affects our perceptions and even our behaviors. Out of necessity, administrators deal with summarized information. Often, they have time only to read report highlights or hear brief presentations. Consequently, the label attached to a measure can seduce and mislead administrators. For example, a harried administrator may remember the findings about the "best" American city, without stopping to learn what criteria were used to rank cities. If you plan to act on findings you have read or heard, you should learn more about the measure used. Then you will be in a better position to decide whether your action will get the intended results.

Establishing a Measure's Operational Validity

Developing measures and amassing evidence of their validity is an ongoing process. Both the developers and users have responsibilities. The developers provide evidence supporting the measure's interpretation, and the users evaluate the evidence. What evidence is needed depends on what is practical and appropriate given a measure's intended use.[11] The evidence may be based on a measure's content and its relationship to other variables.[12] How convincing the evidence has to be depends on the potential impact of the measure. Evidence that shows a measure is inadequate or not working as expected is still a step forward. The evidence provides insight into what the measure is and is not measuring. Investigators can then build on the evidence to improve the measure.[13] In the following sections, we will address evidence based on content and evidence based on the relationship to other variables.

Evidence based on content   An important, and almost obvious piece of evidence of operational validity, is demonstrating that the operational definition is consistent with the conceptual definition. Consider Example 4.1, which measured employee empowerment. To be consistent with the conceptual definition the operational definition needed to measure if employees believe that (1) their work is meaningful, (2) they are competent to do their job, (3) they have autonomy in performing their work, and (4) their work has an impact on the organization. The data produced by the operational definition has merit only if potential users agree on the conceptual definition. In Example 4.2, the engineer and the budget director had different conceptual definitions of productivity. If the budget director had examined the content of the operational definition, he would have raised questions about its validity.

To see how investigators develop evidence based on a measure's content consider personnel selection procedures. A sound selection procedure identifies and ranks applicants based on their ability to do a job. At the simplest level a job description (the conceptual definition) that outlines the knowledge and skills wanted is written. Then staff decides how to evaluate and rank the applicants.

A more elaborate process may occur if positions are numerous, openings are relatively frequent, and the applicant pool is large. Analysts begin by systematically identifying the elements essential to the job. What skills must an employee have? What knowledge does she need? What is the relative importance of the skills and the knowledge? That is, are some skills or types of knowledge more important than others? After this is done, a blueprint for the selection procedures is created; the blueprint outlines the job components and their relative importance. Appropriate measures are developed for each job component, and more important skills or knowledge should receive greater weight than less important ones. The measures may be answers to an objective test, performance in a simulated exercise, or responses to interview questions.[14]

Before using a measure, you need to review the operational definition and any documentation describing its design. You will need to decide if the definition is relevant and representative. A relevant operational definition measures what you want to measure, that is, it captures the essence of the conceptual definition. A representative measure adequately corresponds to the conceptual definition. For example, the representativeness of measures of a nation's wealth has been questioned. Such measures may count all production without regard to its social value. Some critics question whether the measures should consider the cost of depleting a nation's natural resources or if production of weapons, tobacco products, or toxic wastes should be viewed as contributing to its wealth.[15]

Let's consider the relevance of official statistics. While an operational definition may stay the same, it may become less relevant over time. To estimate the inflation rate, governments track the costs of a sample of consumer goods and services. A major problem arises when consumer behavior changes. For many years, the typical American diet was heavy on red meat, eggs, and milk. Americans now eat less of these products and more poultry, fruits, and vegetables. So a measure that tracks the cost of foods eaten by a typical American family in 1950 will not reflect accurately the cost of foods eaten by a typical American family today.

Why not change the measure? First, establishing the typical American diet requires a costly nutritional survey.[16] Second, if the measure is changed, then comparability with the past is lost. To retain comparability, the revisions may be applied to older data, or both measures may be reported for a time.[17] If a measure was changed in the year 2005, data for earlier years may be adjusted to reflect the change; or beginning in the year 2005, data for both measures may be reported. Third, changes in certain measures inevitably bring charges of political manipulation. Can you imagine a politician advocating a change in a measure that would put his administration in a bad light?

Evidence based on relationship to other variables   Reviewing a measure's content does not tell the whole story. Investigators gain additional insight if they correlate the measure with a criterion. *A criterion measures the concept of interest; it may be an alternate or similar measure or a measure of a future outcome.* The investigators look for a similar response pattern between the measure being validated and the criterion. Examples of measures and similar criteria include the following:

Measures	Criteria
Citizen or user satisfaction with a service	Objective measure of service quality
Employee descriptions of a supervisor's management style	Supervisor's description of her management style
Self-report of health status	Medical records or medical examination

Criterion-based evidence of validity can only be produced when a suitable criterion exists and can be applied to the same population. For example, analysts can compare respondents' answers to whether they voted or not (the measure) with actual voting records (the criterion). Finding a weak relationship between a measure and a criterion may be disconcerting, but it may start a valuable exploration of what information a measure is and is not providing. For example, the observation that more people say they voted than actually voted has led to follow-up studies. These studies provide a better understanding of how people report their behavior and the consequences of using a measure instead of its criterion.[18]

In the public sector a similar body of literature examines measures of citizen satisfaction. Example 4.5 draws on two studies to illustrate how criterion-based evidence is gathered and how the evidence contributes to the understanding of what a measure of citizen satisfaction measures. Both studies found a weak relationship between perceived road quality and more objective measures. Do these findings affect how you would interpret satisfaction data? Clearly, satisfaction data do not substitute for determining actual road conditions. What citizens consider quality may be different from what professionals consider quality. Depending on the decision to be made, one will be more appropriate, i.e., operationally valid, than the other.

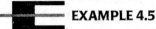 **EXAMPLE 4.5**

Criterion-Based Evidence of Operational Validity: Citizen Satisfaction with Government Services

Study 1

Unit of Analysis: 13 U.S. cities with both citizen survey and performance measurement data

Measure: 100-point scale measuring average satisfaction with a service. Respondents were asked to rate their satisfaction with street maintenance.

Criterion: Percent of lane-miles street engineers assessed as being in good condition

Finding: Weak, but negative relationship ($r = -.36$, $n = 7$), between satisfaction level and city engineers' assessment of street quality. Explanation is that citizens are either poor judges of road quality or engineers have lower quality standards than citizens.

Study 2

Unit of Analysis: 99 Iowa towns, population between 500 and 10,000

Measure: Average of town's surveyed residents' response to rate the condition of streets in [name of town] as "poor," "fair," good" or "very good"

Criterion: Trained observers rated four randomly selected streets in each town based on the physical condition of its surface and curbing and whether it was free of weeds and debris.

Finding: Weak, direct relationship between the measure and the criterion ($r = .49$)

Conclusion: Citizen assessments indicate how citizens view their streets, not their quality.

Lessons

1. Criterion-based evidence may be limited because of lack of a suitable criterion (small n in study 1 was due to the fact that few communities collected both survey and performance measure data) or feasibility (cost in having trained observers gather date in Study 2)

2. Weak or contrary evidence can provide valuable insights about a measure's quality and what it is measuring.

3. These studies are part of a research literature on satisfaction measures. The body of literature confirms the observation that "even if the evidence shows a measure is not working the way it was intended it is a step forward. The challenge is to find the way to make the evidence useful in the next iteration."

SOURCES: Based on studies conducted by D. Swindell and J. M. Kelly, "Linking Citizen Satisfaction Data to Performance Measures: A Preliminary Evaluation," *Public Performance and Management Review* (2000), 30–52; and M. J. Licari, W. McLean, and T. W. Rice, "The Condition of Community Streets and Parks: A Comparison of Residence and Nonresident Evaluations," *Public Administration Review* (2005), 360–368.

A measure may be designed to predict something in the future, e.g., who will succeed in school, be a valuable employee, or commit crimes. The criteria for these respective examples might be grade point average, a measure of employee productivity, or arrests and convictions records. An investigator will need data on both the measure, taken at time one, and the criterion, taken at a later time. Even if an appropriate criterion is identified, a measure's ability to correctly predict a future outcome will be limited. Events and situations concurrent with the criterion may strongly affect the outcome. For example, what happens on a job after a person is hired may explain his productivity more than the selection criterion.

Example 4.6 illustrates the use of predictive evidence to evaluate a measure. The example includes both predicted successes and predicted failures.

 EXAMPLE 4.6

Criterion-Based Evidence of Operational Validity: Predicting Dangerous Behavior

Study

> *Unit of Analysis:* 435 psychiatric patients originally classified as dangerous; 386 recommended for release and 49 others, not recommended for release, but released by court.
>
> *Measures:* Clinical procedures to establish a person's motivation (M), including history of aggression (H), internal inhibitions (I), and situational factors (S). Then, a method to combine these factors, e.g., $(I-(M + H + S)$; if $I > 0$, violent acts are unlikely.
>
> *Criterion:* arrest for a serious assaultive act within five years of release

Findings

1. Eight percent of those considered nondangerous committed an assaultive act (false negative).

2. Sixty-five percent of those considered dangerous did not commit an assaultive act (false positive).

Lessons

Validity of measure is limited by the number of false positives, which must be evaluated in the context of the consequences of labeling incorrectly a person as "dangerous." Roughly two out of three persons considered too dangerous for release were not found to have committed an assaultive act within the follow-up period. Critics have questioned the validity of the criterion measure and have asked how many of the false positives committed violent acts without being caught. Also, questions have been raised about the external validity of generalizing from data gathered in an institutional setting in order to predict behavior in an open community.

SOURCES: E. I. Magargee, "The Prediction of Dangerous Behavior," *Criminal Justice and Behavior* 3 (March 1976): 3–21; and J. Monahan, *The Clinical Prediction of Violent Behavior* (Washington, DC: Alcohol, Drug Abuse, and Mental Health Administration, U.S. Department of Health and Human Services, 1981). Data and procedures adapted from H. Kozol et al., "The Diagnosis and Treatment of Dangerousness," *Crime and Delinquency* 18 (1972): 371–392.

Including both groups is seldom done. For example, universities and employers would be reluctant to accept students predicted to fail or to hire an employee assumed to be less qualified. In the example the measure seemed to do reasonably well at correctly labeling nondangerous individuals, but poorly at labeling dangerous individuals. Incorrectly labeling persons as "dangerous" has serious implications for civil liberties. The example suggests two limitations of using a measure to predict later events. First, the criterion may have limited validity. The criterion "committed an assault" included only those who were caught. Second, unmeasured attributes or external events may have accounted for some of the "false positives" or the "false negatives."

A researcher may show that the measure behaves as expected, that is, it correlates with theoretically linked variables and does not correlate with other variables. If the measures correlate together, they are said to converge; if they do not correlate with each other, they are said to diverge. For example, scores on a quantitative aptitude test should be strongly related to math grades but not to English grades. This validation procedure requires a strong theoretical foundation. If the measures do not correlate, the researcher needs to consider that the theory is wrong.[19]

The Consequences of Measurement

An investigator may show that a measure produces the anticipated consequences. Administrators and policy makers assume positive benefits when a measure is first adopted. After a measure is implemented, it should be monitored to see if the positive benefits were realized and to identify any unintended consequences. One school of thought argues that evidence of a measure's consequences belongs in the realm of professional ethics or political considerations and not operational validity.[20] *The 1999 Standards for Educational and Psychological Testing* included the intended and unintended consequences of measurement as relevant evidence of validity. Consequences may be of utmost importance to administrators who rely on measures to make policy decisions. We include it here because examining the consequences of using a measure is consistent with other empirical evidence of validity.

The more importance decision makers place on one measure or a set of measures, the more they will want to consider its consequences. Consider the No Child Left Behind Act. It was intended to ensure that all American schoolchildren were proficient in mathematics and reading. The act called for annual testing of children in third through eighth grades and remedial action if a school did not meet statewide performance standards. Theoretically, the annual tests would motivate schools to hire qualified teachers, adopt effective teaching practices, and assist children in danger of failing. As a consequence schools may ignore untested subjects such as social studies and arts education. The existence of prescribed standards may discourage teachers from trying new, untested approaches to teaching.

Operational Validity: A Summary for Administrators

Operational validity is not a characteristic of a test; rather, it is the user's judgment that a measure is appropriate. Administrators who work with data should ask themselves: How was the measure operationally defined? Will the operational definition yield useful data? What will these data indicate? What evidence supports an assumption of validity? Below we summarize the major features of operational validity.

Operational validity: evidence that a measure is named correctly and that it measures what it was intended to measure.

Evidence of a measure's operational validity:

Evidence based on content: evidence that the operational definition is relevant (consistent with the operational definition) and representative (adequate).

Evidence based on criterion: evidence that the operational definition is empirically related to a criterion that measures an alternate measure, a similar measure, or a future outcome.

Evidence that the measure is correlated with theoretically linked variables and does not correlate with unrelated variables: requires a strong theoretical foundation explaining why a link between variables is expected to occur.

Evaluating the evidence: evidence based on a measure's content and its relationship to one or more criteria strengthens the argument that a measure is appropriate. Whether a measure is accepted as operationally valid or not depends on the user's purpose and conceptual definition. If the data will drive decisions, investigators should monitor the consequences of using the measure.

When to determine operational validity: operational validity should be determined prior to testing a model, collecting data, or introducing an intervention. Because of the role of judgment the operational definition and evidence supporting its validity should be reviewed with stakeholders.

SENSITIVITY

The *sensitivity* of a measure refers to its precision or calibration. A sensitive measure has sufficient values to detect relevant variations among respondents; the degree of variation captured by a measure should be appropriate to the purpose of the study. Measures that are reliable still may not detect important differences. Consider a salary survey. Suppose employees were asked:

What is your salary? (check appropriate category)

_____ Less than $25,000

_____ $25,000 to $34,999

_____ $35,000 to $44,999

_____ $45,000 to $54,999

_____ $55,000 to $64,999

_____ $65,000 to $74,999

_____ $75,000 or more

The categories included in this measure may be adequate for a survey of entry-level and mid-level city employees. They probably would not be adequate for a survey of city managers or of department heads. The measure is insensitive to variations in city manager salaries, since most top managers will fall in the last category. Thus, in constructing a measure, an investigator wants to avoid having respondents clustered in a single category. If most responses fall into one category, the measure would be considered insensitive. Insensitive measures do not allow investigators to compare respondents. Some investigators prefer to collect uncategorized data and create categories as needed and appropriate throughout the analysis.

Measures developed to study one type of population may be insensitive to differences in other more homogeneous populations. In the previous example, the problem could be solved by creating more and narrower categories, especially at the higher income levels. With complex measures, such as job-satisfaction scales or intelligence tests, different populations may require different sets of indicators to ensure sensitivity. For example, a job-satisfaction measure developed for organizations employing unskilled and skilled laborers, clerical workers, technical, administrative, and professional staff may be a poor choice to study a work unit largely made up of professional employees. If individual differences are of interest, then the measure would not be sufficiently sensitive to identify differences among employees in the more homogeneous group. Sensitivity in policy and administrative research is a relative concept, and no standard for an acceptable level of sensitivity exists.

SUMMARY

Measurement is the process of quantification. Quantification makes it easier to compile, analyze, and compare information on phenomena. Nevertheless, the process of measuring sacrifices the richness of a concept. No measure can describe fully quality of life, employee empowerment, or level of poverty. The information provided by measures has great value, but you also should recognize a measure's limitations.

The measurement process begins with a conceptual definition for each variable to be studied. The conceptual definition indicates what the investigator means by a concept. The conceptual definition should be consistent with the investigator's purpose in developing or selecting a measure and collecting data. The conceptual definition serves as a blueprint for the operational definition. The operational definition details exactly how a concept or variable was measured and its values were determined.

A measure can be classified as nominal, ordinal, interval, or ratio. Nominal scales categorize, but do not rank, data. Ordinal scales rank data, but the exact distance separating two pieces of data cannot be determined. Interval and ratio scales indicate the distance between two pieces of data. Ratio scales, unlike interval scales, have a true zero value.

Measures should be reliable, operationally valid, and sensitive. The reliability, operational validity, and sensitivity of all measures in a model should be established before data collection begins. Reliable measures allow an investigator to conclude that differences between subjects or over time are real differences, and not due to the measure or the measuring process. Reliable measures yield the same results time after time if whatever being measured has not changed. Two or more investigators using a measure should give the same score to the same phenomenon. A careful review using the qualitative method markedly improves reliability. The reviewer makes sure that directions are clear and easy to follow, that items are clearly defined, that given responses cover all likely responses, and that the respondent has access to the requested information. People responsible for data collection or data processing should be trained to avoid inconsistent measurement. A review of the measures and staff training may be adequate to determine reliability. If knowing and limiting the amount of random error are important, an investigator should use mathematical procedures to establish reliability. Unreliable data should be discarded.

A reliable measure is not necessarily operationally valid. An operationally valid measure actually measures the concept of interest. Analysts and data users should examine content- and criterion-based evidence. The evidence informs the judgment of data users; it does not replace it. Evidence based on a measure's content documents that the operational definition is relevant and representative. Criterion-based evidence empirically establishes the relationships between a measure and a criterion. The criterion may be a similar measure, an alternate measure, or a future outcome. Criterion-based evidence focuses attention on what is being measured. Evidence may also be gathered documenting the consequences of implementing a measure. A sensitive measure sufficiently distinguishes cases from each other so that they can be compared.

An administrator who includes quantitative information in her decision making may make an inappropriate decision if the data are unreliable or invalid. Quantitative information may be ignored if administrators consider the measures meaningless or inadequate to support decisions. Administrators should not expect researchers to make all decisions about a measure's appropriateness, nor should they base their decisions upon data without questioning the adequacy of the measures that generated them.

Measurement decisions are tied to other research decisions. The level of measurement determines what statistics the investigator can use. The analysis chapters identify the statistics appropriate to data measured at the nominal, ordinal, or interval level. The data collection chapters explicitly discuss measurement. The number of items and their wording must be considered in conjunction with the data collection method. An investigator who uses existing data must determine the measures' reliability and operational validity.

The next chapter is on sampling. In practice, investigators construct measures and samples independently. Implied links exist. Every measure is not necessarily appropriate for all subjects. The degree of precision can affect the cost of data collection or processing; thus, sample size may limit the sensitivity of measures. Investigators may overemphasize sample construction at the cost of developing high-quality measures.

NOTES

1. For an excellent example of detailed conceptual and operational definitions and the relationship between them, see J. E. Royce, *Alcohol Problems and Alcoholism* (New York: The Free Press, 1981), 15–19.

2. K. W. Thomas and B. A. Velthouse (1990), "Cognitive Elements of Empowerment," Academy of Management Review 15(4): 666–681, cited by S. T. Shelton, "Employees, Supervisors, and Empowerment in the Public Sector," Unpublished Dissertation, North Carolina State University, 2002.

3. J. S. Hunter, "The National System of Scientific Measurement," *Science* 210 (November 1980): 869–874.

4. Frequency distributions may be constructed so that the scales can be considered interval. In general, we do not recommend that you use interval statistics on ordinal scales unless you are sufficiently familiar with the scale and the statistic that you feel you can interpret the statistical findings appropriately. For an excellent summary of the issues see D. J. Hand, *Measurement Theory and Practice: The World Through Quantification* (Ondon: Arnold Publishers, 2004) 72–83.

5. See Susana Urbina, *Essentials of Psychological Testing* (Hoboken: John Wiley & Sons, 2004), chapter 4, for more details on the formulae and their appropriate use.

6. For more detailed discussion on internal consistency and coefficient alpha, see Anne Anastasi and Susan Urbina's *Psychological Testing*, 7th ed. (New York: Macmillan, 1997), 91–102.

7. Other terms, such as *parallel forms*, are also used to describe this type of reliability.

8. R. F. Sparks, *Research on Victims of Crime* (Washington, DC: U.S. Department of Health and Human Services, 1982), 14.

9. This discussion draws on John Cassidy's article, "Relatively Deprived: How Poor is Poor," *The New Yorker*, April 3, 2006, 42–47, and links found at The Census Bureau web page (http://www.census.gov/hhes/www/poverty/poverty.html). The Census Bureau web page includes links to poverty-related definitions, publications on measures of poverty and income, and research on alternative definitions of poverty.

10. "Consumer Expenditures in 2004" (Washingon, DC: U.S. Department of Labor, U.S. Bureau of Labor Statistics, April 2006), Report 992, 3.

11. Urbina, 161.

12. See *Standards for Educational and Psychological Testing* (Washington, DC: American Educational Research Association, 2002), 11–17, for a more detailed discussion of sources of evidence. We have confined our discussion to the sources that readers without more training in tests and measurements are most likely to produce and encounter.

13. Mark Wilson, *Constructing Measures: An Item Response Modeling Approach* (Mahwah, NJ: Lawrence Erlbaum Associates, 2005), 156.

14. M. W. Huddleston, *The Public Administration Workbook*, 4th ed. (White Plains, NY: Longman, 2000), exercise 9.

15. M. H. Maier and Todd Easton, *The Data Game: Controversies in Social Science Statistics*, 3d ed. (Armonk, NY: M. E. Sharpe, 1999), 99–102 discusses problems with Gross National Product (GNP).

16. See USDA's Nationwide Food Consumption Survey, GAO/RCED-91-117 (Washington, DC: General Accounting Office, 1991), which documents the difficulties in collecting these types of data. The contract for the 1987–1988 survey was $6.2 million; however, the survey was largely discredited because of methodological problems.

17. See J. A. Miron and C. D. Romer, "Reviving the Federal Statistical System," and J. E. Triplett, "Reviving the Federal Statistical System: A View from Within" in *American Economic Review* (May 1990), 329–332 and 341–344, respectively.

18. For a discussion of the literature and an extensive bibliography see R. Bernstein, A. Chadha, and R. Montjoy, "Overreporting Voting," *Public Opinion Quarterly* 65 (2001): 22–44.

19. Hand, 133. For an in-depth discussion of patterns of convergence and divergence, see Urbina, 169–181.

20. Urbina, 208–210, discusses and gives sources for the debate on the role of consequences as evidence of validity.

TERMS FOR REVIEW

concept
conceptual definition
operational definition
measurement
measurement scales

reliability
stability
equivalence
internal consistency
test-retest

operational validity
content-based evidence of validity
criterion-based evidence of
   validity
sensitivity

QUESTIONS FOR REVIEW

The following questions should indicate whether you have a basic competency in this chapter's material.

1. Indicate whether each statement represents a conceptual definition, part of an operational definition, or a hypothesis.
   a. The organizational capacity of not-for-profit organizations consists of their relevance, responsiveness, effectiveness, and resilience.
   b. To determine the equity of police services, we asked respondents if they thought there was less, about the same, or more crime in their neighborhoods than in the rest of the city.
   c. The more politically efficacious the respondents, the greater the probability that they will have a favorable attitude toward government services.
   d. Home health care has been defined as an array of therapeutic and preventive services usually provided to patients in their homes or in foster homes because of acute illness or disability.
   e. Controlled inventoried items are those that must be identified, accounted for, secured, segregated, and handled in a special manner.
   f. Uncontrolled, inventoried items have a higher rate of wastage than controlled items.
   g. The rate of school vandalism was measured by counting the number of cracked and broken windows.

2. What type of measurement scale—nominal, ordinal, interval/ratio—does each describe?
   a. Counties in a state (Ash County, Beach County, Maple County)
   b. Number of participants in food stamp programs

c. Reputations of colleges
d. Leadership ability measured on a scale from 0 to 5
e. Divisions within a state agency
f. Inventory broken down into three categories: tightly, moderately, or minimally controlled

3. A job-training program measures its effectiveness by the number of persons placed in a job. Factors such as salary and length of employment are not considered. Comment on the apparent reliability and operational validity of the program's effectiveness measure. How should the program improve its effectiveness measure?

4. Suggest possible operational definitions to test the hypothesis: Parents of elementary-age schoolchildren (5- to 11-year-olds) go to public libraries more often than parents of younger or older children.

5. Evaluate the following statements:
   a. A measure can be reliable for one study but not for another.
   b. A reliable measure will assign the same value to the same subject each time the measure is used.
   c. Test-retest to establish reliability is the same as an experiment's pretest-posttest.
   d. An agency should establish a maximum rate of random error for all the measures it uses.
   e. All measures should be qualitatively reviewed before mathematically estimating reliability.

6. Consider a measure of school vandalism that includes seven indicators of vandalism.
   a. What does a researcher mean when she says that the measure of school vandalism is reliable?

b. What does she mean if she finds that the measure is stable, equivalent, and internally consistent?

c. What does she mean if she says that the measure is operationally valid?

d. What evidence could she produce to demonstrate the measure's validity?

e. What does she mean if she says that the measure is sensitive?

7. Consider the measure of school vandalism. In October, the vandalism at eight schools is determined using the measure. Six weeks later, the vandalism at the same eight schools is again determined using the same measure.

a. What procedure is being used to determine the measure's reliability?

b. The amount of vandalism between the two applications of the measure increased. Should the researcher assume that the measure is unreliable? Explain.

8. A social service agency developed a measure of client satisfaction. What should another agency learn about the measure before using it to survey its own clients?

PROBLEMS FOR HOMEWORK AND DISCUSSION

1. A city department wants to make sure that its user survey to assess program quality contains reliable and operationally valid measures.

a. Present one strategy that you can use to determine that the measures of program quality are reliable.

b. Present one strategy that you can use as evidence that the measures of program quality are operationally valid.

2. To gather information on safety violations in factories, a state agency plans to send investigators to selected factories to obtain safety information.

a. How should the agency determine whether its measure of factory safety is reliable?

b. What content-based evidence would you look for to decide if the measure of factory safety was operationally valid?

c. Suggest a criterion and strategy to produce further evidence of operational validity.

d. If the relationship between the criterion and measure of safety is weak, what would you recommend?

3. Student observers measure traffic flow through a section of the city. They count the number of vehicles that pass through specified intersections. Each observer works for a four-hour period. An engineer notes that observers become careless in counting near the end of the fourth hour. Is this a problem in reliability, operational validity, or both?

4. A planner wants to assess road quality. He sends a questionnaire to a sample of residents and asks them to evaluate road surfaces, repair quality, and amount of traffic. He finds the results of limited value, so he assigns engineers to travel through the neighborhoods to rate the roads. The engineers are given general instructions but no written rating forms. Still dissatisfied, he develops a rating form that lists the number of potholes per mile, the depth of potholes, the thickness of asphalt, the width of the roadway, and similar measures.

a. Comment on the reliability and operational validity of each approach.

b. Which approach would you consider the most operationally valid? Comment on the ways each approach could be modified to improve its reliability and validity.

5. To develop an employment test, two versions of the exam are written and administered. In the morning, one-half of the test takers receive Form A, and the other half receives Form B. In the afternoon, the groups and tests are reversed so that those who took Form A in the morning take Form B and those who took Form B take Form A.

a. What was the agency trying to do?

b. If later administrators learn that people who had passed either Form A or Form B did not correctly interpret information on spreadsheets, is the problem with the examination's reliability or operational validity? Explain.

c. If the testees retook the tests three weeks later and their scores improved, could the administrators assume the tests were unreliable? Explain.

6. Human Resources administers the employment tests to large groups of applicants. To minimize the temptation to cheat, applicants are given different forms of the exams.
a. Why is it important that the reliability of the test be established?
b. Briefly describe how the examiners could establish the reliability of the different forms.

7. A city council wants to learn what the impact would be if it started issuing "tennis licenses" to allow residents to use the tennis court. A sample of players who use public courts are asked, "If the city charged $10 for tennis licenses, would you still use the public courts?" Discuss the operational validity of this question. Do you think that it would give an accurate indication of the effect of a tennis license?

8. Table 4.2 shows the number of people living below the poverty level as determined by two different operational definitions of poverty. Discuss how you would choose one of these definitions as operationally valid. Do you think that your decision would be the same if you were a legislator, a budget officer, or a provider of social services to clients?

9. Go to www.Fedstats.gov and identify an official statistic that interests you. How are key measures defined? How are the data collected? How are they used? What information is available on reliability and validity? Note: You may find the latter information if you enter "reliability" and "validity" as search terms.

TABLE 4.2 IDENTIFYING AN OPERATIONALLY VALID MEASURE OF POVERTY		
Operational Definition	Number Below Poverty Level (2002)	Percentage Below Poverty Level (2002)
Money income (adjusted by household size; $18,556 for family of 4)	34,570,000	12.1%
Money income plus capital gains (losses), less income and payroll taxes, plus value of all noncash transfers	26,750,000	9.4%

SOURCE: U.S. Census Bureau, http://www.census.gov/prod/2003pubs/p60-222.pdf

DISK WORK

1. Using the ORB Research Methods dataset, identify three variables that might be combined to create a single measure of a county's economic status. Using statistical software, check on the internal consistency of these three variables (SPSS refers to this procedure as "reliability"). What do the findings tell you about the reliability of the variables? Can you assume the variables give you an operationally valid indicator of a county's economic position? Why or why not?

2. Choose a different set of three variables, this time seeking to measure a county's poverty. Conduct the same tests. Are the variables reliable? If these were combined, would the index be operationally valid? Given your findings, which indicator, one of economic status or poverty, do you believe is the better indicator? Do they represent the same thing? Why or why not?

RECOMMENDED FOR FURTHER READING

Standards for Educational and Psychological Testing (Washington, DC: American Educational Research Association, 1999). The standards were created by a joint committee of the American Educational Research Association (AERA), American Psychological Association, and National Council of Measurement in Education and approved by their respective governing bodies. The AERA endorsement stated "we believe the *Standards* to represent the current consensus among recognized professionals regarding expected measurement practice. Developers, sponsors, publishers, and users of tests should observe these standards" (*Standards*, viii).

Susana Urbina, *Essentials of Psychological Testing* (New York: John Wiley & Sons, 2004) serves as a basic, accessible resource on psychometrics, that is, measuring characteristics including knowledge, abilities, attitudes, and opinions.

David H. Hand, *Measurement Theory and Practice: The World through Quantification* (London: Arnold Publishers, 2004). The book has a thorough discussion of measurement theory and applications. Its chapter on measurement in the social sciences includes a discussion of performance indicators, customer satisfaction, and crime.

Mark H. Maier and Todd Easton, *The Data Game: Controversies in Social Science Statistics*, 3d ed. (Armonk, NY: M. E. Sharpe, 1999), presents an insightful discussion of social science statistics. They identify and critique health, labor, crime, and educational statistics, among others. Their case-study questions are provocative and highly recommended.

CHAPTER 5

Sampling

In this chapter you will learn

1. The reasons for sampling.
2. Common sampling terminology.
3. How to identify, construct, and interpret common probability and nonprobability samples.
4. The guidelines for determining sample size.

Whether you study groups of 100, 1,000, or 1,000,000, drawing a sample is an economical and effective way to learn about their individual members. This applies if your data come from individual respondents, case records, agencies, or computerized datasets. People unfamiliar with sampling may misunderstand it, mistrust it, and feel that studies should include an entire population.

Consider some practical reasons for sampling. For many groups, it is impossible to identify every member. Thus you cannot contact every member and collect data from him. You cannot realistically collect data on every unit of some populations. Imagine an air-quality control agency collecting data on all the air in an area. The cost of gathering data on an entire group may be prohibitive. Contacting all members of a large or widely dispersed population can require tremendous commitments of time and money. Even with a relatively small group, sampling allows one to gather information on members in a much shorter amount of time.

Investigators draw sample units from a population in order to generalize from the sampled units, which they study, to the other units in the population that they have not studied. Readers should recognize that this involves the concept of external validity. In Chapter 3, we discussed generalizing the results of a study beyond the study itself and defined this as external validity. Generalizing the findings from a sample of units to the population is another instance of external validity. Properly drawn samples allow us to generalize the measures of characteristics from a sample to a large population.

Every 10 years the United States government is required to conduct a census of the nation's population. For the 2000 Census, the Census Bureau proposed sampling the population to improve the accuracy of the count and to reduce expenses. The proposal was controversial—members of Congress debated the issue. Understanding the principles of sampling would help most observers appreciate the Census Bureau's proposal, although it was ultimately rejected by Congress.[1]

Sampling is used in a variety of settings for a number of purposes. Perhaps its most widespread use is in survey research. Sample surveys are used to provide statistical data on a wide range of subjects for research and administrative purposes. A relatively small number of individuals are interviewed in order to gather data that will allow an investigator to find out something about the larger population. Given today's widespread use of surveys, it is somewhat surprising that the sample survey has a relatively short history.[2] Even at the beginning of the 20th century, statisticians debated whether anything less than investigation of a complete population was acceptable.[3] Sampling has since become widely accepted and a number of techniques have been developed.

Sampling involves several interrelated factors. These include the type of sample, its size, the population of interest, the accuracy desired, and the confidence the investigator wishes to have in the results. We will discuss these topics in this chapter. Before describing the methods and techniques of sampling, however, we need to introduce and define a number of terms.

SAMPLING TERMINOLOGY

A *sample* is a subset of units selected from a larger set of the same units. They are the units studied and provide data for use in estimating the characteristics of the larger set. For example, polling organizations, such as the Gallup Poll, use samples of about 1,500 or fewer people to describe the opinions of over 200 million Americans.

The *population* is the total set of units in which the investigator is interested, that is, the larger set from which the sample is drawn. The population's characteristics and the relationships among these characteristics are inferred from the sample data. Investigators wish to generalize from the sample units studied to the entire population of units. A population may be composed of people, but it may also consist of units such as government organizations, households, businesses, records, or pieces of equipment such as police squad cars, and so on.

The *target population* must be specified clearly. The units in a population must conform to a set of specifications, such as "all adults living in Clark County on July 1," so that analysts will know who is considered part of the population and who is not. The interpretation of the results of a study will depend on how the population is defined. Consider a sample survey to assess support for a bond referendum to build a new coliseum in a city. How should the population be defined? Who should be included? Registered voters? Taxpayers? Only people living within the city limits? What should be the minimum age of the population? An investigator may find it useful to start by defining the population as the ideal one required to meet the study objectives. This could be called the target or theoretical population. The definition would then be modified to take account of practical limitations; the modified definition is the *study population.* The study population is a set of units that the investigator can access.

Once the population has been defined, the question arises as to how to draw a sample from it. Many types of samples require a list of all the units in the population. The specific set of units from which the sample is actually drawn is the *sampling frame.* To sample households in a county, for example, one needs a list that identifies every household in the county. Complete lists seldom exist. Whatever list is used is the sampling frame. In the absence of a list, an equivalent procedure may be used to organize the population so a sample can be drawn.

Sampling frames may include units not defined as part of the population or they may fail to include some members. Suppose a sample of households was drawn from a telephone directory. The directory may list businesses, which are not part of the population; it will not include households with unlisted numbers or without land lines. Other potential problems with sampling frames are that some of the listings may be groups of units rather than individual units, and some units may be listed more than once.[4] A list of building addresses, for example, may include apartment buildings in which there are many apartments. If an investigator is interested in individual dwelling units, many would be missed with this frame. We tend to think of sampling frames as being physical or electronic lists of units; however, this need not be the case. For example, you could place grids on a map and select a sample of the grids for further study. The sampling frame would be the gridded map.

The term *unit of analysis* refers to the type of object whose characteristics interest us and whose characteristics we want to measure and study. If data are collected on fire departments, the unit of analysis is "fire department." If data are collected on fires, the unit of analysis is a "fire." Typically, investigators measure something about the unit of analysis. Frequently, administrative studies use agencies, not individuals, as the unit of analysis. A reader who fails to identify correctly the unit of analysis or uses results based on one unit of analysis to make conclusions about a different unit of analysis may reach incorrect conclusions about a study's findings.

A *sampling unit* is that unit or set of units considered for selection at a stage of sampling. The sampling unit may or may not be the same as the unit of analysis. In some sampling procedures, the sampling unit includes several units of analysis. For example, if analysts wanted to interview high school seniors, they might select a sample of high schools across the state. The seniors would be the units of analysis, but the high schools would be the sampling units.

A *parameter* is a characteristic of the population. These are what investigators want to find out about, and finding out about them is the reason for doing the study. The percent of citizens in favor of a bond issue to finance a new coliseum would be a parameter, as would the average age of new police recruits and the range of ages of retirees. A *statistic* is a characteristic of a sample and is developed from information about the members of the sample. We use statistics to estimate parameters. Typically, an investigator will take a sample statistic and estimate that the corresponding parameter of the population is within a certain range of the statistic. For example, the average cost of housing in a sample of residences in the state can form the basis for estimating the average cost of all houses in the state. The investigator does not assume, however, that the statistic exactly estimates the parameter. For the price of housing in the state, she may say that the average cost of all houses in the state is probably within a certain number of dollars of the average cost of houses in the sample.

The difference between the population parameter and the statistic used to estimate it is the *sampling error.* It is the expected error in estimating a parameter for any given sample of a specified size. The *standard error* is a measure of the sampling error and is based on a theoretical sampling distribution. This theoretical sampling distribution is a distribution of the values of a statistic that would result if we were to take an infinite number of samples of the same size and plot those values and their frequency. The standard error is the standard deviation of that theoretical sampling distribution.

Sample bias is a systematic misrepresentation of the population by the sample. The misrepresentation is in one direction and usually comes about because of a flaw in the design or implementation of a sampling procedure. Whereas sampling error is random and its size can be estimated mathematically, sampling bias tends to be in one direction and is difficult to measure.

The *sampling fraction* is the percentage of the population that is selected for the sample. A *sample design* is the set of procedures for selecting the units from the population that are to be in the sample. Two major types of designs are nonprobability and probability sampling designs. The distinction between them is important. With a probability sample, each unit of the population has a known, nonzero chance of being in the sample. Probability samples allow us to avoid selection biases, use statistical theory to estimate population parameters from sample statistics, and evaluate the accuracy of these estimates. Nonprobability designs do not allow the researcher to calculate the probability that any unit in the population will be selected for the sample. In nonprobability sampling designs, other principles take precedence.

We discuss common probability and nonprobability sampling designs in the next section. Both types of designs are useful but typically are used for different purposes and in different situations. A weakness of nonprobability designs is that they allow for an element of subjectivity, thereby preventing the investigator from using statistical theory properly. However, these designs are usually more convenient than probability designs and can be very useful to administrators.

The following application illustrates some of the terms defined above.

An Application of Sampling Terminology

Population: All motor vehicles owned by the state in the current fiscal year.

Sampling frame: All vehicles appearing on the state list of Registered Motor Vehicles prepared July 1 of the current fiscal year by the Department of Motor Vehicles.

Sampling design: Probability sampling.

Sample: 300 motor vehicles randomly selected from the sampling frame.

Unit of analysis: Motor vehicle.

Statistic: Average distance passenger cars in the sample were driven annually: 20,000 miles.

Parameter: The actual average annual mileage of all passenger cars in the state.

PROBABILITY SAMPLING DESIGNS

With a probability sample, each unit in the population has some chance of being in the sample; that chance is greater than zero and can be calculated. Probability samples permit a precise estimate of parameters. If sample statistics are to be used to accurately estimate population characteristics, probability samples are required. Although the reader need not be familiar with the calculation and interpretation of probabilities, it is important to be familiar with the more common probability sampling designs and recognize the situations in which they are likely to be useful. Our purpose here is to describe these designs so that the reader can determine whether sample findings have been interpreted properly and can participate in discussions of alternative ways of selecting a sample.

We discuss four common probability sampling designs: simple random sampling, systematic sampling, stratified *random* sampling, and cluster sampling. While other designs exist, they are often hybrids of these four designs. These designs demonstrate the basic principles of probability sampling.

Simple random sampling requires that each unit of the population has a known, equal, nonzero probability of being included in the sample. The selection of each unit is independent of the selection of any other unit. That is, the selection of one member of the population for the sample should not increase or decrease the probability that any other member of the population will also be chosen for the sample.[5] A common method of constructing a random sample uses either a *lottery method* or a *random number table*. These methods ensure against the inadvertent introduction of a pattern of systematic bias into the procedure. In the lottery method, numbered or named balls, each representing a unit in the population, are placed in a container. The balls are mixed thoroughly, and the number of balls equal to the sample size is removed. For a sample of 100, the investigator would remove 100 balls. The sample then consists of all units of the population corresponding to the selected balls.

While the lottery method is theoretically adequate, usually it is more convenient to use a random number table. To do this, the investigator assigns a number to each unit of the population and consults the table. He then randomly selects a starting place, goes through the table across the rows or down the columns, and lists the numbers as they appear on the table. Members of the population with the selected numbers constitute the sample. The investigator selects a random starting place in order to avoid any preference he may have for beginning at a particular starting spot.

A random number table is a list of numbers generated by a computer that has been programmed to yield a set of random numbers. Computers are used since the typical human is not capable of generating random numbers. For example, a person might have a tendency to list more even numbers or those ending only in 3 or 7. The numbers in a random number table have no particular sequence or pattern. The use of random number tables ensures that the selection will be random and not influenced by any selection bias of the investigator. Computer programs operating on the principle of a random number table for selecting cases are available. Many organizations have computerized records; such records constitute sampling frames, and computer routines can select a simple random sample from them. Even spreadsheets can be used to select simple random samples.

In drawing the sample using a table of random numbers, it is possible for a unit's number to be selected more than once. This possibility does not exist with a lottery method because, when the unit's ball was drawn, it was not replaced and so given another chance to be selected. This sampling method is known as simple random sampling with replacement if a selected unit, or its identifying number, is returned to the population and can be selected again. When the sampling procedures are done without replacement, the method is known as simple random sampling. We will emphasize the method without replacement, as it is used more commonly. Example 5.1 illustrates an application of simple random sampling.

The use of the random number table to select a simple random sample is manageable but can be very tedious. It becomes more so with large populations. Although newer developments for selecting samples, such as random digit telephone dialing, can make the process easier and faster, they cannot be used in many situations.[6] *Systematic sampling* is a widely used alternative to simple random sampling that reduces the amount of effort required to draw a sample and usually provides adequate results. It requires a list of the population units. To construct a systematic sample, the investigator first divides the number of units in the sampling frame (N) by the number desired for the sample (n). The resulting number is called the *skip interval* (k). If the sampling frame consists of 50,000 units and a sample of 1,000 is desired, the skip interval equals 50 (50,000 divided by 1,000). Having determined the skip interval, the investigator then selects a random number, goes to the sampling frame, and uses the random number to select the first case. Next the investigator picks every kth unit for the sample. In the example above every 50th case following the starting place on the sampling frame would be chosen. If the random number 45 was selected, cases 45, 95, 145, and so on would be in the sample. Note that the sampling fraction in this example is 2 percent.

With systematic sampling, the list is treated as circular, so the last listed unit is followed by the first. It is important to go through the entire list that constitutes the sampling frame. If the items on the list occur in a regular pattern and the skip interval coincides with this pattern, the sample will be biased. Consider what could happen in sampling the daily activity logs of a sheriff's department. If the skip interval were 7, the activity logs in the sample would all be for the same day, that is, all Mondays or all Tuesdays, and so forth. A skip interval of 14, 21, or any other multiple of 7 would have the same result. Experienced law enforcement officials tell us that certain days consistently have more activity. If the skip interval matched the cycle, the sample would not represent the population of days accurately.

EXAMPLE 5.1

An Application of Simple Random Sampling

Problem: County officials want to assess the extent of support for a proposed bond issue to fund construction of a new wing to a high school.

   Population: All people eligible to vote in a referendum on the proposed bond issue.

   Procedure:

1. Identify the population: The county's registered voters.
2. Identify and obtain a sampling frame: County Board of Election's list of 40,000 registered voters. The list is on the Board's computer, and names are numbered sequentially.
3. Determine sample size: 500.
4. Select a table of random numbers, pick a random beginning point, use a consistent pattern to go through the list, and list the first 500 five-digit numbers from 00001 to 40000.
5. Select each voter whose name appears next to a number selected from the table of random numbers.

   Discussion: The sampling frame is an accurate list of members of the population, e.g., citizens eligible to vote in a referendum on a bonding request. A simple random sample can be executed relatively easily. A computer-generated sample would be equally good and less time-consuming. A computer program could have printed out a randomly selected sample of names using its own internally generated table of random numbers. Note that each listed voter had the same chance of being in the sample as every other listed voter, and the selection of any one voter did not affect the chance that any other voter on the list would be included.

One way to deal with this problem, known as *periodicity,* is to perform the procedure twice, first doubling the skip interval. In our example we would make 100 the skip interval, randomly select a starting point, and go through the sampling frame once. This provides one-half of the sample. We would then pick another starting point and go through the frame a second time, providing the second half of the sample. Another way is to "mix up" the list before selecting the sample, although this may not be practical. The available evidence indicates that periodicity problems are relatively rare in systematic samples.[7]

In order to sample a population whose size is unknown, such as people attending a community event or clients attending a clinic, systematic sampling may be the only feasible type of probability sample. In such cases one can estimate the probable population size, that is, the number of visitors or patients, determine a skip interval, say 50, and pick a random beginning point, say 6. You would then sample the 6th person to arrive (or depart), the 56th person, the 106th person, and so on, until the end of the sampling period.

Systematic sampling does not result in a truly random sample. Although each unit in the population has the same chance of being selected, the selection of one unit affects the probability of selection of other units. For instance, in the above examples, the probability that both units 1 and 2 will be in the sample is zero. There is some nonzero chance that both units 1 and 50 will be in the sample. There is no possibility that adjacent units within the skip interval will be selected.

In order to apply sampling statistics to systematic samples, the investigator must make certain assumptions about the sampling frame. The major assumption involved is that the units on the list are randomly ordered, or at least approximately so, with respect to variables under investigation. If this is the case, the systematic sample can be treated as a simple random sample. Lists arranged in alphabetical order can be treated this way. Systematic sampling is used widely and works well in practice. You need not be overly concerned about the problems noted here, although it is wise to be aware of them. Systematic sampling is also called quasi-random sampling. Example 5.2 illustrates an application of systematic sampling.

 EXAMPLE 5.2

An Application of Systematic Sampling

Problem: The director of a county Women's Commission wishes to compile a summary describing the characteristics of registrants in the county's Job Bank. The Job Bank has been operating for 10 years.

  Procedure:

1. Identify the population: 6,500 women registered with the county Job Bank.
2. Determine the sampling frame: The set of file folders, one for each registrant, kept for the 10 years of the Job Bank.
3. Decide on sample size: 500.
4. Calculate skip interval: $k = 6,500/500 = 13$.
5. Select a random number between 1 and 13 for a starting place. The number 7 is selected.
6. Pull files from the filing cabinets for the sample. Start by selecting the seventh file, and continue by selecting files number 20, 33, 46, and so forth, through the entire set of files.
7. The 500 files selected constitute the sample for the study.

  Discussion: A systematic sample works well where files are kept. These files were kept in chronological order, providing a useful sampling frame. To go through and number each file and then match them with numbers chosen from a random number table would be tedious. The investigator has no reason to suspect periodicity, so she may pick all members of the sample by going through the sampling frame once. Note: If the skip interval is not a whole number, you may round either up or down. The most important aspects of the procedure are to pick at random a starting place and to be sure to go through the entire list or set of records.

Stratified random sampling ensures that a sample adequately represents selected groups in the population. Analysts use stratified sampling if a group of particular interest is a relatively small proportion of the population, or if they plan to compare groups. This technique assumes some knowledge of the population characteristics. Fortunately, we usually know certain things about the population being studied. Information on demographic characteristics, such as the percentage in various racial groups, ages, percentage employed in manufacturing, and so on, often is available.

The first step in drawing a stratified random sample is to divide or classify the population into strata, or groups, on the basis of some common characteristics such as sex, race, or institutional affiliation such as school or agency. The classification should be done so that every member of the population is found in one and only one stratum. Separate random samples are then drawn from each stratum.

For example, an investigator studying management information systems wanted to compare public with private sector organizations and designed a stratified sampling procedure. He developed two sampling frames, one of public sector agencies and the other of private organizations, and drew separate samples from each.[8] The benefits of stratification derive from the fact that the researcher determines the number of units selected from each stratum. Homogenous populations produce samples with smaller sampling errors than do populations with more diversity. Stratification reduces the diversity in the strata. Hence, stratified samples provide for greater accuracy than simple random samples of the same size.[9]

We will discuss two types of stratified sampling, proportionate and disproportionate. In *proportionate stratified sampling* members of a population are classified into strata, and the number of units selected from each stratum is directly proportional to the size of the population in that stratum. In other words, the sampling fraction is the same for each stratum.

If, for example, an investigator wanted to compare three types of workers—professional staff, technical staff, and clerical staff—she would begin by designating each of these types as a stratum. She would then draw her samples by taking an equal percentage of members from each stratum, say 10 percent of the professional staff, 10 percent of the technical staff, and 10 percent of the clerical staff. The resulting sample would consist of three strata, each equal in size to the stratum's proportion of the total population. A simple random procedure or some other method of probability sampling is used to draw the actual sample from each of the strata. Example 5.3 illustrates an application of proportionate stratified sampling.

The percentage of the members of a stratum selected for the sample need not be the same for each of the strata in the population. In *disproportionate stratified sampling*, a larger percentage is taken from some strata than from others. This is a useful technique when a characteristic of interest occurs infrequently in the population, making it likely that a simple random sample or a proportionate sample may have too few members with the characteristic to allow full analysis.[10] It also is useful when the sizes of important subgroups in the population differ greatly. For example, the State Division of Human Resources wanted to have a sample of employees in all departments of state government. The largest department had

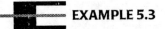 **EXAMPLE 5.3**

An Application of Proportionate Stratified Sampling

Problem: The director of recruitment for the State Law Enforcement Service wanted information about applicants to the service over the previous four years.

Population and sampling frame: All applicants to the State Law Enforcement Service for the past four years.

Procedure: Construct a proportionate stratified sample, using the year of application as the strata. Select a random sample of applications from the total group for each year. The same percentage of each year's total is selected. See the accompanying tabulation in Table 5.1.

TABLE 5.1	CONSTANT SAMPLING FRACTION		
Stratum	Number of Applications	Sampling Fraction	Number in Sample
Year One	400	15%	60
Year Two	350	15%	53
Year Three	275	15%	41
Year Four	250	15%	38
Total	1,275		192

Discussion: The analyst used his knowledge of the population to stratify along yearly groupings and took a 15 percent sample within each subgroup. The information from each year's group can be compared or combined into one sample.

over 18,000 employees and the smallest had 50. In disproportionate stratified sampling, the investigator selects a larger percentage of members from groups likely to be underrepresented in the population. In this fashion the investigator assumes that the number of units included in each stratum of the sample will be large enough to allow for separate analysis of each individual stratum. Since many research projects require sample estimates not just for the total population, but also for various subgroups within the population, this is often a useful technique. It must be emphasized that the samples from each stratum constitute subsamples that can be analyzed separately. Since some strata have been sampled at a higher percentage than others—they have been oversampled—a weighting procedure must be applied to compensate for oversampling before the subsamples are combined to form one sample. To weight the subsamples correctly, the analyst must know the size of each stratum. Example 5.4 illustrates a disproportionate stratified sample and a weighting procedure. One disadvantage of disproportionate stratified sampling is that it may require a larger sample to achieve the same level of accuracy as simple random or proportionate stratified sampling.

EXAMPLE 5.4

An Application of Disproportionate Stratified Sampling

Problem: Identify citizens' transportation needs for a county transportation plan.
   Population: The county's 27,500 residents.
   Sampling frame: List of households from county tax records.
   Procedure:

1. Stratify the population by the county's three townships: Tax records are filed by township, and each township differs in its demographic makeup.
2. Note the number of households in each township.
3. Determine sample size: Approximately 500.
4. Decide between proportionate and disproportionate sampling: Note that a 5 percent sampling fraction would yield a 480-household sample with only 26 households from Southwest Township. Because of the importance of location in developing the plan, analysts decide to oversample Southwest Township.
5. Individual households for the sample are randomly selected from the tax records for each township. One resident in each household is interviewed.

   See the accompanying tabulation.

Stratum	Number of Households	Proportion of Total	Sampling Fraction	Sample Size
North Township	5,760	.60	4%	230
Southeast Township	3,330	.35	4%	133
Southwest Township	510	.05	10%	51
Total	9,600			414

Discussion: Normally, the three groups would be analyzed separately and compared to each other. If the planners wanted to combine the subsamples into one sample, they would weight the subsamples. Specifically, the results of each subsample would be weighted by the proportion of the total population that that strata constituted. The results would then be combined. For example, the average age of residents in North Township would be multiplied by that group's corresponding proportion in the total, .60, Southeast Township by .35, and Southwest Township by .05 to determine the average age of the total population.

Cluster and Multistage Sampling

In many sampling problems, the units of the population exist in groups or *clusters.* For example, if we wanted to survey state residents on their use of certain state services, the unit of analysis would be individual residents. But they could be grouped in clusters in various ways. Each county, city, planning district, or even city block would contain a cluster of residents. We could also view the city block as a unit, in which case each city would have a cluster of city blocks, and each city block would have a cluster of residents. In cluster sampling, we select a sample of groups from the sampling frame and obtain information on all the individual units in the groups selected. If a sample of units is taken from each selected cluster, the design is called a *multistage cluster sample*.

Drawing a sample of a population, such as state residents, can be difficult. You may lack a sampling frame of the population or logistic problems may preclude drawing a sample directly from the sampling frame. A more efficient approach is to design a multistage cluster sample.

Assume that investigators wanted to obtain data on the use and need for mental health facilities in a five-state region. They might design the following multistage cluster sample.

1. Stage One: The investigator takes a sample of large units containing clusters of smaller units. In this case, counties would be a likely choice for the large units.
2. Stage Two: A sample of smaller areas—townships—is selected from the previously chosen counties.
3. Stage Three: A sample of yet smaller geographic areas, designated by population size, is selected from the townships chosen in Stage Two. Census tracts might be used.
4. Stage Four: Select a random sample of dwelling units—houses, condominiums, and apartments—from the census tracts chosen in Stage Three.
5. Stage Five: At this stage the investigators would go to these selected dwelling units and interview a resident. Of course, they would need some procedure for choosing which resident to interview, since many of the dwelling places will have more than one adult resident.

The units selected at each stage are called *sampling units*. The sampling unit may not be the same as the unit of analysis. In this example, the unit of analysis was the resident. However, different sampling units were selected at each stage of the process.

When to Use Cluster Sampling

Cluster sampling is recommended for studies involving a large geographic area. Without the ability to limit the sample to discrete areas, that is, to selected clusters, the costs and logistics would make probability sampling of many widely dispersed populations difficult, if not impossible. If face-to-face interviewing is to be used to collect data, a sample spread thinly over a large area will be extremely expensive to reach. Cluster sampling could help reduce this cost.

Cluster sampling helps to compensate for the lack of a sampling frame. Using cluster sampling in combination with other sample designs allows the investigator to proceed by only developing a sampling frame to draw the specific sample members. In the description above, for example, the investigators did not develop their sampling frame until Step Four, when they listed the addresses of all dwelling units in the selected census tracts. They chose their sample from this list. It would have been very costly and cumbersome if they had begun the process by attempting to find or develop a sampling frame that included addresses of all residents in this five-state region.

Although cluster sampling reduces travel time and costs, it requires a larger sample than other methods for the same level of accuracy. Note that in the multistage process, probability samples are selected at each stage. Each time a sample is selected there will be some sampling error. Since the sampling error accumulates at each stage, a cluster sample requires a larger sample than the other probability samples. Example 5.5 illustrates a four-stage cluster sample. The research staff applied random sampling techniques four times to select the members of the sample.[11]

What happens if the initial clusters to be sampled have very different-sized populations? If one of the clusters contains a significant proportion of the population,

---

 EXAMPLE 5.5

An Application of Multistage, Cluster Sampling

Problem: A state health agency needs to obtain information from high school students living in rural areas.

Population: All high school students attending school in rural areas of the state.

Sampling frames: List of counties, high schools, classes, and students.

Procedure: Construct a four-stage cluster sample.

1. Select a simple random sample of counties from all state counties considered to be rural.

2. Obtain lists of high schools in all selected counties and from these randomly select a sample of high schools.

3. Obtain a list of all classes in the selected high schools. From these, randomly select a sample of classes.

4. From the class lists for the selected classes, randomly select a sample of students.

5. Interview the selected students.

Justification for sampling technique:

1. No obtainable sampling frame of all students attending high school in rural areas existed for the entire state.

2. The study required face-to-face interviews. Cluster sampling allowed research staff to concentrate interviews in fewer locations, thus avoiding costs of traveling all over the state.

a multistage sample could easily miss this cluster and hence a large part of the population. To adjust for this situation, investigators sometimes use a technique called "probability proportional to size" or PPS. A typical application of cluster sampling is a study in which the investigator wants to obtain a statewide representative sample of adult residents. If an accurate list of the number of adults in each county is available, multistage cluster sampling would be appropriate. A probability sample of 10 counties could be the first stage with a sample of residents selected from these counties for the second stage. However, the investigator would want each adult in the state to have an equal chance of being chosen. If one or a very few large counties contain a significant proportion of the state's population, as is the case in many states, the investigator needs to adjust for this. The adjustment must be done in Stage One or the probability of missing the largest county and much of the population would be high.

The investigator must weigh each county by its population. If random numbers are assigned to the counties for the first-stage selection, they would be assigned to the counties in proportion to their population: more numbers assigned to the more populous counties than to the less populous ones. The larger counties would have a greater chance of being selected than the smaller ones. Weighting would ensure that a resident of a large county has the same chance to be selected as a resident of a small county.[12]

A sample taken from a larger group of units, which is itself a sample, is legitimate. For example, students at research universities may have access to databases containing survey responses from a large sample of individuals. Someone wanting to do research on a much smaller sample could instruct the computer to select a random sample to use. This, in effect, would constitute another type of multistage sample.

Probability sampling designs, when used in conjunction with sound statistical methods, allow us to generalize from the sample to the population. The distinguishing characteristic of probability samples is the random selection of the units for the sample. Randomization eliminates biases that may affect the selection of units. It also allows for the correct use of sampling statistics. The principles underlying simple random sampling form the basis for other probability designs. Although other designs are widely used, they are attempts to provide a close approximation to simple random sampling when simple random sampling is either difficult or impossible.

NONPROBABILITY SAMPLING DESIGNS

Investigators also use a variety of nonprobability sampling designs. Nonprobability samples can work well for many types of studies, particularly exploratory studies and those used to generate hypotheses to be more fully tested by further research. The usefulness of the information contained in a nonprobability sample depends on the investigator's purpose, the criteria for selecting the units for the sample, and how well they seem to represent the population of interest. These samples are also useful if it is not important to obtain accurate estimates of population characteristics. A visit to one or two homeless shelters, for example, can provide useful information to housing administrators seeking a change in policy governing the provision of services to the shelters. Since nonprobability samples do not rely on random selection, the results cannot be generalized to a larger population with any accuracy.

Nonprobability sampling designs are used widely. They typically are cheaper and easier to carry out than probability designs. Their major weakness is that in using them one cannot estimate parameters from sample statistics. Obviously, investigators attempt to do this in some fashion. However, with nonprobability samples, statistical theory cannot be applied to make these estimates or to evaluate their accuracy. The adequacy of the nonprobability sample can be evaluated only by subjective means; no mathematical evaluation is possible. With nonprobability samples, one cannot determine the chance that any unit in the population will be selected for the sample. It is therefore impossible to determine, mathematically, how representative the sample is of the population.

The various types of nonprobability samples are named according to the primary criterion used in drawing the sample. *Convenience sampling* involves sampling available units. For example, a researcher may ask a classroom of students to fill out an opinion survey. In so doing, he may hope to find out something about a larger population, such as American youth, but in order to do so, he has to assume that his sample is in fact representative, as there is no way to demonstrate this. Convenience samples are inappropriate for generalizing with any degree of certainty. They can, however, provide illustrative case material or serve as the basis for exploratory studies. One could, for example, use the survey described above to explore whether any items on the questionnaire were difficult for the students to understand.

Examples of convenience sampling include volunteers for a study, interviews conducted in convenient locations such as shopping centers, the respondents to a questionnaire in a newspaper, and telephone calls to a radio talk show. Convenience samples also are known as accidental samples.[13] Although the risk of bias for convenience samples is high, some will be worse than others. Particularly troublesome are those for which subjects select themselves for the sample and in which we would expect only people with strong views to respond. Because of the high risk of bias with convenience samples, it is unwise to use them to make inferences about general populations. Nevertheless, if the purpose is to identify issues of potential concern to a larger population, to pretest forms to be used by an agency, or some similar aim, convenience samples may be economical and appropriate.

A second type of nonprobability sampling is *purposive sampling*.[14] The main criterion for selection of any unit from the population using this sampling procedure is the investigator's judgment that the unit somehow represents the population. Because of this it is also known as judgment sampling. The probability that any unit will be selected is unknown because it depends entirely on the judgment of the investigator. Often units for this type of sample are selected on the basis of known characteristics that seem to represent the population. The investigator assumes that the units selected will represent the population on unknown characteristics as well. Even after collecting the data, an investigator cannot verify the representativeness of the sample on the unknown characteristics. He must therefore be skeptical about the accuracy of estimates.

Local governments use purposive samples when they seek information from cities and counties with a reputation for excellent administration. They may interview the personnel of these governments to ask about their experiences with outsourcing services, what performance measures they use, and how they monitor citizen satisfaction. Similarly, investigators may study school systems that have had the most success and those that have experienced failure in implementing charter schools. Investigators may also be interested in unusual cases, that is, those differing the most from others, and so select them for study. *Expert sampling* is a type of purposive sampling that involves selecting persons with known experience or expertise in an area. A panel of experts is selected to provide the views of persons with specific knowledge and skills.[15] Example 5.6 illustrates the use of purposive sampling.

 EXAMPLE 5.6

An Application of Purposive Sampling

Problem: A county manager plans to purchase a new computer system and wants to find out what experiences similar counties have had with computer systems, specifically their applications, costs, installation, and maintenance problems.

Population: All counties similar to that of the manager.

Procedure: The manager decides to talk at length with personnel in counties similar to hers that have computerized administrative activities.

1. Based on her knowledge of the area, the manager decides to contact five counties similar to her own in population size and makeup, budget, and services provided.

2. County managers and administrative staff in the five counties are interviewed and asked:
   a. What equipment is owned, leased, or shared?
   b. What alternatives were examined? Why was the existing system chosen?
   c. What does the computer system do?
   d. How well does the system perform? How often does it break down?

Sample characteristics: The representativeness of the sampled counties' population size and makeup, budget, and services are known. The representativeness of their computer-related decisions are not known and cannot be determined by this sampling technique.

Discussion: The manager, familiar with her county and its operation, the counties contacted, and the reputation of possible vendors, may reasonably believe that a limited, nonprobability sample will provide adequate information for a good decision.

A third type of nonprobability sampling is *quota sampling.* In this technique the investigator attempts to structure a sample that is a cross section of the population. It is less costly and easier to administer than a comparable probability sample. The researcher attempts to select a quota of individual units with defined characteristics in the same proportion as they exist in the population. If she thinks that gender and age are important characteristics and the population is 55 percent male and 35 percent are over 40 years old, she will require that 55 percent of the units in the sample be men. She will also require that 35 percent of the sample be over 40. The characteristics used to guide the selection of units for the sample may be independent or they may be interrelated. For example, a researcher seeking to interview members for a quota sample of agency employees may be assigned the following quotas:

10 males under the age of 40, 5 males over the age of 40

6 women who have been with the agency for five years or less

7 women who have been with the agency for more than five years

Quota sampling is sometimes used in surveys in which the interviewer selects the specific individuals to be interviewed. Quota sampling has the advantage of not requiring a sampling frame, and it reduces the need for callbacks. With quota sampling, if an eligible person is unavailable when the interviewer calls, the interviewer simply proceeds to the next dwelling or the next eligible respondent.

One purpose in assigning quotas is to reduce the risk of selection biases that might result from giving the interviewer a totally free hand. The biases of the interviewer can reduce the representativeness of a sample since, given a choice, interviewers are likely to interview people with whom they feel most comfortable, who are convenient, or are most willing to be interviewed. Quota samples cannot overcome these biases, however, and, as a result, are likely either to overrepresent or underrepresent traits not specified in the quotas. For this reason stratified sampling is far preferable to quota sampling if it is important that the sample contain an adequate proportion of members of identifiable groups. At one time quota sampling was used widely. Although it may appear to be comparable to stratified sampling, it is not. In stratified sampling, the various strata, or subgroups, are identified in advance and sampling units are selected randomly from each strata.

Snowball or referral sampling is used when members of a population cannot be located easily by other methods and where the members of a population know or are aware of each other. We may want to sample members of professional groups who form informal networks or other elites. Or we may want to sample very small populations who are not easily distinguishable from the general population or who do not want to be identified, for example, drug users. In snowball sampling each member of the population who is located is asked for names and addresses of other members. A bias in snowball sampling is that the more times a given person is mentioned, the more likely that person is to be included in the sample. Those who are most well known may be least typical of the population.

Nonprobability sampling designs have the advantage of being easier, quicker, and usually cheaper than probability sampling. If the purpose is to make accurate generalizations to a larger population, then probability sampling is necessary. If, however, the purpose is to undertake some exploratory investigation, then nonprobability sampling is likely to suffice. If the sample is going to be very small, then a nonprobability sample is likely to be as accurate as a probability sample, and the added inconvenience and cost of a probability sample are not warranted. Here again, this is likely to be the case at the exploratory stages of an investigation.

SAMPLE SIZE

One of the first questions administrators ask about sampling is about appropriate sample size. Those unfamiliar with sampling procedures and theory often assume that a major determinant of sample size is the size of the entire population. But to determine the appropriate sample size, the sampling expert needs to know other information.

Our intuition tells us that larger samples are likely to give better estimates of population parameters. Generally, this is correct. However, additional units also bring additional expense, and increasing the size of the sample beyond a certain point results in very little improvement in our ability to generalize about the population. Thus, in deciding on a sample size, the administrator must balance the need for accuracy against the need to keep costs reasonable. Further, with very large samples, the quality of the data actually may decrease, for example, when a small staff must supervise the interviewing of a large number of people. With a large sample, staff will find it difficult to make many callbacks when respondents are difficult to contact. Each additional case also increases the opportunity for errors in transcribing data.

Note that the following discussion refers only to probability sampling. All of the factors to be discussed here are relevant only when one proposes to use the sample data to estimate population characteristics. Since this cannot be done with nonprobability sampling, the determination of sample size in such cases must be governed by other considerations. In nonprobability sampling, for example, taking a larger sample will not eliminate bias; it may in fact make it worse.

Investigators expect that a statistic will not estimate the parameter exactly. Each possible estimate is likely to be somewhat off its mark. However, if numerous samples were selected, an investigator would expect most of the estimates to be within a specified range of the parameter; otherwise, the estimate would be of little value. The larger the samples, the closer we would expect these estimates to be.

Both *sampling* and *nonsampling errors* contribute to the difference between the value of the statistic and the parameter that it estimates. Sampling error occurs because sampling has taken place; the difference between a parameter and its estimate is random and due to the probability of selecting one unit rather than another. Because of sampling error, every possible sample is as likely to underestimate as it is to overestimate the value of the parameter. Nonsampling error, also called *bias*, is usually due to some flaw in the design or in the way the sampling design is implemented. If nonsampling error is present, all samples selected in the same way will either underestimate or overestimate the parameter. The sources of nonsampling error are discussed later in this chapter.

The size of the sampling error affects the accuracy of the estimate. Since the investigator usually does not know the exact value of the parameter—if he did he would probably not need to draw a sample—the size of the sampling error must be estimated. This is done from the sample itself. The formula for doing this is illustrated in Appendix 5.1.

The appropriate sample size depends on how large of a sampling error an investigator is willing to accept, since accuracy is an important factor in determining sample size. Greater accuracy usually can be obtained by taking larger samples or by accepting less restrictive values for two other factors important in determining the sample size. These are the confidence the investigator wishes to have in the results and the variability within the population from which the sample is selected. They are both related to accuracy.

The formula for calculating the necessary sample size for a study uses sampling error, confidence level, and variability. The formula shown below is specific for a dichotomous variable, that is, a variable with only two values such as a respondent being either For or Against a bond issue. A similar formula is used to calculate sample sizes for studies with interval variables as well. An example of the calculations for an interval variable is shown in Appendix 5.2.

Formula for Determining Sample Size for Population Characteristic Expressed as a Proportion

$$\sqrt{n} = \sqrt{p(1 - p)} \times (z\text{-score for confidence level})/\text{accuracy}$$

where:

n = sample size. (Note: A capital N often is used to indicate population size. The factor to adjust for population size is not included here.)

p = proportion of population in one category of a dichotomous variable. The term $\sqrt{p(1 - p)}$ is the standard deviation for proportions and measures the population variability.

z-score = standard score corresponding to the appropriate confidence level. This is taken from the theoretical distribution of all sample statistics. For a 95 percent confidence level, the z-score would be 1.96, or approximately 2. (Standard scores are discussed in Chapter 12.)

The properties of sample statistics may be derived theoretically by considering what the results would be if all possible samples of a given size were drawn. A certain percentage of these possible samples would estimate the population parameter very closely, some would be less accurate, and a few would be very inaccurate. Figure 5.1 illustrates possible outcomes if several samples were drawn from the population. The parameter is 60 percent, and the statistics from four samples are shown. If a large number of samples were selected, the majority of their estimates would be near the parameter. However, as the figure shows, a few

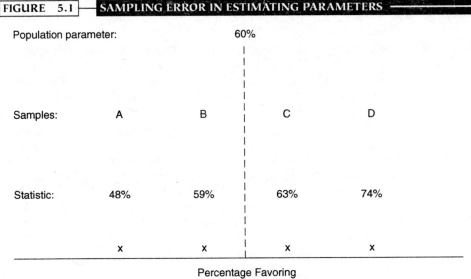

| FIGURE 5.1 | SAMPLING ERROR IN ESTIMATING PARAMETERS |

Population parameter: 60%

Samples: A   B   C   D

Statistic: 48%   59%   63%   74%

x   x   x   x

Percentage Favoring
City–County Consolidation

xxxxxxxxxx
(Most sample estimates would be
about here)

xxx
but some would be
about here

xxx
and some
would be here

would greatly underestimate and some would greatly overestimate the value of the parameter. An investigator, though, draws only one sample. There is always a risk that any single sample will be one of those whose estimate of the parameter is not very accurate. The *confidence level* refers to the confidence the investigator has that the selected sample is one that estimates the population parameter to within an acceptable range. This confidence usually is expressed as the probability that a parameter lies within this range of the sample statistic. The range is called the *confidence interval* and is usually expressed in terms of units of the standard error. The higher the degree of confidence desired by the investigator, the larger the required sample size if no other factors are changed.

Confidence levels usually are discussed in terms of how confident we are of our estimates. When investigators say that they are 95 percent confident that the parameter falls within a certain range of the statistic, this means that 95 times out of 100, using the same sampling procedure, the population parameter will be within that range of the sample statistic. Conversely, 5 times out of 100, the population parameter will be outside the range specified.

The *accuracy* of a sample is how close the sample statistic is to the population parameter. A measure of accuracy is the standard error. If the standard error is small, then the sample estimates based on that sample size will tend to be similar and will be close to the population parameter. If the standard error is large, then the sample estimates will tend to be different and many will not be close to the population parameter.

If we construct an interval of -1.96 to $+1.96$ standard errors around the sample statistic, we can be somewhat confident that the population parameter is located in that interval. That is, we are 95 percent confident that the population parameter falls within -1.96 to $+1.96$ standard errors of a sample statistic. There will be a 5 percent chance that we are wrong; that is, that the population parameter is not within the interval. The confidence level is the extent to which we are confident that the population parameter is within the confidence interval. Table 5.2 illustrates that as the confidence interval is narrowed, that is, the accuracy desired increases, the investigator's confidence that the parameter is within this interval decreases.

If the investigator is not willing to accept a 5 percent risk of being incorrect, he can use a different confidence interval. The chance that the parameter will be within -2.58 to $+2.58$ standard errors of the sample estimate is 99 out of 100. But note that the sample estimate will not be as accurate with the same size sample. The investigator will be 99 percent confident that the estimate is no more than 2.58 standard errors (se's) off its mark rather than no more than 1.96 standard errors off. The width of the confidence interval can be narrower if the researcher is willing to accept a larger risk of being unable to apply the results to the population. For the same size sample, the investigator can have more accuracy but will be less confident in the results. The researcher could use an interval of $-.68$ to $+.68$ standard errors (a very accurate estimate) and have only a 50 percent chance of being correct in assuming that the population parameter is within the interval. To be more accurate without running a larger risk, the investigator needs to take a larger sample.

Usually investigators will say that they want to be at least as accurate as some figure or within a certain number of standard errors of the parameter with their estimate and have a certain level of confidence in their results. That means that a certain size sample is necessary.

The interpretation of confidence levels is difficult because it involves thinking not only about the actual sample but about other samples that could have been drawn. For a 95 percent confidence level, if 100 samples of the same size

TABLE 5.2   THE TRADE-OFF BETWEEN CONFIDENCE LEVELS AND ACCURACY

Confidence Level	Accuracy as Shown by Confidence Interval
99%	$-2.58 - +2.58$
95%	$-1.96 - +1.96$
90%	$-1.65 - +1.65$
50%	$-.68 - +.68$

Note: These figures assume that the sample size remains constant.

EXAMPLE 5.7

Application of Sampling Statistics to a Probability Sample

Problem: State officials want to measure the average earnings of participants in a job training program after they complete the training program.

Population: All participants who have completed the job training program.

Strategy: Construct a probability sample of 100 participants and contact members of the sample to learn each member's annual salary.

Finding: The average (mean) salary of the sampled participants is $16,000 yearly. The standard error is estimated from the sample data to be $250.

Interpretation: The state officials can be 95 percent confident that the average salary of all program participants is between $15,510 and $16,490 (1.96 standard errors below the mean and 1.96 standard errors above the mean).

Explanation: If all possible samples of 100 job training participants were drawn, the average salaries found in 95 percent of them would fall between 1.96 standard errors below and 1.96 standard errors above the true average.

were selected, about 95 percent of them should produce confidence intervals that include the population parameter. The other 5 percent would not.

Example 5.7 illustrates these concepts. The information shows that members of a sample had an average annual salary of $16,000. The standard error of this estimate was $250. The confidence level indicates how likely it is that the population's average salaries are within 1, 2, or 3 standard errors of the sample's average salaries. For the 95 percent level of confidence, the population average would be within 1.96 standard errors of the sample average. Note that the standard error takes on the same unit of measure as the sample statistic; in this example it is measured in dollars. The standard error goes in both directions; that is, the population average may be below or above the sample average.

If the parameter is a proportion, such as the percent of trainees who had completed high school, the standard error is reported as a percent. If 60 percent of the sample had finished high school and the standard error of this estimate was calculated to be 1.5 percent, then an investigator could report that he was 95 percent confident that the proportion of all trainees who had finished high school was between 57 and 63 percent, or within 1.96 standard errors of 60 percent. The specific range depends on the confidence level selected. You would choose the 68 percent confidence level in order to be within 1 standard error of the parameter. To be within 3 standard errors, you would choose the 99 percent confidence level. The standard error of 1.96 corresponds to the 95 percent confidence level. Sometimes 1.96 is rounded to 2. You may be familiar with this measure of accuracy from seeing newspaper reports of the results of polling organizations. Typically, they report the accuracy for a 95 percent confidence level.

If all the units in a population were exactly the same, a sample size of one would be adequate to characterize that population! For example, if everyone in a city earned $45,000 a year, a sample of 1 would be enough to estimate average salary. However, the units within a population usually are somewhat different from each other. *Population variability* is the extent to which members of a population differ from each other on the variables that we want to investigate. The greater this variability, the larger the sample size required to estimate population parameters. A common measure of population variability is a statistic called the *standard deviation*. This measure is used in the formula for determining sample size.

Sample size is a function of the accuracy desired, the confidence level desired, the population variability, and to a lesser extent, the size of the population. These factors are related to each other. The relationship of each to sample size, if the others remain unchanged, is as follows:

1. Accuracy: The greater the accuracy desired, the larger the sample needs to be. This also means that the smaller the sampling error that an investigator is willing to accept, the larger the sample needs to be.
2. Confidence level: The more confidence desired, the larger the sample required.
3. Population variability: The more diversity among the members of the population, the larger the sample size needed.
4. Population size: The larger the population, the larger the required sample size. However, the population size is only a concern if the population is very small. At a certain point, adding more cases to the sample does not add information.

One common misconception about sample size is that a sample must include some minimum proportion of the population. This implies that if the size of the population is larger, the sample size must be increased by a corresponding amount. This is not the case. As you might expect, however, the members of larger populations usually are more diverse than those of smaller populations. In this indirect way, population size affects sample size. Statisticians use the finite population correction (fpc) factor to adjust for population size. If the population is at least five times the size of the sample, however, this factor usually has little impact on the sample size and often is omitted from the formula for calculating sample size. For samples drawn from very small populations, however, the population correction factor is very important.[16] Appendix 5.1 to this chapter shows an example of calculations for a sample drawn from a population of 100. A table illustrating the sample sizes necessary for small populations for selected accuracy and confidence levels is included in Appendix 5.3.

In order to be more accurate and more confident, an investigator needs to take a larger sample. To increase accuracy without increasing the sample size, the investigator must settle for a lower confidence level. To increase confidence and keep the sample size the same, some accuracy must be sacrificed.

The calculation of sample size for simple random samples is relatively straightforward. Determining sample sizes for cluster and stratified samples requires more complex calculations, although the determination is based on the same factors. We suggest that you seek expert advice if you are using either type of sample to estimate population parameters.

Although the accuracy and confidence level can be improved by increasing sample size, the amount of improvement realized with additional units becomes less and less. It is a classic case of diminishing returns. When the sample size is small—say 100—an increase to 400 will greatly improve accuracy and confidence. However, an increase in sample size from 2,000 to 2,300 will bring little improvement, although the additional costs are likely to be the same in both cases. Beyond some sample size, the improvements in accuracy and confidence level from increasing the sample size usually are not worth the cost. For this reason, commonly used limits are around 4 percent for accuracy and 95 percent for confidence.

An example using the formula for calculating sample size follows with information for a dichotomous variable. An investigator attempting to determine the proportion of a population supporting a bond issue, for instance, would analyze a dichotomous variable. The responses would be categorized as either "In Favor" or "Not In Favor." The population parameter would be expressed as the percentage "In Favor."

The example shows the calculations required for a variable in which 50 percent of the population favor an issue and 50 percent oppose it; the confidence level desired is 95 percent, and the accuracy desired is ±4 percent.

$$\sqrt{n} = \sqrt{(.50)(1 - .50)} \times (1.96)/.04$$
$$= (.5) \times (49) = 24.5$$
$$n = 600$$

Table 5.3 shows the relationship of accuracy, confidence level, and sample size for variables that have only two values. In these calculations we assumed that 50 percent of the population was in one category and that 50 percent was in the other. These percentages are expressed as proportions (.50 and .50) and are

TABLE 5.3	SAMPLE SIZES FOR VARIOUS DEGREES OF ACCURACY AND CONFIDENCE LEVELS		
	Confidence Level		
Desired Degree of Accuracy	99%	95%	90%
1%	16,576	9,604	6,765
2%	4,144	2,401	1,691
3%	1,848	1,067	752
4%	1,036	600	413
5%	663	384	271
10%	166	96	68
20%	41	24	17

Computing equation:
$\sqrt{\text{Sample size}}$ = Population variability × z-score for confidence level × 1/degree of accuracy. Where variability is at the maximum for a dichotomous variable, $p = .50$.

used to measure the population variability. This is the maximum variability. A population with a smaller percent in one of the categories, say 30 percent, has less variability and therefore requires a smaller sample size to achieve the same degree of accuracy at a given confidence level. If the investigator has little or no information about the population, the easiest and most conservative approach is to assume that the population is split 50/50.

Table 5.3 provides conservative estimates of required sample sizes; that is, the size shown may be larger than is actually needed. If the population split is anything other than 50/50, the population variability will be less, resulting in a smaller required sample size. Note that a commonly used standard of 4 percent sampling error and 95 percent confidence level requires a sample of 600 units, whereas to have a sampling error of only 1 percent and a 99 percent confidence level requires over 16,000 units. The figures in Table 5.3 also assume that the population is large enough that its size can be ignored as a factor in determining sample size. The reader may wish to compare the sample size figures in Table 5.3 with those in Table 5.4, Appendix 5.3.

The approach described here also is used when calculating sample size for nominal and ordinal variables with more than two categories. The investigator treats the variable of interest as if it were a dichotomy and chooses two proportions for the formula, guessing that a certain percent are in one category, and the remainder in all the others. For example, say the director of the employment division wants to conduct a study in which one of the variables is occupation. This variable includes the following categories: professionals, managers, and skilled workers. To calculate the appropriate sample size, her statistical consultant assumes that 34 percent of the population is in the professional category and that 66 percent is in the other two categories.

Appendix 5.2 illustrates a calculation of sample size for an interval-level variable. Note that the appropriate sample is relatively small compared to those in Table 5.3, which are for nominal and ordinal variables. The variability of interval and ratio variables can be measured more precisely than the variability of nominal and ordinal (categorical) variables, allowing for smaller samples to estimate parameters measured at this level.

The response rate also affects our choice of sample size. In sample surveys, not all of the units selected for the study respond. A large percent of those receiving mailed questionnaires do not return them. Some respondents contacted by telephone or in person will refuse to be interviewed. The percent of those selected to receive the questionnaire or be interviewed who actually complete and return the questionnaire or agree to be interviewed is called the *response rate*. The calculations in Table 5.3 assume that data will be gathered from every unit selected for the sample. Unfortunately, if some units cannot be found or if individuals refuse to respond, the sample's accuracy will be affected in a way that cannot be determined accurately. Thus, factors such as the anticipated nonresponse rate need to be considered and the sample size adjusted accordingly. If a researcher expects to have a high nonresponse rate, he would want to increase his sample size to make sure he has the necessary usable responses. Of course, the amount of time and money available also may set limits on the number to be sampled.[17]

The administrator should keep in mind a study's purpose. Unless the purpose of a study is well defined, and there is reason to be confident that the validity of the measurement of the variables has been established, a preliminary study with a small sample may be more efficient than spending resources on a larger sample. Exploratory studies can be very useful. In quantitative research, just collecting and examining the data frequently give the researcher and the client an opportunity to understand and possibly modify their models. Data collection has its moments of frustration. One is well advised not to spend resources on a large-scale study in the absence of a reasonably well-developed model whose critical measures have been tested for reliability, validity, and sensitivity.

Another important factor in determining sample size is the analysis to be undertaken. Specifically, small samples will not withstand extensive statistical exploration; some statistical procedures require a large sample. If, for example, there are a large number of independent or control variables, working with a small sample may result in the analyst's looking at individual cases rather than true samples. Dividing the sample into many small groups will have the same result. A Southeastern state annually conducts a statewide survey of about 1,300 residents. This size sample is more than adequate for estimating characteristics of the population of the state as a whole. However, the sample is not large enough to allow a meaningful analysis at the county level. For example, too few cases exist for analysts to compare the employment experience of males in all 100 counties of the state.

Sample Size for Different Types of Studies

The minimum sample size necessary for credible research differs from study to study. Public-opinion surveys and epidemiological studies rarely use fewer than several hundred subjects, and sample sizes of over 1,000 are not uncommon. Surveys of the general population spread over a large geographic area tend to have the largest samples. Studies to discover rare events or conditions also tend to require large samples. Sample sizes for other types of studies, such as controlled experiments, can be much smaller.

Samples for Experiments

In experimental studies, sampling seldom is done in order to be representative of the population at large. An important consideration in experiments is that subjects represent the characteristics relevant to the experiment. Units are randomly assigned to the experimental and control groups to ensure that these groups are equivalent at the beginning of the experiment. The main interest is in having a sample large enough so that any difference between the control and experimental groups can be attributed to the independent variable.

A rule of thumb for experimental studies is to have at least 30 subjects for each experimental condition, for example, 30 subjects in the experimental group and 30 subjects in the control group.[18] Experimental designs allow for fewer subjects than do cross-sectional designs for several reasons. Fewer groups are compared; that is, the sample is not divided into as many subsamples as is done often in the analysis of cross-sectional surveys. The experimenter physically controls for more variables, whereas the survey researcher uses statistical controls in the analysis after the data are collected. The survey analyst divides the obtained sample data into many subgroups whose members are equivalent on important variables and compares the different subgroups. In our example of the statewide survey, if the analyst wanted to compare employment experience for various age, sex, and education groups for different counties, she would need a much larger sample than if she wanted only to analyze employment experience.

If possible, experiments should use more than the minimum sample size. If the difference between groups that is expected at the end of the study is small, it might not show up if samples are small. Statistical techniques can be used to estimate required sample sizes for experimental studies. Using these requires knowing or assuming some facts about the population, such as the difference expected between groups and the variability of the dependent variable in the population. A preliminary study can be most helpful in obtaining initial information on these factors.

Sample Size and Statistical Power

Power refers to the ability of a statistical test to detect correctly from a sample a difference in means between two groups or the strength of a relationship between two variables.[19] The smaller the difference between means or the weaker the relationship between variables, the more difficult it will be to detect differences. Tables showing the sample size needed for various levels of accuracy, confidence, and power are available.[20] When testing a hypothesis, the investigator wants to include enough subjects in the sample to demonstrate that the hypothesis probably is true. For example, a sample of 50 may detect a moderate effect of an independent variable on a dependent variable only 46 percent of the time using conventional statistical criteria, whereas, using the same criteria, a sample of 1,300 will detect a very slight effect 95 percent of the time. We explain this in more detail in Chapter 12. On the other hand, an investigator does not want to waste resources by sampling many more subjects than needed.

Consider the following two hypotheses:

H_1:   City managers are paid higher salaries than county managers with the same length of experience.

H_2:   The more hours of training employees receive, the fewer accidents they will have on the job.

To learn whether the hypotheses are probably true in the population of interest, that is, among city and county managers or employees, the investigator may begin by selecting a sample out of the appropriate groups. To decide how many subjects to sample, he needs to decide how great an effect the independent variable is likely to have on the dependent variable.

Let's assume that the investigator anticipates that the difference in pay between city and county managers is relatively small, but he wants to confirm this difference. He also may believe that the impact of longer training on the number of accidents is relatively great, and he may consider his hypothesis to be unsupported if increased length of training brings about only small improvements. In the case of detecting pay differences, then, he will need a larger sample than he will in detecting increased benefits of longer training.

Nonsampling Errors

Sampling errors are errors that come about because we have drawn a sample rather than studied the entire population. They are due to mathematical chance—the probability that we will select those cases not exactly estimating the parameter. If a probability sampling method has been used, the size of the resulting error can be estimated with the use of statistical theory. This is one of the powerful advantages of probability sampling. But other types of errors can cause a sample statistic to be inaccurate. Nonsampling errors usually result from a flaw in the sampling design itself or from faulty implementation. These errors cause a distortion in the estimate of the parameter that cannot be evaluated using statistical theory. Unlike sampling errors, nonsampling errors are likely to cause the difference between the statistic and the parameter to be distorted in one direction. This also is called *bias*. Sometimes we are aware of bias but are not able to estimate its effect, at least not mathematically. Sometimes we are unaware of it. An example of an inappropriate sampling frame causing bias would be the use of the telephone book as a sampling frame for voters. Upper-income individuals are less likely to have a listed number than are those with middle or lower incomes. Younger individuals are less likely to have a land-line telephone (and therefore less likely to have a listed number) than older people. The characteristics related to income and age may also be related to how someone votes.

Nonsampling errors are serious, and their impact on the results of a study cannot be easily or directly estimated statistically. Taking a larger sample may not decrease nonsampling error; such error may, in fact, increase with a larger sample. For example, if coders rush to code and transcribe data, they may make more mistakes than they would have with fewer forms. Similarly, a larger sample size may result in fewer attempts by interviewers to reach respondents who are not at home, thus increasing the nonresponse rate. In short, a larger body of data generated from a larger sample can adversely affect the quality of data gathering and data processing.

People who do not respond to surveys and questionnaires contribute to the nonsampling error of studies in which they are asked to participate. Some people routinely may refuse requests for information; others ignore questionable or poorly conceived surveys. A researcher may be unable to contact a member of a sample; the person may have moved, missed a telephone call, or be otherwise unavailable. The greater the proportion of sample members who do not respond or who do not give usable responses, the greater the nonsampling error.[21] If members of the sample who respond are consistently different from nonrespondents, the sample will be biased. Other nonsampling errors include unreliable or invalid measurements, mistakes in recording and transcribing data, and failure to follow up on nonrespondents. If a sampling frame excludes certain members of a sub-group, such as low- or high-income individuals, substantial bias may be built into the sample. And, as we have already said, taking a larger sample will not necessarily reduce these problems. Careful effort must be given to the proper selection and construction of the sampling frame and other steps in the investigation.

Assessing Sample Quality

Administrators should feel confident in their ability to evaluate the quality of samples encountered in their work. They must frequently rely on studies involving limited samples, such as small samples drawn from a narrowly defined population. For example, a researcher who studied falls suffered by elderly people studied only falls in a geriatric facility, perhaps because she did not have the resources or the contacts to study falls reported to private doctors or hospitals. However, as long as one is aware of the limits of a given sampling design, information thus gathered may prove very useful, and one is not likely to make inappropriate generalizations from it.

In evaluating a given sample, an administrator should consider its size, how representative it is of the population of interest, and the implementation of the design.[22] The size of the sample must be evaluated in light of the purpose of the study. Small samples may be reasonable for a relatively homogeneous population, especially if the investigators do not want to generalize with great accuracy to a larger population. Nevertheless, sample size partially depends on the extent of analysis; a small sample cannot withstand intensive analysis involving investigation of the joint relationships of many variables. If a population parameter is to be estimated from a sample with accuracy and confidence, a larger sample is needed. Similarly, if an analyst intends to divide the sample into many subsamples, the sample must be larger than otherwise. Consider, for example, the *U.S. Current Population Survey*. This survey, which provides statistical estimates of population characteristics for the nation and each state, uses a sample of over 60,000 households. Still, the sample is too small to estimate the characteristics for a single city or county.

The importance of generalizing from the sample to the population depends on the sample and how an administrator plans to use it. A sample representing just one school will be adequate for the principal. It will be of less interest to the head of the State Department of Education, unless it uncovers something amiss or intriguing about that particular school. Awareness of a study's population and its sampling frame may alert an administrator to findings that cannot be generalized to a similar but unsampled population.

Another important consideration is how well the study was implemented; poor implementation of the sample design will cause avoidable nonsampling errors. Evidence of careless data collection, poor staff supervision, inadequate quality control, and low response rate can seriously undermine the most carefully drawn design. Many people understandably refuse to participate in studies that appear poorly conceived and developed. A well-designed sample cannot overcome the flaws in a poorly designed questionnaire. Although sampling is an important part of a study, an administrator should not assume that a well-designed probability sample will ensure a quality study.

SUMMARY

Sampling is an efficient and effective method of studying a population, whether it consists of people, files, agencies, or other units. Probability sampling normally is the preferred sampling method because with it an investigator can apply statistical methods to estimate parameters, and it helps to control biases that inevitably enter into the construction of samples. The four common probability sample designs are simple random, systematic, stratified, and cluster. For simple random sampling, the investigator uses a lottery method or list of random numbers to draw the sample. Each member of the sample has an equal probability of being selected, and the selection of one member does not affect the probability that another member will be chosen. In systematic sampling the population size is divided by the desired sample size to determine a skip interval, a random starting point in the list of the population members is selected, and cases separated by the skip interval are chosen.

In stratified sampling the investigator divides the population into classes or strata and randomly selects units from each class for the sample. Stratified samples may be either proportionate or disproportionate. Proportionate samples include members from the strata in the same proportion as they exist in the population. Disproportionate samples include a higher proportion of the members of some strata than of others. Oversampling of some strata may occur in order to provide sufficient numbers of units from that stratum for detailed analysis. In cluster sampling the investigator randomly selects units that contain members from the population of interest. If sample members are randomly selected from the chosen clusters, the entire sampling is known as multistage cluster sampling.

Nonprobability samples are suitable for exploratory studies. Purposive samples rely on an investigator's judgment; convenience samples rely on ease of access to sampling units. These samples may be adequate if they are free of obvious bias; however, sampling statistics cannot be appropriately applied to them. Quota samples, which specify the number of units with certain characteristics to be selected, are less satisfactory and have little to recommend them. In snowball sampling each respondent in the sample is asked to refer the investigator to another member of the population. Although this method has important biases, it can be useful in reaching a population difficult to contact by other methods.

The appropriate sample size for any given study is a function of the desired degree of accuracy, the population's variability, the desired degree of confidence in the results, and the analysis to be done. Population size is sometimes a factor but usually affects sample size only indirectly. Increased precision, that is, a high degree of accuracy and confidence in the data, requires a larger sample size. However, this also will increase a study's cost and may increase the number of nonsampling errors.

Although sample surveys are perhaps the most well-known use of probability sampling, many other endeavors utilize the principles of probability sampling. Experimental designs seldom use samples to represent a general population. Rather, they use sampling strategies to randomly assign members to experimental and control groups and to assure a sufficient number of members to attribute a change in the dependent variable to the independent variable.

Samples are prone to two types of errors. Sampling errors are a product of the sampling process. One cannot reasonably expect any one sample to be a completely accurate representation of the population, nor can one tell with absolute certainty that the sample has only a low degree of error, but statistical theory provides a basis for estimating the extent of sampling error. Nonsampling error also affects the quality of the sample. Common nonsampling errors include nonresponse bias, careless data collection, and careless data processing. Proper implementation of the sample design is as important as is the design itself in reducing errors.

Next, we will begin to examine data collection techniques. Chapter 6 discusses the process of carrying out a sample survey, while Chapter 7 discusses the design and writing of survey instruments.

NOTES

1. Jennifer D. Williams, Census 2000: *The Sampling Debate, CRS Report for Congress* (Washington, DC: Congressional Research Service, 2000).

2. Graham Kalton, *Introduction to Survey Sampling,* Sage University Paper Series on Quantitative Applications in the Social Sciences, 07–035 (Beverly Hills: Sage, 1983), 5.

3. L. O'Muircheartaigh and S. T. Wong, "The Impact of Sampling Theory on Survey Practice: A Review," *Bulletin of the International Statistical Institute* 49 (1981): 465–493; Kalton, *Introduction.*

4. Leslie Kish, *Survey Sampling* (New York: Wiley, 1965), 53–59.

5. Ibid., 20–21.

6. Because no new principles of sampling are included in Random Digit Dialing (RDD), we discuss it in Chapter 7 along with other data collection methods.

7. Seymour Sudman, *Applied Sampling* (New York: Academic Press, 1976), 56–57.

8. Stuart Bretschneider, "Management Information Systems in Public and Private Organizations: An Empirical Test," *Public Administration Review* 50 (September/October 1990): 536–545.

9. Sudman, *Applied Sampling,* 110, 130.

10. M. Hansen, W. Hurwitz, and W. Madow, *Sample Survey Methods and Theory* (New York: Wiley, 1953), 40–48.

11. Survey Research Center, *Interviewers Manual* (Ann Arbor: University of Michigan, Institute for Social Research, 1969), chap. 8, describes a seven-stage cluster-sampling process used in a nationwide survey.

12. Kalton, *Introduction,* 38–47; E. Terrence Jones, *Conducting Political Research* (New York: Harper & Row, 1971), 61–63 contains a relevant and clear illustration. Also see Earl Babbie, *The Basics of Social Research,* 3d ed. (Belmont, CA: Wadsworth, 2005), 219–220.

13. Kalton, *Introduction,* 90; Kish, *Survey Sampling,* 19. These samples also are called "fortuitous" or "haphazard."

14. William Trochim classifies all nonprobability sampling designs as either accidental or purposive. See William M. K. Trochim, *The Research Methods Knowledge Base* (Cincinnati, OH: Atomic Dog Publishing, 2001), 55–59.

15. Trochim, 57.

16. See Kalton, *Introduction,* 13, 14, 82–84, and William F. Matlack, *Statistics for Public Managers* (Itasca, IL: Peacock, 1993), 132–135 for discussions of the "finite population correction factor" and when to use it. This correction is important if the sample is a large fraction of the population, say 10 percent or over. This is likely when small populations are sampled. If the population is large and the sample is a very small fraction of the population, the correction factor can be ignored with very little effect.

17. Norman M. Bradburn, "A Response to the Nonresponse Problem," *Public Opinion Quarterly* 56 (1992): 391–397.

We discuss the issue of response rate and ways to increase it in Chapter 6.

18. L. R. Gay, *Educational Research,* 4th ed. (New York: Macmillan, 1992), 137.

19. H. C. Kraemer and S. Thieman, *How Many Subjects? Statistical Power Analysis in Research* (Newbury Park, CA: Sage, 1987), 22–29.

20. R. J. Krijcie and D. W. Morgan, "Determining Sample Size for Research Activities," *Educational and Psychological Measurement* 30 (1970).

21. C. A. Mosher, *Survey Methods in Social Investigation* (London: Heineman, 1969), 139–144. Also see pages 246–250 for further discussion of sources of nonsampling error. G. T. Henry, *Practical Sampling* (Newbury Park, CA: Sage, 1990) discusses formulas to adjust for nonresponse. See Chapter 6 references and recommendations for further reading for more on nonresponse rate and effect on sampling errors.

22. See Sudman, *Applied Sampling,* page 27 for a more detailed discussion of these points.

TERMS FOR REVIEW

sample	sampling unit	purposive sampling
population	simple random sampling	quota sampling
sampling frame	systematic sampling	selection bias
parameter	skip interval	snowball sampling
statistic	stratified random sampling	sampling error
sampling error	proportionate stratified	nonsampling error
standard error	sampling	confidence level
sample bias	disproportionate stratified	confidence interval
sample design	sampling	accuracy
sampling fraction	cluster sampling	population variability
probability sample	multistage sampling	standard deviation
nonprobability sample	convenience sampling	

QUESTIONS FOR REVIEW

The following questions should indicate whether you have a basic competency in this chapter's material.

1. What are the advantages of probability sampling over nonprobability sampling? Disadvantages?

2. Explain how systematic sampling violates the principles of simple random sampling.

3. Stratified sampling is said to reduce the variability of the population and hence provide for a smaller required sample size. Explain.

4. "Quota sampling is used by people who don't understand or trust probability sampling." Discuss and explain. What is the appeal of quota sampling?

5. Contrast cluster and multistage sampling. Why are they often used together?

6. Describe the factors that are used to determine sample size. Why is population size often not important?

7. How are the factors used to determine sample size related to sample size and to each other?

8. Distinguish among sampling error, nonsampling error, and bias. What are some common sources of nonsampling error for an investigation using government documents such as police crime reports?

9. How might investigators doing different types of studies, such as sample surveys and experiments, approach the issues involved in determining appropriate sample size?

10. Identify the sampling unit in each of the stages of sampling in Example 5.5.

PROBLEMS FOR HOMEWORK AND DISCUSSION

1. From each description, identify or infer the population, the sampling frame, the unit of analysis, and the type of sample. Assess the adequacy of the sampling strategy.
   a. Problem: To study medical factors related to falls by elderly individuals. Sample: A random selection of 150 of the 311 residents who fell in 2006 while in a particular geriatric facility, and 339 randomly selected from the 850 residents in the same facility who did not fall during that year.
   b. Problem: To study intracity travel patterns. Sample: Council of Governments has computerized dataset of 110,000 trips made in one year; 10 percent of the trips are randomly selected for intensive analysis.
   c. Problem: To see whether employees changed behavior after attending a training program. Sample: Randomly selected five training sessions held in 2003, identified the trainees in the selected sessions, and compared performance reviews of the trainees recorded before the sessions with those developed after.
   d. Problem: To determine the effects of a change in publisher on a newspaper. Sample: Randomly selected seven U.S. cities and identified and studied all newspapers published in these cities over the past century.
   e. Problem: To determine current vacancy rate of rental housing in a city. Sample: Blocks were selected at random within each planning area and the rental units on each selected block were identified. Sampling continued until the sample included 32 percent of the rental units in each area. Units were divided into three categories: buildings completed before 1960 with no more than four units; buildings completed before 1960 with at least five units; buildings completed by 1960 or later. Blocks were removed from or added to the sample until the proportions of units in the three categories were similar to their proportion in the city.
   f. Problem: To determine the total amount of assistance received by welfare clients.

Sample: Thirteen states that represented geographic regions and a full range of payments were selected. One to three counties within a metropolitan statistical area within each of these states were selected. In each selected county, the welfare director gathered data on each of the first 50 clients coming in to recertify eligibility for benefits.

2. You have been contracted by the Office of Continuing Education to construct a sample in order to determine reaction to a public service announcement on your university's night courses. The announcement is intended to attract more adults into night classes. Using publicly available materials:
   a. Design a simple random sample. Identify your population and sample frame. Recommend a sample size and justify it. Give specific directions on how members of the sample would be selected.
   b. Design a systematic sample. Identify your population and sample frame. Recommend a sample size, indicate the skip interval, and select the first 10 members of your sample.
   c. Design a cluster sample. Identify your population and sample frame. Recommend a sample size. Give specific directions on how members of the sample would be selected.
   d. For all three samples, discuss the adequacy of the sample frame.
   e. What sampling design would you recommend? Explain why.

3. Researchers investigated the impact on total salaries of reductions in force in state government agencies by studying a random sample of 20 of 189 abolished positions. The researchers reported that the sample yielded "an accuracy of 69 percent at the 95 percent confidence level." Interpret the researchers' observation.

4. Analysts constructed a random sample of 200 goals and related objectives taken from state health plans in order to evaluate these plans. The analysts reported that 44.4 percent

of the sample objectives were specific and quantified; they reported a sampling error of 6.9 percent. The analysts also found that 26.2 percent of the objectives had no recommended strategies for achieving them; they reported a 6.1 percent sampling error. Explain what the sampling error means in the context of these findings. Explain why the sampling errors are different.

5. Select a confidence level and accuracy level for the studies in Examples 5.1 and 5.2. Justify your choices. As part of your recommendation and justification, you should comment on the cost to sample each person or file.

6. For Example 5.1, what size sample would the county need in order to have the findings within +/−5 percent accuracy at the 95 percent confidence level if the population split about evenly on the proposition? If the community normally splits 60–40 on bonding issues, how could this information modify the choice of sample size?

7. For Example 5.1, what parameter is the study designed to estimate?

8. The local chapter of the National Urban League wants to find out which type of training or education would be most useful to the city's low-income citizens to enable them to obtain higher-paying jobs. The chapter executives want to have focus groups. Design a snowball (referral) sampling procedure to obtain a sample for the focus groups. Identify the populations and describe the sampling procedure.

9. Construct with your classmates a population of 50 members. Indicate the income of each member of the population. Calculate the mean income of the population and its standard deviation. Randomly select five samples of 10 members each and five samples of 20 members each. For each sample compute the mean income and the standard error of its estimate (given by the equation: standard error = standard deviation/n). For each sample size, indicate how many samples come within ±1, 2, and 3 standard errors of the mean. What can you conclude?

10. An intern with the city's Division of Employment and Training is designing a study to evaluate whether three training programs impact future wages of Job Training Partnership Act (JTPA) participants differently. She plans to contact between 25 and 40 participants of each program and is concerned because she knows that sample surveys usually have many more study subjects than this.
a. Write a memo to her explaining why she may have enough subjects for her study. Do you believe that she does have enough? Explain.
b. The intern has decided that if the difference among the post-program wages of the participants in the different groups is less than 15 percent, the difference is not important. Will this affect her sample size? Explain.
c. Discuss how the size of the differences among the post-program wages of the participants and the importance of these differences is an issue of the power of a statistical test.
d. Sketch out a design that the intern might use for the study.

11. Summarize the sampling procedure in the Bretschneider article (Endnote 8). Identify each of the different types of sampling used. Identify or describe each of the following: population, sampling frame, sample size, response rate.

DISK WORK

To see how sample statistics work, load the ORB Research Methods dataset. Use statistical software to determine the frequency distribution for the counties public school enrollment, average SAT total scores, and public school expenditures. Request the mean, standard deviation, and the standard error of the mean for each variable. Then use the software to get a 20 percent sample from the database and determine its frequency distribution for the same three variables. Again, determine the mean, standard deviation, and standard error for each variable.

1. For both the population and the sample, which variable has the most variability? Which has the least? Describe any differences you observe.

2. Compare the means from the 20 percent sample with the means for the entire sample. For each variable determine if the 20 percent sample means come within 1 standard error, within 2 standard errors, or within 3 standard errors of the mean of the entire sample.

3. How does the variability of a variable affect a sample's accuracy? Cite evidence from this exercise to support your answer.

4. Compare the means from your sample with the means from samples gathered by classmates. For each variable determine how many sample means come within 1 standard error, within 2 standard errors, and within 3 standard errors of the mean of the entire survey sample.

RECOMMENDED FOR FURTHER READING

Leslie Kish, *Survey Sampling* (New York: Wiley, 1965), provides an excellent discussion of sampling designs and sampling statistics.

For a clear and practical discussion of many actual applications of sampling designs, see Seymour Sudman, *Applied Sampling* (New York: Academic Press, 1976). The author discusses the strengths and weaknesses of the various designs in different circumstances.

Graham Kalton, *Introduction to Survey Sampling,* Sage University Paper Series on Quantitative Applications in the Social Sciences, 07–035 (Beverly Hills: Sage, 1983), provides good descriptions of various sampling designs, including combinations of those presented here, and discusses the calculations for determining sample size and sampling error for them.

Gary T. Henry, *Practical Sampling* (Newbury Park, CA: Sage Publications, 1990) is a short, readable treatment of sampling with well-developed examples from actual applied research.

Steven K. Thompson, *Sampling* (New York: John Wiley and Sons, 1992) is a very thorough treatment of sampling and sampling designs. Some of the discussion in this book requires knowledge of calculus.

Helena Kraemer and Sue Thieman, *How Many Subjects? Statistical Power Analysis in Research* (Newbury Park: Sage, 1987), discuss the power of statistical tests and provide tables showing sample size for various tests and power. Although much of the book is very technical, Chapter 2 has an excellent general discussion of power for the nonstatistician.

Robert M. Groves, *Survey Errors and Survey Costs* (New York: Wiley Interscience, 1989) is recommended for an excellent treatment of methods to reduce bias and increase response rates, and some of the trade-offs involved.

Jennifer Williams, *Census 2000: The Sampling Debate* (Washington, DC: Congressional Research Service, 2000). This reprint discusses several of the issues surrounding the debate about whether sampling should be allowed for the 2000 Census. The author cites other reports, relevant court cases, and statutes.

APPENDIX 5.1

Calculation of the Standard Error

The three examples in this appendix show the calculation of the standard error when the sample size and the standard deviation (a measure of variability) of the variable in the population are known.

Sampling error is estimated with the standard error formula. One component of the formula is the z-score corresponding to the confidence level desired. For a 95 percent confidence level, the corresponding z-score is 1.96 (often rounded to 2). This also is the most common level of confidence used in administrative and managerial work. For 99 percent and 68 percent confidence levels, the appropriate z-scores are 3 and 1, respectively.

1. The formula for calculating the size of the standard error of proportions is:

$$SEp = \sqrt{p(1-p)/n}$$

where:

SEp = standard error for proportions
p = the proportion of the population in one category of the variable of interest
$\sqrt{p(1-p)}$ = the formula for the standard deviation, the measure of variability of the population
n = the sample size

The reader should note the relationship between this formula and the one for determining sample size presented in the text.

As an example, consider the following situation: A survey was taken to determine the support for city–county consolidation in a city in the Southeast. The following information was developed.

p = the proportion of citizens supporting consolidation = .53

$1 - p$ = the proportion not supporting consolidation = .47
n = sample size = 590

$$SEp = \sqrt{(.53)(.47)/590} = .0205 \text{ or } 2.05\%$$

2. The formula for estimating the size of the standard error for means is:

$$SE\bar{x} = s/\sqrt{n}$$

where:

$SE\bar{x}$ = standard error of the mean
s = standard deviation of the sample; this measures the variability of the population
n = sample size

As an example of the use of the standard error of the mean, consider a sample of county managers drawn in a three-state area to estimate the average age of county managers in these states. The following information was developed.

s = 4.5 years
n = 35
$SE\bar{x}$ = $4.5/\sqrt{35} = 4.5/5.92 = .76$ years

3. The formula for estimating the standard error when sampling from small populations includes the finite population correction factor (fpc). The following example is from a study in which the investigator took a sample out of a population of 100 counties for a study on nursing home care.

$$SEp = \sqrt{p(1-p)/n} \times (N-n)/(N-1)$$

where:

SEp = standard error for proportions
p = the proportion of the population in one category of the variable of interest

$\sqrt{p(1-p)}$ = the formula for the standard deviation, the measure of variability of the population

n = the sample size

N = the population size

$(N-n)/(N-1)$ = the finite population correction factor or fpc.

To facilitate comparison with Example 1, assume the following:

$$p = .53$$
$$1 - p = .47$$
$$n = 60$$
$$N = 100$$

Carrying out the calculations, we have

$$SEp = (.53)(.47)/60 \times (100 - 60)/(100 - 1)$$
$$= (.064)(.404) = .026 \text{ or } 2.06\%$$

For very small populations, investigators may gain little by sampling, even though the fpc has quite an impact. One might wonder if studying all 100 counties wouldn't have been as convenient as taking a sample of 60. In the research from which this example was taken, however, the work involved in studying more counties made the reduction worthwhile. (See Kalton, *Introduction*, pp. 13–16 and 82–84.)

APPENDIX 5.2

Calculation of Sample Size for Means

The example in this appendix shows the calculation for sample size when the variability in the population is known from previous research or is assumed. Researchers often use a pretest or pilot test survey to obtain an estimate of the population variability.

A study similar to that in Appendix 5.1, Example 2, is planned by the Center for Public Affairs. The investigators want to calculate the sample size needed for the study. They wish to be 95 percent confident that they have estimated the average age of county managers to within one year of the actual average of all county managers in the area of study. A 95 percent confidence interval can be placed around this estimate by adding and subtracting a number equal to 1.96 standard errors from the mean estimate. (The z-score corresponding to the confidence level desired is also called the *reliability factor*. In this example, it is 1.96.) The amount of error in the estimate is 1.96 times SE$\bar{x}$.

$$\overline{X} \pm 1.96 \times \text{SE}\bar{x}$$

The problem for the investigators is to determine how large the sample must be to reduce this error to one year.

The formula for calculating sample size is the one given in the chapter:

$$\sqrt{n} = (\text{variability}) \times (\text{reliability factor})/(\text{accuracy})$$

The variability is measured by the standard deviation; the population standard deviation is estimated by sample data, previous knowledge, or is assumed to be a certain value. The investigators have the information from the study done in Example 2.

$$\sqrt{n} = (4.5 \text{ years}) \times (1.96)/(1 \text{ year})$$
$$n = 77.79 \text{ or } 78$$

The investigators will need a sample of 78 managers to reach the desired level of confidence and accuracy.

APPENDIX 5.3

Sample Size for Small Populations

TABLE 5.4   **SAMPLE SIZE FOR SMALL POPULATIONS BY SELECTED ACCURACY AND CONFIDENCE LEVELS**

For 95% Confidence Level

Accuracy Desired	Population Size					
	100	500	1,000	5,000	10,000	20,000
±1%	n.a.	n.a.	n.a.	n.a.	*	*
±2%	n.a.	n.a.	n.a.	1,248	1,825	2,113
±3%	n.a.	n.a.	n.a.	839	953	1,010
±4%	n.a.	n.a.	*	528	564	582
±5%	n.a.	*	237	355	369	377
±10%	*	78	87	94	95	96
±15%	24	40	41	43	43	43

For 99% Confidence Level

Accuracy Desired	Population Size					
	100	500	1,000	5,000	10,000	20,000
±1%	n.a.	n.a.	n.a.	n.a.	n.a.	*
±2%	n.a.	n.a.	n.a.	*	2,427	3,287
±3%	n.a.	n.a.	n.a.	1,163	1,503	1,673
±4%	n.a.	n.a.	n.a.	822	930	983
±5%	n.a.	n.a.	*	575	619	641
±10%	n.a.	111	139	161	163	165
±15%	*	63	68	73	73	74

Note: Where variability is at the maximum for a dichotomous variable.

　　n.a.: Not Applicable.

*Some statisticians report that in the situation illustrated here, a probability sample equal to 50 percent of the population will provide the required accuracy or greater. See, for example, Taro Yamane, *Elementary Sampling Theory* (Englewood Cliffs, NJ: Prentice-Hall, 1967), 398–399. Yamane also suggests that some formulas used for sample size do not apply if sample size, *n*, is more than 50 percent of population size, *N*.

CHAPTER 6

Contacting and Talking to Subjects

In this chapter you will learn

1. How to conduct and use mail, Internet, telephone, and in-person surveys.
2. How to deal with low response rates on mail surveys.
3. Techniques for constructing a random digit dialing sample.
4. The value of intensive interviewing and focus groups.
5. Basic requirements for conducting interviews and focus groups.

After investigators identify the purpose of a study and outline a model, they design a data collection strategy. The design consists of (1) a plan for contacting subjects and obtaining data from them, and (2) a questionnaire or other data collection instrument. Data collection decisions affect the quality of research. Furthermore, in practice, the relationship between the research design and data collection is dynamic. An investigator may change the original research design because of data collection problems. For example, the characteristics of samples affect the feasibility of conducting face-to-face interviews, telephone calls, or mailed surveys. Question wording determines the reliability and operational validity of measures.

Various disciplines have their own way of looking at things and rely on a few data collection methods to answer most empirical questions. Administrative and policy questions can touch on almost any discipline. Consequently, students studying administration may conclude that they need a background in many methodologies. In practice, administrators and policy analysts rely heavily on survey research, experimental and quasi-experimental designs, or economic analysis. These methods produce evidence to answer diverse administrative and policy questions.

Survey research refers to cross-sectional studies in which investigators use questionnaires, forms, or interview schedules to gather data from individual subjects. *Experiments* and *quasi-experiments* refer to studies in which subjects are exposed to deliberately manipulated treatments or interventions that may occur outside of the researcher's control. *Economic analysis* refers to studies in which investigators gather and analyze cost or other economic data; its technical details lie outside the scope of this text. Nevertheless, economic analysis also depends on reliable, operationally valid, and sensitive measures.

Rather than concentrating explicitly on any one research method, we emphasize the processes of organizing data collection, contacting subjects, eliciting their cooperation, writing questions, and designing research instruments. These skills, largely developed by survey researchers, can benefit any empirical investigator. Furthermore, these skills aid even the most basic data collection efforts, such as asking employees to fill out forms reporting organizational and individual performance data.

Chapters 6 through 9 provide an overview of basic data collection techniques. These chapters alert you to the decisions and steps involved in empirical research. Chapter 6 looks at how to contact subjects and collect data from them.

Chapter 7 discusses question writing and questionnaire design. The remaining chapters in this section delve into related data collection topics. Chapter 8 examines the ethical concerns regarding collecting data from, and about, human subjects. Chapter 9 discusses the value of analyzing existing datasets. Chapter 10 shows how to combine several indicators to measure a phenomenon. We included Chapter 10 in the data collection section because of the link between combining indicators and other aspects of data collection.

The chapter begins with a discussion of mailed questionnaires, a relatively unobtrusive and inexpensive method of data collection. Comments about mailed surveys generally apply to other self-administered questionnaires. We then consider Internet and telephone surveys, increasingly common approaches to contacting and interviewing subjects. The telephone survey section includes an explanation of random digit dialing. Next, we discuss in-person interviewing, including focus groups.

Our discussion concentrates on the relationships between data collection methods and the quality of responses, response rates, and costs. Two data-gathering techniques, random digit dialing and unstructured interviewing, have a direct link to other methodological considerations. Random digit dialing was developed to overcome problems of constructing a probability sample for a telephone survey. Intensive interviewing and focus groups serve as a basis for building models, conducting case studies, and developing and evaluating measures.

CONTACTING SUBJECTS

Administrators should work with investigators to decide how to contact subjects and who will contact them. If subjects view investigators as program representatives, an investigator's behavior can affect agency or program reputation. To avoid violating privacy, administrators may not want investigators to make the initial contact with clients or employees. Rather, the agency should contact the clients or employees. As appropriate, the agency either gets their permission to be contacted or notifies them that they will be contacted. In both cases the agency explains the purpose of the survey and how respondents' privacy will be protected.

Typically, an investigator's first contact with research participants is through the mail, over the telephone, face-to-face, or by e-mail. Contacting and interviewing subjects may occur simultaneously. Alternatively, investigators may telephone individuals and arrange a time and place for a personal interview. Potential subjects may receive a letter informing them that they will be called and interviewed in the near future or that they will receive a questionnaire by mail.

Investigators must locate potential subjects and entice them to participate. A low *response rate* may suggest problems with the study's design or implementation. If a large percentage of potential subjects cannot be found, or if they refuse to cooperate, the research findings may be unrepresentative. To determine the response rate and reasons for nonresponses, investigators need the following data:

Total subjects in the original sample

Number of subjects not located (nonexistent address or phone number, undeliverable mail, discontinued phone service, unoccupied housing unit)

Number of subjects not contacted (not at home, unable to understand English or other survey language, illness)

Number of subjects ineligible (sample member does not belong to target population)

Number of subjects refusing to provide information

Deciding how to categorize an uncontacted respondent can be problematic. A ringing phone or unanswered door does not necessarily mean that the telephone works or that the house is occupied. Persons who were not reached may or may not belong to the target population. Conventions for computing response rate vary. A conservative strategy computes the response rate by dividing the number of subjects who provide data by the total number of subjects minus ineligibles. This calculation implies the sampling frame and the data collection effort were adequate.[1]

The development and widespread use of new technologies such as the Internet and cell telephones raise new issues, challenges, and opportunities for survey researchers. Many homes and offices have answering machines and caller identification, which affect telephone surveys. The use of cell telephones has led to a decline in the number of homes with traditional land lines. Some families and individuals rely solely on cell phones, making it more difficult for surveyors to reach respondents even with random digit dialing. Research on polling for the 2004 presidential election showed that about 7 percent of voters relied on cell phones and did not have land lines. Other research showed that this figure may reach 10 percent by 2008. However, the accuracy of the polls seemed not to have been affected by the omission of voters who could be reached only by cell telephones.[2]

The widespread use of the Internet makes available new ways of reaching respondents. Surveys can be administered by e-mail or posted on web sites. With email, the survey is sent in the body of an e-mail message or as an attachment, and the respondent completes and returns it either online or by regular mail. Web-based surveys are becoming more popular, however, than the e-mail survey.[3] Web surveys can handle more complex designs, accommodate skip patterns, and post data directly to a database. Respondents may have more confidence in the anonymity of the web survey since they can go to the site to complete the survey. With an e-mail survey, the form is sent to the respondent, who may feel that confidentiality is compromised. With web surveys, intended respondents are often contacted by e-mail with directions for accessing the web site hosting the questionnaire.

A study comparing mail and web surveys found little difference in response rates of university students to the different methods.[4] The major differences were that the web survey respondents were much younger than the mail survey respondents and the web survey was much cheaper. A prior notice sent to sample members in both groups helped to increase the response rate. Since the study took place on one large university campus, the investigators had the advantage of being able to obtain a sample frame.[5]

PLANNING FOR A SURVEY

Planning for and conducting a survey require many of the same steps and considerations generally completed for any study. Certain components of surveys, however, should receive additional attention. The steps for planning a survey include deciding on the goal of the survey and identifying the target population, how the data will be collected, analyzed, and reported, and other considerations. The process of survey research involves a set of interrelated decisions and activities. These are summarized below. Early decisions will affect activities to be carried out later in the process.

Steps in the Process of Survey Research

1. Conceptualizing: What is the purpose of the survey? What does the researcher want to find out? To whom are the results to apply, e.g. to what set of cases?

2. Study design and data collection method: What is the nature of the sample? What data collection method is most appropriate? Will respondents be surveyed more than once? Are there privacy issues and is Institutional Review Board (IRB) review required? (IRBs are discussed in Chapter 8.)

3. Data analysis and management: How are the data to be managed and analyzed? Will this affect the decision about data collection? Are staff and resources available to do the necessary analysis? (These issues should be considered early in the process. They should not wait until after the data have been collected.)

4. Instrument design: This includes the general layout of the survey instrument as well as the specific questions—type, order, and wording. It deserves a lot of attention.

5. Sampling: The researcher must determine how many respondents are necessary. (If precise estimates are important, a statistician may be consulted to determine the sample size and design.) What data collection method will be used? Will the sample size affect the decision of data collection method?

6. Training: Those who are to collect the data should be well trained.

7. Pretesting: All surveys should be pretested at least once. Often it is wise to conduct several pretests.

8. Pilot study: This is also called a "dress rehearsal." Some respondents are contacted and data obtained and entered into the database. The process and results are reviewed and changes made to eliminate detected problems.

9. Administration: The data and information are collected and documented.

10. Data entry and analysis: Data are organized, entered into a database, and analyzed.

11. Reporting: Remember the audience. The appropriate type of report depends on the purpose of the study and the nature of the audience.

MAILED QUESTIONNAIRES

Often when we talk and write about questionnaires, we think of mailed surveys. At home and work, we receive questionnaires from market researchers, professional associations, university administrators, politicians, and not-for-profit agencies. The mail surveyor does not need to worry about finding respondents at home or contacting them at an inconvenient time. At the same time, he knows that they might put the questionnaire aside and forget it. They may pass it on to someone else to answer. They may answer questions they really do not understand or give cursory answers without attending to their accuracy or completeness.

Mailed surveys cost less than telephone and in-person surveys and cause minimal inconvenience to the respondent. The investigator can collect detailed, thoughtful data, especially information requiring reflective answers or perusal of files and records. At the same time, mailed surveys have distinct disadvantages. Designing an unambiguous questionnaire, mailing it, and having it delivered to the appropriate person, answered, and returned takes time. Mailed questionnaires normally achieve low response rates. Recontacting nonrespondents markedly improves a mailed survey's response rate. Of course, each follow-up adds more time and increases costs.

Investigators conducting mailed surveys cannot tell why a recipient does not respond. A poor sampling frame, e.g., one with out-of-date listings, may lower the response rate. The recipient may not have received the survey or may have forgotten about it or ignored it. The survey may not have applied to the respondent. A postcard enclosure similar to Example 6.1 reduces the uncertainty about why people do not respond. Postcards also keep track of respondents to anonymously answered questionnaires. (Anonymity is different from confidentiality. Anonymity demands that a specific individual cannot be linked to a specific questionnaire or set of data. Confidentiality means that someone on the research team can link an individual to an item in a dataset, but the individual's identity is protected and known only to the researcher.) The postcards are not foolproof. We have had instances where nonrespondents indicated that they had responded and where respondents did not return the postcards.

 EXAMPLE 6.1

Postcards to Monitor Mail Survey Participation

Problem: Investigators surveyed universities to learn about courses in inventory control. Investigators wanted to know which institutions received surveys, which institutions could not answer the surveys because they were not relevant to the respondent, and which institutions refused to respond.

Solution: Include a postcard enclosure:

> The Survey of Educational Opportunities in Inventory Control has been received.
>
>   ( ) We intend to respond by the end of September.
>   ( ) We do not intend to respond
>
>   ( ) because we do not have inventory control courses.
>   ( ) although we do have some inventory courses.
>
> Name:
> Institution:
> City and State:

Notes:

1. Investigators could assume that universities that did not return postcards did not receive the survey. Investigators could concentrate on trying to successfully contact these universities. This strategy reduces the cost of follow-up.

2. The investigators could determine the percentage of the sample who did not respond because the survey was inappropriate. In addition, the investigators had data on which institutions did not offer inventory control courses.

3. The postcard may have acted as an incentive for appropriate universities to respond. Alternative strategies (such as examination of university bulletins) may be adopted to gather data on nonresponding universities with appropriate courses.

The data collection method affects personnel expenses. Mail surveyors do not have to pay for interviewer training, travel, and salary. Still, the benefit of lower cost may be canceled out by the time required to mail a survey and receive the responses. If a respondent must consult records to answer the questions, additional time must be allowed. The timing of the mailing also must be considered; for example, a questionnaire arriving at a government agency during the midst of budget season will not receive immediate attention or be considered a high priority. In the United States, the holidays and other year-end activities probably make December a disastrous time to send surveys to either organizations or individuals.

An effective mailed or other self-administered questionnaire should be easy to understand and answer. To achieve clarity, the designer may oversimplify questions, thus sacrificing operational validity. Respondents cannot turn to the investigator and ask him to interpret the questions and clarify misunderstandings.

Poorly worded questions affect all respondents. In addition, not all populations react the same to a questionnaire. Highly educated groups or people accustomed to forms handle mailed surveys most easily. They can understand and follow directions and deal accurately with a variety of question-and-response formats. Some people routinely express their ideas and opinions in writing, whereas others feel uncomfortable expressing their opinions or writing answers to open-ended questions. Aged or less well-educated individuals may find mailed questionnaires difficult to read and understand. They may fear making mistakes and appearing foolish. Thus characteristics of the sample can affect response rate as much as the questionnaire itself.

Administrators, managers, and other professionals may prefer mailed surveys to the more intrusive telephone interview. Mailed questionnaires and other self-administered reports, such as monthly, quarterly, and annual reports summarizing unit activities, are part of a professional's work environment. Professionals are busy and occupied with the details of their jobs. The surveyor may find reaching them by telephone a time-consuming and costly exercise in logistics. Furthermore, filling out forms, responding to written requests, and writing memoranda constitute normal parts of administrators' work routine, and they can schedule answering a questionnaire at their own convenience to fit in with their other tasks. A mailed questionnaire works well to gather specific information on an agency, such as the number of clients served, their characteristics, and the services received. The addressee may answer parts of the questionnaire and pass it on to another staff member for more detailed completion.

Consciously or unconsciously, an administrator or other respondent decides whether to spend time providing information. Let's assume that most respondents start off willing to answer a survey. What factors may cause them to do otherwise? First, they may postpone answering a survey that seems complicated or asks ambiguous questions. Eventually, the questionnaire sinks to the bottom of a pile of paper, only to reemerge months later and be thrown away.

Second, respondents may ignore questionnaires that ask for inaccessible or hard-to-obtain data. Perhaps no one has time to compile the needed data. Perhaps the respondents resent and resist the expectation that they will gather the data. One of our colleagues received an unanswered questionnaire from a municipality along with a note saying that because of budget cuts the town was no longer responding to questionnaires.

Third, respondents may ignore questionnaires that seem biased. For example, some questionnaires assume a state of affairs inappropriate to the respondent. One questionnaire asked respondents why they had left jobs. The available responses stressed job problems or lifestyle changes. People who changed jobs to take advantage of opportunities for professional and personal growth may have been reluctant to associate their job changes with the listed factors. Although they could fill out the "other" category, they may have been disinclined to take the time. Besides, they may wonder about how much attention the researchers will pay to answers of open-ended questions.

Respondents' perception of a built-in bias may largely center on the appropriateness of the response categories. The less appropriate the listed responses, the less likely the respondent is to complete the survey. Including "neutral," "unsure," or "not applicable" response categories may encourage respondents who feel that checking one of the listed categories would not be an accurate response.

Recipients of mail surveys also may react differently according to the survey sponsor and the survey's apparent purpose. The more recipients believe that the survey will benefit them, the more likely they are to respond—even if they have to spend time compiling data and writing out answers. Conversely, if recipients question whether the survey information will benefit them, complicated questionnaires with ambiguous response categories and a need to look up or compile data will lead them not to respond.

The sponsorship of a survey can affect the rate of responses. In conducting a study for an agency, we have found that a letter from the agency head endorsing the survey and encouraging the recipient to respond helps to establish the legitimacy of the survey. The endorsements also seem to improve response rates. We once sent a questionnaire to university faculty. The questionnaire's cover letter was from the chancellor. We received a 95 percent response rate. One reviewer of this text noted that he got a 99 percent response rate from Massachusetts's school superintendents when he included a cover letter from the dean of Harvard's School of Education.

Sponsorship also can affect the direction of responses. We suspect that this is a particular problem with surveys of work conditions. If an employer conducts or sponsors a survey to learn about employee satisfaction and other components of the work environment, employees may worry about the confidentiality of their responses, and they may distort their responses in line with their perceived self-interest.

The failure to respond is not a trivial problem. Nonrespondents contribute to nonsampling error, therefore undermining the investigator's ability to infer from the sample. We are surprised and appalled at how many published articles report low response rates. Low response rates occur whether the unit of analysis is an individual or an organizational unit.

In considering response rate, we have focused on substantial research issues, that is, the purpose of the survey, its sponsor, and item validity and reliability. In addition, there are "tricks of the trade" that can lessen people's resistance. The length of the questionnaire, the ease in filling it out, respondent interest in the subject matter, the format and design, and a range of other factors, including the color of the paper and the design of the stamps affixed to the return envelope, have been linked to response rates. Further details of research on how to improve response rates are listed below.

Factors Affecting Response Rate

A. Sampling Frame
   1. Accuracy: Sample members may not receive a survey if the sample is drawn from an outdated sampling frame.
   2. Relevance: Survey recipients may not respond if they believe they do not belong to the target population.

B. Questionnaire Design
   1. Questionnaire length: Research shows mixed results, but when salience and follow-up are held constant, shorter surveys have higher response rates than longer ones.
   2. Item content and sequence: Items should be logically arranged by topic.
   3. Questionnaire layout and format: The questionnaire should be attractive and on sturdy, good-quality paper; items should be numbered sequentially, and there should be ample space between items.

C. Delivery
   1. Prenotice: Sending a letter or message in advance alerting the intended respondent that he or she will receive a questionnaire or be contacted about a survey usually improves response rates.
   2. Cover letter: Response rates improve if the cover letter (a) indicates the importance of the study and the value of the respondent's participation, or (b) offers to provide feedback.
   3. Return envelope: Stamped or postage-paid envelopes markedly improve response rate.
   4. Follow-up: Two or more follow-ups are recommended to get higher response rates; including a questionnaire with the follow-up request seems to yield a higher response rate than just a letter follow-up.[6]
   5. Incentives: Including money or another incentive, e.g., entry in a lottery, donation to a charity, or a token item with the initial questionnaire markedly improves response rates.[7]

The above list was generated as part of a study to improve the response rate to an agency survey. The initial survey had a 34 percent response rate. The respondents were police officers, members of a profession notorious for its suspicion of researchers. The questionnaire was complicated. It had a matrix, and embedded in each item were five separate questions. It had not been pretested nor was a follow-up conducted.

The revised questionnaire asked respondents to check the appropriate answer. They could easily and accurately answer the items without reading the directions. A group of police officers reviewed the questionnaire before it was mailed. One follow-up reminder was sent to nonrespondents. The revised survey, sent to different police officers, had a 76 percent response rate.

The problem with the initial questionnaire is familiar to us. We have received and read too many inept surveys; they demonstrate poorly thought-out designs and question wording, inadequate pretesting, and a simple ignorance of sound procedures. If you plan to do a mail survey, do not rely merely on your instincts. Carefully read a how-to-do-it book, either one of the books cited in the bibliography or a similar text; arrange for a variety of people, including members of the study population, to review and comment on the questionnaire; pretest it; and conduct a pilot study.

Follow up mailings will almost always improve response rates and often a second follow-up will improve the rate even more. In anticipation of the year 2000 Census, the Bureau of the Census studied strategies to improve response rates. Just over 40 percent of households responded if they received only the initial cover letter, questionnaire, and postage-paid envelope. Follow-up contact, such as postcard reminders and replacement questionnaires, brought the response rate to over 70 percent.[8]

Example 6.2 shows a postcard reminder that we sent to alumni. We resisted sending a similar reminder to subjects of a university-sponsored study, since some administrators felt it detracted from the seriousness of the survey.

Postcards can be used as inexpensive reminders to subjects. Nevertheless, either on the first or second follow-up, an additional questionnaire and prepaid envelope should be enclosed. Nonrespondents can be contacted by telephone and asked if they received a questionnaire. An additional survey may be sent, or they may be surveyed over the telephone.

Research has shown that incentives included with a survey have a "substantial positive" effect. The groups that received cash, ranging from $1 to $5, had a 19 percent higher average response rate than the control groups. Groups that received a nonmonetary incentive had an 8 percent higher average response rate than controls. Sending an incentive, either monetary or nonmonetary, after a completed survey was received had little or no effect.[9]

Whether an incentive is included with a survey or not, reminders still increase the response rate. Two studies, by the same researchers, found that subjects receiving a $1, $5, or $10 incentive had the same response rate (52 percent) with no follow-up as subjects receiving no incentive and three reminders. On the other hand, subjects that received $20 plus three reminders had a 79 percent response rate.[10]

Not all persons contacted will respond. These people constitute the *nonresponse rate*. An investigator should check the assumption that the nonrespondents are similar to respondents. She can sample nonrespondents and make a special effort to persuade them to answer the questionnaire over the telephone or in person. Thus she can determine whether the assumption of random differences between respondents and nonrespondents holds up. At a minimum she should compare respondents' and nonrespondents' demographics, for example, their

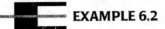

EXAMPLE 6.2

Postcards to Use as Follow-up Reminders

Situation: The authors needed to send an inexpensive, follow-up reminder to people who had not responded to an alumni survey.

Solution: We decided that a humorous postcard would serve as a first reminder to alumni.

CENTER FOR PUBLIC AFFAIRS

HAVE YOU FORGOTTEN SOMETHING?
PLEASE SEND YOUR MPA SURVEY TODAY.*
*If you have not recieved a MPA survey, contact Jay Greene
Center for Public Affairs, 555-3926 or 4006.

Notes:

1. Postcards were inexpensive to reproduce and mail. They were not wordy or heavy-handed.

2. Alumni who did not respond to the postcard reminder were sent a short letter with a duplicate questionnaire. Although not necessary, our next step would have been to telephone nonresponding alumni and to ask key questions.

age, sex, and region of the country, to see whether she can detect a possible bias.[11] Plotting nonresponses on a map can also help identify a regional bias.

INTERNET SURVEYS

Internet surveys are posted on the web or sent as part of an e-mail message. They are faster and cheaper than telephone or mail surveys. No interviewers have to be hired or trained, no postage or printing bills have to be paid, and investigators can avoid having to enter data from paper questionnaires. In other respects Internet surveys are similar to those sent by traditional mail. The researcher needs a sample from a sampling frame of addresses unless he wants to send out a blanket mailing. If the survey is included within an e-mail message, it has to be carefully designed, as completing a survey in a message is tedious. Surveys that are sent as attachments can be completed in much the same way as a mail survey and can be returned online or printed and returned by regular mail. They also must be easy to follow and understand. E-mail surveys can work more quickly and are usually less expensive than mail surveys. Unlike traditional mailed surveys, e-mail surveys raise greater concerns about confidentiality, security of responses, and viruses.[12] Because Internet surveys are a recent phenomenon, questions about their quality remain largely unanswered. Specifically, researchers are only beginning to study ways to improve samples, response rates, and questionnaire design.

Sampling problems are particularly challenging.[13] If a sampling frame with e-mail addresses exists, investigators can choose a sample, send an e-mail message that includes the survey, or, if the survey is on the web, give the address where it is posted. If a list with e-mail addresses does not exist, accessing the target population becomes more difficult. The investigators may publicize the survey through list serves, newsletters, newsgroups, links from relevant web pages, or similar communications. Although access to the Internet is widespread, not everyone has access to it and we cannot assume that a survey using the Internet will reach a representative sample.

If a survey is disseminated through multiple channels, identifying the represented population and the response rate becomes more difficult. A researcher may not know how many people or what groups of people knew about the survey or accessed it. People outside the target population who happen to visit the web site may answer a posted survey. People may send duplicate responses; they may have accessed the survey through more than one link or they may have resubmitted a survey to make sure that it was actually sent out. Researchers may not know how many people begin a survey and then quit without submitting it. The researcher would be unable to define the target population or calculate the response rate because she does not know how many people "received" the survey. Assigning a password that must be used to access the web survey is recommended as a way to control duplicate or other unwanted responses.[14] The password is often assigned in a request to an individual to participate. Sometimes the password is assigned when someone goes to the survey site and attempts to log on. When the survey is submitted the password is no longer active, allowing access to only one copy of the survey. However, this approach still does not allow one to calculate a response rate.

To see if the lessons learned from mail surveys increased the response rate of e-mail surveys, researchers sent a prenotice, letter and survey, reminder, and replacement surveys to randomly selected groups of university faculty. One group received all these materials by e-mail and another group by paper. The response rate for the two groups was virtually identical. E-mail respondents were more likely to complete the survey, to leave fewer items unanswered, to answer open-ended questions, and to give longer answers to open-ended questions.[15]

Other features associated with effective surveys should apply to Internet surveys. Similar to mail surveys, Internet surveys should be easy to access, answer, and return. As is true of any survey, ease of answering and the clarity of the questions should be established through pretesting. A respondent cannot ask an interviewer to clarify a question or write in how she interpreted the question.

Research on the design of web surveys shows that the format and design of the survey affect the response rate and data quality. Many of the characteristics affecting the traditional mail survey apply to e-mail and web surveys. For example, questionnaire length and the ease with which the questionnaire can be followed and completed will also affect response rate and data quality.[16] Respondents to an Internet survey are more constrained by the designer's framework. Unless a comment box is provided, the respondent cannot indicate a more appropriate or precise response. Internet surveys can be more time consuming for the respondent than are the paper-and-pencil versions and, in some instances, e-mail surveys are easier than web-based surveys. For example, this would be the case if respondents have to continually scroll between pages of the web survey to respond to the items. Currently several vendors provide web-based survey software. Before designing their own web survey researchers may want to investigate one or more of these.[17] Some survey software provides almost instant results.

TELEPHONE SURVEYS

In the past, the value of telephone survey data was limited because a sizeable portion of households did not have telephones, nor could investigators reach households with unlisted numbers. Consequently, surveyors could not expect to telephone a representative sample of individuals.

The conditions for telephone surveying have changed dramatically. By the end of the 20th century, census data indicated that roughly 94 percent of U.S. households had regular telephone service. Households without phone service have been described as "outsiders." They have lower incomes, tend to move frequently, and have fewer group memberships and community attachments. Some households, about 3 percent, have intermittent phone service. These households, which discontinue phone service from time to time because of money problems or a move, seem to be similar to nonphone households.[18] More recently the use of cell telephones has become widespread. It is not uncommon to find households that rely completely on cell telephones and do not have land lines.

Researchers estimate that the percent of the population with cell phone only service is growing at about a percent a year and will reach 10 percent by 2008. The increasing number of people who rely on cell phones adds new challenges to survey research. For example, cell phone users may be charged for an incoming call. A survey comparing a cell phone sample with a land line sample found that the cell phone sample members were less likely to be eligible for the survey, usually because they were too young, and they were less likely to cooperate.[19]

Researchers predict that because of the advantages of land lines, a majority of households will continue to have them.[20] Research on the accuracy of polls preceding the 2004 presidential election showed that voters with cell phones only constituted a small segment of the voting population and were similar to others in their age group. The national- and state-level telephone polls conducted in 2004 were quite accurate even though cell phone numbers were not included in the sampling frame.[21]

Random digit dialing techniques, described in the next section, produce samples of randomly generated telephone numbers. Random digit dialing also overcomes the limitations of telephone directories as sampling frames. These techniques have been developed and refined so that investigators can contact households with unlisted telephones. Investigators can be reasonably assured of telephoning a representative sample, including people whose telephone numbers are not listed in a current directory.

In addition to wider telephone coverage and improved sampling, two factors have given impetus to the spread of telephone interviewing. First, face-to-face interviewing has become less feasible. Interviewer time and travel are costly. In some neighborhoods, residents and interviewers worry about safety. Potential subjects refuse to open their doors to strangers, and interviewers also may feel unsafe. Diverse lifestyles mean that people often cannot be contacted during conventional interviewing hours. Second, telephone interviewing can deliver rapid turnaround from survey conception through reporting of the findings. Overnight public-opinion polls reporting reactions to major public events now are commonplace.

Telephone surveying procedures have other distinct advantages. Telephone surveys minimize interview travel time and expense. The interviews can cover a wide geographic area relatively quickly. Interviewers can call from a central location, allowing closer supervision of their work than is possible with face-to-face interviews.

Computerization of surveying processes has accelerated the use of telephone interviewing further. Computers can generate telephone samples and dial the numbers. *Computer-aided telephone interviewing (CATI)* systems have simplified the administration of complex interviews and survey monitoring. The interviewer reads items from a terminal screen and keys in the responses. The computer paces the interview, makes branching decisions for contingency questions, and checks for inconsistent responses. In addition, the computer keeps track of the number of calls made, refusals, completions, and similar data so that at any time, the investigators know the survey's status.

The first questions about telephone surveying center on sampling. How adequate are telephone subscribers as a study population? How can one assemble a representative sample when sampling frames are quickly out-of-date, exclude persons with unlisted numbers, and include households with multiple listings? How does one make sure that the sample units contacted coincide with the intended units of analysis and target population? What has been the nonresponse rate associated with telephone interviewing? The second set of questions centers on questionnaire design. How do telephone questionnaires differ from mailed and other self-administered questionnaires? What types of questions can be asked? How long can telephone surveys be? A third question underlies the other two; that is, how confidential are telephone surveys? Let's consider these questions in turn.

A directory may be an appropriate sampling frame to sample organizations and professionals. Directories of organizations or professionals may be relatively stable and provide few problems. If an investigator plans to draw a sample of the general public from a local telephone directory, however, the sampling frame becomes problematic. A telephone directory does not include cell phone numbers, households with unlisted or unpublished numbers, families who have recently moved into a community, or those who have changed their telephone numbers. Random digit dialing can overcome many of these problems. In addition, random digit dialing reduces the clerical work required to draw a random sample.

As noted earlier, response rates for many types of survey have declined. The rates for many annual surveys conducted by the Survey Research Center (SRC) at the University of Michigan have declined substantially during the last 25 years. This decline has accelerated in recent years. Researchers could not determine how much of the decline was due to an increasing number of refusals to participate and how much was due to failure to contact respondents. Based on their analysis, the authors concluded that nonresponse bias is not as bad as had been feared.[22] The decline in response rates, however, increases the costs of telephone surveying.

Random Digit Dialing

Random digit dialing produces a sample of randomly generated telephone numbers. The sample is an equal-probability sample of all area telephone numbers—listed and unlisted numbers, residential and nonresidential numbers. Pure random digit dialing generates a sample of telephone numbers from seven-digit random numbers. The list will include many nonworking numbers, since some of the random number combinations will be for exchanges that are not operating in the community. To reduce the frequency of nonworking numbers, investigators identify all working telephone exchanges in the target geographic area. The investigators assign four-digit random numbers only to working exchanges. In large communities, certain exchanges may be assigned to nonresidential users, including city or state government offices, universities, and businesses. If individuals or households make up the study population, the investigator omits any nonresidential exchanges before constructing the sample.

After the investigators identify the appropriate exchanges, they select an exchange and complete the telephone number using a variation of random digit dialing. They may select a four-digit random number between 0000 and 9999. Example 6.3 illustrates this procedure. Some telephone companies will provide a list of working exchanges, the number of telephones assigned to each exchange, and an estimate of the proportion of residential telephones assigned to each exchange. With this information the investigator can create a proportional sample as illustrated in Example 6.3.

With faxes, pagers, and telephone lines dedicated to computer use, a researcher using four-digit random numbers may come up with many numbers that do not reach appropriate respondents. Since the telephone company usually assigns telephone numbers in blocks, a researcher may randomly select residential numbers from a telephone directory and replace the last digit with a random number.[23]

EXAMPLE 6.3

Constructing a Random Digit Dialing Sample: A Hypothetical and an Illustrative Example

Problem: Surveyors want to telephone 500 households in a community with three telephone exchanges (111, 112, 555).

Strategy: The telephone company gives the surveyors the number of residential telephones in each exchange.

Exchange	Residential Telephones	Percentage of Total
111	2,000	20%
112	3,000	30%
555	5,000	50%

1. Select 2,000 four-digit random numbers.
2. Assign 20 percent of the random numbers to exchange 111. If the first random number is 8,752, the calling number is 111–8752.
3. Assign 30 percent of the random numbers to exchange 112.
4. Assign 50 percent of the random numbers to exchange 555.
5. Select replacement numbers for nonworking or business telephones from the list of remaining random digits.

Notes:

1. Surveyors expect a large portion of the numbers generated in a random digit sample to be nonworking numbers or business telephones. We have assumed that a surveyor needs four calling numbers to successfully reach one household.
2. If we assigned each exchange the same number of calling numbers, 667 numbers, 1 out of 3 households in exchange 111 would be called and 1 out of 7.5 households in exchange 555 would be called. Thus a household in exchange 111 is 2.5 times more likely to be in the sample than a household in 555. Any unique features of the 111 exchange population will be overrepresented in the sample.

Survey researchers often contract with the telephone company or a private firm to draw a sample meeting certain specifications. For example, only residential telephone numbers may be included in the sample. At least one national firm constructs telephone samples for specific ZIP codes, enabling investigators to study certain population mixes. How representative these samples are depends on the contractor's procedures. Contractors may vary in their policies for including unpublished and unlisted telephone numbers in a sample.

Random digit dialing solves the problem of unlisted numbers but not of multiple telephone numbers. We assume that occurs more frequently as family members acquire cell phones with separate numbers. A household with more than one telephone or listing has a greater probability of being chosen for a sample. To handle multiple listings, interviewers may ask how many telephone numbers and telephone listings the household has. Later, analysts will weight the household's responses. For example, responses may be weighted by the reciprocal of the number of telephone numbers or listings; responses from a household with two telephone numbers receive a weight of 0.5. Investigators may decide to ignore this problem.[24] Nevertheless, one should be aware that households with multiple listings are more likely to be selected, and such households may have distinctive characteristics, such as professional employment or teenagers.

Telephone surveys have the household as the implied unit of analysis. Yet, individuals may be the actual unit of analysis. If the surveyor intends to contact individuals, he should not automatically interview whoever answers the telephone. We assume that family members who answer a telephone differ from those who do not answer. For example, researchers have found that women answer a disproportionate number of telephone calls. For some telephone surveys, the interviewer will have the name of the sample member and will ask to speak to that person. Alternatively, the surveyor may be looking for a particular type of person, for example, the person who last had a doctor's appointment.

When the interviewers can theoretically speak to any household member, they need some way to ensure a representative sample. Various techniques have been developed and tested to select a specific household member for the interview. Some of these techniques are too complex to discuss here. One nonintrusive method is to ask to speak to the member of the household who most recently celebrated his or her birthday. Other surveys ask to speak with the youngest eligible male because young men are least likely to be home when surveyors call.[25] This procedure helps surveyors reach a wider variety of respondents.

The last sample-related question has to do with response rates. In general, telephone surveys have better response rates than mail surveys, although mail surveys with multiple mailings may do nearly as well.[26] Unlike mail surveys, telephone surveyors can distinguish between those they cannot reach (the inaccessible) and those who refuse to participate (the unwilling). As with mail surveys, the response rate to telephone surveys depends on time and money. Because of lifestyle changes, households may be harder to reach than they were in the past. People spend less time at home. They may rely on an answering machine, voice mail, or caller ID to screen calls; however, just because someone screens calls does not mean that she will refuse to answer a survey.[27] Surveyors record machine-answered calls as "not at home," although they may leave a message stating the purpose of the call and the plan to call back.[28] To increase the percent of households successfully reached, a survey organization must conduct calls throughout the week, including weekends, and during daytime and evening hours.

Research on factors affecting telephone refusal rates is limited. A major question that affects survey costs is whether extraordinary efforts to convince respondents to participate bias their responses. A recent study has found that younger and better-educated households are harder to reach; the analysts compared the findings of a five-day survey with an eight-week survey and found few differences in respondents' opinions.[29] Robert Groves, who studies survey research methods, wrote that a high rate of cooperation requires "a population that can be contacted in a reasonable time period, a population measurable using a small set of common languages, a population willing to discuss a wide range of subjects with strangers, and a population trusting of the confidentiality of the answers they supply."[30] These traits may be less common in a nationwide sample. They may be more common in specialized samples, which consist of members who find the study topic interesting or important to them.

Let's turn our attention now to the questioning. Telephone surveys depend on auditory cues. An interviewer has to entice subjects to participate in the study and stay on the telephone to answer the questions. She must rely on her voice and ability to convey key information succinctly. Until recently a pitch to buy real estate or some other product was often preceded by a request to participate in a "survey." Although the availability of "do not call" lists has reduced this sort of marketing, legitimate surveyors may still encounter high resistance to answering questions put by an unknown caller.

In telephone surveys most refusals to participate occur after the introduction and before the first question is asked; therefore, the introduction must be clear and compelling. Consider the typical telephone survey situation. A householder in the middle of other activities is interrupted by an unexpected call by an unknown caller. The interviewer must persuade the subject that it is worth his time to delay whatever he is doing to answer some questions. The interviewer begins by introducing herself and the survey organization. Next, the interviewer explains how the subject was selected, the purpose of the survey, and its approximate length. (See Example 6.4 for wording presenting this information.) The interviewer should be prepared to answer questions about the survey organization, the survey, and the confidentiality of the answers.

In constructing an instrument for a telephone interview, the writer considers the length of the interview and the order, length, and complexity of questions. The questions and possible responses must be clear, so the respondents can correctly figure out what they are being asked. The initial questions should reinforce the purpose of the survey stated by the interviewer. The "wrong" questions may arouse respondent suspicion. As the questions proceed, the respondent should sense the underlying logic; otherwise, he may become confused, lose interest, or question the legitimacy of the study.

Unlike the mail survey, the respondent cannot "read ahead," so investigators should consider how question order will affect later responses. The questionnaire should proceed smoothly, so that the interviewer feels and sounds comfortable moving from topic to topic and the respondent can answer easily. In this regard, all telephone interviewers should be well trained and practice the telephone interview before making the first real contact.

Although the interviewer can repeat questions and responses and clarify the meaning of words, an overdependence on the interviewer burdens both the interviewer and the respondent. The interviewer does not have visual clues to indicate respondent understanding. The person writing the questions should write short, easily understood questions. The writer must watch for wording that may lead a respondent to misconstrue a question. The investigators should not assume that a respondent will ask to have a question repeated or to say that he does not understand what the interviewer is asking.

Response categories must be carefully considered because the respondent does not have the leisure to read over and consider the responses. The respondent

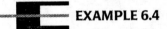 **EXAMPLE 6.4**

Introduction for a Telephone Survey

Situation: A sample of agency employees who participated in the DECIDE management training program were selected for a telephone interview to learn whether they used DECIDE in their work and how they used it.

Step 1: To avoid questions about the legitimacy of the interviewers, a training manager sent a memorandum to the sample explaining that the survey was to find out employee training needs:

To: xxx

From: Joe Doe, Training Manager

Subject: Training Survey

The Human Resources Development Unit will be conducting a phone survey November 7–14, regarding Management/Professional Development courses.

You have been selected in a random sample to participate. Expect a phone call from one of our interviewers during this period. You will be asked to answer a series of questions regarding training you completed, and we ask that you be candid in your responses. The interview should take no more than 10–15 minutes.

I know each of your schedules is full, but to continue to provide quality training, we need your feedback.

Step 2: Three days after the memorandum was sent, the interviewers began calling.

Each interviewer used the following introduction (printed on each survey copy):

Good morning (afternoon). I am John Cooper. I am calling in conjunction with a memo that you should have received from Joe Doe, the Human Resources Development Manager, regarding a training survey. As the memo stated, the interview should take approximately 10–15 minutes and relates primarily to training you completed with Human Resources. We appreciate your taking the time to work with us. Unless you have any questions, I would like to start.

Notes:

1. Introduction does not mention DECIDE, since interviewers did not want to introduce a bias by mentioning it at the beginning. (An early question asked respondents what management decision-making tools they used. If the respondents knew the survey was to study DECIDE, they might have been more likely to mention it.)

2. Interviewer mentioned the probable length of the interview, based on pretest times. This was to prevent being turned down by busy respondents.

3. Introduction was relatively short (as was the memorandum), but interviewer gave respondents a chance to ask any questions.

For Example 6.4 we drew on our work with the DECIDE study and reproduced the memorandum that was sent to members of the sample, and the introductory statement that the interviewers used. An employee from the training division sent a memorandum to the trainees telling them that they would be interviewed. Note that the interviewer mentions the memorandum in his initial comments.

may not remember long lists of alternatives; he may give the last stated alternative just out of convenience or stop the interviewer mid-list to choose an option. Asking the respondent to rank options does not work well, insofar as he has to keep several options in mind prior to ranking them. Instead, a respondent may be asked to rate items on a scale, for example, a scale ranging from a low of 1 to a high of 10.

Open-ended questions work moderately well in telephone surveys if the interviewers can probe beyond a quickly constructed, superficial answer. Open-ended questions work poorly if the interviewers are not well trained about what to listen for, how to probe, and what to record. On occasion we have tried to analyze completed telephone surveys and have found ourselves bewildered by the cryptic wording of the interviewers. This problem is related to problems of reliability where what is noted varies with who conducted the interview.

The length of the survey instrument may affect the decision on how to collect data. Research on telephone surveying has found that few respondents terminate the interview after the first questions. Nevertheless, a telephone interview cannot go on indefinitely. Respondents may tire as it drags on. Remember that the typical survey involves question after question, with the pace controlled by the interviewer. Tired or bored respondents will give unreliable answers. Similarly, respondents may become anxious to get off the telephone and start giving terse, truncated answers.

With longer interviews, costs, including decreased data quality, may make telephone interviewing less satisfactory. Nevertheless, as with mail questionnaires, no absolute rule on questionnaire length can be formulated. The length depends on the study population, the nature of the questionnaire, the motivation to respond, and the skills of the interviewers. One can imagine keeping a professional respondent on the telephone for much more than 20 minutes answering questions relating to her area of expertise.

Confidentiality is the last aspect of telephone surveying we consider. Random digit dialing approximates anonymity; however, respondents reached through random digit dialing are not more likely to disclose sensitive information.[31] If one is calling from a list, the respondent is known. If we plan to telephone individuals who are agency clients or employees, we can have the appropriate agency official write to the individuals explaining the purpose of the study. The letter may discuss provisions for maintaining the confidentiality of the responses. For both clients and employees, the preinterview contact minimizes suspicions about why they were called. Preinterview contact should reduce refusals and avoid lengthy explanations about the purpose of the study and procedures for analyzing and protecting the data.

IN-PERSON INTERVIEWING

In-person, or face-to-face, interviews allow researchers to obtain large amounts of data, perform in-depth probing, ask more complicated or sensitive questions, or contact difficult-to-reach populations, for example, homeless people. Two major types of in-person interviews are (1) structured interviews, where all interviewers ask each respondent the same, closed-ended or short-answer questions in the same order; and (2) intensive interviewing, where interviewers ask general, open-ended questions. In structured interviewing, several interviewers may be involved and each must ask the same questions in the same way. In intensive interviewing, the interviewers must be experienced and often have expertise in topical areas covered in the interviews. Between these two contrasting types we find semi-structured interviews, in which the questions to be asked are the same but the interviewers have flexibility in the order they are asked and in following up on each question. Another type of interview situation is the focus group, in which a facilitator presents questions to a small group whose members then respond to the question and to the comments made by each other.

Studies may combine data collection methods; interviewers may telephone most sample members and meet in-person only with those who either do not have a telephone or are difficult to interview over the phone. In-person interviewers may give respondents a self-administered questionnaire and thus maintain the confidentiality of their responses.

Studies using in-person interviewing may rely on interviewers to solicit subjects' participation. Interviewers who give vague or erroneous explanations of a study's purpose, including information on confidentiality and use of the data, may discourage participation. Variations in asking questions, probing, or recording can contaminate a measure's reliability or operational validity. Interpersonal dynamics may similarly affect response rate, reliability, and operational validity.

Whether an interview is conducted over the telephone or in person, the interviewer cannot help but interject herself into the research environment. Her presence affects what she sees and hears. Her personality affects her observations. Her need to establish rapport, to interpret questions, and to elicit usable answers may influence a respondent's answers. Telephone interviewers working in a central location under supervision are less likely to bias responses. In-person interviewers work largely on their own with limited supervision. Thus they are more apt to bias an interview.

Structured Interviewing

Structured interviews refer to surveys in which all respondents are asked the same questions in the same order by all interviewers. The investigators want different answers to reflect differences among subjects, not differences among interviewers. To minimize the effect of interviewers on the answers, investigators hire and train interviewers to be consistent in how they[32]

1. explain the purpose of the study
2. ask questions
3. handle incomplete or inappropriate answers
4. record answers
5. deal with interpersonal interactions

In-person structured interviewing works well for studies with lengthy or complex instruments. Researchers have noted that respondents become fatigued if they are kept on the telephone too long, whereas in-person interviews can successfully last several hours. The interviewer may elicit the respondent's trust, thus setting the stage for asking sensitive questions. The interviewer can use visual clues to decide whether the respondent understands a question and whether to continue probing the answers to open-ended questions. The interviewer can use visual aids as part of a question. For example, a respondent can study and rank a list of alternative responses.

Structured interviewing depends on standardized interviewers who give the same explanation of the study's purpose; ask questions without changing the wording; probe without directing answers; and record answers verbatim. Furthermore, interviewers focus on the survey and avoid talking about themselves or sharing their opinions about the study or the questions.

Computer assistance is an important component of most large-scale in-person surveys. It allows for more complex instruments, standardized interviews, reduced data entry costs, and decreased time between data collection and data analysis. Interviewers using computer-assisted personal interviewing (CAPI) read the questions presented on the computer screen and enter the data. Interviewers using computer-assisted self-interviewing (CASI) have respondents read the questions or listen to them. Respondents may key in their answers or reply orally. CASI helps in collecting sensitive information and maintains the confidentiality of a respondent's answers. The interviewers give instructions and answer questions; they take care not to observe or overhear a respondent's answers.[33]

Intensive Interviewing

Another type of in-person interviewing is more similar to a conversation, with the interviewer working with a list of general questions. The questions asked, their wording, and order vary from interview to interview. When individuals are interviewed, this type of interviewing is called *intensive interviewing*. One set of experts refers to this type of interviewing as *responsive interviewing* to indicate that the interviewer may change the questions and their order depending on how those interviewed respond.[34] Researchers may apply intensive interviewing techniques when interviewing a group.

For administrative researchers, both structured and intensive interviews accesses rich data to improve a research design or to elaborate on the statistical findings. Before we discuss the intensive interviewing process, let us illustrate its value to a research design. First, both individual and group interviews help develop and test hypotheses. One of this text's authors studied centers for victims of sexual assault; the centers grew out of the radical politics of the 1960s. She began her study of the organization of the centers strongly convinced of the value of unstructured, leaderless organizations. From an interview with staff at a highly structured, traditional social services organization, she learned that it had a large pool of peer counselors. Other centers had scarcely enough volunteers to answer their telephone crisis lines. Furthermore, the traditional center seemed to serve the needs of a wider segment of the community; the unstructured centers rarely worked with children, older victims, or the families of victims. After the interview, she changed her model and postulated that traditionally structured groups were better at providing victim services and that unstructured groups were better at raising the social and political issues associated with sexual assault and victim services.

Second, interviews help identify appropriate measures, especially in program evaluations. Once we did a short study to see the effects of discontinuing free transportation on low-income patients receiving renal dialysis. The administrators wanted to know "if anyone had died as a result." We constructed a sample and called patients or their families to learn whether patients had missed dialysis sessions and their current health status. We spoke with staff at the dialysis centers. One employee mentioned that health status was the wrong outcome measure, "since the patients would do anything to avoid dying." She argued that dietary status and adherence to medication schedules were more valid measures of the impact of termination. Her observation led us to reevaluate how we designed program evaluations; we began to include interviews with program constituents or stakeholders as part of a design.[35]

Interviews help program evaluators to learn about the background of the program, its objectives, its processes, its accomplishments, and its failures. The evaluators identify the people they want to interview and what they want to learn. They compose general questions or outline topics to explore in the interview. The interviewer, for example, might ask why the program was started, what its objectives were, how the program operates to achieve its objectives, how the objectives have changed, and so on.

Effective interviewing requires practice and careful preparation. Specific populations may present special challenges. One colleague, for example, tells about interviewing members of a white supremacist group. He arranged to meet them on street corners, after going through extensive questioning to assure them that he was not conducting a criminal investigation. Furthermore, the respondents insisted on anonymity, which required elaborate procedures for conducting the interviews.

You may occasionally read studies based on intensive, unstructured interviews. Typically, the interviewers have training in clinical interviewing, for example, in counseling, social work, psychology, or a similar therapeutic discipline. The interviewing we advocate here is far more modest. Nevertheless, the interviewer borrows some clinically developed techniques, such as good listening skills. The interviewer needs to have a good understanding of the subject matter of the interview. Finally, the interviewer needs to have had a sufficient amount of interview experience and practice to avoid wasting a subject's time, overlooking important material, or distorting responses. Interviewers conducting intensive interviews must be more well trained, more experienced, and possess more information about the subject matter of the interview than do those doing structured interviewing.

Whom to interview and when to interview them depend on the study and logistics. Some simple guidelines apply to most interviews. First, the interviewer should not speak with the most important respondents first. By most important, we mean the persons whose information, opinions, and insights are expected to be most valuable. Normally, an interviewer can identify her important respondents. They may be more difficult to reach and more protective of their time. She does not expect them to provide basic descriptive or factual information. The rule not to interview important respondents first arises from the logic that one does not want to throw away an important interview by asking the "wrong" questions. Initial interviews also often suggest additional items to be included.

Factual questions covering widely known or easily attainable information constitute a type of question that may be "wrong" for some respondents. Evaluators often start with knowledgeable program staff or constituents willing to describe program operations and accomplishments. These early interviews bring the interviewer up-to-date on the program, its operations, and current issues.

After she has practiced her interview skills for the specific project, identified current issues, and begun to formulate hypotheses, the interviewer can learn more from later respondents. She can test out her hypotheses with these respondents. Furthermore, she may bring insights and observations to the interview that the respondent will find valuable. We often forget that an interview can benefit the respondent. Frequently, in their day-to-day work, managers have little time to reflect upon their programs, why they developed as they did, how they work, and how they could be changed.

Second, interviewers should not avoid talking with respondents who have a different, even hostile, point of view. One does not want to interview them first, but neither should one delay too long. The first interviews serve as a learning period during which the researcher seeks respondents who will be sympathetic to gaps or errors in her information. Delaying interviews with difficult respondents too long has its costs. During the initial interviews, the interviewer is most open and flexible. Later, as the interviewer becomes more convinced of the correctness of her hypotheses, people with a different point of view may be considered "exceptions" and their insights may be ignored or overlooked. Interviewing respondents with a diversity of views is especially recommended to identify unexpected outcomes of programs or policies.

An interviewer needs good listening skills to tap the insights of respondents. Otherwise, she may misinterpret their comments or override them with her own point of view or agenda. Common listening errors include reaching a premature conclusion about the correctness of a respondent's observations. An interviewer who does this may stop listening. Alternatively, the interviewer may become anxious during periods of silence and either begin to fire questions or put words in the respondent's mouth. In both cases the interviewer loses opportunities to learn from the respondent. Other common complaints about interviewers are that the interviewer did not know enough; the interviewer did not use the right vocabulary; and the interviewer interrupted with irrelevant comments or had to have too much explained. These errors tend to put respondents off, and they will become less involved with the interview.

Example 6.5 summarizes a project based on interviews with women police officers. One of us worked with a colleague to learn how women officers participated in a police department: How did they learn about their jobs? In what policing activities were they involved? What were their career goals? How were they planning to achieve them?

We interviewed the women in small groups to minimize the wariness police typically show toward researchers. We felt that the small groups would reduce

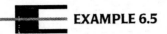 **EXAMPLE 6.5**

Interviews with Women Police Officers

Problem: Academic researchers wanted to learn about the socialization of women police officers, particularly their attitudes toward using force and the military.

Procedure:

1. Obtained permission from the police chief to interview officers.

2. Arranged to interview two or three officers together for approximately 1 hour.

3. Developed an interview schedule:
   a. How are women different from men in their approach to police work?
      (1) Different emphases in law enforcement, service, community relations?
      (2) More/less likely to deviate from department rules?
      (3) More/less committed to a career in police work?
      (4) More/less integrated into the social aspects of police work as a profession?
   b. Once you were out of the academy, who helped you become experienced as a police officer?
      (1) What kinds of partnership arrangements did you have?
      (2) What role did other women play?
      (3) Was your immediate supervisor involved?
      (4) What kinds of problems arose most frequently? Who showed you how to handle them?
      (5) Did you sense antagonism to women as police officers?
   c. What have been your major problems as a police officer?
      (1) Work problems—dealing with the public, other officers, supervisors, handling physical or other aspects of assignments.
      (2) Personal problems—family, social image.
   d. We found that in a survey of this department, most officers who answered said that force was one of the things about policing they liked least. Some people who have studied police, however, have found that the best police officers are those who do not avoid the use of force and are not uncomfortable about the fact that it is sometimes necessary.
      (1) Can you explain why the officers in this department answered that force was the part of the job they liked least?
      (2) Have you ever had to use force in your work?
      (3) Do you think that men handle this part of the job better?
      (4) Is this a problem for policewomen?
   e. How will this job make a difference in your total career?
   f. In your police training and in your work, does the subject of being "professional" come up? What do they mean by that term?
   g. What is most attractive/least attractive about police work for women?

4. Scheduled interviews: placed specialized and senior officers midway in the interviews; scheduling depended on officer availability.

5. Conducted interviews:
   a. The two researchers introduced themselves and the purpose of the study.
   b. Interviews were largely conversational.
   c. Both researchers took notes during the interview and wrote up their notes immediately following.

the tension and encourage free discussion and interaction among the officers. The group interviews seemed to work well for this exploratory study.

At the beginning of the interviews we introduced ourselves and the purpose of the study. We mentioned our criminal justice experience. With most of the officers, the interview proceeded smoothly. We asked the basic questions and followed up with specific questions as needed. Generally, before asking the next question, we glanced at the interview schedule to make sure we had covered all the planned topics. Occasionally we interjected with comments such as, "Could you explain that?" or "Can you give me an example?" to encourage the officers to expand upon their answers. Also, to ensure against projecting our own professional experiences into the answers, we often repeated what the women had said. For example, one of us might say, "Let me repeat what I think you said to make sure I got it right."

Before interviewing, an investigator must decide how to take notes. A method that the interviewer is comfortable with works with most subjects. For example, interviewers who use tape recorders report little subject resistance. Nevertheless, an interviewer who uses a tape recorder may want to jot down the important points of the interview. Transcribing or even listening to an entire interview can be costly in money or time. We still take notes and leave plenty of time immediately after the interview to amplify and organize our notes. Unless we do this promptly, the details fade quickly. The interviewer should not conduct back-to-back interviews. The interviewer may become fatigued, and the content of one interview may merge into the next. Some interviewers work in teams of two, with one person conducting the interview and recording it on tape and the other taking written notes.

Focus Groups

Investigators assemble focus groups to get in-depth information on and reactions to a few topics in any one study. Survey researchers, program evaluators, and program planners often construct focus groups. Surveyors use focus groups to identify appropriate survey questions or to supplement survey findings. Program evaluators use them to delve into the experiences of program clients. Program planners use them to get reactions from potential service recipients. The hallmark of focus groups is group interaction—members of the group can respond to answers given by others in the group. Investigators believe this interaction produces data and insights that would be less accessible if data were collected from separate individuals.

No one focus group represents a population; however, studies include several focus groups to ensure that their insights and observations extend beyond any one group. Recall that the best evidence of external validity is replication, that is, achieving similar results under somewhat varying conditions. Similarly, if several focus groups express similar attitudes or experiences, the investigators may persuasively argue that the groups represent the opinions and experiences of a larger population.

A focus group study involves four major phases: preparing, forming groups, conducting interviews, and analyzing and reporting the results. Preparing for a focus group is similar to preparing for any other empirical research project. The investigators clarify the study's purpose, what information is needed, why, and by whom. They write a limited number of open-ended questions for the group to discuss. Everyone in a focus group should have a chance to discuss each question and to react to each other's comments. Thus the questions must be carefully thought out to ensure that they will spark interest and develop the needed information.

Focus groups bring together a small group, ranging from 4 to 15 members, of unacquainted people who agree to meet for a focused discussion. The group should be small enough for everyone to have a chance to participate but large enough to provide some diversity. In larger groups, some members may dominate the discussion; some members may have little or no chance to talk because there never is a pause long enough for them to speak. Small groups may lack enough diversity to move beyond listless conversation. Experts differ in their recommendations regarding the maximum size of groups. However, the optimal size depends on the topic, the participants, the skill of the moderator, and the purpose of the study.[36] For example, complex topics presented to knowledgeable participants would require and work well with smaller groups.

Researchers recruit focus group members who are homogeneous on some important characteristics. They may have the same occupation, have the same income level, receive services from a public agency, or have a common experience, such as recently losing a job or having heart surgery. Group members must be sufficiently similar to encourage open discussion. If a group represents widely different socioeconomic levels or lifestyles, social dynamics may inhibit free or productive conversations. People with markedly different experiences may not work together effectively in a group. For example, large-scale farmers and family farmers may have an interest in the implementation of new farm legislation, but their different perceptions, concerns, and needs may cause such a group to spend most of its time clarifying and overcoming differences.

Focus group members are selected from lists of persons with the desired characteristics. Potential members are contacted by letter or telephone and are asked if they wish to participate. Potential members are again screened, often in more depth, to make sure that they meet the criteria for participation. For example, each focus group of farmers may consist of farmers who are actually responsible for running the farm, who work on similar-size farms, and whose farms generate similar amounts of revenue annually.

The staff needed to conduct a focus group consists of a moderator and one or two persons to take notes and set up any recording equipment. Other researchers may observe, either behind a one-way mirror or off to the side of the room. The moderator should be familiar with the study's topic; however, she may be less knowledgeable than an intensive interviewer. She may be "brought up to speed" by learning about the questions she will ask and their purpose.

A focus group usually meets for less than two hours. The meeting begins with the moderator's brief description of the study. Then, in a somewhat spontaneous fashion, she leads the group through the list of questions. Her job is to keep the group going and to prevent it from bogging down on unproductive conversations. As soon as the focus group session ends, the moderator and any observers meet to discuss and record their impressions of the group and the interview.

Example 6.6 highlights the focus-group segment of an evaluation of a program offering college courses in prisons. The program director wanted to learn what the inmates thought of the program. Focus groups seemed to be the best way to develop this information.

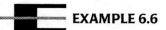 **EXAMPLE 6.6**

Focus Groups with Prison Inmates

Problem: The director of a prison program to provide college education to inmates wanted to know if the program was meeting their expectations. The evaluators decided to survey the prisoners who had taken college courses in the program and to supplement the surveys with information collected in focus groups.

Procedure:

1. Survey forms were created, focus group questions were written, and necessary permissions and authorizations were obtained.

2. The evaluators met with inmates at three prisons. At each prison the evaluators met with the group at one location. The evaluators introduced themselves and the purpose of the study, then the inmates filled out a questionnaire.

3. Randomly selected inmates were asked to stay for a discussion of educational programs.

4. A research team member acted as a moderator and led the inmates through a discussion based on the following questions:
   a. What do you think about the survey?
   b. What do you consider the value of education to be?
   c. What do you think will be the value of the courses you are taking?
   d. What benefits do you expect from taking courses here?
   e. How do prison administrators view the program?
   f. What kinds of courses would you like to see offered?
   g. How would you explain to "John Q. Public" that his taxes help pay for someone who committed a crime to take college courses?

   The discussions proceeded smoothly, with inmates commenting on or reacting to each other's remarks. Security restrictions prevented recording the focus group at the maximum-security prison; the other groups were recorded.

5. The research team met after each session to discuss and record the information; the tapes also were transcribed for further study.

6. The focus group data were included in both the written and oral evaluation reports. Some of the comments supplemented survey data. Discussions on the value of education and the types of courses desired delved into concerns that could not be easily addressed or ascertained by the questionnaire. Comments on the hostile attitudes by the custodial staff addressed an issue that was completely ignored by the survey items.

Discussion: This study violated the focus group model that the participants should not be acquainted. The focus groups elucidated inmates' opinions of the program, and group interaction yielded information that would not have been picked up by a survey or individual information. The survey helped to focus the discussion and to provide summary data.

The team that worked on this project had no previous experience in running focus groups or in prison research. They found that the focus groups provided far superior information than they would have obtained with just a survey. Their judgment mirrors our experience that focus groups add immeasurably to investigators' knowledge of how a program is perceived and how well it is working.

Analyzing Data from Intensive Interviews and Focus Groups

In later chapters we will discuss quantitative analysis. Since intensive interviews and focus groups primarily provide qualitative information, this seems to be an appropriate place to include a few comments about analyzing qualitative information.

Analysis of information from focus groups and intensive interviews depends on the quality of the investigator's records. The investigator should have thorough and accurate notes or recordings of the interviews. He may want to have both. In addition he should leave time after each interview or focus group to write down his observations and to fill in any gaps in his notes. An individual interview or focus group session produces extensive data. When he reviews his notes or recordings, the investigator looks for trends and patterns that reappear among various participants or groups.

The analysis must be systematic and verifiable. Systematic analysis follows a prescribed sequential process. The analysis is verifiable if another researcher can use the same process, information, and documents to reach a similar conclusion.

Analysis of data from focus groups and intensive interviews is driven by the purpose of the study. It also is directly related to the questions asked. Throughout, the analyst must keep the purpose of the study in mind. The objectives should guide the analysis. Researchers clarify and state objectives and ask questions to obtain information according to the purpose of the study. The questions elicit the material that will be analyzed. Clear, well-stated questions related to the study's purpose will make the analysis easier. Responses to complex or confusing questions will be difficult, if not impossible, to analyze. The analyst typically examines each question separately and summarizes the information. He also should consider the context in which comments were made and what triggered them.

To begin with, the analyst may focus on general trends and patterns. He may then do a more detailed analysis in which he codes topics and even phrases and groups those that are similar. He also will consider the range and diversity of information that he heard. After the information is summarized, the analyst interprets it. Of course, the quality of the interpretation relies heavily on the analyst's insights, intellectual talents, and previous experience with the subject matter and with analyzing qualitative data.[37]

SELECTING A METHOD OF DATA COLLECTION

The data collection method selected will depend to a great extent on the nature of the study. The study topic and the required sample interact to suggest the appropriate method. For example, an investigator should consider mailing a complicated questionnaire, or one with many open-ended questions, only to an articulate and highly motivated sample. Studies with inarticulate or socially isolated populations require face-to-face interviews. If the research question requires extensive qualitative information, intensive interviewing or focus groups work best. To explore how stakeholders view program plans or how clients react to an existing program, focus groups may be most effective.

Researchers have compared structured data collection methods, that is, mail, telephone, Internet, and in-person surveys. Their findings suggest that no one factor alone, with the possible exception of cost, automatically points to the desirability of one method over another. Problems such as response rate, questionnaire length, complexity, or sensitivity can be resolved to accommodate the constraints of the data collection method. In our presentation we identified some general advantages and disadvantages of each type of data collection technique. We have summarized these characteristics below.

Comparing Mail, Telephone, Internet, and In–person Surveys: A Review

Costs:

Mail: Relatively low cost (printing, mailing, and postage, incentives for responding)

Telephone: Higher cost (personnel, equipment, telephone charges)

Internet: Low cost

In-person: Highest cost (personnel, travel)

Sampling issues:

Mail: Requires a good sampling frame; can distinguish nonrespondents from nonrecipients if undelivered questionnaires are returned

Telephone: Provides a reasonably good initial sample of general public with random digit dialing; must have a mechanism for selecting respondents within a household to assure generalizability. Sample coverage constrained by increased reliance on cell phones.

Internet: Does not provide a reasonably good sample of general public; a good sampling frame may allow access to specific populations

In-person: No distinctive issues

Response rate:

Mail: Low (follow-up required)

Telephone: Higher (may need to vary calling times to get a representative sample)

Internet: May be difficult to determine; if general population is being surveyed it may have lowest response rate of all

In-person: Highest (problems with not-at-homes)

Turnaround time:

Mail: Slowest

Telephone: Quick

Internet: Quick

In-person: Slow (depends on sample size and dispersion)

Respondent issues:

Mail: Convenient, especially for hard-to-reach professionals; poor if subjects are elderly or poorly educated

Telephone: Most intrusive; allows easy access to dispersed populations

Internet: Requires Internet access, awareness of survey, motivation to access survey

In-person: Convenient, if appointment scheduled; allows access to hard-to-reach populations

Content:

Mail: Highly motivated respondents can look up information, write detailed answers; other respondents require clear, easily answered questions

Telephone: Avoids biases caused by respondent reading ahead; allows for probing and elaboration of answers; may give socially acceptable answers; respondent fatigue if too long

Internet: May have some of the benefits of computer-assisted interviewing; may encounter privacy concerns; respondents limited in their ability to communicate if questions seem ambiguous or responses inappropriate

In-person: Allows for in-depth, probing questions; good source for qualitative detail; valuable for exploratory studies; respondent–interviewer interaction may introduce bias; use of self-administered interviewing may encourage disclosure of embarrassing or sensitive information

Prior to selecting a data collection technique, the investigator should carefully consider the appropriateness of conducting a survey. The rate of refusals of the general public has increased since 1950.[38] Refusal rates of 40 percent for telephone surveys are not uncommon. The ability to successfully contact respondents may further decrease response rates. Overnight and one-day polls may have response rates of less than 30 percent.[39]

Another trend researchers have noted is the incidence of multiple participation; that is, a respondent who participates in more than one sample survey a year. A few years ago, one of the authors was asked to participate in three telephone surveys within a month. One was a political survey and the other two were marketing surveys. Her opinion of how long a telephone survey should take changed when she saw how an interview can interrupt family routine and inconvenience family members who are waiting for a call or who want to use the telephone.

A 1984 study on survey participation found that 23 percent of the respondents interviewed had been surveyed during the year; over half of them had been interviewed more than once during the year. The interview subjects were more likely to be female and younger, wealthier, and better educated than subjects who were not interviewed. The investigators concluded that these differences reflected sampling techniques designed particularly by market researchers to capture the opinions of certain segments of the population. They suggest that oversurveying may increase both refusal rates and multiple participation.[40]

The problems with multiple participation have not been explicitly studied. Investigators wonder whether cooperative subjects overrepresent some characteristics measured in a survey or if multiple participants evolve into "professional respondents," thereby affecting the representativeness of the data.

From our own experience, an analogous case can be made with organizational studies. Just as market researchers target certain populations, trends in administrative studies focus on certain organizations and professions. Imagine how many questionnaires are sent to city managers, municipal police departments, and public administration faculty by students and faculty doing academic research. Add to this professional associations and government agencies that compile statistical data or conduct studies to answer specific questions. Furthermore, city managers and police departments have to contend with inquiries from the public, public officials, and journalists. You may begin to see how repeated requests for information may overwhelm and annoy the most cooperative individual.

Before deciding to conduct an original survey, investigators, especially academic researchers, should attempt to identify and locate existing databases. If no appropriate existing data can be found, the decision to survey should proceed only after carefully pretesting the data collection instrument. The less experience the investigator has with the problem at hand, the more modest should be the research effort. If investigators limit their survey efforts to well-thought-out and carefully designed instruments that respect the time and experience of respondents, refusals to respond by organization members and by members of specific samples should decrease, and the quality of the data should improve.

SUMMARY

The data collection strategy is integral to implementing a research plan. How an investigator contacts potential subjects and obtains data from them may determine the success of a project. Mail, telephone, Internet, or in-person surveys each have strengths and weaknesses. Nevertheless, no one characteristic, with the possible exception of cost, automatically recommends one survey collection method over another. Rather, investigators should consider both the study and its population and choose the data collection method best suited to meet the study objectives.

Mail surveys generally cost the least of any survey method, but the benefit of lower cost must be balanced against the time required for data collection. Mail surveys allow motivated respondents time to look up requested information and to provide detailed answers to open-ended questions. Mail surveys require the investigators to take time to make sure that the final questionnaire is free from confusing or ambiguous items, because no one will be there to answer the respondent's questions about what information is wanted. Complex, multi-part questions also must be kept to a minimum.

Mail surveys work best with educated respondents who are used to working with forms. These respondents will not be intimidated by open-ended questions where they have to express their ideas in their own words. Mail surveys seem appropriate for many organizational studies in which data must be located, and more than one person may be involved in answering the survey. Furthermore, in organizational research the mail survey can be squeezed into the respondents' schedule, whereas telephone or in-person surveys may be disruptive and hard for the investigator to schedule.

The major weakness of mail surveys has been their low response rates. Investigators have found that even in surveys of the general public, who are the least motivated to respond to most surveys, mail surveys perform as well as telephone or in-person surveys if the researchers follow up with nonrespondents. To check the assumption that the nonrespondents are similar to respondents, researchers should compare the known demographic characteristics of the nonrespondents and the respondents. Also, with mail surveys, a random sample of nonrespondents may be telephoned or visited and asked to answer the questionnaire. Their answers may be compared with those of other respondents to assure the investigators that respondents and nonrespondents are not different.

Internet surveys may work well in surveying a discrete group with easy Internet access. The low cost of Internet surveys may be offset by the more common problems of finding a good sampling frame, making potential respondents aware of a survey, and motivating them to answer it. These surveys are becoming more popular and can work well, especially for an identified sample whose members can be sent notices or follow-up contacts. Internet surveys are often conducted with software that provides immediate results on simple items.

Telephone surveys became more common as the cost of in-person surveys increased and the telephone became commonplace in American homes. In addition, random digit dialing solved the inability to reach homes with unlisted telephone numbers and reduces the cost of selecting a representative sample. Telephone surveys can provide rapid turnaround in data collection time and make full use of computerization. Computer-assisted telephone interviewing relies on the computer to help administer a survey. The interviewer keys in the answer; the computer then selects the appropriate next question, reducing the logistical problems associated with making sure the interviewer finds the right follow-up questions. The computer keeps track of inconsistent responses, stores the data, monitors the interviewer's performance, and often uses software that can provide immediate statistical results. The cost of acquiring the equipment, programming each survey, and training interviewers makes computer-assisted interviewing feasible only for organizations that constantly conduct large telephone surveys.

Telephone surveys are most limited in their ability to reach segments of the population who do not have ready access to a telephone. They may not be appropriate for organizational research, where information must be looked up or more than one respondent contacted. Managers and other professionals may be difficult to reach on the telephone, seriously increasing the cost and time involved.

Other limitations of telephone surveys are their length and inability to elicit information on sensitive subjects. Although most nonrespondents have already refused to participate in a survey before the questioning commences, length is the most common complaint about telephone surveys. Long surveys may lead a respondent to refuse later requests for information. In addition, answer quality may degenerate toward the end of a long survey or the respondent may quit answering altogether.

In-person interviews, which approximate telephone interviews, have limited use, insofar as costs and improvements in telephone surveying methods have made them less desirable. Nevertheless, in-person interviews seem to work best for complex studies where interviewer–subject rapport is necessary.

Structured interviewing depends on standardized interviewing. Without standardized interviewing protocols a researcher does not know whether the answers obtained are a product of respondent characteristics or of those of the interviewer. To conduct structured interviews, interviewers must be consistent in how they explain the study's purpose, ask questions, handle inadequate answers, and record information. Above all, the interviewer should not draw attention to his own experiences and opinions.

Intensive interviewing, a type of in-person interviewing, and focus groups can greatly improve administrative studies. The interviews allow investigators to consider the adequacy of their models and the appropriateness of their measures. Furthermore, interviews produce important background information necessary for understanding a problem, how it came to be, what solutions have been tried, and how they have worked.

Effective intensive interviewing requires practice. Some simple steps can minimize common errors. The first interviews usually are informational and focused on factual information. The interviewer normally avoids asking the "most important" subjects for relatively common information and waits to interview key subjects until she has a fuller understanding of the program or the problem at hand. Similarly, the interviewer avoids limiting her early interviews to people who share her own point of view. Unless people with another viewpoint are interviewed early, their insights and information may be inadvertently filtered out.

The interviewer must listen carefully to the subject. Interviewer training often works toward eliminating listening habits that cause interviewers to ignore or misunderstand what a subject is saying. Similarly, interview preparation includes familiarizing oneself with the topic of the interview and the applicable terminology or jargon; otherwise, the subject tends to spend too much time explaining.

Focus groups have the same benefits as intensive interviewing. They also foster group interaction and discussion, which can provide even more information for program evaluation and program planning. Focus group research requires more than one investigator; the responsibilities of moderating and recording should not fall on one person. A major challenge in conducting focus groups is to identify a discrete number of open-ended questions that will elicit discussion consistent with the study's purpose. Because focus group studies involve relatively few individuals who agree to participate, the findings cannot be unambiguously generalized to a larger population. Probably more important than selecting a method of data collection is asking the question, "Are original data needed?" As the number of researchers grows and the value of research findings spreads, people are asked for more and more information. Market researchers target certain groups known to have more discretionary money to spend. Academic and administrative researchers have analogous target groups. The result of all this survey activity may be multiple requests for information, which raises questions as to whether multiple respondents are truly representative and whether in the long run they will continue to answer questions willingly. We assume that the problem is not how many times one is asked, but how worthwhile respondents feel their participation is. If a subject questions the worth of a study or his participation in it, we assume that he either will not answer or will give cursory answers.

In the next chapter, we examine strategies for writing questions and questionnaires. We link questionnaire design to a study's purpose, its model, and the reliability and operational validity of items. Questionnaires that contain unneeded, unreliable, or invalid items waste resources. Failure to include key variables can also waste resources. Consequently, the chapter stresses the need to pilot test any survey and evaluate each question, the proposed data analysis, and planned use of the findings.

NOTES

1. This categorization of potential sample members is drawn from M. A. Hidigoglou, J. D. Drew, and G. B. Gray, "A Framework for Measuring and Reducing Nonresponse in Surveys," *Survey Methodology* 19 (1993): 81–94. See pages 82–84 for a discussion of components and calculations of various rates.

2. Scott Keeter, "The Impact of Cell Phone Noncoverage Bias on Polling in the 2004 Presidential Election," *Public Opinion Quarterly* 70 (1) (2006): 88–98.

3. Katherine Newcomer and Timothy Triplett, "Using Surveys," in J. S. Wholey, H. P. Hatry, and K. E. Newcomer, eds, *Handbook of Practical Program Evaluation*, 2d ed. (San Francisco: Jossey-Bass, 2004), 292–309.

4. M. Kaplowitz, T. Hadlock, and R. Levine, "A Comparison of Web and Mail Survey Response Rates," *Public Opinion Quarterly* 68 (2004): 94–101.

5. The authors followed Dillman's tailored design method. See D. A. Dillman, *Mail and Internet Surveys: The Tailored Design Method* (New York: John Wiley, 2000).

6. See F. J. Yammarino, S. J. Skinner, and T. L. Childers, "A Meta-Analysis of Mail Surveys," *Public Opinion Quarterly* 55 (1991): 613–639 for a more thorough discussion of research on response rates.

7. A. H. Church, "Incentives in Mail Surveys: A Meta-Analysis," *Public Opinion Quarterly* 57 (1993): 62–79.

8. D. A. Dillman, K. K. West, and J. R. Clark, "Invitations to Answer by Phone in Mail Surveys," *Public Opinion Quarterly* 58 (1994): 557–568.

9. A. H. Church, "Incentives in Mail Sureys," 71.

10. J. M. James and R. Bolstein, "Response Rates with Large Monetary Incentives," *Public Opinion Quarterly* 56 (1992): 442–453; and J. M. James and R. Bolstein, "The Effect of Monetary Incentives and Follow-up Mailings on the Response Rate and Response Quality in Mail Surveys," *Public Opinion Quarterly* 54 (1990): 346–361.

11. For a discussion of nonresponse in surveys and how to handle the problem of nonresponse, see N. Bradburn, "A Response to the Nonresponse Problem," *Public Opinion Quarterly* 56 (1992): 391–397. See R. M. Groves, *Survey Errors and Survey Costs* (New York: Wiley Interscience, 2004) for a description of

methods for weighting the responses of a sample of "converted" nonrespondents. I-Fen Lin and N. C. Schaeffer evaluate two models for estimating information from nonrespondents in "Using Respondents to Estimate Nonresponse Bias," *Public Opinion Quarterly* 59 (1995): 236–258.

12. Newcomer and Triplett, "Using Surveys."

13. This section relies on the observations and findings reported by B. K. Kaye and T. J. Hohnson, "Research Methodology: Taming the Cyber Frontier," *Social Science Computer Review* 17 (1999): 323–337.

14. C. Hewson, P. Yule, D. Laurent, and C. Vogel, *Internet Research Methods: A Practical Guide for the Social and Behavioral Sciences* (London: Sage Publications Ltd., 2003), especially chapter 5.

15. D. R. Schaefer and D. A. Dillman, "Development of a Standard E-Mail Methodology," *Public Opinion Quarterly* 62 (1998): 378–397.

16. M. P. Couper, M. W. Traugott, and M.J. Lamias, "Web Survey Design and Administration," *Public Opinion Quarterly* 65 (2001): 230–253. Also see Hewson, et al., chapter 5, "How to Design and Implement an Internet Survey," which addresses several of the issues discussed here.

17. Hewson, et al, chapter 5.

18. Information on nonphone households and households with intermittent service is from S. Keeter, "Estimating Noncoverage Bias from a Phone Survey," *Public Opinion Quarterly* 59 (1995): 196–217. The comment about nonphone households being outsiders is from T. W. Smith, "Phone Home? An Analysis of Household Telephone Ownership," *International Journal of Public Opinion Research* 2 (1990): 369–390, cited by Keeter, 198. The estimate of 3 percent of households with intermittent phone coverage is based on *1992–93 Current Population Surveys* data cited by Keeter, 199.

19. "The Cell Phone Challenge to Survey Research National Polls Not Undermined by Growing Cell-Only Population" (Washington, DC: Pew Research Center, May 15, 2006). Available at http:/ /people-press. org/ reports/ display. php3?PageID=1054.

20. Keeter (2006): 88–98.

21. Ibid.

22. Richard Curtin, Stanley Presser, and Eleanor Singer, "Changes in Telephone Survey Non-Response Over the Past Quarter Century," *Public Opinion Quarterly* 69 (2005): 87–98. The Survey Research Center (SRC) conducts high-quality social science research, including a number of national studies. Among its regular studies are the Survey of Community Attitudes and the National Election Studies.

23. A popular random digit dialing method is described in J. Waksberg, "Sampling Methods for Random Digit Dialing," *Journal of the American Statistical Association* 73 (1978): 40–46. A random number is constructed by adding a two-digit random to a phone bank (a phone bank is the first eight digits of a phone number, starting with the area code). The number is called. If it is a residential number, several other random numbers using the same phone bank are called. If the first phone number is not residential, the phone bank is discarded. J. M. Brick et al., "Bias in List-Assisted Telephone Samples," *Public Opinion Quarterly* 59 (1995): 218–235, identify commercially available lists that categorize phone banks according to whether or not they contain any residential numbers.

24. Backstrom and Hursh-Cesar, *Survey Research,* 115. D. S. Voss, A. Gelman, and G. King, "Review: Preelection Survey Methodology," *Public Opinion Quarterly* 59 (1995): 98–132, gathered data from eight organizations that do presidential polling. Only two organizations reported weighting by the number of phone lines, and both organizations used a weight of 1 for homes with only one phone line and .5 for homes with more than one phone line.

25. See Frey, *Survey Research by Telephone,* 2d ed. (Newbury Park, CA: Sage, 1989): 78–85, for a discussion and evaluation of strategies for selecting persons to interview. See Voss et al., "Review: Preelection Survey Methodology," 110–112, for information on practices of specific polling organizations.

26. D. A. Dillman, *Mail and Telephone Surveys: The Total Design Method* (New York: Wiley, 1978), 248.

27. M. W. Link and R. W. Oldendick, "Is Call Screening Really a Problem?" *Public Opinion Quarterly* 63 (1999): 577–589.

28. Backstrom and Hursh-Cesar, *Survey Research,* 115, suggest that more than three callbacks are inefficient and not worth the benefit of an increased response rate. Dillman, *Mail,* 47–49, has an excellent discussion on substituting sample members in telephone surveys. For how to handle answering machines, see R. W. Oldendick and M. W. Link, "The Answering Machine Generation," *Public Opinion Quarterly* 58 (1994): 264–273; T. Piazza, "Meeting the Challenge of Answering Machines," *Public Opinion Quarterly* 57 (1993): 219–231; and M. Xu, B. J. Bates, and J. C. Schweitzer, "The Impact of Messages on Survey Participation in Answering Machine Households," *Public Opinion Quarterly* 57 (1993): 232–237. The Piazza study, based on California data, considers the probability of getting through, the best times to get through, and the effect of multiple callbacks.

29. S. Keeter et al., "Consequences of Reducing Nonresponse in a National Telephone Survey," *Public Opinion Quarterly* 64 (Summer 2000): 135–148.

30. Groves, *Survey Errors* (1989), 238. See Groves, *Survey Errors* (1989; 2004), chapter 5, for a thorough discussion

on refusals to cooperate, efforts to increase cooperation, and research on noncooperation.

31. W. S. Aquilino and D. L. Wright, "Substance Use Estimates from RDD and Area Probability Samples," *Public Opinion Quarterly* 60 (1996): 563–573.

32. F. J. Fowler, Jr., *Survey Research Methods*, 2d ed. (Newbury Park: Sage, 1993), chap. 7.

33. Research on survey mode and willingness to report sensitive information found that respondents using self-administered surveys seem more likely to disclose embarrassing information. CASI administered in school settings may compromise the accuracy of the responses, if the respondents are physically close to one another. See R. Tourengeau and T. Smith, "Asking Sensitive Questions," *Public Opinion Quarterly* 60 (1996): 275–304, which also summarizes previous research relating survey mode to disclosure of sensitive information; D. L. Wright, W. S. Aquilino, and A. J. Supple, "Comparison of Computer-Assisted and Paper-and-Pencil Questionnaires in a Survey on Smoking, Alcohol, and Drug Use," *Public Opinion Quarterly* 62 (1998): 331–353; Y. Moon, "Impression Management in Computer-Based Interviews: The Effects of Input Modality, Output Modality, and Distance," *Public Administration Quarterly* 62 (1998): 610–622.

34. Herbert Rubin and Irene Rubin, *Qualitative Interviewing: The Art of Hearing Data*, 2d ed. (Thousand Oaks, CA: Sage Publications, 2005).

35. See E. O'Sullivan, G. W. Burleson, and W. Lamb, "Avoiding Evaluation Cooptation," *Evaluation and Program Planning* 8 (1985): 255–259.

36. Richard A. Krueger and Mary Anne Casey, 3d ed., *Focus Groups: A Practical Guide for Applied Research* (Thousand Oaks, CA: Sage, 2000).

37. For additional information and examples on analyzing and reporting results from focus groups, see Krueger and Casey, chapters 6 and 7.

38. Research covering several decades confirms a continuing decline. See C. G. Steeh, "Trends in Nonresponse Rates, 1952–1979," *Public Opinion Quarterly* 45 (1981): 40–57; P. Farhi, "How Would You Answer This One?" *Washington Post*, April 14, 1992, A1, A4; R. Rothenberg, "Surveys Proliferate," A1, A6; and T. W. Smith, "Research Notes: Trends in Non-Response Rates," *International Journal of Public Opinion Research* 7 (1995): 157–171.

39. Farhi, "How Would You Answer," A4.

40. S. Schleifer, "Trends in Attitudes Toward and Participation in Survey Research," *Public Opinion Quarterly* 50 (1986): 17–26.

TERMS FOR REVIEW

response rate
nonresponse rate
random digit dialing

computer-aided telephone
    interviewing (CATI)
Internet surveys

structured interviewing
intensive interviewing
focus groups

QUESTIONS FOR REVIEW

The following questions should indicate whether you have a basic competency in this chapter's material.

1. Why would a low response rate to a survey concern a researcher?

2. What is the value of being able to distinguish between the response rate and refusal rate? Can researchers distinguish between response rates and refusal rates on mail surveys? on telephone surveys? on Internet surveys? on in-person interviews? Explain.

3. Assess the advisability of investigators' assuming that respondents are similar to nonrespondents. What is the value of telephoning a sample of the nonrespondents to a mail or Internet survey?

4. Explain what random digit dialing is and its value for telephone surveys.

5. Compare and contrast information you would collect to pretest a mail survey, a telephone survey, or an Internet survey.

6. When should structured, in-person interviewing be used instead of telephone interviewing?

7. What is the value of intensive interviewing? What type of people would you most likely target for an intensive interview? Why?

8. Some students tend to "wing it" if they have to do intensive interviewing. Assess the dangers of this strategy.

9. What would be the advantage of using focus groups to learn
   a. alumni opinion about the program you are studying?
   b. parents' reactions to a proposed county-wide, after-school program?

10. Suggest and justify a data collection method for each of the following proposed studies:
   a. to find out how many agency employees are attending continuing-education classes.
   b. to understand how parole board members make parole decisions.
   c. to estimate the portion of the voters likely to vote in a referendum who favor issuing a school bond.
   d. to identify the demographic characteristics of city managers in a state.
   e. to find out what corrections officials consider an appropriate measure of "successful rehabilitation."
   f. to learn what constitutes community standards of pornography.

PROBLEMS FOR HOMEWORK AND DISCUSSION

1. Examine an issue of a journal such as *Public Administration Review* or *Administrative Science Quarterly*. For each article based on data collected from individuals or organizations, note
   a. who the research population was.
   b. how the subjects were contacted (mail, telephone, Internet, in person).
   c. what the response rate was.
   d. how the investigators handled subjects who did not respond to the first contact, that is, the number of follow-ups.
   Compare your results with your classmates'. Can you make any generalizations linking the nature of the study population to the method of contacting subjects, and linking the number of follow-ups to the response rate?

2. Try your hand at constructing a telephone sample. Estimate the number of listings in one section of a local telephone directory, for example, listings for one community or residential listings for the city. Develop a procedure for selecting five telephone numbers to serve as the roots for the telephone numbers you will call. (Do not develop a procedure that requires you to count each listing.) Select the five telephone numbers. Note how long it takes you to select the five numbers.

3. Two Internet surveys are designed. Survey 1 asks state, city, and county managers what benefits they offer employees. Survey 2 asks public employees about the benefits they receive from their employer. How would you access respondents for each survey? Contrast the quality of the samples for the two surveys.

4. You want to learn more about research: how projects are selected, models built, measures operationally defined, and new data collected.
   a. Outline what you would ask in an unstructured interview of a faculty member at your university.
   b. Videotape a member of your class interviewing a faculty member. Critique the interview.

5. You decide to construct a study of the effectiveness of your academic program. What data collection method reviewed in this chapter would you use? Whom would you interview or survey (give general characteristics of the potential interviewees or respondents)? How many people would you include? How would you select them? If you tried to cover different groups, say students and faculty, in what order would you interview or survey them? What questions would you ask? Sketch out a research plan for this study. Compare and discuss the research plans in class. Would you base the entire study on your chosen method? If not, what alternative data collection methods would you use, and when would you use them?

6. Identify two web-based software packages available for survey researchers. Write a memo to your supervisor explaining how you would go about using one of them. Also justify why you would choose one rather than the other.

A CLASS PROJECT

Do you think participatory or autocratic groups produce better results? Under what conditions might one management style work better than another? For this project, three groups of students will prepare reports on these questions, using a word factory scenario that is acted out by a fourth group. While the participants operate the word factory, one group of students will observe, one group will prepare a survey, and one group will prepare to interview the factory workers.

1. A group will be assigned to participate in the word factory. Each person brings to the factory one vowel and one consonant. The factory will operate for 20 minutes with a goal of making as many words as possible. (The instructor, class, or factory members set the rules—for example, how members select what letters to bring, whether a letter may be used more than once in a word, and restrictions on permissible words.)

2. One group of about three persons should observe the factory. After the factory ceases operation, they should write a report describing its leadership style.

3. While the factory is operating, another group writes a questionnaire to learn about the group's leadership style and its output. (The questionnaire may have been assigned previously.) After the factory ceases its operations, the members answer the questionnaire. The group then analyzes the answers and writes a report describing the factory's leadership style.

4. While the factory is operating, the third group of students will decide how to interview members on the subject of the factory's leadership and output. After the factory ceases operations, conduct the interviews and write up a report describing the group's leadership style. Now compare the three reports. What are your conclusions?

RECOMMENDED FOR FURTHER READING

Many how-to-do-it books on survey research are available. The following two go through the entire process from designing a study to analyzing the results: Louis M. Rea and Richard A. Parker's *Designing and Conducting Survey Research: A Comprehensive Guide*, 2d ed. (San Francisco: Jossey-Bass, 1997); Arlene Fink, *How to Conduct Surveys: A Step-by-Step Guide*, 3d ed. (Thousand Oaks, CA: Sage, 2006). Also recommended for public administrators is David Foltz, *Survey Research for Public Administration* (Thousand Oaks, CA: Sage Publications, 1996). A classic reference on surveys is D. A. Dillman's *Mail and Telephone Surveys* (New York: Wiley, 1978). Also see his *Mail and Internet Surveys: The Tailored Design Method* (New York: John Wiley, 2000). The following is recommended as a volume that brings together chapters on how-to-do surveys and practical advice with theoretical underpinnings of survey research: *Survey Methodology* (Hoboken, NJ: Wiley Interscience, 2004) by R.M. Groves, F. Fowler, M. Couper, J. Lepkowski, E. Singer, and R. Tourangeau.

An excellent resource book examining and comparing errors in mail, telephone, and in-person interviewing is R. M. Groves, *Survey Errors and Survey Costs* (New York: Wiley Interscience, 2004).

For information on unstructured interviewing, a classic text is L. A. Dexter's *Elite and Specialized Interviewing* (Evanston, IL: Northwestern University Press, 1970). Herbert Rubin and Irene Rubin's *Qualitative Interviewing: The Art of Hearing Data*, 2d ed. (Thousand Oaks, CA: Sage Publications, 2005) is also informative.

For a how-to-do-it guide on focus groups, see R. A. Krueger and Mary Ann Casey, *Focus Groups: A Practical Guide for Applied Research*, 3d ed. (Thousand Oaks, CA: Sage Publications, 2000).

Readers interested in focus groups also should consult *The Focus Group Kit* by David L. Morgan and Richard A. Krueger (Thousand Oaks, CA: Sage Publications, 1998). The entire kit contains six volumes covering all aspects of focus-group research including planning, question development, moderating, and analyzing and reporting results, among other topics. The volumes are available individually.

For up-to-date research findings on surveying strategies, see *Public Opinion Quarterly*, the journal of the American Association of Public Opinion Research, published by the University of Chicago Press. *Social Science Computer Review*, published by Sage Publications, provides timely information on web-surveying and data collection software.

CHAPTER 7

Data Collection: Questions and Questionnaires

In this chapter you will learn

1. The role of model building and the model in designing a survey.
2. Proper roles for open-ended and closed-ended questions.
3. How question content and wording affect reliability and operational validity.
4. Ways to avoid asking unnecessary questions and forgetting important ones.
5. Pretesting methods to prevent wasting resources on surveys.

Writing questions and designing questionnaires are important research skills for administrative investigators. Agencies use questionnaires in program planning, monitoring, and evaluation. Surveys help agencies plan programs by identifying problems, assessing support for policy alternatives, and learning what services are needed. Administrators may use questionnaires to monitor programs by compiling information on client characteristics and what services clients use, when, and how often. Evaluators use questionnaires to gather information from clients about their satisfaction with a program, its actual practices, and its effectiveness. Social scientists rely on questionnaires to collect a wide range of data on individuals and organizations.

Writing questionnaires seems easy. Yet, as we implied in our discussion of cross-sectional designs, poor-quality questionnaires are common. Poor questionnaires may result in low response rates, unreliable or invalid data, or inadequate or inappropriate information. In our classes we have observed that students identify a problem for which they need data and begin immediately to write a questionnaire. Potential questions flow quickly as they brainstorm. We believe that similar behavior occurs in offices, when someone wants information about other people or organizations.

What is wrong with a questionnaire that comes out of such a session? The questionnaire may be inappropriate for the study's purpose. It may ask too few questions or the wrong questions. Unless it is adequately pretested, serious errors affecting reliability, such as ambiguous questions or confusing directions, may not be detected. The underlying concepts may not be clarified, resulting in invalid measures.

Quality questionnaires require well-worded questions, clear responses, and attractive layouts. In addition, investigators must use systematic procedures to decide exactly what to ask. First, the investigators must clarify the study's purpose, ascertain that the proposed questions are consistent with its purpose, and determine whether the administrators believe that the survey information will be adequate. Second, the investigators want to make sure that the questions and the overall data collection strategy will yield reliable and operationally valid data. Third, they want to verify that the data meet the needs of the intended users.

Investigators may meet with intended users to confirm that the study will produce appropriate and adequate information for their needs. For example, a city may contract for a citizen survey to find out what services citizens most want and who wants them. Staff who plan to use the survey data should meet with the survey designer to discuss how they want to use the data and to review the survey draft. If a survey designer fails to ask respondents where they live or how old they are, staff will not know if demands for better recreational facilities vary by neighborhood or age group. Alternatively, a designer may ask about potential services that the city has no intention of providing. Unneeded questions increase the burden on respondents. The questions may falsely imply planned changes in city services, irritating those who feel the city is doing too much and misleading those who think the city is not doing enough.

This chapter examines strategies for developing questionnaires that yield useful data. It begins by considering strategies for making sure that an instrument asks the right questions. It presents techniques for writing effective questions and questionnaires. It suggests a strategy for mapping out the questionnaire to confirm that it is complete. The chapter discusses how to pretest questionnaires. Investigators cannot accurately assess the clarity of the questionnaire or its completeness without a pretest. This chapter stresses the necessity of thoroughly pretesting all questionnaires before using them to collect data and conducting a pilot study to see how a questionnaire and the data collection strategy actually work.

QUESTIONNAIRE AND QUESTION CONTENT

A questionnaire with short, easily answered questions may seem to have required little effort to write. But, in fact, questionnaire writing can be tedious, involving several drafts and more than one pretest. A clear, uncluttered questionnaire may be a testament to the time and effort of its writers. Questionnaire writing involves deciding what variables to measure; writing questions that accurately and adequately measure the variables; assembling the questions in a logical order on a questionnaire; and pretesting the questions and conducting a pilot study.

In deciding what to include in a questionnaire, researchers need to identify the variables they want to measure, the type of questions that will measure the variables, and the number of questions needed to ensure reliability and operational validity. Many analysts, including ourselves, have labored on questionnaires only to discover later that they asked questions that were not used in the analysis. Some questions were not needed; others were useless because the respondent misunderstood them. Researchers also fail to ask questions critical to the study. Over time, we have become philosophical about this failure—nobody is perfect.

The first component that defines a survey's content is the model. We are certain that many surveys are written with no reference to a model. It may have faded into memory, but more likely, no one ever constructed an explicit model for the study. Model building requires investigators to identify and link variables needed to answer a question or solve a problem. Prior to building a model, investigators need to know why it is being built, that is, its purpose. Similarly, investigators need to know a survey's purpose. They also should be convinced that a study is necessary and that a survey is better than alternative methods of data collection.

The investigators identify those variables for which data are needed. They must find or develop measures for each variable in the model. Other variables should be included only if they serve a clear purpose. Next, the investigators decide what linkages among variables need to be studied. Explicitly listing the variables and the linkages of interest should guide the debate about whether a specific question is necessary.

As useful as we find model building, for some projects developing a coherent, integrated model may be inefficient. Some users may actively resist efforts to build a fully articulated model. Investigators conducting a study for a specific user, for example, an administrator or a legislator who wants the information to help make a decision, may prefer to focus on the specific questions that the user wants to have answered. Michael Patton, in a classic program evaluation text, suggests that investigators first identify the purpose of the study and its primary users. Next, the investigators ask the primary users to indicate how they plan to use the study to answer their questions or to solve a problem.[1] The discussion between the investigators and primary users should detail exactly what information they need, how they will use it, and whether it will be adequate. With this information, questions can be formulated to yield the needed data.

Decisions on what questions to include may extend over the planning period. Later in the chapter, in Example 7.7, we show a procedure to track how each question in a questionnaire will be used. The procedure should prevent asking unneeded questions and failing to include necessary questions. The investigators also should analyze the data gathered during pretests or pilot studies. The data analysis may help the investigators and users to evaluate the adequacy of the questionnaire.

The second component of content is the type of question being asked. Knowledge of question type can help you decide the operational validity of a measure. Survey analysts may categorize questions as gathering information on:

Facts

Behaviors

Opinions

Attitudes

Motives

Knowledge

Factual questions elicit objective information from respondents. The most common factual questions are demographic questions, such as sex, age, marital status, education, income, profession, and occupational history. Factual questions may be asked about anything on which someone wants information. How much money does a participant in a charity walk-a-thon raise? How long does it take a city to issue a building permit? How many miles of highway does a state pave annually?

Behavior questions, which are a type of factual question, ask respondents about things they do or have done. For example, residents may be asked how far they travel to work or whether they have ever attended a public hearing. They may be asked if they have volunteered and, if so, for how many hours a month.

Opinion questions ask people what they think about a specific issue or event. Opinions are said to be the verbal expressions of attitudes. *Attitude questions* try to elucidate more stable, underlying beliefs or ways of looking at things. *Motive questions* ask respondents to evaluate why they behave in a particular manner or hold certain opinions or attitudes.

Knowledge questions, which are similar to test questions, determine what a person knows about a topic and the extent or accuracy of the information. Knowledge questions may act as filters to eliminate the answers of uninformed respondents. Knowledge questions commonly appear in evaluations of training programs to find out whether subjects learned what was taught. Knowledge questions can measure what a population knows about a policy or issue. They can indicate whether citizens know that a particular service or program exists.

Investigators who know a model's purpose and understand how different types of questions produce different information avoid collecting the "wrong" data. Consider a problem in program evaluation. Participants may be asked their opinions of a program. For example, trainees may be asked to rate the quality of a training program they had completed. Administrators, however, may want to know whether training increased participants' knowledge or changed their behavior on the job. The administrators may question retaining a program that does not produce these results. They may find opinions interesting, even helpful. Respondent opinions may lead to future program changes. Still, the opinions do not indicate whether the program has performed as desired.

Question wording, emphasis, and order have a greater effect on opinion and attitude questions than on factual questions. For any type of question, the respondent must understand what information is wanted. For example, in a housing survey, respondents may report fewer bedrooms than their houses contain because they do not think of a den, a playroom, or a home office as a "bedroom." If the questionnaire writer wanted to count such converted rooms as bedrooms, she may be stuck with unreliable data.

The third component of content is the number of questions to be asked to measure each variable. Recall that the number of questions or indicators affects a measure's reliability. To avoid burdening respondents, we should keep the number of questions to a minimum. Thus we have to consider the trade-off between lower reliability and higher response rates.

The number of questions also affects operational validity. Many variables cannot be adequately measured with only one indicator. Recall our Chapter 4 example of employee empowerment. Empowerment was measured by four variables. They were employees' belief that (1) their work was meaningful, (2) they were competent to do their job, (3) they had autonomy in performing their work, and (4) their work had an impact on the organization. Examining satisfaction with a police department may involve asking citizens to rate the department's response time; its ability to prevent crime and to solve crimes quickly; how fairly officers treat all citizens, especially young people and minorities; and the department's general competency.

The number of questions and operational validity problems are of special concern when gathering organizational data. To determine organizational or program effectiveness requires more than a single indicator. Imagine if the only information collected on the performance of a job training program was the percentage of trainees placed. Relying on this one piece of data may inaccurately measure program effectiveness. Information on the quality of trainees' jobs—for example, pay rate, skills required, and stability of employment—gives a more complete and valid picture. Furthermore, measures that have inadequate content may seriously distort staff behavior. Staff members may focus on the one measured indicator, for example, the percentage placed, and accept only trainees with a high placement potential, or they may place graduates in low-paying or temporary jobs to keep the placement rate up.

QUESTIONNAIRE STRUCTURE

Open-ended Questions

Questions may be either open-ended or closed-ended. *Open-ended* questions require the respondent to answer in her own words. *Closed-ended* questions ask the respondent to choose from a list of responses. For example, respondents may check whether they "strongly agree," "agree," "disagree," or "strongly disagree" with a statement, or they may indicate a number representing the most appropriate answer.

Researchers ask open-ended questions for at least five reasons. They help a researcher identify the range of possible responses. They avoid biases that a list of responses can introduce. They yield rich, detailed comments. They give respondents a chance to elaborate on their answers. Just as "a picture is worth a thousand words," a comment can add immeasurably to an investigator's information. Finally, respondents can more easily answer some questions with a few words rather than by selecting an answer from a long list of possible responses. For example, the question, "In what state do you live?" is easier to answer by writing a state name than by looking for the state on a list. Open-ended questions have two major drawbacks. First, they are often unanswered. Respondents with little time or limited communication skills may ignore them. Second, they complicate data compilation. Categorizing and counting the answers can be a formidable task.

Open-ended questions are most valuable during the early stages of questionnaire design. When we studied how trainees used DECIDE, a management training program, we did not know how the trainees used the decision-making techniques nor did we know if trainees had found unique uses for the techniques. We asked trainees for an example of how they applied DECIDE. Some respondents could not give a work-related example, but they did give examples of using DECIDE to make personal decisions. If we had written a list of responses, we would not have included personal applications, and we would have overlooked one reason why the course was popular with employees. From the examples, we categorized and summarized how employees used DECIDE. With the uses identified and responses categorized, we later wrote appropriate closed-ended questions. For example, we asked, "How often do you use DECIDE to help you make budget request decisions?" "How often do you use DECIDE to help you make purchasing decisions?" "How often do you use DECIDE to help you make personnel allocation decisions?" In constructing the questions, we selected specific decisions from our list of common uses.

In political polling the movement from open-ended to closed-ended questions is well established. Long before American political parties and voters express any formal preference for a presidential candidate, pollsters may ask respondents to name whom they prefer for the next president. This procedure allows pollsters to identify candidates with early support. It avoids the possibility that respondents will simply choose a familiar name, in which case the poll is measuring name recognition rather than support. As Election Day approaches, open-ended questions have long since disappeared, replaced by closed-ended questions that focus on actual, active candidates.

A similar pattern occurs as decision makers study policy alternatives. Administrators may ask constituents to indicate policies that they want adopted. Example 7.1 presents several open-ended questions from a state health planning survey of county health directors. State health planners asked the directors to suggest programs and policies to address the problem of teenage pregnancy. Question 1 asks for a description of the problem of teenage pregnancy in the director's county. From the descriptions, the planners can learn about local conditions and programs, agency attitudes about teenage pregnancy, and acceptable programs. For example, what information is selected to show that teenage pregnancy is a problem? What, if any, causes of teenage pregnancies are cited? Are the needs of young teenage parents distinguished from the needs of older teenage parents?

Question 2 asks directors to suggest programs or policies to address problems of teenage pregnancy in their counties. From the comments, the planners can hypothesize which programs will be acceptable and which ones will be unacceptable. Innovative solutions or programs may be suggested, and unanticipated benefits or costs of possible programs may be mentioned. The answers to Questions 1 and 2 help the planners find out more about the policy environment. They

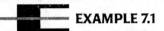 **EXAMPLE 7.1**

Application of Open-ended Questions

Problem: State planners are developing policies and programs to address the problem of teenage pregnancy. County health agencies will administer the programs.

Strategy: To make sure planned programs are acceptable, the planners write a series of questions to get needed information and survey county health directors. The following questions are included:

1. Describe the problem of teenage pregnancy in your county.

2. In your opinion, what programs or policies would help with the problems of teenage pregnancy? Make any additional comments on the strengths and weaknesses of these solutions. Your comments will help us formulate statewide plans.

3. What is the size of your annual budget?

Discussion: Initially, planners informally reviewed the answers to select the most feasible programs and policies. The planners also compiled the answers and presented them systematically in a report. The answers to Question 1 disclose how the directors view teenage pregnancy; the question avoids distortions introduced by a set of responses. The answers to Question 2 may reveal innovative programs or policies; later closed-ended questions and responses may be developed from the answers. Categorizing the answers can be tedious. Reliability problems may occur if directors either describe similar programs with different terms or use similar terms to describe different programs.

Question 3 was open-ended because the planners did not know the range of possible responses. A list of responses could have been either insensitive to actual variations or too long. The answers are relatively easy to categorize and present quantitatively.

may learn how much time county directors have spent thinking about and learning about teenage pregnancy programs; whether any programs have been planned or implemented; and what local conditions would affect the success of a program.

Including open-ended questions during the process of questionnaire design may reduce the biases introduced by the responses attached to a closed-ended question. Respondents may stick to the available responses or they may use characteristics of the response to decide the most appropriate answer. In the case of DECIDE, a list of work-related uses would not have captured personal uses. Questions asking respondents to rate effects of global warming might encourage them to rate effects that had never occurred to them and ignore unlisted concerns that bothered them a lot.

Answers to open-ended questions provide the rich detail that puts a mass of collected data into context. If a policy is being planned or evaluated, a comment may add immeasurably to an investigator's understanding about the policy and how the public views it. The answers may help explain the findings and how the respondent interpreted a question. Respondents may be invited to explain their answers to a preceding question. For example, respondents may be asked whether they are doing better, worse, or about the same economically this year as last. Then, they will be asked to explain why they answered the way they did. From the explanations, investigators learn how respondents evaluate their economic situation and what factors they believe contribute to their economic well-being. Comments from open-ended questions are normally incorporated into a report. The comments add to its readability and keep the interest of less quantitatively oriented readers.

A survey gives the respondent the ear of the investigator or study sponsor. The respondent may wish to comment on related issues and bring them to the attention of others. We ended our survey of DECIDE trainees by asking respondents whether they had comments that they wanted us to pass on to the training department. Several did; one respondent had a lengthy complaint about problems with computer training. In community surveys, respondents can comment on the policies being considered, comment on other policies, or mention related concerns they have about local government or agency operations.

The answers to broad, open-ended questions may add to the administrator's general information. They may contribute to respondents' positive feelings about surveys. Soliciting a respondent's opinion may serve as minimal compensation for his time, effort, and cooperation.

You can infer the problems of open-ended questions from Example 7.1. First, a respondent must be motivated to spend the time and effort to answer an open-ended question. We may assume that the survey about teenage pregnancy was important to the directors and that they took the time to write thorough, thoughtful answers. The directors were probably motivated by more than the content of the survey. Since the survey was sponsored by a state health department, the directors may have assumed that their answers would affect state policy. More often than not, respondents will not be so motivated.

We may assume that in many studies, the investigators have more at stake in the survey and its findings than the individual respondents. Thus investigators tend to overestimate the importance of their work and respondents' willingness to provide detailed answers. We assume that generally respondents prefer to avoid questions that require a long written response. This assumption may not apply if the answers will affect a policy decision important to the respondent.

Respondents may answer open-ended questions more readily if they are asked over the telephone or in person. The interviewers must be well trained. Otherwise, they may add their own interpretation to respondents' answers, amplify the question in a way counter to the investigator's intentions, or fail to record the comments accurately.

The other problem of open-ended questions is how to use the information effectively. If relatively few people are surveyed, the answers may be carefully read, analyzed, and quoted. If many people are surveyed, the probability of carefully reading the answers diminishes. One solution is to select a random sample of open-ended responses for detailed analysis.

Whether all the answers or merely a sample are studied, categorizing and counting the answers is difficult, time consuming, and requires thoughtful attention.

A perusal of the questionnaires by someone familiar with the study's model should help create appropriate categories. The difficulty rests in assigning responses accurately and consistently. To ensure reliable data based on open-ended questions, the investigators should apply a test/retest procedure to a random sample of cases. If several analysts are categorizing responses, inter-rater reliability also should be established. To do so, each analyst categorizes the same sample of cases. Then, an investigator compares the work of the analysts to see if they reported similar results.

Closed-ended Questions

Closed-ended questions come in several formats. All closed-ended questions require a respondent to select one or more appropriate responses from a list. The reliability and operational validity of closed-ended questions partially depend on the list provided.

A list may include several options with instructions to "check all that apply." While such a list may burden respondents less, they may not actually check all that apply. An unchecked item may (1) not apply or (2) have been overlooked. More items may be reported if a respondent is asked to check an appropriate response for each item, for example, "yes" or "no."[2]

Including an "other" category does not guarantee that additional appropriate responses will be mentioned. Some respondents may limit themselves to the list. They may do this out of laziness, because they have identified a desirable response, or because the list has led them to accept the investigators' frame of reference. Even if they answer the "other" category and write in a response, the investigator may be stuck interpreting and categorizing these responses.

Some response lists do not include "other," "no opinion," "not sure," or "not applicable" as choices. Alternatively, the question may include an even number of possible responses. This prevents a respondent from taking a more neutral position. Both types of questions are called *forced choice questions.* Of course, respondents cannot be forced to choose, and some will pen in their own answers or ignore the question. In general respondents should be given the option to express "no opinion" or indicate that the question isn't applicable. Otherwise the investigator does not know why a question was skipped. If a web-based survey does not allow a respondent to proceed without answering, we assume that she may quit or randomly select an answer. Similarly, including a neutral response, such as "neither agree nor disagree" may increase reliability. Research has found that the ratio between positive and negative responses is the same whether or not a neutral response is provided.[3]

Example 7.2 takes a selection of questions from a survey that a state employees' association (SEA) sent to its members. The questions illustrate some common formats used in closed-ended questions. You should visualize how easily an investigator can compile the responses. At the same time, you may think of how the responses could be misinterpreted. For example, some respondents may answer the questions on why others do not join the association by reflecting their own dissatisfaction with SEA or a similar organization. Members who have tried to recruit others to join may have more accurate perceptions. As the

---

EXAMPLE 7.2

Application of Closed-ended Questions

Situation: A state employee association (SEA) wants to survey its members to learn their opinions about SEA and state employment.

Strategy: Develop a closed-ended questionnaire to survey members. Format should be chosen to facilitate quick responses by members and easy tabulation. The questions include:

1. What is your opinion of why some employees do not join SEA? Check all that apply.

   _____ Money (dues)
   _____ Dislike organizations
   _____ SEA doesn't adequately represent employees
   _____ Don't consider their jobs permanent
   _____ Don't care
   _____ Don't know

2. How much influence do you believe the average SEA member has in SEA?

   _____ Very much
   _____ Quite a bit
   _____ Some
   _____ Very little
   _____ None
   _____ Don't know

3. Number the following in order of priority, 1 being highest, 2 next highest, etc. SEA should work for

   _____ payment of sick leave upon separation from the service.
   _____ collective bargaining.
   _____ payment of time and one-half for overtime.
   _____ reduction in retirement contributions.
   _____ dental insurance.
   _____ higher salaries.
   _____ increased mileage and per diem rates.

---

questionnaire is written, the analyst cannot separate the two types of respondents, and their answers will be grouped together.

Another type of closed-ended question asks the respondent to rank or rate items. Look at Question 3 in Example 7.2. Respondents are asked to rank organization activities proposed for an employee association. Inevitably, some respondents select several items and rank each item with a "1." A few may appear to reverse the rating scale. In the example, they would give a "7" to the highest-priority item and a "1" to the lowest-priority item. Some will rate all items; others will ignore all but a few items. Similar to ranking questions are questions that ask people to assign percentages to how much time they spend on a list of activities. A surprising number of people assign values that add up to well over 100 percent.

Note also that Question 3 does not include an "other" option. Consequently, respondents who wanted the organization to pursue on-site day care or flexible work schedules did not have an opportunity to voice their opinion.

The limitations of closed-ended questions are best understood by thinking of the strengths of open-ended questions. Closed-ended questions encourage the respondent to accept the investigator's response categories. Investigators may assume that they and the respondents interpret the questions and response choices the same way. Once we asked agency heads about volunteer characteristics. The question asked respondents to note how many volunteers in their agency had certain characteristics. Included among the response categories was "Native Americans." When we wrote Native Americans, we were referring to American Indians, Hawaiians, Eskimos, and Aleutians. Only after we received several surveys indicating that "all" volunteers were Native Americans did we realize that our terminology was interpreted differently by our respondents.

To minimize misinterpretation of responses and inadequate or inaccurate response lists, closed-ended questions should be carefully pretested. Investigators also should satisfy themselves that their testing included procedures to review item reliability and operational validity.

The decision as to whether to choose an open-ended question over a closed-ended question depends on the type of information needed, who is supplying the information, the data collection method, and the time available for completing the study. Open-ended questions are important in the first stages of questionnaire design. They help with question wording and creating appropriate response categories. The type of respondent and the data collection method may affect the choice. Questions that require longer, thought-out answers, such as in Example 7.1, may work best on mail surveys if the survey is sent to a targeted sample of interested respondents. Less-interested and less-motivated respondents may avoid answering open-ended questions that require more than a few words. Interviewers may be more successful in getting complete responses to open-ended questions; however, unless the interviewers are well trained, the information may be unreliable or invalid. Closed-ended questions can be compiled and analyzed far more quickly. Investigators should not waste respondents' time by asking open-ended questions unless they have budgeted time for the proper analysis of the answers.

Filter Questions

Filter questions identify respondents who should answer follow-up questions, and direct the respondent or the interviewer to the appropriate parts of a questionnaire. Filter questions are nearly always closed-ended. A filter question in a housing survey might be:

Do you own or rent the house in which you now live?

_____ Own (answer Question 10). Visual cues should lead a respondent to the questions he should answer.

_____ Rent (skip to Question 11).

Can you imagine one or more questions that apply to homeowners but not renters? For example, questions on mortgages, interest rates, and property taxes would apply to owners but not directly to renters.

An effective format leads a respondent to the questions he should answer. It should prevent him from missing questions that apply to him and from answering questions that do not apply to him. The above filter question has written directions next to each response category, telling respondents the next question they should answer. Visual coding is especially effective. Arrows may direct the respondent to the appropriate questions. In designing filter questions care must be taken to keep the questionnaire simple and the instructions clear. Example 7.3 is an example of visually coded filter questions.

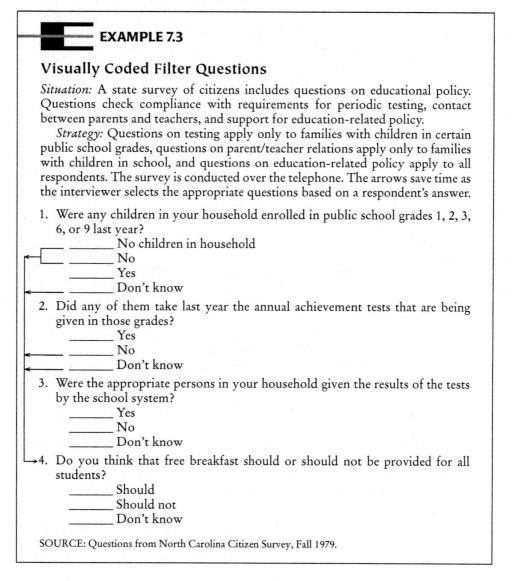

EXAMPLE 7.3

Visually Coded Filter Questions

Situation: A state survey of citizens includes questions on educational policy. Questions check compliance with requirements for periodic testing, contact between parents and teachers, and support for education-related policy.

Strategy: Questions on testing apply only to families with children in certain public school grades, questions on parent/teacher relations apply only to families with children in school, and questions on education-related policy apply to all respondents. The survey is conducted over the telephone. The arrows save time as the interviewer selects the appropriate questions based on a respondent's answer.

1. Were any children in your household enrolled in public school grades 1, 2, 3, 6, or 9 last year?
   _____ No children in household
   _____ No
   _____ Yes
   _____ Don't know

2. Did any of them take last year the annual achievement tests that are being given in those grades?
   _____ Yes
   _____ No
   _____ Don't know

3. Were the appropriate persons in your household given the results of the tests by the school system?
   _____ Yes
   _____ No
   _____ Don't know

4. Do you think that free breakfast should or should not be provided for all students?
   _____ Should
   _____ Should not
   _____ Don't know

SOURCE: Questions from North Carolina Citizen Survey, Fall 1979.

QUESTION AND RESPONSE WORDING

Question Wording and Formatting

Respondents must see the value of a question. Respondents providing information for performance appraisals, program evaluations, or other management studies may resist spending time collecting and recording data that they do not value. They may distort data that they believe can adversely affect them. They may estimate or make up data to conform to management expectations or to get a form off their desk. Administrators and others who are frequently surveyed may also show resistance. They may start to answer a questionnaire and stop if it is too time consuming or if they perceive it will produce worthless information. We suspect that respondent perceptions are shaped as they read the specific questions.

Each question should be worded so that the respondent accurately understands its meaning and answers honestly. An investigator wants to make sure that she and the respondent view a question as asking for the same information. Imagine a question asking, "Do you own stock?" People can interpret stock as an investment instrument, livestock, or broth. We have discussed misunderstood questions in the context of reliability and operational validity. The ambiguity of the term "stock" illustrates the importance of precisely defining critical terms.

Questions should be clear, short, and specific. Words in common usage and not subject to different interpretations add to question clarity. Long questions tend to be complicated and confusing; they may be easily misinterpreted. Frequently, a respondent will consider part of a long question in his answer and ignore the question's broader meaning.

Specific questions leave little room for interpreting the time, place, or amount involved. For example, to estimate clinic usage in a town, investigators may ask, "How many visits did you make to a medical clinic in Middletown between September 1 and December 31 of this year?" If "Middletown" did not appear in the question, respondents might count out-of-town clinic visits. If the question said "recently" instead of "between September 1 and December 31," each respondent could answer the question with a different time interval in mind. Some respondents may think of the number of visits within the last month; others may think of the number of visits within the past year.

The advice to keep questions short and specific may conflict. A vague term may confuse respondents and lead to unreliable data. Asking teenagers how many hours they worked, or asking adults how many hours they exercise, may raise questions about what constitutes work or exercise. The researchers must know exactly what they want to measure. They must know if their conceptual definition defines baby-sitting as work or not, or if working in the yard constitutes exercise. To solve this problem, the definition may be incorporated into the instructions. Alternatively, the definition may be incorporated into the body of the question. Example 7.4 illustrates (1) including definitions in the instructions, and (2) including a definition in the question. In practice strategy 2 would include parallel questions about the behavior of top administration and the work group.

Separate questions including different components of the conceptual definition may be written, thus improving a measure's operational validity. Example 7.5

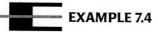 **EXAMPLE 7.4**

Two Strategies for Defining Ambiguous Terms in a Survey

Strategy 1: Key terms are defined as part of the instructions. Actual wording and format included on cover page:

The following terms are used in the survey:

TOP ADMINISTRATION means the President/CEO and Vice Presidents, or Senior Administrators

SUPERVISOR means the person to whom you report on a daily basis

WORK GROUP means the people you work with on a daily basis

Strategy 2: Define terms as part of the question. Actual wording and format included in question:

"How often, if at all, does your supervisor, that is, the person to whom you report on a daily basis, overrule the findings or conclusions of a report and require that changes be made?"

1[ ] Never, or almost never

2[ ] Some of the time

3[ ] About half the time

4[ ] Most of the time

5[ ] Always, or almost always

SOURCE: Strategy 2 item adapted from *Federal Personnel Management: OPM Reliance on Agency Oversight of Personnel System Not Fully Justified* (Washington, DC: General Accounting Office, GAO/GGD–93–94, December 1992), 51.

---

illustrates a list of separate questions used to ask employees to rate their satisfaction with employee benefits. An alternative, and preferred,[4] format has respondents react to specific statements. For example, employees may indicate their degree of agreement with statements such as, "I am satisfied with the medical benefits I receive on my job," "I am satisfied with the life insurance I receive on my job," "I am satisfied with the pension benefits I receive on my job." Possible responses may range from "strongly disagree" to "strongly agree." Asking people about their satisfaction with various components of their benefits package yields data that better represents overall satisfaction with benefits. Nevertheless, at some point the cost of obtaining more accurate information must be weighed against the benefits. An example of erring by seeking too much specific information occurred in the Nationwide Food Consumption Survey. Respondents were asked to keep a two-day record of what they ate and whether it was eaten at home or away, how it was prepared, and the size of the portion. Data were collected on extensive checklists, which included 350 foods. By putting the responses together, the investigators could learn that one day Jane Doe ate at home and had a boneless, roasted slice of chicken breast, 2-by-1½-by-¼-inch. The survey's low response rate of 34 percent was partially blamed on the burdensome questionnaire.[5]

EXAMPLE 7.5

Dividing a Question into Separate Questions

Strategy: Rather than ask one broad question, the investigator may divide a question into a series of questions. The following questions ask respondents to indicate their level of satisfaction with various employee benefits. The survey directions told respondents to X-out the number that corresponded to their response. The directions included a sample item with an X covering one of the numbers.

Actual wording and format: In these questions, please indicate how satisfied you are with each of the following employee benefits (1 = very dissatisfied; 2 = dissatisfied; 3 = slightly dissatisfied; 4 = indifferent; 5 = slightly satisfied; 6 = satisfied; 7 = very satisfied).

How Satisfied Are You With:

Medical—Employee coverage	[1]	[2]	[3]	[4]	[5]	[6]	[7]
Medical—Family coverage	[1]	[2]	[3]	[4]	[5]	[6]	[7]
Dental insurance	[1]	[2]	[3]	[4]	[5]	[6]	[7]
Life insurance (Employee)	[1]	[2]	[3]	[4]	[5]	[6]	[7]
Dependent life insurance	[1]	[2]	[3]	[4]	[5]	[6]	[7]
Long-term disability	[1]	[2]	[3]	[4]	[5]	[6]	[7]
Pension plan	[1]	[2]	[3]	[4]	[5]	[6]	[7]

Notes: This question did not include a "Not applicable" category, which may affect the accuracy of the results. Employees who have neither dependent medical insurance nor life insurance may check "indifferent" or not answer the question. Either response is subject to misleading interpretations.

In constructing a list of responses, investigators need to list all probable responses. Recall that this is a qualitative indicator of reliability. Respondents may resent response categories that seem to exclude them. For example, listed responses may not allow a young adult to report that her job is only temporary or a disabled respondent to indicate that he depends on public transportation. The respondents may become frustrated or annoyed; they may toss out the questionnaire. Agencies may react similarly. For example, an agency that has volunteers deliver client services may question the motives of a surveyor who lists fund-raising and office work as volunteer tasks but does not mention delivering services.

The question or the list of responses should indicate how precise an answer is expected. A county official wanted to estimate how user fees would affect the use of county recreational facilities. He surveyed recreation department heads and asked them, "How much did the implementation of user fees impact the use of recreation facilities and programs?" The answers received were "very much," "very little," and so forth. A closed-ended question that gave the possible responses "less than 10% decrease in use of facilities," "10–25% decrease in use of facilities," and so forth, would have avoided this problem.

Related to amount specificity is the need to ask a respondent for information she has or can easily get. A demand for specific information may require a respondent to calculate or search out data with which she could give a reasonably accurate estimate. The questioner needs to keep in mind the purpose of the research and the trade-off between precision and the cost of information gathering.

Writing Questions for Self-Reports of Behavior and Opinions

Question and response wording are especially important in surveys that ask people to report their behavior, attitudes, or motives. Clearly defined questions requesting accessible information can produce reasonably accurate organizational information, for example, the number of full-time staff or the size of the budget. Furthermore, investigators can verify the accuracy of such information. Self-reports by individuals are harder or even impossible to verify; consequently, investigators have far less confidence in its reliability and operational validity.

People have models of how they should act, and their answers may be more in line with how they think they should act than with how they actually act. Alternatively, the answers people give may depend on how they store and retrieve information. Consider information on who votes. From time to time, researchers check voting records to establish the validity of the self-reports of voting. They have found that roughly 15 percent of the people surveyed after an election misreport whether or not they voted, and a higher percent of those polled after an election report having voted for the winning candidate than indicated by actual votes.

The direction of misreports is not random. Typically, nonvoters "erroneously" report voting. Three reasons have been proposed to explain why misreporting occurs. First, misreporters may wish to give a socially desirable answer. Second, they may be people who usually vote, and they forgot that they did not vote in the most recent election. Third, voting records may be in error. For example, a check of records may miss a voter whose name on the voters' rolls differs from the name she gave to the surveyor.[6] The accuracy of voting information has been studied extensively, because self-reports can be validated and because the relatively large number of misreports may have distorted knowledge of American voting behavior. Because an act as straightforward and uncontroversial as voting is consistently misreported, we recommend interpreting all self-reported information with caution.

Similar problems of social desirability and misreporting occur with opinion questions. Uninformed or disinterested respondents may express an opinion. Including "don't know" as a response choice may alleviate this problem; however, investigators cannot infer what a "don't know" indicates. Respondents may answer "don't know" because they have problems answering the question. They may be ambivalent, that is, they may have thought about the issue but have yet to reach a firm opinion. Some respondents may become distracted while hearing a question or have trouble understanding it. They will answer "don't know" to avoid the trouble of having the question repeated or trying to decipher its meaning. Thus investigators must examine any question that generates a high proportion of "don't knows" to make sure it is not ambiguous or otherwise flawed.

To get a snapshot of the public's opinion, the distinction between disinterested and ambivalent respondents may be less necessary.[7] If an investigator wants to identify disinterested respondents, she may ask a filter question. For example, respondents may be asked, "How interested are you in the bond referendum to build a civic center?" An alternative solution, illustrated below, asks a dichotomous question and follows up with an intensity question. Since asking a series of questions may tax respondents' patience, respondents may be simply reminded that "not interested" is an appropriate response.

1. Do you support or oppose the bond referendum to build a civic center?

_____ Support

_____ Oppose

_____ Don't know

2. How interested are you in the bond referendum to build a civic center?

_____ A lot

_____ Somewhat

_____ Not much

_____ Not interested

Among the respondents who answered "don't know" to Question 1, investigators may assume that disinterested respondents answered "not much" or "not interested" to Question 2, and ambivalent respondents answered "a lot" or "somewhat" to Question 2.

Questions asking respondents how often they do something should cover a limited time span. Someone may accurately remember how many times he used a library in the past month. If he is asked about the past year, he may multiply the number of visits in the past month by 12. He is unlikely to adjust his estimate to indicate that he used the library more than usual or less than usual. A response list may serve as a frame of reference, and a respondent may alter his answers if they seem atypical.[8]

If a measure includes a series of questions with similar answers, such as "agree" and "disagree," the respondent may answer all questions in the same way regardless of content. Serious distortions may occur if a respondent guesses the purpose of the questions. For example, a survey to identify opinions about community development may have a number of questions about types and levels of development. A respondent who is generally opposed to development may answer all questions with a "disagree" and ignore the content of the specific questions. This problem can be reduced if all questions do not go in the same direction. In other words, for some questions a "disagree" would be a pro-development choice and for others a "disagree" would be an anti-development choice. Nevertheless, the respondent may become annoyed or confused with a questionnaire in which questions change direction capriciously. Some questions may be misread or misunderstood simply because the respondent missed a key word such as "not."

The items below, taken from a client satisfaction survey, illustrate how questions are worded to avoid set responses. Investigators conducted the survey to see how agency clients rated support staff. The respondent ranked each statement on a scale ranging from "strongly agree" to "strongly disagree."

1. The agency staff can answer my questions.
2. The agency staff is polite when I telephone.
3. The agency staff is accessible by telephone.
4. The agency staff is rude when questions are asked.
5. The agency staff interrupts me when I talk with them.

A person who is pleased with agency staff should agree to items 1 through 3 and disagree with items 4 and 5. The shift from "agree" to "disagree" is referred to as a change in direction. The shift is achieved without resorting to awkward wording. A respondent should quickly and accurately grasp the meaning of each question. Still no solution ever works all the time. One group of researchers grouped similar items together on a web survey. They found respondents were more likely to give the same answer for each item, including those items worded in the opposite direction.[9]

A major problem with changing the direction of items may occur when the data are compiled. The direction should not be changed when the data are coded and entered into a computer file. By keeping the original direction, the analyst reduces the risk of data-entry errors. Instead, she can easily change the direction as part of the computer programming.

Biased Questions

A *biased question* is worded so that it encourages respondents to give one answer over another, eliciting inaccurate information. Although questions may be intentionally worded to lead the respondent to give a specific answer, biases also may be introduced unintentionally. A response list is often a source of question biases. Responses should cover the range of plausible options. One error is to use a rating scale with a disproportionate number of positive (or negative) ratings. For example, a four-point rating scale with responses of "excellent," "good," "satisfactory," and "poor" has three positive responses out of four possible responses. This increases the probability that a person will express some degree of positive satisfaction. The failure to include a particular response on a list of responses also may create biases. Instead of penning in the appropriate information, a respondent may settle for checking off the next-best answer.

Loaded questions are worded so that a respondent gives an acceptable answer. Some adjectives or phrases tend to have a positive or negative value, thus leading a person to ignore the major content of the question. For example, labeling a proposed policy as "liberal," "permissive," or "bureaucratic" will tend to measure respondents' reactions to these words and not their general opinions about the policy. Also, questions may include an assumption affecting answers. For example, if we ask people whether they agree or disagree that the "state should build more prisons in order to decrease violent crimes," we are assuming that building prisons will decrease violent crime. The question may unwittingly lead respondents concerned about violent crime to support building more prisons.

Another common, unintentional bias is to ask two questions in one. These questions are easily identified by the conjunction "and." Consider the question, "Are you in favor of tightening the state's DUI (Driving Under the Influence) laws and making it illegal for parents to serve liquor to minors in their homes?" A person may favor tightening up the DUI laws but not agree with making it illegal for parents to serve liquor to their minor children. How should the person accurately report her attitude?

Another source of bias occurs if the available responses do not fit the question asked. For example, we received a questionnaire with the following item:

Do you think that state annexation statutes need to be changed, or do you think that they are appropriate as they are?

_____ Yes

_____ No

The question writer was following the professional practice of wording the question so that it did not favor either changing the statutes or leaving them alone. Unfortunately, the responses were not appropriate. There was no way we could accurately report our opinion unless we went to the trouble to write an answer. This problem is easily solved by altering the response wording. The two responses to this item could be:

_____ Yes, statutes need to be changed.

_____ No, statues are appropriate as they are now.

Other Considerations

Whereas inexperienced question writers unintentionally write biased questions, special-interest groups may intentionally word items to encourage a particular answer. A *New York Times* article reported on a study contrasting an interest-group question with questions written by professional surveyors.[10] An example of a leading question and a balanced version of the same question is:

Version 1: Should laws be passed to eliminate all possibilities of special interests giving huge sums of money to candidates?

Version 2: Should laws be passed to prohibit interest groups from contributing to campaigns, or do groups have a right to contribute to the candidate they support?

The differences in wording should leap out at you. The first question has charged phrases "special interests" and "huge sums of money." It also lacks the feature of stating a contrasting choice in the question in order to keep the item neutral. Of course, Version 2 could not "work" if the response categories were "yes" and "no." Rather, response choices included "laws should be passed to prohibit interest groups from contributing to campaigns" and "groups have a right to contribute to the candidate they support."

We cannot contrast the responses to the two questions because the first question was answered by a voluntary sample. Version 2, which was administered to a random sample, found 40 percent favored prohibiting contributions. Another version of the question that asked, "Please tell me whether you favor or oppose the proposal: The passage of new laws that would eliminate all possibility of special interests giving large sums of money to candidates," found 70 percent favored prohibiting contributions. The example suggests how question wording can affect the response pattern and how fragile one question is at measuring attitudes and opinions.

Questions that ask respondents how much they would be willing to pay for something are particularly sensitive to wording. If the respondent feels that her answer will affect service cost, she may cite an amount lower than what she would pay. Consider a question from a city's recreation department that asks people whether they would pay $10 for a tennis license to play on the city's public courts. A tennis player, who may be quite willing to pay $10, might try to influence the policy outcome by answering "no." Alternatively, people asked how much they would pay for various environmental programs are likely to overestimate their willingness to pay.[11]

Some studies involve sensitive subjects, and one must be aware of the probability that a respondent will distort his or her answers. Questions on drug use and other activities that are illegal or widely criticized may bring about inaccurate responses. A naive schoolchild may report drug use to make herself appear knowledgeable, whereas a drug user fearful of the consequences of accurately reporting her behavior will deny or underreport her drug experience.

Each of us has feelings about what we have accomplished and how we have failed. Surveys to learn about individuals undoubtedly will have questions that make some respondents uncomfortable. Questions that seem likely to create respondent discomfort should be carefully considered. First, such questions may raise ethical concerns; that is, the research may harm the subjects. (Ethics and the avoidance of harming human subjects are discussed in Chapter 8.) Second, the questions may cause respondents not to participate in a study and may even result in a negative attitude toward research in general. Third, the questions may lead respondents to give inaccurate information.

Knowing which questions are potentially threatening depends on the subjects. Observers should not assume that their perceptions of what is a sensitive subject or a threatening question agree with a respondent's perceptions. The pilot test may identify sensitive questions. Alternatively, investigators familiar with the subject population may be aware of inappropriate questions. An acquaintance from India observed that Americans seemed to talk freely about their feelings toward family members but refused to discuss their salaries. Conversely, he noted that Indians talked about their earnings openly but virtually never discussed their feelings about family members.

Stating a question so that it suggests to the respondent that any possible answer is acceptable not surprisingly helps reduce threat. For example, such questions may be introduced with the phrase, "Some people find . . ." Question order also can reduce the discomfort associated with a question. Potentially threatening questions should not be asked at the beginning of a questionnaire or interview, where they may make a respondent suspicious and less willing to cooperate. On the other hand, a sensitive question should not be placed at the end either, where it may cause a person to finish a survey feeling anxious and wondering if the survey had a hidden purpose. Finally, as we discussed in Chapter 6, respondents are more likely to share sensitive information on self-administered questionnaires, including those that a respondent answers on a computer or with paper and pencil while an interviewer waits.

QUESTION SEQUENCING AND QUESTIONNAIRE DESIGN

Question Sequencing

Obviously, one cannot put questions on a form in random order. Questions should be logically ordered. The initial questions can affect a respondent's willingness to answer a questionnaire. If the early questions are confusing, threatening, or time consuming, a respondent may not complete the survey or cooperate with the interviewer. Self-administered questionnaires and interview schedules follow a general sequence.

Introduction

An introduction states the nature and purpose of the survey. It identifies the person or organization conducting the survey. The introduction should be short and to the point. An overly long explanation of the purpose of a survey may bias results. Introductions to web-based surveys that extend over one screen may seem burdensome right off and consequently discourage participation.

Subjects must be told what, if any, risks may be associated with participating in a study. Subjects must understand that their participation is voluntary, they may decline to answer any question, and they can withdraw from a study at any time. Regulations on "protection of human subjects" cover requirements for informing subjects of their rights and the risks of participation. The regulations and related ethical issues are discussed in Chapter 8.

Example 7.6 illustrates two questionnaire introductions. The first is from a survey given to town employees. The second is from a phone survey of the general public. Each introduction indicates the purpose of the study. Each introduction encourages respondents to participate by indicating the importance of their answers. Note that both introductions failed to mention how long it will take to respond. As people become oversurveyed, this information may be critical in deciding whether to participate. Each introduction implies voluntary participation. In the case of mail or telephone surveys, voluntary participation is often implied because subjects usually feel no compunction about not returning the survey or hanging up the phone.

▐▐ EXAMPLE 7.6

Examples of Survey Introductions

Sample 1: The introduction is from a survey given to town employees. The surveys were given directly to employees, and they could mail their responses back to the investigators.

Actual wording: This questionnaire is designed to find out how you and others feel about the Town of Oaks as a place to work. The data collected will provide information needed to better understand how people feel about the quality of working life in the organization.

If this questionnaire is to be useful, it is important that you answer each question frankly and honestly. There are no right or wrong answers to these questions. We are interested in what you think and feel about your life at this organization.

Your answers to these questions are completely confidential. All questionnaires will be taken to State University for analysis. No one in the Town of Oaks organization will ever have access to your individual answers.

For analysis and data collection purposes, a number has been put on this questionnaire that can be matched with your name on a list at the university. It would be appreciated if you would leave this number intact.

Thank you in advance for your cooperation and assistance.

Sample 2: This survey introduction is from a telephone survey of community residents. The purpose of the survey was to learn their opinion of the town police force.

Actual wording:

INTRODUCTION: Hello, my name is (interviewer name), and I'm calling from the Town of Oaks.

PURPOSE: In conjunction with State University, we are calling about 500 homes in Oaks to find out how you feel about police services in Oaks. (TO INTERVIEWER: IF CALLING BETWEEN 5 and 6:30 p.m., ADD: Is this a convenient time to call you, or should I call back later this evening?)

CONFIRMATION: Do you live within the town limits of Oaks? (If the answer is no, END THE CALL.) Is this a home phone or a business? (If a business, END THE CALL.)

The introduction to the survey sent to employees fully detailed how the investigators planned to protect respondents' confidentiality. Such surveys are particularly sensitive because employees are suspicious about what will be done with the information. The other survey informs the respondent that the survey is anonymous.

Sampling frames are not perfect. A sample may include inappropriate respondents who should be screened out immediately. The introduction or the first question should establish whether the respondent should complete the survey. In Example 7.6, Sample 2, the respondents were asked whether or not they lived in the town. In Example 6.1, an enclosed postcard allowed inappropriate respondents to quickly excuse themselves from replying. Respondents who do not fall within the sample population are usually asked to return the uncompleted questionnaire. An interviewer will have a parallel set of directions that also tell him if and how he can replace an ineligible respondent.

First Questions

Following the introduction, relevant, easily answered questions appear. These involve the respondent in the study. During an interview, this section builds rapport between the interviewer and the respondent. In a self-administered questionnaire, the questions draw the respondent into making a "psychological commitment" to complete the questionnaire.

For the recipient of a mailed or web-based survey, the first questions keep her from putting the survey aside and forgetting it; however, if the survey becomes unduly complex or confusing, the benefits of good first questions may be lost. In a telephone survey, the first questions may be important in getting cooperation from a wary respondent who may suspect that the caller is really going to sell him something.

In the questionnaire sent to employees of the town of Oaks, the first three questions, each answered on a strongly agree to strongly disagree scale, were:

1. I get a feeling of personal satisfaction from doing my job well.
2. I work hard on my job.
3. If I had the chance, I would take a different job within this organization.

Major Questions

The distinction between the initial questions and the major questions may be virtually nonexistent. Many questionnaires ask a few introductory questions, then group questions in sections addressing the major issues of the survey. In the sections, the question order may be important. In-person interviewers start with more general questions, followed by specific questions. Care must be taken to avoid sequences that can bias answers.

The introduction of the DECIDE study told respondents that the survey's purpose was to learn more about management training needs. The questionnaire started with questions about respondents' management responsibilities. The next grouping of questions asked respondents about management decision-making tools: What tools were they familiar with? What tools did they commonly use? What were some of the problems with the tools?

The following section asked about DECIDE as a decision-making tool. In Question 5 respondents were asked, "What decision-making tools do you commonly use?" A note to the interviewers told them, "If a prompt is needed, use value analysis." The first mention of DECIDE was in Question 7, after respondents had been asked about management decision-making tools. Nearly

90 percent of the respondents who said they used DECIDE several times a month had mentioned it earlier as a decision-making tool. If we had mentioned DECIDE early in the study, we would have been more suspicious of the level of reported use.

Sequencing to avoid bias is not as effective in self-administered questionnaires. The respondent can read the entire questionnaire before answering any questions, or he can go back and change answers.

Demographic Questions

The final section typically asks personal questions about income, age, race, education, or employment. Analogous questions are asked in organizational surveys. By the end of the interview, the respondent may feel less reluctant to answer personal questions. Personal questions at the beginning of a survey may make a person wonder about its real purpose. We suspect that this reaction is especially likely in areas where telephone salespersons use the guise of a survey to keep a potential customer on the telephone.

Some investigators get into the habit of asking a standard set of demographic questions at the end. For example, they may routinely include questions about age, sex, race, education, and income. These questions increase the burden on respondents, may go unanalyzed, and risk compromising an individual's confidentiality. Surveying consumes resources, including respondent goodwill. Thus we prefer to stick to information appropriate to the study and to eliminate questions that are not in the analysis plan. In addition, too many personal questions may disturb respondents who worry about the anonymity of their answers.

Questionnaire Design

Question wording and sequencing are elements of questionnaire design; they affect the clarity and validity of the responses. The physical layout of the questionnaire or interview schedule affects its utility. In organizing a questionnaire, the designer must consider its impact on the person filling it out and the person compiling or coding the information.

An interviewer needs a form that is easy to read and to follow while speaking to a respondent and recording responses. A respondent needs a questionnaire that is easy to follow and does not overwhelm her. A questionnaire that can be easily and quickly answered reduces the possibility that it will be put aside and forgotten. Factors such as the design of the pages also may affect the response rate and the quality and quantity of the information obtained. Furthermore, a well-designed questionnaire may communicate to the respondent the seriousness of the research effort and favorably affect her inclination to respond.

We have listed on the next page a partial "instrument checklist" to guide you in constructing a survey. You may wish to add to this checklist as you read other materials or review various data collection instruments.

A Checklist for Constructing Surveys

Self-administered surveys:

The purpose is clearly stated in the introduction.

Directions on how to answer are clear.

Recipients who do not belong to the target population are quickly identified, for example, by the use of a screening question, and are told what to do with the survey.

Survey instrument deadline date and return address should appear on survey instrument.

Interviewer-administered surveys:

Interviewer's introduction clearly indicates the purpose.

Directions on how to ask questions and record answers are clear.

Recipients who do not belong to the target population are quickly identified, and interviewer instructions indicate if and how he should look for a replacement respondent.

On all surveys and data-collecting instruments:

Critical terms are defined.

Abbreviations are not used.

Conjunctions such as *and* are avoided, because an answer may not apply to both parts of the question.

Response choices must be adequate, appropriate, and mutually exclusive.

Requested data must be easily accessible.

Item groupings are logical.

For opinion questions:

Question wording should be neutral, such as, "Do you favor or oppose?"

Responses should be balanced, for example, there should be an equal number of positive and negative responses.

Questionnaire Efficiency

Trying to make certain you need every question you ask and ask every question you need is difficult. The more you can visualize the information a survey will produce and how you will use it, the better off you are. Working with a model serves as a beginning point in deciding what questions to ask and how to ask them, yet it may be insufficient. Identifying the output the survey will produce should improve its efficiency and suggest ways to improve it.

The researchers should describe how they plan to analyze the data. Then, they link the plan with the questionnaire to double-check that each question is needed. The team can review the plan with the study users to show them what information the study will produce. To help users visualize what information they will receive, they may be shown formatted tables or charts with dummy data. The review should help users identify gaps in the planned survey as well as information not needed. After the data are collected, the researchers can refer to the plan to guide their data analysis.

Example 7.7 shows a partial outline produced to help design a questionnaire to learn how agency managers trained in DECIDE used the technique. The DECIDE training program required two licensed trainers to conduct weeklong training seminars of 16 agency managers. During the week, teams of trainees systematically analyzed problems, identified and evaluated possible solutions, selected a solution, and developed an implementation plan. The agency needed the information to help it decide whether the benefits of the training justified the costs.

 EXAMPLE 7.7

Using Planned Output to Guide Questionnaire Content

Situation: Investigators plan to survey managers who received DECIDE training and ask them how they used the training in their jobs.

   Step 1: Describe planned analysis. Indicate what outputs will be produced, identify the questions that will be included to produce each output, and indicate the value of each output to the study. Note the number of categories that are needed to perform analysis.

   Outline of Planned Output:

   Univariate Output: Trainees' use of DECIDE

   Frequency of use (Question 3)
   Impact on present job (Question 5)
   Types of use (Question 4)
   Specific examples of use (Question 4; categorize and analyze open-ended responses)

   Bivariate Output: Factors associated with how often trainees use DECIDE, how they use it, and problems with the use. Tables will be created to examine the following relationships:

1. Frequency of use by
   a. years since training
   b. management functions
   c. position
   d. division
   e. education

Continued

EXAMPLE 7.7 *Continued*

2. Type of use by
   a. years since training
   b. management functions
   c. position
   d. division
   e. education
3. Problems with use by
   a. years since training
   b. management functions
   c. position
   d. division
   e. education

Value and use of bivariate output on use: If patterns of use are related to years since training, the pattern may be attributed to decay (training forgotten over time); changes in the types of persons trained over the years; changes in trainees' jobs. (Note: Should we include questions to measure the latter explanations?)

If patterns of use are related to management functions, the number of employees supervised or position pattern may show whether variations in use are associated with either a specialized or generalist management focus. Information could be used to limit training to groups identified as frequent or effective users of DECIDE.

If patterns of use are related to work unit, the pattern may suggest that DECIDE is more suited to the work of specific units, or that some unit managers are more supportive of the technique. Information could be used to limit training to units identified as frequent or effective users of DECIDE. If supervisor training in DECIDE is related to frequent or effective use, managers may suggest the need to train supervisors before training their staff.

Step 2: Check outline against draft questionnaire to make sure it contains all items needed for analysis; consider deleting questions that are not noted on outline.

Step 3: Review questionnaire and outline with study users to see if they can identify unnecessary information or overlooked information.

Planning, Pretesting, and Piloting Surveys

Good data collection instruments that yield useful and used information emerge from an iterative process. The first stage, which has been the focus of the chapter, involves planning and writing the instrument. As ideas are fleshed out to form an actual survey, investigators better understand the purpose of the study and what it can find out or accomplish. The planning process brings critical actors together to decide what information they want, whether a survey is needed, and if it will yield the desired information. From the various discussions, the investigators should be able to identify a list of variables. With this list they can develop measures and design an instrument. Finally, the contents of the questionnaire are outlined as in Example 7.7 to evaluate if all the proposed items are needed and if all needed items have been included. Once it is outlined, further feedback may be solicited from critical actors.

Next, the questionnaire should be reviewed by researchers and their colleagues. They should determine if the questions seem reliable: Are there any ambiguous items? Are the response choices appropriate? Is the information easily available to respondents? Human nature may lead the writers to disagree with their critics and argue that an item is not ambiguous, that the response choices are fine, or that the respondents will be motivated to find the information. Nevertheless, in our experience, reviewers tend to identify the same items that study subjects find troublesome.

Writing questions takes time and effort. Participants need a thick skin because good questionnaires emerge only after a lot of criticism and argument. Good questionnaire design takes place among equals, with everyone's comments getting consideration. In our experience, not only do participants act as equals, but they become intense and pointed in their comments. To illustrate the process of question writing, we have selected just one question from the DECIDE survey. Example 7.8 shows the changes that question underwent through various drafting sessions.

After the questionnaire is redrafted, it should be *pretested*. (Note that this use of *pretest* refers to evaluating how questions actually work. It is different from the use of *pretest* to refer to data gathered prior to an intervention.) To conduct a pretest, one asks a small group to answer the proposed questionnaire. These pretest subjects should represent common variations found in the target population. For example, a survey of city employees should be pretested on employees ranging from unskilled laborers to senior management. The investigators also may want pretest subjects who represent various city departments, such as public works, public safety, planning, and finance.

Pretests normally involve face-to-face contact with the subjects. The investigators determine if subjects understood and could answer the questions, and if their answers showed enough variation for the planned analysis to be conducted. The investigators should record how long it took individuals to answer the survey and if it held their interest and attention. If a survey does not engage respondents, the information may be less reliable, incomplete questionnaires may be more common, or, in the case of mail questionnaires, the response rate may be lower.

After answering the questionnaire, the pretest subjects may be interviewed or debriefed about their answers and reactions to the questions and the survey as a whole. The investigators use their own observations, the subjects' comments, and their responses to the survey questions to determine how coherent the questionnaire is: Are directions clear? Is the question order logical? The survey should be redrafted based on the pretest findings. Common changes include changing or clarifying unclear terms, rewording or dropping ambiguous questions, changing response categories, and shortening instruments.

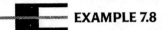 **EXAMPLE 7.8**

The Evolution of a Question

Situation: Questionnaire on DECIDE training was designed to learn how trainees felt it affected their jobs.

Stage 1: Group of three wrote a questionnaire. First questionnaire had several questions on DECIDE's effect and use on the job. Questions 1 and 2 were both open-ended.

1. Were DECIDE course objectives related to your job needs?

2. Do you use any DECIDE processes on the job? If not, why?

Stage 2: Questionnaire map drawn up and questionnaire redrafted by another team member.

1. In general how would you rate DECIDE's impact on your present job? (responses: excellent, good, fair, poor, no impact, unsure)

2. About how often do you use any DECIDE process on your job? (responses: 1 time a week, several times a month, about once a month, several times a year, rarely or never, don't know)

3. Let me know if DECIDE helps you think about any of the following: (responses included: setting priorities, setting objectives, identifying alternatives)

4. Give me a specific example of how you have used the DECIDE approach on your job.

5. In applying the DECIDE process, what, if any, problems have you encountered?

Stage 3: Team of seven reviewed the draft and made the following changes:

1. In general, how would you rate DECIDE's effect on your job performance? (changed "no impact" response to "no effect")

2. Question kept the same. Placed "rarely and never" responses into separate categories. Respondents who answered "never" were directed to a later question.

3. Question kept the same. Deleted two response categories.

4. Give me a specific example of how you have used the DECIDE process on your job.

Stage 4: Questionnaire pretested. Sample of 10 called. Frequency of responses to each question reviewed. The only change in the above questions was to further reduce the number of response categories for Question 3.

The final stage is the *pilot study,* or dress rehearsal. One text in questionnaire design contains the statement, "If you do not have the resources to pilot test your questionnaire, don't do the study."[12] Even lack of time should not justify skipping a pilot test. In modest studies the pilot study and the pretest may overlap, but at a minimum investigators should test the instrument on potential subjects, check that items have sufficient variation, and conduct minimum analysis to assess whether the survey will produce useful information. Pretesting and pilot testing are most effective at detecting technical problems associated with questions and questionnaires, e.g., questions that are misunderstood. They do less well at detecting measurement problems, especially operational validity. Focus groups, asking subjects to talk aloud as they answer questions, and other techniques are being developed to better capture what questions are actually measuring.[13]

The amount of resources wasted on poorly designed or inadequate questionnaires is staggering. More astonishing is how many questionnaires are sent out without a commitment of resources for data analysis. Consider an actual survey that resulted in 33,000 responses. The office, which did not normally conduct or process surveys, spent a frantic few weeks simply coding 21 closed-ended and two open-ended questions. Each questionnaire took approximately one minute to code, for a total of 550 hours. Staff also read the responses to four other open-ended questions. The data analysis was less of a drain on resources; the questionnaire's content didn't allow for much analysis beyond counting and categorizing the responses to each question. Two questions could not be analyzed; because of ambiguous wording, the responses were uninterpretable. We assume that the poor ratio between the survey's cost and the meager amount of information it yielded could have been avoided if the survey had been pretested and piloted. It wasn't.

The pilot study involves conducting the entire study as planned on a small sample representing the target population. The questionnaire is administered as planned, that is, either in person, through the mail, or over the telephone. The planned analysis is conducted on the returned surveys. Any special procedures to be used in collecting or compiling data, for example, computer-assisted interviewing, are used during the pilot study.

By the time of the pilot study, questionnaire problems should be minimal. Investigators pay closer attention to the feasibility of the sampling, data collection, and analysis procedures. The dress rehearsal should identify any problems in contacting sample members and getting their cooperation. The investigators can estimate the average amount of time required to answer a survey, to organize the information, and to prepare the data. The adequacy of data preparation and analysis plans can be checked. Previously unnoticed, unreliable, or invalid measures may be detected. Problems encountered in the pilot study should be resolved prior to implementing the final study design.

Earlier in this chapter, we mentioned the Nationwide Food Consumption Survey, which had a response rate of 34 percent. The problems with that survey illustrate two common situations. First, identifying problems in a pretest or dress rehearsal is not enough. An effective solution to the problems identified in the pilot study must be put in place. Second, without a dress rehearsal the serious problems may be missed or underestimated. Two pretests of the food consumption survey had been conducted. Interviewers and subjects complained of fatigue with a survey that took as long as 5½ hours to complete. As a result, the computer-assisted interviewing procedures were supposed to be improved. The pretest of the improved computer-assisted interviewing methods found that interviewers required rigorous training. To save money, the planned dress rehearsal was canceled. Note that the dress rehearsal would have evaluated the effectiveness of the interviewers' training. The long survey was not shortened, and interviewer training was not sufficiently rigorous. As a result, a study that cost $7.6 million yielded seriously flawed data.

SUMMARY

Questions and questionnaires constitute basic elements of data collection. Writing questions and designing questionnaires require one to understand their effect on the implementation of a research design. Each question or series of questions has implications for reliability and operational validity.

A first step in questionnaire construction is to outline its content. An investigator wants to avoid a questionnaire that asks trivial questions or fails to ask important ones. To prevent a mismatch between the research purpose and a survey instrument, each question's role in the research should be explored and justified. One also should determine whether the types of questions asked elicit the desired information. Asking the wrong type of question—for example, asking an opinion question where a behavior question is needed—affects operational validity. Common question types ask about facts, behaviors, opinions, attitudes, motives, and knowledge.

A second step is deciding on whether to ask open-ended or closed-ended questions or to include filter questions. Open-ended questions require respondents to write their answers. These questions work well during questionnaire development, when investigators want to learn the range of possible responses. Open-ended questions provide rich, detailed information; they may be asked in conjunction with closed-ended questions. Because open-ended questions are difficult to quantify, may unnecessarily tax respondents, and may lower the response rate, researchers prefer closed-ended questions. Closed-ended questions have a respondent select an appropriate response from a list. These questions work well if the questionnaire has been carefully pretested to ensure that the questions are understood and the response categories are appropriate.

Filter questions or screening questions direct subgroups of respondents to appropriate follow-up questions. For example, renters may answer one set of questions and home owners another set. On mailed questionnaires, arrows may direct respondents to applicable questions. Interviewers may use the same tools or they may use computer software that "automatically" goes to the appropriate follow-up questions.

Question wording is a major component of measure reliability and operational validity. In general, questions should be clear, short, and specific. The respondent should understand what information the question is asking for. Questions can be biased, either intentionally or unintentionally. A biased question increases the probability that a respondent will choose one answer over another. Words that respondents perceive as positive or negative may bias answers. Response lists that have disproportionately more positive or negative alternatives also introduce bias. Questions on sensitive subjects must be handled with special care. Respondents may distort their answers; furthermore, such questions can raise ethical concerns if confidential information is not adequately protected.

The order in which questions are asked affects response rate and the operational validity of the questions. Nevertheless, ordering questions to avoid bias works better if subjects are being interviewed. Respondents answering self-administered questionnaires may be able to read ahead or change their answers, reducing the value of the sequence.

Questionnaires start with an introduction. Any needed demographic questions are usually placed at the end. Some researchers get in the habit of routinely asking a set of demographic questions, without considering which demographic variables are needed for the planned analysis. Asking needless questions should be avoided; furthermore, demographic questions may raise the distrust of respondents who wish to remain anonymous.

One would be well advised to approach any survey asking, "Is this survey necessary?" To assure oneself that it is and that it does not squander resources, one should first determine that the needed data do not yet exist. (See Chapter 9 for a discussion of secondary data. Various web sites such as fedstats.com identify accessible databases.) If the data do not exist, then the survey should proceed only after a pilot study. A pilot study rehearses the research plan, including the analysis. In analyzing a pilot study, researchers may focus on question wording, the sensitivity of the response categories, the response rate, and the time required to answer. Researchers may be tempted to ignore the opportunity to evaluate their planned analysis. Yet, a review of the planned analysis may be most helpful in avoiding unnecessary surveys or questions.

The next chapter looks at the ethical concerns raised by gathering data from human subjects. We will review some key incidents that led to federal regulations and professional guidelines for protecting human subjects. The regulations dominate data collection. The requirement for informed consent dictates what potential research subjects must be told about a planned study and its effects. Furthermore, the provision that research participation must be voluntary challenges researchers to design studies that respect the respondents' privacy and entice their participation.

NOTES

1. M. Q. Patton, *Utilization-Focused Evaluation*, 3d ed. (Thousand Oaks, CA: Sage, 1997).
2. K. A. Rasinski, D. Mingay, and N. M. Bradburn, "Do Respondents Really 'Mark All that Apply' on Self-Administered Questions?" *Public Opinion Quarterly* 58 (Fall 1994): 400–408. J. C. Smyth et al., "Comparing Check-All and Forced-Choice Question Formats in Web Surveys," *Public Opinion Quarterly* 70 (Spring 2006), 66–77.
3. N. Bradburn, S. Sudman, and B. Wansink, *Asking Questions*, rev ed. (San Francisco: Jossey-Bass, 2004), 141–142, 162–163. For discussion on neutral responses

and their placement see Don A. Dillman, *Mail and Internet Surveys: The Tailored Design Method*, 2d ed. (New York: John Wiley and Sons, 2000), 58–60.
4. Dillman, *Mail and Internet Surveys*, 102–104.
5. *USDA's Nationwide Food Consumption Survey*, Washington, DC: General Accounting Office, GAO/RCED–91–117. The GAO report on why the survey yielded poor-quality data is highly recommended; it vividly points out several errors that can occur in a major survey project. For more detailed and recent information on nutrition surveys and a link to articles examining their reliability and validity, go to the web

page of the Food Surveys Research Group: http://www.ars.usda.gov/main/site_main.htm?mode-code=12-35-50-00.

6. Most of the information on validating voting data are from S. Presser and M. Traaugott, "Correlated Response Errors," *Public Opinion Quarterly* 56 (Spring 1992): 77–86. For a discussion on voter records as a source of error, see P. R. Abramson and W. Claggett, "The Quality of Record Keeping and Racial Differences in Validated Turnout," *Journal of Politics* 54 (August 1992): 871–880.

7. Researchers have reported that the ratio of positive to negative responses remains the same whether or not "don't know" is offered as a response alternative. For further discussion of "don't know," see L. F. Feick, "Latent Class Analysis of Survey Questions That Include Don't Know Responses," *Public Opinion Quarterly* 53 (1989): 525–547; J. M. Converse and S. Presser, *Survey Questions: Handcrafting the Standardized Questionnaire*, Sage University Paper Series: Quantitative Applications in the Social Sciences 63 (Beverly Hills: Sage Publications, 1986): 35–39, and M. Gilljam and D. Granberg, "Should We Take Don't Know for an Answer," *Public Opinion Quarterly* 57 (Fall 1993): 348–357.

8. S. Sudman, N. M. Bradburn, and B. Wansink, *Asking Questions*, rev. ed. (San Francisco: Jossey-Bass, 2004), 103–104.

9. R. Tourangeau, M. P. Couper, and F. Conrad, "Spacing, position, and order: Interpretative Heuristics for Visual Features of Survey Questions," *Public Opinion Quarterly* 68 (Fall 2004): 368–393.

10. D. Goleman, "Psychologists Offer Aid on Bias in Polls," *New York Times*, September 7, 1993, B5, B7. The article relies heavily on information included in an article in the June 1993 issue of *The Public Perspective.*

11. See P. Passell, "Polls May Help Government Decide the Worth of Nature," *New York Times*, September 6, 1993, for an example of a question to ask how much a respondent would be willing for the government to pay to clean up an oil spill.

12. For a thorough discussion on pretests and pilot studies, see Converse and Presser, *Survey Questions*, 51–75 and F. J. Fowler, Jr. "Presurvey Evaluation of Questions," *Improving Survey Questions: Design and Evaluation* (Thousand Oaks, CA: Sage, 1995), chap. 5. Fowler discusses the use of focus groups, intensive interviewing, and field pretests.

13. S. Presser et al., *Methods for Testing and Evaluating Survey Questionnaires* (Hoboken: Wiley-Interscience, 2004) provide in-depth coverage of various techniques. A shorter discussion of the various techniques is found in Groves at al., *Survey Methodology* (Hoboken: Wiley-Interscience, 2004), chap. 8.

TERMS FOR REVIEW

open-ended questions
closed-ended questions
forced-choice questions

filter questions
biased questions
loaded questions

pretest
pilot study

QUESTIONS FOR REVIEW

The following questions should indicate whether you have a basic competency in this chapter's material.

1. List the steps required to write a questionnaire.

2. How would you decide the content of a questionnaire?

3. Imagine you are writing a questionnaire to evaluate training given to new employees. (The training introduces employees to the agency, its purposes, and major policies.)
   a. Write a factual, behavior, opinion, motive, and knowledge question that you could include on the questionnaire.

   b. How valuable do you imagine each type of question (factual, behavior, etc.) would be in determining the quality of the training?

   c. On reflection, would you include all the questions you listed in part a?

4. A young researcher believes that questionnaires tend to be too long and adopts a rule of asking only one question to measure a variable. Evaluate the advisability of such a rule.

5. Compare and contrast the value of open-ended questions and closed-ended questions.

6. In general, would you recommend asking respondents ranking questions? Justify your answer.

7. What characteristics of question wording affect reliability? Explain.

8. Should you always include questions asking for demographic information? Why or why not? If you choose to include them, where would you place them in the survey?

9. Compare and contrast pretesting and piloting a questionnaire.

10. An investigator has written a questionnaire asking police officers about their career satisfaction. She pretests the questionnaire on students in an undergraduate criminal justice class. Comment on the adequacy of her pretesting strategy.

11. You are interested in neighborhoods and communities. You find a questionnaire that was used in metropolitan New York. The questionnaire covers topics that you are interested in studying in a moderate-size midwestern city. What would you do in order to decide that the questionnaire was appropriate for your study?

PROBLEMS FOR HOMEWORK AND DISCUSSION

1. The following is from an actual town survey. Identify the different parts of the survey. Identify the type of questions asked. Consider the value of findings from this questionnaire. Assess the wording of the questions.

    Questions a–d could be answered "yes," "no," or "no opinion." Questions f–h were open-ended.

    > Hi, I am _____. I am helping to conduct a census for Wind Valley. Would you mind answering a few questions? It will take only a few minutes.

   a. Are you a resident of Wind Valley? (if yes, continue; if not, thank him/her and leave)
   b. Would you support redevelopment of the downtown business area?
   c. Would you favor once-a-week garbage collection in order to keep service charges down?
   d. Would you be willing to accept fewer services for a reduced tax rate?
   e. If city services had to be reduced in one area, which would you choose? (responses were: streets, fire, sanitation, parks and recreation, police, library, other, none)
   f. How long have you lived in Wind Valley?
   g. How many people are living in this household?
   h. How many people are over 60 years of age?

2. The following questions are taken from a draft of a survey to identify stereotypes that social service workers may have of American Indian people. Review each question and then the five questions together. Assess the wording of the questions. Consider whether the questionnaire seems to risk a set response pattern problem. Note: All questions were to be answered "yes" or "no."
   a. Do you put down Indians for their lifestyle?
   b. Are the Indian people losing their culture?
   c. Do you feel white society in general has labeled Indians to be lazy, uneducated, and drunk?
   d. What is it to you to be an Indian today?
   e. Do you provide support through staff who have knowledge and understanding of reservation or urban Indian needs?

3. Evaluate questions a and b from a "Job Turnover Questionnaire" sent to public administrators. What changes would you recommend?
   a. Most important reasons for leaving your last job (check two only):
      _____ Lack of job satisfaction (e.g., lack of achievement, recognition, growth potential)
      _____ Disagree with agency policy/administration
      _____ Poor interpersonal relations on job
      _____ Salary insufficient
      _____ Poor physical conditions
      _____ Discrimination
      _____ Workload
      _____ Sexual harassment
      _____ Continue education

_____ Family reasons (e.g., spouse moving, birth of child)

_____ Termination (end of contract, position defunded, reorganization)

_____ Other, specify

b. Type of job (check one only):

_____ Administration

_____ Counseling/social work

_____ Research/technical

_____ Secretarial/clerical

_____ Teaching

_____ Other; specify

4. A community survey sent interviewers to residents' homes. The respondent, any adult living in the household, was asked to supply the following information for each person in the household. Evaluate this question.

The Major Source of Income

	Person 1	Person 2
Salary	_____	_____
Hourly wages	_____	_____
Investments	_____	_____
Retirements/pensions	_____	_____
Parent support/inheritance	_____	_____
Welfare	_____	_____
Self-employment	_____	_____
Refusal	_____	_____
Don't know	_____	_____

5. Evaluate the following question: "Do you oppose measures promoting the abolition of the death penalty?"

6. Evaluate the following question and response categories on a survey given to nursing home residents. What changes in wording, if any, would you recommend?

How much do you use or participate in the following services or activities?

a. The Beauty and Barber Shop

_____ Often

_____ Occasionally

_____ Rarely

_____ Never

b. Crafts

_____ Often

_____ Occasionally

_____ Rarely

_____ Never

c. Card and Game Night

_____ Often

_____ Occasionally

_____ Rarely

_____ Never

d. Religious Services

_____ Often

_____ Occasionally

_____ Rarely

_____ Never

7. Draft a survey to determine needs and preferences of part-time students enrolled in your degree program. The survey should identify changes the program could make to better serve the needs of part-time students. Create and use the mapping forms to determine what questions to ask, how they will be used, and the value of the information.

8. Imagine 600 members of a statewide professional association responded to a survey. It included an open-ended question on the effectiveness of the association's activities. Perusal of the questionnaires suggests that most members answered the question.

a. You are asked to make an initial report on the survey findings. You will not have time to examine all the open-ended questions. Suggest a strategy so that you can include information from the open-ended questions in your report.

b. Describe how you would analyze the question for your final report.

9. Contrast the value of (a) finding questionnaires that have questions you can adapt and (b) writing questionnaires with a group of colleagues.

10. Investigators are often tempted to add questions that they may or may not get around to analyzing. Evaluate this strategy.

11. Review and evaluate a software package to design questionnaires.

DISK WORK

Limitations of a questionnaire and the resulting dataset may become obvious only as you analyze the data. To get a feel for this role of analysis, this exercise asks you to use the ORB Research Methods dataset.

The Governer is planning a series of statewide town meetings to connect with the public and wants to be well prepared. She would like to know how population characteristics vary by region of the state. Unfortunately, she needs the information immediately, and your office only has the information in the Research Methods dataset on hand.

1. Explore the differences in average population density, social security beneficiary popula-

tion, Medicaid eligible population, and crime indexes across the three state region.

2. Based on your analysis, write a memo (no longer than one page, single-spaced) to the Governor presenting your key findings. Make appropriate recommendations for topics the Governor may wish to discuss or avoid.

3. Based on your analysis, what information should be added to the office database for the staff to be better prepared for such a request were it to come again? Write a memo to your office director summarizing your suggestions (one page, single-spaced).

RECOMMENDED FOR FURTHER READING

There are a number of excellent books on survey research and questionnaire design. We recommend that you review one of these or a similar book before writing a questionnaire.

Don A. Dillman, *Mail and Internet Surveys: The Tailored Design Method*, 2d ed. (New York: John Wiley and Sons, 2000).

Floyd J. Fowler, Jr., *Survey Research Methods*, Sage Applied Social Research Methods Series, 3d ed. (Thousand Oaks, CA: Sage, 2001).

Norman M. Bradburn, Seymour Sudman, and Brian Wansink, *Asking Questions: The Definitive Guide to Questionnaire Design*, rev ed. (San Francisco: Jossey–Bass, 2004).

Ellen J. Westland with Kent W. Smith surveys research on response accuracy and a meta-analysis in *Survey Responses: An Evaluation of Their Validity* (San Diego: Academic Press, 1993).

Professional associations and researchers publish guides for designing questionnaires and conducting surveys. Two guides that review major points covered here and provide additional examples are H. P. Hatry et al.,

Customer Surveys for Agency Managers: What Managers Need to Know (Washington, DC: The Urban Institute, 1997), and Thomas I. Miller and Michelle A. Miller, *Citizen Surveys: How to Do Them, How to Use Them, What They Mean*, ICMA's Special Report Series, 2d ed. (Washington, DC: International City Management Association, 2000). Other how-to-do-it books can help refresh your memory of key points; for example, see Mildred L. Patten, *Questionnaire Research*, 2d ed. (Los Angeles: Pyrczak Publishing, 2001); and a very helpful basic brochure series called *What is a Survey?* provided by the American Statistical Association's Survey Research Section.

To keep up-to-date with current research on survey research topics such as question wording, questionnaire design, data collection, and data analysis, see *Public Opinion Quarterly*, the journal of the American Association for Public Opinion Research, published by the University of Chicago Press. S. Sudman, N. M. Bradburn, and N. Schwarz, *Thinking about Answers* (San Francisco: Jossey-Bass, 1996), provide a good review of research findings.

CHAPTER 8

Protection of Human Research Subjects and Other Ethical Issues

In this chapter you will learn

1. Some of the major cases informing ethical practices in conducting research on human subjects.
2. Elements of ethical practice in conducting research on human subjects.
3. Requirements for obtaining informed consent from a research subject.
4. What to consider in protecting confidential information.
5. Federal requirements for protecting human subjects.
6. What administrators should consider before permitting research on their employees or agency's clients.

The nature of research creates a special relationship between researchers and their human subjects. Researchers require the cooperation of humans to conduct investigations. At the same time, subjects rely on researchers to treat them respectfully and ethically. Subjects do not expect to be harmed by merely participating in research. Nevertheless, some research projects may expose participants to risks, including physical injury, psychological discomfort, or loss of privacy.

Administrative students may believe that administrative or policy research rarely puts a *subject at risk*. While the subjects seem unlikely to experience physical harm or life-threatening effects, the risks may be more than trivial. Apparently innocuous studies may leave participants feeling angry, upset, humiliated, or otherwise worried. They may be less willing to participate in other studies. They may tell others of their experience and further decrease support for research endeavors. Sound, ethical research practices can greatly lessen such negative effects.

Administrators should be sensitive to the issues surrounding research with human subjects and recognize how research participation can cause a subject distress. Otherwise, administrators may fail to adequately protect their agency, its employees or clients, or themselves. Administrators who work in hospitals, schools, prisons, and social services agencies should be particularly vigilant since their employees, patients, students, or clients often interest researchers. An administrator is responsible for protecting the rights of employees and clients whether she is conducting the research, contracting with outside researchers, or cooperating with other researchers. If she agrees to provide investigators requested access to employees or clients, she should ensure that a study conforms to ethical research practice and does not reflect badly on the agency.

In this chapter we begin by highlighting some well-known cases. The cited cases are dramatic examples, but they were not necessarily aberrations from contemporary research practices. For one reason or another, they achieved notoriety and shaped current thinking about ethical research on human subjects. Since the last cited case occurred in 1963, you may reasonably conclude that ethical missteps no longer occur. This is not true. From 1993 to 2001 four different medical studies resulted in the deaths of eight research subjects. As a result, bio-ethicists began to review policies intended to protect research volunteers.[1] Ethical concerns are not limited to medical research. In 1999 parents filed a lawsuit claiming that a student survey which asked questions about teenagers' lifestyles violated their children's privacy.[2]

As you read the cases, put yourself in the place of the judges, hospital administrators, or others who have a role in approving research. Put yourself in the position of the patient, juror, or an observed citizen. Imagine how you would react to a survey asking about your management style. As you think about these different scenarios, you may realize that protection of human subjects can directly involve you even if you never conduct research in your professional career.

The second part of the chapter focuses on principles of ethical treatment of human subjects, e.g., obtaining informed consent. The administrator familiar with what constitutes informed consent has a firm foundation for deciding on the appropriateness of research involving agency personnel or clients. The chapter considers privacy and confidentiality and presents strategies to protect confidentiality. Next, the chapter summarizes current federal regulations on protecting human research subjects. The chapter concludes with a discussion on administrative concerns, which should guide a decision whether or not to cooperate with a research effort.

ILLUSTRATIVE CASES

The Tuskegee Syphilis Study is the best-known U.S. example of an egregious abuse of human subjects.[3] Begun in 1932 by the U.S. Public Health Service, its researchers monitored the health of two groups of African American males. One group had untreated syphilis; the other group was free of syphilis symptoms. The research documented the course of untreated syphilis. At the time the study began, treatments for syphilis were potentially dangerous, so denying treatment might have been rationalized. However, from the mid-1950s on, penicillin was known to be an effective treatment for syphilis and was widely available. Yet by 1973, when the study was discontinued, the participants had not received penicillin and had been actively discouraged from seeking treatment elsewhere.

The failure to treat the subjects was particularly disturbing because the study continued unchallenged despite the findings of the Nuremberg Trials and a later lawsuit against the Jewish Chronic Disease Hospital. At the end of World War II, disclosure of Nazi atrocities included reports of abuses committed by doctors and scientists performing human experiments. The Nuremberg Military Tribunal judgment against these doctors and scientists listed 10 principles of moral, ethical, and legal medical experimentation on humans. The principles, referred to as the "Nuremberg Code,"[4] formed the basis for later regulations protecting human subjects.

The Tuskegee study did not comply with the Nuremberg principles. The violated principles included free and informed consent from the subjects, the researcher's obligation to avoid causing unnecessary physical suffering, the subject's ability to terminate his or her participation at any time, and the researcher's obligation to discontinue an experiment when its continuation could result in death.

In 1963 the issue of informed consent again received public attention. A lawsuit and investigation questioned whether 22 patients at Brooklyn's Jewish Chronic Disease Hospital (JCDH) had given informed consent when they agreed to be injected with live cancer cells.[5] The patients were asked if they would consent to an injection for research on immune system responses. They were not told that the experiment was unrelated to their disease or its treatment. They were not told that the injection contained live cancer cells. The investigation concluded that asking a patient to consent to a vaguely described procedure could not be considered informed consent. Still the publicity surrounding the JCDH case did not change the course of the Tuskegee study, which continued until 1973, when an ad hoc advisory committee to the Secretary of Health found that the study did not meet requirements for informed consent.

The knowledge of Nazi medical experiments, the Tuskegee study, and other reported cases has had a lasting effect. Most notably, withholding beneficial treatment from control-group subjects is considered unethical. Several controlled studies have been discontinued when a marked improvement occurred in the experimental group. For example, a five-year clinical trial was stopped after two and a half years. The researchers learned that the study drug was decreasing the rate of breast cancer recurrence by nearly half.[6] Alternatively, if some treatment may be beneficial, but the most beneficial treatment remains unknown, the control-group subjects are assigned to a form of treatment. For example, in a study of depression, all subjects were assigned to some form of treatment. Each form of treatment was believed to be better than no treatment, but the relative effectiveness of the treatments was unknown.

The Tuskegee study left as a legacy African Americans' distrust of medicine. African Americans are less likely to participate in medical research or to donate their organs for transplant. Polls conducted in 1990 found that roughly a third of African Americans thought it was at least possible that AIDS was a genocidal plot to infect them.[7]

The lack of informed consent is a theme that runs through most of the reported abuses of human subjects. The following cases illustrate other themes that have helped define ethical research practices. In 1954, researchers from the

University of Chicago Law School secretly recorded jury deliberations. The investigators wanted to learn more about the jury processes, processes that were known only by anecdotes, post-trial interviews with jurors, and jury simulations. The researchers believed that open recording would affect and distort the deliberations. They conscientiously developed procedures to obtain undistorted information while protecting the rights of the parties involved. Only juries deliberating civil cases were studied, and the presiding judge and the attorneys representing the litigants gave their permission for the recording. After the recordings were made, they were kept with the judge until the case was closed.

As word of the jury study spread, a U.S. Senate subcommittee held a hearing to learn more. Despite the researchers' precautions to protect the jury members and other parties to the case and to avoid influencing the judicial processes, the research compromised the secrecy of jury deliberations. A comment by the subcommittee's chairman identified the potential harm: "Would a member of a jury hesitate to frankly express his opinion if he thought there might be a microphone hidden, taking down what they said? . . . [H]ow is he going to know whether in that particular case there is a microphone or not?"[8]

Research participants may lose their privacy. *Privacy* refers to an individual's ability to control the access of other people to information about himself. A loss of privacy may occur in deceptive research, where a participant is not told a study's real purpose. While few public administrators become directly involved in deceptive research, it is an issue associated with social science research. In a well-known deceptive study, a doctoral student, Laud Humphreys, studied men who engaged in casual, anonymous sexual activities with other men. He found that these men were indistinguishable from other members of the community, rather than stereotypical deviates.

Humphreys offered to act as a lookout for men who were using a public rest room for sexual encounters. He recorded the license plate numbers of the unsuspecting, and nonconsenting, subjects. He traced the licenses and linked them to the subjects' names and addresses. A year later he changed his hairstyle and manner of dress and took on the role of surveyor. He visited the homes of the previously identified subjects and asked them to participate in an anonymous public-health survey.

Critics questioned whether the benefits of Humphreys' research outweighed the costs.[9] Even if the risks of disclosing the subjects' identities were negligible, the extent of other risks was unknown and inestimable. Given the publicity surrounding the study, one can imagine the men figuring out that they were the subjects, experiencing a loss of privacy, and feeling used and betrayed by Humphreys.

Some social scientists argued that Humphreys had a right to pursue knowledge, that his strategy was appropriate to the question at hand, and that the subjects benefited from the revelation that they did not fit any commonly held, unsavory stereotype. Others believed that deceptive practices were morally wrong and demeaning to subjects. Some critics worried that knowledge of deceptive research studies might result in a general reaction against social science research.

Another deceptive research study illustrates the possibility that research subjects may gain unwanted information about themselves. Psychologist Stanley Milgram designed a study to see how ordinary people could be induced to obey authority. The research question was sparked by his interest in understanding how the Holocaust happened. The subjects were told that the experiment was to study learning theory. As part of the experiment, the subjects were told to administer what they believed were electric shocks to other participants. The other participants were actors, who vividly acted out the pain of the (nonexistent) "shocks."

Some subjects refused to continue administering the shocks and withdrew from the study. Others continued but were clearly distressed at their participation. The ethical problem that critics noted was that the subjects had learned that they would follow orders and seriously harm others. This self-knowledge may have never been gained without their participation in the experiment.

In addition, without their knowledge, subjects were forced to choose between two strong and competing values. On the one hand, they had an implied contract with the researcher to carry out the research as designed. On the other hand, they held the value of not harming another person.

Milgram was conscious of the study's potential to disturb the subjects, and his study included a careful debriefing procedure. A sample of participants was interviewed by a psychiatrist, who was experienced in outpatient treatment; he reportedly found no evidence of injurious effects.[10] Milgram's own and others' follow-up research found that the self-knowledge had no lasting ill effects, and that some participants reported benefiting from the insight. Nevertheless, the case stands as a landmark in the history of deceptive research.

PRINCIPLES OF ETHICAL TREATMENT OF HUMAN SUBJECTS

In response to these and other reported abuses, the Belmont Report, written by the National Commission for the Protection of Human Subjects of Biomedical and Behavioral Research, identified three basic ethical principles: respect for persons, beneficence, and justice. Respect for persons requires that subjects enter into research voluntarily and with adequate information. Beneficence requires doing no harm and maximizing possible benefits and minimizing possible harm. Justice requires that research subjects are not selected "simply because of their easy availability, their compromised position, or their manipulability, rather than for reasons directly related to the problem at hand." To implement these principles requires that subjects give informed consent, that benefits and risks be identified and weighed, and that selection of subjects be fair.[11] Informed consent demonstrates respect for persons, assessing risks and benefits demonstrates beneficence, and fairly selecting subjects demonstrates justice.

Informed Consent

Informed, voluntary consent is a cornerstone of ethical research practice. Voluntary consent is based on respect for individual autonomy and personal dignity. A potential subject must be given adequate information so he can make an informed, voluntary decision to participate. First, potential subjects need to know the general purpose of the study. This information provides a foundation for a subject's assessment of the costs and benefits of participating. Second, federal guidelines and common ethical practice require that subjects be informed about the procedures, their purposes, and possible risks, including risks that are unknown. In other words, subjects should be told what they will be expected to do and what will be done to them. This information on risks should include mention of possible discomfort, anxiety, unwanted information about oneself, or inconvenience. In low-risk studies subjects may be more concerned about the time involved than they are about the procedures.

Deceptive studies, such as the Milgram experiment, misinform subjects about a study's purpose or procedures. Deceptive research pits two values against each other: the potential value of a study's findings and respect for individual autonomy. Although the debate about the acceptability of deceptive research continues, existing procedures can minimize informed consent concerns. For example, a subject may be told that deception is part of the research and that he is being asked to agree to participate without knowing the full details of the study's purpose.[12]

Third, potential subjects should be told why they were selected. While this is not required or even implied in the federal regulations, this practice strengthens the subject's understanding of a study's purpose, his importance to the study, and the fairness of the selection process.[13]

Fourth, potential subjects should be told what will be done with the collected information and any limitations on its confidentiality. Who will receive the information from the study? What type of information will be disseminated? What steps will be taken to protect the identity of the subject? What will happen if a researcher learns of an illegal act or identifies a health risk? If photos, movies, recordings, or similar research records are being produced, the subject should know what will be done with them. We know of one student who was shocked to learn that an interview tape, produced as part of an experiment, was being shown to classes at her college.

Providing information about a study's purpose, procedures, and risks is only part of ensuring voluntary participation. Other factors can compromise the voluntary nature of research participation. First, the subjects must understand the potential risks and the probable benefits. The way the risks and benefits are communicated must be appropriate to the subject population and the study. For example, in a research project that puts a subject at risk, oral consent is not adequate. Nor is just signing a statement adequate. Rather, the researcher needs to select words and techniques to ensure that subjects actually appreciate what is being asked of them.

Second, the relationship between the researcher and the potential subject may cloud the subject's judgment. For example, imagine a teacher who asks students to participate as research subjects. The teacher may state that participation is voluntary and will have no effect on class grades. Nevertheless, students may volunteer because they imagine that declining to participate may influence the teacher's feelings about them. The question is not whether a decision to participate or not to participate affects the teacher's grading or other class-related behaviors. Rather, if a student feels that his or her academic progress could be affected, then the decision to participate may not be voluntary.

Third, specific circumstances may impede a subject's ability to make a voluntary decision. Prisoners, members of the military, and schoolchildren, all of whom are in controlled settings, may interpret requests for information or participation as commands. Research involving prisoners is closely scrutinized. Current federal policy limits research involving prisoners to studies that address questions associated with criminal behavior or incarceration.[14] The regulations remind researchers that even modest incentives can compromise a prisoner's ability to assess the risks of participation and may preclude a voluntary decision to participate.

Patients may mistakenly believe that their research participation will have a therapeutic benefit. Voluntary research participation requires clear, realistic information on the benefits and risks of participation. Participants should be told how research interventions may affect their present treatment. Still, the ability of seriously ill persons to give informed consent, no matter what they are told, is questionable. A *New York Times* article summed the problem as follows:

> Potential participants are often desperately ill and may grasp at any straw—even signing a document without reading it. For this reason, many say there is no such thing as informed consent—only consent.[15]

Fourth, care must be taken in working with vulnerable populations, such as children, aged people, and mentally disabled people, who may not be fully capable to make an informed decision or to protect their own interests. In general, researchers try to get informed consent from such subjects and from a legal guardian.

Finally, voluntary participation requires the ability to withdraw from a study at any time. The potential subject must be told this as part of informed consent. Furthermore, potential subjects must be told that other benefits they are entitled to will not be affected by their decision to participate or to discontinue their participation. For example, a client receiving public assistance must be told that his continued eligibility for assistance does not depend on participating in a research study.

Informed consent and an informed consent form are not one and the same. A subject must be free to make her own decision about whether she wishes to participate or not. To make this decision she must be informed about the study and give her consent to participate. A signed informed consent merely documents what information was given, that the participant received and understood the information, and that she consented to participate. The greater the risk to a subject, the more extensive the informed consent procedures required. To obtain informed consent for online surveys subjects may read a statement describing the research and then indicate their willingness to participate by clicking on an "accept" button. For projects where a subject experiences no risks beyond the risks of everyday life or ordinary professional responsibilities, signed statements may be reasonably viewed as unnecessary. Just because the recipient of a mail or telephone survey does not sign an informed consent form does not relieve the surveyor from giving the subject sufficient information so that she can give her informed consent to participate.[16]

Identifying and Weighing Costs and Benefits

People may not agree on the costs and benefits of research participation. Individuals' commitment to research and their educational, social, and professional backgrounds contribute to what they see as risks and benefits and their importance. Consequently, informed consent requires that researchers, impartial reviewers, and potential subjects separately assess a proposed study and decide if the benefits outweigh the risks. Researchers may incorrectly assume that a proposed study presents minimal or no risk. They may overestimate the benefits of a study. Researchers are expected to be especially vigilant if potential subjects represent a distinctly different population from themselves. For example, researchers may underestimate the potential harm in studying recent immigrants. In such cases the researcher is more likely to misjudge what constitutes a risk or a benefit for a participant. She may erroneously assume that the way she requests consent is unbiased and informative.

To minimize the potential of overlooking risks, overestimating benefits, and assuming consent is informed and voluntary, an investigator should solicit the opinion of others. Most university-based research or biomedical research is reviewed by an Institutional Review Board (IRB), which determines that a proposed project adequately protects its human subjects. (IRBs are discussed in more detail later in this chapter.)

What are the benefits of participating in research? Sometimes the research involves a treatment that may relieve a physical or psychological problem. Sometimes the research may seem to benefit a group that a potential subject values. For example, alumni may agree to participate in research on the effectiveness of their education because they believe that the findings will help future students. For some studies, perhaps most, the subject may participate because the research question seems somewhat interesting and the inconvenience is minimal.

For some studies, remuneration is a valuable benefit. We know of a few graduate students who subsidized their incomes by participating as subjects for biomedical research projects. Paying subjects for the inconvenience of participating is not unethical, unless the remuneration is so large that it may be considered as a bribe or questionable inducement to participate. What distinguishes reasonable reimbursement from "undue inducements"? Federal regulations offer no guidance, and opinions vary as to whether participants should be paid more than their direct costs for participating. The federal regulations are not silent about partial payments. The Food and Drug Administration requires that paid subjects who withdraw from a study receive a prorated payment.[17]

What are the risks of participating in research? The most commonly cited risks are physical harm, pain or discomfort, embarrassment, loss of privacy, loss of time, and inconvenience. A study could potentially uncover illegal behavior.

Other risks, alluded to in the illustrative cases, include undermining confidence in public institutions and lessening interpersonal trust.

As part of informing a subject, he must be told what risks may occur during the study or as a result of the study. If the risks are unknown, or if researchers disagree on the risks, this information must be communicated to the subject. Terminally ill patients may agree to participate in a study that promises to lead to a future cure. Nevertheless, a researcher must inform potential subjects only of benefits that can be reasonably expected. Theoretically, a study may be groundbreaking; however, most studies are not. Consequently, a subject should not be told that a study has a probability of generating significant knowledge. Nor should potential subjects be led to believe that they will gain benefits that are possible but unlikely.

Although not usually covered in informed consent, administrators may wish to consider that risks and benefits may apply beyond individuals. For example, families may be affected by the time a family member spends participating in a study, his reactions after sharing information, or the outcome of study intended to increase skills. The jury study example suggested a project that would neither harm nor benefit its participants, but which could have had a serious negative effect on an important social institution.

Selection of Subjects

Selection of research subjects should be unbiased and take into account who will benefit from the study. Examples such as the Tuskegee study and the Jewish Chronic Disease Hospital raised questions about studying vulnerable populations. Subsequently researchers and IRBs are expected to be especially diligent in reviewing work that relied on subjects from vulnerable populations and to make sure that appropriate measures are taken to solicit informed consent. The perspective on selection of subjects has shifted from exclusion to inclusion. Excluding certain groups from studies is also viewed as ethically questionable, because the group excluded does not benefit from the research. For example, prior to the 1990s women were routinely excluded from clinical trials. Much more was known about men's health and how males reacted to various therapies than was known about women's health.[18] A major consequence was that women and men with heart disease were treated the same. Subsequent research has found gender differences in women's symptoms, response to treatment, and outcomes.[19]

Recruiting subjects is the first step in ensuring informed consent. Announcements should state that participants are sought for a research project. They should avoid terms that oversell potential benefits or emphasize inducements for participating. The words appearing on flyers, media advertisements, Internet sites, and letters to potential subjects may act as a questionable inducement. Consider the attractiveness of being asked to test out a "new" or "exciting" treatment, to participate in a "free" program, or to receive "$1,000 for a weekend stay in our research facility." If participants are recruited through personal contact, the investigator must be particularly sensitive to not pressuring participation.[20]

The recruitment process may also raise privacy concerns. Later in this chapter we write about privacy in the context of confidentiality, i.e., the ability to control disclosure and dissemination of information about oneself. Another dimension of privacy is physical privacy, that is not having to endure unwanted intrusions.[21] Ethical concerns about intrusion vary. If a person is likely to wonder, "How did they get my name?" there may be an ethical problem. For example, before contacting recipients of social services to evaluate a program, someone in the agency who is familiar with the clients should ask their permission to be contacted. Along the same lines, agency clients should be assured that whether they choose to participate or not will not affect services they normally receive.

The key principle in the ethical selection of a study population is distributive justice: equitably distributing research benefits and risks, treating like situations the same way, and offering equal access to participate in research.[22] Currently, the ethical debate on subject selection is confined to biomedical research where both the individual risks and benefits can be quite high. Because each population is different, a general rule will not cover different racial and ethnic groups, institutionalized people, and international studies. Rather, researchers should be aware of why they are studying a particular group and the ethical dimensions of their choice.

Selection of individual subjects should be fair. For example, in medical experiments people assigned to a placebo group may feel cheated and lobby to receive the experimental treatment. Placing a favored subject in a more beneficial treatment group or placing a disliked subject in a more risky treatment group is unethical. Note that good research practice coincides with ethical practice.

Sample size is not included as a component of informed consent nor is it discussed in behavioral and social science texts on research ethics. Still, the number of desired subjects may affect how vigorously subjects are recruited and open the door for subtle coercion. The American Statistical Association includes sample size in its ethical guidelines. Its guidelines state that statisticians making informed recommendations should avoid allowing an excessive number of subjects or an inadequate sample.[23] An inadequate sample can affect the quality of the statistical analysis, e.g., decisions about whether findings occurred by chance. Conversely, an overly large sample may squander resources, including participants' time, and should not be gathered just to alleviate distributive justice concerns.

PROTECTING PRIVACY AND CONFIDENTIALITY

Understanding the terms *privacy, confidentiality, anonymity*, and *research records* provides a basis for ethical research practice.[24] As we noted earlier, *privacy* refers to an individual's ability to control the access of other people to information about himself. *Confidentiality* refers to protection of information, so that researchers cannot or will not disclose records with individual identifiers.

Anonymity refers to collecting information so that researchers cannot link any piece of data to a specific, named individual. *Research records* refers to records gathered and maintained for the purpose of describing or making generalizations about groups of persons. Unlike administrative or clinical records, research records are not meant to make judgments about an individual or to support decisions that directly and personally affect an individual.

The requirements of voluntary participation and informed consent uphold the individual's right to have control over information about himself. While a researcher may promise anonymity or confidentiality, a potential subject may not necessarily trust her to follow through. Guarantees of confidentiality neither ensure candor nor increase propensity to participate in research; rather, limited research has found that respondents tend to view promises of confidentiality skeptically.[25] Nevertheless, researchers must respect participants' privacy and maintain confidences as part of their professional responsibilities to subjects.

Some research questions may seem unduly intrusive. Questions may stir up unpleasant recollections or painful feelings. Such topics include research on sexual behaviors, victimization, or discrimination. People who read pornography, have poor reasoning skills, or harbor controversial opinions may prefer to keep this information to themselves. Disclosure of behaviors such as drug use, child abuse, or criminal activity may cause a respondent to fear that she will be "found out." For a study of a sensitive topic to be ethical, (1) the psychological and social risks must have been identified, (2) the benefits of answering the research question must offset the potential risks, (3) the prospective subjects must be informed of the risks, and (4) promises of confidentiality must be maintained.[26]

To avoid the problems associated with confidentiality, the researcher may gather anonymous information. Anonymous participation occurs if no records are kept on the identity of subjects, and data cannot be traced back to a specific individual. If researchers are conducting a study for an agency, an approach that approximates anonymity is for the agency to collect information and delete any information that directly identifies the respondents. This approach may be taken if revealing a client's identity to outsiders compromises the client's privacy. An agency may select the sample, distribute questionnaires, or collect data from agency files. Alternatively, an agency may ask clients' permission to give their names to the researchers.

Often anonymity is impossible. Researchers must know and record subject names to follow up on nonrespondents or to compare respondents and nonrespondents; to combine information from a subject with information from agency records; to carry out panel studies and collect information from an individual at different points in time; or to conduct a study audit to verify that the research was done and that accurate information was collected and reported. Auditors may need access to identifiable records. Auditing can present problems of confidentiality, but without the possibility of conducting an audit, incompetence or malfeasance may go undetected and potentially cause even greater harm.

Exactly how much care to take in protecting the identity of respondents varies from topic to topic. Some topics and some information require stringent safeguards. For the most part, social science researchers record individual information only to keep track of respondents and their data. They should take adequate safeguards to prevent disclosing identifiable information about an individual. Normally, at a minimum disclosure may be disquieting. Removing identifying information from the data and strictly limiting access to lists with subject names are sufficient for studies requiring stringent safeguards to protect confidentiality.

Confidentiality may be breeched by carelessness, legal demands, or statistical disclosure. To avoid accidental disclosure of personal information a researcher should separate identifying information from an individual's data. A code can be assigned to each record and a list of names and matching codes kept separately in a secure place. Lists with names of subjects may be kept separate from information collected on them. For longitudinal studies or other studies that combine information from more than one source, each person may be assigned an alias so that the information can be combined. A respondent may choose her own alias, that is, information that others could not easily obtain, such as her mother's birth date. The success of having respondents choose their alias depends on their ability to remember it each time they are asked. The list of names and aliases should be kept separately from the collected data. Theoretically, researchers can have their records subpoenaed. Federal policies offer some protections to participants and researchers. The Confidential Information Protection and Statistical Efficiency Act (CIPSEA), passed in 2002, requires that federal statistical agencies inform respondents and get their informed consent if the information is to be used for nonstatistical purposes.[27] Certificates of confidentiality by and large protect researchers investigating sensitive subjects, e.g., mental illness or drug abuse, from having to provide identifying information. The U.S. Department of Health and Human Services offers certificates to researchers whose subjects might be harmed if they were identified. The Department of Justice offers certificates to researchers conducting criminal justice research. A certificate cannot be obtained after data collection is completed.[28]

When reporting data, one should be sensitive to inadvertent disclosures. For example, if a state has very few female city managers, tables distinguishing between the responses of male and female city managers may compromise the confidentiality of the female managers. Similarly, case studies may require more elaborate procedures to protect identities, including pseudonyms, and alteration of some personal information, such as occupation.

Sharing research records constitutes special problems for confidentiality. As we discuss in the following chapter, data sharing and secondary analysis may reduce research costs and increase research quality. Nevertheless, once records leave the control of the researcher, issues of informed consent and confidentiality become a particular concern. In regard to informed consent, the subject may have agreed to participate in research for a specific purpose without giving blanket authorization for other uses. Researchers should inform potential subjects of anticipated future uses of the data, including their availability for independent verification of the study's implementation and replication of its analysis.[29] Before releasing data, the researcher should remove identifiers such as names, addresses, and telephone numbers.

A more formidable problem is that of *deductive disclosure.* If the names of participants in a research project are known, someone may be able to sort through the data to identify a specific person. Imagine a study of employee satisfaction in a state agency. With a list of respondents, someone may sort the data by age, race, sex, and position and deduce a respondent's identity. One way to protect against such abuses is to not disclose the list of respondents.[30] Deductive disclosure is a concern with publicly available electronic databases. For example, if Census data were released as reported, one could learn detailed information about the three Hispanic families in a county or a state's six female-owned utilities companies. To prevent such abuses the Census bureau has developed procedures to release as much information as possible without violating respondents' privacy. One procedure is to suppress the data if the number of cases falls below a minimum threshold.[31] As is true with many of the Census Bureau's statistical practices, these procedures can serve as a model for other researchers.

An emerging concern is Internet research. Research might be done on web sites and their content, on communications on electronic bulletin boards, on listservs, in chat rooms, and in similar venues. There are disagreements about what online communications should be considered public as opposed to private and how researchers should treat the information. In the absence of specific requirements, common sense should lead to ethical decisions. Information found on a web site may be treated the same as other textual material, and one would not normally seek informed consent or be concerned about privacy. On the other hand, participants on a listserv may not expect to read their comments in a research article. Although it may be naïve to assume that any communications sent out into cyberspace are private, we cannot agree that one should forgo obtaining informed consent. The challenge in obtaining consent may be in locating current e-mail addresses and obtaining consent to use information from an individual's postings.

FEDERAL POLICY ON PROTECTION OF HUMAN SUBJECTS AND INSTITUTIONAL REVIEW BOARDS

In 1991 a uniform federal policy, the Common Rule for the protection of human subjects, was published.[32] Its hallmark was a requirement that every institution receiving federal money for research involving human subjects create an *Institutional Review Board (IRB)* and appoint its members. The IRB determines if a proposed project meets the following requirements: (1) risks to subjects are minimized, (2) risks are reasonable in relation to anticipated benefits, (3) selection of subjects is equitable, (4) informed consent will be sought and appropriately documented, (5) appropriate data will be monitored to ensure the safety of subjects, and (6) adequate provisions exist for ensuring privacy of subjects and confidentiality of data.[33] Two of these criteria merit further mention. First, the long-range effects of the knowledge gained from the research are explicitly excluded in determining the risks and benefits of participation. Second, the policy reflects concern with possible abuses of vulnerable populations. IRBs are reminded to consider whether research on a specific population is consistent with an equitable selection of subjects and to make sure that these populations' vulnerability "to coercion or undue influence" has not been exploited.

To perform these tasks, an IRB as a whole should be professionally competent to adequately review the proposals it commonly receives and sensitive to general ethical issues, especially issues affecting "vulnerable" populations, for example, prisoners, children, pregnant women, people with mental or physical disabilities, and otherwise disadvantaged people. An institution should consider each appointee's training, race, gender, cultural background, and sensitivity to community attitudes.

Failure to comply with the Common Rule can result in termination or suspension of federal support, which is a powerful incentive to ensure that the IRBs are created and follow through on their responsibilities.

An IRB reviews all research involving human subjects under the purview of the institution. To review only publicly or privately supported research implies that only funded projects have to conform to ethical practices. To understand what an IRB does requires knowledge of what constitutes research and what constitutes a human subject.

> Covered research is "a systematic investigation, including research development, testing and evaluation, designed to develop or contribute to generalizable knowledge."[34]

> A *human subject* is a "living individual about whom an investigator (whether professional or student) conducting research obtains (a) data through intervention or interaction with the individual, or (b) identifiable private information."[35]

The IRB chair or the chair's designee first determines if a project is exempt from further review, appropriate for an expedited review, or must be subject to full review. Exempt and expedited projects receive less close scrutiny. These categories allow research involving minimal risk to avoid the long delays associated with a full IRB review. Minimal risk applies to those projects where the risks of participating in the research are similar to the risks of daily life.

The Common Rule exempts demonstration projects that study or evaluate public benefit or service programs, procedures for obtaining benefits or services under these programs, changes in or alternatives to the programs or procedures, and changes in the level or method of payment.[36] The U.S. Department of Health and Human Services wanted demonstration projects exempt because needed studies could not be conducted if subjects could withdraw at any time or if they could receive entitled benefits if they refused to participate. A 1972 study required an experimental group of employable welfare recipients to accept public-sector employment; if they refused to work, their benefits were discontinued. Clearly, such a study would have problems with internal validity if subjects could change their experimental-group status at will. The study ended up in federal court, which ruled that the experiment was acceptable because it was consistent with the Social Security Act's objective to remove people from the welfare rolls and move them into gainful employment.[37]

The Common Rule implicitly allows IRBs to waive written documentation of informed consent for surveys and observation of public behaviors. Waivers are not permitted if responses could be traced to a specific individual and if disclosure could result in civil or criminal liability or damage subjects' financial standing, employability, or reputation.

The federal regulations are more detailed than we have presented here. Furthermore, practices are still evolving and the regulations receive frequent scrutiny.[38] The 1999 death of an 18-year-old participant in a federally funded gene therapy study led to an examination of the IRB system. He suffered from a disorder that was controlled by diet and drugs; he was not terminally ill. One of the immediate reactions was to pay more attention to informed consent forms, and to stress that having people sign informed consent forms was not sufficient evidence that they understood the information, especially the risks.

Federal agencies, advisory commissions, and research organizations have drafted and reviewed policies, which may culminate in "a unified, comprehensive federal policy embodied in a single set of regulations and guidance . . . that would apply to all types of research involving human participation." The policies have been drafted by persons in the fields of bio-ethics and biomedical research. Nevertheless, these proposed policies will affect social science research, and social science organizations are monitoring and evaluating them.

To what extent do you have to concern yourself with IRB review? Federal policies protecting human subjects require compliance by federal agencies, institutions, and individual researchers. If you are a student or an employee of a university, a medical facility, or other institution that receives federal research funds, you should consult with your IRB before proceeding to conduct research that has you interacting with people, manipulating them, or using identifiable private information. Public administration students and professionals are most likely to conduct "research on individual or group characteristics or behavior . . . or research employing survey, interview, oral history, focus group, program evaluation, human factors evaluation or quality assurance."[39] All of these may be eligible for an expedited review.

BEYOND INFORMED CONSENT AND CONFIDENTIALITY: ISSUES OF INTEREST TO ADMINISTRATORS

As an administrator, you may not work in settings that have an IRB. Nevertheless, you should adhere to standard practices as presented in the Belmont Report, discussed earlier in this chapter. Recall that these are respect for persons, beneficence and justice or getting informed consent, having a favorable cost-benefit ratio, and fair subject selection. Even if you never conduct your own research on human subjects, you may be approached by researchers who want to study your clients or employees. Administrators who work in educational, penal, or health care institutions are especially likely to be approached by researchers. In considering the ethical aspects of research, the administrator's major interest is to make sure that the researcher implements standard procedures to reduce risks.

First, an administrator should get an overall picture of the planned study. Why does the researcher want to study her agency's clients or employees? How will the research subjects be chosen? Will they be anonymous or confidential? What steps will be taken to protect their identities? What will they be asked to do? How much time will it take? What are other potential risks? She will want to make sure that selection of research subjects or assignment into different experimental groups is fair and will be seen as equitable to both participants and nonparticipants.[40] To protect the identity and privacy of clients and employees, an agency representative should contact the affected people, explain the nature of the research, and seek their permission to give their names to the researchers. The researchers should not initiate contact with clients, and the agency representative should take care in using noncoercive language in approaching potential subjects. Public announcements, such as posters, may be used to recruit employees or clients. Voluntary participation is less likely to be compromised with posted announcements than by personal solicitation.[41]

Second, the administrator should make certain that contacted clients understand that their eligibility for agency programs or services will not be affected by a decision to participate. Research with employees may be problematic. For employee participation to be voluntary, whether or not employees decide to participate should not affect performance ratings or pay decisions, and this should be clearly communicated to them.[42]

Third, the administrator should review the informed consent procedures. If subjects will be at risk, the administrator should remember that signing an informed consent form is not sufficient evidence that the subjects understood what was asked of them and the risks involved. The administrator may want to learn whether the researcher has submitted the research for review to an IRB. The administrator may want to learn who reviewed the proposal to ensure that the researchers are not blinded by their hopes for the research. Input from representatives of the participant community is especially valuable in identifying potential concerns. For example, prisoners, ex-convicts, and prison guards might review proposals involving prisoners.

The administrator may want to engage the researcher in a discussion of potential risks. This lets the administrator decide whether the researcher has considered the ethical implications of the research. The administrator may learn more about research risks and improve his or her ability to judge the risks involved in later projects that come to the agency. Similarly, the administrator should check to see that subjects will be debriefed, if appropriate, at the end of their participation. For example, subjects who perform some task may be disappointed or frustrated about their performance. A debriefing offers the researcher an opportunity to observe any negative effects of the research and to answer questions or concerns that a subject may have.

Fourth, if the study involves creating a program, the administrator may want to find out what the researcher plans to do when the research is finished. In prisons or psychiatric hospitals, the subjects may participate in a research project, such as a therapy group, that seems to end prematurely because the researcher's data collection has ended. Employees or students may participate in an experimental course only to find that their new skills are not wanted by their employer or do not fit into their school's curriculum.

A sticky issue is what will become of the findings. Does the researcher plan to put the data into an archive? If so, the subjects should be told where the data will be stored and how individual identities will be protected. If the agency expects to receive the research data, it should work out the details beforehand. This must be done if the researcher is going to act ethically and inform subjects of what will become of the information. If the agency, whether it employs the subjects or provides them with benefits, is going to get individual information, then the subjects must be told this as part of giving their informed consent. What information will the subjects or the agency receive? Will they receive the final report? What about interim reports? What will be done with the completed questionnaires, recordings, or other research documents?[43]

Fifth, the administrator should consider how the proposed research may affect the agency's reputation. No matter what the agency's role, its reputation may be enhanced by research that others consider valuable and harmed by research that they consider worthless or intrusive. An administrator may question whether a planned study will unduly infringe on respondents' privacy or abuse their time. He should decide if a study requiring agency resources, including time, represents a good use of the public's money. He should be convinced that a study will yield valued information. Unreliable items and items that serve no clear purpose cannot yield valued information. Studies that assume others will act on the findings should be reviewed by relevant actors, or at least the investigators should try to anticipate their reactions realistically. Unreliable items, unwanted items, or unwanted studies waste respondents' time. Items not operationally valid may abuse respondents' goodwill, insofar as their responses contribute to incorrect or misleading conclusions. To ensure that a proposed study provides usable and useful information, administrators should review research instruments, and make sure that the researchers pilot tested all instruments, establishing their reliability and operational validity.

The detrimental effects of an unwanted or poorly designed study go beyond the respondents. Future studies also are affected. Seeking too much information or seeking it too often can build resistance to future requests for information. Consider the complaints of businesses and state and local governments that must churn out data only to meet federal information requests. A similar outcome may occur if respondents perceive that the data are merely collected but not used.

SUMMARY

Whether they are conducting research or permitting researchers to gather data on their organization, employees, or clients, administrators must make sure that all research participants are treated ethically. They should adhere to the dictates of the Belmont Report and ensure that all participants are treated with respect, beneficence, and justice.

Obtaining informed consent is central to most research on humans. Informed consent means that a subject agrees to participate after receiving information on the purpose of the study, the potential risks associated with participating, and the probable benefits associated with participating. The information should be clear; the investigators should not oversell the benefits of participating nor discount social or psychological discomfort. Subjects must be told what will be done to them and what will be expected of them. Although informed consent may need to be documented, this should not take precedence over making sure that subjects understand what is being asked of them.

Selection of research subjects should be unbiased and take into account who will benefit from the study. The participation of subjects must be voluntary. Participants may receive incentives, but they should not be so large or attractive that they act as an "undue inducement." Researchers who maintain a professional or personal relationship with potential subjects must be aware that the relationship may make a request to participate in research exploitative and preclude the possibility of voluntary participation. Potential subjects must be told that their eligibility for benefits, other than benefits associated directly with participation, does not depend on participation. Similarly, their continued eligibility for benefits cannot be affected if they decide to withdraw from a study. As part of the informed consent process, the potential subject must be informed that he or she can withdraw from the research at any time.

Potential subjects should be told what will be done with the information after the study is completed. The research records should not be made available to others, including a subject's parents, physician, or employer, without the subject's explicit permission. This prohibition does not preclude allowing authorized auditors to examine records to verify the integrity of the research; however, the procedures for an audit must take proper precautions to maintain confidentiality, and disclosure to auditors should be part of the informed consent. If data are to be sent to a databank, the researcher should remove identifying information and take precautions to prevent deductive disclosure of a person's identity.

Agencies that receive federal money for research involving human subjects must have an Institutional Review Board (IRB), which reviews and approves all research involving human subjects. The IRB may expedite review of research involving minimal risk to subjects and waive certain aspects of informed consent for research involving surveys, observations of human behavior, and social experiments sponsored by a government agency or government officials. Whether IRB approval is required or not, researchers and project sponsors should satisfy themselves that a study adequately protects human research subjects.

The administrator who agrees to have research conducted with an agency's cooperation should interview the researcher and ascertain that the researcher will employ standard ethical practices and use appropriate procedures to get informed consent. Procedures for selecting subjects and assigning them to experimental groups must be perceived as fair by both participants and nonparticipants. Care must be taken that clients recognize that participation will not affect services they receive from the agency, and employees must know that their participation does not affect their working conditions. The administrator will want to learn, as appropriate, whether subjects will be debriefed and how research programs, such as therapy groups, will be terminated. If the agency expects to have access to the research data, this must be worked out beforehand and included in the information given to obtain a potential subject's informed consent.

Chapter 9 discusses the use of data that have been gathered earlier and stored. Acquisition of preexisting, or secondary, data eliminates the time and cost required to design and implement a data collection instrument. Use of existing data also decreases the burdens placed on the people and agencies that are queried for information. The chapter covers how investigators may locate secondary data; what information is required to acquire, verify, and document them; and the content of some major studies conducted by the Bureau of the Census. While secondary data have distinct benefits, they may be inadequate or inappropriate for the planned study. Furthermore, as this chapter has indicated, ethical considerations may rule out the use of existing data.

NOTES

1. L. K. Altman, "Volunteer in Asthma Study Dies After Inhaling Drug," *New York Times,* June 15, 2001.

2. K. Sucato, "Education; Student Survey's Unexpected Lessons," *New York Times,* February 5, 2001.

3. N. Hershey and R. D. Miller, *Human Experimentation and the Law* (Germantown, ND: Aspen Systems Corporation, 1976), 8–10, summarizes the bureaucratic history of the Tuskegee study. Hershey and Miller made the observation that the Tuskegee study continued during this period when protection of human subjects was receiving so much attention.

4. An Internet search should locate a text of the Nuremberg Code. The code is included in many research ethics texts, including R. Amdur and E. Bankert, *Institutional Review Board Management and Function* (Sudbury, MA: Jones and Bartlett Publishers, 2002).

5. Jay Katz, *Experimentation with Human Beings* (New York: Russell Sage Foundation, 1972), 10–65, reproduced a slightly edited version of the record from the investigation. Hershey and Miller, *Human Experimentation,* on 6–7, summarize the issues.

6. Richard Friedman, "Cases: Long-Term Questions Linger in Halted Breast Cancer Trial," *New York Times,* October 21, 2003.

7. J. H. Jones, *Bad Blood: The Tuskegee Syphilis Experiment* (New York: Free Press, 1993), 221. Other research on patient trust and willingness to participate in research can be found at http://www.phrusa.org/research/domestic/race/race_report/subsections/20_pttrust/chart.html

8. Katz, *Experimentation,* 68–103, reproduced material from the hearings. The subcommittee chairman was Senator James O. Eastland. His quote is found on page 80 of Katz's book.

9. This summary of the critics' points of view is based on information from T. L. Beauchamp, et al., *Ethical Issues in Social Research* (Baltimore: Johns Hopkins University Press, 1982), 11–15. Edited versions of key criticisms also are found in Katz, *Experimentation,* 325–329.

10. Katz, *Experimentation,* 358–365, reprints Milgram's description of the study; on pages 403–405 Katz has reprinted some of the reactions to the Milgram study.

11. *The Belmont Report: Ethical Principles and Guidelines for the Protection of Human Subjects of Research* (Washington, DC: The National Commission for the Protection of Human Subjects of Biomedical and Behavioral Research, April 1976), 4–6.

12. Standard 6.15 in *Ethical Principles of Psychologists and Code of Conduct* (Washington, DC: American Psychological Association, 2002) covers the use of deceptive research. Two articles in Donald N. Bersoff, *Ethical Conflicts in Psychology,* 3d ed. (Washington, DC: American Psychological Association, 2003) are recommended: J. E. Sieber, et al., "Deception Methods in Psychology: Have They Changed in 23 Years?" 406–407, and D. J. Pittenger, "Deception in Research: Distinctions and Solutions from the Perspective of Utilitarianism," 408–415. The Siebert et al. article evaluates the potential ethical objections to seven strategies for obtaining informed consent.

13. This suggestion is made by Hershey and Miller, *Human Experimentation,* 33.

14. E. D. Prentice et al., "Research Involving Prisoners," in Amdur et al., *Institutional Review Board,* pp. 394–398.

15. L. K. Altman, "Fatal Drug Trial Raises Questions about 'Informed' Consent," *New York Times,* October 5, 1993, B7.

16. R. M. Groves, et. al., *Survey Methodology,* (Hoboken, NJ: John Wiley, 2004), 352–355; a summary of research on informed consent is found on pp. 364–366. See also J. M. Oakes, "Survey Research," in Amdur and Bankert, 430.

17. See B. G. Gordon et al., "Paying Research Subjects," in Amdur and Bankert, 183–190. This article covers the arguments for and against reimbursing subjects and models for reimbursing subjects.

18. N. Kass, "Gender and Research," in J. P. Kahn, A. C. Mastroianni, and J. Sugarman, eds., *Beyond Consent: Seeking Justice in Research* (New York: Oxford University Press, 1998), 67–87.

19. See http://www.ahrq.gov/research/womheart.htm (accessed July 22, 2006).

20. For further discussion of ethics and recruitment procedures, see the following articles in R. J. Amdur and E. A. Bankert, *Institutional Review Board.* F. A. Khin-Maung-Gyi and M. D. Whalen, "Recruitment of Research Subjects," 176–179; R. Homer, R. Krebs, and L. Medwar, "Advertisements for Research," 180–184.

21. For further discussion including references, see H. Cho and R. LaRose, "Privacy Issues in Internet Surveys," D. de Vaus, ed., *Social Surveys,* vol. II (Thousand Oaks, CA: Sage, 2002), 206–222. J. M. Oakes, "Survey Research," p. 430, also discusses privacy and recruitment.

22. C. R. McCarthy, "The Evolving Story of Justice in Federal Research Policy," in J. P. Kahn, A. C. Mastroianni, and J. Sugarman, eds., *Beyond Consent: Seeking Justice in Research* (New York: Oxford University Press, 1998), 11.

23. American Statistical Association, "Ethical Guidelines for Statistical Practice" (1999). The guidelines are available on the association's web site (www.amerstat.org/profession/ethicalstatistics.html).

24. R. F. Boruch and J. S. Cecil, *Assuring the Confidentiality of Social Research Data* (Philadelphia: University of Pennsylvania Press, 1979), 23–27.

25. A. G. Turner, "What Subjects of Survey Research Believe about Confidentiality," in *The Ethics of Social Research: Surveys and Experiments,* ed. J. E. Sieber (New York: Springer-Verlag, 1982), 151–165. For a summary of more recent research on the public's attitude about the confidentiality of data, see *Expanding Access to Research Data: Reconciling Risks and Opportunities* (Washington, DC: National Academies Press, 2005), 52–54.

26. For an extensive discussion of procedures to protect privacy, applicable federal laws, and an extensive bibliography, see *Protecting Human Research Subjects,* 3-27–3-37, 3-56. Readers interested in strategies for identifying and questioning subjects about sensitive topics may wish to read the cases in C. M. Renzetti

and R. M. Lee, eds., *Researching Sensitive Topics* (Newbury Park: Sage Publications, 1992).

27. For a brief, but fuller, discussion of Federal legal protections, see *Expanding Access to Research Data,* 56–59. The report also considers threats to confidentiality associated with national security concerns.

28. Ibid., 56.

29. T. E. Hedrick, "Justifications and Obstacles to Data Sharing," in *Sharing Research Data,* eds. S. E. Fienberg, M. E. Martin, and M. L. Straf (Washington, DC: National Academy Press, 1985), 136. Hedrick cites sources that discuss this issue in more depth. See also the *Ethical Guidelines in Statistical Practice,* D4, (Alaxandria, VA: American Statistical Association, 1989).

30. For strategies to prevent deductive disclosure, see J. Steinberg, "Social Research Use of Archival Records: Procedural Solutions to Privacy Problems," in *Solutions to Ethical and Legal Problems in Social Research,* eds. R. F. Boruch and J. S. Cecil (New York: Academic Press, 1983), 249–261: and Boruch and Cecil, *Assuring the Confidentiality of Social Research Data,* chap. 7.

31. For information on specific strategies and when they are applied, see http://factfinder.census.gov/jsp/saff/SAFFInfo.jsp?_pageId=su5_confidentiality

32. U.S. Science and Technology Policy Office, "45 Code of Federal Regulations 46 (45 CFR 46) Federal Policy for the Protection of Human Subjects: Notices and Rules," *Federal Register* 56. (June 18, 1991): 28002–28018.

33. 45 CFR 46 Section 46.111.

34. 45 CFR 46 Section 46.102(d).

35. 46 CFR 46 Section 46.102(f).

36. 45 CFR 46 Section 46.110.

37. Breger, "Randomized Social Experiments and the Law," 104–105, citing material from *Aguayo* v. *Richardson,* 352 F. Supp. 462 (S.D.N.Y. 1972).

38. An excellent source of current activity is the Office of Human Research Protections web page (http://www.hhs.gov/ohrp/). For social science concerns, see "Protecting Participants in Social, Behavioral, and Economic Science Research: Issues, Current Problems, and Potential Solutions," *Responsible Research: A Systems Approach to Protecting Research Participants* (Washington, DC: National Academies Press, 2003), Appendix B.

39. "Categories of Research that May be Reviewed by the Institutional Review Board (IRB) through an Expedited Review Procedure" (Washington, DC: Office of Human Research Protection), November 1998, 63 FR 60364-60367.

40. For a more detailed discussion on recruiting volunteers, employees, and vulnerable populations, see

Protecting Human Subjects, chap. 6, and A. J. Kimmel, *Ethical Issues in Behavioral Research* (Cambridge, MA: Blackwell Publishers, 1996), 215–235.

41. *Protecting Human Subjects,* 6–53.

42. Ibid, 6–55.

43. Paul Oliver, *The Student's Guide to Research Ethics* (Philadelphia: Open University Press, 2003), chapt. 4 has a useful discussion related to these concerns.

TERMS FOR REVIEW

subjects at risk	privacy	research records
informed consent	confidentiality	Institutional Review Board
voluntary research participation	anonymity deductive disclosure	human subject

QUESTIONS FOR REVIEW

The following questions should indicate whether you have a basic competency in this chapter's material.

1. What four main pieces of information must a potential research subject have to give informed consent? Explain why each is needed.

2. How are informed consent and voluntary participation related?

3. To learn if traumatic events are associated with drug abuse, researchers propose to interview drug abusers about their childhood and adolescence. The researchers know that the interviews may be painful and cause participants emotional distress. What should an IRB consider before allowing the research to be conducted?

4. What types of benefits should a potential participant be told about? How expansive should an investigator be when informing potential participants about the benefits of participation?

5. What types of risks should a potential participant be told about? How expansive should an investigator be in informing potential participants about the risks of participation?

6. Why is debriefing subjects important? What is the role of debriefing in lessening the risks to the subject? In teaching the researcher more about the risks of participation?

7. Explain why the following may be considered inappropriate:
   a. A principal asking teachers in her school to participate in a study she is doing for a graduate class.
   b. Giving each return envelope in an "anonymous" survey a different box number so that each participant can be identified.
   c. Explaining in English the planned research to potential participants who recently immigrated from Asia.
   d. A social agency turning over a list of clients to researchers who are studying how clients view agency services.
   e. Conducting research on developmentally disabled adults based on the consent of their guardians and not the subjects.

8. Explain the difference between collecting confidential and anonymous information. Under what circumstances will a researcher prefer confidential information? Under what circumstances will a researcher prefer anonymous information?

PROBLEMS FOR HOMEWORK AND DISCUSSION

1. Imagine you head a large agency, such as a school district. Outline a protocol for approving research involving agency employees and/or clients.

2. How does a researcher identify the risks associated with his or her studies?

3. A researcher proposes testing an accelerated math program on talented third graders in

a school system. The program will last for one year, although data collection on participants may continue through elementary school. What risks do you foresee for children who participate in the program?

4. A young researcher contends that never putting subjects at risk is the only ethical way to conduct research. Comment on this position.

5. The American Statistical Association ethical guidelines imply that having too many subjects or too few are ethical concerns. Why do you think that this is so?

6. Does your college or university have an IRB? Who is on it? Obtain a copy of its policies for human subjects research. How is survey research handled? How is research involving agencies (such as program evaluations) handled?

7. Find a consent form and identify the components critical to giving informed consent.

Are any pieces of critical information missing?

8. A researcher is studying the effectiveness of educational programs offered to prisoners. In his interviews with prisoners, he learns that several of them smuggle drugs. Should he inform the prison authorities? Why or why not?

9. A researcher conducts genetic tests on subjects. One genetic test shows that Mary Doe carries the gene for Huntington's disease. What should the researcher tell Mary Doe?

10. Investigators are conducting a 24-month demonstration project to study the effectiveness of a job-training project. The investigators propose to randomly assign persons eligible for job training to either an experimental or control group. Control group members will neither receive training nor will project staff inform them of other training opportunities. Comment on the ethics of this proposal.

RECOMMENDED FOR FURTHER READING

Paul Oliver, *The Students' Guide to Research Ethics* (Philadelphia: Open University Press, 2003), is a good introduction to ethical concerns.

For up-to-date information on federal policies affecting human subject research, the Office of Human Subjects Research, National Institutes of Health home page is recommended (http://ohsr.od.nih.gov). The section on "Regulations and Ethical Guidelines" contains copies of regulations and other documents. *Responsible Research: A Systems Approach to Protecting Research Participants* (Washington, DC: National Academies Press, 2003) evaluates the current federal framework for protecting human subjects and makes recommendations for reform.

A valuable resource is R. Amdur and E. Bankert, *Institutional Review Board: Management and Function* (Sudbury, MA: Jones and Bartlett, 2002). It includes copies of major policies and short presentations on the IRB process, components of informed consent, vulnerable populations, and issues associated with various research approaches.

As this chapter was being revised, a study recommending changes in research involving prisoners was released. It provides an excellent review of the Belmont principles,

concerns with confidentiality and privacy, and the application of federal policy. L. O. Gosten, C. Vanchicri, and A. Pope, eds., *Ethical Considerations for Research Involving Prisoners* (Washington, DC: National Academies Press, 2006).

Celia B. Fisher, *Decoding the Ethics Code: A Practical Guide for Psychologists* (Thousand Oaks, CA: Sage Publications, 2003) covers both research ethics and other ethical concerns of non–research psychologists. Other professional associations including those of historians, anthropologists, statisticians, sociologists, and program evaluators have ethical guidelines (available on their professional societies home pages), which are worth consulting to get a better understanding of the ethical issues.

Expanding Access to Research Data: Reconciling Risks and Opportunities (Washington, DC: National Academies Press, 2005) focuses on competing demands for data access to microdata and maintaining confidentiality.

R. F. Boruch and J. S. Cecil, *Assuring the Confidentiality of Social Research Data* (Philadelphia: The University of Pennsylvania Press, 1979), covers issues associated with confidentiality, strategies for maintaining confidentiality, and legal issues.

Secondary Data Analysis: Finding and Analyzing Existing Data

In this chapter you will learn

1. Advantages and disadvantages of secondary data analysis.
2. Strategies for identifying, accessing, and evaluating the quality of secondary data.
3. The general content of major U.S. Census Bureau population surveys and vital records.
4. About using census data.

In our eagerness to get a study under way, we may overlook the possibility that appropriate data may already be available. Similarly, we may avoid examining problems with data needs that exceed our data-gathering capacity. Secondary data can provide inexpensive, high-quality data adequate to define or solve a problem.

Secondary data are existing data that investigators collected for a purpose other than the given research study. Secondary data may result from the research efforts of an individual researcher, a research team, an agency division, or a research organization. The data may have been collected for a specific study or as part of a database. The data may have been collected as part of a routine record keeping or to monitor agency performance. Investigators with differing backgrounds, needs, and questions regularly consult and use secondary data.

Typically, researchers collect more data than they analyze for the purpose at hand. They ask questions that turn out to be unreliable or not operationally valid. They find some data are helpful while others are not. In writing a questionnaire, the investigators may act as if information is free. They add questions with vague plans to analyze the responses later, but typically investigators run out of time and their interests shift.

Organizations collect and store data for many purposes. Managers consult data to monitor spending, personnel activity, resources acquired and spent, and productivity. Managers review specific pieces of data, such as performance indicators, at regular intervals as part of their management responsibilities. Managers depend on data to track the performance of agency subdivisions. They use existing data to estimate demand for services and the resources needed to meet the demand. No matter why data are collected and stored, they may be retrieved and combined to answer a range of questions beyond those originally asked.

Statistical organizations, including the U.S. Census Bureau, state offices of vital statistics, public opinion firms, and university research groups, such as the InterUniversity Consortium for Political and Social Research, based at the University of Michigan, exist to collect, compile, and interpret data. Professional associations, such as the International City/County Management Association (ICMA), and public interest groups routinely collect and publish survey data on topics of interest to their members. For example, each year ICMA publishes *The Municipal Year Book*. Investigators with differing backgrounds, needs, and questions consult and use such data regularly.

In this chapter we survey the benefits and costs of using secondary data and how to identify appropriate databases, gain access to them, and evaluate their quality and applicability to a study. Next, we introduce you to a few important data sources. The chapter gives an overview of the contents of the Census of Governments and two population surveys conducted by the U.S. Census Bureau.

WORKING WITH SECONDARY DATA

The Benefits and Costs of Secondary Data Analysis

Secondary data analysis markedly reduces a researcher's costs. She can dispense with the costs of instrument design, data collection, and compilation. It has other benefits as well. Secondary data analysis enables researchers to conduct studies that are otherwise unfeasible. It opens up research to public scrutiny, thereby allowing for verification, refinement, or refutation of the original results. It can improve research quality.

Secondary data analysis may be necessary if investigators want comparative or longitudinal data. Consider a study to analyze the feminization of poverty, that is, the perception that women and children make up a disproportionate segment of the poor. The investigators examined patterns of women's labor force participation, the availability of social welfare, and the diffusion of single-parent households in the United States and other industrialized nations.[1]

The investigators could not have conducted their study without government statistics. They would have had to dig through records, some in languages other than English, to compile the data. Searching records requires time and money; hiring translators adds even more expenses. One also must locate the appropriate records and get permission to review them. If records do not exist, a cross-sectional study might have been tried. Logistic requirements would have restricted the study population. Including time-series data seems out of the question.

Relying on government statistics has limitations. The researchers have to determine that the data are sufficiently reliable and comparable. The design may have to be modified if data for certain years or for some countries are missing or unattainable. Such modifications may introduce bias. For example, we assume that there is a difference between those countries that share their data and those that do not.

There is a dramatic difference in the ability of various countries to gather and disseminate data. One of the authors worked on a study of international income inequality. Wage data reported by some countries were more reliable than data on income. To increase the number of countries included in the study, the research team decided to use the wage data rather than income. Even by using the proxy measure of wages to expand the scope of the study, large areas of the world, such as the Middle East and most of Africa, were still missing data.

In a similar vein, different levels of government or organizations have much more data than other levels. More data are available on a national level than on the state level, and on the state level than on the local level. For example, comparing recent data between two states on the average manufacturing wages paid may be possible; comparing the same data between two cities in these same two states may be impossible. It would be a questionable assumption that the wages in the cities reflected the same relationship as between the states.

Secondary analysis is a necessary component for open science; it allows others to scrutinize a researcher's work. In the field of public policy, scrutiny can be especially important. Secondary analysis may be undertaken if the investigator's veracity is questioned; however, it is more likely to occur within the context of challenging and improving research that affects policy decisions. Some academic journals, notably in health fields, require public access to the data used in a study as a condition of publishing the results. For example, before it even reviews an article, the journal *Molecular Systems Biology* requires that all data be submitted to a public database. This is a common requirement for certain research studies published in prominent journals such as *Science* and *Nature*.

Analysts working with existing data may reexamine the findings by including supplemental data, adapting the measures, or applying new or different statistical models. Their efforts may confirm and extend the research findings. If their work contradicts the original research, their findings may contribute to greater insight into the complexity of the policy issue and its solution.

Ideally, secondary analysis should improve the quality of data collection and documentation. The researcher who knows that her work will be scrutinized may pay more attention to documenting the research process: the decisions that were made about which variables to include and how to measure them; the results of pretests; the sampling design and possible nonsampling errors; and the details of how data were compiled and analyzed. An investigator working with secondary data may have his mind jogged. He may think creatively about the research design and have insights on better ways to measure the concepts or to analyze the data. His experience is analogous to most researchers' reactions when they analyze their own data and find themselves rethinking the research design, including their model and how they measured the variables.

The ability of researchers to share data electronically has made outside scrutiny easier, with more cases of fraud being exposed as a result. Between 1995 and 2000, Karen Ruggiero of Harvard University became a national expert on the psychological effects of race and sex discrimination. Ruggiero was exposed as a fraud after she refused to share her raw data, which turned out to be made up. In 2006, for the first time in U.S. history, a university researcher was sentenced to prison for using false data to obtain federal research grants.[2]

While secondary data reduce the costs of the secondary analyst, they can increase the costs to the initial investigators.[3] They may incur costs in increased data preparation and documentation. In modest studies many of the details are carried in the investigator's memory. Modest studies have their place, but investigators conducting them should not absolve themselves of proper documentation and retention of research records. Later analysis of existing data can prevent needless requests for information from subjects or replication of earlier mistakes. One of the authors kept the original surveys from her master's thesis for 15 years. Two months after they were destroyed, another researcher requested the surveys in order to update the analysis.

M. H. Maier's book *The Data Game* demonstrates the use of secondary analysis to investigate policy questions and the value of scrutinizing reported findings. The book includes thumbnail sketches of policy controversies fueled by analysis of publicly available data; for example, "Does capital punishment deter murder?" "Are the rich getting richer?" "Is the workplace safe?" Maier concludes that the misuse of statistical data (for example, by treating a short-term change as a long-term trend) and different conceptual definitions of such phenomena as white-collar crime, illiteracy, and a nation's economic health contribute to policy debates.[4]

Finding Secondary Data

If you want to find out whether data exist to meet your needs, where do you begin? Technology is rapidly changing search techniques, and the number of databases available electronically is constantly expanding. Official statistics, national surveys, and other data can be accessed through the Internet. Internet search engines may help identify potential databases. Nevertheless, any given search engine may "miss" obvious web sites. A search engine can direct you to an out-of-date, biased, or poorly maintained database. As we write, no surefire, efficient method exists to locate needed data. For example, in an earlier edition, we spent several hours searching for smoking data for a homework problem in Chapter 2. Years later, it took only moments to locate the original data and update the problem. With changing technology, such as improvements in constructing and maintaining web pages, and variations in licensing agreements, a reference librarian may be the best source of suggestions on how to conduct an online search.

Published works should indicate where their data came from, alerting you to databases you may wish to examine. Some works cite privately held data, that is, data owned by the researcher or a private organization. You may infer that a database contains variables of interest from the description of its sample, purpose, general content, or from the identity of the agency sponsor(s). You may or may not have access to these data, depending on the willingness of the researcher or her sponsors to make them available or to perform requested analyses for you. Even your access to public data may be limited by confidentiality guarantees to the respondents.

Reference librarians can alert you to other resources for locating databases. Some databases are located almost by luck. Throughout agencies and universities, there are individuals who hold data. Administrators or analysts may conduct a survey, analyze the data, and write up the findings. The data may have been entered into a computer file with little or no formal documentation of their existence, or paper questionnaires may be stored on an office shelf. Inventories of agency databases may reduce the waste of underanalyzed data and redundant studies; however, the cost of documenting, storing, and protecting confidentiality may offset the benefits.

Database Access

Identifying a database is only half the battle. The researcher must determine whether he can access it, and he must review its documentation. Poor documentation or the inability to access a database may eliminate it from consideration. In some cases, technology is a double-edged sword. One of the authors spent a year working with a consultant on gaining access to data locked in customized, out-of-date software.

For some research questions, investigators may be able to confine themselves to aggregated and published data. Example 9.1 shows how a researcher compiled

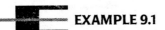 **EXAMPLE 9.1**

Combining Aggregated Databases

Problem: Academic researchers wanted to identify factors associated with work stoppages from strikes, walkouts, and lockouts.

Strategy:

1. Collect data for one year (1973) measuring: number of public-employee work stoppages, number of public employees involved, and number of public employee–days lost.

2. Identify sets of variables measuring state social and economic characteristics; local government structure and finance; local government workforce characteristics; state policies regarding local government collective bargaining.

3. Identify data sources measuring variables.

4. Conduct analysis: Use factor analysis to combine variables into summary measures (see Chapter 10); covary summary measures with numbers of work stoppages, employees participating in work stoppages, and employee-days idle from work stoppages.

EXAMPLE 9.1   *Continued*

Unit of analysis: States of the United States
Sample: All 50 states
Variables measuring state social and economic characteristics:

1. Percentage of state population urban, 1970
2. Percentage of nonagricultural workforce that has union membership, 1972
3. Right-to-work law
4. Percentage of state population below low-income level, 1969
5. State per capita income, 1973
6. State median family income, 1969
7. Percentage of state population of African Americans, 1970
8. Percentage of state population employed in nonagricultural establishments, 1973
9. Employee-days idle/million nonagricultural employees, 1972
10. State population density, 1970

Data sources for variables in study:

1. Council of State Governments, *The Book of the States* (Lexington, KY: Council of State Governments).
2. U.S. Dept. of Labor, *Summary of State Policy Regulations for Public Sector Labor Relations* (Washington, DC: U.S. Government Printing Office, 1973).
3. U.S. Census Bureau, *Public Employment in 1972* (Washington, DC: U.S. Government Printing Office, 1973).
4. ——, *Statistical Abstract of the United States* (Washington, DC: U.S. Government Printing Office).

Illustration of data compilation procedures for Alabama:

1. From *Summary of State Policy Regulations,* determine whether Alabama has right-to-work law; code "yes" or "no."
2. From *Public Employment in 1972,* copy data for Alabama on percent nonagricultural workforce that has union membership and employee-days idle/million nonagricultural employees.
3. Copy Alabama data on other variables from specified data sources.

Discussion: First, actual study collected data on 40 variables. Second, all data were collected or aggregated at the state level. A preferable unit of analysis would have been local governments. The researchers did not sample local governments because statistics on some variables of interest were not published for local governments. Third, all the dependent variable data were for 1973, and independent data variables were for 1973 or earlier. Earlier data were the most recent available statistics and were assumed to be the best estimate of 1973 values.

SOURCE: J. L. Perry and L. J. Berkes, "Predicting Local Government Strike Activity," *Western Political Quarterly* 30(4): 1977.

information from four published sources to study factors associated with public-employee work stoppages. The researchers studied variations in work stoppages among the states because local government statistics were not published at the time the research was conducted.

Compiling aggregated data can be tedious. A researcher who relies on aggregated and summarized data is limited in the analysis he can perform. For maximum flexibility, investigators require access to individual records for their analysis. They may get access in one of three ways:

1. Through extracted files, containing a portion of the data, such as
   a. a sample of cases, or
   b. a subset of variables on all cases
2. Through direct access to the database via
   a. a purchase of CD-ROMs or other electronic media
   b. a direct link allowing the investigator to access the database
3. Through an agreement for the database holder to perform the requested data extractions and manipulations

Of course, the investigator has no guarantee that he can access the database at all, especially if it is held by a nonpublic agency. Agency policy and his affiliation with the agency affect whether he can access data stored on an agency information system. The goodwill of the original researcher largely determines whether he can access individually held data. Contractual agreements may either guarantee or prohibit public access. Furthermore, confidentiality considerations may limit his access to the database or his ability to perform certain tabulations.[5]

Locating and accessing public data is becoming easier all the time. The University of Michigan's Document Center (http://www.lib.umich.edu/govdocs/stats.html) has a comprehensive list of publicly available data and databases organized by subject matter. FedStats (http://www. fedstats. gov) is similar to the Michigan site. FedStats directs users to publicly available federal data. Users can track trends and access official statistics. At either of these sites a user can easily locate needed data and receive information on how to access them. Some databases can be analyzed or downloaded online. Other databases are available for purchase. In addition, each state has a state data center that provides users with technical assistance in accessing and using Census and other public data.[6]

One should be sure to retrieve database documentation along with the actual data. It is a common mistake to download data without the appropriate coding key to variable names, dates data were gathered, original sources, and data definitions. In addition, researchers should always document when they accessed a database. Many databases are like living things—they are updated on a regular basis, and data previously listed are modified.

Verifying the Database

After a database is downloaded, its content and scaling should be verified. Analysts need to understand how the original data were collected, cleaned, and prepared for analysis.

We suspect some problems in using secondary data are most likely to occur in working with older databases, databases where information was transferred from one medium to another, or databases developed or used by smaller organizations. We know of instances where investigators put a dataset aside until they were ready to do the analysis, only to discover the dataset was seriously flawed. To verify a database's content, an analyst confirms that (1) the number of cases or records conforms to the number indicated in the documentation; (2) variables listed in the documentation have actually been downloaded on disk or CD-ROM; and (3) summary statistics reported in the documentation can be confirmed. An error may have been made in downloading the data, or the wrong data may have been sent. Furthermore, the possibility that errors can be traced and resolved decreases as time passes, and people involved in the collection, documentation, and compilation of the original database can no longer be reached.

Next, the scaling should be verified. This may have been done as part of documenting the content, but, if not, the researcher should review the variables of interest or a sample of variables. He should check that codes used in the database conform to the codes found in the documentation. For example, if the documentation indicates that males are coded as "1," females as "2," and missing data as "9," no other codes should appear in the database. We have found discrepancies occur because of errors in transferring the data into the computer file or typographical errors in the documentation. In working with a database, variables can be dropped or lines deleted with the unintended (and perhaps unnoticed) keystroke. After one author's analysis of thousands of lines of federal budget data, she discovered data from a small federal agency were missing. It had been skipped in the data download. The error was not discovered for weeks, and the analysis had to be redone. Typographical errors may be especially serious since an analyst may be manipulating the wrong variable or assuming the wrong values for a variable.

If an analyst is unfamiliar with the database, or unsure about the quality of the original survey or the accuracy of the documentation, he may wish to verify the accuracy of the sample. The analyst may apply techniques to answer the question, "Could the data here have been produced by the methodology described in the documentation?" The analyst may want to note the frequency of nonresponses and missing data. Sample verification may be especially important when databases are being merged and the study will be used to estimate parameters.

Special care should be taken in merging data series from different databases. Even something as simple as unseen formatting can cause different series to be misaligned. In merging databases, and eliminating cases where observations are missing for some of the variables, the number of cases may be reduced, altering the representativeness of the original samples. The techniques for sample verification can become quite complex. The reader interested in learning more about how to verify a sample should consult the article by J. C. Fortune and J. K. McBee and the references they cite.[7]

Evaluating the Database

Quantitative researchers are continually reminded about their vulnerability to having "the tail wag the dog." They may unconsciously define a problem so that they can solve it using their methodological skills. Similarly, they may radically alter a problem to make it conform to available secondary data. In working with secondary data, some shifts in the original research question may be necessary. Nevertheless, a researcher should determine the impact of the shift and whether the change will undermine his ability to accomplish the study's original purpose.

In working with secondary data, a researcher must first remember that secondary data can be no better than the research that produced them. Analytical sophistication cannot compensate for poorly conceived measures and sloppy data collection. Investigators may be wary of working with data accompanied by haphazard documentation. To decide whether the secondary data meet his needs, the researcher needs to know the following:

1. What constituted the sample?
   a. What was the population?
   b. What was the sampling frame?
   c. What sampling strategy was used?
   d. What was the response rate?
2. When were the data collected?
3. How were the data collected?
4. How were the data coded and edited?
5. What were the operational definitions of measures?
6. Who collected the data and for what purpose?

Information on the sample population lets the researcher know whether the data represent the population of interest. If the population of interest and the database's population do not coincide, the researcher must decide the impact of the difference. This is especially important to researchers working in public administration or studying nonprofits. For example, data for smaller units of government are often not available. If they are not, and a researcher is interested in a local government issue, she must decide if regional or state data can be used with any confidence. In the research on work stoppages, the researchers decided to settle on state data rather than collect local data; they reasoned that state data would uncover patterns of association that could be investigated later. Similarly, nonprofits vary by size and type. A database representing national nonprofits may not tell the researcher about what goes on in grassroots organizations.

Information on the sampling frame, sampling strategy, and response rate all affect the quality of the sample. Furthermore, a low response rate may render the data inadequate for the researcher's purpose. He also may decide that a low response rate indicates low research quality.

Knowing when the data were collected can be extremely important in correctly interpreting some study findings. Consider school data. Achievement scores gathered on fourth graders in October should be interpreted differently from achievement scores gathered in May. Time can affect public opinion data. Investigators examining public concern about environmental warming may hypothesize that the public's opinion is linked to weather patterns. Consequently, investigators would want to know when surveys were conducted, so they could learn if, and how, extreme temperature or weather-related disasters were associated with variations in the public's opinions.

Information on how the data were collected helps an investigator make inferences about data quality. He wants to know if respondents were surveyed by mail, over the Internet, telephone, or in person, and how interviewers were trained and supervised. Information on data coding and editing procedures also relates to data quality. Specifically, the investigator wants to know whether someone checked for errors in coding data or entering them into a computer. He also wants to learn how atypical responses, missing responses, and atypical answers were handled. In evaluating the information, the investigator uses his judgment to decide whether the evidence suggests sound research procedures.

Knowing the operational definitions of measures allows the investigator to determine the reliability, operational validity, and sensitivity of the measures. Ideally, the documentation explains and evaluates the measures used. Studies generated with the database also may provide evidence of the quality of the measures. Finally, a copy of the instrument used to collect the data helps the investigator to reach his own conclusions.

Data published by the Bureau of the Census are accompanied by fairly detailed documentation. In Example 9.2 we have quoted sections of the appendices of an issue of *Current Population Reports.* The purpose of the example is to

 EXAMPLE 9.2

Documenting Secondary Data: An Example from the Annual Demographic Survey

Situation: Each March the Current Population Survey (CPS) conducts an Annual Demographic Survey, which supplements its monthly data on labor force participation with data on money received the previous calendar year, education, household and family characteristics.

Population and sample: The Annual Demographic sample consists of the CPS sample of 60,000 housing units, 2,500 additional units with at least one Hispanic member, and members of the Armed Forces, which are excluded from the CPS labor force survey.

Sampling frame and strategy: The sampling frame was selected from 1990 Census files and updated to reflect new construction. Current CPS sample is located in 754 areas; an area consists of a county, several contiguous counties, or minor civil divisions in New England and Hawaii.

Response rate: About 50,000 occupied households were eligible for interview. Interviews were not obtained from about 3,200 occupied units, because the occupants were not found at home after repeated calls or were unavailable for some other reason. Between 92 and 93 percent of households provide basic labor force information; between 80 and 82 percent complete the Annual Demographic Survey supplement.

Continued

EXAMPLE 9.2 *Continued*

When data were collected: March 19–March 27, 1996.

How data were collected: Face-to-face interviews, with the interviewer using a laptop computer, were conducted with households that had not been interviewed previously, with poor English language skills, or without telephone access. Telephone interviews were conducted with other households.

Conceptual definition of involuntary part-time: Individuals who give an economic reason for working 1 to 34 hours during a week. Economic reasons include slack work or unfavorable business conditions, inability to find full-time work, and seasonal declines in demand. Those who usually work part-time must also indicate that they want and are available to work full-time to be classified as part-time for economic reasons.

Operational definition (partial): In the weeks that (name/you) worked, how many weeks did (name/you) work less than 35 hours in 1995? What was the main reason (name/you) worked less than 35 hours per week? (1) Could not find a full-time job, (2) Wanted to work part-time or only able to work part-time, (3) Slack work or material shortage, (4) Other reason.

SOURCE: Information drawn from Current Population Survey web site (http://www.bls.census.gov)

show you what to look for in reviewing documentation and to provide you with a model of what to include when you write up your own research.

Changes can occur to data sources that reflect new uses for the original data. For example, in 2001 the Census Bureau expanded the sample used for the Annual Demographic Supplement, a part of the Current Population Survey. It did so primarily to improve state estimates of the number of children without health insurance. Why was this necessary? Federal funds for the State Health Insurance Program (SCHIP) are based on these estimates. States wanted better estimates so funding needs would be more accurately identified. Thus the original data source was expanded. If a researcher using SCHIP funding data noted an increase in the estimate, she might think there was a rise in the number of children eligible for the program or that benefits were increased. In reality, the increase might just be due to the change in how the sample used for the estimates was selected.

Knowing who collected the data and why can be valuable. Imagine you find data supporting the health benefits of eating chocolate. Would you be skeptical if the report was from a trade association of chocolate manufacturers? What information would convince you that the data were not biased or misleading? The answers to questions about the sample, the operational definitions, and how the data were coded and analyzed might lessen your suspicions.

U.S. CENSUS DATA

Official statistics, statistics collected by governments, are a major source of secondary data. In the United States, most federal cabinet-level agencies regularly collect data needed for policy making. Important agency producers of statistical series include the Departments of Education, Health and Human Services, Agriculture, Justice, Labor, and Commerce. Major federal databases can be accessed at four main web sites:

- www.fedstats.gov
- www.fedworld.gov
- www.gpoaccess.gov
- www.firstgov.gov

The U.S. Census Bureau conducts periodic and special studies to describe the characteristics of the American people, their governments, and their businesses. The periodic studies include:

Census of Governments

Decennial Census of Population and Housing

Current Population Survey (CPS)

American Community Survey[8]

Survey of Business Owners

Economic Census

We limit this chapter to U.S. Census Bureau surveys because of the extensive use of Census data and the Bureau's longstanding efforts to reduce nonsampling errors. The data are critical to political and policy decisions. Census data users include federal agencies, state and local governments, nonprofit associations and businesses, and private citizens pursuing business and personal interests.

This chapter discusses the Census of Governments and the Bureau's two major population surveys. We summarize how the Bureau decides on questionnaire content and documents data. The methodological discussion should improve your knowledge of data collection and your appreciation of Census Bureau procedures. You may wish to note that the Census Bureau and other federal agencies do not do public opinion polling. Official statistics document information about governments, other organizations, and individuals.

The U.S. Bureau of the Census

The U.S. Bureau of the Census traces its origins back to the Constitutional requirement that the U.S. population be counted every 10 years. The head count forms the basis for reapportioning the number of seats a state holds in the U.S. House of Representatives. By law, within nine months of "Census Day," the Census Bureau must give the President a count of state populations so that congressional delegations can be apportioned. Within a year, state legislatures must receive population totals for specified political subdivisions so they can draw legislative districts.

A hallmark of the Census Bureau has been its record for protecting the confidentiality of the information it collects. The principle of confidentiality has contributed to its success in getting people and businesses to answer questions about themselves. Current law on confidentiality states:

Census data may be used only for statistical purposes.

Publication of census data must not enable a user to identify individuals or establishments.

Every person with access to individual data is sworn for life to protect the information.

The Bureau releases its information on an individual only with that person's specific consent. For example, some individuals have asked for census records to corroborate their ages and demonstrate their eligibility for Social Security benefits. Census officials must anticipate how computer users can manipulate data to uncover the identity of and private information on specific individuals or establishments.[9] To respond to this threat, the Bureau uses statistical methods to avoid unanticipated disclosures, including suppressing or modifying some data, to screen out any that might identify a specific business or individual. It also has an internal Disclosure Review Board to determine if any risks to confidentiality exist before data are released.

The Census Bureau is not restricted to collecting data on and from individuals. It also collects data on the nation's economic activity, including manufacturing, agriculture, transportation, and government. The Bureau protects the confidentiality of business information. Data on governments are based on public records and are not confidential.

After census data are compiled, the immediate interest is in the snapshots they supply of the nation and its economic activity. Nevertheless, the real importance of the census statistics is their role as time-series data. Thus the Bureau is concerned with producing high-quality data and ensuring their comparability over time.

Censuses of Governments

In years ending with two or seven, the Census Bureau's Government Programs Division conducts a Census of Governments. In addition, it conducts annual sample surveys to gather data on government finances and public employment. Data from the censuses are used to estimate the government-sector economic activity in the United States. These estimates are incorporated into the National Income and Product Accounts, the account that measures the Gross Domestic Product.[10] The census collects information on four major areas—governmental organization, taxable property values, governmental employment, and governmental finance.

Public officials and scholars may cite these data when comparing governments or looking for patterns of fiscal health. Regularly reported data can answer questions such as:

How much revenue does California realize from state-run lotteries? What percentage goes to prizes? How does its profitability compare with New York's state-run lotteries?

In how many counties in Iowa can the public do business with the county government via the Internet? What percent of municipalities offer the same service? How does this differ between large cities and small towns?

What percentage of state and local government employees work in corrections? What percentage of payroll goes to corrections? How does this differ by state?

Rules governing statistics collected by the Government Division differ from typical census operations in two respects. First, as mentioned, governmental information is not confidential; the Bureau regularly publishes statistics for individual governments. Second, the sovereignty of the American states exempts them and their subdivisions from the U.S. code (Title 13) requirement to supply the Bureau with requested information. Therefore, this is a voluntary survey. In the 2002 Census of Governments, 30 percent of governmental units did not respond.

A major challenge for the Bureau's Government Division is to procure comparable data. Achieving high response rates and receiving comparable information necessitate developing data collection procedures that do not burden respondents. The Bureau collects some data from reports submitted to other federal agencies. The Bureau receives some financial data for individual local governments from state governments. Some information is based on responses to earlier surveys or other Census databases. All these strategies avoid having a state or local government receive more than one request for the same information.[11] To further decrease respondent burden, staff review existing documents and rely on information available via the Internet. If necessary, they will use mail-out/mail-back surveys.

Staff manually reviews responses for completeness and consistency. A computer check is performed to identify improbable data and to show differences from previous years. Staff may conduct extensive follow-ups with the governments to fill in incomplete data, to clarify ambiguities, or to verify questionable responses.

Publication of the data is relatively quick. The Census Bureau constantly updates contact and legal status information in preparing for the coming government census. For the 2002 Census of Governments, the official survey period was November 2001 to April 2002. Preliminary results were released in July of the same year. More detailed results were published periodically in the years following. For government finances, tax information and pension system information are typically the first forms of information available. For employment, preliminary data are released in the same year, with updates, more details, or revisions taking place periodically. Because the data are not confidential and largely consist of publicly available information, errors are constantly being identified and the data refined. A city manager or mayor who sees her city's revenue has been misreported is unlikely to let it pass without comment.

The Census of Population and Housing

The mainstay of the Census Bureau is the *Decennial Census of Population and Housing,* the constitutional reason for its existence. As we have suggested, counting the population is neither an easy task nor one that can be done with complete accuracy. From the first census, government officials added to the work of census takers and asked them to collect additional information about the population. Thus the Census Bureau has had to develop procedures to accurately count the population and to determine what additional information to gather and from whom.

The Census Bureau, government officials, and researchers have given considerable attention to how the census can obtain an accurate population count. In 1990 census forms, including late returns, were returned by 75 percent of occupied housing units compared to an 83 percent response rate in 1980. The lower rate of cooperation increased costs and decreased quality. More census takers had to be hired and trained.[12] Plausible explanations for the low response rate included reluctance of people living in nontraditional households to disclose household composition, an aversion to surveys instilled by repeated telephone and mail surveys, increased concern with privacy, and a growing non-English-speaking population.[13]

In preparation for the 2000 Census, the Census Bureau focused on containing costs and increasing the response rate. The Bureau studied ways to increase the return rate for the mailed Census form.[14] Follow-up questionnaires were mailed out. Citizens could fill out and mail back the questionnaires or answer online or over the telephone. States and advocacy groups urged citizens to respond. The 2000 Census was the first time the government used a paid advertising campaign to urge response. The following statement from the State of Ohio's home page illustrates the appeals made to citizens and some of the official uses of Census data.

> Census 2000 is critical to assuring Ohio's success in the next millennium. Census data will be used to allocate federal funds for communities throughout the State of Ohio. Results of the 2000 census are crucial to planning local community services including: schools, employment services, housing assistance, road construction, hospital services and special programs for children and the elderly. Businesses will decide where to locate and to invest with assistance of Census 2000 data. An accurate 2000 census will guarantee Ohio is properly represented and prepared for the future.

The result was a slight reverse (or at least stabilization) of the trend of declining return rates. For the 2000 Census, 78.4 percent of occupied housing units mailed back a response (including late responses). This was seen as a major success of the 2000 Census.

The phenomenon of the Census missing people completely is referred to as the *undercount.* The problem of undercounting goes beyond underestimating the total size of the U.S. population. Certain groups, particularly urban minorities, are more likely to be missed, and their need or demand for services may be seriously underestimated. Urban areas with a sizeable uncounted population may end up shortchanged in their number of legislative representatives or in the size of their allotment of government program funds. To address the problem of the undercount and to keep costs in line, the Bureau recommended sampling a portion of the households that did not return their forms. The plan to sample, however, ran into Congressional resistance. Court challenges resulted in a Supreme Court decision in 1999 stating that the Census could not use sampling for Congressional seat apportionment, and in 2000 the Bureau was stuck with the costs of attempting to contact every nonresponding household.[15] In the end, the 2000 Census had an estimated undercount of 1.18 percent, or slightly over 3 million people. More than $100 billion in federal programs alone are allocated by using census data. A report to Congress from the U.S. Census Monitoring Board estimated that the 2000 Census undercount will lead to a net loss of almost $.5 billion to the states between 2002 and 2012.[16]

What to include in the Census requires negotiation and evaluation. Other federal agencies, state and local government users, interest groups, and individual citizens suggest questions. To decide what additional questions to ask, census officials assess whether the proposed information will serve a broad public interest. Census officials approach the issue of the public interest by deciding whether the information justifies the expenditure of public monies. The criterion of public interest commonly leads to the elimination of questions primarily of interest to businesses, such as information on the number of pet owners in the United States.

One way the Census Bureau avoids overburdening respondents is to limit the number and content of questions so a respondent can complete the form within a reasonable amount of time. The Decennial Census used to have two forms, a short and long form. The short form asks all households to answer no more than two facing pages of questions. A sample of about 1 in 6 households used to receive a longer form. The longer form asked the same questions as the short form; plus one-and-a-half pages of housing questions and two additional pages of information on each household member.

In an effort to address some problems of earlier censuses, the 2010 Census is introducing a major change: It is discontinuing the use of the long form and relying only on the short form. Information previously gained through the long form is now gathered through the American Community Survey, a more frequent sample survey.[17] The Census Bureau plans to use more technology to reduce the cost of the Decennial Census, such as using handheld computers to record information. Even with all the changes, however, as of 2006, estimates of the cost of the 2010 Census exceed $11 billion.

The 2010 Census will ask only each household member's name, relationship to the respondent, sex, race, ethnicity, and age. In asking its questions, the Bureau considers historical comparability. If a question is reworded or response categories are altered, the change affects the answers. The Bureau must weigh whether the benefit of a change balances the loss of comparability of information from one census to another.

The history of the race and ethnicity questions, as shown in Example 9.3, illustrates the trade-off between consistency and the need to make question changes that reflect current social conditions. From this abbreviated summary, you can infer the social conditions that gave rise to the particular data-gathering strategy and the problems in comparing racial or ethnic changes from one census to the next. For example, note that until 1960 racial classification was not based on self-identification; rather, by asking specific questions on parentage or by observation, census takers decided a household's race. In 1960 and 1970, households that received a mailed form identified their own race, but if a census taker collected data, he or she decided, based on observation, the appropriate racial category. By 1980 the race question included 15 categories, mixing traditional concepts of race

EXAMPLE 9.3

Comparability among Censuses

Summary of the Recent History of Racial and Ethnic Questions

1920: Census taker decided appropriate category. Categories: White, Negro, Mulatto (Black–White mixture), Chinese, Japanese, Indian, Other

1930: Mulatto category dropped; a person identified as Mulatto counted as Negro

1940: Mexican (Mexican birth or Mexican parents) added; persons who qualified as Mexican but who were identifiable as Negro, Chinese, Japanese, or Indian were no longer counted as Mexican

1960: Self-identification of race on mailed census forms. If data collected by a census taker, the census taker observed and filled in the racial data.

1970: Combination of self-identification and census taker observation continued. Categories: White, Black or Negro, Japanese, Chinese, Filipino, Korean, Vietnamese, Indian (Amer.), Asian Indian, Hawaiian, Guamanian, Samoan, Eskimo, Aleut, Other

1980: Question added to 100 percent count, "Is this person of Spanish/Hispanic origin or descent? Categories: No (not Spanish/Hispanic); Yes, Mexican-Amer.; Yes, Chicano; Yes, Puerto Rican; Yes, Cuban; Yes, Other

1990: Changed the "other" response category in both the race and Hispanic questions to allow the respondent to name the specific Asian or Pacific Islander or Spanish/Hispanic group

2000: Allowed respondent to check more than one racial group; allowed respondent to select "some other race" with space to write in an answer.

SOURCE: C. F. Citro and M. L. Cohen, eds., *The Bicentennial Census: New Directions for Methodology in 1990* (Washington, DC: National Academy Press, 1985), 205–214; 1990 Census Questionnaire. 2000 Information from Census 2000 form available on Census Bureau web site.

with ethnic or geographic identities. Also in 1980, respondents in all parts of the country could identify themselves as Eskimos or Aleuts; previously, these groups were listed only on census forms distributed in Alaska. The 2000 form simplified the directions on how to identify the applicable Hispanic group, e.g., Colombian or Peruvian. An analysis of the New York City data found a sharp increase in the number of "other Hispanics" since 1990. At the same time, city agencies had overestimated the size of specific Hispanic groups. Explanations for the change, other than the wording, could not be ruled out. One critic speculated that younger, U.S.–born Hispanics might not identify with a specific nationality.[18]

Deciding on racial categories was a major controversy in planning for the 2000 Census.[19] People who had more than one racial background expressed their resentment at having to choose one racial group over another. Adding "bi-racial" and "multi-racial" as categories was considered. This strategy was opposed by those who feared that many African Americans would choose these categories and diminish the ability of analysts to identify patterns of discrimination. The final decision was to allow respondents to check more than one racial group.[20] The respondent could also have marked "some other race" and filled in an answer. The controversy over wording of this question continued after the 2000 Census. The Census Bureau found that in 2000, when people responded "some other race," they did not always identify what that race was. So the Bureau investigated dropping the option, effectively forcing people to choose one of the stated options or skip the question. However, the decision was taken out of its hands. In an example of the direct intervention Congress can make, the 2005 Consolidated Appropriations Act included language directing the Census Bureau to use the "some other race" option with all future censuses.

Approximately five years before "Census Day," a series of census pretests begin. The pretests gather data on diverse aspects of the census process. Analysts evaluate the questionnaire, any computer-assisted interviewing techniques, and response rates. For the 2010 Census, dress rehearsals will take place in 2008 in Fayetteville, North Carolina, and San Joaquin County, California. These rehearsals are major affairs—each will generate thousands of local temporary jobs. Other tests have already taken place throughout the country, from Texas to Alaska.

The Bureau conducts post-census evaluations of the census coverage and content. The evaluation findings indicate data quality and suggest future changes. Post-census evaluations largely consist of information supplied by respondents, who are re-interviewed. The Bureau also checks administrative records. For example, public utilities records have been compared with respondents' reports of utility expenditures. Medicare, income tax returns, and similar governmental records have been used to improve the accuracy of the population count.[21] The Census Bureau conducted 87 evaluations in the wake of the 2000 Census, covering everything from the impact of the paid advertising campaign to focus groups to explain respondent behavior. For 2010, the Bureau will keep up the emphasis on post-enumeration work, but this time distinguishing between auditing data for coverage and veracity and outcome-focused evaluations of Census programs.

The Census Bureau does not escape data-collection problems, but in general it does as well as or better than other organizations that collect data. The

Bureau's resources, including its reputation, add to its advantage. In general, people are more willing to respond to government requests for information; consequently, census surveys have lower nonresponse rates than similar surveys conducted by nongovernment agencies and researchers.

Current Population Survey (CPS)

The *CPS* is a monthly household survey to gather current population and labor force data. The U.S. Bureau of Labor Statistics releases the CPS data each month in its report on the nation's employment and unemployment rates. The Census Bureau analyzes the population data and reports them in *Current Population Reports.*

The data describe the personal characteristics of the labor force, including the age distribution, race, and sex of American workers. Data on who works, who works full-time, who works only part-time, and who is unemployed give us a picture of who gets ahead or falls behind in the labor force. For instance, the CPS reports separately the employment patterns for whites and African Americans, for men and women, for teenagers and adults, and for rural residents and urban dwellers. What will be done with this information depends on one's responsibilities. Interest groups, journalists, and legislators cite data to document social problems or to advocate policy changes. Program managers, especially in education and job-training programs, consult the data to structure programs to meet their clients' needs or simply to give their clients accurate information and advice.

Planners in programs delivering services to specific age groups, such as schoolchildren or the elderly, need current data on the population's age distribution so that they can estimate demand for services. Business analysts examine the data to identify population trends that may change the demand for products and services; administrators can undertake similar studies to improve their program planning or implementation.

Census analysts construct the CPS sample, consisting of approximately 60,000 households, so that it is representative of the nation's population. The sample is large enough that one can estimate parameters for individual states, Los Angeles, New York City, and the District of Columbia.[22] Example 9.4 reviews sampling statistics and illustrates why you may be able to use a given database to estimate parameters for a state but not for its communities.

In reviewing Example 9.4, you may wish to note what a small standard error means at the national level. In 2001 the size of the civilian labor force was 141.8 million. If the unemployment rate was estimated to be 5 percent, then 7,090,000 persons were believed to be unemployed. If an analyst assumed a 95–5 split between employed and unemployed, the standard error would be .0009 (0.09 percent). This means that at the 95 percent confidence level the estimate of the percent unemployed would be off by plus or minus 0.18 percent (0.09 times 1.96). The actual number of unemployed could be as high as 5.18 percent, e.g., 7,345,240 or as low as 4.82 percent, e.g., 6,834,760. Thus a very low standard error, less than 0.1 percent, can yield an estimate off by as many as 510,480 persons.

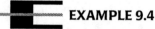 **EXAMPLE 9.4**

Estimating Parameters from the CPS: A Hypothetical Example

Problem: Can an analyst use CPS data to estimate the proportion of a city's households with a certain characteristic? What will be the size of standard error if the characteristic is split 50–50? 75–25?

Sample	*n*	*SE* 50–50	95% Confidence Interval	*SE* 75–25	95% Confidence Interval
National	50,000	.0022	49.55–50.45%	.0019	74.63–75.37%
Regional	11,000	.0048	49.06–50.93%	.0041	74.19–75.81%
State	1,700	.012	47.65–52.35%	.0105	72.94–77.06%
City	85	.054	39.37–60.63%	.047	65.79–84.20%

Discussion: Recall that to establish a 95 percent confidence interval, the *SE* is multiplied by 1.96. The standard error will be larger for interval data because they are more variable. This example assumes that the analyst is manipulating data for all city households included in the subsample. The sample sizes become considerably smaller, and the standard error larger, when one tries to estimate the distribution of the characteristic among a specific group, for example, income of Hispanic families.

USING CENSUS DATA

The Census Bureau aggregates and releases data from the Decennial Census by political and statistical areas. The political areas are states, counties, minor civil divisions (such as townships and New England towns), and incorporated places. Statistical areas have been created to describe functionally integrated areas that are relatively homogeneous in population characteristics, economic status, and living conditions. Most important of these are the *census tract* and the *block.* Census tracts are large neighborhoods, averaging 4,000 in population and generally with a population between 1,500 and 6,000. Census tracts are not to cross county lines. As of the 2000 Census, all counties had census tracts, even rural areas. Blocks are sub-units of tracts and are the smallest geographical unit for which the Census Bureau collects 100 percent data—that is, data on all the households, not a sample. Over 8 million blocks were used in the 2000 Census.[23]

Traditionally, census data have been publicly available as *macrodata,* that is, data aggregated by political or statistical area. Beginning with the 1940 Census, samples of individual records, called *microdata,* have been made available for public use. These used to be the systematic, stratified samples of the long questionnaires filled out by individuals. The American Community Survey is now the source for microdata information through its Public Use Microdata Sample.[24] A microdata record includes the responses reported to the Census Bureau with all personal identifiers removed. Information on geographic locations and data on very small and visible subgroups also may be eliminated to protect the confidentiality of respondents.

The advantages of the microdata are that the user can access individual records and design cross-tabulations of the variables in these records. Users can analyze variables in any combination they choose, something not possible with the summary data files. Since the microdata represent a sample, users must deal with the issues associated with making inferences from samples to populations. These files also are large, and users need adequate computer support to do the analysis. These days, virtually all census data are available online and can be downloaded electronically. Menu-driven applications make it simple to access information on almost any geographic level from almost any survey through www.Census.gov. In addition, researchers are continuously constructing new databases and sharing information. For example, the Minnesota Population Center at the University of Minnesota has developed the Integrated Public Use Microdata series, which has pulled together a variety of high-precision samples over time for social science and economic research.[25]

The most immediate and obvious uses of the decennial data are for legislative reapportionment, funding allocations, and policy decisions. The national, state, and local government data give politicians, administrators, and journalists a snapshot of the nation's population on one day. The population can be viewed cross-sectionally or longitudinally. Cross-sectional studies look at the patterns among variables in the census dataset; longitudinal studies measure changes from one census to another.

One outstanding feature of census data is that the same types of data are provided in the same format for so many different places. Users can analyze any state in the nation, any of the nation's over 3,000 counties, or any city or neighborhood. Data are in a standardized format for every place, so the same analysis can be easily repeated for any jurisdiction. Another important characteristic of census data is its coverage of small geographic areas. As we implied in our discussion of the CPS, at best, national surveys estimate population characteristics of individual states and large metropolitan areas. Example 9.5 illustrates how a smaller community can use census data to select an area for a pilot project serving impoverished preschoolers.

Census data are important components of demographic analysis, such as studies of patterns of fertility, mortality, and the population's age distribution. Public services rely on demographic data to help with planning. School planners attempt to provide advance notice that school capacity is greater or less than needed for the anticipated number of children that the community must educate. In recent years communities have paid more attention to the needs of their aging populations. Communities with an increasing proportion of elderly persons may experience a marked change in demand for certain services—for example, an increased need for nursing homes and specialized medical care.

An obvious problem with decennial data is its timeliness. Over the course of a decade, the accuracy of the counts declines substantially. Population changes at the block level can be rapid and dramatic. Within a matter of months, vacant lots,

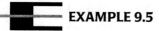 **EXAMPLE 9.5**

Using Census Data on Census Tracts to Select a Site for a Program

Situation: A local human services program plans to launch a pilot program for impoverished preschoolers. The program will combine a full-day nursery school program with nutritional and health services. A human services analyst has reviewed data on city census tracts to identify communities where the program could be located; see Table 9.1.

TABLE 9.1   HOUSEHOLDS BELOW POVERTY LEVEL IN SELECTED CENSUS TRACTS

	Census Tract				
	A	B	C	D	E
Population below poverty level	4,390	3,458	2,670	5,262	3,417
Number of related children less than six years old	151	114	91	173	41
Number of related children less than six years old in a household with no husband	77	51	56	63	12
Percentage population below poverty level	28	25	29	21	16

Decision: Look for a site in Census Tracts A or D. Indicators for both communities show a high level of need: number of young children living in poverty; number of young children living in a female-headed household; large percentages of population below poverty level. Census Tract E is an inappropriate site for the community project because of the small number of children in the target population and a distinctly lower level of need evidenced by indicators.

fields, and wooded areas may be replaced by residential housing. Conversely, housing of marginal quality may be condemned and disappear. The switch from the long form previously used in the Decennial Census to the American Community Survey (ACS) may alleviate this problem. About three million households are surveyed each year with the ACS. In 2004, data for most metropolitan areas of 250,000 population or more, all 50 states, and the District of Columbia were available. According to a 2005 update on the ACS web site, data for all areas with 20,000 population should be available, and within five years, data should be available for smaller units.

Each state has an agency called a State Data Center that helps disseminate census data to other state agencies and local governments and aids those wishing to use census data. State data centers are the main contact between the Census Bureau and state and local governments. Many of these centers also coordinate the collection, documentation, and dissemination of data by all state government agencies. They can update the ACS population count for the state and major subdivisions, such as counties and cities. States may also project or estimate the state's future population and that of its subdivisions, particularly counties. If you have good reason to believe that an agency in your state collects certain data, chances are that the state data center can tell you if it is available and how to obtain access to it.[26]

We have only scratched the surface in our description of census data and their uses. We have only touched on data gathered in the census of governments and the economic censuses conducted every five years. And we have not mentioned many of the products derived from the Decennial Census. Similarly, we have ignored many other important statistical collections and agencies. Federal agencies regularly gather statistics describing the nation's health, education, agriculture, crime, and criminal justice systems.

We had three reasons for writing at length about census data. First, we wanted to alert you to their availability and potential. Second, the Bureau of the Census continually appraises its data collection and compilation procedures; thus, it is an important source of information on current developments in survey research methodology. Third, the information accompanying Census Bureau data serves as a model for documenting primary data; researchers need similar information to decide if a data set is suited to their needs. The Census Bureau continually strives to make the census data more available and easier to use. With the Internet and other advances in technology, more people can access this important source of secondary data.

VITAL STATISTICS

Vital records are another important secondary data source used by investigators from different disciplines and with different interests. Vital records and the resulting *vital statistics* give information on births, deaths, marriages, divorces, abortions, communicable diseases, and hospitalizations. Most countries have a system for recording vital statistics. These data were among the first collected by governments and nongovernmental organizations. Before national censuses were conducted, these records were used to estimate populations.

In the United States, federal, state, and local government agencies cooperate to collect, compile, and report vital statistics. Data are collected by individual counties and states. The state data are forwarded to the National Center for Health Statistics, which compiles the data. The center publishes U.S. vital statistics reports and provides technical assistance to state agencies and other data users. As is standard with much secondary data, much of the data are online.[27]

Investigators use vital statistics to assess the state of a community's mental and physical health. Policy makers can examine vital statistics to evaluate the effectiveness of current programs, change policies or programs to better meet existing needs, and forecast future needs.

Typically, a county collects data required by state statute and reports them to the state. Hospital administrators, physicians, funeral directors, and medical examiners may collect the actual data. In most states the state health department maintains vital records and releases them to the public in printed form or on computer media after removing information that identifies individuals. State offices of vital statistics also issue periodic statistical reports describing the health of the states and their communities.

The information gathered on a live birth illustrates the extensive information included in vital records:

where birth occurred

institution of delivery

mother's residence

mother's marital status

mother's race

mother's total pregnancies

mother's previous number of live births

mother's previous number of fetal deaths

date of mother's last live birth

date of mother's last fetal death

outcome of mother's last delivery

mother's number of previous children still living

prenatal care

baby's Apgar score (a medical rating scale done at birth)

complications with this pregnancy

congenital malformations

At first vital records may appear to be objective, and a user may not doubt the quality of the data. Actually, the accuracy of any one vital record is subject to many possible errors. Think of distortions that can occur in the information on a live birth. For example, information on previous pregnancies may be misreported. Fear of censure may cause a woman not to tell her physician or midwife about previous pregnancies that resulted in an abortion, miscarriage, or adoption. Many women may not have recognized miscarriages early in a pregnancy. Added to the problem of misreporting are possible errors in recording the data and different standards in diagnoses; considering these factors, you can begin to appreciate the difficulties of maintaining data quality.

Similarly, social values affect death reports. Vital statistics on causes of death are obtained from death certificates and are coded according to an international code. Consider the current problems in getting accurate data on deaths from AIDS. AIDS patients and their families may fear the social stigma attached to the disease. Physicians sensitive to the feelings of patients and their families have admitted to indicating cancer or another related disease on the death certificate rather than AIDS. Similarly, accurate reporting of suicide varies widely. Societies that consider suicide a shameful act are likely to under-report its occurrence. Depending on community mores, then, a physician may decide to attribute a death to diseases or events that cause a family less embar-rassment.

Vital statistics and some other health records are based on complete counts of all relevant individuals. The Center for Health Statistics attempts to count all births and deaths, and the Centers for Disease Control and Prevention attempts to collect a complete count of many diseases and causes of death. However, a great deal of useful health-related information is collected with sample surveys. The National Center for Health Statistics, several other U.S. government agencies, and many private organizations conduct extensive surveys on health-related topics. Large amounts of health survey data are available.[28]

SUMMARY

Secondary data are existing data that investigators collected for a purpose other than the given research study. Secondary data can be inexpensive, high-quality data adequate to define or solve a problem. Analyzing an existing database requires fewer resources than collecting original data. Some data-bases have higher-quality data than a researcher can hope to gather. Organi-zations specializing in collecting data typically have well-trained, professional staff to check the reliability and operational validity of measures; to design, implement, and document a sound sampling procedure; and to col-lect and compile data.

One may argue secondary analysis contributes to the quality of primary data-bases. First, secondary analysis requires that the original researchers fully document a database. Second, secondary analysis enables researchers to see whether they can replicate the original researcher's findings. The need to document and the ability to check findings will encourage researchers to attend to research quality.

As documentation becomes routine, data archives are kept, and access to secondary data becomes easier, investigators may increasingly turn to existing data to conduct preliminary research and to hone their research questions. Whether or not secondary data are appropriate for the final research question depends on the question and the data. As investigators work on a research problem, they begin to understand what population and what measures are needed to answer their questions. Sometimes they may modify the question so that it is consistent with the existing database. Such adjustments should be made only after the investigators fully consider what is lost in making such a shift.

The U.S. Bureau of the Census is a major source of data on the country's population, governments, and businesses. Investigators find census data valuable because of their content and the quality of the data collection. Census data may be analyzed by geography, by demographic characteristics, and over time. Maintaining comparability and reducing respondent burdens have been especially challenging in a changing society.

Other federal bureaus, state offices of vital statistics, survey organizations, and professional associations routinely collect data that others study. Virtually any organization is a potential source of data, as are individual researchers. Internet sites may help you locate existing data. Occasionally, by asking agency personnel, individual investigators may uncover a fugitive or unknown database.

Once investigators locate a database, they have to find a way to access it. Some questions can be answered by working with published statistics, but often one needs access to the database. Depending on who holds the database, and the contractual provisions for releasing data, a researcher may either access the database or a portion of it directly or have the database holder perform the analysis. Nevertheless, researchers cannot assume that access to a database is guaranteed. Organizational policies, contractual guarantees, and researcher inclination may become important factors in any agreement to allow someone to access data.

If access is obtained, the investigators need to verify the content of the database. Occasionally, the wrong database is accessed or information about a variable and its coding is incorrect. The researchers also need to review information on the sample, the measures, when the data were collected, how they were collected, and coding procedures to infer data quality.

Chapter 10 examines techniques to combine indicators to form a single measure. Data are collected on each indicator and stored as separate variables in a database. Investigators may, and often do, analyze each variable separately. Nevertheless, as you should observe, combining variables can give a more accurate, fuller picture of the phenomenon under consideration. Examining a long list of single variables can easily mislead a busy decision maker, who may be mistakenly impressed by one or two striking findings.

NOTES

1. G. S. Goldberg and E. Kremen, *The Feminization of Poverty: Only in America?* (New York: Praeger, 1990).

2. "Former UVM researcher sentenced for falsifying work," *Boston Globe*, June 28, 2006, accessed at http://www.boston.com/news/local/vermont/articles/2006/06/28/former_uvm_researcher_sentenced_for_falsifying_work/ on August 1, 2006.

3. For more discussion of the costs of secondary analysis, see Committee on National Statistics, Commission on Behavioral and Social Sciences and Education, National Research Council, *Sharing Research Data*, eds. S. E. Fienberg, M. E. Martin, and M. I. Straf (Washington, DC: National Academy Press, 1985), 15–18.

4. M. H. Maier with T. Easton, *The Data Game*, 3d ed. (Armonk, NY: M. E. Sharpe, 1999).

5. J. S. Cecil and E. Griffin, "The Role of Legal Policies in Data Sharing," in *Sharing Research Data*, discuss laws that affect researchers' access to data.

6. See http://www.census.gov/sdc/www/, accessed August 1, 2006.

7. J. C. Fortune and J. K. McBee, "Considerations and Methodology for the Preparation of Data Files," in *Secondary Analysis of Available Data Bases*, ed. D. J. Bowering (San Francisco: Jossey-Bass, New Directions for Program Evaluation, 1985).

8. By 2010, the American Community Survey intends to provide current data on an annual basis for all levels of geography, including the smallest for which aggregate data are generally available—census tract and block groups. It will replace the traditional "long form" of the Decennial Census of Population and Housing.

9. For a further discussion of confidentiality, see C. P. Kaplan and T. L. Van Valey, *Census '80: Continuing the Factfinder Tradition* (Washington, DC: U.S. Bureau of the Census, 1980), 65–79; "Plenary Session V: Confidentiality Issues in Federal Statistics,"

First Annual Research Conference Proceedings (Washington, DC: U.S. Bureau of the Census, 1985), 199–233.

10. For information on the National Income and Product Accounts, see Stratford and Stratford, *Major U.S. Statistical Series,* 64–66.

11. Each major Government Division report includes a section on data collection, including any sampling, in its introduction. The fiscal surveys are more complicated and tend to use the full array of strategies described here.

12. *Decennial Census: 1990 Results Show Need for Fundamental Reform* (Washington, DC: General Accounting Office, GAO/GGD-92–94, 1992), chaps. 2–5.

13. Ibid, 37–38.

14. *2000 Census: Progress Made on Design, but Risks Remain* (Washington, DC: U.S. General Accounting Office, GAO/GGD-97–142, July 14, 1997).

15. To learn more about the politics surrounding the Census Bureau's plans to sample, see M. J. Anderson and S. E. Fienberg, *Who Counts? The Politics of Census-Taking in Contemporary America* (New York: Russell Sage Foundation, 1999). I. I. Mitroff, R. O. Mason, and V. P. Barabba, *The 1980 Census: Policymaking Amid Turbulence* (Lexington, MA: Lexington Books, 1983), detail the political, legal, and statistical aspects of the undercount.

16. See final report by PriceWatershouseCoopers at http://govinfo.library.unt.edu/cmb/cmbp/reports/final_report/fin_sec5_effect.pdf.

17. For an excellent overview of the changes and continuing design issues, see *2010 Census: Cost and Design Issues Need to Be Addressed Soon* (Washington, DC: GAO-04-37, January 15, 2004).

18. J. Scott, "A Census Query is Said to Skew Data on Latinos," *New York Times,* June 27, 2001.

19. For an excellent discussion of the issues involved in the racial categories, see L. Wright, "One Drop of Blood," *New Yorker,* July 25, 1994, 46–55.

20. A March 14, 2001, press release, "Questions and Answers for Census 2000 Data on Race," discusses issues associated with categorizing racial data and comparing the races over time. The press release is available at the Bureau's web site, www.census.gov/Press-Release/2001/raceqandas.html.

21. N. L. Stevens, *Census Reform: Major Expansion in Use of Administrative Records for 2000 is Doubtful* (Washington, DC: General Accounting Office, GAO/T-GGD-92–54, 1992), 4–6.

22. *Design and Methodology: Technical Paper 63* (Washington, DC Current Population Survey, March 2000): H–1.

23. Dowell Myers, *Analysis with Local Census Data: Portraits of Change* (San Diego: Academic Press, 1992), 16–17. Those interested in doing research with census data, particularly for the investigation of local areas, should see this book. Beginners as well as those with considerable experience working with census data will find it useful.

24. See http://factfinder.census.gov/home/en/acs_pums.html, accessed August 9, 2006.

25. See http://www.ipums.umn.edu/, accessed August 9, 2006.

26. For example, see North Carolina State Data a Center at http://sdc.state.nc.us/, accessed August 9, 2006.

27. See http://www.cdc.gov/nchs/nvss.htm, accessed August 9, 2006.

28. ICPSR, the Inter-University Consortium on Political and Social Research, is another good source for computer-accessible secondary data. Its web address is www.icpsr.umich.edu.

TERMS FOR REVIEW

secondary data
Current Population Surveys
Decennial Census of Population
   and Housing

American Community Survey
census undercount
census tract
census block

macrodata
microdata
vital statistics

QUESTIONS FOR REVIEW

The following questions should indicate whether you have a basic competency in this chapter's material.

1. What is the value of secondary data? When would you recommend collecting original data instead of relying on secondary data?

2. A regional agency plans to study the relationship between highway features and accident rates.
   a. Briefly describe how you would go about locating existing databases.

b. Briefly describe how you would decide whether existing databases were adequate for the planned study.

c. Assume that you have obtained a computerized copy of a database. What information would you need to be able to use and interpret the data?

3. You analyze a computerized database. You examine it and note that it reports 70 managers and 200 nonmanagers. The documentation indicates the data represent 60 managers and 210 nonmanagers. What would you do?

4. Why is an undercount of the population during the Decennial Census treated as a serious problem?

5. In conducting a survey regularly, such as the Decennial Census, what are the trade-offs between changing a question's wording or its responses and keeping the wording the same?

6. Why did the Census Bureau switch from using a long-form survey every 10 years as part of the Decennial Census to the American Community Survey, conducted every year?

7. How can local government planners use American Community Survey data?

PROBLEMS FOR HOMEWORK AND DISCUSSION

1. Refer to Example 9.5. In Census Tract A:
   53 percent of the adults are high school graduates
   100 percent of the population over 5 years of age speak English
   1,105 rent housing
   Median family income of female householder with no husband present and children under 18, $8,774
   Median family income in census tract, $12,580

   a. A program in Census Tract A compiles information on community services. Which of the following should receive highest priority—information on tenants' rights, high school equivalency requirements and resources, or English language resources? Justify your recommendation.

   b. Based on the above data, what types of eligibility requirements would you initially suggest adopting to make sure that those needing the services the most will receive them? (Your recommendations will be tentative, and they will be refined as you become more familiar with the community.)

2. Use the Internet or your university's library to obtain census data on the following for the state and city of your choice:
   a. Number of people over age 65
   b. Number of people under age 5
   c. Number of households with incomes between $35,000 and $75,000
   d. Median value of owner-occupied homes
   e. Percent of labor force employed in public administration

3. Assume that a hospital located in your community is assessing the need to open a long-term care facility (nursing home). Gather census data on no more than five variables. Based on these census data, what would be your initial recommendation? What other data would you want?

DISK WORK

The state legislature has funded a limited project to aid the state's poorest areas in economic development. You work for the agency that will implement and oversee the project monies. You have been asked to select no more than six counties to receive project funds. The primary criterion for the selection must be based on income.

1. Decide on an operational definition to measure a county's need for this program. The ORB Research Methods dataset contains several possible variables: mean family income, median household income, the percent of persons in poverty, median family income, and number of families in poverty.

a. Of those, identify which definition of county poverty you would choose to use. Make a preliminary argument for its operational validity.

b. Use your operational definition to select the project counties.

c. By examining the data, identify at least three other variables that would support your choice of these particular six counties.

d. Write a short memo (no more than one page, single-spaced) for the state legislature identifying your county choices and providing evidence to justify them.

e. Compare your recommendations with those of your classmates. Can the class as a whole reach a consensus on which counties should receive funding?

2. We have found that students make some common errors when working with macro-data. To illustrate these errors, examine the following relationships in counties using the ORB Research Methods dataset:

a. the relationship between median family money income and number of families in poverty. Are these two indicators measuring the same concept? Why or why not?

b. the number of families in poverty and the number of violent crimes. Are these two variables related? According to these data, what can you say about the hypothesis that poverty is the root of violent crime?

c. the crime index and median family income. Are these two variables related? Is this a better test of the hypothesis that poverty is the root of violent crime? Why or why not?

d. median family income and the number of child abuse and neglect cases. Can one conclude from the evidence that children from poorer parents are more likely to abuse or neglect their children? Justify your answer.

RECOMMENDED FOR FURTHER READING

For information on secondary analysis, see *Secondary Analysis of Available Data Bases*, ed. D. J. Bowering (San Francisco: Jossey-Bass, New Directions for Program Evaluation, 1984). This collection includes J. C. Fortune and J. K. McBee's detailed essay on merging and verifying databases.

The Committee on National Statistics, Commission on Behavioral and Social Sciences and Education, National Research Council, *Sharing Research Data*, eds. S. E. Fienberg, M. E. Martin, and M. I. Straf (Washington, DC: National Academy Press, 1985), includes the committee's report and essays. Its essays discuss data sharing in the social sciences, with a list of data-sharing facilities and legal policies covering data sharing.

M. H. Maier with T. Easton, *The Data Game*, 3d ed. (Armonk, NY: M. E. Sharpe, 1999), is an excellent compendium of some commonly used databases and their limitations. The book is especially strong in identifying common problems of misinterpreting data.

J. S. and J. Stratford, *Major U.S. Statistical Series: Definitions, Publications, Limitations* (Chicago: American Library Association, 1992) is another work that identifies major databases and measures.

Descriptions of Census Bureau products, data, and methodology may be found at its web site (www.census.gov). The reports prepared by the General Government Division of GAO are a good source of various details (www.gao.gov). Census staff also report on census research activities at professional conferences, including the American Statistical Association's sections on survey research methods. Stephen E. Fienberg and Margo J. Anderson, *Who Counts? The Politics of Census-Taking in Contemporary America* (New York: Russell Sage Foundation, 1999), have a discussion of the controversy surrounding the undercount and sampling and racial classifications.

On understanding the issues surrounding the changes to the Decennial Census, see *Reengineering the 2010 Census: Risks and Challenges*, Daniel L. Cork, Michael L. Cohen, and Benjamin F. King, eds., Panel on Research on Future Census Methods, Committee on National Statistics Division of Behavioral and Social Sciences and Education National Research Council (Washington, DC: National Academies Press, 2004).

CHAPTER 10

Combining Indicators: Index Construction

In this chapter you will learn

1. The reasons for using indices.
2. Issues involved in the development of indices.
3. Some common methods of developing indices.
4. Ways to standardize measures for use in indices.
5. The uses of index numbers.

Administrators often find it useful to combine several indicators to form a single measure. For example, one indicator is rarely adequate to measure a community's need for health services, the amount of crime in a neighborhood, or the level of sanitation. To measure the health status of a neighborhood, an administrator would want to use more than one indicator of a disease or condition and would combine several indicators into a composite measure called an index. *Index* is a term for a set of variables used as a measure for a more abstract concept. Each variable is called an item or indicator; an index will be composed of two or more items or indicators.

We are all familiar with a number of commonly used indices, such as the consumer price index (CPI), the National Association of Security Dealers Automatic Quotations (NASDAQ), which tracks stock market activity, and students' grade point averages (GPA). The consumer price index is used to measure the prices of goods that consumers purchase. Obviously, the price of more than one good must be included to obtain an accurate and valid measure. The prices of a basket of representative goods are combined to arrive at a value for the CPI. The NASDAQ provides an indicator of the performance of the stock market by combining a measure of the performance of a set of selected stocks. And we are all familiar with the grade point average illustrated in Table 10.1. Grades are assigned a numerical value and combined to provide a measure of academic performance.

TABLE 10.1   **EXAMPLE OF AN INDEX: THE GRADE POINT AVERAGE (GPA)**

Course	Letter Grade	Numerical Grade	Credit Hours	Points (grade × hours)
Math	C	2.0	3.0	6.0
History	A	4.0	3.0	12.0
Economics	B	3.0	4.0	12.0
Total			10.0	30.0

GPA = Total points divided by total credit hours
= 30/10
= 3.00

The value of the index is computed using an equation that includes all the items that are part of the index. The result is a composite of two or more numbers, each representing an item in the index. A more operationally valid and reliable measure can usually be obtained if several components of an attribute, rather than only one, are used. A measure of crime in a neighborhood that combines the rates of several different crimes including burglaries, assaults, homicides, and robberies will be more valid and reliable than one that uses only one crime, such as the rate of home burglaries. Indices are often constructed so that seemingly different things can be combined and described by a single number. For example, an index of environmental health included measures of child mortality, water quality, adequate sanitation, and indoor air pollution.[1]

Researchers often do not distinguish between indices and scales and use the terms interchangeably. A *scale* combines indicators according to rules that are designed to reflect only a single dimension of a concept.[2] Strictly speaking, a scale assigns a number to a case based on how that case fits into a previously identified pattern of indicators. An index usually refers to any combination of indicators. True scales can be difficult and complex to construct and their operational validity and reliability difficult to establish. Numerous published scales are available for the study of attitudes, opinions, beliefs, and other mental states. They range from some developed for specific projects to standardized (and copyrighted) scales for the measurement of common concepts such as managerial stress and job satisfaction. Readers interested in these or in the various types of scaling procedures should consult the books listed at the end of the chapter. We discuss only index construction and will not delve into scaling as such.

Some indices have been validated through long and varied experience. Before constructing a new index, analysts should attempt to locate and review indices that others doing similar kinds of research have developed. We will discuss four important issues in developing indices. These are:

1. Defining the concept to be measured
2. Selecting the items to be included in the index
3. Combining the items to form an index
4. Weighting the separate items

DEFINING THE CONCEPT

A clear understanding and definition of the concept to be measured are needed. The analyst should be able to explain what the concept means and, theoretically, what its components are. In Chapter 4 we discussed conceptual and operational definitions. The first step in developing a measure is to define and describe the concept to be measured. The literature should be reviewed to find definitions used by others. We should define a concept in the same way that others have unless there is good reason for not doing so.

An operational definition of a concept details how the concept is to be measured; this is done in the remaining steps. However, the conceptual definition will determine the appropriateness of each possible measure included in the operational definition. We want the correspondence between the conceptual and operational definitions to be close. When selecting items for a measure, the analyst should be able to discuss how each item measures the concept as defined.

SELECTING THE ITEMS

Choosing items carefully for a composite measure is important. The analyst should be concerned about four things. First, use the right items—those that represent the dimension of interest and no other. Second, include enough items to distinguish among all the important gradations of a dimension and to improve reliability. The emphasis here is on thinking of lots of items. Items that do not result in any variation when applied are not useful and should not be included. Such items would classify all cases as the same even if there are differences among them. Third, decide whether every item is supposed to represent the entire dimension of interest or whether each is to represent just part of the dimension. Fourth, keep costs down and reduce unnecessary complexity by excluding items that provide no additional information.

Recall that an operationally valid measure should be relevant and representative. The items selected for the index should cover the characteristic being measured in a balanced way. An analyst constructing an index to measure management performance for an agency would include those aspects that he felt were important. For example, if personnel turnover, absenteeism, and the number of grievances were all thought to be important, a measure leaving out any of these may be biased.

One's knowledge of the subject matter related to a topic being measured can be very important in selecting items. Items should not be picked arbitrarily; they should be theoretically or conceptually related to what the analyst wants to measure. Those that logically relate to the concept being measured should be given top priority. Evidence from other sources that indicates an item is related to the concept being measured should be considered. For each item the analyst should be able to write at least a few sentences explaining why she thinks it should be included.

Analysts may use several methods to choose items for an index. They may rely on their own judgment. Or they may talk to people who are knowledgeable in the area and to potential users of the index to determine what they think is important. One danger in talking to too many users, however, is that if they think that they will ever have a use for an item, they may suggest including it. You must guard against including unneeded items.

Analysts may prefer methods that make it possible to assess how well a set of items "hangs together", that is, whether each item in a set contributes significantly to the reliable measurement of a well-defined concept. Items hang together when each of them reflects the underlying dimension in roughly the same way. They also hang together when several measures are all associated—correlated—with each other. When this happens the separate measures may all be tapping the same concept, and the analyst may prefer to drop some items. One method for reducing a large number of associated items and combining them into fewer indices is factor analysis. Later in the chapter we discuss factor analysis and how it can be used to select among variables to be included in an index. For an index analysts want measures that are related to each other but not too highly related. Two measures that are perfectly related, that is correlated, with each other would not both be included.

The validity of a measure is greatly dependent upon the items selected for the index. The validity of an index's content can be evaluated by reviewing the items involved in measuring the concept. In developing an index to measure performance of personnel, a supervisor would want to be sure that the items in the index represented the content of the performance being evaluated. That is, the content of the index should match what is thought to be important about the employee's performance. Example 10.1 illustrates the construction of an index and the content-based evidence of its operational validity.

 EXAMPLE 10.1

Index Construction and Operational Validity

Problem: A supervisor wants to develop an index to appraise the performance of her subordinates.

Procedure: After reviewing her agency's personnel policies and the job descriptions of those she supervises and discussing the task with other supervisors, she determines that the following characteristics are most important: accuracy in filling out standard forms, production (the number of forms completed and entered in the office database in a week's time), knowledge of her office's filing system, ability to use the filing system in her office, and facility with computer software. The supervisor then selects items for the index to measure the employee's performance in these areas.

Comment: The items that the supervisor selects must measure the employee's performance in these areas in order for the index as a measure to be relevant and representative. If one or more of these criteria were not included in the index, a critic could argue that it is not operationally valid based on its content. If evaluation of other characteristics were included, such as the employee's attitude or dress, this also would affect the validity of the index.

COMBINING THE ITEMS IN AN INDEX

An administrator can use a variety of methods to combine the values for separate measures into an index. The simplest and most common procedure is simply to add the values of the separate items. A City Stress Index provides an example of simple adding, using rankings on four separate items. The authors of this index obtained data on four indicators of psychological stress for cities. These were the rates for each of the following: alcoholism, divorce, suicide, and crime. They then ranked the 300 largest cities in the nation on each of the four indicators and added the ranks together for a composite ranking for each of the cities.[3] Another common procedure is to find an average of the values of the separate items. Items for an index also may be combined by a more complicated equation to compute a single value. The individual values may be multiplied or divided by each other, for example.

Ranges for indices include absolute ranges, such as items with a minimum and maximum value. Others use a relative standard, such as the degree to which each individual case has attained the group average on an item. Using the literacy rate for a country to measure development would be an example of the first. Literacy can range from zero to 100 percent. The extent to which a country's average life span reaches the average life span for all countries would be an example of the second.[4]

The values of each separate item may need to be transformed to be combined. Often the separate items will be in different units and have different ranges of values. For example, in an index to determine grant eligibility for a community, one cannot meaningfully add the percent of unemployed adults to the per capita income of residents. Methods of transforming measures so that they can be combined to accurately measure the characteristic of interest are discussed later in the chapter.

WEIGHTING THE SEPARATE ITEMS

Each item should contribute to the index in proportion to its importance. For some indices we will want each item to have the same influence. For others we may decide that some items are more important and want them to have greater influence on the final index. We can *weight* the separate items differently if we want them to have different influence on the index. You may create an index to evaluate the desirability of different job offers, for example, and decide that the following items are important: salary, location, and vacation time. Assume that you need to decide between two jobs and construct the following index.

Job Offer A		Job Offer B	
Salary	= 1	Salary	= 2
Location	= 2	Location	= 1
Vacation	= 1	Vacation	= 2

The numbers are the ranks of each of the items for each job offer; the higher the number, the better the job. The number 2, for example, means that the job ranks higher on that item than the other job does. Salary for Job B is preferable to the salary for Job A, but the location for Job A seems better to you than the location for Job B, and so on. You also decide that salary is by far the most important thing that you are looking for in a new job and that the amount of vacation time is not nearly as important. So you decide to weight each item by how important it is and multiply the rank of each item by its weight.

The index provides a higher value for Job B than for Job A. If you have included the proper items and weighted them accurately, you would choose Job B over Job A.

Job Offer A	Weights	Job Offer B	Weights
Salary = 1	× 4 = 4	Salary = 2	× 4 = 8
Location = 2	× 2 = 4	Location = 1	× 2 = 2
Vacation = 1	× 1 = 1	Vacation = 2	× 1 = 2
Total Index Value	9		12

The Uniform Crime Index adds together the number of crimes per 100,000 people for each of a wide variety of crimes including murder, manslaughter, rape, and burglary. Table 10.2 gives an example of the crime rate index for two cities. Note that the level of crime in the two cities is the same on the index, although the cities have different rates for each of the crimes in the index. Each crime in the index is treated as having the same importance. Since the Crime Index is dominated by property crimes, changes in the rates of other, more violent crimes have less impact on it.[5]

Sometimes administrators may want to assign varying weights to separate items when combining several into an index. The weight is determined by the importance of an item to the attribute being measured. If an index is described as being "unweighted," it typically means that each item comprising it is weighted the same. We need to be careful that we do not unintentionally allow some items to have undue influence on the index. This might happen if we tried to combine items whose values had much different scales or ranges. An item with values that range from 1 to 50 differs considerably from an item whose values range from 1 to 10. The difference between 5 and 10 on the first item is probably not as important as the difference between 5 and 10 on the second. However, if we simply added them together, they both would have the same influence on the index.

TABLE 10.2 THE CRIME RATE INDEX FOR TWO CITIES

City A		City B	
Crime	Rate	Crime	Rate
Homicide	5	Homicide	8
Manslaughter	7	Manslaughter	6
Rape	13	Rape	10
Burglary	35	Burglary	36
Total	60	Total	60

EXAMPLE 10.2

Community Financial Stress Index

Item 1. Percentage of population applying for any kind of public assistance. Lowest community = 10; highest = 50; Community C = 14; Community D = 20.

   Item 2. Percent increase in the number of business failures from previous year. Lowest community = 1; highest = 10; Community C = 7; Community D = 1.

Financial Stress Index Values:

	Item 1	Item 2	Total
Community C =	14%	7%	= 21%
Community D =	20%	1%	= 21%

Both communities have the same total value on the index. However, the difference between the values for Item 1 is likely to be much more important than the difference between the values for Item 2. Although both items are measured in the same units—percents—they have greatly different ranges and simply adding them together gives greater weight to the first item.

The index to measure financial stress in communities, discussed in Example 10.2, gives an example of this situation. In Item 1 of the index, the range of values obtained went from 10 to 50, and in Item 2 the range was from 1 to 10.

CREATING STANDARDIZED INDICATORS FOR INDICES

Separate items in indices must be included so that each is in comparable units and contributes appropriately to the composite measure. It is often necessary to *standardize* the individual measures so that each is based on the same scale and items measured in different units may be combined. If this is not done, one item may contribute more to the final index than another simply because of different values or ranges. Combining, transforming, and weighting the separate items in an index are related issues. Transforming the items will often reduce the risk that any one item will have undue influence in the index. We can then decide how we want to weight the separate items; if we want some to have more weight, we can multiply the values of those items by a factor before combining them, as in the job-offer example. In building an index the analyst should address the two issues of transforming the measures and weighting the items separately.

   As an example, consider an index of intercity hardship created by combining six measures including the unemployment rate and dependency, that is the percentage of persons under 18 or over 64.[6] Although the second figure could vary more among cities, the first may be more important, and a few points' difference in the unemployment rate may be very important. To measure each variable using the same units and to prevent the second measure from having undue weight, researchers standardized the variables. Example 10.3 presents a detailed example drawn from the research mentioned above.[7]

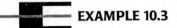

EXAMPLE 10.3

Creation of an Intercity Hardship Index
Quantifiable Measures and Definitions

1. *Unemployment:* percent of civilian labor force unemployed
2. *Dependency:* percent of persons under 18 or over 64
3. *Education:* percent of persons 25 years of age or older with less than a 12th-grade education
4. *Income level:* per capita income
5. *Crowded housing:* percent of occupied housing units with more than one person per room
6. *Poverty:* percent of families below 125 percent of low-income level

Note that the range of each of these variables could differ considerably. Also, the income level variable is not a percent as are the other five. In order to standardize them, each of the variables was treated in the following manner: The lowest value of the variable was assigned the value 0; the highest was assigned a value of 100. The value for cities in between was determined by the following formula:

$$x = ((y - y_a)/(y_b - y_a)) \times (100)$$

where:

x = standardized value to be created for each city
y = value on a specific measure of need for each city
y_a = value of y indicating least need
y_b = value of y indicating greatest need

Thus, for each measure, the city with the greatest need (the highest unemployment, the lowest per capita income, and so on) was assigned a score of 100, and the city with the lowest need was assigned a score of 0. Consider unemployment and per capita income as examples.

Unemployment: The city having the lowest unemployment is Fargo, with 1.5 percent; the highest rate occurs in El Centro, California, with 17.6 percent. Determine the standardized value for El Paso with an unemployment rate of 11.1 percent.

$$x = ((\text{El Paso rate} - \text{lowest})/(\text{highest} - \text{lowest})) \times 100$$
$$= ((11.1 - 1.5)/(17.6 - 1.5)) \times 100 = 59.63$$

Income: Per capita income: highest = Newport Beach at $63,000; lowest = Newark at $13,100. Lower per capita income indicates greater need. Determine standardized value for El Paso, with per capita income at $15,300.

$$\text{Standardized measure of income for El Paso} =$$
$$(($15,300 - $63,000) \div ($13,100 - $63,000)) \times 100 = 95.59$$

■■■■■■ **EXAMPLE 10.3** *Continued*

Since a higher income level is considered to be more desirable than a lower one, the lowest value for income is given the value of 100. This city then has the highest value of need on the per capita income measure. Both variables are now standardized to a range of 0 to 100 and are measured in the same units. (The units, of course, are percents. They are not the amounts of unemployment or of income.) The standardized measures for each variable can be added together to obtain an index value for each city.

Each separate variable in the index is standardized in the fashion described and summed for each city. Table 10.3 shows the low and high values for each variable and the standardized value for the example city, El Paso.

TABLE ■ **10.3**   **DEVELOPING STANDARDIZED VALUES FOR THE ITEMS IN AN INDEX FOR CITIES**

			El Paso	
Variable	High	Low	Unstandardized	Standardized
1	17.6%	1.5%	11.1%	59.63
2	42%	7%	41%	97.14
3	31%	5%	31%	100.00
4	$13,100[a]	$63,000[b]	$15,300	95.59
5	39%	10%	29%	65.52
6	35%	14%	21%	33.33
Total				451.21

[a]greatest need
[b]lowest need

Note that the highest possible value for the index would be 600. A city would have this value only if it were the highest on each of the separate variables.

The separate factors in an index such as this can be averaged. That is, the total value for each case would be divided by the number of factors in the index. For this index, the total for each city would be divided by 6. For El Paso, the six-item average would be 75.20. The maximum average for the index would be 100.

Indices like the one described above have been developed to measure city stress and community need to determine allocation formulas for grants. Each of the indicators in this index was standardized and weighted equally. However, different weights could have been assigned to each. Another method of creating standardized measures is to calculate the z-scores of cases on each of a series of separate measures and then add the z-scores. An example of this approach is included in Appendix 10.1 at the end of this chapter.

EXAMPLES OF CREATING INDICES

Likert Scaling

A common method of building indices is called *Likert scaling*.[8] Likert scales also are called summated rating scales. The procedure is relatively easy to use. To develop an index using Likert scaling, the analyst selects a set of statements, each of which reflects favorably or unfavorably on some aspect of the characteristic that he wants to measure. A rating form is provided for each item with several ranked responses. The dimension is then rated on each item according to the responses provided. A numerical value is assigned to each response, and the values are summed to obtain a single numerical value. An alternative is to sum the separate ratings and divide by the number of items to provide an average of the responses to each item.

Likert scaling is often used to measure opinions or attitudes of individuals. If it is used in an interview or survey, respondents are asked to indicate on the rating scale the degree to which they agree or disagree with each statement. The agreement scale may have only two choices (Agree–Disagree), or it may have more choices, permitting a respondent to indicate a level of agreement or disagreement. Five categories are commonly used: Strongly Agree, Agree, Neutral or No Opinion, Disagree, and Strongly Disagree. Some forms omit the neutral category, and some add even more categories to permit finer distinctions. An equal number of positive and negative statements is recommended. An unequal number of positive or negative response categories may bias responses. For positive statements the categories are scored 1, 2, 3, 4, 5, with 1 indicating "Strongly Disagree" and 5 indicating "Strongly Agree." If the statement is unfavorable toward the subject, the scoring is reversed, as in Example 10.4. The respondent's

---

■ EXAMPLE 10.4

An Example of a Likert Scale Index

The following was developed to assess client satisfaction with a public agency.

Item 1. The staff of this agency always treat me with respect.

_____ Strongly Agree   _____ Agree   _____ Neither Agree nor Disagree
     (5)   (4)   (3)

_____ Disagree   _____ Strongly Disagree
     (2)   (1)

Item 2. I never have to wait longer than 20 minutes for service at this agency.

_____ Strongly Agree   _____ Agree   _____ Neither Agree nor Disagree
     (5)   (4)   (3)

_____ Disagree   _____ Strongly Disagree
     (2)   (1)

EXAMPLE 10.4 *Continued*

Item 3. I am often told to come on the wrong day by staff of this agency.

_____ Strongly Agree   _____ Agree   _____ Neither Agree nor Disagree
            (1)   (2)   (3)

_____ Disagree   _____ Strongly Disagree
            (4)   (5)

Item 4. I am not satisfied with the services provided by this agency.

_____ Strongly Agree   _____ Agree   _____ Neither Agree nor Disagree
            (1)   (2)   (3)

_____ Disagree   _____ Strongly Disagree
            (4)   (5)

The numbers under the responses are the values for each item. They can be added together to obtain a value for the index. Of course, more items would usually be included. The numbers representing the values of each response category would not necessarily appear on the questionnaire. Notice that the direction of Items 3 and 4 is reversed from that of Items 1 and 2. Items 1 and 2 are positive statements, and if the client agrees with them a higher value is given. Items 3 and 4 are negative statements, and if the client agrees with them a lower value is given. People often get into the habit when answering questions of this nature of either agreeing or disagreeing without giving the item adequate thought. It is therefore wise to change the direction of some of the items so that the client is more likely to think through an answer before responding. Note also the "Neither Agree nor Disagree" category. This response is often included in Likert scaling.

Two alternatives are used to combine the responses to these items into an index. The first is to add the numerical value of the response to each item. Assume that a client gave the following responses to the questionnaire in this example.

Item	Response	Numerical Value of Response
1.	Agree	4
2.	Agree	4
3.	Strongly Disagree	5
4.	Strongly Disagree	5
Total		18

The total would be the index value. If one of the items did not apply to this agency, or if the client did not respond to one or more of the items, adding the total responses would be inappropriate. The alternative is to add the total values of each response and divide by the number of items answered. This would give an average value for each item and would be more accurate if some items were not answered. Using this approach for the client above would result in an index value of 18/4 = 4.5.

Continued

EXAMPLE 10.4 *Continued*

If we used the index in another agency where Item 3 did not apply, we might find a client giving the following responses:

Item	Response	Numerical Value of Response
1.	Agree	5
2.	Agree	4
3.	(No answer. Clients come in at their convenience.)	NA
4.	Strongly Disagree	5
Total		13

To compare this total to the total for the first agency would be inappropriate and inaccurate. Dividing the total by the number of items answered gives a more accurate value and one that can be compared to the average of the first agency.

Total/number of items answered = 13/3 = 4.33.

index value is the sum of the values on the separate items. Example 10.4 shows an example of a typical Likert scale used as an index to assess clients' satisfaction with agency service.

The first stage of constructing a Likert scale is the selection of the items. Although no definitive set of procedures exists, we offer the following general suggestions. First, understand the concept to be measured. The analyst should be able to write a few paragraphs about the concept and why each item is chosen and explain how she thinks each item relates to the concept being measured. Much of what applies to writing good questions for questionnaires applies to the construction of items for Likert scales. Once statements have been selected, they should be pretested. The relationship of each item to the total score should be examined. In general, one wants items that are highly associated with the total scores. The items in a Likert scale need not be weighted equally. However, in practice most Likert scales treat items with parity. One criticism of Likert-type indices is that the same total score can be obtained in a variety of ways. One of the main advantages is that they are easily constructed.

Indices based on the Likert scaling technique do not always use the "Strongly Agree" to "Strongly Disagree" continuum. And although each item has the same number of response categories, every item may not have the same responses. Example 10.5 shows such an index.

A Likert-type index represents an ordinal level of measurement. The items do not really measure the quantity of a characteristic, but we can use the items to rank the cases. However, by adding together the numbers assigned to the response categories for each item or by calculating the mean for the scale, we are treating the measurement as if it were interval. This practice allows us to use more statistical techniques for analysis.

EXAMPLE 10.5

Example Index

A city's Public Works director wishes to evaluate the cleanliness of neighborhoods surrounding the city's solid-waste transfer and materials recycling stations. He prepares an index for inspectors to use once a month. Inspectors are to check one rating for each item.

Neighborhood Cleanliness Index

1. The entire area looks like a pleasant residential neighborhood.

    _____Very much   (A)
    _____Somewhat   (B)
    _____Not at all   (C)

2. Loose trash such as paper, bottles, and cans are visible.

    _____Not at all   (A)
    _____Somewhat   (B)
    _____Very much   (C)

3. Grass is neatly trimmed and weeds are kept out.

    _____Very much   (A)
    _____Somewhat   (B)
    _____Not at all   (C)

4. Streets and sidewalks are dusty or dirty.

    _____Not at all   (A)
    _____Somewhat   (B)
    _____Very much   (C)

Numerical values are assigned to each response in the following manner:

$$A = 3; B = 2; C = 1$$

If an inspector rated a neighborhood as shown below, the corresponding numerical values would be assigned:

Item	Rating	Numerical Value
1.	B	2
2.	A	3
3.	A	3
4.	B	2

The total would be 10. The inspector could divide this by 4—the number of items—to obtain a cleanliness index value of 2.5 for the neighborhood. This number could be used to compare the cleanliness of the neighborhood with other neighborhoods or with the same neighborhood at some previous time.

Continued

EXAMPLE 10.5 *Continued*

Note that the higher the value of the index, the cleaner the neighborhood. If the value of the index falls below a certain level, the director would probably wish to address the problem and take corrective action.

The operational validity and reliability of the index also should be determined. If the items comprising the index were known to be the factors that most concerned nearby residents, then it would probably be a content-valid measure. However, the director would need to verify that each inspector used the index in the same way and that the index allowed the inspectors to assess cleanliness accurately.

FACTOR ANALYSIS

Factor analysis is a technique used to investigate the relationship between theoretical concepts and empirical indicators. It also is used to reduce a large number of items to a smaller, more manageable number of indices. Analysts use it to select items and determine their importance to an index. One method of factor analysis transforms a set of variables into a new, smaller set of composite variables. It can show which items should be used in an index and how they should be weighted. The technique involves a large number of calculations. However, computer programs can quickly do the computations and provide the necessary information. You are likely to see the application of factor analysis in reports using or developing indices.

Factor analysis was developed to help construct indicators of abstract concepts. The basic ideas were developed in the context of using examination grades to measure general intelligence. Suppose we have a large number of students' exam grades on six courses taken during a semester. We would expect that a student's exam grades in the different courses would be related to each other. The original investigators suggested that the link among the exam grades was the individual's general level of intelligence and was not directly observable. The investigators suggested that grades in all subject areas would depend to some extent on this factor. General intelligence could be considered a factor common to the performance on all of the tests. The several exam grades can then be used as a measure of this factor.

When factor analysis is used to condense a large number of items into a smaller number of indices the composite should have greater reliability and operational validity than the items taken separately. Factor analysis also can be used to identify individual variables to combine in order to measure a complex concept and thus help select the variables to include in an index. Factor analysis calculates how closely a large number of variables, assumed to be associated with each other, are related to a common dimension or factor. The analyst can pick variables that seem to be most closely associated with that factor and then use them in the index. The factor analysis results can also help in showing how to combine the separate variables.

For example, assume an analyst has data on several characteristics of counties in his state. These might include utilization of public services such as hospitals and parks; measures of conditions such as prevalence of diseases, the number of high school graduates and dropouts, and the number of handicapped; and measures of per capita income, employment, types of jobs, assessed evaluation of county real property, and so on. The analyst wants to develop indices of human service needs and financial condition. A factor analysis could help determine which of the separate indicators best measure these two dimensions. It would show the analyst how the individual measures are related to the two conceptual dimensions of human service needs and financial condition. The analysis will help him pick out the indicators to use in the two indices and in the weighting of these indicators.

Factor analysis is based on the concept of association. Associations among variables are assumed to reflect the extent to which the variables measure the same trait or factor. Factor analysis begins by calculating association measures between each pair of variables of interest. Then, a factor that maximizes the associations among the variables in the set is created mathematically. Next, coefficients measuring the association between each variable and the factor are calculated. These coefficients, called *factor loadings,* vary between zero and 1; the closer the loading is to 1, the more closely the variable is associated with the factor. Variables showing high loadings with a factor are considered to be measures of that factor. The analyst using factor analysis to help build an index would use as items in that index those variables that had the highest loadings with the factor.

Factor analysis is also used to determine which underlying dimensions are measured by a group of separate indicators. In an effort to learn more about which local governments were likely to suffer strikes by public employees, James Perry and William Berkes conducted a factor analysis of a large number of government characteristics of communities.[9] Perry and his colleagues did not know what factors would emerge from the analysis. They had a large number of separate variables and wanted to use them to create indices to predict how likely it was that localities would experience strikes.

These authors analyzed the following "public-employment variables":

a. Ratio of local government employee earnings to private-sector employee earnings

b. Ratio of local employee earnings to teacher earnings

c. Local government employment as a percentage of nonagricultural employment

d. Ratio of local employee legal policy to teacher policy

e. Number of teacher strikes in one year

f. Number of public employees involved in work stoppages over a 10-year period

g. Public-sector employee-days idle, 10-year period

TABLE 10.4	PREDICTING PUBLIC-EMPLOYEE STRIKE ACTIVITY: DETERMINING AND MEASURING THE IMPORTANT FACTORS

Factors and Factor Loadings[a]

Variable	Local Employee Status	Past Strike Activity
a	.97	−.01
b	.99	−.02
c	.93	−.02
d	.69	.05
e	−.05	.46
f	.05	.99
g	.08	.97

[a]Remember that the factor loadings are measures of how closely a variable is associated with the underlying factor.

SOURCE: James Perry and William Berkes, "Predicting Local Strike Activity," *Western Political Quarterly* (Spring 1979), pp. 501–517.

The factor analysis generated two factors from these variables. The authors named the factors based on the variables with the highest loadings on that factor. The first was called "Local Employee Status" and the second "Past Strike Activity." The factors with the factor loadings of the variables on each are shown in Table 10.4. The authors used these loadings to create indices of "Local Employee Status" and "Past Strike Activity." These composite indices were used to assess how likely it was that any local government would experience a public-employee strike in the near future.

An analyst also can use the results of factor analysis to determine a value for each case for the index. The factor-analysis program provides a second coefficient, called a *factor score coefficient*, for each variable. These are the weights to be used; the analyst multiplies each by the original value of the case on that variable. The results are added to obtain the index value for each case. This value is called a *factor score*. Example 10.6 shows an index developed with factor analysis and the factor score coefficients used. (See Appendix 10.2 for the details on how to calculate a factor score.)

In an effort to develop several indices of urban needs, researchers used factor analysis to select items for each index. They wished to develop indices of health, social service, recreational, environmental, public safety, and transportation needs and analyzed a large number of separate measures of community characteristics.[10] The factor analysis showed how the individual variables were associated with five different factors. Five indices were developed from the loadings on these five factors. Example 10.6 shows the items selected to form an index of health needs for cities because of the high loading of each of these items with the factor named "Health Needs." The factor score coefficients also are shown. Computer programs that perform factor analysis also will produce the factor score coefficients and can also calculate the composite value, the factor score, for each city.

EXAMPLE 10.6

Need Index

Factor	Composite Variables	Factor Score Coefficients
Health needs	1. Local suicide rate	.73
	2. Infant mortality rate	.64
	3. Birth rate	.55
	4. Death rate	.51
	5. Families with income below $7,500	.44

The composite value computed for each city on the index, the factor score, is obtained by multiplying the coefficient for each variable by the value that the city has for that variable. The formula that is applied in each case is:

factor score = .73 × (value on variable 1) + .64 × (value on variable 2) + .55 × (value on variable 3) + .51 × (value on variable 4) + .44 × (value on variable 5).

In combining the values for each separate item, it is usually necessary to use the cities' z-scores for each variable rather than the cities' actual value. Appendix 10.1, at the end of this chapter, shows how to do this and calculates the index value for an example city. The z-score is used to account for different units of measurement and different ranges of the separate items.

Factor analysis requires interval level measurement, although analysts sometimes use it when the variables are measured at ordinal and even nominal levels. A large number of cases is also needed to develop reliable factors.

INDEX NUMBERS

Index numbers express the relationship between two figures, one of which is the base, and are used to describe changes over time in such things as prices, production, wages, and unemployment. Indices such as the CPI are used extensively in the analysis of economic conditions. The CPI combines prices for a large number of separate items to measure the cost of living and to describe changes in economic variables over time. This index produces a summary statistic called an *index number*.[11] The CPI, as an index number, provides information on (1) a composite price of a standard set of goods and services, and (2) the percent change that has occurred in the composite over a given time. To facilitate comparison, the index is expressed as a percentage, a proportion, or a ratio.

The CPI, probably the most commonly used and well-known index number, has many subcomponents. It groups the prices of more than 400 commodities

TABLE	10.5		CHANGES IN THE CPI OVER TIME					
Year:	1 (Base)	2	3	4	5	6	7	8
Index:	100	101.9	105.5	109.6	111.2	115.7	121.1	127.4

SOURCE: U.S. Department of Labor, *CPI Detailed Report for March 1993* (Washington, DC: Bureau of Labor Statistics).

and services into eight categories.[12] The index measures price changes from a designated reference date, which is set equal to 100. An increase of 50 percent, for example, is shown by the index as 150. This change also can be expressed in dollars as follows: The price of a set of goods and services in the CPI has risen from $10 in the base year to $15. One can treat the index number as a percent to determine by what percent the price of goods and services has increased since the base year. Currently, the period 1982–1984 is used as the base for the components of the CPI. Table 10.5 illustrates how index numbers show the relative increase in a factor of interest, such as prices. The index number for year 5, for example, shows that the prices of goods and services have increased by 11.2 percent since the base year.

Administrators often wish to assess growth in the amount of money spent by the organizations they direct. However, they usually like to separate increases in expenditures due to increased services and activities from growth due to inflation. An index number helps them to do that. For example, the administrator of a county hospital can use a component of the CPI to compare increases in the cost of hospital and health care goods and services to increases in the hospital's budget.

SUMMARY

When a single indicator is inadequate to measure a concept, investigators often use multi-item measures called indices. Three important, related issues in constructing indices are (1) selecting items to be included in the measure, which involves being very clear about what you want to measure and not omitting any important aspect; (2) combining items to form an index, which requires you to think about strengths of indices, the categories of the index, and type of index; and (3) weighting the separate items so the index satisfactorily represents the concept you had in mind when you started. Procedures and methods for accomplishing each of these were discussed. These include Likert scaling, factor analysis, and procedures for standardizing variables.

Likert scaling is most likely to be used when the cases can be rated on several items. It is easy to do and can be done even if only a few items are available. Although each item represents an ordinal scale, by assigning a numerical value to each category and adding the values for each, analysts treat the index as an interval-level measurement. The resulting index value is often treated as an interval value as well. This has the advantage of allowing the analyst to apply statistics that assume interval-level measurement.

If the separate items measure the case's attributes on an interval scale, you may prefer one of the other methods. Factor analysis is used to reduce a large number of measures to a few underlying common factors. The variables associated with each factor can be combined in a composite index. The factor analysis provides information to help in choosing the variables for the index and weights to use for each variable. Factor analysis requires a large number of cases and requires that the measures be interval level.

If separate items in the index are measured in different units, the measures must be standardized. Even if the items are measured in the same units, if the range of values for the items differs greatly, the scale or range should be standardized. If not, the greatly differing ranges may cause some of the items to have a greater impact than others, contrary to the intent of the analyst.

In constructing indices, one should determine whether each item measures the variable appropriately and then decide how to weight each item. If the ranges or units used to measure items are different, the analyst should first standardize them and then separately apply a weighting procedure.

The consumer price index (CPI) is an example of an index number. Index numbers typically express the change in some factor relative to a designated date called the base year. The CPI is set to 100 for the base year, and the number for each succeeding year indicates the percent change in prices since that year.

The previous three chapters have discussed data collection and related issues. The next chapters consider what to do with the data from a study once they have been collected. Chapter 11 discusses managing data and analyzing single variables, Chapter 12 covers statistical significance, and Chapters 13 and 14 deal with measures of association.

NOTES

1. Daniel C. Esty et al., *Pilot 2006 Environmental Performance Index* (New Haven: Yale Center for Environmental Law and Policy, 2006).
2. R. A. Singleton, B. C. Straits, and M. M. Straits, *Approaches to Social Research*, 2d ed. (New York: Oxford University Press, 1993), 397. Earl Babbie, *The Basics of Social Research*, 3d ed. (Belmont, CA: Wadsworth, 2005) Chapter 6 discusses scales and indexes and the differences between them.
3. Robert Levine, "City Stress Index: 25 Best, 25 Worst," *Psychology Today* (November 22, 1988), 52–58.
4. Allen C. Kelley discusses these issues in describing and critiquing a human development index. See Allen C. Kelley, "The Human Development Index: 'Handle With Care'" *Population and Development Review* 17, No. 2 (June 1991): 315–324.
5. The Uniform Crime Reports are described in the Federal Bureau of Investigation, U.S. Department of Justice, *Crime in the United States 1987* (Washington, DC: U.S. Government Printing Office, 1988). Also see Mark H. Maier, *The Data Game*, 3d ed. (Armonk, NY: M. E. Sharpe, 1999), Chapter 6. Maier discusses the Crime Index and how reporting methods can cause

it to be biased. He also reports on other sources of crime statistics as well as their shortcomings.
6. See Robert W. Burchell, David Listokin, George Sternlieb, James W. Hughes, and Stephen C. Casey, "Measuring Urban Distress: A Summary of the Major Urban Hardship Indices and Resource Allocation Systems," in *Cities under Stress: The Fiscal Crises of Urban America*, eds. R. Burchell and D. Listokin (Rutgers: The State University of New Jersey, 1981), 159–229. The specific index on which Example 10.3 is based was developed by Richard P. Nathan and Charles F. Adams, Jr. They measured city hardship using 1970 Census data in "Understanding Central City Hardship," *Political Science Quarterly* 91 (1), 1976, and updated the study with 1980 Census data in "Four Perspectives on Urban Hardship," *Political Science Quarterly* 104 (Fall 1989), 483–508.
7. Nathan and Adams, "Four Perspectives," 504–506; Burchell et al., *Cities Under Stress*, 159–229.
8. Although other common scaling methods, such as Thurstone, Guttman, and the semantic differential are used in basic research, most administrators are seldom likely to use them. Readers interested in pursuing these

topics will find them discussed in Andy B. Anderson, Alexander Basilevsky, and Derek P. J. Hum, "Measurement: Theory and Techniques," in *Handbook of Survey Research*, eds. Peter H. Rossi, James D. Wright, and Andy B. Anderson (New York: Academic Press, 1983), 231–287. For an extensive discussion of the distinction between indices and scales, see Earl Babbie, *The Practice of Social Research*, 9th ed. (Belmont, CA: Wadsworth/Thompson Learning, 2001), 149–152. Other sources for these topics are listed in "Recommended for Further Reading" at the end of this chapter.

9. James Perry and William Berkes, "Predicting Local Strike Activity," *Western Political Quarterly* (Spring 1979), 501–517.

10. Gregory Schmid, Hubert Lipinski, and Michael Palmer, *An Alternative Approach to General Revenue Sharing: A Needs Based Allocation Formula* (Menlo Park, CA: Institute for the Future, 1975).

11. Wayne Daniel and James Terrel, *Business Statistics*, 7th ed. (Boston: Houghton-Mifflin, 1995), 69–81. See David S. Moore, *Statistics: Concepts and Controversies*, 5th ed. (New York: W. H. Freeman and Company,

2001), 308–327, for a thorough but accessible discussion of the CPI, trends, and how to convert the purchasing power of a dollar at one time to another. The reader should note that the CPI received a great deal of criticism in 1997, and a major revision of the methodology for calculating it was discussed and researched. CPI data can also be found at http://www.bls.gov/cpi.

12. For a more detailed discussion of the Consumer Price Index, see U.S. Department of Labor, Bureau of Labor Statistics (BLS), *Handbook of Methods*, Vol. II, "The Consumer Price Index," Bulletin 2134–2, April 1984; and "The Consumer Price Index: 1987 Revision," BLS Report 736, January 1987. Also see the Department of Labor's monthly publication *CPI: Detailed Report and the Department of Commerce's Survey of Current Business* for current and historical values of the CPI and other indexes. See David Ammons, *Tools for Decision Making* (Washington, DC: CQ Press, 2002), 108–114, for a discussion of the Implicit Price Deflator (IPD), an index number appropriate for use by local governments. Ammons has clear instructions for using the IPD.

TERMS FOR REVIEW

index
weighting
Likert scaling

factor analysis
factor loading
factor score coefficient

factor score
index number

QUESTIONS FOR REVIEW

The following questions should indicate whether you have a basic competency in this chapter's material.

1. What benefits does using an index to measure a characteristic provide to an investigator?

2. How does operational validity apply to index construction?

3. Explain why an index should provide a more valid and reliable measure than a single indicator.

4. Give an example of an index for which using unweighted items is not likely to cause any problem. (Unweighted items means that all items are weighted the same.)

5. Give an example of a second index for which unweighted items are likely to result in an invalid measure.

6. Explain why transforming variables so that they are in comparable units and weighting the items are usually accomplished separately.

7. Consult a library to obtain a recent copy of the United States Department of Labor's *CPI: Detailed Report* or access the Department's web site at http://www.bls.gov/cpi. Determine how much goods and services costing $50,000 in 1982 would cost in the current year or in the year of the report. What is the CPI for the year used?

PROBLEMS FOR HOMEWORK AND DISCUSSION

1. Develop a Likert index to rate the quality of a public transportation system. List 10 items that could be included. Use the index to evaluate the bus system in a town or city with which you are familiar.

2. Refer to Example 10.4 to answer the following: Assume that a client gave the following responses to the items in the index: Agree, Disagree, Strongly Disagree, No Opinion.
   a. Calculate the index value for this client.
   b. What other item(s) would you consider adding?

3. In Example 10.3, work out the calculations for Items 2, 3, 5, and 6. (Items 1 and 4 are done in the text.) Check your answers against those listed in the example.

4. Pick a sample of five cities in your state, and apply the index discussed in Example 10.3. Remember that the lowest and highest levels of need will be based on the values from your sample, not on those in the example.

5. Name five indicators of health needs that may have been included in the set of measures factor-analyzed in the research reported in Example 10.6. Which of these indicators do you think would be most closely associated with a factor called "Community Health Needs"?

6. Find examples of indices using each of the following:
   a. Likert scaling
   b. Factor analysis

   c. Different weights for at least some of the items
   d. A method of standardizing items that measure characteristics in different units such as dollars, years of education, and percent unemployed.
      Describe how each was used and what it was intended to measure. Do you think that another technique would have been better? If so, why?

7. Consult a recent edition of the County and City Data Book and develop an index of "city hardship" using three of the following indicators: percent unemployed, average level of education, income level, amount of crowded housing, percent of residents under age 18 and over age 64. Copies of the Data Book can be found on the Internet at http://fisher.lib.Virginia.edu/ccdb. Most academic libraries also have printed copies.

8. For one of the examples found for Question 6, discuss the validity and reliability of the index. Evaluate the index in general. What criticisms, if any, do you have of the index?

9. If your class updated and gathered the James Perry and William Berkes data as suggested in Chapter 9, do a varimax factor rotation on the dataset, and compare your findings with those of Perry and Berkes.

DISK WORK

1. Refer to Example 10.3 and how the Hardship Index was constructed. Using variables in the ORB dataset, follow the same formula to create a hardship index for the 100 counties. In some cases, you will first have to create new variables using existing variables. Before carrying out this exercise, you should have worked out Problem 3 in Problems for Homework and Discussion. Based on this index, which five counties have the greatest hardship; which five counties have the least hardship?

2. Now, using at least three of the variables in the ORB Research Methods dataset, create your own county hardship index. With your new index, which five counties have the greatest hardship; which five counties have the least hardship?

3. Produce a frequency distribution for the hardship index calculated according to Example 10.3 and for your own index.

4. For each of the three counties with the greatest hardship and the three counties with the

least hardship, identify the percent of labor force employed in: manufacturing; retail trade; and service industries. Put your findings in a table similar to Table 9.1. Do these data suggest what types of economic development might be most beneficial? Write a brief memo (no more than one-page, single spaced) suggesting types of economic development activity which should be explored in more depth to benefit less-well-off counties.

RECOMMENDED FOR FURTHER READING

D. C. Miller and Neil Salkind, *Handbook of Research Design and Social Measurement: A Text and Reference Book for the Social and Behavioral Sciences,* 6th ed. (Thousand Oaks, CA: Sage Publications, 2002). Miller and Salkind list and review many existing indices covering a variety of subjects. Although the majority of these are used in basic research, many others reviewed are likely to be of interest to managers and administrators. These include measures of organizational structure, organizational effectiveness, community services, leadership in the work organization, morale, and job satisfaction.

For an extensive discussion of job-satisfaction scales and similar indices, see J. P. Robinson, R. Athansiou, and K. Head, *Measures of Occupational Attitudes and Occupational Characteristics* (Ann Arbor: Institute of Social Research, 1969). A publication similar to Robinson et al. reviews and discusses a large number of scales and indices measuring social, psychological, and related attitudes. See J. P. Robinson and P. P. Shaver, *Measures of Social Psychological Attitudes* (Ann Arbor: Institute for Social Research, 1973).

I. McDowell and C. Newell, *Measuring Health: A Guide to Rating Scales and Questionnaires* (New York: Oxford University Press, 1987), review and evaluate several indices of health and well-being.

For an extended discussion of the development and application of a new index, see *Methods and Applications in Mental Health Surveys: The Todai Health Index,* eds. S. Suzuki and R. Roberts (Tokyo: University of Tokyo Press, 1991).

Guttman scaling is discussed in R. L. Gordon, *Unidimensional Scaling of Social Variables* (New York: Macmillan, 1977).

Craig Mertler and Rachel A. Vannatta, *Advanced and Multivariate Statistical Methods,* 3d ed. (Glendale, CA: Pyrczak Publishing, 2005). Chapter 9 has an easy-to-follow discussion of factor analysis with examples of computer output.

Factor analysis is also discussed in the following (the Kim and Mueller booklet is more technical than the others):

B. B. Jackson, *Multivariate Data Analysis: An Introduction* (Homewood, IL: Richard D. Irwin, 1983).

J. Kim and C. W. Mueller, "Factor Analysis: Statistical Methods and Practical Issues," Sage University Paper Series on Quantitative Applications in the Social Sciences, 07–014 (Beverly Hills and London: Sage, 1978).

M. Hamburg, *Basic Statistics,* 2d ed. (New York: Harcourt, Brace, Jovanovich, 1979). Chapter 14 discusses index numbers and procedures for combining and weighting items.

For more information on the CPI—Consumer Price Index—see the Bureau of Labor Statistics web site: www.stats.bls.gov/cpihome.htm; and David S. Moore, *Statistics: Concepts and Controversies,* 5th ed. (New York: W.H. Freeman and Company, 2001).

APPENDIX 10.1

Using z-Scores to Standardize Measures for Indices

The z-score is calculated by the following formula:

((value of a case for a specific measure)
− (average value of the measure for all cases))/
(standard deviation of the measure)

In an index developed to measure the fiscal strain of cities, five quantifiable variables were used, and z-scores for each city on each of the measures were calculated. The variables were:

Population change, 1972 to 1976

Per capita income change, 1969 to 1974

Own-source revenue burden change, 1969 to 1974

Long-term debt burden change, 1972 to 1976

Change in local full market property value, 1971 to 1976

Statistical z-scores were developed for each city for each indicator. The five z-scores were summed for each city to obtain a Total Fiscal Strain value.[1]

You should note that each standardized measure can be given greater weight than others if desired. In the example used here, some of the z-scores were given greater weight as the analysts thought that these indicators were more important than others. The z-scores for each city were multiplied by the following weights before summing:

Variable	Weight
Population change	.37
Per capita income change	.27
Revenue burden change	.12
Long-term debt burden change	.12
Change in full market value	.12

Population change was given more weight than any other indicator in the index.[2]

Notes

1. Robert W. Burchell, David Listokin, George Sternlieb, James W. Hughes, and Stephen C. Casey, "Measuring Urban Distress: A Summary of the Major Urban Hardship Indices and Resource Allocation Systems," in *Cities under Stress: The Fiscal Crises of Urban America,* eds. R. Burchell and D. Listokin (Rutgers: The State University of New Jersey, 1981), 159–229.
2. Ibid.

APPENDIX 10.2

Calculating Factor Scale Scores

In Example 10.6, factor score coefficients were used to construct an index. This appendix gives more detail on that procedure and calculates the index value for a city using the items in the example. The z-score is calculated:

z value for each city = ((city's value for a variable) − (average value of the variable for all cities))/(standard deviation of the variable)

The z-score is a standardized measure for each variable. The mean and standard deviation for each variable are provided by the factor analysis program, and most programs also will calculate the z-scores. Commonly used factor analysis programs also have routines that will provide the factor scores for each of the cases so that this does not have to be done separately by the investigator.

The following calculates the factor score for one city.

Variable	City A's Values	z-Scores for City A	z-Score × Coefficient
1.	3 per 1,000	.5	$.5 \times .73 = .365$
2.	5 per 1,000	−.2	$-.2 \times .64 = -.128$
3.	9 per 1,000	1.0	$1.0 \times .55 = .550$
4.	2%	.5	$.5 \times .51 = .255$
5.	5,000	2.0	$2.0 \times .44 = .880$
Total			1.922

City A's value on the index is 1.922.

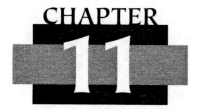

CHAPTER 11

Univariate Analysis

In this chapter you will learn

1. How to prepare and organize data for analysis.
2. About computer programs for managing and analyzing data.
3. About displaying data in graphs, tables, and charts.
4. About statistics for analyzing a single variable.
5. To calculate and interpret measures of relative frequency.
6. To calculate and interpret measures of central tendency and measures of dispersion.

An early step after collecting and assembling a set of data is to get a sense of its nature: What are the values of individual variables? How similar are the values for different cases? How different are the cases? Over what range are values distributed? Even if the analyst's purpose is to evaluate associations between variables, he also should describe the values for individual variables. Often the main purpose of a study, however, is to obtain data on individual variables, for example when the fire chief or city manager wants to find out the dollar amount of fire damages in the city over the past year.

Many of the questions we ask as administrators, analysts, and researchers require us to describe the distribution of a single variable: How many individual programs were funded last year by the county budget? What percent of welfare recipients have lived in the county for less than two years? How much do the per capita expenditures for police differ among cities in the state? How does the tax rate in my county compare to the most common rate?

Two important distinctions in statistics are (1) between descriptive and inferential statistics, and (2) between statistics for univariate and those for multivariate distributions. *Descriptive* statistics are used to summarize and describe the data on cases included in a study. *Inferential* statistics are used to make inferences to larger populations, to use data from the cases studied to conclude something about the cases not studied. *Univariate* statistics tell us about the distribution of the values of one variable. *Multivariate* statistics measure the joint distribution of two or more variables and are used to assess the relationships between and among variables. *Bivariate* distributions are special cases of multivariate distributions; they are the joint distributions of two variables.

In this chapter we discuss descriptive statistics for univariate distributions and several other quantitative measures for describing single variables and their distributions. We also discuss tables and graphs—important tools for analyzing and illustrating the nature of variable distributions—and computer programs for managing, analyzing, and presenting data.

The availability of computers has eased the burden of calculating statistical measures. However, the full potential of statistical packages to aid in understanding and using statistics often is not realized. Although more people are likely to use computers to obtain statistical measures, they may not understand the statistics or use them correctly. All users need to understand basic statistics. We discuss several—such as the arithmetic mean, the median, and the mode—useful to administrators and analysts. New analytical techniques allowing for useful visual presentations of data have been combined with the power of personal computers to provide additional tools.

Our purpose in these chapters on statistics is to discuss application in a way that is useful. We do not intend for these chapters to substitute for courses in statistics. We provide formulas for the statistics and, in some cases, worked-out examples. The main reasons for providing these examples, however, are to clarify the nature and purpose of statistical measures and to illustrate their applications. An appendix to this chapter includes additional information and worked-out examples of some of the statistics. A second appendix includes an example and discussion of preparing data for computer analysis.

COMPUTER SOFTWARE FOR DATA MANAGEMENT AND ANALYSIS

A variety of computer programs are available for managing and analyzing data. These include statistical analysis programs, spreadsheets, database managers, and geographic information systems (GIS). The most powerful and versatile types of software for statistical analysis are *statistical software packages*. These were developed to analyze large datasets and include numerous statistical routines. After the data are prepared and entered, the user can easily conduct many types of analysis. Statistical packages calculate various statistics and allow the user to subdivide the dataset, combine the values of different variables, create new variables from earlier calculations, and change the values of variables. Three widely used statistical packages for administrative and social science data are *SPSS*, Statistical Package for the Social Sciences; *SAS*, Statistical Analysis System; and *Stata*. Students and practitioners may have to encounter SPSS as it is easy to use, often taught in undergraduate and graduate courses, and performs most routines that practitioners are likely to need.[1]

Administrators are more likely to have spreadsheets and database managers available on their desktop computers than they are to have a statistical package. Spreadsheet programs are used extensively for managing numerical information. They can be used to calculate many of the statistics discussed in this and the following chapters.

A *spreadsheet* is a matrix of rows and columns. A spreadsheet program shows on the computer screen a form on which data can be entered in an array, usually with each row as a case and each column as a variable. The user can enter labels for columns and rows. He can change column widths to accommodate lengthier pieces of information, enter and manipulate data, and perform statistical and other mathematical analysis. Numbers, text, formulas, and logical statements are used. A spreadsheet is useful for entering data and creating datasets, for recording budget and expenditure data, and for doing arithmetic and algebraic calculations. The data input form for some statistical programs also uses a spreadsheet format.

While spreadsheet programs generally do not perform advanced statistical calculations, most have built-in functions for basic and intermediate-level statistics. Users can write formulas to perform others. Managers and students who have never used a statistical program but have considerable experience with spreadsheets often ask why university instructors require them to learn how to use a statistical program. The answer is essentially this—although spreadsheets provide for some statistical analysis, their capacity is limited. Statistical software packages are faster, permit easier alteration of variables and their values, handle larger datasets, provide a wider range of statistical tools, and allow more sophisticated data analysis. Spreadsheets, however, are especially useful for managing small datasets, calculating univariate and some multivariate statistics, providing graphics, and entering data.[2] After a dataset has been entered into a spreadsheet program, a user can easily import it into a more powerful statistical analysis program for extensive analysis.

Even fairly large data files are sometimes available as spreadsheets.[3] Many datasets released by U.S. government agencies are made available in spreadsheet format. Others, including some census data files, are released in a database format, which can be transferred to a spreadsheet program and then to a statistical package.

A *database management system (DBMS)* is a program through which the user enters and stores large amounts of data under different headings. These systems can store textual information for each case. Forms containing the outline of a questionnaire or other data-collecting instruments can be shown on the screen. Information stored in a database can be edited and manipulated easily and specific information located quickly. Database management systems can sort and report large amounts of data quickly. They can handle text, numbers, labels, and formulas and manage related files. If the database has more than one file, the files must be related to each other. A database with two or more files with common variables, or fields, that allow information to be linked across files is called a *relational database.* The most powerful and useful database managers for personal computers are relational database managers. These help the user manage information in new ways and can be used to organize data from separate files for reports and statistical analysis.

Relational databases have several advantages. Old information does not have to be reentered when a new file is created. The first file does not have to save space for records in succeeding files that might have blank fields. Databases are often developed for multiple purposes and the data shared by many users. For example, a county government may have records on personnel, financial information (such as revenues and expenditures), and budget information in a large database accessible to all departments. Several different files may contain information about employees. One may contain employment history, another may contain benefit records, and a third may contain information on training and volunteer activities. Many include a data dictionary function that names and describes each piece of information and its location in the database. The dictionary aids users by letting them know what information is available and how it can be obtained.

Relational database managers can produce summary information, basic statistical analysis, and graphs. Database managers are not powerful tools for statistical analysis. For this reason, analysts often transport the data to a statistical analysis package. If data from more than one file are used, transporting usually requires that the analyst create a new file containing those variables that he wishes to analyze further. The database manager program will do this easily. The resulting file is then transported (exported) to the analysis program. The major statistical analysis programs also provide for easy transfer of data from database programs, as they do with spreadsheets.[4]

Separate data dictionaries should be developed for each file in a database to explain the codes, labels, and location of each data item. The planning for this should be done before data entry. The quality of the data is paramount to a good database. The structure of the database makes little difference if the quality of the data or the documentation is poor. Throughout this book we have emphasized the importance of ensuring high-quality data. As data files are linked in databases and their use expands, the quality of the data becomes even more important.

A *geographic information system (GIS)* is a special type of relational database. Its unique and defining characteristic is that it records data that can be displayed geographically. Many data records stored by government agencies include important geographic location information. A few examples are property valuation and taxes, residence information, and locations of streets, water mains, buildings, utility lines, and crimes. A GIS has the ability to display this information on maps produced by the computer.

Examples of location information collected by governments and private organizations include data on individuals: taxpayers, clients of various services, school-age children, homeowners, and users of public facilities. Such information may be kept in separate files in a relational database. With the addition of geographic location information, a GIS can show these data in various ways on maps and provide an important method for analyzing them.[5] The method of analysis provided by a GIS is called *analytic mapping*.[6] A GIS has the ability to map on a geographic display the values and distributions of variables. For example, a GIS can show the locations of users of services, of existing and proposed school district lines, and numbers of school-age children. A GIS can present data so that the analyst can literally see the relationship between location and values of a variable. An important and powerful use of GIS is in combining census data with mapping capability.

Analytic mapping using geographic databases has developed rapidly in recent years with advances in microcomputer technology, software, and improved collection and dissemination of geographic data. With this tool the analyst can relate the values of variables to areas or locations. Although a GIS map shows the relationship of variables to locations rather than to each other, the distribution of several variables can be overlaid. For example, a city analyst working with a GIS could map crime data and unemployment data on the same map. The same map could also show where the city government spends its money.[7]

The statistical capability of GIS programs has been expanded along with their increased use and sophistication. Univariate and multivariate statistical techniques have been developed to analyze spatial relationships in new ways. Statistical analysis modules have been included in GIS allowing more thorough statistical analysis of variables.[8] These statistical routines allow the calculations of average distances between residents and facilities such as fire stations; the extent to which objects, such as houses with specified characteristics, are clustered; and locations of houses valued at a certain level.

In their 1992 book, G. David Garson and Robert Biggs discussed the uses of GIS in social science, public administration, and public policy and the relationship of statistical analysis to GIS and analytic mapping. They emphasized that statistical and GIS approaches are complementary. The substantial developments in GIS technology and statistically related tools have made these relationships even more important and useful today. The relationship between statistical analysis and GIS approaches is easier to accomplish and provides more powerful results than ever before. Given the importance and growth of this technology in the public sector, we agree with Garson and Biggs that a generalist knowledge of research methods should include information about GIS.[9] In the Recommended for Further Reading section, we cite four of the many books describing GIS now available, including the Garson and Biggs book.

ANALYZING AND PRESENTING THE DATA

Tabular Presentation

A straightforward way to present data is to report the measurements associated with each case. This is done in an *array*—a listing of each case along with the classification or value for each of the variables measured. An array provides useful information concerning the individual cases but does little to facilitate the analysis of the variables. For example, a researcher may be less concerned with the fire rates of individual cities than with how many cities have high rates and an average rate for the group of cities. The frequency of high or low values or what

| TABLE 11.1 | DATA ARRAY FOR THREE VARIABLES: COUNTY, CAUSE, AND SEVERITY OF INJURY |

Case	County	Cause	Severity
01	Baker	Fall	3
02	Charlie	Car	4
03	Charlie	Violence	6
04	Able	Car	4
05	Charlie	Violence	5
06	Baker	Fall	9
07	Charlie	Car	10
08	Baker	Fall	1
09	Able	Violence	5
10	Charlie	Violence	5
11	Charlie	Fall	7
12	Able	Car	4
13	Charlie	Car	7
14	Baker	Fall	6
15	Able	Fall	3
16	Baker	Car	5
17	Charlie	Car	5
18	Baker	Fall	6
19	Able	Car	4
20	Charlie	Violence	7

constitutes a typical rate cannot be easily ascertained from a data array with a large number of cases. Table 11.1 is a data array for three variables and 20 cases from an Injury Protocol (see Appendix 11.2). It would be unusual, by the way, to see a data array included in a report except as an appendix. Data arrays are often so large that they are seldom included in a report. Increasingly, if readers want to analyze the data further, the data array may be provided electronically.

The first step in organizing data in an array for analysis is to group cases with the same or similar values, and count them. This process is called *enumeration* and is the starting point for analysis. If the analyst's concern is with the variable distribution itself, rather than with the value of individual cases, then developing a frequency distribution is the next step. A *frequency distribution* lists the values or categories for each variable and the number of cases with each of the values. A *univariate distribution* is the distribution of a single variable. If the variable is the number of fires per 1,000 households per year and the population is the 340 towns and cities of a state, then the distribution consists of the 340 separate fire rates, as shown in Table 11.2. Remember, however, that one table may include several univariate distributions.

The categories in the frequency distribution must be exhaustive and mutually exclusive. The categories for any variable must be defined or set up in such a way that each case will be counted in only one category. Also, there must be a category into which each case will be counted.

TABLE 11.2   FREQUENCY DISTRIBUTION OF FIRE RATES FOR CITIES IN SOUTHEASTERN STATES 1998

Fire Rates (Number of fires per 1,000 buildings)	Number of Cities	Percentage
0–1.99	49	14.4
2–3.99	87	25.6
4–5.99	112	32.9
6 and above	92	27.0
Total	340	100.0

Percentages do not add up to 100% because of rounding.

Percentage or relative frequency distributions are often included in the same table with frequency distributions and, as in Tables 11.2 and 11.3, show what proportion of the total number of cases has a particular value or is within a given category. A frequency distribution should show the total number of cases. If a percentage distribution is presented without the accompanying frequency distribution, enough information should be given so that the reader can determine the number of cases represented by each of the percentages.[10]

The letter f, for frequency, indicates the number of cases with each value or category of the variable. The letter N stands for the total number of cases in the distribution and equals the sum of the category frequencies. Developing a frequency distribution for a variable often requires the analyst to decide how many categories of the variable to present and how wide to make these categories, called *class intervals*.[11] If there are a large number of cases and many individual values, the values may be grouped into a smaller set of class intervals. A distribution for income, for example, could have so many values that presenting them all separately would not be very useful. Rather, an analyst would group, or collapse, the cases into a smaller number of income categories.

In the example of the fire rates for a number of cities, the investigator may have nearly 340 different values, because the rates include decimal values—for example, 5.75 fires per 1,000 buildings. The analyst needs to reduce the large number of separate rates, presented in a data array, to a much smaller number of categories for the frequency distribution. Table 11.2 illustrates this.

TABLE 11.3   FREQUENCY AND PERCENTAGE DISTRIBUTION FOR COUNTY OF INJURY

County	Frequency	Percentage
Able	5	25
Baker	6	30
Charlie	9	45
Total	20	100%

The intervals should allow the reader to make comparisons among them. If the variable being grouped is discrete, the highest value of one category is clearly distinct from the lowest of the next. If the variable is continuous, the values of the categories could seem to overlap. For continuous variables, class intervals include the left endpoint but not the right. In Table 11.2, the first interval contains 0 and up to, but not including, 2; a city with a fire rate of 1.99 would be in the first group, whereas a city with a fire rate of 2.0 would be in the second group. The intervals should not be so broad that important differences are overlooked. Nor should they be so narrow that too many intervals are required. The number of cases in the data array and the range of values in the data suggest to the researcher how to set up the class intervals.[12] The analyst may need to experiment with different widths and choose according to how well the shape of the distribution is best communicated.

Table 11.3 is a frequency and a percentage distribution for the variable "county of injury" developed from the array in Table 11.1. The frequency distribution lists each value or category of the variable in one column and the number of cases with that value—the frequency—in another. Note how this table is fully labeled.

Cumulative Frequency Distribution

A cumulative frequency distribution shows how many cases are below a certain value of the variable. Table 11.4 shows a frequency and cumulative frequency distribution for the ages of a number of employees.

The entries in the Cumulative Frequency column are obtained by adding the number of observations in an interval to the total number of observations from the first interval through the preceding one. For example, Table 11.4 shows that 39 employees are under 50 years of age.

Tables are commonly used to present data arrays and frequency and percent distributions. Students have produced and interpreted tables since grade school. However, tables can be easily misinterpreted and are sometimes confusing. Analysts must make certain that their tables can be easily and correctly understood. Administrators must take care to interpret correctly the various tables they are presented.

TABLE 11.4	FREQUENCY AND CUMULATIVE FREQUENCY DISTRIBUTION OF AGES OF EMPLOYEES	
Age in Years	Frequency	Cumulative Frequency
20–29	9	9
30–39	14	23
40–49	16	39
50–59	21	60
Total	60	

Conventions important in constructing tables are:

1. Provide a descriptive title for each table. This applies as well to charts, graphs, and figures.
2. Label variables and variable categories. All rows and columns should also be fully labeled.
3. All terms open to interpretation should be defined in the footnote section below the table.
4. The source of the data should be indicated in the footnote section.

More detail regarding the preparation of tables is provided in Chapter 15 of this text. Chapter 15 discusses preparing and communicating results of studies.

VISUAL PRESENTATION OF DATA

Visual presentations of data often can illustrate points more clearly than do verbal descriptions. In addition to tables, charts and graphs help the analyst see what is in the data as well as present them to an audience. The analyst should prepare a picture of the data for his own use. Visual presentations can be more precise and revealing than conventional statistical computations. Maps showing the distribution of variable values and frequencies are also very useful and easily produced with GIS software. The injury data from Table 11.1, for example, could be shown on a map of the counties involved. Visual displays should:

show the data.

entice the reader to think about the substance of the information.

avoid distorting what the data have to say.

make large datasets coherent.

encourage the eye to compare different pieces of data.

serve a clear purpose—to describe, explore, tabulate, or elaborate.

enhance the statistical and verbal descriptions of the data.[13]

Develop the habit of fully labeling each table, graph, and other display. Although each graph, table, and figure in a report should be discussed, if only to identify it and its purpose, readers should be able to comprehend and interpret each without reference to the discussion.

Several conventions have been developed for tables showing the joint distribution of two variables. Usually the independent variable is the column variable, with its label and categories along the top of the table. The dependent is the row variable, with its categories forming the rows. The frequencies in each column of the independent variable are then totaled at the bottom. The frequencies in each row of the dependent variable are added across and shown at the right side of the table. We discuss two-variable tables in more detail in Chapters 12 and 13.

Bar Graphs and Histograms

Bar graphs are a particularly effective and simple way to present data. A *bar graph* shows the variable along one axis and the frequency of cases along the other. The length of the bar indicates the number of cases possessing each value of the variable. Figure 11.1 is a bar graph for the variable "county of injury" from Tables 11.1 and 11.3. It is a graphical representation of the frequency distribution for that variable.

The bars in a bar graph should be of the same width for all categories of the variable. It can be misleading to show bars of different widths for different categories. In fact, that technique is used at times to intentionally mislead the reader.[14] Bar graphs also are used to present percentage distributions for variables.

Bar graphs are sometimes developed with the bars displayed horizontally so that the frequency is indicated by the length of the bar. In this case the value labels for the variables would be placed along the side of the vertical axis, as in Figure 11.2. Many computer programs generate bar graphs with horizontal rather than vertical bars, and some authors prefer this. Whether the bars are presented vertically or horizontally depends on several factors, including the number of categories of the variable, the length (or height) of the bars, and the amount of variation in frequency that must be displayed. The horizontal format is useful when there are many categories as it provides more room for the category labels. The choice of horizontal or vertical bars depends on which display communicates more effectively and clearly.

| FIGURE 11.1 | BAR GRAPH FOR COUNTY OF INJURY |

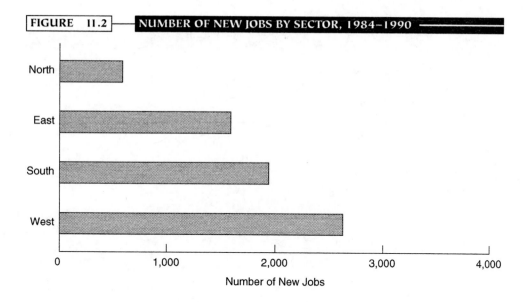

FIGURE 11.2 — **NUMBER OF NEW JOBS BY SECTOR, 1984–1990** —

A *histogram* is a bar graph made by plotting frequency of occurrence against the values obtained for interval- and ratio-level variables. It is the common way of representing frequency distributions in statistics and also is used for relative frequency distributions, that is, those showing percents. With the histogram, the width of the bar also portrays information so that the width of the bar and its length or height are related.[15] Each column of the histogram represents a range of values, and the columns adjoin one another because the range of values is continuous. The variable and its values are displayed along the horizontal axis, and the frequency or percentage is displayed along the vertical axis of a histogram. Figure 11.3 is an example of a histogram. A histogram represents numbers by area, not height. Histograms differ from bar graphs in that the width of the bars represents specific quantitative values or ranges of values. Although histograms are used for percentage distributions, the percents are not plotted unless the class intervals are equal.[16]

Pie Charts

A *pie chart* represents a complete circle—indicating a quantity—that is sliced into a number of wedges. This graph conveys what proportion of the whole is accounted for by each component and facilitates visual comparisons among parts of the whole. The portions usually are expressed as percentages of the whole. Financial information, such as source of revenue, category of expenditure, and so on, is often displayed in this manner. The circle represents 100 percent of the quantity of the resource or other factor displayed. The size of each wedge or "slice of the pie" corresponds to a percent of this total. Consult the budget document for your city or county and you are likely to see information displayed in

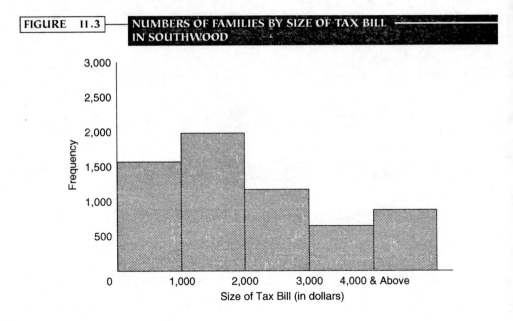

FIGURE 11.3   NUMBERS OF FAMILIES BY SIZE OF TAX BILL IN SOUTHWOOD

one or more pie charts. Figure 11.4 is a pie chart showing the sources of revenue for a city government. Some authors advise that when possible the largest slice of the pie should begin at the 12 o'clock position, and the other slices should follow in a clockwise direction according to size, with the smallest slice last. Analysts may violate this rule when two pie charts are used for comparison.[17]

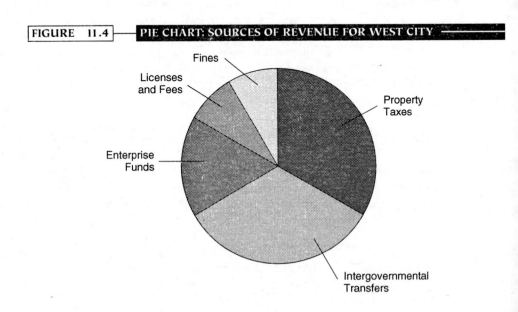

FIGURE 11.4   PIE CHART: SOURCES OF REVENUE FOR WEST CITY

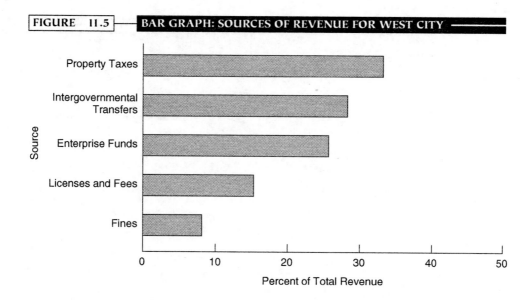

FIGURE 11.5 — **BAR GRAPH: SOURCES OF REVENUE FOR WEST CITY**

The same information also can be shown by a bar graph, as in Figure 11.5; however, the pie chart more effectively illustrates the relationship of parts to the whole and allows the reader to more readily see the relative sizes of various categories. Pie charts are commonly used to enhance presentations. Many computer programs, such as spreadsheets and data analysis programs, can generate them.[18]

On Figure 11.5, note how the bars are arranged in declining order of magnitude. The longest bar is at the top, indicating the largest source or frequency, and the other bars become shorter as we look down the chart. This makes it easy to spot the largest and smallest revenue sources. Arranging bars this way is particularly effective in charts with numerous bars.[19]

Line Graphs

Line graphs used for displaying frequencies are primarily of two types: the frequency polygon and the time series. We will discuss each here, but recall that we introduced the time series in Chapter 2.

Frequency Polygon A *frequency polygon* has as its horizontal axis a scale showing the values of an interval-or ratio-level variable. Frequencies or percentages are placed on the vertical axis. The frequency polygon is closely related to the histogram in the type of information and in the way that it is presented. The area under the line—the polygon—has important implications. The line is formed by marking a position, a "dot" over the value of the variable at the height corresponding to the number of cases—frequency—possessing that value. The line is formed by connecting these dots. For a distribution with many individual values, the line will appear continuous and smooth. Alternatively, the height of

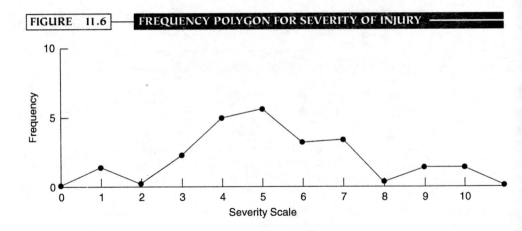

FIGURE 11.6 — FREQUENCY POLYGON FOR SEVERITY OF INJURY

the line could indicate the percentage of cases possessing any value of the variable. The values of the variable indicate quantities measured with an interval or ratio scale.

Figure 11.6 is a frequency polygon illustrating the distribution of the variable "severity of injury" from Table 11.1. For example, there are five cases of injury with a severity rating of 4, one with a severity rating of 9, and none with a severity of 8. Figure 11.6 does not look much like a polygon. However, with more and more cases, a smoother curve, such as that in Figure 11.7, would result.

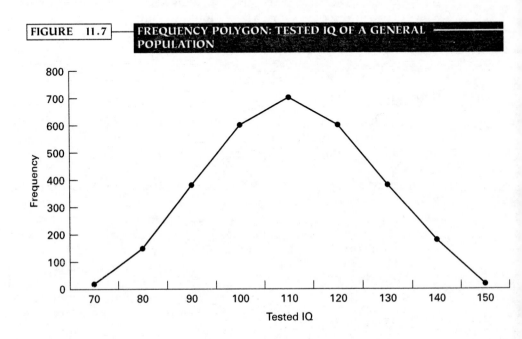

FIGURE 11.7 — FREQUENCY POLYGON: TESTED IQ OF A GENERAL POPULATION

FIGURE 11.8 COUNTY PROPERTY TAX LEVY BY YEAR

The polygon in Figure 11.7 is an example of an important type of distribution, the normal curve. It can be described by a mathematical formula that allows analysts to make precise observations about this population.[20] The normal curve will be discussed in more detail near the end of this chapter.

Time Series   In a time series, the units of time are displayed along the horizontal axis, and the frequency of some occurrence or the values of a variable are scaled along the vertical axis. The time scale marks the passage of time in units such as days, months, or years. Figure 11.8 shows a line graph of a time series—county property tax levy by year.

For many time series, the occurrences being enumerated are given in *rates*. Time-series graphs of accident rates, crime rates, unemployment rates, and so forth, allow the analyst to compare these factors from year to year without worrying about changes in population, because these changes are accounted for in the process of calculating rates.

QUANTITATIVE MEASURES

Numerous measures are available for summarizing and comparing datasets as well as for measures of individual quantities. These include traditional statistical measures such as arithmetic means as well as newer measures used for specific purposes.

Percentage or Relative Frequency Distribution

The most well-known relative frequency is the percentage. Almost everyone is familiar with percents and can quickly understand presentations based on them. A *percent* reports the number of units as a proportion of 100. It is calculated by dividing the frequency of one category of the variable by the total number of cases in the distribution and multiplying the result by 100. Percents are especially useful when the analyst wants to compare the frequency of the part to the whole or compare frequency distributions with different numbers of cases.

Proportion

Parts of a whole are sometimes given as proportions. A *proportion* is the same as a percentage, except we do not multiply it by 100. The formula for a proportion is: proportion = f/N. For example, the proportion of all injuries in the distribution in Table 11.3 that occurred in Able County is .25.

Percent Change

Analysts are often interested in the degree of change in the frequency or amount of something over time. The changes in budget amounts, tax collections, population, unemployment, and so forth, are important to track over time. A relative frequency that provides a useful measure of change is the *percent change*. This converts to a percentage the amount of change in the value of a variable between two points in time for a case. The formula is:

$$\text{percent change} = ((N_2 - N_1)/N_1) \cdot (100)$$

The value of the variable at the earlier time (N_1) is subtracted from the value at the later time (N_2), and the difference is divided by the earlier value. The result is multiplied by 100 to produce a percent. For example, over a 10-year period the population of Mecklenburg County increased from 511,433 to 695,454. This is a 36 percent increase in population.

$$N_1 = 511,433; N_2 = 695,454$$
$$\text{percent change} = ((695,454 - 511,433)/511,433) \cdot 100$$
$$= (184,021/511,433) \cdot 100 = 35.98 = 36\%$$

Of course, the percent change could be negative, indicating a decrease in the frequency or value. Recently in one small city in Texas, property-tax collections declined from $13,300,000 to $12,700,000 from one year to the next. This is a 4.5 percent decrease.

Do not attempt to find an average yearly rate of change by dividing the percentage change over a period of time by the number of years involved. Think of the percentage change as an interest rate that is compounded at the end of each year. The base on which each succeeding year's growth is calculated changes.

In the previous example of population change in Mecklenburg County, for example, it would not be accurate to calculate an average yearly growth rate by dividing the total percent change for the decade by 10. The appropriate statistical measure to use in this case is the geometric mean. We will discuss this after discussing the arithmetic mean. Logarithms can also be used to determine the yearly average growth.

Ratio

A *ratio* compares the frequency of one variable category to the frequency of another variable category. Patient-to-physician ratios and student-to-teacher ratios are common. Often the denominator is reduced to 1; for example, the patient-to-physician ratio for a state may be 240 to 1, or the student-to-teacher ratio for a school system may be 30 to 1. Administrators can compare these ratios for different years or for different communities. We may also compare the number of cases in one category of a variable to that in another. For example, assume we found that an organization employed 45 men and 15 women; we would express this as a ratio of male to female employees of 3 to 1.

Rates

Rates are defined as the number of actual occurrences of an event divided by the number of possible occurrences of that event over some period of time. To compare the number of occurrences of an event, such as crimes or traffic accidents in a year for different cities or states, the number of occurrences must be evaluated by standardizing the measure. This is usually done by dividing the frequency of the occurrence of an event in a jurisdiction by the total population of that jurisdiction.

For example, in one year Perth County had only 24 automobile accidents, whereas Maltiby County had 384. Which county has the greater accident problem? Directly comparing the number of accidents would not be useful since Perth County had only 14,800 inhabitants, while Maltiby County had 307,700 inhabitants. A more useful comparison is the frequency of automobile accidents in each county relative to the population of the county.

Dividing the number of automobile accidents by the population for each county results in ratios of 24 to 14,800 or .001621 to 1 for Perth County and 394 to 307,700 or .00128 to 1 for Maltiby. The large imbalance between the numerator and the denominator makes it difficult to comprehend these figures. The decimal values are so small that readers and analysts find it hard to understand them. These problems can be corrected by multiplying by a base number that will convert the numerator from a decimal to a whole number. Multiplying by 1,000 as a base number produces 1.62 accidents per 1,000 of population for Perth County and 1.28 per 1,000 of population for Maltiby County. This is clearer and makes the comparison of these rates between counties over time much more meaningful. Table 11.5 illustrates this.

TABLE 11.5	AUTOMOBILE ACCIDENTS FOR TWO COUNTIES, 1990		
County	Number of Accidents	Population	Rate
Perth	24	14,800	1.62 per 1,000 of population
Maltiby	394	307,700	1.28 per 1,000 of population

A *rate* divides one frequency count N_1, by another frequency count, N_2, and multiplies the result by a base number. The numerator, N_1, in the rate formula contains the count for the variable of interest; for an accident rate, it is the number of accidents; for the murder rate, it is the number of murders. The denominator, N_2, is the population size or another indicator of the number of cases at risk. The formula for a rate is as follows:

$$rate = (N_1/N_2)(base\ number)$$

The selection of the denominator for the rate is very important but somewhat arbitrary. For many rates the denominator is the size of the population. However, an analyst could compare the frequency of automobile accidents in a county relative to the number of automobiles in the county. Automobile death rates also are expressed in terms of millions of miles driven. Rates also are given for the size of the population at risk. The rate of a childhood disease, for example, means more if it is given relative to the number of children in the population rather than for the entire population. Example 11.1 illustrates how the choice of a denominator for the rate can influence our perspective of the subject variable.

The following conventions apply in selecting an appropriate base number. Remember that these are guidelines, not rigid rules.

1. Be consistent with rates already in general use for given properties. Be consistent in your own use of rates for the same properties. Crime rates, for example, are usually given as crimes per 100 of the population. Birth and death rates, however, are usually given per 1,000 of the population.

2. The base number should produce a rate with a whole number of at least one digit and not more than four digits.

3. The base number is usually an exponent of 10 (10, 10^2, 10^3, and so forth).

4. Use the same base number when calculating rates for comparison. For instance, in the above case, you would not use a base number of 1,000 for Maltiby County and a base number of 100 for Perth County.

Rates are reported for birth, death, crime, accident, illness, unemployment, and countless other variables. Note that a rate is meaningful only if it is specified for a particular time period, usually a year. Many of the terms used in the discussion of rates come from the various fields of health care. Incidence and prevalence are two of the most common rate measures developed by health care professionals. *Incidence* is defined as the number of people who get a disease over a specified period of time, usually a year. *Prevalence* is defined as the total number of people

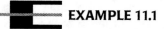 **EXAMPLE 11.1**

Selecting a Denominator for a Rate

Policy analysts in a large southeastern state investigated the potential impact of a proposed law requiring hunters to wear orange reflective clothing. Opponents of the proposal pointed out that the rate of hunting deaths in the state was very low and did not differ from states with a reflective-clothing law. They used the state's population as the denominator for the rate calculation. A more useful denominator might have been the number of hunting licenses issued. This would provide a more useful rate to compare with other states having a law requiring hunters to wear orange clothing.

Consider the following information from states A and B.

State	A	B
"Wear orange" law:	No	Yes
Number of hunting fatalities:	9	5
State's population:	5,500,000	3,200,000
Number of hunting licenses issued:	18,100	16,900

Calculate the following rates for both states (use 100,000 as the base number):

1. Number of hunting fatalities per population
2. Number of hunting fatalities per licensed hunter

Do you think that the "wear orange" law is a good idea? Do you see how the choice of a denominator for the rate calculation influences the perspective?

Rate calculation answers:

1. **A.** 16 per 100,000 population   **B.** 15 per 100,000 population
2. **A.** 49.7 per 100,000 hunters   **B.** 29.6 per 100,000 hunters

SOURCE: *The Charlotte Observer* (Charlotte, NC, December 28, 1986).

---

who have a disease at a given time. We can apply these concepts to the occurrence of conditions other than disease, for example, being a victim of a crime, having an accident, being unemployed, and so on.

An incidence rate would be calculated by dividing the number of people who get a disease or a condition over a specified period of time relative to the total number who are at risk of getting the disease or condition in the same period of time. In calculating incidence, only the new cases for the time period in question are included. If we are investigating the incidence of a chronic disease, such as diabetes, for 2006, we would include in our rate calculations only the number of new cases occurring in 2006. Cases carrying over from 2005 or previous years would not be counted.

In measuring prevalence, cases carrying over from previous years are included in the count. Those individuals who developed diabetes prior to 2006 and in 2006 and still had the condition would be included in the 2006 prevalence count. Incidence and prevalence rates are usually calculated for a year's time. The number of people in the population of interest at midyear is then used as the denominator. Prevalence rates can be determined using a cross-sectional design; incidence rates typically require a longitudinal design. Usually a panel or a cohort design is used, with a cohort design the more common. Ideally, to determine incidence, an analyst would follow a population over time.[21]

All of us are aware of the danger of AIDS. Public health and other officials are concerned with both the number of new cases each year and the total number of people with AIDS. The first of these concerns involves incidence and the second involves prevalence. Another example is the statistics on epilepsy in Olmsted County, Minnesota, where one year the incidence was 30.8 cases per 100,000 of population and the prevalence was 376 cases per 100,000 of population.[22]

CHARACTERISTICS OF A DISTRIBUTION

In summarizing a distribution of values, analysts usually want to provide several kinds of information. They want to indicate how similar the individual values are to each other and also how different they are. Two types of statistics are ordinarily used to describe the distribution of one variable: (1) measures of central tendency, and (2) measures of dispersion. These categories represent two important things that an analyst usually wants to show about a group of values: how similar the individual values are and how different they are. Several measures are included in each of these categories. The choice of which to use depends on the level of measurement of the variable and the information the analyst wants to obtain. Other types of measures also are used by statisticians, but we do not discuss them here.

The measures of central tendency indicate what a typical value or case in the distribution is like. One might ask how well the measure of central tendency reflects the overall nature of the distribution. This leads to measures of the variability of the values in a distribution. Measures of variability include those of spread, variation, and dispersion. These, along with measures of central tendency, are useful for measuring and comparing groups.

Measures of Central Tendency

Measures of central tendency are used to indicate the value that is representative, most typical, or central in the distribution. These measures include mode, median, and arithmetic mean.

Mode   The simplest summary of a variable is to indicate which category is the most common. The *mode* is that value or category of the variable that occurs most often. In a frequency distribution, it is the value with the highest frequency. Table 11.6 shows the distribution of a nominal-level variable. The mode for this

TABLE 11.6	FREQUENCY AND PERCENTAGE DISTRIBUTION FOR TYPE OF CITY GOVERNMENT	
Type of Government	Frequency	Percentage
Strong mayor	22	25
Council manager	45	51
Weak mayor	17	19
Commission	4	5
Total (N)	88	100

variable is "Council manager": More cities in the table have this form than any other. Remember that we find the mode by determining which category or value has the highest frequency. The mode can be determined for all levels of data: nominal, ordinal, interval, and ratio. A mistake that students often make is to confuse the frequency of the modal category with the mode. For instance, the mode for Table 11.6 is "Council manager"; it is not 45. For nominal and many ordinal variables, the category that occurs most often will have a name; for interval and ratio variables, the value of the mode will be a number.

Median The *median* is the value or category of the case that is in the center of the distribution. It is the value of the case that divides the distribution in two; one-half of the cases have values less than the median and one-half of them have values greater than the median. The median requires that variables be measured at the ordinal or interval level. It can be determined only if the values can be ordered. It makes no sense, by the way, to find the middle case if the cases have not been ordered according to their values on the variable of interest.

To find the median, we must locate the middle case in a distribution. To find the middle case we add 1 to the number of cases and divide by 2, or: $(N + 1)/2$. If the number of cases (N) is odd, then the median will be the value of a specific case. If N is even, then the median is estimated as the value that is halfway between two cases. For example, if N is 21, then the median is the value of the 11th case. If N is 22, then the median would be halfway between the value of case number 11 and case number 12. Several examples follow.

Table 11.7 shows the distribution of an ordinal variable from a sample survey. The table also includes a column showing the cumulative percent, that is, the percent of cases with a particular value or less. The middle case is the case $(629 + 1)/2 = 315$.

TABLE 11.7	RATING OF COUNTY GOVERNMENT		
Rating	Frequency	Percentage	Cumulative Percentage
Poor	36	5.7	5.7
Fair	206	32.8	38.5
Good	287	45.6	84.1
Excellent	100	15.9	100.0
Total (N)	629	100.0	

TABLE 11.8	YEARLY INVESTMENT INCOMES OF SEVEN EMPLOYEES (IN DOLLARS)						
(1) Unordered:	17,000	25,000	30,000	12,000	24,000	18,000	27,000
(2) Ordered:	12,000	17,000	18,000	24,000	25,000	27,000	30,000

This case is in the rating category "Good." The median for this variable, then, is "Good." One-half of the cases rated county government as "Good" or better, and one-half rated it as "Good" or worse. Note that the cumulative percent reaches 50 in the "Good" category. Cumulative percent information allows us to quickly locate the category containing the middle case.

Table 11.8 shows the distribution of a small number of values—the amount of investment income for a year for a number of employees. We will discuss how to calculate the median income for this group. The first part of Table 11.8 shows the income data as it was collected; that is, the values are not in any particular order. To find the median, the cases must be ordered according to increasing or decreasing values. Sometimes, people unfamiliar with calculating the median overlook this. The second part of Table 11.8 orders the amounts from lowest to highest. The median is the amount of the middle case in the ordered set. Since the number of cases N in the distribution is 7, the middle case is $(N + 1)/2 = 8/2 = 4$. The value of the median is the investment income of that case, $24,000.

Consider how the median would be affected if one more case were added. Table 11.9 shows the same distribution as does Table 11.8 with one income figure added. In Table 11.9, N is 8, an even number, so the middle of the distribution is between case number 4 and case number 5. We would place the median value halfway between the values of these cases. This value would be

$$(24,000 + 25,000)/2 = 24,500$$

Notice how little the extreme value of the highest amount in the distribution affects the median. In Table 11.9, the one income amount of $58,000 is substantially higher than any of the others. However, the median is only $500 higher than the median of the distribution in Table 11.8. This is one of the most important characteristics of the median. An additional property is that when used with interval and ratio variables, the median is closer to all other values than any other point in the distribution.

The median should be used as the measure of central tendency for ordinal variables. It is also useful for interval variables if the distribution has a few extreme values, as in Table 11.9. A distribution such as this with a few extreme

TABLE 11.9	YEARLY INVESTMENT INCOMES OF EIGHT EMPLOYEES (IN DOLLARS)						
12,000	17,000	18,000	24,000	25,000	27,000	30,000	58,000

TABLE 11.10	AGES OF EMPLOYEES IN CENTRAL AGENCY	
Age (in years)	Frequency	Cumulative Frequency
20–29	9	9
30–39	14	23
40–49	16	39
50–59	21	60
Total	60	

values is said to be skewed. The most serious problems of skewing seem to occur with variables measuring resources. These include income, in particular, but also the values of stock, land, and other real estate owned by individuals and families. Since the median is affected little by extreme numerical values, it gives an accurate picture of central tendency even for highly skewed distributions.

Computing the Median from Grouped Data   It is often necessary to compute the median from grouped data, that is, data already organized and presented in a frequency distribution with class intervals more than one unit wide. Table 11.10 shows such a distribution. Since the individual values in the frequency distribution are not identifiable, we cannot find the exact value of the median. One method of estimating the median is to find the class interval containing the middle case and take the midpoint of that interval as the median. The middle case is in the third class interval, the interval with ages 40–49. The midpoint of this interval is 44.5 years; thus 44.5 is the estimated median.[23] A more exact procedure for estimating the median from grouped data is explained in most introductory statistics textbooks.[24]

Arithmetic Mean   A third way of measuring central tendency is with the arithmetic average or arithmetic mean. This is probably the most commonly known measure of central tendency. The *arithmetic mean* (mean or $\overline{X}$) is the arithmetic balance point or center of the distribution. By that we mean that the sum of the differences from the mean for values above the mean is equal to differences from the mean of the values below the mean. Although the mean is sometimes the middle of the distribution and has the same value as the median, we cannot always expect this to be so. To use the mean requires variables to be measured at the interval or ratio level.

The mean is created by mathematical calculations involving the values of each case. It is useful by itself as a measure of central tendency but is also an important component of many other statistical formulas. To calculate the arithmetic mean, add the value of the variable for each case and divide by the number of cases. The following is the formula for the arithmetic mean.

$$\text{arithmetic mean} = \overline{X} = \Sigma X_i / N$$

The symbol Σ means to sum the value of the variable for each individual case. X_i is the value of the variable for each case. The distribution in Table 11.9 would have the arithmetic mean as follows:

$$\Sigma X_i = 12{,}000 + 17{,}000 + 18{,}000 + 24{,}000 + 25{,}000 + 27{,}000$$
$$+ 130{,}000 + 58{,}000$$
$$= 211{,}000$$
$$\text{arithmetic mean} = 211{,}000/8 = \$26{,}375$$

For a frequency distribution, the following formula is more useful:

$$\overline{X} = (\Sigma f_i x_i)/N$$

This directs you to multiply each value of the variable by the frequency of that value (f), then add these values and divide by the total number of cases (N).

Calculate the mean for the distribution in Table 11.8. You should obtain $21,857. This illustrates how a few extremely high or low values will greatly affect the value of the mean. The reason that the mean for distribution 11.9 is so much higher than the mean for distribution 11.8 is the one very high earnings figure of $58,000. If a distribution has a few extreme values, the mean is not as useful a measure of central tendency, and the median is the preferred measure. Providing both the mean and the median for distributions of interval and ratio variables is often useful, and we recommend it.

Computing the Mean from Grouped Data   As with the median, analysts often want to have the mean for data grouped in class intervals and presented in tables. In this situation the analyst multiplies the value of the midpoint of each interval of the variable by the frequency of that interval.[25] The resultant values are added and divided by the total number of cases to obtain the mean. The procedure is demonstrated in Table 11.11, which reproduces the data from Table 11.10. The arithmetic mean for this distribution is 42.7. The reader should compare this to the value of the median.

Geometric Mean   The *geometric mean* is used to average ratios and rates of change. Assume that an agency's budget increased from $100,000 to $150,000 over a period of five years. The change is 50 percent during this time. But how much has the budget grown on a yearly basis? If we used the arithmetic mean

TABLE 11.11	AGES OF EMPLOYEES IN CENTRAL AGENCY		
Age (in years) (X)	Frequency (f)	Midpoint of Interval (m)	(f) × (m)
20–29	9	24.5	220.5
30–39	14	34.5	483.0
40–49	16	44.5	712.0
50–59	21	54.5	1,144.5
Total	60		2,560.0

and divided the total percentage change by the number of years—five—the average yearly change would be 10 percent. However, this would be too high. If you start out with the beginning budget of $100,000 and increase it by 10 percent each year, the ending budget will be larger than $150,000. (It is a useful exercise to do this.) The actual average yearly growth is less than 10 percent. The geometric mean is used to calculate this. Several sources are available for those who wish to pursue this topic.[26] Our concern here is that the reader understand that the geometric mean is used with ratios and rates of change, especially in calculating the mean percentage change over time, giving the annual average growth rate.

Guidelines for Selecting an Appropriate Central Tendency Measure Spindel County was applying for a Community Improvement Grant for one of its low-income neighborhoods. "But the average income in that neighborhood is over $25,000," said County Commissioner Crane. "Yes," agreed Hap, the county's grants manager, "but one-half of the families earn less than $15,000." Charlie, a member of the neighborhood, commented, "The most common income level here is around $20,000." The grant application required the reporting of an "average income figure." Which average or measure of central tendency should the grants manager include?

The analyst needs to be aware of which appropriate measure of central tendency to use. Since each of the measures provides somewhat different information, she must take care to choose the proper one. The appropriate measure of central tendency depends on the level of measurement, the nature of the resulting distribution, and the information the analyst wants to present. The following guidelines should be considered:[27]

1. The median and the mean require ordinal and interval levels of measurement, respectively. If the variable is nominal, only the mode can be used. Nevertheless, the mode is appropriate when the purpose is to report an actual typical figure. In Spindel County, Charlie is reporting that $20,000 is a typical income. If the distribution has two or more modes, both of these should be reported.

2. In a distribution of an interval or ratio variable, if the distribution is unimodal and symmetrical, or nearly so, the mean is the preferred measure of central tendency. In such a distribution, the mode, median, and mean will be the same or nearly so. If, however, the distribution has a few extreme values, either high or low, the mean will be distorted, and the median should be used. Such a distribution is said to be *skewed*.

   Distributions of the measures of income tend to be skewed. For example, in any community, most people will have relatively low or moderate incomes. But a few people, or families, will have very high incomes. These high values will distort the mean. This has probably happened in the neighborhood in Spindel County. The grants manager

FIGURE 11.9 — EXAMPLES OF SKEWED DISTRIBUTIONS

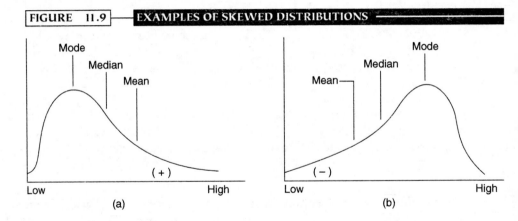

would want to report the median, as it will be affected less by any extreme income values.

3. The geometric mean has an explicit application. It is used primarily to average rates of change and does not apply to the Spindel County example.

Unimodal distributions that are not symmetrical are skewed. Extremely high or low values in a skewed distribution pull the mean away from the median toward the extreme value. The more the degree of skew, the greater the difference between the values of the mean and the median. The mean may give a misleading figure for a skewed distribution. The median also should be given, and the analyst should compare the median and the mean to judge if the distribution is skewed.

Figure 11.9(a) shows a distribution positively skewed or skewed to the right. The mean is higher than the median and the mode. The distribution in Figure 11.9(b) is negatively skewed or skewed to the left. The mean is lower than the median and the mode.

Measures of Variation and Dispersion

Two distributions may have similar means yet very different values overall. So in addition to measures of central tendency, analysts present measures of dispersion and variation that indicate the extent to which individual values in a distribution are different from each other. *Measures of dispersion* describe the uniformity of the data. Relatively smaller values on the measure of dispersion for a variable imply more uniformity, whereas relatively larger values imply more diversity or variation. Some measures indicate only the difference between two observations in an ordered set of values. Other measures consider all observations in a distribution.

In comparing distributions of income for two groups of employees, measures of central tendency would be used. The average incomes of the two groups shown in Table 11.12 are nearly equal, but, as a visual inspection of the data will confirm, the individual incomes are very different. Measures of dispersion must be calculated to provide complete information.

TABLE 11.12	DATA AND ARITHMETIC MEANS FOR INVESTMENT INCOMES OF TWO GROUPS OF EMPLOYEES (IN DOLLARS)

Group A: 12,000; 17,000; 18,000; 24,000; 25,000; 27,000; 30,000; 58,000
$\overline{X}$ = 26,375

Group B: 22,500; 24,500; 25,000; 26,000; 27,000; 28,000; 28,500; 29,000
$\overline{X}$ = 26,312.50

Maximum variation for ordinal, interval, and ratio variables is defined as occurring when all cases are equally divided between two extreme categories or values. Maximum variation for nominal variables occurs when cases are evenly distributed across all categories. The more the cases are clustered in one category, the less the variation. If all cases were in one category, then variation would be zero.[28]

Common measures of dispersion for interval and ratio variables are the range, midranges (such as the inter-quartile range), standard deviation, and variance. Somewhat less common but useful as quantitative measures are the average deviation and median absolute deviation.

Range   The simplest measure of dispersion is the *range*. It is the difference between the highest value and the lowest value in a distribution and indicates the range over which the values are spread. However, it has many disadvantages, since one extreme value will greatly affect its size. Note the ranges for the investment income distributions from Employee Groups A and B from Table 11.12.

Group A Range = Highest value − Lowest value = $58,000 − $12,000
= $46,000

Group B Range = Highest value − Lowest value = $29,000 − $22,500
= $6,500

These range figures make it obvious that although the two distributions have similar arithmetic means, they are different in other respects.

Because the extreme values in a distribution affect the size of the range, statisticians have developed a number of midrange measures that eliminate some portion of the low and high ends of a distribution. Whereas the range is very sensitive to extreme values, the midrange measures are not. The most common of these is the *inter-quartile range*. It is also known as the midspread.[29]

Inter-quartile Range (IQr)   This specifies the range of values within which the middle 50 percent of the observations are found. The first quartile is that value below which 25 percent of the cases are found. The third quartile is that value below which 75 percent of the cases are found. The second quartile, of course, is the median. In determining the inter-quartile range, the lowest 25 percent of the observations and the highest 25 percent are omitted. The resulting range is less affected by extreme values than is the range. Note the inter-quartile ranges for the incomes of the two groups of employees shown in Table 11.12.

> IQr (distribution A): Range of the middle 50 percent of values, e.g., the four values between $18,000 and $27,000. To find the first quartile, drop the lowest 25 percent of the cases, that is, the two cases with the lowest values. To find the third quartile, drop the upper 25 percent of the cases, that is, the two cases with the highest values. For this distribution the inter-quartile range = $27,000 − $18,000 = $9,000. The spread of the middle 50 percent of the cases is $9,000. Compare this to the IQr for distribution B.
>
> IQr (distribution B): $28,000 − $25,000 = $3,000. The middle 50 percent of the cases are spread over a range of $3,000.

The inter-quartile range indicates the extent of variation among individual values. It is useful as a means of comparing the variation or spread of two or more distributions measuring the same variable. Many analysts use it to compare distributions over time or to compare the distributions for two or more groups. For example, in a quality-improvement program, we might record the number of errors made by accounting clerks. To show success, we would expect that the inter-quartile range would become smaller over time and that those involved in the program would show a smaller variation than those not involved. By itself, however, without a context or perspective, the inter-quartile range has little meaning. A more precise method for calculating quartiles and the inter-quartile range is shown in Appendix 11.1.

In reporting on frequency distributions with a large number of cases, investigators often quote percentiles of the distribution. A *percentile* is a value below which a certain percent of the ordered observations in a distribution are located. The 90th percentile of a distribution of applicants' job-registry ratings is the rating value below which 90 percent of the applicants fall. Only 10 percent of the applicants equal or exceed the 90th percentile. The 50th percentile, of course, is the same as the median: 50 percent of the values are lower and 50 percent are higher. The 25th percentile and the 75th percentile are the first and third *quartiles,* respectively, and mark the endpoints of the inter-quartile range. Students are usually familiar with instructors "curving" the exam scores from large classes to assign grades. Those students at the 90th percentile or above get As; those between the 80th and 89th get Bs, and so forth. *Quartiles, percentiles,* and similar measures are called location parameters because they help locate a distribution on the axis showing the variables' values when the distribution is graphed.[30]

Standard Deviation and Variance   Analysts also need a measure that includes all values in a distribution. Two such measures for quantitative variables are the standard deviation and the variance. The *standard deviation* is a measure of the average distance of values in a distribution from the arithmetic mean of the distribution. The *variance* is the square of the standard deviation. Both of these measures are used in higher-level statistical tests; they are two of the most important of all statistical measures. Unfortunately, it is difficult to obtain an intuitive understanding or interpretation of them. The following calculations will help explain them.

The formula for the variance is given first, as we usually calculate the variance and then take its square root to find the standard deviation:

$$S^2 = \text{variance} = \frac{\Sigma(X_i - \overline{X})^2}{N}$$

The formula for the standard deviation is the square root of the variance:

$$S = \sqrt{\Sigma(X_i - \overline{X})^2/N}$$

The steps for calculating the variance and standard deviation are these:

1. Subtract the mean $(\overline{X})$ from each individual value $(X_i - \overline{X})$. This shows how much the value of each case deviates from the mean of the distribution.
2. Square each deviation value $(X_i - \overline{X})^2$.
3. Add the squared deviations $\Sigma(X_i - \overline{X})^2$.
4. Divide the total of the squared deviations by the number of cases $\Sigma(X_i - \overline{X})^2/N$. This is the variance.
5. Take the square root $\sqrt{\Sigma(X_i - \overline{X})^2/N}$. This is the standard deviation.

The variance and standard deviation of the salaries in Group A, Table 11.12, are $173.23 and $13.16, respectively.

The formulas presented above are to be used with a population. If you are working with a sample, the denominator, N, is replaced with $n - 1$. n is the number of cases in the sample, whereas N denotes the number in the population. Many calculators and computer packages have $n - 1$ programmed in the equations used for the variance and standard deviation.[31] If the means of two distributions are about the same and the standard deviations differ, the larger standard deviation indicates greater dispersion in the distribution.

Alternative formulas for calculating the standard deviation and variance are given and illustrated in Appendix 11.1. Although they do not demonstrate as well the principles underlying the measures, the alternative formulas are easier to use with calculators than is the one shown here.

Other Deviation Measures

The *average deviation* and the median absolute deviation are two useful quantitative measures, although they lack mathematical properties necessary for inclusion in other statistics. Unlike the standard deviation, which is used as a component in the formula for many other statistical measures, the average and median absolute deviations are not used in formulas for other statistics.

Average Deviation The *average deviation* measures how far, on average, the cases deviate from the arithmetic mean. To calculate it, add the absolute value of the deviation of each case from the mean of the distribution and divide by the number of cases. The formula is:

$$\text{Average Deviation} = \frac{\Sigma \, | \, X_i - \overline{X} \, |}{N}$$

For most people the average deviation is more intuitively appealing than is the standard deviation. Forecasters use it to estimate the accuracy of models. In a normal distribution, the average deviation is about 20 percent smaller than the standard deviation.[32] The average deviation is less sensitive to extreme values than is the standard deviation.

Median Absolute Deviation This measure calculates the average deviation of a set of cases from the median of the distribution. A property of the median is that the total deviations and the average deviation from the median are smaller than from any other point in the distribution. This fact makes the median absolute deviation useful in some financial applications, such as measuring the uniformity of property tax assessments of local governments.[33]

The Standard Deviation and the Normal Curve

The standard deviation is used extensively in inferential statistics. It allows us to estimate population parameters, such as means and variances. From our knowledge of the distribution of sample means, we can use the standard deviation to estimate how close any particular sample characteristic is to the corresponding population parameter.

The standard deviation is a key part of an important type of distribution in statistical analysis. This distribution is the *normal curve* and has the following characteristics:

1. It is bell-shaped and symmetrical.
2. The mode, median, and arithmetic mean have the same value at the center of the distribution.
3. A fixed proportion of the observations lie between the mean and any other point.[34]

This last characteristic is very useful. If a distribution is normal, or approximately so, we know what proportion of observations found in it lie between any two values of the variable measured. Typically, these values are measured in standard deviation units above and below the mean. This is illustrated in Figure 11.10.

The mean of the distribution divides it exactly in half: 50 percent of the observations are above it and 50 percent are below. Between the mean and one standard deviation above it lie 34.13 percent of the observations. The same proportion is between the mean and one standard deviation below the mean. Exactly 68.26 percent of all observations in the distribution are between one standard deviation below the main and one standard deviation above the mean.

FIGURE 11.10 — **PROPORTIONS FOR THE NORMAL CURVE**

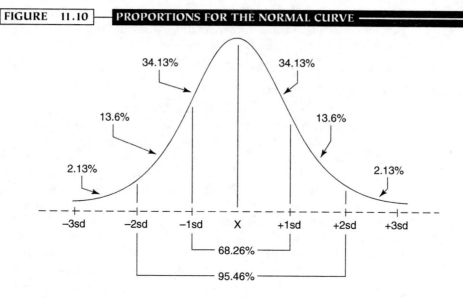

Standard scores, also called z-scores, are used to measure the values of the individual observations in a normal curve. Standard scores express the values in terms of units of the standard deviation. A z-score of 1.5, for example, indicates that a case's value is 1.5 standard deviations above the mean; a z-score of −2.0 shows that the value is two standard deviations below the mean, and so on. An observation with a z-score of −2.0 would be an unusually low observation relative to the rest of the observations. Standard scores are calculated by the following formula:

$$z = \frac{X_i - \overline{X}}{S}$$

where:

   z = standard or z-score = number of standard deviation units
   X_1 = an observation
   $\overline{X}$ = arithmetic mean of the distribution
   S = standard deviation of the distribution

For example, if the mean of the distribution in Figure 11.10 is 100, the standard deviation is 20, and an individual observation, x, has the value 115, the z-score for that individual would be:

$$z = (115 - 100)/20 = .75.$$

If the observations in the distribution are the means of all possible samples, we can determine how likely it is that any particular mean is within a certain distance of the center of the distribution. The center of such a distribution is the mean of all sample means; it also is the population mean. This information is very useful in inferential statistics as discussed later in the book. And as discussed in chapter 5, it allows us to calculate the size of the standard error and to determine how likely it is that the confidence interval around any particular sample estimate encompasses the population parameter.

EXPLORATORY DATA ANALYSIS

The topics of central tendency and variability are among the oldest in statistics. In addition to traditional ways of treating them, newer techniques have been developed in recent years. Based on the work of statistician John Tukey and others, the field of applied statistics has developed many techniques of exploratory data analysis, often abbreviated as EDA.[35] EDA emphasizes becoming thoroughly familiar with a set of data, rather than just computing one or two summary statistics. The adherents of this approach have introduced new terms and devised new measures of center and spread. New diagrammatic and graphical means of displaying distributions also have been developed and adapted for personal computers.

New measures of central tendency include order-based measures and some variations of the arithmetic mean, such as *trimmed means*.[36] These measures are helpful in understanding the central part of the distribution of a variable. Variations of the arithmetic mean, such as trimmed means, are not influenced by cases with extreme values, or outliers, as these means are calculated after adjusting or removing such cases. The 5 percent trimmed mean, for example, drops the top 5 percent and the bottom 5 percent of cases before calculating the mean. The mid-mean uses only the middle 50 percent of the cases. Although these means are useful in comparing the centers of distributions without influence from outliers, some authorities feel that they pay too little attention to extreme values. Also, remember that these measures do not enter into the calculation of other statistics.

Several new graphic procedures have been created for data exploration in recent years. They appear to have been motivated both by developments in EDA and by the enhanced graphics capabilities of computers. These techniques and computers provide opportunities for visual analysis of distributions in ways not generally used before.[37]

One popular technique is the *box plot,* also called a box and whisker diagram. This shows in the same graphic the median of a variable, its minimum and maximum values, quartile locations, inter-quartile range, and in some cases, outliers. Box plots give a quick and clear view of both central tendency and spread.

Figure 11.11 illustrates a box plot for the 1999 murder rates from 23 western and southern states in the United States. The horizontal axis gives the possible values of the variable. The extreme left part of the plot, the end of the whisker, shows the minimum value in the distribution. The maximum value is marked by the extreme right of the plot. The box enclosed by two vertical bars and two horizontal bars marks the middle 50 percent of the cases in the distribution. This, of course, is the inter-quartile range, with the left vertical bar marking the first quartile and the right vertical bar marking the third quartile. The median is marked within the box by an asterisk. Some graphics programs will show the median as another vertical bar.

The minimum, maximum, median, first quartile, and third quartile values are called the *Tukey five-number summary* after the statistician who developed

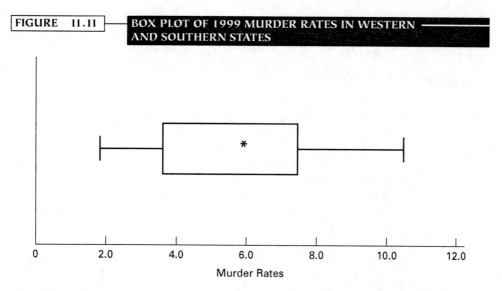

FIGURE 11.11 — BOX PLOT OF 1999 MURDER RATES IN WESTERN AND SOUTHERN STATES

several EDA measures. These are readily shown on the box plot and often are included in the computer output. For the set of data illustrated by the plot in Figure 11.11, these values are:

$$\text{minimum} = 2.0; \text{maximum} = 10.7; \text{median} = 6.0;$$
$$\text{first quartile} = 3.4; \text{third quartile} = 7.8.$$

Figure 11.12 shows two box plots on the same diagram—one for western states and the other for southern states. Comparison of the two reveals much about

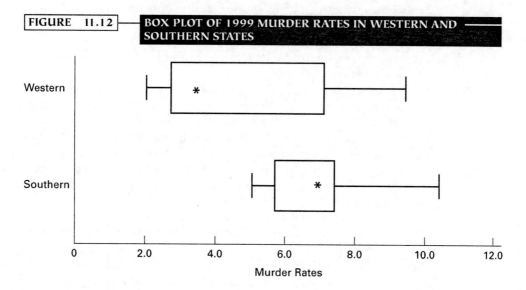

FIGURE 11.12 — BOX PLOT OF 1999 MURDER RATES IN WESTERN AND SOUTHERN STATES

murder rates in the two groups of states. The data for these box plots are included in Problem 9 at the end of the chapter.

SUMMARY

After data are collected, appropriate ways of managing and analyzing them must be found. This chapter discusses preparing and organizing data for analysis. Data are usually coded and entered into a computer file. A data dictionary enables the user to interpret the meaning of the data codes without having to go back to the original collection forms.

With the increased availability, versatility, and use of personal computers, hundreds of programs to manage, analyze, and store data are available. Three types of computer software available for the administrator and the analyst to manage and analyze data are statistical packages, spreadsheets, and database managers. Statistical packages are perhaps the most useful for thorough statistical analysis of large datasets. Spreadsheets can assist in the entry of small datasets, as a medium of data transfer between application programs, and for some simple statistical calculations. Geographic Information Systems (GISs) use geographic data and allow users to show the distribution of other variables on maps produced by the computer. Newer GIS programs are capable of calculating numerous statistics, and new statistical techniques have been developed to take advantage of the spatial characteristics of geographic data.

Investigators typically organize data in frequency distributions for further analysis and presentation. In frequency distributions, cases are grouped by their variable value and the number of cases with each value is shown. Relative frequencies, especially percents, also are included in frequency distributions. Percents, rates, rates of change, ratios, and proportions communicate information about a variable quickly and effectively. Most people can easily visualize and interpret percentage data. Ratios facilitate comparisons between groups or jurisdictions, whereas percent changes and rates of change indicate how the values of a variable change over time.

Various graphs and tables are used in analyzing and presenting data. Bar graphs and histograms show the frequency of cases for each variable value with a bar whose height or length indicates the number of cases. Histograms are limited to interval and ratio variables. Line graphs also are used to summarize and display interval- and ratio-level variables. Time-series and frequency polygons are two types of line graphs. Frequency polygons show the frequency of cases with each value of a variable. Time-series graphs show how the value of a variable changes over time.

Measures of central tendency describe one aspect of a frequency distribution. The mode, a nominal measure, is the most frequently occurring value in a distribution. The median, an ordinal measure, is the value at the center of a distribution's cases. It should be used with interval and ratio variables when the distribution is skewed, as its value is not affected by extreme values. The arithmetic mean, an interval measure, is preferred to summarize those interval variables that are neither bimodal nor skewed. The mean has properties that make it an important measure for many statistical procedures.

Measures of dispersion indicate how well the measure of central tendency describes a variable. A number of measures of spread, such as the range and inter-quartile range, help assess the configuration of a distribution. The variance and standard deviation describe the degree of variation in the distribution of interval and ratio variables. The variance and standard deviation are important components of other statistical measures and are useful in estimating population parameters.

Recent work in statistics has produced measures for exploratory data analysis. This approach emphasizes the benefit of becoming thoroughly familiar with a set of data. Graphic techniques, such as box plots, based on this approach are readily produced by computers, providing additional visual means of analyzing data.

Chapter 12 discusses hypothesis testing and the concept of statistical significance. Chapter 13 discusses the analysis of relationships between variables. It discusses contingency tables and presents statistics for analyzing the relationships among variables in contingency tables. In addition, in Chapter 13 we discuss analysis of variance, a method for analyzing the differences between groups as measured by the arithmetic means of variables. Chapter 14 treats correlation and regression analysis—techniques for the analysis of relationships among interval and ratio variables.

NOTES

1. L. B. Bourque and V. Clark, *Data Processing: The Survey Example*, Sage University Paper Series on Quantitative Applications in the Social Sciences, series no. 07–085 (Newbury Park, CA: Sage, 1992), 45–48. Several introductory manuals for SPSS are available. Some focus on using SPSS software; others are for the purpose of teaching SPSS and statistical analysis. For an example of the latter see Samuel Green and Neil Salkind, *Using SPSS for Windows and Macintosh: Analyzing and Understanding Data*, 3d ed. (Upper Saddle River, NJ: Prentice Hall, 2003).

2. D. L. Harnett and J. F. Horrell, *Data, Statistics, and Decision Models with Excel* (New York: John Wiley and Sons, 1998).

3. Larry D. Hall and Kimball Marshall, *Computing for Social Research* (Belmont, CA: Wadsworth, 1992), 230–232.

4. Bourque and Clark, *Data Processing*, 46–47.

5. Andy Mitchell, *Zeroing In: Geographic Information Systems at Work in the Community*, Environmental Systems Research Institute Press (Redlands, CA, 1997–1998).

6. G. David Garson and R. S. Biggs, *Analytic Mapping and Geographic Databases*, Sage University Paper Series on Quantitative Applications in the Social Sciences, series no. 07–087 (Newbury Park, CA: Sage, 1992), 2–3.

7. Ibid., 2.

8. Andy Mitchell, *The ESRI Guide to GIS Analysis, Vol. 2: Spatial Measurements & Statistics* (Redlands, CA: ESRI Press, 2005); David Wong and Jay Lee, *Statistical Analysis of Geographic Information With ArcViewGIS and ArcGIS* (Hoboken, NJ: John Wiley and Sons, 2005). The Wong and Lee book is the more advanced of these two.

9. Garson and Biggs, 76.

10. Remember that the percent is calculated by dividing a part by the whole and multiplying by 100. For example, the percent of injuries in Table 11.3 occurring in Able County is the number of injuries in that county divided by the total, then multiplied by 100: $(5/20) \times 100 = 25\%$.

11. Wayne Daniel and James Terrell, *Business Statistics for Management and Economics*, 7th ed. (Boston: Houghton-Mifflin, 1995), 19.

12. See Daniel and Terrell, 18–21, for discussion of a formula, Sturgis' Rule, used to guide analysts in deciding on the number of intervals. An alternative is the Rice rule which puts the number of intervals as twice the cube root of the number of observations. See David Lane for a discussion of Sturgis' and Rice rules, http://cnx. org/content/m10160/latest. (accessed December 20, 2006).

13. Edward R. Tufte, *The Visual Display of Quantitative Information* (Cheshire, CT: Graphics Press, 2001), 13.

14. Ibid., 54–58; Darrel Huff, *How to Lie with Statistics* (New York: Norton, 1954) is an older yet entertaining, relevant, and informative treatment of techniques used intentionally and unintentionally to mislead and misrepresent data.

15. David Freedman, Robert Pisani, and Roger Purvis, *Statistics* (New York: Norton, 1978), 25–31.

16. Ibid., 30–31.

17. Ibid., 39–40.

18. For example, see "Microsoft Excel" in Gary Shelley, Thomas Cashman, and Misty Vermaat, *Microsoft Office 2003: Introductory Concepts and Techniques* (Cambridge, MA: Course Technology, 2005).

19. An effective example is a bar graph of the murder rates of the fifty states in descending order with horizontal bars indicating the murder rate. See "The Curse of the South," *The Charlotte Observer*, August 2, 1998, 1C, 4C.

20. Frequency polygons of a particular shape are called normal curves or normal distributions. These have characteristics that are extremely useful in statistics. See Freedman, Pisani, and Purvis, *Statistics*, 69–87, and Joseph F. Healey, *Statistics: A Tool for Social Research*, 3d ed. (Belmont, CA: Wadsworth, 1993).

21. For information on measures of incidence and prevalence and a discussion of formulas, see a basic text in epidemiology, for example, Gary D. Friedman, *Primer of Epidemiology* (New York: McGraw-Hill, 1980), especially Chaps. 2 and 6, or Charles H. Hennekens and Julie E. Buring, *Epidemiology in Medicine* (Boston: Little-Brown and Company, 1987). For a comprehensive list of concepts and definitions used in epidemiology see John Last, ed., *A Dictionary of Epidemiology*, 3d ed. (New York: Oxford University Press, 1995).

22. Rochester, Minnesota, the home of the Mayo Clinic, is in Olmsted County. The medical conditions of its population are among the most thoroughly studied of any county in the nation.

23. H. F. Weisberg, *Central Tendency and Variability* (Newbury Park, CA: Sage, 1992), 26–27.

24. For example, see K. J. Meier, J. L. Brudney, and J. Bohte, *Applied Statistics for Public and Nonprofit Administration*, 6th ed. (Belmont, CA: Thomson-Wadsworth, 2006), Chapter 5 and B. P. Macfie and P. M. Nufrio, *Applied Statistics for Public Policy* (Armonk, NY: M. E. Sharpe, 2006), Chapter 4. Weisberg also demonstrates this on page 11.

25. In the calculation of the median we assumed that the lower limit of the class interval was the whole number ending in 0. We make that assumption here as well. In this case the midpoint of the interval is then halfway between two numbers. If the true lower limit of the interval 20–29 is 20, for example, then the midpoint of the interval is 24.5.

26. See Weisberg, *Central Tendency*, 41–43, or one of the other "Recommended for Further Reading" suggestions for a formula to calculate the geometric mean. Logarithms also can be used, and readers familiar with the mathematics of finance will have used present-value and interest-rate tables that can be used to determine the geometric mean.

27. These criteria consider the major properties of measures of central tendency but are not the only ones. See Weisberg, *Central Tendency*, 35, for a more extensive list.

28. Healey, *Statistics: A Tool for Social Research*, 93–97, discusses the calculation of IQV, a measure of variation for nominal and ordinal variables.

29. Weisberg, *Central Tendency*, 63–64.

30. Daniel and Terrel, *Business Statistics*, 65–66.

31. For a more detailed discussion of the difference between N and $n - 1$ in the formulas for computing the variance and standard deviation, consult one of the statistics texts listed under "Recommended for Further Reading"; see especially Hubert Blalock, *Social Statistics* (New York: McGraw-Hill, 1972), 81, 185–193.

32. Richard Chase and Nicholas Aquilano, *Production and Operations Management: A Life Cycle Approach*, 5th ed. (Homewood, IL: Irwin, 1989), 250–254.

33. See Weisberg, *Central Tendency*, 66, for more information about this measure and its calculation. For application to property tax procedures, see John Mikesell, *Fiscal Administration: Analysis and Applications for the Public Sector*, 7th ed. (Belmont, CA: Thomson-Wadsworth, 2007), 439–443.

34. For more discussion of the normal curve, see "Recommended for Further Reading," especially Freedman, Pisani, and Purvis, *Statistics*, 69–87, and Healey, 120–130.

35. See the following for discussions of exploratory data analysis. John Tukey, *Exploratory Data Analysis* (Reading, MA: Addison-Wesley, 1977); D. Hoaglin, F. Mosteller, and J. W. Tukey, eds., *Understanding Robust and Exploratory Data Analysis* (New York: Wiley, 1983); Frederick Hartwig and Brian E. Dearing, *Exploratory Data Analysis* (Newbury Park, CA: Sage, 1979); Herbert

Weisberg, *Central Tendency and Variability* (Newbury Park, CA: Sage, 1992).

36. Tukey, *Exploratory Data Analysis*; Hartwig and Dearing, *Exploratory Data Analysis*; Weisberg, *Central Tendency*.

37. See Tufte, *The Visual Display of Quantitative Information.* Two books by William S. Cleveland are also recommended: *Visualizing Data* (Summit, NJ: Hobart Press, 1994) and *The Elements of Graphing Data* (Summit, NJ: Hobart Press, 1994).

TERMS FOR REVIEW

descriptive statistics	frequency distribution	median
inferential statistics	univariate distribution	arithmetic mean
univariate statistics	class interval	measures of dispersion
multivariate statistics	bar graph	range
bivariate statistics	histogram	inter-quartile range
statistical software packages	frequency polygon	percentile
spreadsheet	pie chart	quartile
database management system	rate	standard deviation
relational database	incidence	variance
GIS	prevalence	average deviation
data array	ratio	normal curve
	percentage change	box plot
	mode	data dictionary

QUESTIONS FOR REVIEW

The following questions should indicate whether you have a basic competency in this chapter's material.

1. How does a bar graph differ from a histogram?
2. Describe the differences between a frequency polygon and a graph of a time series.
3. Why are pie charts used so often in budget documents?
4. Compare percentages to rates. How are they similar? How are they different?
5. When would the median be preferred to the arithmetic mean as a measure of central tendency? In what situations would you recommend using both?
6. "The standard deviation can be used as a measure of how adequate the arithmetic mean is as a measure of central tendency." Explain.
7. Compare the uses of the standard deviation and midrange measures of variation or dispersion. What are the advantages and disadvantages of each?
8. When would an analyst use the inter-quartile range for interval or ratio-level data instead of the standard deviation?
9. When is the average deviation best used?
10. Discuss the criteria to use for choosing a measure of central tendency.
11. What statistics are used to construct a box plot? When would you use box plots to present your data?

PROBLEMS FOR HOMEWORK AND DISCUSSION

1. Develop a data dictionary for the following data collection instrument. You will need to anticipate the responses to Part E, an open-ended question.

Library Users' Study

A. Do you currently have a County Public Library card?

Yes. 1   No. 2

B. How often have you visited the Public Library within the past 12 months?

At least once a week 1
Less than once a week but at least once a month 2
Less than once a month but at least once every three months 3
Less than once every three months but at least once a year 4

C. Which of the following keeps you from using the Public Library more frequently?

Hard to find parking 1
Hours are inconvenient 2
Too far away from home 3
I use another library 4
Lack of time 5
No need for library services 6
Library doesn't have what I need . . . 7
I'm not a reader. 8
Other (please specify) 9

D. Do you usually find the materials you need?

Yes. 1   No. 2

E. What subject area or types of materials would you like to see the library add to its collection? (please specify)

F. What is your age?

16–20 years. 1
21–30 years. 2
31–50 years. 3
51–65 years. 4
Over 65 years 5

G. What is your gender?

Male. 1
Female. .2

2. Write the data record for a case having the following answers to the Library Users' Study survey.

Item	Response
A	Yes
B	At least once a week
C	Hours inconvenient
D	Yes
E	Architectural history
F	31–50 years
G	Female

3. Obtain a copy of a recent budget for a city, town, or county and answer the following questions concerning it. Which types of graphical presentations are used? For what purposes? Which type is most effective? Would you change any of them in order to improve them? How?

4. Change one of the graphical displays from the budget you obtained by using a different format. That is, change a pie chart to a bar graph. Or change a bar graph to a pie chart to show the same information.

5. A users' survey to determine the number of personal computers owned by government agencies in a five-county planning region generated the data shown in Table 11.13. Construct a frequency polygon using these data. Write a short paragraph describing the results of the survey.

TABLE 11.13   DATA ARRAY FOR NUMBER OF PERSONAL COMPUTERS

Agency ID Number	Number of Computers	Agency ID Number	Number of Computers
01	1	16	3
02	4	17	4
03	9	18	2
04	7	19	5
05	7	20	8
06	7	21	11
07	10	22	6
08	6	23	6
09	4	24	4
10	5	25	8
11	9	26	5
12	10	27	7
13	5	28	3
14	1	29	5
15	2	30	3

6. Use the data array given in Table 11.14, which is a slightly revised version of Table 11.1, to work the following:

a. Calculate injury rates for Able and Charlie counties. (The population of these counties is 15,300 for Able and 79,200 for Charlie.) Which is the most dangerous county in which to live?

TABLE	11.14	**DATA ARRAY FOR THREE VARIABLES: COUNTY, CAUSE, AND SEVERITY OF INJURY**

Case ID	County	Cause	Severity Index
01	Baker	Fall	3
02	Charlie	Car accident	4
03	Charlie	Violence	6
04	Able	Car accident	4
05	Charlie	Violence	5
06	Baker	Fall	9
07	Charlie	Car accident	10
08	Baker	Fall	1
09	Able	Violence	5
10	Charlie	Violence	5
11	Charlie	Fall	7
12	Able	Car accident	4
13	Charlie	Car accident	7
14	Baker	Fall	6
15	Able	Fall	3
16	Baker	Car accident	5
17	Charlie	Car accident	5
18	Baker	Fall	6
19	Able	Car accident	4
20	Charlie	Violence	7

b. What is the ratio of injuries due to violence to those due to falls in Charlie County?

c. What is the mode for "cause of injury"?

d. For "severity index," calculate the following: mode, median, arithmetic average, range, 90th percentile, variance, and standard deviation. Also calculate the z-score for case 07.

7. The population of Mecklenburg County in 1970 was 354,000. In 1980 it was 404,270. Calculate the percent change in population during this time. Compare the change in population in this period to the change worked as an example in the text. (The 1990–2000 population percent change was used in the text example.)

8. Draw box plots illustrating how the distributions from the following figures in the chapter might look: Figure 11.9 (a) and (b); Figure 11.10.

You will not be able to get precise values from the figures. The purpose is to approximate the distribution by drawing a box plot to show the various locational measures of center and spread.

9. Table 11.15 shows murder rate data for 12 southern and 11 western states for 1997 and 1999. These include murder and non-negligent manslaughter and show the number of crimes per 100,000 of population.

a. Calculate the arithmetic average for the data for each year, and determine the following: minimum, maximum, median, first and third quartiles, and inter-quartile range. Draw a box plot for the dataset from each year and label the components corresponding to the Tukey five-number summary.

TABLE	11.15	**MURDER RATE DATA FOR SELECTED STATES, 1997 AND 1999**

State	1997 Murder Rate	1999 Murder Rate	State	1997 Murder Rate	1999 Murder Rate
Alabama	9.9	7.9	Montana	4.8	2.6
Arizona	8.2	8.0	Nevada	11.2	9.1
Arkansas	9.9	5.6	New Mexico	7.7	9.8
California	8.0	6.0	North Carolina	8.3	7.2
Colorado	4.0	4.6	Oregon	2.9	2.7
Florida	6.9	5.7	South Carolina	8.4	6.6
Georgia	7.5	7.5	Tennessee	9.5	7.1
Idaho	3.2	2.0	Utah	2.4	2.1
Kentucky	5.8	5.4	Virginia	7.2	5.7
Louisiana	15.7	10.7	Washington	4.3	3.0
Maryland	9.9	9.0	Wyoming	3.5	2.3
Mississippi	13.1	7.7			

SOURCES: FBI "Uniform Crime Reports for the United States—1997 edition" (U.S. Government Printing Office, November, 1998) and *Statistical Abstract of the United States.*

b. Construct a frequency distribution of the rates for 1997. Group the values into intervals of 5, that is, 0–4.99; 5.0–9.99; and so on. Draw a histogram from the frequency distribution.

c. Review the box plots in Figure 11.12, and write a page describing the differences between the two groups of states in their murder rates.

d. Draw separate box plots for southern and western states for the 1997 rates.

e. Write a memo comparing the rates in southern and western states. Discuss how these rates have changed from 1997 to 1999 (see Figures 11.11 and 11.12).

DISK WORK

These exercises require you to become familiar with statistical software and its outputs. Begin by using the ORB Research Methods dataset from the disk.

1. This exercise requires you to use a statistical software package or spreadsheet to learn about variation in counties' net migration.

   a. Get the following information on net migration across the counties: frequency distribution, relative frequency distribution, and cumulative percents.

   b. Produce a bar graph (for both number of counties and percent of counties) and a pie chart describing counties' net migration. Which would you include in a report? Justify your choice.

   c. If you were including the information on migration in a report to the state's governor, what class intervals would you use? Justify your choice.

   d. Get information on the mode, median, and mean for counties' net migration. Use the procedure "Computing the Mean from Grouped Data," described in the chapter to calculate the estimated mean. Compare this with the mean on the output. Can you conclude that either mean is accurate? Why or why not?

2. This exercise asks you to analyze variations in the demographics in counties, using them to make decisions about allocating health care resources.

   a. With data on the counties' population, use spreadsheet formula functions to calculate the number of active primary care physicians and social security beneficiaries per 1,000 population in each county. Produce a histogram and frequency polygon for these variables. Experiment with creating additional visuals communicating the distribution of each variable. Which would you be most likely to include in a report? Justify your choice. Would you consider using bar graphs or pie charts to present these data? Why or why not?

   b. For the variables Average SAT total and Average public school expenditure per 1,000 population (which you must calculate), produce a frequency distribution and obtain the following statistical information: mode, median, mean, minimum, maximum, range, first quartile (25th percentile), third quartile (75th percentile), standard deviation. What do these statistics tell you about the similarities and differences between the two distributions?

3. Do counties with high fiscal stress tend to spend in a different fashion than those with low fiscal stress? Explore this relationship by creating the variable of county debt service per person to represent county fiscal stress. Create a new variable that codes each county as high or low fiscal stress.

   a. Create two sets of box plots for high and low fiscal stress counties. Have one set of box plots compare cultural and recreation spending per person. Have the other set of box plots compare human services expenditures. Can you comment on the initial question? Do county spending patterns differ?

   b. Write a one-page single-spaced memo for the state Association of Counties, reporting your findings and their implications.

RECOMMENDED FOR FURTHER READING

H. M. Blalock, Jr., *Social Statistics,* 2d ed. (New York: McGraw-Hill, 1972) is the standard source of details on statistics commonly used by social scientists.

J. F. Healey, *Statistics: A Tool for Social Research,* 3d ed. (Belmont, CA: Wadsworth, 1993) is an excellent introductory statistics text covering a wide range of topics.

K. J. Meier, J. L. Brudney, and J. Bohte, *Applied Statistics for Public and Nonprofit Administration,* 6th ed. (Belmont, CA: Thomson Wadsworth, 2006) presents excellent examples and problems suggesting how administrators can use statistics in decision making. The calculations for statistics are worked in detail and easily followed.

Several works discuss preparation of charts and graphs, theory of graphic design, visualization techniques, and the research supporting these principles. The following five are recommended: G. T. Henry, *Graphing Data: Techniques for Display and Analysis* (Thousand Oaks, CA: Sage Publications, 1995); E. R. Tufte, *The Visual Display of Quantitative Information,* 2d ed. (Cheshire, CT: Graphics Press, 2001); William S. Cleveland, *The Elements of Graphing Data* (Summit, NJ: Hobart Press, 1994); William S. Cleveland, *Visualizing Data* (Summit, NJ: Hobart Press, 1994); H. Wainer, *Graphic Discovery: A Trout in the Milk and Other Visual Adventures* (Princeton, NJ: Princeton University Press, 2005). Tufte and Wainer provide interesting histories of the development of techniques with examples from history and modern times.

J. W. Tukey, *Exploratory Data Analysis* (Reading, MA: Addison-Wesley, 1977), discusses several techniques for exploratory data analysis, illustrates their use, and provides examples.

H. F. Weisberg, *Central Tendency and Variability* (Newbury Park, CA: Sage, 1992) is a thorough and accessible discussion of these two topics.

For preparing survey data for analysis by a statistical package, see L. B. Bourque and V. Clark, *Data Processing: The Survey Example,* Sage University Paper Series on Quantitative Applications in the Social Sciences, series no. 07–085, (Newbury Park, CA: Sage, 1992); and D. H. Folz, *Survey Research for Public Administration* (Thousand Oaks, CA: Sage, 1996), Chaps. 5 and 6.

For GIS see the following: Laura Lang, *GIS For Health Organizations* (ESRI Press, Redlands: CA, 2000). This inexpensive book includes a tutorial compact disk for the beginner. ESRI (Environmental Systems Research Institute) has numerous publications describing GIS applications (www. esri. com). An excellent treatment of GIS and statistics is David Wong and Jay Lee, *Statistical Analysis of Geographic Information With ArcView GIS and ArcGIS,* 2d ed. (Hoboken, NJ: John Wiley and Sons, 2005).

William E. Huxhold, *An Introduction to Urban Geographic Information Systems* (New York: Oxford University Press, 1991) provides an excellent introductory overview of GIS and is a good source for a discussion of the development of a GIS for urban government applications. He describes various types of computer files and the similarities and differences among them. David Garson and Robert Biggs, *Analytic Mapping and Geographic Databases,* Sage University Paper Series on Quantitative Applications in the Social Sciences, series no. 07–087 (Newbury Park, CA: Sage, 1992), discuss the application of GIS to public policy and administration.

For a brief yet more detailed overview of the following types of applications programs—word processing, statistical packages, spreadsheets, and database managers—see L. D. Hall and K. P. Marshall, *Computing for Social Research* (Belmont, CA: Wadsworth, 1992).

D. B. Wright, *Understanding Statistics: An Introduction for the Social Sciences* (London: Sage, 1997) is a very readable text in which the author integrates output from SPSS with his discussion of a variety of statistics.

APPENDIX 11.1

Statistical Calculations

Finding Quartiles

The following is a more precise method than the one discussed in the text for determining the value of quartiles of a distribution. For ungrouped data, as in the example array shown in Table 11.16, reprinted from Table 11.12, the first and third quartiles may be found as follows:

First Quartile or Q1:

$$\text{Value of the ordered observation number} = (N + 1)/4$$

TABLE 11.16	YEARLY INCOME OF EIGHT EMPLOYEES (IN DOLLARS)		
12,000	17,000	18,000	24,000
25,000	27,000	30,000	58,000

For the array in this example, this would be $(8 + 1)/4 = 2.25$. This would put the value of the quartile between two observations. Case number 2 has the value 17,000, and case number 3 has the value 18,000. The quartile would be 25 percent of the way between 17,000 and 18,000, or 17,250.

Third Quartile or Q3:

$$\text{Value of the ordered observation number} = 3(N + 1)/4.$$

For this example it would be $3(8 + 1)/4 = 6.75$. This value also comes between two observations, cases number 6 and 7. The third quartile would be 75 percent of the way between the values of these two cases, 27,000 and 30,000. This would make it 29,250.

The inter-quartile range is the distance between the third and the first quartiles and would be $29,250 - 17,250$, or 12,000.

From this it follows that the formula for the second quartile, the median, also may be written:

$$\text{Median} = Q2 = \text{value or ordered observation}$$
$$\text{number} = 2(N + 1)/4 = (N + 1)/2.$$

Variance and Standard Deviation Calculation

The following illustrates the calculation of the variance and standard deviation. Formula 1 is the formula given in the text and is the definitional formula for each. Formula 2 is an alternative that works better if you have a large number of cases and a calculator. Of course, many calculators have a standard deviation routine built in.

Find the variance and standard deviation of the distribution in Table 11.17. The calculation table setup is useful.

TABLE 11.17	CALCULATION TABLE FOR VARIANCE AND STANDARD DEVIATION		
X	X^2	$(X - \overline{X})$	$(X - \overline{X})^2$
13	169	-14.4	207.36
18	324	-9.4	88.36
19	361	-8.4	70.56
25	625	-2.4	5.76
26	676	-1.4	1.96
28	784	.6	.36
31	961	3.6	12.96
59	3,481	31.6	998.56
Σ 219	7,381		1,385.88

Formula 1:

$$S^2 = \frac{\Sigma(X - \overline{X})^2}{N}$$

$$S = \sqrt{S^2}$$

$$S^2 = \frac{1385.88}{8} = 173.2$$

$$S = \sqrt{173.2} = 13.2$$

Formula 2:

$$S^2 = \frac{\Sigma X^2 - \frac{(\Sigma X)^2}{N}}{N}$$

$$S^2 = \sqrt{\frac{\Sigma X^2 - \frac{(\Sigma X)^2}{N}}{N}}$$

$$S^2 = \frac{7381 - \frac{47961}{8}}{8} = 173.2$$

$$S = \sqrt{173.2} = 13.2$$

These formulae apply to a population. If the data are from a sample, then $n - 1$ replaces N in the denominator.

APPENDIX 11.2

Data Preparation

Data are usually coded for storage and analysis by computers. Before collecting the data, project staff should consider how it will be coded, stored, and analyzed, as these concerns may affect the number of variables included in the study and their operationalization. Coding should be kept simple. Data must be in a form that can be entered in a computer file and the desired analysis can be done easily. Usually, this means assigning a number to each value of a variable.

For an example, consider a data collection form used by a state-supported regional emergency medical service (EMS). Individuals suffering head injuries in a multi-county area were taken by ambulance to the emergency room of a regional hospital associated with the EMS. An attendant recorded several pieces of information on each case, including the county where the injury occurred, the cause of the injury, the severity of the injury, and other information about the individual who was injured.

Preparing a data dictionary, also called a codebook, is an important step in organizing and preparing the data. In a *data dictionary,* the analyst lists the items, labels the valid codes for a variable's values, names each variable, and gives the location of the variable in the file. Given the data and the dictionary, an analyst should not need to consult the original data collection forms. Coding all information as numbers is useful for statistical analysis, although it is not always necessary. However, data analysis with a statistical package will be easier with numerical coding.

Data dictionaries typically contain the following information:

1. *Item number*
2. *Item description* This may include the actual question from a questionnaire or the instructions that were used for collecting a particular piece of data.
3. *Item codes* This is the most important part of the dictionary. These show the numbers, letters, or other codes assigned to each possible value of the item. It is a good idea to assign a code for unavailable data. Analysts usually try to use the same code, such as 9 or 99, for missing information for all items. Similarly, the same code may be assigned to all "Don't Know" responses. In a survey, for example, the number 8 might be consistently used to code an answer of "Don't Know," and 9 to indicate missing information.
4. *Variable or field name* Most statistical computer programs require that a name be assigned to each variable. The variable name is used in instructions to the program for manipulating and analyzing the data. Sometimes the variable name is determined early in the process and printed on the data collection form.

A dictionary for the Injury Protocol Data Collection Form is represented in Table 11.18. This questionnaire and the data from it were used for some examples and exercises in this chapter. Note that the unit of analysis for this example is the injured individual.

An identifying number should be assigned to each case and placed on the data collection form for that case. This number should be included in the data record and in the data file.

Computerized data collection systems display a collection form on the computer screen, and the researcher enters the data directly. When

TABLE 11.18	DATA DICTIONARY FOR INJURY PROTOCOL DATA COLLECTION FORM		

Item	Description	Codes	Variable Name
1	Case identification number	001 -total	ID
2	County of injury	01 = Able	County
		02 = Baker	
		03 = Charlie	
		.	
		.	
		.	
		99 = Unknown or not answered	
3	Cause of injury	01 = Car accident	Cause
		2 = Fall	
		3 = Violence	
		.	
		.	
		.	
		99 = Unknown or not answered	
4	Severity scale	Include actual score: 1–10	Severity
		1 = Least severe	
		10 = Most severe	
		99 = Unknown or not answered	

complete, the information on the form is transmitted directly into the computer and stored, and a blank form takes its place on the screen.

One form is used for each case. This system is often used in telephone surveys and is called CATI—computer-assisted telephone interview.

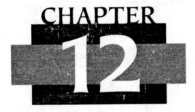

CHAPTER 12

Examining Relationships among Variables: Tests of Statistical Significance

In this chapter you will learn

1. The meaning of the terms *null hypothesis, statistical significance, Type I* and *Type II* errors, and *power*.
2. How to determine the statistical significance of research results.
3. When to use chi-square and *t*-tests.
4. How to apply and interpret tests of statistical significance.
5. The distinction between statistical significance and practical significance.

Deciding how to analyze data involves many choices. The researcher chooses from an array of analytical tools and statistics. The choice is based on her knowledge of specific tools and statistics, the questions she wants to answer, and the properties of the variables and the sample. She learns the tools common to her profession on the job and in her professional reading and training. Investigators have identified certain tools as appropriate for typical questions and data in her profession. Consequently, planners, psychologists, engineers, financial analysts, and administrators may prefer different approaches to analysis and work with different statistics. In carrying out management and policy-making tasks, public administrators rely on analytic approaches favored by social scientists. They use the tools of sociologists and political scientists in working with cross-sectional data, the tools of economists and statisticians in working with time series, and the tools of psychologists in working with experimental and quasi-experimental designs.

The following three chapters should guide public administrators in selecting methods of data analysis and interpreting statistics. We include only the statistics commonly encountered by administrators. Chapter 12 focuses on tests of statistical significance. Chapter 13 looks at two major approaches to examining the relationships among variables: contingency tables and measures of association, used to study cross-sectional data; and the basic analysis of variance model, used to study experimental findings and to compare means among groups. Chapter 14 discusses.

linear regression. Our discussions are not intended to teach you statistics. Rather, we emphasize what you need to consider in selecting a data analysis method or in interpreting statistical findings. The chapters focus on the questions that a statistic helps to answer, its data requirements, and its correct interpretation and application.

In examining data, the researcher may have two general questions: (1) What is the probability that a particular finding arose by chance? and (2) How strong is the relationship between an independent and a dependent variable? To answer the first question, the researcher works with tests of statistical significance. To answer the second, he works with measures of association, comparison of means tests, analysis of variance, and regression.

Before you start reading, we want to alert you that respected social science researchers argue that tests of statistical significance are overrated and misunderstood. We agree. Nevertheless, we decided to begin our discussion of statistical analysis with them. We did this because introductory statistics courses typically focus on testing the null hypothesis. Consequently, you may be familiar with the steps in significance testing, and the chi-square and *t*-test statistics. You may encounter these statistics in professional reports and research journals.

Statistical significance can be difficult to understand. We have found in our classes that students feel frustrated if we rush through it during the last week of classes. Furthermore, the term *significance*, the time spent on hypothesis testing in statistics courses, and the frequent appearances of significance tests in research reports all suggest that tests of statistical significance are extremely important. To counter this misperception, we point out the limitations of significance tests and suggest alternative statistical information and procedures that provide additional information about a hypothesis test.

Tests of statistical significance are a type of inferential statistic. *Inferential statistics* allow an investigator to infer population characteristics from sample data. To use inferential statistics correctly, the investigator must have a probability rather than a nonprobability sample. (The reader may find it useful to review parts of Chapter 5 before completing this chapter.)

Recall that probability samples allow an investigator to use inferential statistics to estimate parameters. A parameter can be estimated for a single variable or a relationship among variables. With sample data, one can state the probability that a parameter falls within a specified range, called the *confidence interval*. From a sample, one cannot tell exactly what portion of the population has a certain characteristic, but one can say with 95 percent confidence that the parameter falls within ±1.96 standard errors of the sample's estimate. Remember that a 95 percent confidence level indicates that 95 times out of 100 the sample design will allow the investigator to correctly estimate a parameter.

Another use of inferential statistics is to learn the probability that the observed relationship between variables in a sample could have occurred if the two variables are *randomly related* in the population. "Randomly related" means that the two variables are independent of each other or not related to each other. Asking if variables are randomly related in the population is the same as asking, "Could this relationship have occurred by chance?" If we examined the entire population or another sample, would a relationship between the variables still be found? The two variables are the independent and dependent variables of a hypothesis. If a statistical test suggests that in the population the relationship between the two variables is nonrandom, the relationship is said to be *statistically significant.*

Just because the relationship between two variables is statistically significant does not mean that the relationship is important or strong. Nor does it mean that all or any of the previous research steps were conducted correctly. An important, valuable, or useful research finding is said to have *practical significance.* Just because a finding is statistically significant does not mean that it is practically significant.

Statistical significance simply tells us something about the statistical relationship between variables. For example, with a large sample, many relationships will be statistically significant. Yet, the independent variable may do a poor job of explaining the variation in the dependent variable; large samples often lend statistical support to trivial relationships.

The traditional process of determining if two variables have a nonrandom relationship requires the researcher to carry out four steps:

1. State the null and research hypotheses.
2. Select an alpha level.
3. Select and compute a test statistic.
4. Make a decision.

You may have learned this four-step process or a similar one in a statistics course. We use it here to organize our discussion. Nevertheless, strict adherence to these steps may not be appropriate in social science research.[1] The term *significance* and the logical process in applying tests of statistical significance imply that these tests are more informative than they are. They provide evidence that may support a hypothesis, but they may be inadequate for making a final decision whether to accept or reject a hypothesis.

Before we explain each step, we want to assure you that many people are bewildered the first time they study hypothesis testing. It is probably one of the most complicated topics in statistical analysis. Furthermore, hypothesis testing has its own terminology. Hypothesis testing has developed from careful statistical and epistemological thinking, and this attention is reflected in the terminology. Nevertheless, the phrases may seem convoluted.

With careful reading you should be able to follow the reasoning behind hypothesis testing and to interpret a finding of statistical significance. Rather than slowly reading, digesting, and thoroughly understanding each section, you may find it better to read through the chapter and then go back and review the specific sections.

STATING THE NULL HYPOTHESIS

A *hypothesis* states a relationship between two variables. The *research hypothesis* is the hypothesis that an investigator is studying. Typically, through model building, the investigator formulates a plausible research hypothesis; then he initiates research to see if it is supported. The *null hypothesis* postulates no relationship, or a random relationship, between the same two variables. The following examples state three sets of research (H_1) and null (H_0) hypotheses:

Examples of Research and Null Hypotheses

H_1: Some job training programs are more successful than other programs in placing trainees in permanent employment.

H_0: All job training programs are equally likely to place trainees in permanent employment.

H_1: The more clearly written a research report, the more likely it will be used.

H_0: The clarity of a research report is not related to the probability that it will be used.

H_1: Male planners earn higher salaries than female planners.

H_0: Gender is not related to planners' salaries.

To "prove" that a hypothesis is true requires two types of evidence: confirming evidence, based on inductive reasoning, and disconfirming evidence, based on deductive reasoning. Consider the hypothesis that participants in on-the-job training (OJT) programs are more likely to find jobs than are nonparticipants. If one study is conducted, and it shows that OJT participants have more placements, can a researcher argue that her hypothesis is true? Evidence confirming her hypothesis would include her ability to demonstrate that the study design satisfies the criteria for establishing causality, including eliminating alternative hypotheses. The subjects of one study represent one sample. If investigators consistently find higher placement rates among OJT trainees, the hypothesis receives stronger support. When just one study is conducted, one has to entertain the possibility that sampling error accounts for the higher placement rates of OJT trainees. One must entertain the possibility that another sample from the same population may not show a higher placement rate for OJT participants.

Hypothesis testing and tests of statistical significance rely on disconfirming evidence to support a hypothesis. An investigator does not directly assert that her data support the research hypothesis. Rather, she states that her data show that the null hypothesis is probably false. She confirms the research hypothesis by disconfirming the null hypothesis.[2] Let's outline that process:

Stage 1: Investigator states research hypothesis that OJT has higher placement rates.

Stage 2: Investigator states null hypothesis of no relationship between OJT training and placement rate.

Stage 3: Data from sample support hypotheses, i.e., the data show that a relationship exists.

Stage 4: Investigator rejects the null hypothesis as false.

Stage 5: Investigator argues that because the null hypothesis is false, OJT affects placement rate.

If her data did not show a difference in placement rates, she notes that she failed to reject the null hypothesis. For the same reasons that she cannot prove the research hypothesis, she cannot prove the null hypothesis. She cannot use failure to reject her null hypothesis to argue categorically that OJT training does not affect placement rates.

In conducting a hypothesis test, the researcher selects a statistical test to determine the probability that the hypothesized relationship in the population is random; this is the same as saying that the null hypothesis is true. The investigator uses data from a sample to make a guess about the population. In our example, the investigator found higher placement rates among OJT trainees; she selects a hypothesis test to determine the probability that the type of training program does not affect placement rates in the population.

In guessing about what is true in the population of interest, a researcher risks making one of two types of errors. She may decide to reject the null hypothesis, when in reality the null hypothesis is true, or she may decide not to reject the null hypothesis, when in reality the null hypothesis is untrue. Each of these errors has a name. Rejecting a true null hypothesis is a *Type I* error. Failure to reject a false null hypothesis is a *Type II* error. Table 12.1 illustrates the linkage among the researcher's decision, the state of nature (what is "really" true), and the types of errors.

With a Type I error, we have concluded from sample data that the research hypothesis is true, when in fact the research hypothesis is untrue. In general, researchers try to minimize the probability of a Type I error. This bias rests in their desire to minimize the risk of promoting research findings that may have occurred by chance. Conversely, researchers want to accept only findings that were unlikely to have occurred by chance. A Type I error may be thought of as a false alarm; in other words it alerts one to the possibility of a relationship or situation, yet in reality the relationship or situation does not exist. A Type II error may be thought of as a failure in signal detection; it fails to alert the researcher to an existing relationship or situation.

Prior to beginning the analysis, the investigator decides on a criterion for rejecting a null hypothesis. This criterion is a probability value and is referred to as the *alpha* (α) *level*. The alpha level is a number between 0 and 1. Common alpha levels for hypothesis testing are .05, .01, and .001.[3]

TABLE 12.1	TYPE I AND TYPE II ERRORS	
	State of Nature	
Decision Based on Sample	**H_0 True**	**H_0 Untrue**
Reject H_0	Type I error	Correct decision
Do not reject H_0	Correct decision	Type II error

The interpretation of the alpha levels is as follows:

$\alpha = .05$, 5% chance of committing a Type I error

$\alpha = .01$, 1% chance of committing a Type I error

$\alpha = .001$, 0.1% chance of committing a Type I error

If alpha is set at .05, and an investigator tests 100 hypotheses where the null hypothesis is true, he can expect to make five Type I errors.

Closely related to Type I and Type II errors is the concept of power. Just as we know that not all of the hypotheses we accept are true, some of the null hypotheses we do not reject are untrue. *Power* refers to the probability that a test of significance results in the rejection of false null hypotheses, which you may think of as the probability that an investigator will accept a true research hypothesis.

The power of a test of significance is 1 minus the probability of a Type II error (β); if the probability of a Type II error is 20 percent, the power of the test of significance is 80 percent, or .80. If the power of the test is .80, an investigator knows that 80 times out of 100 she will correctly reject the null hypothesis, and 20 times out of 100 she will fail to reject an untrue null hypothesis.[4] Determining the probability that the null hypothesis is false requires calculating the probability of a Type II error, a tedious procedure. The hypothesis must be exact, that is, the hypothesis must state the strength of the anticipated relationship. In the absence of an exact hypothesis, an administrator can consider sample size and the anticipated magnitude of the effect to estimate the power of the test.

We debated whether to include a discussion of power in this text; most readers may rarely apply the concept of power directly in their work or encounter it in their professional reading. We decided to discuss power, because it captures the relationship among the criteria for establishing significance (alpha-level), sample size, and the strength of a relationship.

If we hypothesize that OJT programs have higher placement rates than other training programs, how big a difference do we think there is? If we expect that the difference is very small, we may need a relatively large sample; otherwise, we risk failing to reject a false null hypothesis. If we expect to find a large difference, a relatively small sample may be adequate. For example, a sample of 1,300 will detect a very slight effect 95 percent of the time at an alpha level of .05. A sample of 50 will detect a moderate effect only 46 percent of the time if alpha is set at .05.[5]

SELECTING AN ALPHA LEVEL

The specific alpha level selected depends on the practical consequences of committing a Type I error or a Type II error and on the anticipated strength of the relationship. Sorting out the consequences of Type I and Type II errors involves thinking through the hypothesis and the null hypothesis and the actions that will result from accepting or rejecting the null hypothesis. Example 12.1 describes how one might think through the practical consequences of committing a Type I or Type II error.

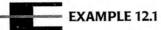 **EXAMPLE 12.1**

Practical Consequences of Type I and Type II Errors

Case 1

H_1: Gamma cars are less safe than other cars.
H_0: Gamma cars are as safe as other cars.

Situation: You have an opportunity to buy a Gamma car for an excellent price. You collect accident data on a sample of Gamma cars.

To select an alpha level, you need to think through what will happen if you commit a Type I error or a Type II error. If you conclude from the data in your sample that Gamma cars are less safe than other cars when in fact Gamma cars are as safe as other cars, you will commit a Type I error. The practical significance? You miss out on a bargain.

If you conclude from the data in your sample that Gamma cars are as safe as other cars when, in fact, they are less safe, you will have committed a Type II error. The practical consequence? You may purchase and drive a car that is less safe than other cars. Eventually, this decision may lead to a serious personal injury that could have been avoided.

Your decision in this situation? In analyzing the data you collect on cars and safety, you want to minimize the probability of committing a Type II error. Specifically, you will select a higher alpha level, that is, a value closer to zero. Alternatively, you will select a test with high power, that is, a low probability of accepting a false null hypothesis.

Case 2

H_1: Some job training programs are more successful than others.
H_0: All job training programs are equally successful.

Situation: Data on job training programs and placement outcomes are gathered and analyzed. What happens if a Type I error is committed? Some job training programs are erroneously assumed to be more successful than other programs. What are the practical consequences? Program continuation or cessation may depend on the findings. Programs that in reality are as successful as other programs may come to an end.

What happens if a Type II error is committed? Less effective programs will continue to offer training.

Your decision? It may depend on your point of view. If you represent training programs, you may want to minimize Type I error, which could result in effective programs closing. If you are a trainee, you may be concerned about being assigned to a less effective program. If you are a legislator, you may want evidence of the success of the programs you have supported.

The findings may reduce ambivalence about minimizing one type of error or the other. A small, but significant, difference in placement rates may not be worth the disruption of discontinuing programs.

The examples should lead you to question the wisdom of accepting a specific, rigid criterion, such as $\alpha = .05$, and applying it to a wide range of studies. The examples also illustrate that acceptable levels of Type I or Type II errors are affected by point of view and other practical concerns.

The alpha level is one of four parameters that should be considered in testing statistical significance. The other parameters are the power of the test, the sample size, and the size of the effect. A small effect is unlikely to be detected with a small sample and the traditional $\alpha = .05$ cutoff. Manipulating the alpha level can change the probability of Type I and Type II errors. If the alpha level is raised, the probability of Type I errors will increase, and the probability of Type II errors will decrease. If the alpha level is lowered, the probability of Type I errors will decrease, and the probability of Type II errors will increase. Type I and Type II errors both decrease with added cases.

How do these considerations apply to public administrators? While administrators may want to know the probability that an observed relationship is non-random in the population, the size of the effect is of far greater concern. For some situations, reacting to a "false alarm" or even responding to minor, nonrandom differences may be undesirable. Segments of the population may differ in their opinions about public policies or their experiences with public services. Nevertheless, administrators may prefer to ignore small differences. If older people are less satisfied with recreational facilities than other respondents, or if the police respond less quickly to calls from the south side of town than from other parts of town, administrators may not address these variations if they do not suggest indisputable patterns of discrimination or other problems. The political and economic costs may render resolving small differences infeasible or undesirable.

A test of significance is an inadequate criterion of a program's effectiveness. Evaluations based on small sample sizes and programs with modest effects may result in the erroneous conclusion that an effective program is ineffective. When social programs were first evaluated, researchers were disappointed in how little such programs accomplished. The disappointment was misplaced. It now seems naive to assume that a limited social program is going to markedly change behavior. We may have to be satisfied with smaller changes, albeit changes in the desired direction.

To limit research costs, evaluations of experimental programs may involve relatively few subjects. If a study has few subjects, and the program's effect is not expected to be strong, the probability of a Type II error is larger. If the measures have poor reliability, more random error will be introduced, further increasing the probability of a Type II error.[6] If a limited number of measures are used, other effects may be missed. Let's imagine an evaluation of a job training program. If a Type II error occurs, which is far more likely than a Type I error, a program that has a modest impact on participants may be judged to make no difference. If the program is canceled or phased out, trainees lose tangible benefits associated with program participation. They also may become more cynical or discouraged if a program that seemed to offer a brighter future no longer exists. Because of the higher probability of a Type II error and its consequences for program clients, evaluation students have been encouraged to consider the need to minimize Type II errors.

SELECTING AND COMPUTING A TEST STATISTIC

In this text we discuss two common tests of statistical significance. If you need only a basic understanding of the research findings, you should find the information provided here adequate for your needs. The first test statistic we consider is *chi-square* (χ^2). Chi-square is a statistic for nominal level data, although as is true with other statistics for nominal data it may be used to analyze ordinal and interval level data. It is often used to analyze contingency tables. (Contingency tables are covered in Chapter 13.) The second test statistic is the *t-test*. The *t*-test examines the differences between the means of two groups, that is, the relationship between an interval dependent variable and a nominal independent variable.

Chi-Square

The chi-square test compares the observations contained in a dataset with the observations expected if the relationship between variables is random in the population. Chi-square only indicates the probability that in the population the variables are unrelated; it does not indicate the direction of a relationship. Table 12.2 contains data gathered to test a hypothesis that specific job training programs achieved different outcomes. Table 12.2 (top) compares three job training programs and outcomes; the table contains the frequencies observed (f_o) in the collected data. Table 12.2 (bottom) shows what the data would look like if there were no relationship between a program and trainees' outcomes. The figures in Table 12.2 (bottom) represent the frequencies expected (f_e) if the null hypothesis were true.

TABLE 12.2   **OBSERVED AND EXPECTED FREQUENCIES**

CURRENT STATUS BY TRAINING PROGRAM ATTENDED: OBSERVED FREQUENCIES (f_o)

	Program			
	Vocational Education	On-the-Job Training	Work Skills Training	Total
Working	19	109	164	292
In school	19	82	31	132
Unemployed	26	82	54	162
Total	64	273	249	586

CURRENT STATUS BY TRAINING PROGRAM ATTENDED: EXPECTED FREQUENCIES
IF PROGRAM AND STATUS ARE UNRELATED (f_e)

	Program			
	Vocational Education	On-the-Job Training	Work Skills Training	
Working	31.9	136.0	124.1	292
In school	14.4	61.5	56.1	132
Unemployed	17.7	75.5	68.8	162
Total	64	273	249	586

Note: To calculate frequency expected (f_e) for each cell, multiply the column total and the row total for that cell and divide by the table total. f_e (cell 1,1): $(64 \times 292)/586 = 18,688/586 = 31.9$.

In the observed frequencies, we see that nearly 50 percent of all subjects were working (292 of 586). If the work status and program categories were not associated, the same percentage of participants in each program would be working. Hence, in Table 12.2 (bottom) nearly 50 percent of the clients of each program are assigned to the category "working." The ratios in the overall group for in-school and unemployed are similarly applied to the subgroups. A little less than 25 percent are assigned to the "in school" category, and somewhat more than 25 percent to the "unemployed" category. The footnote in Table 12.2 explains how the values for the table of expected frequencies are calculated.

The next step is to calculate chi-square. Each cell from the table of frequencies observed is subtracted from its counterpart in the table of frequencies expected $(f_o - f_e)$. The result is squared and divided by the frequency expected $((f_o - f_e)^2/f_e)$. For example, for the cell "Working" and "Vocational Education," the calculation would be $(19 - 31.9)^2/31.9 = 5.22$. Chi-square (χ^2) equals the sum of these figures. Thus the equation is

$$\chi^2 = \Sigma(f_o - f_e)^2/f_e$$

for the example $\chi^2 = 50.57$.

The "significance level" of a χ^2 value is typically reported by statistical software programs. The programs perform the calculations and report the χ^2 value and its "significance level." This significance level is the *associated probability*, that is, the probability that the specific value of χ^2 will occur if the null hypothesis is true in the population. (In the appendix to this chapter we show how to calculate chi-square and the relationship between its value and common alpha levels.) In interpreting computer program output, the investigator determines if the associated probability level is equal to or smaller than the alpha level he set. In this example, if $\alpha = .05$, $\chi^2 = 50.67$ indicates that the relationship is statistically significant. (The associated probability of a χ^2 value of 50.67 for this size table is less than .001.) Chi-square is a widely used and understood test of statistical significance. You should be aware of three of its characteristics. First, because chi-square is a statistic for variables measured at the nominal level, it does not provide information on the direction of any association. In our example, the chi-square evidence indicates that the relationship between type of training program attended and current status is probably nonrandom. It does not indicate which program is the most effective.

Second, the numerical value of chi-square tends to increase as the sample size increases. Thus the chi-square value is partially a product of sample size. A larger chi-square value is more likely to be statistically significant, even if the practical effect is small. It does not directly measure the strength of the association between variables and should not be used as a measure of association. Some statistics to measure the strength of a relationship are based on chi-square, but they take into account and adjust for sample size and number of rows and columns. We present one such statistic, Cramer's V, in Chapter 13.

Third, chi-square does not reliably estimate the probability of a Type I error if the expected frequency of a cell in a table is less than 5. Research has found that violating the expected frequencies criterion causes relatively small errors; a researcher can easily ignore this problem if it occurs in relatively few cells. If most cells have few cases, the investigator may consider combining categories.[7]

Let's review with an example the steps taken thus far to test the hypothesis that the training program was related to program outcomes:

1. State the hypothesis and the null hypothesis:

   H_1:   Different job training programs achieved different outcomes.

   H_0:   The job training programs did not differ in their achievement of outcomes.

2. Select an alpha level: Set alpha at .05, the default value which is common. Alternatively, a lower alpha level, e.g., .01, may be selected because of the relatively large sample size and desire to detect only a marked difference between program outcomes (making changes based on small differences would be costly).

3. Select a test statistic: Chi-square is selected because the table had nominal data.

4. Determine the value of test statistic: $\chi^2 = 50.57$.

5. Determine if the value of χ^2 meets alpha-level criterion: From the associated probability reported in the output, associated probability must be less than or equal to .05.

6. Decide if statistical evidence supports the research hypothesis: If associated probability is no more than .05 the statistical evidence supports the research hypothesis.

t-Tests

Assume that you want to learn whether men earn more than women or whether children at School A obtain higher state achievement test scores than children at School B. One way you could test these hypotheses is to rearrange the data into contingency tables and perform a chi-square test. Of course, to create contingency tables you must change the dependent variable information from interval to ordinal and would lose information. And you might rightfully wonder whether the finding of significance or lack of significance was associated with how the values were combined. Alternatively, you could hypothesize that the average achievement test grades at School A are higher than at School B.

The t-test is an interval statistic that can test hypotheses that two groups have different means. Each group is considered a sample, and the test is a two-sample t-test. The two-sample t-test can test a hypothesis (a) that two groups have different means or (b) that one group's mean is higher than the other's. The first type of hypothesis has no direction; a two-tailed t-test is used to test nondirectional hypotheses. The second type of hypothesis has direction; such hypotheses are tested with a one-tailed t-test.

The degree of variability in each sample affects the choice of formula used to calculate the t-value. One formula is used if the variances of each population represented by the sample are assumed to be equal. Another formula is used if the populations are assumed to have unequal variances.

A third formula is used if data for both groups come from the same subjects. For example, a researcher may compare analysts' error rates when entering data on laptop computers as opposed to desktop computers. A single group of analysts would enter data into both laptop and desktop computers. The dependent variable would be error rate, and the independent variable would be type of computer.

The t-test can also test a single sample hypothesis, for example, that a group's mean is greater or less than a specified value. The single sample t-test is useful for staffing studies.[8] For example, a university library may assume that its reference desk handles an average of 25 inquiries per hour on weekends. The assumption determines the level of staffing at the reference desk on weekends. Periodically, data may be gathered and the average number of inquiries per weekend calculated. A single sample t-test is performed to evaluate the hypothesis that the average number of inquiries is greater or less than 25.

To illustrate a t-test, we test the hypothesis that male planners earn higher salaries than female planners. We assume unequal variances of the salaries of the two groups. Assuming unequal variances is less likely to result in a Type I error, and consequently is more conservative than assuming equal variances, i.e., it is less likely to result in accepting an untrue hypothesis.

Step 1. State the hypothesis and the null hypothesis.

H_1:   The average salary of male planners is higher than the average salary of female planners.

H_0:   The average salary of male planners is the same as or less than the average salary of female planners.

The above hypothesis requires a one-tailed test. In a one-tailed test, the null hypothesis is expanded to include a finding in the "wrong" direction. Thus, if the data showed that the average salary of female planners was more than that of male planners, the researcher would not reject the null hypothesis. Alternatively, with a two-tailed test, the hypothesis only indicates a difference in salaries. It does not specify which gender earns more. The null hypothesis only notes no differences in the average salaries of male and female planners. So a researcher could find that the average salary of female planners is greater than that of male planners and still reject the null hypothesis.

Step 2. Select an alpha level; $\alpha = .05$ often serves as a default alpha level. It simply suggests that the relationship probably did not occur by chance, directing the investigator to examine the size of the difference in salaries.

Step 3. Select a test statistic: A t-test is selected because the hypothesis postulates that the two samples have different means. A one-tailed test is selected because the hypothesis postulates which sample mean is greater than that of the other.

Step 4. Calculate the test statistic. An assumption about the variances must be made. The formula for unequal variances will have produced slightly higher associated probabilities. Consequently, assuming unequal variances is a more conservative test and reasonable. When the study was done women had only recently entered the planning profession. Thus they were less likely to have salaries consistent with extensive experience, and one can expect that their salaries would have less variance than the salaries of males. With this assumption that the variances are unequal, the formula to calculate *t* is:

$$t = \frac{\overline{X}_1 - \overline{X}_2}{\sqrt{\dfrac{s_1^2}{n_1 - 1} + \dfrac{s_2^2}{n_2 - 1}}}$$

where:

For the Male Sample

$n_1 = 403$
$\overline{X}_1 = 17{,}095$
$s_1 = 6{,}329$
$s_1^2 = 40{,}056{,}241$

For the Female Sample

$n_2 = 132$
$\overline{X}_2 = 14{,}885$
$s_2 = 4{,}676$
$s_2^2 = 21{,}864{,}976$

$$t = \frac{17{,}095 - 14{,}885}{\sqrt{\dfrac{40{,}056{,}241}{402} + \dfrac{21{,}864{,}976}{131}}}$$

$$= \frac{2210}{\sqrt{99{,}642 + 166{,}908}}$$

$$= \frac{2{,}210}{\sqrt{266{,}550}}$$

$$= 4.28, \, df = n_1 + n_2 - 2 = 533$$

Step 5. Determine if the value of *t* meets the alpha-level criterion: From the associated probability in the computer output, associated probability must be less than or equal to .05. (Table 12.13 in Appendix 12.1 shows the relationship between values of *t* and common alpha levels.)

Step 6. Decide if statistical evidence supports the research hypothesis: If associated probability is no more than .05 or if *t* equals at least 1.645, the alpha-level criterion, statistical evidence supports the research hypothesis. In this case, $t = 4.28$, which is much higher than the level we need, and we can reject the null hypothesis. The research hypothesis is supported. In other words, from this study, the researcher has support for saying that the average salary for male planners is higher than the average salary for female planners.

The Normal Distribution

Students who have studied statistics may wonder why we do not use the normal distribution (z-scores) to test hypotheses about sample means. To use z-scores properly, the population variance must be known. If the population variance is not known, it is estimated by the standard deviation, in which case t-tests as opposed to z-scores are appropriate. With larger samples, t-scores approximate z-scores. While using z-scores introduces little error with larger samples ($n = 60$), social scientists tend to report t-tests.

MAKING A DECISION

Making a decision based on a test of statistical significance is relatively straight-forward. The strategy we have presented thus far has the investigator (1) setting the alpha-level criterion to reject the null hypothesis, (2) selecting a test statistic, (3) comparing the associated probability to the alpha-level criterion, and (4) rejecting the null hypothesis if the calculated value yields an associated probability equal to or less than the alpha level—otherwise, the null hypothesis is not rejected. In our examples an investigator would reject the null hypotheses and accept the research hypotheses that different job training programs achieved different outcomes and that male planners earned more than female planners. The associated probabilities for χ^2 and t are less than the selected alpha level of .05.

An alternative strategy begins with the associated probability. The investigator looks up the specific probability (p) associated with the calculated value of χ^2 or t. If this associated probability is no larger than the alpha-level criterion, the researcher rejects the null hypothesis and accepts the research hypothesis. Statistical software programs usually report associated probabilities. Example 12.2 reproduces computer output examining the relationship between respondent age and the grade given to a local police department. The output is from a popular statistical software program, SPSS, and identifies the relevant χ^2 information. Note that if an investigator had decided on an alpha level of .05 or .01, she would accept the research hypothesis. If she had decided on an alpha level of .001, she would not reject the null hypothesis.

The associated probability does not indicate the probability of a Type I error, nor does it imply that a relationship is "more significant" or "stronger." Its contribution is more modest. It indicates the probability of a specific χ^2 or t-value occurring if the null hypothesis is true.[9] Researchers combine information on the associated probability with the other evidence to make inferences about hypotheses. Such evidence may include evidence of internal validity or findings from previous studies.

Tests of statistical significance may appear to constitute a "pass/fail" test. Should they play this role? No, not in our examples or in similar situations. The investigator is only testing a statistical model. The data represent many decisions, including whom to sample, how to sample them, what information to gather, how to gather it, and when to gather it. The investigator applies statistical tests to a set of numbers; he obtains an answer even if he violates all the statistical assumptions and ignores sound methodological practice.

If the methodological decisions are sound and the statistics are applied correctly, the data still represent a single sample out of all the possible samples from

EXAMPLE 12.2

Interpreting χ^2 Information on SPSS Output

Situation: A probability sample of 830 citizens graded a city's police department. The investigators hypothesized: The younger the respondent, the lower the grade he or she gave the police department. (The null hypothesis was that age had no relationship to the grades given.)

Findings: An SPSS program is run, and Table 12.3 and statistics are reported. Note that relatively more of the oldest respondents gave the department an A or B, and that relatively more of the youngest respondents gave the department a D or F.

TABLE 12.3   GRADE BY AGE

		Age			
Grade Column %		**Under 18**	**18–59**	**60 or older**	
		1.00	2.00	4.00	Row Total
A or B	1.0000	50.0	72.7	82.0	615
					74.1
C	2.0000	41.7	22.0	14.8	174
					21.0
D or F	4.0000	8.3	5.3	3.3	41
					4.9
	Column	24	623	183	830
	Total	2.9	75.1	22.0	100.0

Chi-Square	Value	*df* (Degrees of Freedom)	Significance
Pearson	13.90036 [calculated value of χ^2]	4	.00762 [associated probability]

Notes:
1. "Pearson" refers to "Pearson's chi-square," which is the chi-square equation used in this text.
2. The χ^2 information would be reported as follows: "$\chi^2 = 13.9$, $df = 4$, $p = .00762$." One may round p to .008.
3. The column labeled "significance" is actually reporting the associated probability. Some researchers do not report the specific associated probability; instead, they indicate if the hypothesis was supported based on the preset alpha level. For example, if the researcher set $\alpha = .01$, he would report "$\chi^2 = 13.9$, $df = 4$, $p < .01$."
4. If the researcher changes the number of rows or columns in the table, chi-square must be recalculated.

the population. A test of significance alone should not bear the burden of demonstrating the value of a hypothesis. It is far more realistic and reasonable to consider each statistical finding as part of a body of evidence supporting the truth or error of a hypothesis. We doubt that any administrator would decide the effectiveness of a program or the fairness of salaries based on one piece of statistical evidence.

In some situations, investigators can appropriately use tests of statistical significance to make definite decisions. The tests establish interrater reliability, verify whether shifts in time series can be assumed to be random, and demonstrate the probability that respondents and nonrespondents are similar to one another.[10] Tests of statistical significance have been particularly valuable in quality control, where a sample of "products" is inspected to locate systematic problems. For example, a quality control unit may review a sample of public assistance cases. An analyst reads a case record and notes any errors. Working with small samples, she applies tests of statistical significance to determine the probability that the errors she finds are random. If it is highly likely that the errors are not random, the agency should take corrective action, such as retraining the caseworker.

REPORTING TESTS OF STATISTICAL SIGNIFICANCE

In most reports, tests of statistical significance may be inconspicuous. The reader unfamiliar with them may scarcely notice that they are mentioned. Readers with a serious interest in the research topic refer to them to evaluate research and its findings.

The researcher should report the test statistic used and its value, the degrees of freedom, and the associated probability. Citing the statistic allows readers trained in statistics to determine whether the researcher used the appropriate statistical test. The statistic's value and degrees of freedom (df) are needed to determine the associated probability. With this information, a reader can identify mathematical or recording errors, and she can visualize how the data were analyzed. The associated probability allows the reader to make her own independent determination of the findings' "significance." To report this information in the text, the researcher encloses the statistical details in parentheses. For example:

The type of job training received is related to participants' current employment status ($\chi^2 = 50.57$, $df = 4$, $p < .001$).

The average salary of male planners is higher than that of female planners ($t = 4.28$, $df = 533$, $p < .001$).

If contingency tables are included in a report, the same information is reported immediately beneath the last row of table cells. Table 12.4 illustrates a common format for presenting a series of t-tests, which compares means for two values for each independent variable. The table reports the average (mean) values for male and female planners on nine variables. Underneath the mean values are the values of the standard deviation. The third column reports the values of the t-test. Note that marital status and race are dichotomous variables and the means represent the percent of married planners and the percent of white planners. The interested reader has all the information she needs to compute the values of t herself. The asterisks next to the t values direct the reader to the table footnotes, where she can find the associated probability rounded to the nearest commonly used alpha level. One asterisk represents $p = .1$, two asterisks represent $p = .05$, and three asterisks represent $p = .01$. The relationship between the number of asterisks and value of p varies from author to author. Usually, the more asterisks, the lower the value of p.

At the present time, no one convention for reporting associated probability has emerged. Using a preset alpha level to report the significance of all values is least

TABLE 12.4	TESTS COMPARING MEN AND WOMEN IN PLANNING		
	Men $\overline{X}$ (s)	Women $\overline{X}$ (s)	t
Individual characteristics			
Age	32.43 (8.28)	30.11 (7.72)	2.93[c]
Marital status (1 = married)	.75 (.41)	.61 (.49)	3.00[c]
Race(1 = white)	.93 (.26)	.81 (.34)	2.05[b]
Organization characteristics			
Agency size	4.78 (2.88)	5.29 (2.99)	−1.70[a]
Centralized management	5.01 (2.61)	5.25 (2.73)	−.85
Career behavior			
Job turnover	.51 (.37)	.60 (.39)	−2.19[c]
No. of roles	7.98 (1.67)	7.88 (1.79)	.53
Yrs. experience	3.67 (5.31)	3.42 (2.57)	7.26[c]
Career attainment			
Income	17,095 (6,329)	14,885 (4,676)	4.28[c]

[a]Significant at the .10 level.
[b]Significant at the .05 level.
[c]Significant at the .01 level.

SOURCE: M. Mayo, Jr., "Job Attainment in Planning: Women Versus Men," *Work and Occupation* (May 1985): 152. (Copyright © 1985 by Sage Publications, Inc. Reprinted with permission: Sage Publications, Inc.)

common. In Table 12.4 the author distinguished among three levels of significance rather than reporting all the significant findings as significant at $p = .10$. Whether the specific associated probability is reported or not seems to depend on the researcher's ability to present the information in an uncluttered table. The asterisks in Table 12.4 would not work if the author wanted to report the exact associated probability. This author's strategy is the most common, that is, to round the associated probability up to .10, .05, .01, or .001 and report the rounded-up p value.

A researcher may simply note that a relationship was found to be "statistically significant." This observation merely means that the value of a specific statistical test met the researcher's alpha-level criterion. If the value did not meet the alpha-level criterion, the relationship is said to be "statistically insignificant." In order for such information to have any value, the researcher must indicate the statistical test and alpha level that he used.

MODIFICATIONS AND ALTERNATIVES TO TESTS OF STATISTICAL SIGNIFICANCE

Let us reiterate some important misconceptions about tests of statistical significance.[11] They cannot remedy a flawed design. They only test a statistical hypothesis, not the theoretical hypothesis. The analyst applies an equation to a set of numbers, comes up with a statistical value, and makes a decision. Nothing prevents someone from dividing a set of random digits into groups, calculating a test statistic, and finding a statistically significant relationship. One researcher summed up the situation aptly with the phrase "the numbers don't remember where they came from."[12] The numbers do not know if the data represent a carefully designed study with reliable measures and a sample free of nonsampling errors or if the sample was biased and the measures unreliable.

The information produced by a test of statistical significance is modest. It simply indicates the probability that a relationship exists in the population. The relationship may be weaker, or stronger, than the one found in the sample data. Depending on the sample size and the α-level, statistically significant differences may be too slight to be of theoretical interest or practical use. Social scientists have recommended four alternatives to the traditional significance test. First, the null hypothesis can include a specific difference. Let's go back to an earlier example. We will assume that administrators do not want to fund more on-the-job training programs unless they place at least 10 percent more of their trainees than other training programs. To test this preference, the hypothesis and null hypothesis would be stated as:

H_1: On-the-job training programs place at least 10 percent more of their trainees than other training programs.

H_0: On-the-job training programs place less than 10 percent more of their trainees than other training programs.

Second, instead of reporting significance, researchers may report confidence intervals. (To refresh your memory on the standard error and computation of confidence intervals, see Chapter 5.) Proponents argue that confidence intervals are more informative. They provide information on the estimated size of parameters, differences between them, and the direction of the differences.[13] To illustrate how this works, Table 12.5 is based on the data comparing male and female planners.[14]

TABLE 12.5	MEAN AGE AND INCOME OF MALE AND FEMALE PLANNERS	
Age	Mean	95% Confidence Interval
Males ($n = 300$)	32.43	31.49–33.37
Females ($n = 132$)	30.11	28.8–31.42
Income		
Males ($n = 300$)	17,095	16.379–17.811
Females ($n = 132$)	14,885	14.087–15.683

Table 12.5 shows that male planners on average are older and earn more than female planners. These differences continue even when sampling error is taken into account. The confidence interval avoids implying that the sample means provide a precise estimate of the differences. Rather, the population means probably fall somewhere within the range indicated by the confidence intervals.

The third strategy is to report a measure of association. Chapters 13 and 14 cover statistics that quantify the effect of an independent variable on a dependent variable. These statistics, not tests of statistical significance, measure the strength of a relationship.

The fourth alternative is replicating studies. One author states, "The results from an unreplicated study, no matter how statistically significant . . . are necessarily speculative . . . Replications play a vital role in safeguarding the empirical literature from contamination from specious results."[15] Replications do not have to duplicate previous research exactly. Investigators may implement the research using a different population or another setting and see if the findings generalize to other populations or settings. Findings that go in the same direction, whether or not they attain a specified α-level, or that have overlapping confidence levels provide more confirmation than a simple significance test.

With the exception of measuring the size of the effect of the independent variable on the dependent variable, each alternative has constraints. A researcher may have inadequate knowledge or understanding of the question at hand to specify a relationship beyond anticipating some difference. Confidence levels work with interval data, but setting confidence levels for proportional data can become unwieldy. Replication requires the opportunity and resources to repeat a study.

Tests of statistical significance can serve as a provisional test of a hypothesis. The term *provisional* avoids inferring that any one hypothesis test is definitive. On the other hand, investigators may use them as an initial screen to filter out the weakest relationships and to identify relationships meriting closer examination. In using significance tests as a filter, an investigator should recall that with an alpha level of .05 and a small sample, a test of statistical significance will have low power and will probably identify only strong relationships as statistically significant.

One author surveyed the technical and theoretical arguments for and against using tests of statistical significance. While he found little support for the tests, he gave two justifications for their continued use. First, the tests allow a researcher to argue that he found a low probability of random error or chance. Second, since the tests yield "pure numbers," they standardize findings, allowing researchers to easily scan findings to identify results that are too weak for further study.[16]

Neither a test of statistical significance nor an alternative approach can indicate that a supported hypothesis is interesting or of any apparent importance. The findings may have no practical significance. Statistically significant findings may be uninteresting and unimportant. A practically significant finding is one that piques people's interest and leads to follow-up investigations, spurs policy decisions, or causes change in behavior. *Practical significance* is what most people mean by the term *significant* in everyday conversation.

Over the years professionals have become more educated about statistics and more sophisticated in using them. Researchers typically report statistical significance along with measures of association. The readers are given sufficient information to decide whether they agree with the researcher's conclusions or to apply different statistical criteria and reach other conclusions. The researcher and the reader are both likely to understand that statistical significance is not the same as practical significance.

SUMMARY

Tests of statistical significance allow a researcher to determine the probability that variables related in a random sample are not related in the population. A test of statistical significance cannot indicate that a relationship is strong or important; it may not even indicate if the direction is as hypothesized. Nor does a finding of statistical significance imply that other parts of the research were carried out correctly. The test only makes a statistical statement about the nature of a relationship.

To carry out a test of statistical significance, a researcher

1. states the null and the research hypotheses.
2. selects an alpha level.
3. selects and computes a test statistic.
4. makes a decision.

The null hypothesis postulates that an independent and a dependent variable are not related. For some statistical tests, the null hypothesis may state that the relationship goes in a certain direction or does not exceed a specific value.

In hypothesis testing, a researcher runs the risk of making two errors. First, he may reject a null hypothesis that is actually true. The researcher, then, has accepted an untrue research hypothesis. This error is called a Type I error. Second, the researcher may accept a null hypothesis that is untrue. The researcher has failed to accept a true research hypothesis; that is called a Type II error.

In practice, researchers are more likely to make a judgment about a hypothesis based on the associated probability, the sample size, the magnitude of the effect, and the practical consequences of their decisions than they are to decide on a specific alpha level set a priori. The associated probability is the probability of a specific χ^2 or t value occurring if their relationship does not occur in the population, that is, if the null hypothesis is true. To detect small effects, the investigator will tend to set higher alpha levels, accept higher associated probabilities, or use larger samples. With a larger sample and an interest in detecting moderate or strong effects, the investigator will want to work with lower alpha levels or prefer lower associated probabilities.

Depending on the nature of the data and the hypothesis, the researcher selects a test of significance. Chi-square and t-tests are two commonly used tests. The major piece of information needed is the probability that a given statistical value would occur if the null hypothesis were true, indicated by the xx value in the notation $p < xx$.

Tests of statistical significance are easily misinterpreted and produce modest information. Researchers are urged to put aside the traditional process of focusing solely on testing a null hypothesis of no difference. Rather, they should provide alternative or additional information supporting the merits of a hypothesis. Researchers may include a specific difference in the null hypothesis, report confidence levels, and report measures of the strength of the relationship between variables. Replication of studies provides the best test of a hypothesis. Occasionally, administrative investigators base a decision on a single test of significance, for example, in deciding whether respondents and nonrespondents are similar, or if shifts in a time series are greater than shifts that can be attributed to long-term trends, cycles, seasonal effects, or random fluctuations.

NOTES

1. For discussion on uses of tests of statistical significance in social sciences, see J. Cohen, "Things I Have Learned (So Far)," *American Psychologist* 45 (December 1990), and M. Oakes, *Statistical Inference: A Commentary for the Social and Behavioral Sciences* (New York: Wiley, 1986).

2. For clear explanations of the epistemological reasons for working with and rejecting null hypotheses, see A. Kaplan, *The Conduct of Inquiry* (San Francisco: Chandler, 1964), and R. E. Henkel, *Tests of Significance* (Beverly Hills: Sage, *Quantitative Applications in the Social Sciences*, 07–004, 1976), 34–40.

3. See D. B. Wright, *Understanding Statistics: An Introduction for the Social Sciences* (London: Sage Publications, 1997), 42–43, for a short but informative discussion of the nature and philosophy of probability or *p* values and the link to power analysis.

4. Wright, *Understanding Statistics*, 42–43; 77–83.

5. J. Cohen, "Things I Have Learned," 1309.

6. E. J. Posavac and R. G. Carey, *Program Evaluation: Methods and Case Studies*, 5th ed. (Englewood Cliffs, NJ: Prentice-Hall, 1997), 97.

7. Henkel, *Tests*, 48–49.

8. T. H. Poister, *Public Program Analysis* (Baltimore: University Park Press, 1978), 213–214, illustrates the one sample *t*-test with a worked-out example.

9. For a discussion on how to interpret the associated probability, see M. Oakes, *Statistical Inference* (New York: Wiley, 1986), 15–19.

10. Statistical tests in time-series analysis are key in model building, and the findings from a specific test determine subsequent decisions. See R. McCleary and R. A. Hay, Jr., *Applied Time Series Analysis for the Social Sciences* (Beverly Hills: Sage, 1980), 97–100. Homework Problem 5 shows how tests of statistical significance are used to compare respondents and nonrespondents.

11. This section is based on the several works critiquing tests of statistical significance. The consulted works were: *What if There Were No Significance Tests?* edited by L. L. Harlow, S. A. Mulaik, J. H. Steiger (Mahwah, NJ: Erlbaum Associates, Publishers, 1997), especially "Significance Testing Introduction and Overview" by L. L. Harlow; M. N. Branch, "Statistical Inference in Behavior Analysis: Some Things Significance Testing Does and Does Not Do," *The Behavior Analyst* 22 (1999): 87–92; Hubbard and Ryan, "The Historical Growth of Statistical Significance Testing in Psychology—and Its Future Prospects," *Educational & Psychological Measurement* 60 (2000): 661–681.

12. This phrase is cited by Oakes, *Statistical Inference*, 173, and Cohen, "Things I Have Learned," 1310. Curiously, the citations differ slightly. Oakes quotes it as "don't remember" and Cohen as "don't know." The original is found in F. M. Lord, "On the Statistical Treatment of Football Numbers," *American Psychologist* 2 (1953): 750–751.

13. Observations about the value of using confidence intervals are not covered here. For information on using confidence intervals, see H. Rothstein and M. C. Tonges, "Beyond the significance test in administrative research and policy decisions," *Journal of Nursing Scholarship* 32 (2000): 66–70. For a critique of using confidence levels see J. M. Cortina and W. P. Dunlap, "On the logic and purpose of significance testing," *Psychological Methods* 2 (1997): 161–172.

14. The standard error, used to compute the confidence level, was estimated by dividing the standard deviation by the square root of the respective samples.

15. Hubbard and Ryan, "The Historical Growth of Statistical Significance Testing in Psychology."

16. Henkel, *Tests*, 87. On pages 78–87 he summarizes the literature on the utility of tests of statistical significance. He divides the literature into two categories: technical issues and philosophy of science issues.

TERMS FOR REVIEW

randomly related	null hypothesis	*t*-test
statistical significance	Type I error	associated probability
practical significance	Type II error	
hypothesis	chi-square	

QUESTIONS FOR REVIEW

The following questions should indicate whether you have a basic competency in this chapter's material.

1. What is meant by statistical significance? How is it different from practical significance?
2. What are the steps in hypothesis testing?
3. Distinguish among Type I error and Type II error. What two strategies are available to reduce the probability of a Type I error? What two strategies are available to reduce the probability of a Type II error?
4. The common wisdom among social scientists is that tests of statistical significance are overrated. What is the value of tests of statistical significance? What are their limitations?
5. Evaluate the soundness of using an alpha level of .05 as a minimal cutoff point for rejecting a null hypothesis.
6. Discuss the adequacy of tests of statistical significance as evidence supporting a hypothesis.

PROBLEMS FOR HOMEWORK AND DISCUSSION

1. A parents' group has charged that minority students are more likely than other students to be suspended for breaking school rules. For example, minority students are more likely to be suspended for fighting. The school superintendent has a random sample of 200 cases drawn from the list of all students in grades 7 through 12 who have been cited for serious school infractions. For each sample, student data are gathered on the student's racial or ethnic group, nature of offense, and action taken.
   a. State a hypothesis that the superintendent may have tested.
   b. What would be the practical consequences of committing a Type I error? What would be the practical consequences of committing a Type II error?
   c. Should the superintendent seek to minimize a Type I or a Type II error? Justify your answer.
   d. What contribution would power make in deciding if the parents had a legitimate concern?

2. The data given in Table 12.6 are reported in a study of soup kitchen users. (Note: Soup kitchens serve free meals to homeless or very poor people.)
   a. State the hypothesis and the null hypothesis that these data may have been testing.
   b. If you set $\alpha = .05$, what is the probability that you committed a Type I error? Would you reject the null hypothesis?

TABLE 12.6   NUMBER OF MEALS EATEN DAILY BY SOUP KITCHEN USERS

	Age of Soup Kitchen User		
Number of Meals Eaten Daily	Less than 31 Years Old (n = 66) %	31–54 Years Old (n = 213) %	Over 54 Years Old (n = 144) %
1	37.9	29.1	27.1
2	47.0	49.3	40.3
3	15.2	21.6	32.6

Note: $\chi^2 = 10.4$, *df* = 4, $p < .05$.

c. If you set $\alpha = .01$, what is the probability that you committed a Type I error? Would you reject the null hypothesis?

d. What is the value of knowing whether age is related to the number of meals a soup kitchen user eats daily? Assess the adequacy of using only the information provided by a χ^2 test to decide if these two variables are related.

3. The data given in Table 12.7 were reported in a study of children's knowledge of the effects of smoking. The column headed "χ^2 probability" reports the associated probabilities.

a. How many hypotheses are being tested?

b. Explain what information the associated probabilities reported in the chi-square analysis provide.

c. State the hypotheses that you would probably accept based on the associated probabilities results.

d. What other information would you include, if any, to support your hypotheses? Justify your answer.

4. Consider the data in Table 12.8:

a. How different are male and female planners?

b. What alpha level would you suggest for this dataset? Why did you select it?

TABLE 12.7 PERCENTAGE OF CORRECT ANSWERS BY GRADE LEVEL

	6th (265)	9th (125)	12th (120)	χ^2 probability
Lung cancer is higher among pipe smokers	10.2	5.6	10.8	.593
Smoking constricts blood vessels	38.2	70.8	57.7	.0001
Smoking helps circulation	43.3	65.8	61.3	.0001
Smokers live longer than nonsmokers	77.0	90.8	84.9	.0189

SOURCE: T. T. L. Chen and A. E. Winder, "When is the Critical Moment to Provide Smoking Education in Schools," *Journal of Drug Education* 16 (1986): 121–132.

TABLE 12.8 COMPARISONS BETWEEN MALE AND FEMALE PLANNERS ON SELECTED CHARACTERISTICS

	Men $\overline{X}$ (s)	Women $\overline{X}$ (s)	t
Age	32.43 (8.28)	30.11 (7.72)	2.9[b]
Agency size	4.70 (2.88)	5.29 (2.99)	−1.7[a]
Job turnover rate	.51 (.37)	.60 (.39)	−2.19[b]
Number of planner roles	7.98 (1.67)	7.88 (1.79)	.53
Years of professional experience	3.67 (5.31)	3.42 (2.57)	7.26[b]
Income	17,095 (6,329)	14,885 (4,676)	4.28[b]

[a]Significant at the .1 level.
[b]Significant at the .01 level.

SOURCE: J. M. Mayo, Jr., "Job Attainment in Planning: Women Versus Men," *Work and Occupation* (May 1985): 152. (Copyright © 1985 by Sage Publications, Inc. Reprinted with permission: Sage Publications, Inc.)

Which null hypotheses would you fail to reject?

c. What information does a *t*-test give that chi-square doesn't?

5. A random sample of 407 adults was asked to participate in a study; 283 agreed to participate. Can the researchers conclude from the data in Table 12.9 that the participants were similar to the nonparticipants? Justify your answer.

6. Use $\alpha = .05$ to interpret the findings in Table 12.10.

TABLE 12.9   COMPARISON BETWEEN PARTICIPANTS AND NONPARTICIPANTS ON SELECTED CHARACTERISTICS

Race	Participated %	Did Not Participate %
White	70 (186)	30 (81)
African American	88 (97)	12 (13)
$\chi^2 = 14.25, df = 1, p < .001$		
Gender		
Male	85 (115)	15 (21)
Female	70 (168)	30 (73)
Education		
12 years or less	73 (101)	27 (37)
13–15 years	82 (80)	18 (17)
16 years or more	72 (102)	28 (39)
Age		
18–39 years	80 (177)	20 (43)
40 years or older	67 (105)	33 (51)
$\chi^2 = 8.36, df = 1, p < .005$		

SOURCE: D. Linz et al., "Estimating Community Standards," *Public Opinion Quarterly* 55 (Spring 1991): 93.

TABLE 12.10   DIFFERENCES BETWEEN EARLY AND LATE ADOPTERS OF SPREADSHEET SOFTWARE

	Early Adopters		Late Adopters			
	Mean	s	Mean	s	t-value	Significance Level
Age	28.3	(7.3)	30.3	(10.1)	−1.91	.059
Years of education	16.2	(1.7)	15.4	(1.8)	3.06	.002
Number in prof. assoc.	2.6	(3.5)	2.6	(4.9)	.05	.956
Number of professional journals read	8.2	(4.5)	6.7	(5.3)	2.21	.028
Size of work group	2.6	(1.2)	2.5	(1.1)	.65	.516

SOURCE: J. C. Brancheau and J. C. Wetherbe, "The Adoption of Spreadsheet Software: Testing Innovation Diffusion Theory in the Context of End-User Computing," *Information Systems Research* 1 (June 1990): 129.

DISK WORK

1. Test the hypothesis that public safety expenditures vary by county median family income level.
   a. State the research hypothesis and null hypothesis
   b. To test the hypothesis would you use chi-square or a t-test? Justify your choice.
   c. Using the ORB Research Methods dataset, carry out the appropriate statistical procedure. Based on the analysis would you reject your null hypothesis? Why or why not? What evidence did you use to make your decision?

2. Analyze the data to see if county expenditures on cultural or recreation services vary by school enrollment. To conduct your analysis, categorize expenditures and school enrollment into three categories: high, medium, and low. Test two hypotheses.
   a. Report your findings in a table similar to 12.7
   b. State the hypotheses you tested.
   c. Were your hypotheses supported? Give evidence to support your decision.

3. Some of the counties in the ORB dataset had reformed their welfare systems in the past ten years. An assumption of experimental design is that random assignment controls for differences between groups. In this case, assume counties were randomly assigned to reform their welfare system or to maintain the status quo. Use the t-test (independent samples) to see if a county's welfare reform status influenced the unemployment rate. Remember that to perform a t-test the independent variable must be dichotomized. Report your findings in statements similar to those found in the section on reporting tests of statistical significance. Does the assumption of random assignment make sense in this example? Why or why not?
   a. Calculate the percent of the total registered voters who are Hispanic. Consider the assumption that this percentage, a measure of political activity, is associated with unique characteristics of each region of the state. Use region as an independent variable and the percent of registered voters being Hispanic as a dependent variable.
      i. State a research hypothesis and null hypotheses.
      ii. What is the associated probability? What does it indicate about the relationship between region and politically active Hispanic population?

RECOMMENDED FOR FURTHER READING

Theoretical orientation for this chapter was drawn from the insights of Michael Oakes in *Statistical Inference: A Commentary for the Social and Behavioral Sciences* (New York: Wiley, 1986). This book will challenge and reward readers interested in statistical inference.

What if There were no Significance Tests? Edited by L. L. Harlow, S. A. Mulaik, J. H. Steiger (Mahwah, NJ: Erlbaum Associates, Publishers, 1997). An excellent source on current thinking about tests of statistical significance. "Significance Testing Introduction and Overview" by L. L. Harlow is especially recommended.

J. Cohen, "Things I Have Learned (So Far)," *American Psychologist* 45 (December 1990): 1304–1312, is an accessible work that identifies common misconceptions in interpreting and working with tests of statistical significance.

Helena Kraemer and Sue Thieman, *How Many Subjects? Statistical Power Analysis in Research* (Newbury Park: Sage, 1987), discuss the relationship between sample size and the power of statistical tests.

APPENDIX 12.1

Calculating Chi-Square and Two-Sample *t*-Tests

This appendix reviews the equations for chi-square and *t*-tests and how to use the tables for their respective distributions.

Chi-Square

The equation for chi-square is

$$\chi^2 = \Sigma \, (f_o - f_e)^2/f_e$$

The data contained in Table 12.11 show the values for the observed frequency (f_o) and the expected frequency (f_e). The symbol f_e is the frequency expected if the independent and dependent variables are randomly related. To obtain its value for a cell, the frequency of the row total is multiplied by the frequency of the column total and divided by the total n represented in the table.

For the three cells under "Vocational Education," the calculations to derive f_e are:

$$f_e \text{ (voc. ed. \& working)} = (64 \times 292)/586 = 31.9$$
$$f_e \text{ (voc. ed. \& in school)} = (64 \times 132)/586 = 14.4$$
$$f_e \text{ (voc. ed. \& unemployed)} = (64 \times 162)/586$$
$$= 17.7$$

The next step is to subtract the value of f_e from the value of f_o for each cell, square this figure, and divide it by f_e. For the three cells under vocational education, these calculations are

Cell 1,1 $(f_o - f_e)^2/f_e = (19 - 31.9)^2/31.9 = 5.22$
Cell 1,2 $(f_o - f_e)^2/f_e = (19 - 14.4)^2/14.4 = 1.47$
Cell 1,3 $(f_o - f_e)^2/f_e = (26 - 17.7)^2/17.7 = 3.89$

TABLE 12.11 OBSERVED AND EXPECTED FREQUENCIES

CURRENT STATUS BY TRAINING PROGRAM ATTENDED: OBSERVED FREQUENCIES (f_o)

	Program			
	Vocational Education	On-the-Job Training	Work Skills Training	Total
Working	19	109	164	292
In school	19	82	31	132
Unemployed	26	82	54	162
Total	64	273	249	586

CURRENT STATUS BY TRAINING PROGRAM ATTENDED: EXPECTED FREQUENCIES
IF PROGRAM AND STATUS ARE UNRELATED (f_e)

	Program		
	Vocational Education	On-the-Job Training	Work Skills Training
Working	31.9	136.0	124.1
In school	14.4	61.5	56.1
Unemployed	17.7	75.5	68.8

TABLE 12.12	CHI-SQUARE DISTRIBUTION			
	Probability			
df	**.10**	**.05**	**.01**	**.001**
1	2.706	3.841	6.635	10.827
2	4.605	5.991	9.210	13.815
3	6.251	7.815	11.345	16.266
4	7.779	9.488	13.277	18.467
5	9.236	11.070	15.086	20.515
6	10.645	12.592	16.812	22.457

SOURCE: Adapted from R. E. Walpole and R. H. Myer, "Critical Values of the Chi-Square Distribution," *Probability and Statistics for Engineers and Scientists*, 3d ed. (New York: Macmillan, 1985), 577.

To obtain the value of chi-square, all the values for $(f_o - f_e)^2/f_e$ are summed. For this example, $\chi^2 = 50.57$.

The degrees of freedom (*df*) equal the number of columns minus 1 multiplied by the number of rows minus 1 $((C - 1)(R - 1))$. For the example, the degrees of freedom $= (3 - 1)(3 - 1) = 4$. Next, the investigator consults a chi-square distribution table, such as Table 12.12.

If the investigator has selected a specific alpha level, for example, $\alpha = .05$, he notes the value in the column headed ".05" and the row for 4 degrees of freedom (*df*), that is, 9.488. For $\alpha = .05$, he will reject the null hypothesis if the value of chi-square is equal to or greater than 9.488.

Alternatively, he can find the associated probability for $\chi^2 = 50.57$. He goes to the row for 4 degrees of freedom and looks for the value that is closest to, but not greater than, 50.57, that is, 18.467. He identifies which column 18.467 is in, .001; thus, .001 is the associated probability for $\chi^2 = 50.57$ with 4 degrees of freedom.

If he includes the table in the report, he puts the χ^2 value, the degrees of freedom, and the associated probability underneath the table. (For an example, see Tables 12.6 and 12.9.) If the investigator combines two columns or makes another change in the table, he must recompute chi-square.

Two-Sample *t*-Tests

To test hypotheses that compare two means, an investigator chooses between two equations of *t*. If she assumes the variances for the two groups are unequal, she calculates *t* using the equation

$$t = \frac{\overline{X}_1 - \overline{X}_2}{\sqrt{\dfrac{s_1^2}{n_1 - 1} + \dfrac{s_2^2}{n_2 - 1}}}$$

If she assumes the variances of the two groups are equal, she calculates *t* using the equation

$$t = \frac{\overline{X}_1 - \overline{X}_2}{\sqrt{\dfrac{n_1 s_1^2 + n_2 s_2^2}{n_1 + n_2 - 2}} \cdot \sqrt{\dfrac{1}{n_1} + \dfrac{1}{n_2}}}$$

How does she decide between the two models? She may prefer to assume unequal variances, since the appropriate use of the equation does not require unequal population variances.[1] If she wishes, she can test the hypothesis that the variances of the two groups are unequal. If she fails to reject the null hypothesis (H_0: the variances are equal), she will calculate *t* with the second equation; if she rejects the null hypothesis, she will use the first equation.

For either equation, the degrees of freedom equals the sum of the number of observations in the two samples minus 2. Next the investigator consults a *t*-distribution, such as Table 12.13. If she has hypothesized a direction, she uses the columns reporting probabilities for a one-tailed test. Otherwise, she uses the columns reporting for a two-tailed test.

Let's consider the example of planners' salaries. We hypothesized that female planners would have lower salaries than male planners; thus, we would want to perform a one-tailed *t*-test. If we select a specific alpha level, for example, $\alpha = .01$, we note

TABLE 12.13   DISTRIBUTION OF *T*-VALUES

df	Probability for One-Tailed Test		Probability for Two-Tailed Test	
	.05	.01	.05	.01
1	6.314	31.821	12.706	63.657
2	2.920	6.965	4.303	9.925
3	2.353	4.541	3.182	5.841
4	2.132	3.747	2.776	4.604
5	2.015	3.365	2.571	4.032
6	1.943	3.145	2.447	3.707
7	1.895	2.998	2.365	3.499
8	1.860	2.896	2.306	3.355
9	1.833	2.821	2.262	3.250
10	1.812	2.764	2.228	3.169
11	1.796	2.718	2.201	3.106
12	1.782	2.681	2.179	3.055
13	1.771	2.650	2.160	3.012
14	1.761	2.624	2.145	2.977
15	1.753	2.602	2.131	2.947
16	1.746	2.583	2.120	2.921
17	1.740	2.567	2.110	2.898
18	1.734	2.552	2.101	2.878
19	1.729	2.539	2.093	2.861
20	1.725	2.528	2.086	2.845
21	1.721	2.518	2.080	2.831
22	1.717	2.508	2.074	2.819
23	1.714	2.500	2.069	2.807
24	1.711	2.492	2.064	2.797
25	1.708	2.485	2.060	2.787
26	1.706	2.479	2.056	2.779
27	1.703	2.473	2.052	2.771
28	1.701	2.467	2.048	2.763
29	1.699	2.462	2.045	2.756
30	1.697	2.457	2.042	2.750
60	1.671	2.390	2.000	2.660
∞	1.645	2.326	1.960	2.567

SOURCE: Adapted from R. A. Fisher and F. Yates, *Statistical Tables for Biological, Agricultural, and Medical Research*, 6th ed. (New York: Hafner, 1968), Table III, 46.

the value in the column headed ".01" and the row for the appropriate degrees of freedom (*df*). In the example, the degrees of freedom was 533. So we go to the row marked with ∞ (infinity) and find that if the value of *t* is equal to or greater than 2.326, we will reject the null hypothesis.

Note that *t*-values may be negative. The negative sign indicates which group has the larger mean. In reading and interpreting the *t*-distribution tables, the associated probability is the same whether *t* is negative *t* or positive *t*.

Notes

1. For a discussion of these two equations, see H. M. Blalock, *Social Statistics* (New York: McGraw Hill, 1972), pp. 220–228.

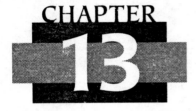

Examining Relationships among Variables: Contingency Tables with Measures of Association, Analysis of Variance

In this chapter you will learn

1. How to construct and interpret contingency tables with two or three variables.
2. How to select and interpret common measures of association for variables measured at the nominal or ordinal level.
3. How to analyze data from experiments.
4. A technique for determining the statistical significance and strength of a relationship between a nominal independent variable and an interval dependent variable.

This chapter discusses two alternative approaches to data analysis: contingency tables with measures of association and analysis of variance. In practice, analysts tend to work with one or the other approach. Investigators who conduct surveys and work with cross-sectional designs tend to rely on tests of statistical significance, contingency-table analysis, and measures of association. Depending on the level of measurement, they select specific statistics appropriate to their data. The measures of association generated from contingency tables or from regression analysis, discussed in Chapter 14, provide evidence of the strength of a relationship.

Analysis of variance is frequently encountered in connection with the analysis of experimental data. Its primary output is a test of statistical significance, the *F*-test. With one additional calculation, a measure of association, eta, also can be produced. We discuss analysis of variance in this chapter for four reasons. First, it parallels contingency-table analysis. A researcher who chooses analysis of variance may seldom use contingency-table analysis to analyze a dataset. The reverse also is generally true. Second, contingency-table analysis and regression dominate research conducted by social scientists doing nonexperimental research. Analysis of variance dominates research conducted by experimental researchers. Researchers may be familiar with one set of techniques and have only passing knowledge of the other. While the discussion in this chapter does not give a balanced coverage of both techniques, it should give you a better idea of their separate roles.[1] Third, analysis of variance involves a specific statistic to determine the significance of a relationship and a specific statistic to determine its strength. Consequently, discussing these features of analysis in separate chapters seems inefficient. Fourth, analysis of variance can be used to compare means of several groups, that is, to analyze the relationship between an interval dependent variable and a nominal independent variable.

If you are reading this chapter before the material on tests of statistical significance, you may wish to concentrate only on the contingency-table section. The analysis of variance discussion will be of more value if you understand tests of statistical significance.

CONSTRUCTING AND INTERPRETING CONTINGENCY TABLES

Often the analyst wants to investigate the joint occurrence and distribution of the values of two or more variables. He may want to know how the distribution of the values of one variable differs for different levels or categories of a second variable. To find out he may organize his data into a contingency table. A *contingency table* shows the frequency or relative frequency of each value of the dependent variable for each value of the independent variable. An analyst may use measures of association to summarize the relationship depicted in the contingency table. *Measures of association* are statistics that indicate the strength of the relationship between a dependent and an independent variable.

Contingency tables and measures of association help test hypotheses. Chapter 12 suggested that accepting a research hypothesis required empirical evidence that the relationship between variables was (1) nonrandom, (2) in the anticipated direction, and (3) sufficiently strong given the sample size. Contingency tables indicate the direction of the relationship and provide information so one can judge the strength of the association. Measures of association serve as standardized indicators of the strength of a relationship; some measures also indicate the direction of the relationship. Tests of statistical significance indicate the probability that a relationship occurred by chance.

Table 13.1 shows how residents of Large County reacted to a proposal to consolidate the county government with the government of the county's largest city. Analysts wanted to display how residents inside the large city and residents outside of the city differed in their responses.

By convention, the values of the independent variable head the columns and the values of the dependent variables head the rows. If the variables are ordinal, the values are arranged along a continuum. In this table, "no opinion" was put in the middle or neutral position. The research model guides analysts in deciding which values to

| TABLE 13.1 | SUPPORT FOR CITY–COUNTY CONSOLIDATION BY RESIDENCE |

| | Residence | | | |
| | Inside City | | Outside City | |
Support for Consolidation	N	%	N	%
For	273	54	54	37
No opinion	134	27	34	23
Against	98	19	57	39
Total (% rounded)	505	100	145	100

Note: Percentages may not add up to 100% because of rounding.

include and how to include them. The study's purpose should dominate their decisions, but other factors, such as the distribution of the values and the clarity of the table, may be considered as well. In Table 13.1 the analysts examined the values "inside city" and "outside city" and "for," "against," and "no opinion." Support for consolidation opinions originally included "strongly for" and "strongly against." In the table, the analysts defended combining "strongly for" with "for" and "strongly against" with "against" on the grounds that their job was to estimate the proportion of residents for and against consolidation, and that more specific information was not needed. If relatively few residents were strongly against consolidation, the analysts may appropriately decide to report four categories: "strongly for," "for," "no opinion," and "against." Depending on the purpose of a report, such an arrangement may provide fully adequate information without adding to a table's clutter.

The percentages are computed "in the direction of the independent variable." That is, if the independent variable heads the columns, as in Table 13.1, the column percents sum to 100 percent; if the independent variable heads the row, the row percents sum to 100 percent. Occasionally, a report will focus on the percentage of respondents in each category. For example, 54 percent of the respondents who live inside the city support consolidation. In this study local government officials were most interested in the difference between city and non-city residents. Each group's total was treated as 100 percent, and the relative frequency of each group who responded "for," "no opinion," and "against" was computed.

To interpret contingency tables, analysts focus on the percentages and the percentage difference between the values of the independent variable. In Table 13.1 the population of city residents is so much larger than that of non-city residents that directly comparing the frequencies for any particular response would be inappropriate. Using percentages corrects this. The *percentage difference,* the difference in percentages when subtracting across the rows, indicates the strength of relationship between two variables. The analyst begins by reading across a row and noting how the percentages change. The difference can range from 0, for no difference, to 100, indicating maximum difference. The analysis is clearest when there are only two columns, that is, two columns for the independent variable.

In comparing the two groups in Table 13.1, we find that 54 percent of city residents supported consolidation, but only 37 percent of non-city residents did, a percentage difference of 17. Nineteen percent of city residents and 39 percent of non-city residents were against consolidation, a percentage difference of 20. We can conclude that city residents differ from non-city residents in the distribution of opinions toward consolidation.

The joint distribution of the values of two variables is a *bivariate distribution.* Table 13.1 shows the bivariate distribution between residence and support for consolidation. In Example 13.1, Table 13.2 shows the bivariate distribution between the evaluation of city services and support for consolidation. The table

 EXAMPLE 13.1

Organizing and Interpreting Contingency Tables

Situation: City and county residents were surveyed about their evaluation of local government services and whether they favored city–county consolidation. The researchers' implied hypothesis was: Support for city–county consolidation is directly related to respondents' evaluation of their local services.

Analysis: The data are organized into a contingency table, Table 13.2. The values of the independent variable head the columns, and the values of the dependent vari-

TABLE 13.2 SUPPORT FOR CONSOLIDATION BY EVALUATION OF LOCAL SERVICES

	Evaluation of Local Services			
Support for Consolidation	Excellent or Good (%)	Fair (%)	Poor (%)	Total (N)
For	55	47	36	331
No opinion	24	25	34	161
Against	21	28	31	155
Total (N)	387	224	36	647

Note: Percentages may not add up to 100% due to rounding.

able head the rows. Either the highest or lowest value can go in the first column or first row. To avoid clutter, only the percents are shown in the body of the table.

To determine the direction of the relationship, an analyst looks across the rows: From left to right along the "For" row, the percentages drop; and from left to right along the "Against" row, the percentages increase. The data are consistent with the hypothesis. The higher the rating that respondents give to local services, the more likely they are to favor consolidation; the lower they rate local services, the less likely respondents are to favor consolidation. Another way to view the table is to look at how the "center of gravity" changes along the values of the independent variable. The "Excellent or Good" column has the highest center of gravity and the "Poor" column the lowest. This strategy helps to quickly identify nonlinear relationships, where a middle value will have the highest or lowest center of gravity.

Continued

> **EXAMPLE 13.1**   *Continued*
>
> A test of statistical significance establishes the probability that the distribution in the contingency table occurred by chance. The percentage distributions provide further support for a hypothesis, although whether one judges the relationship strong enough to support the hypothesis based on the percentage distributions is a matter of judgment.

shows that those who gave a higher evaluation to city services were more likely to support consolidation. The example's discussion spells out how the table was constructed and interpreted.

Earlier in this book we addressed control variables. This refers to a situation in which a third variable is included in the analysis to see if it influences the relationship between the other two variables. For example, we may wish to see whether the relationship between service rating and support for consolidation is the same for city residents as it is for non-city residents. We would divide the original group of cases into two subgroups—city residents and non-city residents—and create two additional tables, one for each group. We would then analyze the relationship for each subgroup. In doing so, we would have controlled for place of residence. Table 13.3 shows the relationship among three variables: support for consolidation, rating of local services, and place of residence. Inspection of the percentages in the table shows that those in the city were likely to be in favor of consolidation if they rated service as "good" (65 percent), whereas non-city residents were very unlikely to be for consolidation if they rated service as "good" (1 percent). The number of variables displayed in a table can be expanded to three, four, and even more. Although occasionally we see a table with four variables, very few tables show the relationships among more than three.

Tables also are described by their *size* and *dimensions*. A table's size is indicated by the numbers of rows and columns in the table. The number of rows is the number of categories of the dependent variable, and the number of columns

TABLE 13.3   **SUPPORT OF CONSOLIDATION BY RATING OF LOCAL SERVICES BY PLACE OF RESIDENCE**

	Residence					
	City Service Rating			Non-city Service Rating		
Support for Consolidation	Good (%)	Fair (%)	Poor (%)	Good (%)	Fair (%)	Poor (%)
For	65	46	30	1	49	35
No opinion	20	25	35	45	25	34
Against	15	29	35	54	25	31
Total (*N*)	329	161	15	59	63	21

is the number of categories of the independent variable. The dimension of a table refers to the number of variables whose joint distribution is being displayed. A table showing the joint distribution of two variables is a two-dimensional table; one with three variables is a three-dimensional table, and so on.

SELECTING AND USING MEASURES OF ASSOCIATION

The percent distributions in a contingency table suggest the strength of the relationship between two variables; however, what constitutes a "strong" or a "weak" relationship partially depends on the observer. Measures of association are descriptive statistics that indicate the strength of a relationship between two variables. They provide a standard criterion to summarize the relationship in a table. Statisticians have developed specific measures of association to summarize the relationships between nominal, ordinal, and interval variables. Nominal and ordinal measures of association are most useful when investigators want to see the effect of a control variable. Investigators may use them to compare tables examining the strength of different independent variables.

Perfect and Null Relationships

Each measure of association has a criterion for *perfect relationship*. A perfect relationship is one in which a change in the independent variable is always associated with a change in the dependent variable. An analyst may observe a direct relationship in which an increase in the value of the independent variable always coincides with an increase in the dependent variable. Alternatively, she may observe an inverse relationship in which an increase in the value of the independent variable always coincides with a decrease in the dependent variable. Typically, measures of association designate a perfect relationship with an absolute value of 1.00.

Similarly, each measure of association has a criterion for a *null relationship*. A null relationship occurs if a change in the independent variable is as likely to coincide with an increase as with a decrease or no change in the dependent variable. Typically, measures of association designate a null relationship with a value of 0.00.

The values of nominal measures of association vary between 0.00 and 1.00. The values of ordinal measures of association vary between 0.00 and ±1.00. The closer a measure of association is to 0.00, the weaker the association; the closer it is to 1.00, the stronger the association. The sign, a plus or a minus, indicates the direction, not the strength or weakness, of a relationship. A +1.00 represents a direct relationship, and a −1.00 represents an inverse relationship.

Tables 13.4 and 13.5 illustrate two models of perfect relationships. Table 13.4 illustrates a perfect direct relationship, and Table 13.5 illustrates a perfect inverse relationship. A nominal measure of association for both of these tables would have a value of 1.00; an ordinal measure of association would have a value of 1.00 for Table 13.4 and −1.00 for Table 13.5.

TABLE 13.4	LENGTH OF JOB-TRAINING PROGRAM AND PLACEMENT SUCCESS		
	Length of Job-Training Program		
Placement Rate (%)	≤ 1 Month	2–3 Months	> 3 Months
Low (< 50)	100%		
Moderate (50–75)		100%	
High (> 75)			100%

TABLE 13.5	LENGTH OF JOB-TRAINING PROGRAM AND PLACEMENT SUCCESS		
	Length of Job-Training Program		
Placement Rate (%)	≤ 1 Month	2–3 Months	> 3 Months
Low (< 50)			100%
Moderate (50–75)		100%	
High (> 75)	100%		

Table 13.6 illustrates a model of a null relationship. Measures of association for the table would have a value of 0.00.

Most, if not all, readers would agree that Tables 13.4 and 13.5 represent perfect relationships and that Table 13.6 represents a null relationship. One would anticipate that measures of association for the respective tables would be 1.00, − 1.00, and 0.00. What about Table 13.7? This table illustrates why one needs to understand a statistic's model for a perfect or null relationship. Does this seem to be a null relationship? Some measures of association would consider it null and produce a value of 0.00. Alternatively, readers may argue that it shows a direct relationship. As the length of job training increases, the placement rate also increases.

Selecting a Measure of Association

The first criterion for choosing a measure of association is the consistency between the statistic and the level of measurement. If the variables are measured

TABLE 13.6	LENGTH OF JOB-TRAINING PROGRAM AND PLACEMENT SUCCESS		
	Length of Job-Training Program		
Placement Rate (%)	≤ 1 Month	2–3 Months	> 3 Months
Low (< 50)	20%	20%	20%
Moderate (50–75)	40%	40%	40%
High (> 75)	40%	40%	40%

TABLE 13.7	LENGTH OF JOB-TRAINING PROGRAM AND PLACEMENT SUCCESS		
	Length of Job-Training Program		
Placement Rate (%)	≤ 1 Month	2–3 Months	> 3 Months
Low (< 50)	40%	30%	20%
Moderate (50–75)	40%	40%	40%
High (> 75)	20%	30%	40%

at the nominal level, the analyst must use a nominal statistic. If they are measured at the ordinal level, the analyst may use a nominal or an ordinal statistic. If the relationship includes one nominal and one ordinal variable, the analyst may use a nominal statistic or choose a measure of association designed to examine a relationship between nominal and ordinal variables. It would not be appropriate to use a measure designed for ordinal variables.

Note that dichotomous nominal variables, variables with two categories, may be analyzed using ordinal measures of association. The two categories may be visualized as endpoints of a continuum. For example, male and female may be categorized as male and non-male (or female and non-female). Conventionally, one category of the variable is assigned a "1," and the other category is assigned a "0."

The second criterion for selecting a measure is its criteria for a null and perfect relationship. The analyst should choose a statistic that is consistent with her theoretical purposes. She should select a measure that assigns values of "1" to relationships that she considers perfect and assigns a value of "0" to relationships that she considers random or null.

The third criterion for selecting a measure is its sensitivity. A *sensitive measure of association* is a statistic that detects small differences between the strengths of relationships. When we introduced measures of association, we argued that they helped the investigator quickly distinguish between stronger and weaker relationships. An insensitive measure assigns the same or nearly the same numerical value to relationships that an investigator would judge differed in their strength. A sensitive measure assigns different numerical values to relationships that may have slight, even subtle, differences in strength.

The fourth criterion is familiarity with the statistic. An analyst needs to be familiar with a statistic to know how sensitive it is and to decide if he agrees with its criteria for a null and perfect relationship. Furthermore, familiarity helps an analyst to judge the strength of a specific relationship.

The answer to what constitutes a strong relationship depends on the statistic and the research question. First, because of having different criteria for null and perfect relationships, some measures of association tend to have much lower values than others. Second, the factors affecting some dependent variables are well known. If a researcher were analyzing such a well-studied dependent variable, even moderate associations might be of limited value because stronger relationships may have been identified and explained. On the other hand, some dependent variables are not well studied or understood, and even relatively weak relationships may suggest research questions worth pursuing.

To compare one relationship with another, we use a single measure of association. We cannot directly compare two different statistics measuring association, as each has its own criteria for perfect and null relationships. These criteria as well as the strength of the association affect the numerical value. Thus we cannot assume that a relationship with a Cramer's V of .10 is weaker than a relationship with a gamma of .45. If, however, different measures of association all suggest a strong or weak relationship between two variables, we can be more confident in our conclusions.

Comparisons using a single statistic should be done with caution. Some ordinal measures of association may underestimate or miss nonlinear relationships, so a measure that primarily identifies a strong direct or inverse relationship may completely miss a strong nonlinear relationship. Exact comparisons between tables of different sizes should be avoided, because the number of rows and columns in a table can affect the value of a measure of association.

The Logic of a Measure of Association

Rather than survey specific nominal and ordinal measures of association, we present one nominal measure of association to give you a better idea of what a measure of association does. We also outline the major features of an ordinal measure of association to demonstrate how ordinal measures incorporate the additional information contained in ordinal variables and to alert you to some common problems encountered in working with ordinal measures of association. With this understanding you can refer to a statistics text to study and select a measure appropriate to your needs. In addition, you can find the calculations for the nominal and ordinal measures mentioned in this chapter in the chapter appendix.

We look at lambda, a simple nominal measure, to illustrate measures of association. Lambda is a *proportional reduction in error (PRE) measure* and is based on the mode. All PRE measures indicate how much that knowledge of the distribution of the independent variable reduces the error in predicting the distribution of the dependent variable. How much error is there in predicting the distribution of the dependent variable without knowing the independent variable? Lambda calls this error *original error*. Original error for lambda is equal to the number of nonmodal responses.

Consider the analysis of the ratings of the performance of a city's human resources department produced in Table 13.8. Imagine that you were to meet all 95 survey respondents but only knew the total number giving each rating. You know that 38 of the respondents rated the human resources department as "poor," 32 rated the department as "satisfactory," and 25 rated the department as "good." You guess how each individual rated the human resources department. To meet the assumptions of lambda, you guess that each person rated the department as "poor." In other words, you guess the most common response, or the mode, for each individual. With this guessing rule, you are wrong 57 times. Fifty-seven is the

TABLE 13.8	RATINGS OF THE HUMAN RESOURCES DEPARTMENT'S PERFORMANCE BY RESPONDENT DEPARTMENT				
	Police	Fire	Public Works	Planning	Total
Poor	10	15	5	8	38
Satisfactory	5	10	15	2	32
Good	15	5	5	0	25
Total	30	30	25	10	95

original error—the sum of the nonmodal responses. If you guessed that everyone gave the department either a "satisfactory" or "good" rating, you would be wrong more than 57 times.

Does including data on an independent variable reduce the original error? Lambda considers the error for each value of the independent variable as *new error*. New error for lambda is equal to the nonmodal responses for each value of the independent variable. Let's return to our example. Note that the table gives you the distribution of the independent variable, that is, the distribution of ratings given by each department's respondents. You use this additional information and ask each respondent in which department he or she works. You then guess that a respondent's rating was the same as the modal response for his or her department. You guess a police department employee rated the human resources department as "good," fire and planning employees rated it as "poor," and public works employees rated it as "satisfactory." In our example, you have incorrectly labeled 15 police employees, 15 fire employees, 10 public works employees, and 2 planning employees. With knowledge of a respondent's department, you made 42 errors. The 42 errors, based on the distribution of the independent variable, make up the new error.

To compute lambda, subtract the new error from the original error and divide the result by the original error. The solution for our example is:

$$\text{lambda} = (\text{original error} - \text{new error})/\text{original error}$$
$$= (57 - 42)/57$$
$$= .263$$

The .263 indicates that by knowing respondents' departments, we have reduced the error in guessing the ratings by 26.3 percent. This demonstrates that knowing department affiliation can improve our guess. There seems to be a relationship.

Lambda is an insensitive measure. That is, it does not detect small shifts or differences in the strength of a relationship. You can infer this by looking at its criterion for a null relationship. Lambda is calculated in such a way that many relationships with a discernible pattern between the independent and dependent variables have a lambda equal to 0.00. Consequently, even though lambda equals 0.00, an analyst or audience may see a relationship between the variables. Let's illustrate this by arranging our dataset on perceptions of the human resources

TABLE 13.9	RATINGS OF THE HUMAN RESOURCES DEPARTMENT'S PERFORMANCE BY RESPONDENT DEPARTMENT				
	Police	Fire	Public Works	Planning	Total
Poor	12	15	9	8	44
Satisfactory	6	10	8	2	26
Good	12	5	8	0	25
Total	30	30	25	10	95

department a little differently. In Table 13.9, do you see any departmental trends in the perception of the human resources department?

The majority of respondents in the planning department rate the human resources department as "poor." Exactly half of the employees in the fire department and fewer than half the employees in the police and public works departments give a similar rating; in fact, 40 percent of the police employees rated human resources as "good." Lambda for these data equals 0.00. The lesson is not that your perception was wrong. Rather, it is to demonstrate that lambda is insensitive and ignores relationships if the mode of every value of the independent variable is the same category of the dependent variable.

Salient Features of an Ordinal Measure of Association

Ordinal measures of association summarize relationships between ordinal independent and dependent variables. These measures take into account the additional information provided by ordinal measures. If an analyst has hypothesized a direct relationship, an increase in the value of the independent variable should be associated with an increase in the value of the dependent variable. If she has hypothesized an inverse relationship, an increase in the value of the independent variable should be associated with a decrease in the value of the dependent variable.

Ordinal measures of association vary in their statistical models of what constitutes a perfect relationship. Gamma is an ordinal measure with a generous criterion for detecting perfect relationships. Consequently it may overestimate the strength of a relationship between two variables. An analyst who wishes to identify potentially interesting relationships may prefer to work with gamma, which will screen out fewer relationships than other ordinal measures.

Ordinal measures cannot effectively estimate the strength of nonlinear relationships. If the analyst has hypothesized or suspects a nonlinear relationship, she may prefer to use a nominal measure of association. Nominal measures evaluate each category of a variable without assuming a rank ordering, and they will assign the same numerical value no matter how the categories are arranged. Ordinal measures assume a monotonically increasing or decreasing pattern; that is, two variables either steadily increase or decrease together.

Table 13.10 relates years of working experience to perceptions of the human resources department's effectiveness. Note the nonlinear pattern. Employees

TABLE 13.10	RATINGS OF THE PERFORMANCE OF THE HUMAN RESOURCES DEPARTMENT BY YEARS OF FULL-TIME WORKING EXPERIENCE		
	< 2 years	2–5 years	> 5 years
Poor	20	0	5
Satisfactory	10	10	20
Good	5	20	5

Note: Gamma = .29.

with the least working experience are most likely to rate the human resources department as "poor." Employees with between two and five years of working experience are most likely to rate the department as "good." Employees with more than five years experience are most likely to rate the department as "satisfactory." The data indicate a relationship that is neither distinctly direct nor inverse. The gamma value, suggesting a weak direct relationship, underestimates the strength of the relationship because it ignores the nonlinear pattern. A good analyst will examine tables analyzing hypothesized or anticipated relationships even if the measures of association suggest a weak relationship.

Measures of association can be characterized as symmetric or asymmetric. *Symmetric measures* have the same value no matter which variable is designated as the independent variable. *Asymmetric measures* may have different values depending on which variable is designated as the independent variable. Lambda is an asymmetric measure. Gamma is a symmetric measure of association. Cramer's V, which appears in several examples in this chapter, also is a symmetric measure.

Some Common Nominal and Ordinal Measures of Association

Nominal measures of association can be categorized as chi-square–based measures and Proportional Reduction in Error (PRE) measures. Chi-square, an inferential statistic discussed in Chapter 12, is the basis for several nominal, symmetric measures, including Cramer's V. As mentioned above, lambda is a PRE measure.

PRE measures tend to have lower values for a given relationship than do chi-square–based measures. Instead we might choose a chi-square–based measure to screen a set of contingency tables for further analysis. Chi-square–based measures will normally result in more tables being reviewed, and the investigator is not apt to miss an interesting relationship.

PRE measures are less likely to overestimate the strength of an association. In fact, PRE measures may underestimate them. An investigator summarizing the effects of a large number of independent variables might choose a PRE measure. Thus, the investigators reduce the risk of assuming that a trivial or nonexistent relationship is important.

Ordinal measures also are called rank order measures. Three common ordinal measures for contingency tables are *gamma, tau,* and *Somers' d*.[2] Gamma

TABLE **13.11**		COMMON MEASURES OF ASSOCIATION FOR DATA MEASURED AT THE NOMINAL OR ORDINAL LEVEL
Measure	**Type Data**	**Characteristics and Comments**
Lambda (λ)	Nominal	Asymmetric, PRE measure; may report 0.00 even if variables are statistically related
Cramer's V	Nominal	Symmetric; chi-square–based; values of .20–.40 range suggest a moderate relationship; values over .80 are rarely encountered[a]
Gamma (γ)	Ordinal	Symmetric; reaches ± 1.00 for relationships that seem less than perfect; values of .30–.40 range suggest a moderate relationship[b]
Tau (τ)	Ordinal	Symmetric; tau_b used for square tables, tau_c for rectangular tables (tau_b cannot reach ± 1.00 for nonsquare tables); values of .30–.70 range suggest a moderate relationship[c]
Somers' d	Ordinal	Asymmetric; values normally fall between gamma and tau[d]

[a]Interpretation of values is from T. H. Poister, *Public Program Analysis: Applied Research Methods* (Baltimore: University Park Press, 1978), 443.

[b]Interpretation of values is from Poister, *Public Program Analysis*, 456, citing J. A. Davis, *Elementary Survey Analysis* (Englewood Cliffs, NJ: Prentice-Hall, 1971), 49.

[c]Interpretation is from B. D. Bowen and H. F. Weisberg, *An Introduction to Data Analysis* (San Francisco: W. H. Freeman, 1977), 76.

[d]Poister, *Public Program Analysis*, 457.

and tau are both symmetric measures, while Somers' d is asymmetric. If the variables in a contingency table are ordinal, researchers normally prefer ordinal measures of association over nominal measures. They are more likely to detect relationships, since they make fuller use of a table's information. Nominal statistics ignore the ranking inherent in an ordinal scale. However, in a table with one nominal and one ordinal variable, the analyst usually must rely on a nominal statistic.

Table 13.11 summarizes major characteristics of common measures of association for data measured at the nominal and ordinal levels. As you review this table, remember that the measures of association should add information to a contingency table. If the independent and dependent variables are ordinal, then gamma, tau, or Somers' d should be examined; however, if the relationship is nonlinear, these measures underestimate the strength of the relationship. Recall that what constitutes a "strong" or "moderate" relationship partially depends on the study topic. If an investigator has found few independent variables that are associated with the dependent variable, a weak relationship may merit attention. Furthermore, while ordinal measures of association assign negative values to inverse relationships, the sign indicates only the direction, not the strength, of the relationship.

MEASURES OF ASSOCIATION WITH CONTROL VARIABLES

Depending on the model, an investigator may add a control variable to eliminate a rival hypothesis or to explore further the original relationship. Including a control variable in a contingency table is relatively easy. The dataset is divided into subsets. Cases are assigned to subsets on the basis of their values of the control variable. For example, for the variable *gender*, the subsets are male and female. All the females in the dataset are assigned to one subset and all the males are assigned to the other.

The model guides the number of subsets created and studied. For some variables, such as gender, the content of subsets is clear-cut. For other variables, the analyst may have to decide what categories are appropriate for the planned study. He needs to avoid having so many subsets that they contain too few cases for meaningful analysis. He may limit the subsets to the values of interest or combine similar values. The control variables he chooses and the way he arranges them depend on the purpose of the study. For example, if education were the control variable, with the values less than 12 years, high school graduate, bachelor's degree, and graduate degree, the analyst does not have to study each category. He may use all the existing values, combine some values, or examine select values. Listed below are three possible ways of treating education as a control variable:

Option 1: (1) Less than 12 years, (2) high school graduate, (3) associate's degree, (4) bachelor's degree or graduate degree

Option 2: (1) Less than 12 years, (2) high school graduate, (3) post-secondary degree

Option 3: (1) Less than 12 years, (2) high school graduate (includes those with a post-secondary degree)

A relationship between two variables is considered spurious if it disappears when a control variable is added to the analysis. A *spurious relationship* is one where the independent variable has been falsely assumed to cause the dependent variable.

Example 13.2 gives a vivid, homey example of a spurious relationship. Table 13.12 lends credence to the hypothesis based on the folk legend that storks deliver babies. Counties with large numbers of storks have high birth rates; conversely, counties with few storks have low birth rates. Undoubtedly, no reader of this text believes the hypothesis to be true. An alternative hypothesis that explains why the relationship was observed is that population density is related to both the independent and dependent variables. Specifically, rural areas may have both large numbers of storks and high birth rates, and urban areas may have few storks and low birth rates. Table 13.13, introducing the control variable, county population density, shows that most rural counties have high birth rates no matter how many storks are present and most urban counties, with typically few storks, have low birth rates. You may be familiar with similar examples, such as ice cream sales being related to violent crimes (the control variable that explains the association is outdoor temperature).

Administrators usually want to learn how a relationship changes if other variables are considered. This is referred to as *specifying* or *elaborating* a relationship. They want to understand how three variables interact. In other words, they

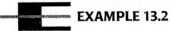 **EXAMPLE 13.2**

An Example of a Spurious Relationship. *Hypothesis:* Storks Deliver Babies

TABLE 13.12 BIRTH RATE OF COUNTY BY NUMBER OF STORKS SIGHTED IN COUNTY

	Stork Count	
Birth Rate	High (n = 100)	Low (n = 100)
High	82%	18%
Low	18%	82%

Note: lambda = .36; Cramer's V = .64; gamma = .91; χ^2 = 82; *df* = 1, *p* < .001.
Control variable: County population density.

TABLE 13.13 BIRTH RATE OF COUNTY BY NUMBER OF STORKS SIGHTED BY POPULATION DENSITY OF COUNTY

Rural Counties Stork Count			Urban Counties Stork Count		
Birth Rate	High (n = 90)	Low (n = 10)	Birth Rate	High (n = 10)	Low (n = 90)
High	90%	90%	High	10%	10%
Low	10%	10%	Low	90%	90%

Note: For statistics involving rural and urban counties, lambda = 0.00; Cramer's V = 0.00; gamma = 0.00; χ^2 = 0, *df* = 1, *p* > .90.

SOURCE: J. B. Williamson, D. A. Karp, and J. R. Dalphin, *The Research Craft* (Boston: Little, Brown, 1977), 417–418.

want to learn if the original relationship changes under different conditions. The conditions are represented by the values of the control variables.

An analyst normally looks for one of four outcomes in elaborating a relationship. First, the original relationship may continue with little change in each category of the control variable. Second, the original relationship may become stronger or weaker in some, but not all, categories of the control variable. Third, the original relationship may disappear in some or all categories of the control variable. Fourth, the relationship may change direction in some or all categories of the control variable.

If an investigator finds that the relationship disappears in all categories of the control variable, the relationship is considered spurious. Occasionally, the control variable may reveal an association between two variables that was not observed when the relationship between only the independent and dependent variables was analyzed.[3]

Measures of association decrease the work required to determine the effect of a control variable. By looking at a measure of association, an analyst can quickly visualize how the control variable affects the original relationship. The analyst looks at the measure of association summarizing the relationship between independent and dependent variables for each value of the control variable to see how it varies among the values. To illustrate this role of control variables, we analyzed data on municipal employees to identify characteristics associated with the type of position employees held. The dependent variable, position type, was assigned three values: administrator, supervisor, and nonmanager. Four independent variables that might account for variations in employee positions were examined: employee department, number of years with the city, sector of previous job (private or public), and education. The analyst controlled for the variable gender to see if it affected the relationship between any of the independent variables and the dependent variable, position type.

Table 13.14 reports the statistical findings. The column "Among All Employees" shows the relationship between each independent variable and whether a person worked as an administrator, supervisor, or nonmanager. To examine the table we used Cramer's V, a statistic for nominal-level variables, which has values ranging from 0.00 to 1.00. Cramer's V is a chi-square–based measure which takes into account the sample size. It is more sensitive than a PRE measure. Consequently, it is less likely to report a value of 0.00 and more likely to pick up variations in relationships. The Cramer's V statistic suggests that an employee's department and the years worked with the city are most closely related to the employee's position type. If we could examine the individual tables (not shown here), we would find that employees of the finance and planning departments were most likely to be administrators. Police and fire department employees were most likely to be supervisors. Employees with master's degrees were more likely than employees without master's degrees to hold either administrative or supervisory positions. Whether a person had previously worked in the private sector had little relationship to whether he or she currently held a managerial position.

The columns "Among Males" and "Among Females" report the relationship between the dependent variable (position type) and the three independent variables. The column "Among Males" shows the values of Cramer's V for the relationship between the dependent variable and each independent variable when only the data

---

TABLE 13.14	ASSOCIATION BETWEEN POSITION TYPE AND SELECTED EMPLOYEE CHARACTERISTICS CONTROLLING FOR GENDER		
	Measure of Association (Values of Cramer's V)		
	Among All Employees	Among Males	Among Females
Department	.26	.30	.36
Years with city	.30	.30	.22
Sector of previous job	.09	.10	.10
Education	.17	.19	.08

on men are analyzed. Similarly, the column "Among Females" shows the values when only the data on women are analyzed.

An analyst can quickly determine the influence of the control variable by reviewing a measure of association. Since Cramer's V is a statistic for nominal data, we had to check the tables relating each independent variable to the dependent variable to understand the exact nature of the relationship. Without having the tables to look at, we can only guess which departments had relatively more administrators or supervisors and whether certain departments were more likely to employ women in managerial positions. Only finance and planning departments had women administrators. Women were most likely to work as supervisors in public safety and public works departments. The tables confirmed that the number of years spent working with the city seemed to benefit women less than men. Men were more likely to hold administrative positions the longer they worked for the city.

With an ordinal measure, an analyst can more clearly visualize the content of the table by just reviewing the measure of association. Let's look at the relationship between years with the city and management position in more detail. Table 13.15 shows the relationship separately for men and women.

The tables show that for both men and women, the longer they work with the city the more likely they are to have a managerial position. Nevertheless, both the tables and gamma values imply that men are more likely than women to be promoted the longer they stay with the city. The tables and measures of association are said to show an interaction between gender and length of city employment. Being both male and employed by a city for more than 10 years increases the probability of working as either an administrator or supervisor.

Recall the early chapters of this text in which we wrote about the importance of an explicit research model. At the same time, we encouraged you to consider a model as tentative. The tentativeness of a model is apparent as an analyst examines

TABLE 13.15   **MANAGEMENT POSITION BY YEARS EMPLOYED WITH CITY BY GENDER**

	Males: Years Employed by City				
	< 1 (72)	1–2 (153)	3–6 (208)	7–10 (243)	> 10 (830)
Nonmanager	81.9%	79.7%	79.8%	68.5%	35.5%
Supervisor	12.5%	16.3%	13.5%	27.2%	57.0%
Administrator	5.6%	3.9%	6.5%	4.5%	7.5%

Note: Gamma = .56.

	Females: Years Employed by City				
	< 1 (19)	1–2 (45)	3–6 (41)	7–10 (51)	> 10 (72)
Nonmanager	100.0%	91.1%	87.8%	84.3%	76.4%
Supervisor	0.0%	6.7%	12.2%	5.9%	22.2%
Administrator	0.0%	2.2%	0.07%	9.8%	1.4%

Note: Gamma = .39. Percentages may not add to 100% due to rounding.

table after table of bivariate relationships. Then he or she explores the *effect of control variables*. For many analysts the process is compelling. Each table raises more questions and possibilities. The analyst might wonder where to stop. The purpose of the study should suggest which control variables are worth examining. The purpose also may imply how exhaustive an investigation is warranted.

TESTS OF STATISTICAL SIGNIFICANCE AND MEASURES OF ASSOCIATION

Measures of association summarize the strength of the relationship between two variables; that is, a measure of association indicates the magnitude of the effect. It serves as a criterion for labeling an effect as weak, moderate, or strong. A measure of association that suggests a weak relationship may motivate a researcher to discount a relationship found to be statistically significant. Indeed, a relationship may be nonrandom, but it also can be too small or trivial to merit any action. Recall that what constitutes a weak effect or a strong effect depends on the statistic, its criteria for a perfect relationship and a null relationship, and the degree of existing knowledge about the research question. Effect size is related to the power of a statistical test. Power depends on the size of the effect that has been measured and on the number of cases in the dataset being studied. Other things being equal, the larger the effect and the larger the sample, the more powerful the test. When a test with low power fails to show a statistically significant relationship, one should not necessarily conclude that there is no effect.[4]

Tests of statistical significance are inferential statistics. They indicate the probability that an observed relationship occurred by chance. A researcher uses inferential statistics to infer from a sample to the population. Appropriate use of tests of statistical significance requires a random sample. Measures of association are descriptive statistics. A researcher uses descriptive statistics to summarize data, whether or not they represent a random sample. Taken together, measures of association and tests of statistical significance produce evidence supporting or disconfirming a hypothesized relationship.

The more knowledge an investigator has about an entire research effort and the details contained in a contingency table, the more confident he can be in interpreting the study's statistics. The tests of statistical significance and measures of association may confirm his conclusions or lead him to look at some of the evidence more carefully. The statistics can elucidate the research findings, reinforce decisions about their implications, and help to summarize and communicate them effectively to an audience.

COMPARISON OF MEANS AND ANALYSIS OF VARIANCE

For many situations contingency-table analysis is inadequate. It ignores the statistical advantages of experimental designs, misses the clarity of comparing the means of two or more groups, and fails to utilize information available when means and variances can be calculated. For example, suppose school system administrators wanted to compare the number of days missed by children who attend schools outside their neighborhood with the number of days missed by children attending neighborhood schools. An analyst can create several categories of days missed, for example, none, 1–5, 6–10, and so on, and construct a contingency table. Alternatively, the analyst can average the number of days missed by children who attend schools outside their neighborhood and compare it with the mean number of days missed by neighborhood children.

The primary statistical tool for analyzing experimental data and the differences between group means is analysis of variance, abbreviated ANOVA. *ANOVA* provides information on both the strength and statistical significance of a relationship. Analysis of variance was developed early in the 20th century by R. A. Fisher, a British statistician, who wanted a method for analyzing data collected in carefully structured experiments. He primarily studied agricultural practices. Hence, many of the early textbooks and experts treated analysis of variance in the context of agricultural research. The main statistical test used in ANOVA, the *F*-test, is named for Fisher.[5]

In an experiment the subjects may be drawn from the same population and randomly assigned to an experimental or control group. The experimental and control groups constitute separate samples. Just as differences between a random sample's statistics and its parameters are due to chance, pretest differences between the means and variances of the experimental and control groups should be due to chance.

Analysis of variance has the following assumptions: (1) dependent variables are interval or ratio level; (2) variances and standard deviations for each group are equal or close to it; (3) the independent variable or variables should be normally distributed for each group; (4) the values of the dependent variables are independent of each other.[6] Correctly designed experiments fulfill these assumptions.

After the experimental intervention takes place—the independent variable of the experiment—the means of the groups may differ. Experimenters expect an experimental intervention to cause differences between the experimental and control groups. ANOVA is designed to determine whether the posttest differences between the experimental and control groups are large enough that they probably occurred for a reason other than chance.

Analysis of variance examines two types of variances: within-groups variances and between-groups variances. *Within-groups variances* refers to how each member within an experimental or control group varies from the group mean. *Between-groups variances* refers to how the mean and variances of each group differ from those of other groups. If experimental and control group subjects are assigned correctly, the between-groups and within-groups variances of pretest groups should be equivalent. If the experimental treatment had no effect, the statistics for the posttest groups also will be equivalent.

ANOVA begins by establishing whether the differences between the experimental and control groups could have occurred by chance. Analysis of variance has the following basic research and null hypotheses:

H_1:   The arithmetic means of two or more groups are unequal.

H_0:   The arithmetic means of two or more groups are equal.

In experiments the investigators compare the means of the posttest experimental and control groups to see whether the data support the research hypothesis. Analysis of variance determines whether differences between the groups (that is, between-group variance) are greater than differences within any of these groups (that is, within-groups variances).

To judge whether the difference between two means is large enough to be statistically significant, we use the *F-test,* which is based on the following ratio:

Between-groups variance/Within-groups variance

If the value of the ratio is much greater than 1, the difference between group means is likely to be statistically significant. The ratio will be greater than 1 if the difference between group means is a relatively large value, and the variability within groups is relatively small. If the researcher obtains a large enough value for the *F*-ratio, he rejects the null hypothesis of the equality of the means and accepts the research hypothesis.[7]

ANOVA has widespread applications apart from experimental designs. It is used to assess the results of multiple regression, a topic covered in the next chapter.[8] It may be used to analyze cross-sectional data if the dependent variable is interval or ratio and the independent variable is nominal.[9] Remember that an ordinal variable can be treated as a nominal variable. To use ANOVA appropriately, the data must come from random samples. The assumption that variances in all groups in the population must be equal is often ignored if the number of cases in each group is similar. The analyst may wish to check this assumption, especially if the group sizes are markedly different.[10]

To clarify the points we have made thus far, let us consider a study conducted by an analyst with Majesty City's Division of Training and Job Placement.[11] The analyst wanted to compare three programs sponsored by the agency: (1) Basic Skills, (2) Classroom Training, and (3) On-the-Job Training (OJT). The agency assigned clients to one of the three programs. At the end of the training program, clients were placed in jobs.

The analyst wanted to see if clients trained in the OJT program were earning more than clients trained in either of the other two programs. Previous research suggested that OJT participants were more successful. Furthermore, from her own observations, she knew that OJT participants were normally more "job ready" than other trainees, and therefore were more likely to receive better job placements. The analyst collected data on trainees' monthly earnings during their first year of work. Her research and null hypotheses were:

H_1:   The average earnings of OJT trainees will be greater after one year than the earnings of trainees in the Basic Skills and the Classroom Training programs.

H_0:   The average earnings after one year will be equal for trainees in all three programs.

A sample of clients attending each program was selected from agency records. Interviewers telephoned the members of the samples and asked them for

TABLE 13.16	AVERAGE MONTHLY EARNINGS BY PROGRAM			
		Program		
		Basic Skills	Classroom Training	On-the-Job Training
Average monthly income ($)	$\overline{X}$	433.5	528.7	765.1
Sample size	n	11	21	8

Note: Average for all participants = grand mean = 549.8; total number of participants = 40.

wage information. Table 13.16 shows the average monthly earnings for each group. The grand mean refers to the average monthly earnings for all 40 persons included in the study.

Figure 13.1 supplements the table information and visually represents the data. The graph shows the average earnings and the range, a measure of variability, for each group. The asterisk indicates the average income, and the ranges are enclosed with the boxes.[12]

The data in Table 13.16 and the graph support the research hypotheses. To supplement these findings, the analyst uses statistics to answer two questions:

1. Are the differences among average salaries for the groups statistically significant? That is, are the differences larger than would be expected to occur by chance?

2. How strong is the relationship between type of program and average income?

The *F*-test answers the first question. A measure of association, *eta*, answers the second question.

| FIGURE 13.1 | AVERAGE MONTHLY EARNINGS BY PROGRAM |

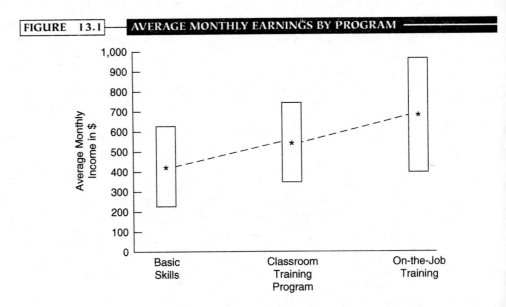

FIGURE 13.2	ANALYSIS OF VARIANCE TABLE

ONEWAY

	Variable	MWAGE	Monthly salary and wages
By	Variable	PROGRAM	Program participant enrolled in

ANALYSIS OF VARIANCE

SOURCE	D.F.	SUM OF SQUARES	MEANS SQUARES	F-RATIO	F-PROB.
BETWEEN GROUPS	2	528,965	264,482.5	5.2	.0100
WITHIN GROUPS	37	1,869,230	50,519.7		
TOTAL	39	2,398,195			

If all three groups were equal on the dependent variable (earnings), then the between-groups and within-groups variances would be equal and the value of the F-ratio would be 1. If the F-ratio is larger than 1, the investigator determines its statistical significance by consulting a table of F-values or obtaining the statistics from a computer program. To use a table of F-values, the analyst must know the value of the F-ratio and the degrees of freedom for the numerator and the denominator. In our example the degrees of freedom for the numerator is 2, the number of groups minus one, and for the denominator it is 37, the total sample size minus the number of groups.

The data from the Majesty City study were analyzed by a computer program, SPSS, using analysis of variance. Figure 13.2 shows the printout from this program. We will comment only on portions of the printout that help you decide whether the data support your hypothesis. The "Source" column identifies the two types of variance, between groups and within groups. "D.F." is the degrees of freedom for each group. The "Sum of Squares" measures the between-groups variation and the within-groups variation. The "F-Ratio" is between-groups mean square divided by the within-groups mean square. The "F-Prob." refers to the associated probability of F. In this case the probability that an F-ratio as large as 5.2 would have occurred if the means of the three groups were equivalent is .01, or 1 percent.

The F-test, in this example, tells the investigator that at least two of the groups differ significantly from each other. To learn which pairs of means are significantly different, separate t-tests must be performed. t-tests of the example's data found a significant difference between the earnings of trainees who received Basic Skills training and those in the OJT group.

An F-test does not measure the strength of the relationship between variables. A measure of association, eta or E, based on analysis of variance, is used for this purpose. Eta can vary between 0.00 and 1.00. The formula for eta is:

$$E = \sqrt{SS_b/SS_t}$$

where:

SS_b = Between-groups sum of squares
SS_t = Total sum of squares

For the example's data:

$$E = \sqrt{528,965/2,398,195}$$
$$= .47$$

Analysts square eta to interpret it.[13] In the example $(.47)^2$ equals .22, which indicates that 22 percent of the variation in monthly income after one year of work is associated with the independent variable, that is, the program in which the client was trained.

This discussion focused on the basic analysis of variance model. In one-way analysis of variance, the analysis involves one independent variable and each case contributes one score to the analysis. In the school example mentioned at the beginning of this section, the independent variable was whether a student attended school in the neighborhood or elsewhere, and the piece of data contributed by each subject was the number of days missed from school. In the job training example, the independent variable was type of job training program, and the contributed score was each subject's monthly earnings.

The basic model can be adapted to include other variables. Analysis of variance models including more than one independent variable are called multivariate analysis of variance (MANOVA) or, depending on the number of independent variables, two-way analysis of variance, three-way analysis of variance, and so on. Analysis of variance models also may include more than one measure on a subject; these are called repeated measures models.[14]

SUMMARY

Administrators are normally comfortable with contingency tables and the information conveyed by percents. They also may be familiar with tests of statistical significance, especially chi-square, which indicate the probability that the relationship occurred by chance. Measures of association associated with contingency tables are less familiar to administrators and generally are of interest only to the analyst.

Contingency tables illustrate the relationship between variables. If the independent variable heads the table column, a user may compare the relative distribution of the dependent variable for each value of the independent variable. With the comparison he sees how the percentage values of dependent variables differ for each category of the independent variable. The comparison, then, suggests if the data support a given hypothesis.

Measures of association reduce the table data to a single metric. All measures of association indicate a null relationship with a value of 0.00. Nominal measures of association indicate a perfect relationship with a value of 1.00. Ordinal measures of association assign +1.00 or −1.00 to a perfect monotonic relationship; they will miss or underestimate the strength of nonlinear relationships. The closer a measure is to ±1.00, the stronger the relationship. The closer a measure is to 0.00, the weaker the relationship.

To compare contingency tables with measures of association, an analyst must use the same measure for all comparisons. In choosing a measure she should select a measure she is familiar with and consider the level of measurement of the variables and the measure's criteria for a perfect and a null relationship. Comparisons must be made with caution, especially if the number of rows and columns varies from table to table.

The criteria for a strong or weak relationship depend on the measure of association and the nature of the research question. In general, ordinal measures produce higher values than nominal measures. Symmetric measures produce higher values than asymmetric measures. Similarly, some variables have been extensively studied, and moderate associations without a theoretical basis may not add to our knowledge. Other dependent variables are poorly understood, and weak relationships may generate some productive leads.

Measures of association help an analyst to determine the effect of control variables. The control variable may suggest that the original relationship is spurious or that the control variable has no effect. More often the control variable elaborates the relationship by showing how a relationship changes for different values of a control variable—it may become stronger for some values, it may disappear for some values, or it may change directions in some or all values.

Analysis of variance, originally developed for experimental studies, may be used to analyze hypotheses with an interval dependent variable and a nominal independent variable from nonexperimental studies. The subjects must constitute a random sample, however. Analysis of variance provides information on both the statistical significance and the strength of a relationship. To determine statistical significance the F-ratio is calculated. If it is markedly larger than 1, the relationship probably is statistically significant. The statistic eta is calculated to measure the strength of association. The values of eta range from 0.00 (a null relationship) to 1.00 (a perfect relationship). Eta squared indicates the amount of variation in the dependent variable that is explained by the independent variable.

One-way analysis of variance applies in designs with one independent variable in which each subject contributed one piece of data. Other models of analysis of variance are used to analyze designs with more than one independent variable or which collect data from the subjects more than once over the course of the study.

Chapter 14 parallels this chapter and examines techniques for studying the linear relationship between variables measured at the interval level. Nominal and ordinal measures of association act primarily to identify relationships for closer study. Interval statistics are widely reported and provide investigators with valuable information to explain, describe, or predict relationships.

NOTES

1. D. B. Wright, *Understanding Statistics: An Introduction for the Social Sciences* (London: Sage Publications, 1997) discusses the relationship between ANOVA and regression and cites seminal work in the social sciences on this topic. See page 132 especially.

2. There are other useful measures for ordinal variables in situations where there are many cases and many categories of the variables but data are not in contingency tables. We do not discuss these measures of association here. See Sidney Siegal, *Nonparametric Statistics for*

the Behavioral Sciences (New York: McGraw-Hill Book Company, 1956), 202–239 and Hubert M. Blalock, Jr., 2d ed. *Social Statistics* (New York: McGraw-Hill Book Company, 1972), 415–421.

3. For a complete discussion on how a control variable can affect the relationship between an independent and dependent variable, see T. Poister, *Public Program Analysis: Applied Research Methods* (Baltimore: University Park Press, 1978), 153–171. Also see M. Rosenberg, *The Logic of Survey Analysis* (New York: Basic Books, 1968).

4. R. S. Pindyck and D. L. Rubinfeld, *Econometric Models and Economic Forecasts*, 4th ed. (Boston: Irwin/McGraw-Hill, 1998), 43–45.

5. Poister, *Public Program Analysis*, 463.

6. Wright, *Understanding Statistics: An Introduction for the Social Sciences*, 131–133; G. W. Bohrnstedt and D. Knoke, 2d ed., *Statistics for Social Data Analysis* (Itasca, IL: F. E. Peacock, 1988), 232–233. These assumptions are for between subjects ANOVA. Other models require somewhat different assumptions; see Wright, 141.

7. L. Meyers and N. Grossen, *Behavioral Research: Theory, Procedure, and Design* (San Francisco: W. H. Freeman, 1974), 78–79. Also see Bohrnstedt and Knoke, 232–233.

8. Wright, *Understanding Statistics: An Introduction for the Social Sciences* (London: Sage, Inc., 1997), 132, 183–184.

9. See Bohrnstedt and Knoke, *Statistics for Social Data Analysis*, 240–244.

10. J. F. Healey, *Statistics: A Tool for Social Research*, 3d ed. (Belmont, CA: Wadsworth, 1993), 287–293. Wright, 131–133 discusses using SPSS to test for equality of variances.

11. H. Livengood, *JPTA: Follow Up and Evaluation of Selected Programs in Charlotte, N.C.* (Charlotte: University of North Carolina at Charlotte, 1993).

12. To help visualize the data and the model, you also could draw a box plot for each group and indicate in it the location of the mean instead of the median. Remember that ANOVA requires the calculation of the arithmetic mean. Wright, *Understanding Statistics*, 116–119.

13. Bohrnstedt and Knoke, *Statistics for Social Data Analysis*, 234–236 and 290–294 discuss eta.

14. Wright, *Understanding Statistics*, 116–145 is recommended for an introductory discussion of ANOVA and MANOVA models. Wright includes the SPSS printout for several of these.

TERMS FOR REVIEW

contingency table
measure of association
percentage difference
bivariate distribution
perfect relationship (between two variables)
null relationship

sensitive measure of association
proportional reduction in error (PRE) measure
original error
new error
symmetric measure
asymmetric measure

spurious relationship
effects of a control variable
ANOVA
F-test
within-groups variance
between-groups variance
eta

QUESTIONS FOR REVIEW

The following questions should indicate whether you have a basic competency in this chapter's material.

1. Use the data array in Table 13.17 to:
   a. Create a contingency table showing the relationship between county and causes of injury. Write a sentence describing the relationship.
   b. Create a contingency table showing the relationship between cause of injury and its severity. Note that you will have to group together values of the severity

index. Write a sentence describing the relationship.

2. Table 13.18 was constructed in an evaluation of a pilot project conducted by a city to encourage citizens to recycle more of their trash. Calculate percentages for this table. Write a short report to the head of the Engineering Department summarizing the results.

3. In a related activity, the city obtained information regarding the support of a sample of citizens for bond financing for a waste-to-energy facility. Table 13.19 shows support

TABLE 13.17	DATA ARRAY FOR THREE VARIABLES: COUNTY, CAUSE, AND SEVERITY OF INJURY		
Case ID	County	Cause	Severity Index
01	Baker	Fall	3
02	Charlie	Car accident	4
03	Charlie	Violence	6
04	Able	Car accident	4
05	Charlie	Violence	5
06	Baker	Fall	9
07	Charlie	Car accident	10
08	Baker	Fall	1
09	Able	Violence	5
10	Charlie	Violence	5
11	Charlie	Fall	7
12	Able	Car accident	4
13	Charlie	Car accident	7
14	Baker	Fall	6
15	Able	Fall	3
16	Baker	Car accident	5
17	Charlie	Car accident	5
18	Baker	Fall	6
19	Able	Car accident	4
20	Charlie	Violence	7

TABLE 13.18	RECYCLING PARTICIPATION BY NEIGHBORHOOD		
	Number of Times Participated in Recycling Program		
Neighborhood	0–2	3–6	7–10	11–13
---	---	---	---	---
Steel Creek	13	16	8	5
Hidden Valley	6	15	17	12
East Side	2	5	14	19

TABLE 13.19	SUPPORT FOR BONDS TO FINANCE WASTE-TO-ENERGY FACILITIES BY INCOME LEVEL	
	Income Level	
Support for Bonds	Below $14,500	Over $14,500
Oppose	185	153
Favor	95	167

by income level. Table 13.20 shows the support for two areas of the city.

a. Calculate the percentages for Table 13.19 and use the percentage difference to describe the variations in support.

b. Calculate the percentages for Table 13.20 and describe what happens.

c. What control variable was used in this analysis? What was its effect?

4. List the criteria one should use to choose a measure of association.
5. Consider the hypothesis: "Employers who are trained during their second quarter on the job make the greatest use of computer software." The variables were categorized as: extent of use (limited, moderate, extensive) and time of training (1st quarter of employment, 2nd quarter, 3rd quarter, or 4th quarter).

a. If time of training and extent of use have a perfect relationship, what would the data look like?
b. If time of training and extent of use have a null relationship, what would the data look like?
c. Would you be more likely to consider using a nominal or an ordinal measure of association to study this hypothesis?

TABLE 13.20 **SUPPORT FOR BONDS FOR WASTE-TO-ENERGY FACILITIES BY INCOME AND PLACE OF RESIDENCE**

	Residence			
	West Side Income Level		East Side Income Level	
Support for Bonds	Below $14,500	Over $14,500	Below $14,500	Over $14,500
Oppose	158	79	27	74
Favor	42	21	53	146

6. Explain why a rule of thumb such as the following is poor: "Any measure of association with a value greater than .45 depicts a strong relationship."
7. For Example 13.2, explain what Table 13.13 shows. What happens when a control variable is included in the analysis? What could explain this outcome?
8. Tables 13.21 through 13.23 present data collected on soup kitchen users. The tables related age to the number of meals eaten in a day.
   a. Write a sentence describing the relationship depicted in each table.

b. What is the control variable? How does it affect the original relationship?
c. Which measure of association did you use to compare the tables? Why did you select it?
9. Discuss when an investigator would use analysis of variance and eta to evaluate a relationship instead of Cramer's V or gamma. When would she use analysis of variance instead of a t-test?
10. The average murder rate for western states is lower than the average murder rate for southern states. Is murder rate in states related to region? Explain.

TABLE 13.21 **NUMBER OF MEALS EATEN DAILY BY RESPONDENT'S AGE**

	Age		
Number of Daily Meals	< 30 (66)	31–54 (213)	> 55 (144)
1	38%	29%	27%
2	47%	49%	40%
3	15%	22%	33%

Note: Cramer's V = .11; lambda = .002; gamma = .18. Percentages may not add up to 100% because of rounding.

TABLE   13.22   NUMBER OF MEALS EATEN DAILY BY AGE FOR RESPONDENT MALES

	Age		
Number of Daily Meals	< 30 (48)	31–54 (172)	> 55 (108)
1	35%	32%	31%
2	50%	48%	41%
3	15%	20%	29%

Note: Cramer's V = .09; lambda = .000; gamma = .12. Percentages may not add up to 100% because of rounding.

TABLE   13.23   NUMBER OF MEALS EATEN DAILY BY AGE FOR RESPONDENT FEMALES

	Age		
Number of Daily Meals	< 30 (18)	31–54 (38)	> 55 (35)
1	44%	18%	17%
2	39%	53%	40%
3	17%	29%	43%

Note: Cramer's V = .21; lambda = .070; gamma = .34. Percentages may not add up to 100% because of rounding.

11. Draw a graph similar to Figure 13.1 that would illustrate that (a) the average murder rate decline for regions in the following order: South, Northeast, West, Midwest, and (b) the variance in murder rates declines in this order: Northeast, West, Midwest, South.

PROBLEMS FOR HOMEWORK AND DISCUSSION

1. An investigator is curious about whether respondent characteristics were associated with completion of a lengthy questionnaire. Seven contingency tables were produced; their measures of association are given in Table 13.24.

   a. Which characteristics of respondents seem clearly to be randomly related to completion of the survey?
   b. Which characteristics appear to be associated with whether a person completed the questionnaire?

TABLE   13.24   ASSOCIATIONS BETWEEN COMPLETION OF SURVEY AND RESPONDENT CHARACTERISTICS

	Lambda	Cramer's V	Gamma
Years worked for city	.00	.12	.14
Department	.00	.14	−.19
Sector of previous employment (public, private, first job)	.00	.00	−.01
Age	.00	.08	−.14
Gender (M/F)	.00	.01	−.04
Position (management, nonmanagement, unskilled, clerical)	.00	.14	−.375
Degree (MPA, BS/BA, Other)	.00	.09	.18

c. What criterion did you use to answer a and b?

d. For what relationships (independent variables), if any, does lambda appear to be an inappropriate measure of association? Explain.

e. For what relationships (independent variables), if any, does gamma appear to be an inappropriate measure of association? Explain.

f. For this particular study, do you think that the investigator should use lambda or Cramer's V as a screen to identify tables for further examination? Explain.

g. Do you need to consult the tables to interpret the measures of association? Explain.

2. Tables 13.25 through 13.30 are from a printout examining data on people who volunteer for direct service activities.

a. Write a sentence describing the findings of each table.

b. Does education or age seem to play a greater role in whether a person decides to volunteer? Justify your answer.

c. Interpret the gammas for those tables. If you were reporting the findings, would you keep the signs for gamma the same as on the printout, or would you reverse them? Justify your answer.

d. Briefly discuss how you would use the above information to recruit volunteers.

TABLE 13.25 **VOLUNTEERING BY RESPONDENT AGE**

	Age			
Volunteers	18–29 (331)	30–49 (529)	50–64 (301)	>65 (181)
Yes	25%	35%	20%	18%
No	75%	65%	80%	82%

Note: Lambda = 0.00; Cramer's V = .16; gamma = .14.

TABLE 13.26 **VOLUNTEERING BY RESPONDENT EDUCATION**

	Years of Education				
Volunteers	< 8 (203)	9–11 (238)	12 (504)	13–15 (206)	16 (178)
Yes	8%	19%	28%	34%	48%
No	92%	81%	72%	66%	52%

Note: Lambda = 0.00; Cramer's V = .26; gamma = −.41.

TABLE 13.27 **VOLUNTEERING BY EDUCATION FOR RESPONDENTS AGED 18–29**

	Years of Education				
Volunteers	< 8 (11)	9–11 (56)	12 (162)	13–15 (67)	16 (33)
Yes	18%	14%	25%	27%	42%
No	82%	86%	75%	73%	58%

Note: Lambda = 0.00; Cramer's V = .17; gamma = −.26.

TABLE 13.28   VOLUNTEERING BY EDUCATION FOR RESPONDENTS AGED 30–49

Volunteers	Years of Education				
	< 8 (31)	9–11 (98)	12 (212)	13–15 (95)	16 (91)
Yes	6%	18%	34%	41%	60%
No	94%	82%	66%	59%	40%

Note: Lambda = 0.04; Cramer's V = .31; gamma = −.46.

TABLE 13.29   VOLUNTEERING BY EDUCATION FOR RESPONDENTS AGED 50–64

Volunteers	Years of Education				
	< 8 (89)	9–11 (56)	12 (89)	13–15 (31)	16 (30)
Yes	6%	23%	23%	23%	37%
No	94%	77%	78%	77%	63%

Note: Lambda = 0.06; Cramer's V = .25; gamma = −.39.

TABLE 13.30   VOLUNTEERING BY EDUCATION FOR RESPONDENTS OVER AGE 64

Volunteers	Years of Education				
	< 8 (72)	9–11 (28)	12 (41)	13–15 (13)	16 (24)
Yes	10%	25%	20%	38%	21%
No	90%	75%	80%	62%	79%

Note: Lambda = 0.08; Cramer's V = .21; gamma = −.29.

DISK WORK

1. Using the ORB Research Methods dataset, create ordinal variables representing low, medium, and high spending per capita on public safety, human services, and cultural/recreational expenditure for each county. Analyze these variables to see if there is a relationship between region of the state and county funding levels per capital for these services.

   a. Use computer software to create contingency tables for each type of expenditure, similar to Table 13.1 or Table 13.2, to examine the relationship between region and spending per capita in each area.

   b. Write a very brief report (no more than one page, single spaced) identifying the relationships you studied, the resulting contingency tables, and a summary of what you found.

2. As the number of cells in a contingency table increases, the difficulty of interpreting the table also increases. This exercise is meant to improve your table reading skills and to demonstrate the role of measures of

association. Create a new variable, designating each county as under fiscal stress or not, depending on whether the county's debt service payments per capita are higher or lower than the median. Take one of the tables used in problem 1. For each region, designate high and low fiscal stress counties, and prepare a new contingency table. If available on the statistical software, request lambda, Cramer's V, and gamma.

i. Interpret the values of lambda, Cramer's V, and gamma.

ii. Write a very brief (no more than one page, single-spaced) report of your findings: identify the relationship you studied and your operational definitions (including recodes); produce a contingency table to report the findings; and summarize what you found.

3. This exercise gives you some experience in applying analysis of variance. Create new income variables by taking at least three measures of county wealth (by income or poverty measures) and categorizing each county as low, medium, and high. Analyze the data to see if income, the independent variable, is related to political activity as measured by percent of registered voters who actually vote.

a. Create a graphic similar to Figure 13.1.

b. Generate an analysis of variance table similar to Figure 13.2.

c. Compute eta.

d. What does your analysis tell you about the relationship between county wealth and political activity?

RECOMMENDED FOR FURTHER READING

K. Elifson, R. P. Runyon, A. Haber, *Fundamentals of Social Statistics*, 3d ed. (Boston: McGraw Hill, 1998) discuss the construction and interpretation of contingency tables and calculation of measures of association for contingency tables and analysis of variance.

K. J. Meier, J. L. Brudney, and J. Bohte, *Applied Statistics for Public and Nonprofit Administration*, 6th ed. (Belmont, CA: Thomson Wadsworth, 2006) presents excellent examples and problems suggesting how administrators can use statistics in decision making. Calculations for statistics are worked out in detail and are easily followed.

M. Rosenburg, *The Logic of Survey Analysis* (New York: Basic Books, 1968). Rosenburg thoroughly discusses the use of control variables in the analysis of survey data. He covers virtually all possible situations in a very readable fashion. Readers should note that the only measures of association he uses are percentages. A useful appendix on how to read contingency tables is included.

F. N. Kerlinger and H. B Lee, *Foundations of Behavioral Research*, 4th ed. (Fort Worth: Harcourt College Publishers, 2000) has an excellent, nonstatistical discussion of analysis of variance. D. B. Wright, *Understanding Statistics: An Introduction for the Social Sciences* (London: Sage Publications, 1997), Chapter 6, contains an excellent introductory discussion of analysis of variance models and statistics.

G. Keppel and T. D. Wickens, *Design and Analysis: A Researcher's Handbook*, 4th ed. (Englewood Cliffs, NJ: Prentice-Hall, 2004) provides a thorough discussion of the experimental design, analysis of variance, and related topics, including details on statistical calculation and interpretation. His discussion is more accessible than that available in other excellent but more technical works.

13.1

Some Measures of Association
for Nominal and Ordinal Data

This appendix presents the equations and shows the calculations for a few common measures of association for variables measured at the nominal and ordinal levels. To illustrate the calculations, we use a Chapter 12 table, repeated here as Table 13.31, relating citizens' rating of the police department to their ages. If we were actually selecting a measure of association for this table, we would use an ordinal statistic because both variables are ordinal and the relationship is linear.

TABLE 13.31	RATINGS OF POLICY DEPARTMENT BY RESPONDENT'S AGE		
	Age		
Rating of Police Department	< 18 yrs.	18 − 59	> 59
Poor (D to F)	2	33	6
Satisfactory (C)	10	137	27
Good (A or B)	12	453	150

Nominal Measures

Nominal measures of association are required if the independent and dependent variables are nominal. If only one of these variables is nominal and not dichotomous, the analyst would need to use a nominal measure or a measure specifically intended for nominal-ordinal combinations.

The chapter discusses lambda, also known as Goodman's lambda, at length, and nothing needs to be added here.

Cramer's V, a chi-square–based measure, also is used with nominal measure of association. The equation for Cramer's V is

$$V = \sqrt{\frac{\chi^2}{n \cdot \min(\text{row} - 1, \text{column} - 1)}}$$

For the data in Table 13.31: $\chi^2 = 13.9$, $n = 830$, $\min(\text{row} - 1, \text{column} - 1) = 2$. The value of $\min(\text{row} - 1, \text{column} - 1)$ is either the row minus 1 or the column minus 1, whichever yields the lower figure. If Table 13.31 had four rows and three columns, the $\min(\text{row} - 1, \text{column} - 1)$ would still equal 2.

$$V = \sqrt{\frac{13.9}{830 \cdot 2}} = 0.0915$$

The measure of association, phi (ϕ), is used for 2×2 tables. It has essentially the same equation as Cramer's V. Since the $\min(\text{row} - 1, \text{column} - 1) = 1$, the equation reduces to

$$\phi = \sqrt{\frac{\chi^2}{n}}$$

Ordinal Measures

This section includes three common ordinal measures of association for data in contingency tables: gamma, Somers' d, and Kendall's tau_b and tau_c. This chapter considers measures of association in two roles: (1) to filter out trivial relationships and (2) to show the effects of control variables. All three measures have the same numerator, so we will start by explaining how to calculate its components. First, the values of the variables must be in rank order; that is, they must be ordered along a continuum. The analyst begins the calculations by identifying the number of cases that are in agreement (A) or disagreement (D) with the rank ordering of both variables. The rank order suggested by Table 13.31 is: "The older the respondent, the higher the rating." Note the placement of the values of the variables, particularly those of the dependent variable.

To calculate A, we start with 2 in the upper, left-hand corner and count how many respondents are older than 17 who rate the police as better than "poor"; that is, $137 + 453 + 27 + 150 = 767$. We then go to 10 and count the 603 ($453 + 150$) cases where people are older than 59 and rate the police as better than "poor." We repeat the procedures in the remaining columns. The value of A is based on the calculation:

$$
\begin{aligned}
A &= 2 \cdot (137 + 453 + 27 + 150) + 10 \cdot (453 \\
&\quad + 150) + 33 \cdot (27 + 150) + 137 \cdot 150 \\
&= 1,534 + 6,030 + 5,841 + 20,550 \\
&= 33,955
\end{aligned}
$$

To calculate D we go through a similar procedure, but we begin with the top, right-hand cell. Starting with 6 we count the number of people who are younger than 60 and rate the police as better than "poor"; that is, $137 + 453 + 10 + 12 = 612$. The value of D is based on the calculation:

$$
\begin{aligned}
D &= 6 \cdot (137 + 453 + 10 + 12) + 27 \\
&\quad \cdot (453 + 12) + 33 \cdot (10 + 12) + 137 \cdot 12 \\
&= 3,672 + 12,555 + 726 + 1,644 \\
&= 18,597
\end{aligned}
$$

Gamma is an ordinal measure of association. It is a PRE measure and symmetric; that is, it makes no difference which variable is identified as the independent variable and which is the dependent variable. To calculate gamma (γ) the equation is

$$
\begin{aligned}
\gamma &= \frac{A - D}{A + D} \\
&= \frac{33,955 - 18,597}{33,955 + 18,597} \\
&= .29
\end{aligned}
$$

Somers' d (d_{yx}) is an asymmetric measure that builds on the gamma calculation. To calculate Somers' d, the independent variable must be identified. The analyst calculates the number of ties,

that is, the number of cases with the same value of the dependent variable as the cases being observed. Starting with 2 we count the number of people older than 17 who also rated the police department as "poor"; that is, $33 + 6 = 39$. The value of T_r is based on the calculation:

$$
\begin{aligned}
T_r &= 2 \cdot (33 + 6) + 33 \cdot (6) + 10 \cdot (137 + 27) \\
&\quad + 137 \cdot 27 + 12 \cdot (453 + 150) + 453 \cdot 150 \\
&= 78 + 198 + 1,640 + 3,699 + 7,236 \\
&\quad + 67,950 \\
&= 80,801
\end{aligned}
$$

To calculate Somers' d, the equation is

$$
\begin{aligned}
d_{yx} &= \frac{A - D}{A + D + T} \\
&= \frac{33,955 - 18,597}{33,955 + 18,597 + 80,801} \\
&= .12
\end{aligned}
$$

The calculations for T_r assume that the independent variable heads the columns of Table 13.35. (The subscript r refers to rows. Note that we counted ties in the rows. In the next paragraph we show how to count ties in the column.) A table can be organized so that the dependent variable heads the columns and T_c, column ties, can be substituted for T_r.

Tau$_b$ is another ordinal measure of association. It considers both ties on the dependent variable and the independent variable; hence, it is a symmetric measure. The discussion of gamma and Somers' d has covered all but one component of the equation to calculate tau$_b$. We have shown you how to calculate agreements, disagreements, and ties on the dependent variable, leaving only ties on the independent variable to be covered. To calculate the ties on the independent variable (T_c), we start again with 2 and note how many people younger than 17 rated police as better than "poor"; that is, $10 + 12$. The value of T_c was based on the calculation:

$$
\begin{aligned}
T_c &= 2 \cdot (10 + 12) + 10 \cdot 12 + 33 \cdot (137 + 453) \\
&\quad + 137 \cdot 453 + 6 \cdot (27 + 150) + 27 \cdot 150 \\
&= 44 + 120 + 19,470 + 62,061 + 1,062 \\
&\quad + 4,050 \\
&= 86,807
\end{aligned}
$$

To calculate tau_b the equation is

$$Tau_b = \frac{A - D}{\sqrt{A + D + T_c} \sqrt{A + D + T_r}}$$

$$= \frac{33,955 - 18,597}{\sqrt{33,955 + 18,597 + 86,807} \sqrt{33,955 + 18,597 + 80,801}}$$

$$= \frac{15,358}{373.3 \cdot 365.2}$$

$$= .113$$

For nonsquare tables tau_c, a symmetric ordinal measure, should be used. Tau_c is not a PRE measure. The equation for tau_c is:

$$Tau_c = \frac{2(\min(\text{row, column}))(A - D)}{N^2(\min(\text{row} - 1, \text{column} - 1))}$$

Similar to Cramer's V, "min(row, column)" is replaced with the number of rows or the number of columns, whichever is lower. For the sake of simplicity, we will calculate tau_c for Table 13.31:

$$Tau_c = \frac{2 \cdot 3 \cdot (33,955 - 18,597)}{830^2 \cdot (3 - 1)}$$

$$= \frac{6 \cdot 15,358}{1,377,800}$$

$$= .067$$

CHAPTER 14

Regression Analysis and Correlation

In this chapter you will learn

1. How to interpret a linear regression equation with one or more independent variables.
2. About tests to determine how well a linear regression model fits a dataset.
3. Common mistakes in interpreting a linear regression equation.
4. How to interpret logistic regression statistics.
5. Use of regression to analyze time-series data.

Once administrators go beyond studying a single variable, their interest lies in studying the relationships among variables. Examining bivariate relationships is typically only a first step in studying complex relationships. With a little practice, administrators can easily interpret contingency tables. Nevertheless, these tables quickly become cumbersome as more variables are added to the analysis. None of the contingency tables in our Chapter 13 examples had more than three variables, and the control variables only had two values. Try to visualize what the tables would look like if you wanted to control for several variables at the same time or if you were studying a control variable that had eight or nine values. Interpretation becomes elusive. Furthermore, contingency tables may not be the best way to analyze interval-level data.

Administrators who study multivariate relationships desire simplicity while maintaining statistical accuracy. Statistics for interval-level data offer an attractive alternative to contingency-table analysis. The major advantage of these statistics is their ability to make full use of the information contained in interval variables and to come up with more precise descriptions of the relationships in a model. These statistics greatly facilitate complex analysis and allow research findings to be reported in relatively direct, easily understood formats.

Furthermore, statistics to measure associations among interval variables are versatile. They can be used to

summarize or describe the distribution of interval variables.

infer population characteristics from a sample.

argue, by statistically manipulating variables, that variables are causally linked.

forecast outcomes.

In this chapter we limit our presentation of interval statistics to linear regression and correlation. Both are widely used. Furthermore, they are fundamental to understanding analogous statistical models and more sophisticated linear models that have been developed to analyze complex relationships.

An administrator can use and interpret regression findings profitably and appropriately with an understanding of a few basic principles. The chapter endnotes present equations for deriving the basic regression statistics. The references and our recommendations for further reading direct you to some excellent texts appropriate for the administrative analyst.

ANALYZING TWO-INTERVAL VARIABLES

Although administrators and analysts typically want to learn about the relationships among several interval variables, we will begin with the two-variable model. The principles of bivariate regression analysis and correlation apply to multiple regression models, that is, models containing more than one independent variable. The major benefit of starting with a two-variable example is that we can illustrate the logic of linear regression with graphs. We cannot produce similar graphs for more than two variables. Similarly, some of the statistics are easier to explain and understand in the two-variable case.

To examine the relationship between two-interval variables, an analyst produces a *regression equation* and a *correlation coefficient*. The regression equation describes the relationship between two-interval variables. The correlation coefficient, a measure of association, indicates the amount of variation in the dependent variable associated with the independent variable.

The Regression Equation

The regression equation is the equation for the straight line that best describes a set of data points. The equation is asymmetric; therefore, the independent and dependent variables must be designated before calculating the equation. Deriving a regression equation involves four steps:

1. Obtaining data on two-interval variables
2. Plotting the data on a graph:
   a. The dependent variable, Y, is graphed on the vertical axis
   b. The independent variable, X, is graphed on the horizontal axis

3. Determining whether the relationship between the two variables represented by the plotted data can be appropriately summarized by a straight line
4. Calculating the regression equation

To see how these steps are carried out, let's consider a simple study, reported in Table 14.1, to learn how cumulative car mileage is related to annual repair costs. We randomly selected 10 cars from a motor pool and we collected data on each car's mileage on the first of January and its repair costs over the following 12 months.

Next, we plotted the data on the graph. The dependent variable, the Y of the regression equation, was placed on the vertical axis. The independent variable, the X of the regression equation, was placed along the horizontal axis. The graph of plotted points is called a *scatterplot* (Figure 14.1). Examining the scatterplot is necessary so that the analyst can decide if he should use a linear model to summarize the relationship between the two variables. A linear model assumes that the relationship between the variables can be appropriately described by a straight line.

The two scatterplots in Figures 14.2 and 14.3 illustrate cases where a straight line or linear model is inappropriate. Figure 14.2 shows no discernible pattern; the relationship between the two variables appears random. Figure 14.3 illustrates a nonlinear pattern. Use of linear regression to analyze the scatterplots in Figures 14.2 and 14.3 is a mistake because the analyst forces a linear model onto nonlinear data.

If a linear model is deemed appropriate, then the regression equation is calculated. (See the appendix to this chapter for equations and calculations.) In practice, analysts rely on computer programs or calculators to carry out the actual calculations.

TABLE 14.1	DATA ON CAR MILEAGE AND REPAIR COSTS	
	Total Miles on Odometer (X) January 1	Repair Costs (Y) from January–December
Car 1	80,000	1,200
Car 2	29,000	150
Car 3	42,000	600
Car 4	53,000	650
Car 5	73,000	1,000
Car 6	80,000	1,500
Car 7	60,000	600
Car 8	13,000	200
Car 9	14,500	0
Car 10	45,000	325

The regression equation has the general format

$$Y = a + bX$$

where:

a = the constant or Y intercept
b = the regression coefficient or slope
Y = predicted value of Y, the dependent variable
X = the independent variable

| FIGURE 14.1 | SCATTERPLOT OF CAR REPAIR COSTS AND MILES DRIVEN |

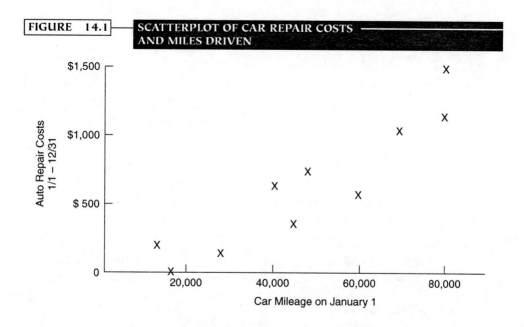

Car Mileage on January 1

| FIGURE 14.2 | SCATTERPLOT OF A RANDOM RELATIONSHIP |

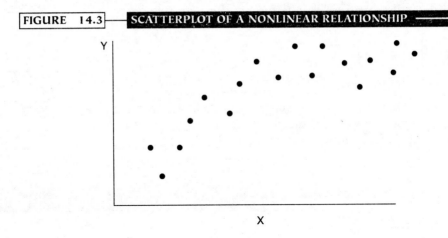

FIGURE 14.3 — SCATTERPLOT OF A NONLINEAR RELATIONSHIP

For our example the equation of the regression line is

$$Y = -267 + .018X$$

where:

   Y = repair costs from 1/1 through 12/31
   X = car mileage in thousands of miles on 1/1

From the *regression coefficient*, we learn how a unit change in X, miles driven, affects Y, repair costs. For example, for every 100 miles driven, we expect the next year's repair costs to increase by $1.80. We obtained the figure $1.80 by multiplying .018 by 100. For every 1,000 miles driven, we expect repair costs to increase by $18.

Figure 14.4 shows the relationship between the regression line and the plotted points.

On the graph you can locate the point with an X value of 60,000 and a Y value of 600. The 600 is the cost of auto repairs for a car in the dataset that has been driven 60,000 miles. The Y equal to 600 is referred to as an *actual value of Y*.

Now, recall your algebra. For a given value of X, you can substitute its value in the equation and calculate the value of Y. For a car driven 60,000 miles, you would perform the following calculation:

$$Y = -267 + .018 (60,000)$$
$$= 813$$

The 813 is the predicted value of the cost of a year's car repairs, Y, for a car that has been driven 60,000 miles. The *predicted value of Y* is the Y value on the regression line at the point where it intersects with X equal to 60,000.

The actual value of Y is often designated by Y_i, and the predicted value of Y by $\hat{Y}$. Specifically, Y_i means the actual value of Y when X equals X_i, and $\hat{Y}$ means

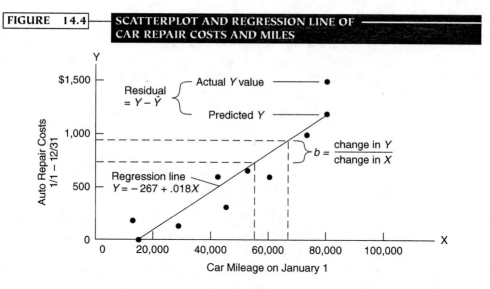

FIGURE 14.4 SCATTERPLOT AND REGRESSION LINE OF CAR REPAIR COSTS AND MILES

the predicted value of Y when X equals X_i. The difference between Y_i and $\hat{Y}$ is referred to as the *residual.* In the example, the residual is -213 ($600 - 813$). The "$-$" indicates that Y_i falls below the regression line; in other words, the regression equation overestimated the repair costs for the specific car. For any case you may calculate the residual with the equation

$$\text{Residual} = Y_i - \hat{Y}$$

A major use of the regression equation is to estimate population characteristics.[1] It is said to be the best estimator of the linear model because on the whole it yields the smallest residuals. If any other straight line were placed on the scatterplot, the sum of the squared residuals, the distance between the Y_is and $\hat{Y}$s would be larger.

Values of the dependent variable are estimated from the regression line. The predicted $\hat{Y}$ represents the expected value of Y for a specific value of X. Values can be predicted for values of X that do not appear in the dataset; however, predictions should not be made for values that are higher or lower than values of X in the dataset. To predict the repair costs for the entire motor pool, an investigator calculates the values of $\hat{Y}$ for each car in the pool and then adds all the $\hat{Y}$s together.

Tests of *goodness of fit* let an analyst decide how well the linear regression equation fits the data. A poor fit implies that the equation does a poor job of describing the data. One goodness of fit test is the visual evidence provided by a scatterplot. An analyst should routinely examine the scatterplot and satisfy himself that a linear model is reasonable.[2]

The Correlation Coefficient

A second test of goodness of fit is the correlation coefficient. The correlation coefficient is a measure of association for interval-level data. Common terms used to identify the correlation coefficient include *Pearson's r*, *r*, and the *zero order correlation coefficient*. We shall refer to it as "*r*." An *r* of 1.00 or −1.00 indicates that every point on the scatterplot falls on a straight line, the regression line. An *r* equal to 1.00 indicates a direct relationship; an *r* equal to −1.00 indicates an inverse relationship. Similar to other measures of association, *r* equal to 0.00 designates a null linear relationship similar to Figure 14.2. The closer the value of *r* is to 1 or −1, the stronger the relationship. (The equation for *r* and a worked-out example are given in the appendix to this chapter.)

A valuable and intuitively attractive interpretation of *r* is given by r^2, formally called the coefficient of determination. The r^2 value indicates the proportion of the variance in the dependent variable associated with or explained by the independent variable. In the example, *r* equaled .93. The r^2 equaled .87, indicating that 87 percent of the variation in annual car repair costs was explained by knowing a car's cumulative mileage. The only value of reporting the *r*, instead of r^2, is that *r* gives direction.

The question of what size *r* is sufficiently large to merit attention does not have a definite answer. Instead, the value of a particular finding depends on the nature of the subject. An acquaintance who is a geneticist considers an *r* less than .95 to be worthless. Few, if any, social science studies approach that level of association. Values of *r* between .40 and .60 seem quite strong. In some studies a modest *r* may be considerably larger than previous findings and therefore warrant attention. Nevertheless, remember that an *r* equal to .30 explains less than 10 percent of the variation in a dependent variable.

Other Factors in Interpreting a Linear Regression Equation

Four other factors affect the correct interpretation of a linear regression equation. They are the size of the regression coefficient, the standard error of the regression coefficient, the range of X values used to calculate the regression equation, and the time interval between the measurement of X and Y.

The size of the regression coefficient does not necessarily imply the strength of a relationship. The size of the regression coefficient is partially a function of the measurement scale. In the motor pool example, if the X value was measured in thousands of miles, the regression equation would be Y = −267 + 18X. Remember, when X represented actual miles, the equation was Y = −267 + 0.018X. Eighteen is 1,000 times larger than .018; however, the two equations describe the same relationship and yield the same $\hat{Y}$ and the same *r*.

Not only does the measurement scale affect the size of the regression coefficient, but it also may cause estimation errors. Users who ignore the specific measurement of a variable may substitute the wrong value for X in predicting Y. Students commonly puzzle over how to handle Xs that represent a percentage value. A percent should be treated as a whole number (10 percent, not 0.1). However, if the predicted values of Y do not make intuitive sense, you may investigate whether the calculations were based on proportions and not percents.

In Chapter 5 we used sample statistics to estimate population proportions and means. Similarly, we can estimate the relationship between two variables in a population. The *standard error of b (se_b)*, also called the *standard error of the slope,* estimates the variability of the regression coefficient from sample to sample. The se_b has two uses. Analysts use it to estimate the true value of the regression coefficient. Se_b also determines whether the relationship is statistically significant, that is, the probability that *b* in the population equals 0.00.

The specific values of both the constant and the regression coefficient normally vary from sample to sample. In the motor pool example, the se_b equaled .0025. At the 95 percent confidence level, an investigator estimates that the actual regression coefficient for the entire motor pool falls between .013 and .023. From the original equation, we stated that car repair costs would increase by $1.80 for every 100 miles driven. We can refine this statement. For the motor pool as a whole, we can estimate at the 95 percent confidence level that the repair costs range between $1.30 and $2.30 for every 100 miles driven. Recall that with a 95 percent confidence level we assume that 5 out of 100 samples will fall outside this range.

The se_b also is used to calculate the *t*-statistic and determine the statistical significance of the regression coefficient. The value of *t*, the *t*-ratio, equals the regression coefficient (*b*) divided by the se_b. One can use a *t*-table to determine the associated probability. The null hypothesis is that the actual regression coefficient is 0.00; that is, there is no relationship between car repair costs and the number of miles driven. In the motor pool example, the *t*-statistic equals 7.2 and the associated probability is less than .001. If the actual slope were 0.00, the probability of obtaining a slope as large as .018 would be quite small. A convenient rule of thumb to remember is that if the *t*-ratio is greater than 2, the regression coefficient is significant at the .05 level.[3]

The regression equation is computed for a specific dataset from the data in it. One should not estimate a value of Y for values of X that are well below the minimum or well above the maximum X values in the dataset.

To illustrate the danger of estimating the value of Y for an X value outside the range of values used to compute the regression equation, let us return to the motor pool example. Consider a car that had been driven 160,000 miles by January 1. The predicted repair bill for the following year would be $2,613. In fact, the actual car repair bill was far less, only $100. Such "junkers" tend to stay in use as long as the costs of repairs do not get out of hand. In our dataset the most miles a car had been driven was 80,000, which was half as much as the junker. Clearly, the dataset did not reflect the repair record of superannuated cars!

In a small dataset the regression equation and correlation coefficient may show substantial changes with the addition or deletion of a single case. One should be especially careful in drawing implications from a small dataset. For example, the addition of just one car can have a marked impact on a regression equation. If the car with 160,000 miles and repair costs of $100 had been included in the original dataset, the regression equation would have changed from Y = −267 + .018X to Y = 404 + .003X. The r^2 would drop from .87 to .06. Such marked changes are most likely if the one case has an extreme value.

Points well outside the range of the other data are called *outliers.* In addition to checking the scatterplot for random or nonlinear patterns, you also must look for outliers. An outlier will bias the statistics. The scatterplot in Figure 14.5 illustrates an outlier that may yield a regression equation and correlation coefficient that make the relationship appear stronger than it actually is.

Conversely, an outlier can draw the line away from the other points and make the relationship appear weaker than it actually is.

To handle outliers one may

1. limit the analysis to the appropriate values of X, and note that the model does not apply to other values of X.
2. consider if a nonlinear model would better describe the data.[4]
3. look for reasons why the particular case is different from other cases and decide how to handle the case. For example, if the data for the case were collected at a different time, one might seek data that were contemporaneous with the other cases. Alternatively, the case might be deleted from the analysis. If so, the decision and the reasoning behind it should be documented.[5]

Another consideration is the time relationship between the independent and dependent variable. In many studies time order may be of little concern, but sometimes it is important. *Lagging a variable* means that X is measured at a time preceding Y, and that the time interval between X and Y is sufficient for X to have affected Y. In our example, we assumed that the cumulative mileage on a car affected its next year's repair costs. X was measured on January 1, and Y, representing repairs over the following 12 months, was measured on December 31, one year later. Similarly, one may assume a change in tax rate will affect spending three months later or that habits in one's youth will affect an aspect of his or her old age. In the case of tax rate, Y may measure spending three months after the tax rate change. In the case of tracing the effect of youthful habits, an interval of 40 or more years may be created.

| FIGURE 14.5 | SCATTERPLOT OF A RELATIONSHIP WHERE AN OUTLIER STRENGTHENS A WEAK RELATIONSHIP |

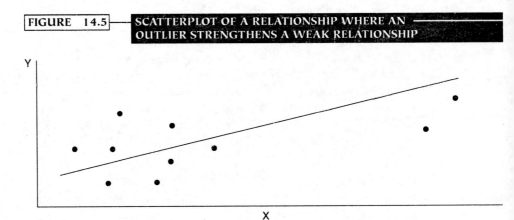

REGRESSION ANALYSIS: THE MULTIVARIATE CASE

The Multiple-Regression Equation

Multiple regression has many advantages when compared to contingency tables. The analyst can present several variables in one equation. Furthermore, the regression equation gives the independent effect of each variable while controlling for the other variables in the equation. A common format for the regression equation is:

$$Y = a + b_1X_1 + b_2X_2 + b_3X_3 + b_4X_4$$

A more elaborate equation, which helps illustrate the information provided by multiple regression, is:

$$Y = a + b_{y1 \cdot 234}\, X_1 + b_{y2 \cdot 134}\, X_2 + b_{y3 \cdot 124}\, X_3 + b_{y4 \cdot 123}\, X_4$$

where:

Y = dependent variable

a = constant

$b_{y1.234}$ = regression coefficient for X_1 associated with Y, while controlling for X_2, through X_4

X_1 = independent variable X_1

$b_{y2.134}$ = regression coefficient for X_2 associated with Y, while controlling for X_1, X_3, and X_4

X_2 = independent variable X_2

$b_{y3.124}$ = regression coefficient for X_3 associated with Y, while controlling for X_1, X_2, and X_4

X_3 = independent variable X_3

$b_{y4.123}$ = regression coefficient for X_4 associated with Y, while controlling for X_1 through X_3

X_4 = independent variable X_4

The equation is normally written without the string of subscripts under each b, but viewing the subscripts may help you to understand the information in the equation. Each b, a *partial regression coefficient,* indicates the effect of the independent variable on the dependent variable while controlling for all other variables in the equation. The dot in the equation with subscripts separates the two variables being related from the variables being controlled.

$$Y = a + b_1X_1 + b_2X_2 + b_3X_3 + \ldots + b_nX_n$$

We arbitrarily chose to include four independent variables in the equation. We could have included fewer or more variables. The basic equation remains the same. A given independent variable would be related to the dependent variable while controlling for the other independent variables.

The easiest way to explain the multiple-regression equation is to look at an example. A study published in 1986, despite its age, clearly illustrates aspects of multiple regression.[6] The author gathered data on selected employee characteristics from a sample of federal government personnel records to derive a regression equation to explain a person's grade level of entry into the federal career service. The regression results are given in Table 14.2.

To interpret the results, we first examine the variables. Several of the variables do not represent interval measures. Years of education, potential experience, and veteran's preference are the only variables measured at the interval level. The other variables represent dichotomies.

Dichotomous variables also are called *dummy variables.* A person either has the indicated characteristic or not. If the person has the characteristic, the variable is assigned value "1"; otherwise, the value "0" is assigned. In Table 14.2, major field of study was broken into a series of dummy variables, including business or management, law, and the social sciences. For each variable, a person was assigned the value 0 or 1. Although regression is intended for interval-level data, use of dichotomous independent variables in regression equations is a common and acceptable practice.

Potential experience represents the author's attempt to measure previous working experience of a newly hired federal employee. Potential experience was the difference between the person's age when he or she completed school and age upon starting federal employment. Veteran's preference is a bonus added to certain applicants' scores; some applicants may be entitled to a 5- or 10-point veteran's preference.

TABLE 14.2   REGRESSION EQUATION TO PREDICT ENTRY GRADE INTO U.S. CIVIL SERVICE ($n = 2,146$)

Variable	Regression Coefficient
White female	−.08
Minority female	−.29
Minority male	−.17
Years of education beyond high school	.50
Major field of study	
Biology, agriculture, or health profession	.97
Business or management	.82
Engineering, mathematics, or physical sciences	1.59
Law	4.37
Social sciences	.36
Other	.06
Potential experience	.17
Veteran's preference	.10
Constant	2.42
$R^2 = .69$	

SOURCE: G. B. Lewis, "Equal Employment Opportunity and the Early Career in Federal Employment," *Review of Public Personnel Administration,* Summer 1986, 1–18.

The equation shows that female or minority status has a slight negative effect on a person's entry grade. Education has a positive effect, and degrees in either law or the physical and mathematical sciences markedly boost a person's entry grade. The coefficients for minority and female status control for years of education, veteran's preference, and specific degrees.[7]

Example 14.1 shows how the equation can be used to find a predicted entry grade for specific cases. We use the word "predicted" advisedly. The predicted value represents the estimated mean Y value for persons with the given characteristics.

The regression equation predicts or estimates the average entry grade for people in the population, that is, persons with records in the sampled personnel files. The dataset used to calculate the equation did not include persons who applied for the federal civil service but either were never selected or turned down a federal position. Also excluded from the dataset were persons who never applied for the federal civil service. Furthermore, the dataset represented federal personnel policies during a specific time period. Over time, policies may change or demand for specific skills may change, consequently, estimates based on an old dataset may become less accurate. If you are familiar with current civil service entry-level grades, you may find that the estimate for your civil service grade level is too low. Grade inflation isn't confined to universities.

We expect that the example helps you to appreciate the value of multiple regression. With the equation you could identify the factors affecting entry grades for people in the civil service. The equation is easy for most people to work with, it generates useful data, and it requires little mathematical ability to understand or to estimate values of Y.

You may have wondered why we kept the information on women and minorities in the equation since they seemed to make so little difference in predicting entry grade. By far the most important reason for keeping these variables in the equation was the purpose of the study. The study was to see what, if any, patterns of discrimination occurred in entry-level employment. Including the sex and race variables meant that the researcher could document how sex or race affected placement after eliminating the effects of education, previous experience, academic discipline, and veteran's preference. If race and sex were eliminated a reader would not know if they had any impact. If the sex and race variables were deleted, the regression equation would be recalculated, since it no longer controls for sex or race. If sex and race were removed, the other regression coefficients should change only slightly since sex and race had a weak statistical association with entry-level grade.

Measure of Association for Multiple Regression

How good were the predictions from the equation? The $R^2 = .69$ means that the equation explains 69 percent of the variation in entry grade. R^2, formally called the *coefficient of multiple determination*, is a multivariate measure of association. R^2 indicates the degree of variation in the dependent variable explained by the model, that is, the independent variables included in the equation. By convention, r is used to indicate a bivariate relationship, while R indicates a multivariate

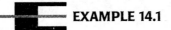 **EXAMPLE 14.1**

Predicting Individual Entry Level Grade from a Multiple Regression Equation

Case 1: What entry level grade would you predict for a white male, law school graduate, who has no veteran's preference, was 26 when he finished school, and is now 28?

Recall that potential experience is the difference between school-finishing age and entry-level age.

The predicted grade level can be calculated by substituting the data from Case 1 into the equation that can be derived from the data in Table 14.2. The equation may be fully written with the zero values or without them. Keeping the same order for the variables as given in Table 14.2, the equation is written:

Predicted Entry Grade = 2.42 − .08(0) − .29(0) − .17(0) + .50(7) + .97(0) + .82(0)
+ 1.59(0) + 4.37(1) + .36(0) + .06(0) + .17(2) + .1(0)

The 0 values may be deleted in calculating the equation. The equation would then look like this:

Predicted Entry Grade = 2.42 + .50(7) + 4.37(1) + .17(2) = 10.63

Case 2: What entry grade would you predict for an African American female with an M.S. degree in biology, who has no veteran's preference, was 24 when she finished school, and is now 25?

Predicted Entry Grade = 2.42 − .29(1) + .50(6) + .97(1) + .17(1) = 6.27

Case 3: What entry grade would you predict for yourself?

Discussion: This example shows how to use the equation to calculate predicted values for the dependent variable. You actually predicted the average value of Y for people with a given set of characteristics. When you tried to apply the equation to yourself, you may have wanted to know more about how the variables were operationally defined. For example, if you studied engineering in school, graduated 10 years ago, and are now studying administration in an evening program, you may want more details on how the researcher defined potential experience and major field of study. The sample consisted of employees who had entered the federal civil service shortly after leaving school. Thus you may fall outside the range of Xs included in calculating the equation.

one. Unlike *r*, which indicates direction, *R* can only be positive. Thus reporting *R* as opposed to R^2 gives the user no additional information.

With the addition of variables, R^2 may either stay the same or become larger. The addition of a variable will never make R^2 smaller. This observation implies that with enough variables one can explain a large portion of the variation in a dependent variable. Trivial relationships may add .03, .02, or even smaller amounts to R^2.

With experience you will find that few variables, often five or less, will explain much of the variation in the dataset. For example, in the civil service study, the author found that when years of education was the only independent variable, R^2 equaled .60. When the dummy variables measuring field of study were added, the R^2 increased to .68. The remaining variables brought the value of R^2 up to .69. In other words, potential experience, gender, race, and veteran's preference explained an additional 1 percent of the variation in a person's entry-level grade.[8]

A serious mistake is to have more independent variables than cases or a large number of independent variables to analyze a relatively small dataset. The model then explains virtually all the variation in the dataset, but it is worthless because the equation is literally custom-designed to fit the dataset.

To avoid being misled and misleading others, researchers may report the adjusted R^2. The adjusted R^2 equation "shrinks" the value of R^2 by "penalizing" for each additional independent variable, k (k = number of independent variables). The adjusted R^2 cannot be larger than R^2. It may be noticeably smaller if the model applies a relatively large number of independent variables to a small number of cases.[9]

$$\text{Adjusted } R^2 = 1 - (1 - R^2)(n - 1)/(n - k - 1)$$

You might wonder when to stop adding variables to a model. The best strategy is to follow the example of the researcher in the civil service study and include the variables that are theoretically important to the model.[10] As you may infer from the discussion above, simply seeking the highest value for R^2 is not recommended. Some investigators eliminate variables that are not statistically significant; however, with a large enough sample, even the smallest regression coefficients may be "statistically significant."

The Importance of Each Independent Variable: Beta Weights

Note that with the information in Table 14.2, you cannot rank the independent variables in order of their contribution in explaining the dependent variable. Remember that the regression coefficients are affected by how the independent variable is measured. Thus the .5 for years of education has a far greater impact on a person's entry grade than the .97 for a degree in a life science such as biology. Why? The independent variable, life science, has the value of either 0 or 1. The largest impact it could have is .97 (1 times .97). Years of education after high school could easily range between 0 and 10, that is, from only high school to a Ph.D, and the impact of education could range between 0 and 5. So, in the equation, a degree in biology raises a person's predicted entry grade by roughly one grade. Two years of school have the same effect, and a college degree would raise a person's predicted entry grade by two grades.

Beta weights, the standardized regression coefficients, allow one to rapidly and precisely compare the relative importance of each variable. Beta weights are calculated by normalizing the variables, that is, rescaling a variable so that its mean equals 0 and its standard deviation equals 1. In other words, all the variables are in the same standard units.

The larger the Beta weight, the stronger that variable's relationship to the dependent variable. Beta weights are usually calculated as part of the regression statistics produced by computer software. You need not understand how the variables are normalized to correctly rank the strength of the association between the dependent variable and the various independent variables.

Example 14.2 illustrates the use of a regression equation in a study of student admissions. The researcher studied students admitted to a graduate business

 EXAMPLE 14.2

Developing a Regression Equation to Quantify Admissions Criteria

Background: The analysts developed a 12-point scale to summarize personal qualities, such as previous work experience and evidence of undergraduate leadership. They calculated scale scores for admitted students and then computed a regression equation to see whether the scale would improve the quality of admissions decisions. Graduate school performance was the dependent variable. Two sets of equations were calculated. One equation examined performance throughout the graduate degree program; the other examined performance during the first semester.

The first-semester equation is reported in Table 14.3.

TABLE 14.3   REGRESSION MODEL TO PREDICT STUDENT GRADE POINT AVERAGE

	Unstandardized Regression Coefficient	(s.e.)	Beta Weight
Undergraduate average	.367	(.088)	.371
GMAT score	.00099	(.00045)	.188
Admissions scale	.036	(.016)	.188
Sex	−.019	(.080)	−.021
Years since college graduation	.014	(.012)	.104
Prior graduate work	−.055	(.054)	−.088
Constant	1.437	(.080)	
R^2	.188		

Note: GMAT = Graduate Management Admissions Test.

Discussion: To predict a student's first-semester grade point average, the equation with the unstandardized regression coefficient would be used. To determine which admissions factors are most closely associated with first-semester grades, the standardized regression coefficients, Beta weights, would be examined. Probably most striking is the importance of the Graduate Management Admissions Test (GMAT) score's tie with that of the admissions scale; the size of the unstandardized regression coefficient might lead one to conclude that GMATs had little to do with predicting a person's first-semester grades.

SOURCE: M. G. Sobol, "GPA, GMAT, and Scale: A Method for Quantification of Admissions Criteria," *Research in Higher Education* 20 (1984): 77–88.

program to determine whether adding a scale quantifying personal achievements would improve admissions decisions.

In the example you can observe the role of Beta weights and compare the information they give to the information given by the unstandardized regression coefficients. Note particularly the unstandardized regression coefficient for the GMAT score. The coefficient is so small that one might erroneously conclude that GMAT scores had no relationship to GPA. The coefficient of .00099 represents the impact of a 1-point increase in GMAT; at the time the data were collected, the GMAT had a minimum score of 200 and increased in 10-point increments.

Some studies report both pieces of information. Beta weights alone tend to appear in studies where the meaning of the regression coefficient cannot be clearly interpreted. For example, neither the analyst nor the user will have a clear image of what a unit increase in an ordinal variable, such as satisfaction with a policy, means.

The standard errors of b also were reported in the example. Recall the rule of thumb that if the t-ratio, b divided by se_b, is larger than 2, the relationship is statistically significant at the .05 level. Five times out of 100, a regression coefficient as large as the one obtained may occur if the value of the slope in the population is zero. The regression coefficients for undergraduate average, GMAT scores, and admissions scales were the only ones that had a t-ratio greater than 2; these also were the variables with the largest Beta weights.

To refine the scale further, the authors checked how R^2 improved as different variables were entered into the admissions criteria. The findings are shown in Table 14.4.

The Beta weights, the t-ratio, and the changes in R_2 with each additional variable all supported the researchers' conclusion that only undergraduate grade point average, GMAT scores, and the score on the admissions scales should be considered in predicting success in graduate school.

The regression equation shows that the score assigned on the basis of undergraduate grade point average, GMAT scores, and the admission's scale explains only 18 percent of the variation in first-semester grades. In other words, 82 percent of the variation in first-semester grades is associated with some other factor(s) not present in the model.

TABLE 14.4   RELATIONSHIP BETWEEN FIRST-SEMESTER GRADES AND ADMISSIONS CRITERIA

Regression Equations	R^2
Undergraduate average (UA)	.104
UA + GMAT	.148
UA + GMAT + admissions scale (AS)	.181
UA + GMAT + AS + Sex	.184
UA + GMAT + AS + Sex + Previous graduate study	.188

Note: GMAT = Graduate Management Admissions Test.

SOURCE: M. G. Sobol, "GPA, GMAT, and Scale: A Method for Quantification of Admissions Criteria," *Research in Higher Education* 20 (1984): 77–88.

Two tests of statistical significance, the t-ratio and the F-ratio, are commonly reported along with regression findings. The t-ratio tests the hypothesis that the regression coefficient does not equal 0.00. A researcher may report t-ratio (b/se_b), its associated probability, or se_b. If se_b is reported, the t-value can be computed by dividing the regression coefficient by its standard error.

The F-ratio tests the model, as represented by the equation, as a whole. The F-ratio is the ratio between explained and unexplained variance. It indicates the probability that the regression equation could have occurred by chance. (See Chapter 13 to review the F-ratio and use of the table of F-values.) The null hypothesis is $b_1 = b_2 = b_3 = \cdots = b_k = 0.00$; k equals the number of independent variables. The hypothesis is that at least one of the independent variables is not equal to 0. The equation for the F-ratio is

$$F = R^2(n - k - 1) \div (1 - R^2)(k)$$

where:

R^2 = coefficient of multiple determination

n = number of subjects

k = number of independent variables

When several models are tested, the Beta weights, R_2, and significance data are examined to decide which model best describes the data. Example 14.3 shows three models developed to identify factors associated with the frequency with which management reports are used. Note that the statistics reported for Equations 2 and 3 are similar. A researcher may decide that Equation 2 is the better model. Equation 2 explains the same amount of variation as Equation 3 but with less information; consequently, it is more efficient. Variable X_4, which is not included in Equation 2, is statistically significant, but it has the lowest level of significance and it has the weakest relationship with the dependent variable.

MULTICOLLINEARITY

Sometimes in postulating a regression model, independent variables that are highly related will be incorporated into the model. The problem of having highly correlated independent variables in a regression model is termed *multicollinearity*. When two independent variables are highly correlated, the regression equation cannot accurately estimate their independent effects on the dependent variable. A variable that actually is related to a dependent variable may appear to be unimportant. Multicollinearity can affect the decisions of policy makers. In his data analysis text, E. R. Tufte gives an example of trying to study the relationship of family income and air quality on health.[11] If the family income and neighborhood air quality of subjects are closely related, an analyst cannot determine how much the variation in health was associated with air quality and how much was due to

EXAMPLE 14.3

Statistical Significance and Multiple Regression

Situation: An investigator wants to identify management report characteristics associated with their actual use. He measured several variables:

Y = average frequency that a manager discussed report information with others

X_1 = report frequency (e.g., 1 = annual, 12 = monthly, 52 = weekly)

X_2 = medium (0 = distributed printed report, 1 = accessible by terminal display)

X_3 = technical quality of the report

X_4 = accessibility of report information

X_5 = perceived value of the report

Strategy: Evaluate alternative exploratory models using multiple regression analysis (see Table 14.5).

TABLE 14.5   BETA WEIGHTS FOR THREE MULTIPLE-REGRESSION EQUATIONS

	Beta Weights		
Independent Variables	Equation 1	Equation 2	Equation 3
X_1	.41[c]	.39[c]	.39[c]
X_2	−.30[c]	−.27[c]	−.28[c]
X_3		−.26	−.29
X_4			.11[a]
X_5		.31[c]	.27[b]
R^2	.10	.16	.16
F-Ratio	10.94[c]	9.02[c]	7.53[c]

[a] $p < .05$.
[b] $p < .01$.
[c] $p < .001$.

Discussion: The first model, Equation 1, includes just two independent variables, X_1 and X_2; the model explains 10 percent of the variation in the frequency of report usage. In the second model, Equation 2, two additional independent variables are added to the model, X_3 and X_5. The addition of the new variables changes the Beta values for X_1 and X_2 slightly. With the addition of the two variables, the model now explains 16 percent of the variation in the frequency of report usage.

The researcher found that Equation 2 was the best model. It produced the highest R^2 value. Equation 3 did not improve upon Equation 2. Equations 2 and 3 each explained 16 percent of the variation. Thus the addition of variable X_4 to Equation 3 did not add to the explanation already provided by the other variables.

Continued

EXAMPLE 14.3 *Continued*

The Beta weights indicate that report frequency is the most strongly related to frequency of use and that the perceived value of the report also is strongly related. The footnotes imply that a *t*-ratio was computed, and the researcher concluded that the relationships between frequency of use and report frequency, value, and medium were probably nonrandom (Beta not equal to zero). The lack of statistical significance suggests that the technical quality of the report may not be associated with the frequency of use.

The *F*-ratio corroborates the other information. There is a low probability that any of three equations happened by chance. The *F*-ratio and the *t*-test findings strongly imply that the regression coefficients for frequency of use, medium, and perceived quality were not equal to 0.00. All three equations are statistically significant at the .001 level.

SOURCE: E. B. Swanson, "Information Channel Distribution and Use," *Decision Sciences* 18 (1987): 131–145.

socioeconomic factors. Yet, an administrator will want this information to decide whether investing in improving air quality is necessary.

The analyst will be particularly concerned with identifying multicollinearity. Symptoms of multicollinearity can be identified, and an investigator should review the analysis to make sure that it is free of these symptoms. Two symptoms of multicollinearity are that (1) the multiple regression equation is statistically significant, but none of the *t*-ratios is statistically significant, and (2) the addition of an independent variable radically changes the values of the Beta weights or the regression coefficients. If you review Table 14.5 in Example 14.3, you may note that neither of these conditions exist. Although all three equations are statistically significant, none of the equations has nonsignificant Beta weights. Similarly, the addition of new independent variables did not markedly change the value of Beta weights in the equations. Researchers commonly examine the data matrix that contains the correlation coefficient (*r*) for each pair of independent variables. If any *r* is ≥.80, the researcher may suspect multicollinearity. Nevertheless, this strategy is not perfect; multicollinearity may occur with lower correlation coefficients, and it is not necessarily present when *r* is as large as .80.[12]

Multicollinearity is considered a problem of sampling; that is, the type of selected cases does not allow estimates of each variable's independent effects.[13] Including cases that represent areas with wealthier families and poor air quality will reduce the association between these variables and may help a researcher to estimate each variable's effects on health. With more cases the problem may disappear, but gathering more data is normally infeasible. Sometimes, the researcher can do no better than note the problem of multicollinearity and her inability to solve it.

Sometimes a researcher can modify the original model. She may decide two variables are measuring the same underlying concept and drop one of the variables.

She may combine the variables into a single measure.[14] If a researcher includes city budget and number of full-time municipal employees as independent variables, she may find that the personnel costs constitute a sizable portion of the city budget and that the two variables are highly correlated. She may argue that the two variables represent the financial investment in city services and drop one of the variables. She may create a new variable, number of full-time employees for each $100,000 in the city budget.

Multicollinearity is not a problem if the purpose of the regression analysis is to forecast. When forecasting, the user is concerned with the accuracy of the prediction and not necessarily the accuracy of a specific regression coefficient. The accuracy of forecasting depends on past conditions interacting in the future the same way they did at the time the data were gathered.

REGRESSION AND NON-INTERVAL VARIABLES

One of the assumptions of regression is that the variables are measured at the interval level. In reading social science journals, you will often see ordinal variables in regression equations. If the values of an ordinal variable form a uniform scale, the assumption may be relaxed. There are different rules of thumb. A classic psychometric text suggests an analyst can treat ordinal variables with 11 or more values as interval. This is not a hard and fast rule. Level of education measures that may have only seven categories seem to work reasonably well.[15] If an ordinal variable has few values, the analyst should examine contingency tables or scatterplots to see that important dynamics of the relationship are not being missed.

As we pointed out earlier, interpreting dichotomous variables as interval measures is acceptable. Dichotomous variables may be included as independent variables in a regression equation. If the dependent variable is dichotomous, linear regression should not be used. Rather, an analyst may choose logistic regression or another statistical model analogous to linear regression. Logistic regression provides the advantages of the computational and interpretational ease of regression analysis without violating its assumptions.

Logistic Regression: An Application

The details of *logistic regression* are beyond the scope of this text.[16] Nevertheless, a review of how to interpret the *logistic regression coefficients* and a strategy for determining the goodness of fit of the model may be valuable. The review should enable you to identify situations where logistic regression could yield valuable information and to understand logistic regression findings.

As an example we will use data from a pretrial release program.[17] Pretrial release involves releasing a defendant from jail until his or her trial is held. Program staff wanted to learn if their criteria for recommending pretrial release were effective. To make their recommendation, the staff weighed 24 factors including age, sex, marital status, employment history, nature of current charges, previous convictions, treatment for substance abuse, and ability to verify the defendant's information.

They considered their program successful if released defendants appeared at scheduled hearings.

The dependent variable was "appeared in court" (1 = defendant appeared in court, and 0 = defendant did not appear in court). Table 14.6 reports the logistic regression coefficients.

To determine the probability (prob) of an event, the following equation is used:

$$\text{Prob (event occuring)} = 1/(1 + e^{-Z})$$

where $Z = \text{Constant} + b_1X_1 \ldots + b_iX_i$

e is the natural logarithm, a constant equal to approximately 2.71828.

Specifically, the equation predicts the probability that the event or outcome scored with a 1 will occur. To find the probability of the event not occurring, the probability of the event occurring is subtracted from 1, that is:

$$\text{Prob (event not occuring)} = 1 - \text{Prob (event occuring)}$$

Let's apply the equation derived from the results in Table 14.6 to two individuals. First, we apply the equation to an individual who appears to be a poor risk for pretrial release. She is charged with driving while impaired, is being treated for substance abuse, has a prior conviction for a violent misdemeanor, has no current employment, has another pending charge, and information on her residency cannot be verified.

$$
\begin{aligned}
Z &= -.318 + .853(0) - .624(1) - 1.125(1) + .908(1) + .008(0) - .843(1) \\
&= -.318 - .624 - 1.125 + .908 - .843 \\
&= -2.002
\end{aligned}
$$

$$
\begin{aligned}
\text{Prob (appearing in court)} &= 1/(1 + e^{-(-2.002)}) \\
&= 1/(1 + e^{2.002}) \\
&= 1/(1 + 7.404) \\
&= 1/8.404 \\
&= .119
\end{aligned}
$$

TABLE 14.6   EFFECT OF DEFENDANT CHARACTERISTICS ON PROBABILITY OF MAKING COURT APPEARANCES

Variable	Logistic Regression Coefficient
Verified information (1 = yes)	0.853
Charged with driving while intoxicated (1 = yes)	−0.624
Treatment for substance abuse (1 = yes)	−1.125
Prior conviction for violent misdemeanor (1 = yes)	0.908
Time employed (in months)	0.008
Other pending charges (1 = yes)	−0.843
Constant	−0.318

The probability that she will appear in court is less than 12 percent (.119 = 11.9%); she probably is not a good candidate for pretrial release.

Next, we apply the equation to an individual charged with something other than driving while intoxicated. He is not a substance abuser, has no previous arrests (thus no previous convictions nor pending charges), has worked for 24 months, and his residency and employment have been verified.

$$Z = -.318 + .853(1) - .624(0) - 1.125(0) + .908(0) + .008(24) - .843(0)$$
$$= -.318 + .853 + .192$$
$$= .727$$

$$\text{Prob (appearing in court)} = 1/(1 + e^{-.727})$$
$$= 1/(1 + .483)$$
$$= .674$$

The probability that he will appear in court is 67 percent. Clearly, he is a better candidate for pretrial release than our first example.

What about the other criteria the staff used? Their regression coefficients were not reported because they appeared to have a random (p > .10) relationship with whether or not a defendant appeared in court. The findings suggest that far fewer than 24 criteria were needed to select good candidates for pretrial release. Since verifying information has a large role in predicting success, the staff may continue collecting some information, such as residency, that does not appear in the final model. (The ability to verify information may actually measure a defendant's community ties, which are not directly captured by the other variables in the model.)

The next step is to evaluate how well the model works. Table 14.7 compares the outcomes predicted and the actual outcomes. How good was the model? Note that 50 percent of the defendants failed to appear in court and 50 percent appeared in court. A coin toss could have just as well predicted 50 percent of the outcomes correctly. The logistic regression model yielded empirical evidence that the decision criteria were better than tossing a coin. Nevertheless, the staff could expect to be wrong in 33 percent of the cases. The statistics confirmed that the staff was collecting data that were not helping them to predict correctly whether or not a defendant would appear in court. Based on the findings, the staff might identify and test other variables that may improve the accuracy of their predictions.

REGRESSION MODELS TO ANALYZE TIME-SERIES DATA

A researcher can use regression to analyze longitudinal data. Time-series data are particularly valuable for making forecasts. Administrators commonly forecast future demands to make hiring, scheduling, and purchasing decisions. Economic decisions depend on forecasts; governments forecast tax revenues, while businesses forecast demand for their products.

TABLE 14.7	MODEL'S ABILITY TO CORRECTLY PREDICT COURT APPEARANCES	
	Predicted	
Actual	**Appeared in Court**	**Failed to Appear**
Appeared in Court	84	46
Failed to Appear	39	91

Percent "Appeared in Court" Correctly Predicted

$$= \frac{84}{84 + 46} \cdot 100 = 65\%$$

Percent "Failed to Appear in Court" Correctly Predicted

$$= \frac{91}{39 + 91} \cdot 100 = 70\%$$

Percent of Cases Correctly Predicted

$$= \frac{84 + 91}{260} \cdot 100 = 67\%$$

The linear regression model is appropriate for forecasting if over time the variable's values can be reasonably described by a straight line. Nevertheless, predictions based on linear regression may be inaccurate. First, the basic *linear regression model* fails to react to changes in direction or in the rate of change. Second, short-term estimates, such as estimates of demand for tax forms in any given month, may be highly inaccurate if a model ignores seasonal and cyclical data.

Example 14.4 presents a model to illustrate this use of the linear regression; the model was built to forecast the size of the local government workforce in the United States. Our example is rather elementary. It involves few years and ignores seasonal and cyclical fluctuations.

Before analyzing time-series data to determine the relationships among variables measured over time, a researcher needs to determine if autocorrelation is present. *Autocorrelation* refers to a nonrandom relationship among a variable's values at different time periods. A monograph on time series uses the variable "U.S. defense budget" to illustrate autocorrelation. The author posits two scenarios. In one scenario, the defense budget follows a consistent pattern of feast or famine. If the budget is quite large at Time 1, one may expect a decrease at Time 2. At Time 3 the defense budget again increases to offset the period of relative deprivation. In another scenario, if the defense budget is quite high, the forces in favor of keeping the spending high may thwart efforts to decrease spending; conversely, if spending is low, those favoring less defense spending may be able to successfully forestall efforts to increase spending. Either scenario is symptomatic of autocorrelation; that is, the defense spending at one time is associated with defense spending at a later time.[18]

EXAMPLE 14.4

Forecasting the Value of a Variable with Linear Regression

Situation: A policy analyst wants to estimate the size of the local government workforce in the United States two years from now.

Strategy: He examines employment data for the previous nine years.

Number of Local Government Employees in 1,000s (Y)	Year
2,357	1
2,423	2
2,434	3
2,467	4
2,494	5
2,541	6
2,570	7
2,569	8
2,642	9

Scatterplot:

FIGURE 14.6	**NUMBER OF LOCAL GOVERNMENT EMPLOYEES (IN 1000s) BY YEAR**

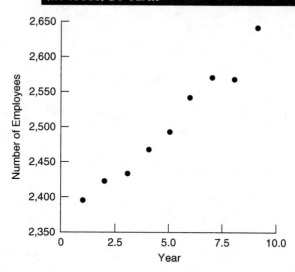

Regression model:

$$Y = 2{,}357 + 29 \text{ (Year)}$$

To estimate the size of the local government workforce in two years, that is, Year 11:

$$Y = 2{,}357 + 29(11) = 2{,}676 \text{ or } 2{,}676{,}000 \text{ employees}$$

SOURCE: U.S. Bureau of the Census, *City Employment, 1990,* Series GE-90–2. (Washington, DC: U.S. Government Printing Office), vi.

Autocorrelation violates an assumption of the regression model that the residuals are independent of one another. If autocorrelation is present, the model will produce biased t-ratios, confidence limits, and tests of statistical significance.[19] To check for autocorrelation, researchers begin by plotting the residuals.[20] If autocorrelation is present, the plot of residuals will have a distinctive pattern. For example, if the first scenario accurately describes the pattern of defense spending, every other residual will lie beneath the regression line. If the second scenario accurately describes the pattern of defense spending, the size of the residuals may increase for awhile, then decrease for a time, and then begin to increase again.

Autocorrelation may be eliminated if the researcher can identify and include an independent variable that explains some of the unexplained variance. One author notes that an apparently strong relationship between the number of suicides and the number of persons unemployed between 1900 and 1970 may have been due to population growth during the time period. If population size were included as a variable, the problem of autocorrelation might disappear.[21] If autocorrelation cannot be eliminated, a researcher should use a statistical model other than the ordinary least squares (OLS) regression model, the model described in this chapter.[22] Analyzing time-series data presents other challenges. One rule of thumb suggests at least 30 cases for a stable regression model. Working with 30 years' worth of data may introduce other problems. A complete set of data may not be available, or the operational definitions or the measurement intervals may have changed. To add cases, an analyst may divide the data into months or quarters, but this strategy may introduce seasonal variations. The OLS model is inappropriate if seasonal variations or autocorrelation occur. Statistical methods exist that take into account autocorrelation and seasonal variations. An investigator with time and patience can work through practical examples, such as those found in L. J. McCain and R. M. McCleary's text, and develop the skills and understanding necessary to analyze time-series data.[23] In addition, in working with social data, one may question how consistent the relationship between two or more variables is over a long time period.[24]

REGRESSION AND CAUSALITY

Many topics of interest to administrators and policy analysts cannot be studied experimentally. Multiple regression techniques, e.g., path analysis and structural equation modeling, have been employed to produce statistical evidence of causality.[25] A major value of these techniques is in their ability to eliminate alternative hypotheses by statistically controlling for possible causal variables. The quality of the theoretical model affects the accuracy of the statistical model. For example, control variables, which can demonstrate the spuriousness of the model, may not have been included; thus a causal relationship may be erroneously assumed. Control variables, which interact with other variables, may have been left out, affecting the accuracy of the estimated relationships.

In general, administrators are well advised to remember the shibboleth "Correlation does not equal causality." An assumption of causality seems defensible only after extensive model building, testing, and refinement.[26] Alternative models should have been tested and refined. Control variables believed to have an impact on the other variables should have been identified and tested. Nonlinear relationships should have been identified and the linear model modified. The surviving model should have been theoretically and statistically challenged. A thoroughly tested statistical model can improve the efficiency of experiments; it avoids wasting time and resources on poorly conceived models.

SUMMARY

Regression analysis is a statistical technique that efficiently describes complex relationships. A regression equation allows the user to describe a dataset, to estimate population parameters, to infer causality, and to forecast.

The linear regression equation for the two-variable case is the equation for the straight line that is the best linear description of a dataset. An estimated value of the dependent variable for specific values of the independent variables can be calculated from the equation. The regression coefficients estimate the amount of impact of the independent variable.

To assess the adequacy of the linear-equation model, the analyst should examine the scatterplot to make sure that the relationship is reasonably well described by a straight line. Furthermore, the analyst should look for outliers that may bias the statistics.

The correlation coefficient, r, measures the strength and direction of the association between variables. The r^2 value represents the percentage of variation in the dependent variable that is explained by the independent variable.

Multiple regression extends the two-variable regression model. Partial regression coefficients estimate the impact of an independent variable while controlling for the other independent variables in the equation. Beta weights, the standardized regression coefficients, indicate the relative strength of the association between each independent variable and the dependent variable. The user who assumes that the size of the unstandardized regression coefficient indicates an independent variable's importance in the model may be seriously misled.

The R^2, similar to r^2, reports the variation in the dependent variable that is explained by the variables included in the model. The R^2 may increase slightly with the addition of even trivial variables. Consequently, the analyst should be skeptical of the models with large values of R^2 and many variables. To determine what variables to include in a model, the analyst should first consider the purpose of the model and each variable. Secondly, the analysis should examine the statistical evidence supporting each variable's relationship to the dependent variable. The analyst also needs to check for multicollinearity, that is, when two variables vary together. If unresolved, the effects of the related variables will not be correctly estimated. Whether a particular value of r^2 or R^2 merits attention depends on the nature of the study. Physical science researchers generally expect far higher values for these statistics than do social scientists. The differences reflect the disciplines' research questions and models. High R^2 values may occur if a dataset contains more variables than cases; the model is essentially hand-tailored. When examining a regression model, one should not assume that a low R^2 value is offset by statistical significance. If the model is based on a large sample, a nonrandom relationship may be very weak.

Although regression techniques have been used in forecasting and to infer causality, the administrator should be skeptical of such inferences. In forecasting, the length of the series, changes in the longer-term trends, and other fluctuations in the series may distort the estimate. A model that suggests a causal relationship based on time-series data may not be credible if the investigators did not test for autocorrelation and make appropriate adjustments.

Regression statistics assume that the variables are measured at the interval level. If ordinal variables can be assumed to form a uniform scale, the assumption is relaxed. Regression appears to work reasonably well if an ordinal variable has at least 11 values. Dichotomous independent variables may be used in multiple regression. Regression should not be used to analyze dichotomous dependent variables; rather, logistic regression may be used. Logistic regression predicts the probability that an event will occur and indicates the statistical model's ability to correctly categorize the values of the dependent variable.

At this point we have surveyed the major approaches that administrators use to examine and analyze data. Chapter 15 discusses the last stage of the research process—how to report the findings. In addition, the chapter considers two serious issues—ethical considerations in reporting findings and requirements for keeping research records.

NOTES

1. For a further discussion on using regression to estimate parameters, see L. L. Giventer, *Statistical Analysis for Public Administration* (Belmont, CA: Wadsworth, 1996), Chap. 13, which is organized around estimation. The Giventer chapter and K. J. Meier, J. L. Brudney, and J. Bohte, *Applied Statistics for Public and Nonprofit Administration*, 4th ed. (Belmont, CA, 2006), Chap. 18, cover the standard error of the estimate (used to calculate confidence limits around Y for a specific value of X), which we do not include in this chapter.

2. In addition to problems of randomness or a nonlinear relationship, the analyst should look for patterns suggesting that statistical assumptions have been violated. For a discussion on the statistical assumptions, illustrated with scatterplots, see Meier and Brudney, 324–332. Giventer has a similar discussion on pages 360–364. T. H. Poister, in *Public Program Analysis* (Baltimore: University Park Press, 1978), 523–525, has a clear discussion on how plots of the residuals can be evaluated to determine goodness of fit.

3. M. S. Lewis-Beck, *Applied Regression: An Introduction* (Newbury Park, CA: Sage University Paper, Quantitative Applications in the Social Sciences, no. 22, 1980), 32–33.

4. See Meier Brudney, and Bohte, 354–357, for illustrations of nonlinear scatterplots. A common strategy is to use logarithmic transformations. For a detailed discussion of logarithmic transformations, see E. R. Tufte, *Data Analysis for Politics and Policy* (Englewood Cliffs, NJ: Prentice-Hall, 1974), 108–131.

5. See Giventer, *Statistical Analysis*, 361, for an elaboration of this point.

6. G. B. Lewis, "Equal Employment Opportunity and the Early Career in Federal Employment," *Review of Public Personnel Administration* (Summer 1986): 1–18.

7. Ibid., 8. The regression coefficient for minority female status was statistically significant at the .01 level. In other words, if the actual coefficient was 0, there was a less than 1 percent chance of obtaining a regression coefficient as high as 2.29. The regression coefficients for white females and minority males were not significant at the .05 level.

8. Technically, the percentage of contribution of potential experience, gender, race, and veteran's preference depends on how the analyst built the model. If these had been entered before the education variables, the strength of their relationships might have been greater. This aspect of model-building strategies is beyond the

scope of this text, but you should recognize that the analyst makes decisions that determine the specific values in a multiple regression equation.

9. This equation for adjusted R^2 is from J. Cohen and P. Cohen, *Applied Multiple Regression/Correlation Analysis for the Behavioral Sciences*, 2d ed. (Hillsdale, NJ: Erlbaum 1983), 105–106.

10. This issue is discussed as specification error, that is, omitting an important variable or including an irrelevant variable. See C. H. Achen, *Interpreting and Using Regression* (Newbury Park, CA: Sage University Paper, Quantitative Applications in the Social Sciences, no. 29, 1982), 51–56, or W. D. Berry and S. Feldman, *Multiple Regression in Practice* (Newbury Park, CA: Sage University Paper, Quantitative Applications in the Social Sciences, no. 50, 1985), 18–26.

11. E. R. Tufte, *Data Analysis for Politics and Policy* (Englewood Cliffs, NJ: 1974), 150.

12. Berry and Feldman, *Multiple Regression*, 43. Two common symptoms are high intercorrelations between independent variables or very large standard errors of *b*. For further discussion on symptoms of multicollinearity and possible solutions, see Tufte, *Data Analysis*, 148–155, Lewis-Beck, *Applied Regression*, 58–63, and Berry and Feldman, *Multiple Regression*, 42–50.

13. Tufte, *Data Analysis*, 150.

14. If multicollinearity is suspected, the analyst may increase the size of the sample, combine the involved variables to form a single variable or keep only one of the variables, or consider an experimental design. For further discussion, see Tufte, *Data Analysis*, 148–155, and S. Welch and J. C. Comer, *Quantitative Methods in Public Administration* (Homewood, IL: The Dorsey Press, 1983), 215–216.

15. Jum C. Nunnally and Ira H. Bernstein, *Psychometric Theory*, 115–116. Observation about uniform scales is from Giventer, *Statistical Analysis*, 162.

16. The SPSS manual, *SPSS Advanced Statistics™ User's Guide* (Chicago: SPSS Inc., 1990), by Marija J. Norusiis, has an accessible explanation of logistic regression. D. W. Hosmer and S. Lemeshow's *Applied Logistic Regression* (New York: John Wiley, 1989) is recommended as an introduction to the method.

17. The example is based on T. Benton et al., "A Comparison of Differences between Successful and Unsucessful Participants in ReEntry's Pretrial Release Program" (Raleigh: Department of Political Science and Public Administration, North Carolina State University, Unpublished paper, 1986).

18. C. W. Ostrom, Jr., *Time Series Analysis: Regression Techniques*, 2d ed. (Newbury Park, CA: Sage University Paper, Quantitative Applications in the Social Sciences, no. 9, 1990), 11.

19. For discussions on detecting autocorrelation and its effects, see Ostrom, *Time Series Analysis*, 12–17, 25–35. S. Makridakis and S. G. Wheelwright, *Forecasting Methods for Management*, 5th ed. (New York: John Wiley, 1989), has a relatively clear discussion on autocorrelation, 126–130, 192–194.

20. Statistical tests, such as the Durbin-Watson, will test for autocorrelation.

21. M. M. Mark, "The Causal Analysis of Concomitances in Time Series." In *Quasi-Experimentation: Designs and Analysis Issues for Field Settings*, eds. T. D. Cook and D. T. Campbell (Boston: Houghton-Mifflin, 1979), 323.

22. For discussion of alternate models, see Mark, "The Causal Analysis," 321–339, or Ostrom, *Time Series Analysis*. The works of S. Makridakis and S. G. Wheelwright, Armstrong, and McCleary and Hays (cited in Recommended for Further Reading section) provide more detailed information.

23. L. J. McCain and R. M. McCleary, "The Statistical Analysis of the Simple Interrupted Time-Series Quasi-Experiment." In *Quasi-Experimentation: Designs and Analysis Issues for Field Settings*, eds. T. D. Cook and D. T. Campbell (Boston: Houghton-Mifflin, 1979), 292–293.

24. The 30 rule of thumb is from S. Makridakis and S. G. Wheelwright, *Forecasting Methods*, 208. For more elaboration on this discussion of the drawbacks of using linear regression, see Mark, "The Causal Analysis," 335–339.

25. See J. Cohen and P. Cohen, *Applied Multiple Regression*, Chap. 9; R. D. Cook and D. T. Campbell, *Quasi-Experimentation* (Boston: Houghton-Mifflin, 1979), Chap. 7.

26. This argument is effectively made by Tufte, *Data Analysis*, 146–147.

TERMS FOR REVIEW

regression equation	outliers	multicollinearity
correlation coefficient	lagging a variable	linear regression model
scatterplot	partial regression coefficient	logistic regression
residual	dummy variables	logistic regression coefficient
goodness of fit	coefficient of determination	autocorrelation
regression coefficient	Beta weights	

QUESTIONS FOR REVIEW

The following questions should indicate whether you have a basic competency in this chapter's material.

1. Data are gathered on 40 countries to study variations in birth rate. Consider an equation derived in the study:

$$Y = 32 - .0018X$$

$$r = -.78$$

$$se_b = .00024$$

where:

Y = birth rate per 1,000 population
X = per capita income

a. Identify the following:
   the independent and dependent variables
   the regression coefficient
   the constant
   the correlation coefficient
   the coefficient of determination
   the standard error of the slope (se_b)
   the linear regression equation

b. What percent variation in birth rate is associated with per capita income?

c. What is the direction of the relationship between per capita income and birth rate? What evidence supports your answer?

d. What goodness of fit information is provided? How should you interpret this information?

e. Calculate the t-ratio. What can you infer about the relationship between per capita income and a nation's birth rate?

f. A country has a per capita income of $2,000. Estimate its birth rate.

g. Per capita income in the dataset ranges from $400 per year to $12,000. Can you estimate the birth rate for a country with a per capita income of $20,000 per year? Justify your answer.

h. If per capita income is measured as "per capita income in thousands of dollars," the regression equation is Y = 32 − 1.8X. Is this a better model of the relationship? Justify your answer.

i. Should you examine the scatterplot for this data? Why or why not? What pattern would you need to decide that the linear regression model is appropriate? What would you do if you found a curvilinear pattern or no pattern at all?

j. Should you examine a scatterplot of residuals for this data? Why or why not? What would you hope to find?

2. The equation is recalculated to include information on the percentage of the population living on farms:

$$Y = 36 - .0018X_1 - .186X_2; R^2 = .67$$
$$ (.00023) \quad (.066)$$

where:

Y = birth rate per 1,000 population
X_1 = per capita income
X_2 = percentage of population living on farms
se_b reported in parentheses

a. Interpret the information provided by "−.0018" and "−.186" in the equation.

b. What does the se_b indicate about the relationships between birth rate and per capita income and percentage of the population living on farms?

c. What variation in birth rate is explained by the multiple regression model? Do you consider this high, low, or in between? Explain.

d. What is the direction of the relationships between birth rate and per capita income and percentage of the population living on farms? What evidence supports your answer?

e. Predict the birth rate for countries with the following characteristics:
   i. Per capita income of $10,100 and a farm population of 13%
   ii. Per capita income of $1,230 and a farm population of 35%
   iii. Per capita income of $4,100 and a farm population of 4%

f. What additional information would Beta weights provide that you do not currently have?

3. Use the equation below to predict values of Y for the following cases:
   a. a department with an average grade point of 2.5 and no placement assistance
   b. a department with an average grade point of 2.5 and formal placement assistance
   c. a department with an average grade point of 2.7 and no formal placement assistance

$$Y = 5 + 20X_1 + 10X_2; R = .5$$

where:

Y = percentage of department graduates placed within a month of graduation

X_1 = mean grade point average of department graduates

X_2 = formal placement assistance ($X_2 = 1$ if formal assistance; $X_2 = 0$ if no formal assistance)

   d. What variation in placement success is explained by the multiple regression model?

4. What is meant when we note that the linear regression line is asymmetric?

5. Why should you learn the range of values of X that are used to calculate the regression equation?

PROBLEMS FOR HOMEWORK AND DISCUSSION

1. The following two problems refer to the multiple regression equation given in Review Question 3.
   a. If the data had been collected last year, how would they affect the ability of the university to forecast placement outcomes for this year's graduates?
   b. The original model included X_3, average aptitude test scores, for example, Scholastic Aptitude Tests (SATs) and Graduate Record Exams (GREs). The variable was dropped because of a problem with multicollinearity. Explain what is meant by multicollinearity in this context. How could it have been detected?

2. Table 14.8 appeared in a study of the income of planners. Note that planners' income is the dependent variable.
   a. Compare how well the model explains the variation of income among male and female planners.

TABLE 14.8	PLANNERS' INCOME BETA COEFFICIENTS BY GENDER	
	Men	Women
Age	.02	.08
Education[b]	.25[a]	.30[a]
Marital (married = 1)	.05[a]	.01
Race (white = 1)	.01	.02
Agency size	.19[a]	.17[a]
Centralization	.04	−.03
Job turnover	−.14	−.10
No. planner roles	.03	−.01
Yrs. professional experience	.53[a]	.37[a]
R^2	.600	.426

[a]Significant at the .05 level.

[b]Education rescaled: (1) high school; (2) 1–2 years college; (3) 3 or more years college; (4) bachelor's degree; (5) 1 or more years graduate work; (6) master's degree; (7) 1 or more years graduate work after master's; (8) doctorate.

SOURCE: J. M. Mayo, Jr., "Job Attainment in Planning: Women Versus Men," *Work and Occupation* (May 1985): 152. (Copyright 1985 by Sage Publications, Inc. Reprinted with permission: Sage Publications, Inc.)

b. What factors have the greatest effect on the income of male planners? On female planners? What information did you use to reach this conclusion?

c. Does the evidence suggest that job turnovers were associated with higher incomes? Briefly explain how you reached this conclusion.

d. Does the evidence suggest planners' salaries were affected by racial considerations or marital status? Briefly explain how you reached this conclusion.

e. What does the evidence suggest about the value of taking on many different planner roles?

f. What is the difference between the starred (*) regression coefficients and the other coefficients?

3. To study factors associated with frequency of managers' use of report information, a researcher examined five linear models, reported in Table 14.9. The independent variables consisted of:

Frequency of report (annual = 1; monthly = 12; weekly = 52; daily = 260)

Medium (printed = 1; terminal screen = 0)

Technique (factor score representing objective information quality, for example, data reliability, precision, and timeliness)

Accessibility (factor score representing ability to obtain and interpret information)

Value (factor score representing value of information to specific user)

a. Based on the above information, which model best explains variations in managers' information use? Why did you choose this model?

b. Based on the above information, should an agency go to the extra expense of printing reports? Justify.

c. Based on the above information, should an agency concentrate on continually improving the quality of its information? Explain.

d. Which variable has the greatest association with the frequency of report use?

e. "Technique" has a Beta weight of $-.07$ in Equation 2 and a markedly higher value in Equations 3 through 5 ($-.17$, $-.26$, and $-.29$). Briefly explain.

4. The following model was used to study variations in water consumption (measured as total sales) in communities:

$$Y = 600 + .019X_1 - 15X_2 - .02X_3 - 6X_4 - 682D_1 - 736D_2 - 626D_3 - 356D_4 + 40D_6 + 244D_7 + 226D_8 + 2D_9 - 183D_{10} - 532D_{11} - 720D_{12}$$

where:

Y = total water sales
X_1 = community population
X_2 = average yearly rainfall (in inches)
X_3 = public relations costs
X_4 = real price/acre
$D_1–D_{12}$ = January–December

TABLE 14.9	STANDARDIZED (BETA) REGRESSION EQUATIONS				
	1	2	3	4	5
Independent Variables					
Frequency of report	.41	.42	.41	.39	.39
Medium	−.30	−.2	−.31	−.27	−.28
Technique		−.07	−.17	−.26	−.29
Accessibility			.19		.11
Value				.31	.27
R^2	.10	.10	.12	.16	.16

SOURCE: E. B. Swanson, "Information Channel Disposition and Use," *Decision Sciences* 18 (1987): 131–145.

Adapted from L. J. Mercer and W. D. Morgan, "Impact of a Water Conservation Campaign," *Evaluation Review* 4 (1980): 112.

a. What would be the predicted water consumption in January for a community of 50,000 with an annual rainfall of 10 inches, $1,000 in costs for public relations, and real price of $80/acre?

b. What is the effect on water consumption of every $100 spent on public relations?

c. What month is water consumption the highest? The lowest?

5. Table 14.10 reports data on verbal SAT scores and average daily attendance for 15 high schools.

The equation for the regression line is:

$$Y = -46 + 4.4X \quad r = .66$$

where:

Y = verbal SAT score
X = average daily attendance

Note: Percents were entered as whole numbers; for example, the value entered for X was "20" for a school with 20 percent daily attendance.

a. Create a scatterplot for the data in Table 14.10.

b. Plot the regression line.

c. Calculate the residuals for Adams, Day, and Lee.

d. Do the data indicate that students who attend school regularly do better on their verbal SATs than students who do not? Justify your answer.

e. Interpret the relationship between school attendance and SAT verbal scores.

6. Researchers created an accounting test to replace a standardized test. They wanted to validate the test and to establish that the test did not discriminate against minority or female job applicants. To validate the test, the researchers tested agency accountants and gathered data on two criteria:

Criterion 1 (C1): Behavioral scale demonstrating job knowledge

Criterion 2 (C2): Rating of overall job performance

Table 14.11 reports the correlation coefficients (r) between each test and validation criteria for various types of subjects. For instance, the .56 at the bottom of column 1 represents $r = .56$

TABLE 14.10	AVERAGE VERBAL SCHOLASTIC APTITUDE TEST (SAT) SCORES AND AVERAGE DAILY ATTENDANCE FOR COUNTY HIGH SCHOOL	
School	**Average Verbal SATs**	**Average Daily Attendance**
Adams	281	77%
Bell	312	75%
Clark	439	96%
Day	282	91%
Edwards	294	81%
French	316	83%
Grant	365	84%
Hill	294	80%
James	308	79%
Key	257	85%
Lee	308	76%
Mann	387	95%
Nash	287	71%
Parr	394	91%
Rhodes	319	88%

TABLE 14.11 CORRELATIONS BETWEEN PERFORMANCE ON TWO JOB TESTS AND TWO PERFORMANCE MEASURES BY SUBJECT CHARACTERISTICS

Test	Created Test		Standardized	
	C1	C2	C1	C2
All subjects	.44	.28	.12	− .18
Male subjects	.41	.20	− .03	− .14
Female subjects	.48	.56	.25	.11
Minorities	.37	.26	.18	− .21
Nonminorities	.56	.29	.20	− .10

SOURCE: G. A. Kesselman and F. E. Lopez, "The Impact of Job Analysis on Employment Test Validation for Minority and Nonminority Accounting Personnel," *Personnel Psychology* (1979): 99.

for the relationship between the score on the behavioral scale demonstrating job knowledge (C1, a dependent variable) and the score on the created test for all nonminority subjects.

a. What type of validation did the researchers conduct?

b. Which test does the data suggest the agency should use to hire accountants? Why? Do you see any weaknesses in this test that should be rectified? What are they?

c. Based on the data, would you recommend using both criteria to validate future tests? Justify your answer.

7. Tables 14.12 and 14.13 were reproduced from a General Accounting Office report, "Infant Formula in the WIC program." The study estimated the effects of various factors on the cost of infant formula in the federal Women, Infant and Children's (WIC) program.

a. Estimate the cost of infant formula in a program in the West that uses sole-source bidding, has an average WIC population of 5,000, serves approximately 60 percent of the eligible population, and does not have an infant formula manufacturing facility in the state.

b. What percent of the variance in the cost of infant formula is explained by the model?

c. Based on these data, would you recommend that a WIC program use sole-source competitive bidding or multisource? Justify your answer.

d. Do states that have an infant formula manufacturer in their state benefit? Justify your answer.

TABLE 14.12 DEFINITION OF VARIABLES USED IN REGRESSION ANALYSIS

Variable	Description
SOLE_BID	Equals 1 if WIC agency uses sole-source competitive bidding, 0 otherwise
MULTI_BID	Equals 1 if WIC agency uses multisource competitive bidding, 0 otherwise
WICPOP	Average monthly WIC infant population (June 1988 to May 1989) in thousands
MFGSTATE	Equals 1 if infant formula manufactured in the state, 0 otherwise
ELIG89	Proportion of the eligible population served by the WIC agency in fiscal year 1989
INDIAN	Equals 1 if the WIC agency represents an Indian tribe, 0 otherwise
MIDWEST	Equals 1 if the WIC agency is located in the Midwest, 0 otherwise
WEST	Equals 1 if the WIC agency is located in the West, 0 otherwise
SOUTH	Equals 1 if the WIC agency is located in the South, 0 otherwise
PRICE	Wholesale price minus rebate amount per 13-ounce can of formula as of June 1, 1989

TABLE 14.13	REGRESSION RESULTS		
Variable	Parameter Estimate (*B*)	Standard Error	*T*-stat
INTERCEPT	0.53	0.10	5.39
SOLE_BID	− 0.36	0.05	− 7.91
MULTI_BID	− 0.24	0.09	− 2.85
WICPOP	0.0002	0.00082	− 0.25
MFGSTATE	− 0.01	0.07	− 0.11
ELIG89	0.40	0.15	2.64
INDIAN	0.27	0.06	4.45
MIDWEST	− 0.04	0.06	− 0.66
WEST	0.03	0.06	0.58
SOUTH	0.01	0.06	0.12

Notes: Number of observations, 56.
Adjusted *R*-square, 0.824.
F-statistic, 29.67.
Probability of *F*-statistic, 0.0001.
WIC = Women, Infants and Children.

DISK WORK

1. Researchers continuously try to understand why people do or do not vote in elections. Using the ORB Research Methods dataset, examine the relationship between the dependent variable percent of the population voting and independent variables of your own choice representing education, poverty, unemployment, crime, and income. Use all interval data for this exercise.
   a. Write a hypothesis about the relationship between the dependent variable and each independent variable; remember to indicate an anticipated direction.
   b. Create a scatterplot for each relationship. Do the data fit a linear model? Explain why or why not.
   c. Use a statistical software program and obtain the following statistics for each relationship: constant, slope or regression coefficient, *r*, standard error of the slope.
      i. Write the regression equation for each relationship.
      ii. How well is each relationship described by the linear regression model? Cite evidence to support your observation.
   iii. For each relationship decide whether or not it supports the hypotheses you postulated in 1.a.
2. Using the same variables and data, use a statistical software program to test a multiple regression model that tests these relationships simultaneously.
   a. Obtain the overall R^2, the b (unstandardized regression coefficient), B (standardized regression coefficient), and standard error of b or value of *t* for each independent variable.
   b. Report your findings in a table similar to Table 14.3.
   c. Report your findings as an equation (for an example see problem 4 for homework and discussion).
   d. How much variation in political activity across counties, as measured by the percent of the population voting, is explained by the model?
   e. Would your model be better if unemployment was dropped from the model? Justify your answer.
3. Add the independent variable region to your model using dummy variables, one dummy for each region (remember to only use two dummies in the model, leaving the third

region as the benchmark). Report your findings in a table similar to Table 14.3.
  a. Which variables have the strongest relationship to percent of the population which voted? What criteria did you use to select these variables?
  b. Which variables have the weakest relationship to percent of the population which voted? What criteria did you use to select these variables?
4. Use the regression model in exercise 2 and report separate equations for each region. Compare the models for the three regions.
5. Use the variables in the ORB Research Methods dataset to create and test a multiple regression model of our own design.

  a. Write up a verbal model which includes four to five independent variables. Your write-up should suggest the value of studying the relationships, anticipate the direction of the relationships, and provide evidence supporting the hypothesized direction. (For this exercise the evidence may be modest and based on experience or "common wisdom.")
  b. Test your model and present your findings in a table or equation.
  c. Write a verbal summary of your findings. If your hypotheses were not supported suggest possible reasons for the lack of support.

RECOMMENDED FOR FURTHER READING

E. R. Tufte, *Data Analysis for Politics and Policy* (Englewood Cliffs, NJ: Prentice-Hall, 1974). This is a classic text with excellent examples and valuable observations about the interpretation of regression findings. Our discussion owes much to Tufte's presentation. He provides more detail and considers a variety of statistical models, such as logarithmic transformations.

For accessible explanations of regression statistics along with worked-out examples, see L. L. Giventer, *Statistical Analysis for Public Administration* (Belmont, CA: Wadsworth, 1996), Chaps. 12–14, and K. J. Meier, J. L. Brudney, and J. Bohte, *Applied Statistics for Public and Nonprofit Administration*, 6th ed. (Belmont, CA: Thomson*Wadsworth, 2006), Chaps. 18–19, 21, 23). Both texts include computer printouts. Meier, Brudney and Bohte also cover cubic and quadric transformations.

J. Cohen and P. Cohen's *Applied Multiple Regression/ Correlation Analysis for the Behavioral Sciences*, 2d ed. (Hillsdale, NJ: L. Erlbaum, 1983), is a comprehensive guide to multiple regression, including causal modeling. The Sage Series, Quantitative Applications in the Social Sciences, has several monographs on regression.

Information on forecasting and analyzing interrupted time-series designs can be found in Meier, Brudney, and Bohte, Chapters 20 and 22 C. W. Ostrom, Jr., *Time Series Analysis: Regression Techniques*, 2d ed. (Newbury Park, CA: Sage University Paper, Quantitative Applications in the Social Sciences, no. 9, 1990); R. McCleary and R. A. Hay, Jr., *Applied Time Series Analysis for the Social Sciences* (Beverly Hills: Sage, 1980) provide more sophisticated discussions of how to analyze time-series data.

G. David Garson's online stat book, *Topics in Multivariate Analysis* provides an accessible discussion of advanced regression models. See http://www2.chass.ncsu.edu/ garson/pa765/statnote.htm

Calculating Regression Statistics for Bivariate Relationships

This appendix reviews the equations for deriving a simple linear regression equation, the correlation coefficient (r), standard error of the estimate of the regression coefficient (se_b), and the t-ratio. (See Table 14.14.)

The calculations to obtain the regression equation involve two major steps. First, the value of the slope, or the regression coefficient, symbolized by b, is calculated. The equation to calculate the regression coefficient is:

$$b = \frac{\Sigma(X_i - \overline{X})(Y_i - \overline{Y})}{\Sigma(X_i - \overline{X})^2}$$

where:

X_i = the value of each X
$\overline{X}$ = the mean value of all the Xs
Y_i = the value of each Y
$\overline{Y}$ = the mean value of all the Ys

Second, the value of the Y intercept, or constant, symbolized by a, is calculated. The equation to calculate the intercept is:

$$a = \overline{Y} - b\overline{X}$$

Using the same figures, we can calculate the correlation coefficient r with the equation:

TABLE 14.14 CALCULATIONS FOR b, a, AND THE LINEAR REGRESSION EQUATION

Car	Miles (1000s) (X)	Repair Costs (Y)	$X_i - \overline{X}$	$Y_i - \overline{Y}$	$(X_i - \overline{X})(Y_i - \overline{Y})$	$(X_i - \overline{X})^2$	$(Y_i - \overline{Y})^2$
1	80	1,200	31.05	577.5	17,931.38	964.10	333,506.3
2	29	150	− 19.95	− 472.5	9,426.38	398.00	223,256.3
3	42	600	− 6.95	− 22.5	156.38	48.30	506.25
4	53	650	4.05	27.5	111.37	16.40	756.25
5	73	1,000	24.05	377.5	9,078.88	578.40	142,506.3
6	80	1,500	31.05	877.5	27,246.38	964.10	770,006.3
7	60	600	11.05	− 22.5	− 248.62	122.10	506.25
8	13	200	− 35.95	− 422.5	15,188.88	1,292.40	178,506.3
9	14.5	0	− 34.45	− 622.5	21,445.13	1,186.80	387,506.3
10	45	325	− 3.95	− 297.5	1,175.13	15.60	88,506.25
Sum	489.5	6,225			101,511.29	5,586.20	2,125,562.8
Mean	48.95	622.5					

$b = (101511.3)/5586.225 = 18.17$
$a = 622.5 - 18.17(48.95) = -266.92$
$Y = -267 - 18X$

$$r = \frac{\Sigma(X_i - \overline{X})(Y_i - \overline{Y})}{\sqrt{\Sigma(X_i - \overline{X})^2 \, \Sigma(Y_i - \overline{Y})^2}}$$

$$r = \frac{(101,511.3)}{\sqrt{(5,586.225)(2,125,563)}}$$

$$r = .93$$

To calculate the se_b, the equation is

$$\sqrt{\frac{\Sigma(Y_i - \overline{Y})^2/(n-2)}{\Sigma(X_i - \overline{X})^2}}$$

Table 14.15 uses the data from Table 14.10 to show the calculations for obtaining the value se_b for the car repair dataset.

$$se_b = \sqrt{(281,800/8)/5,586.225} = 6.31$$

The t-ratio $= b/se_b$; in our example, the t-ratio is $18/2.5 = 7.2$. A table of the t distribution shows that the associated probability for $t = 7.2$, $df = n - 2 = 8$, is less than .01. In other words, a t-ratio as great as 7.2 would occur less than 1 time out of 100 if the regression coefficient in the population were 0.

TABLE 14.15 DATA AND CALCULATIONS FOR SE_B

Car	Miles (1000s) (X)	Repair Costs (Y)	$\hat{Y}$	Residual	Residual²	$(X_i - \overline{X})^2$
1	80	1,200	1,173	27	729	964.1025
2	29	150	255	−105	11,025	398.0025
3	42	600	489	111	12,321	48.3025
4	53	650	687	−37	1,369	16.4025
5	73	1,000	1,047	−47	2,209	578.4025
6	80	1,500	1,173	327	106,929	964.1025
7	60	600	813	−213	45,369	122.1025
8	13	200	−33	233	54,289	1,292.403
9	14.5	0	−6	6	36	1,186.803
10	45	325	543	−218	47,524	15.6025
Mean	48.95	622.5				
Sum					281,800	5,586.225

CHAPTER 15

Communicating Findings and Completing the Project

In this chapter you will learn

1. The information to include when presenting research findings.
2. How to include tables and graphs in a presentation.
3. Elements of effective oral briefings and written reports.
4. Ethical considerations in reporting research findings.
5. Guidelines for storing data.

Most investigators find conducting quantitative research engaging and satisfying. From building the initial model through to the statistical analysis, they get caught up in the excitement of testing and refining their ideas. After they have received the last set of data and completed the analysis, the researchers prepare to report the findings. They report their findings in informal meetings, formal briefings, project reports, and academic papers. Their audiences rarely share the investigators' level of enthusiasm or interest in the research. If researchers want their efforts to influence policy decisions, they must tailor their presentations to engage audience interest.

This chapter examines the last stages of a research project. It focuses on the components of quantitative reports and how to present them. The chapter argues for clear, focused presentations tailored to the needs of a particular audience. The desire to be relevant and to enhance one's reputation can conflict with ethical practices. The last section of the chapter discusses ethical considerations in reporting research findings and in storing research data. Administrators should review the data storage section; failure to establish ownership of the data and determine where they will be kept and for how long wastes resources and prevents efforts to validate or refine findings. Administrators who lose track of information risk serious problems if promised confidentiality is compromised.

VARIATIONS IN AUDIENCES AND THEIR NEEDS

In presenting a report and its findings, investigators focus on the presentation's purpose and the characteristics of its intended audience. Whether preparing a briefing or writing a report, researchers have expectations of an audience. Even the modest expectation of interest in a study is hard to satisfy in an age when professionals are bombarded by requests for their time and attention. Researchers have to contend with the ability of administrators and policy makers to protect their time and to ignore information that they do not want. Beyond getting an audience's attention, investigators want listeners and readers to correctly identify important findings and implied actions.

Technical communications texts consider audience analysis as preparatory to drafting oral or written presentations. One text points out that academic paper writing gives students unrealistic expectations. The student writer can assume that instructors are knowledgeable, that they read each paper in its entirety, and that they try to understand unclear sections. "Real-world" readers may not understand the paper, they may not care about the topic, they may ignore unclear discussions, or they may browse through a few sections. "Real-world" listeners may let their minds wander, they may fall asleep, or they may slip out of the room. Of course, these behaviors may be witnessed in the classroom as well.

To counteract the freedom of audiences to ignore or misunderstand information, researchers identify their audiences and their audiences' characteristics and anticipated needs. The following five-step procedure for audience analysis seems well suited to administrative researchers.[1]

Step 1: Identify all possible audiences, including future audiences for a communication.

Step 2: Identify the uses of a communication and the route it will travel.

Step 3: Identify an audience's concerns and needs.

Step 4: Make communications clear and accessible.

Step 5: Identify arguments and approaches that will be effective with an audience.

Step 1 identifies probable audiences and suggests how they will use the information. Step 2 applies primarily to written communication. Once a report is written and released, its routing is uncertain. Administrators may give a report or handouts to their supervisors, staff, agency analysts, interest-group members, professional acquaintances, legislators, students, or the agency library. To satisfy diverse audiences, researchers need to write clear reports that fully document procedures and distinguish objective findings from opinions.

Step 3 is recommended so that researchers can learn if their perspective differs from that of an audience. To appreciate differences between themselves and their audiences, the researchers may wish to identify an audience's educational background and experience, knowledge of the subject, and expectations about the report presentation. Then the researchers should identify the same information about themselves.[2] This information will help them critique the clarity of a planned presentation and avoid making unwarranted assumptions about an audience's interests and values.

Step 4 recognizes the competition for an audience's attention. You may wonder if Steps 1 and 2 conflict with Step 4. Providing full information can diminish a presentation's clarity or accessibility. Researchers resolve the dilemma by putting important information first and placing lengthy complicated or technical details in footnotes or appendices.

Step 5 builds on the information developed with the preceding steps and requires the investigators to consider how to tailor their presentation so that they communicate effectively to an audience. As part of this step, they may look for models for organizing a presentation. To learn agency preferences for organizing and presenting information, researchers may attend oral briefings or ask agency contacts to identify especially effective reports. The researchers use this information to infer what features of reports or briefings generate audience interest and involvement. As you read professional reports, save ones that seem particularly well done. You also may want to save an example of a poor report to remind yourself of features to avoid. When you attend oral presentations, note what seems to work and what does not.

COMPONENTS OF THE QUANTITATIVE REPORT

A quantitative research report includes a summary of the report, a discussion of the study's background, a review of the literature, a description of the methodology, and the findings. Recommendations, references, and a bibliography are included as appropriate. We assume that readers are familiar with standard documentation requirements, so we will not discuss them in this section.

Example 15.1 reproduces a table of contents for a report on citizen attitudes toward a local police department. It is typical of quantitative reports. As is true of all reports, the specific sections and their content depend on the nature of the study. The study was designed to meet accreditation requirements. Its background section was brief and included as part of the discussion of purpose. The methodology was straightforward and could be communicated clearly in the body of the report. If the methodology is complex or a detailed discussion is needed, the investigators may place the technical details in an appendix. This study did not make recommendations to the police department; if it had, the recommendations would normally appear in the executive summary and at the end of the body of the report.

Executive Summaries and Abstracts

The *executive summary* highlights a report's content. The intended audience is the executive who has little time to read reports. Busy administrators and policy makers scan an executive summary to decide if and when to read the entire report

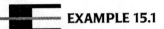

EXAMPLE 15.1

Sample Table of Contents for a Quantitative Report

Executive Summary   i
  Purpose of Study and Accreditation Requirements   1
  Sample Survey Design
      Survey instrument   1
      Sample design   2
      Instrument implementation   3
      Respondent characteristics   4
  Findings
      Overall agency performance   5
      Overall competence of employees   8
      Citizen perceptions of officer behavior and attitudes   9
      Concerns about safety and security within the city   10
      Concerns about safety and security within the neighborhood   13
      Citizen recommendations for improvement   14
  Summary and conclusions   17
  Appendix A: Survey instrument with frequencies   18
  Appendix B: Approval from human subjects' committee   25
  Appendix C: Selected indicators of citizen perceptions by district   26
  Tables
      Table 1: Respondent characteristics   4
      Table 2: Reason for and date of most recent policy contact by district   6
      Table 3: Rating of police department by district   8

Comments: The report does not have some sections that commonly appear in quantitative reports. Specifically, it does not include a background discussion, recommendations, bibliography, or methodological appendices. The purpose of the study was to conduct and report on a citizen survey to meet accreditation requirements. This tended to focus the study and enable investigators to skip some of the detail that is found in other papers. The actual paper had more than three tables, but we wanted to give you an idea of what information was included.

SOURCE: J. Barlow et al., "An Analysis of Survey of Citizens' Opinions of City Police" (Raleigh: North Carolina State University, Unpublished paper, 1992).

or to refer it to an associate. Administrators with a limited interest in the topic may skim a summary to keep themselves current. Policy actors may distribute summaries to communicate and endorse the report's findings. Investigators doing literature reviews can use the executive summary to infer if a report is appropriate to their needs.

The executive summary is the last part of the report to be written. It includes only information in the report, but it can be read and understood independently of the report. The researchers condense the report. They decide what they want a reader, who will spend just a few minutes learning about the study, to know. They may visualize the impatient administrator who asks: "What's the headline?" The researchers go through the report and find sentences that concisely describe why the study was done, who the subjects were, how the data were collected, limitations in the methodology or its implementation, and what the major findings were. An executive summary may include recommendations.

Example 15.2 reproduces the executive summary for the report on citizen attitudes toward the police department. The summary relies on clear, direct sentences and visual cues to allow an individual to read it quickly. Its length and

---

 EXAMPLE 15.2

An Executive Summary

Purpose: To meet accreditation standards, the police department must annually survey citizen attitudes and opinions. The department may combine survey findings with other information to aid departmental decision making. This report analyzes data gathered during the 1992 citizen survey.

Methodology: A telephone survey was conducted during October 1992 to gather opinion data from a sample of 898 city residents. The respondents were randomly selected from the city directory so that the same percentage of people came from each police beat.

Police department personnel took the lead in writing the survey questionnaire. The questions focused on how citizens felt about the department in the following areas: overall agency performance, competence of agency employees, officers' attitudes and behaviors toward citizens, concerns over safety and security.

Major findings:

In all districts among respondents who have contact with officers:

- More than 90 percent agree or strongly agree that police officers are competent.
- More than 80 percent agree or strongly agree that police officers have good attitudes.
- More than 85 percent agree or strongly agree that the overall performance of the officers present was good.
- City residents (91 percent) feel safe moving around the city, but 69 percent do not feel safe in downtown at night.
- Twenty-eight percent of respondents feel unsafe in the Southern District.
- Over 50 percent of Southern District respondents expressed safety and security concerns. The most frequently mentioned concerns were related to drug problems.
- The most frequently mentioned concern in the rest of the city was break-ins.

SOURCE: J. Barlow et al., "An Analysis of Survey of Citizens' Opinions of City Police" (Raleigh: North Carolina State University, Unpublished paper, 1992).

degree of detail are consistent with the length and complexity of the report, agency expectations, and the importance of the findings. In preparing an executive summary, the writer avoids compressing as many details as possible into the summary; otherwise, its benefits are defeated.

Journal articles have abstracts instead of executive summaries. Abstracts and executive summaries have a similar purpose and content. Abstracts are shorter, about 200 words, with highly condensed writing. They may liberally use technical jargon. In addition to prefacing articles, abstracts are reprinted in various compilations, such as *Sage Public Administration Abstracts.*

Background Information

Background information, which puts the study in context, may be included in the introduction as a separate background section or in a review of the literature. The report should include sufficient information for the audience to understand why the study was designed the way it was. The specific information needed depends on the report's audience and the study's purpose. A knowledgeable audience may need little background information.

Management and administrative research studies typically start with a problem or a question to be answered. The background information includes a definitive statement of the study's purpose and a history of the problem or the source of the question. If the study involves a program or policy, the report may discuss its origins, implementation history, goals, relevant constituents or stakeholders, resources, and processes. If a formal research proposal was written, the investigators may include its background material in the final report instead of writing a new version.

To develop the background information, investigators rely on interviews, documents, and the research literature. In applied research reports, information from the literature may be woven into the background presentation, assigned to an appendix, or abbreviated in an annotated bibliography. In academic research the literature review may appear as a separate section.

The *literature review* establishes the value of the research and how it fits in with other research. It brings the reader up-to-date on previous research that applies to the given study. In academic publications, the literature review demonstrates that the research (1) addresses a question not investigated in previous studies, (2) fills in a gap in previous research, (3) tests a model under different conditions, (4) corrects for errors in previous research, or (5) resolves conflicting research findings.

Three literature review formats are common. The review may discuss previous research in chronological order. This strategy works best if there is a discrete body of studies that build upon each other. Or the literature review may organize the discussion around key variables or concepts. An article on citizen satisfaction with the police organized its literature review around three sets of independent variables. The authors first discussed studies that linked demographic variables (age, race, gender, and education) to attitudes about the police. Then, they considered studies that investigated the effect of individual political variables, such as political efficacy. Finally, they wrote about studies that examined the effect of objective delivery of services.[3] An analogous approach organizes the discussion around theoretical or methodological approaches. Organizing the discussion around variables, theories, or methodologies works best if there are diverse studies examining the same dependent variable.

The third format may be visualized as a set of concentric circles. The discussion begins by identifying studies relating to the general research topic; this is the outermost circle. In each subsequent section, the researcher moves closer and closer to the literature that generated the specific research question. In a study on incentives and response rates to mail surveys, the author first identified literature that confirmed the widespread use of mail surveys. He next cited a source documenting problems with response rates. He worked his way through research on the effectiveness of incentives in increasing response rates, on comparisons between the effectiveness of monetary versus nonmonetary incentives, and whether incentives should be mailed with a survey or sent after the response is received. At this point the stage was set for his study on the combined effects of timing and type of incentive on response rate.[4] This format seems to work best for research that is narrowly focused and fills in a research gap or applies a model under different conditions.

The amount of space devoted to any particular article depends on its relevance to the given project. At a minimum a researcher cites an article, establishes its relevance, and summarizes its major finding. For articles that directly apply to the study, the researcher gives more details. These details allow a reader to compare and contrast the research findings with other research. Such details may include information on the model (what variables were included), the methodology (characteristics of the measures, sample, or research design), the method of analysis, and the findings.

Methodology Section

The methodology section describes a study's measures, sample, and research design. The amount of detail it contains varies widely depending on the audience. At a minimum it should have enough information so that audience members can decide if the findings are credible. The final project report should be comprehensive enough for others to verify the findings or replicate the research.

The measurement section implicitly or explicitly discusses the operational definitions, how numerical values were assigned and combined, how indices and scales were created, and evidence supporting the reliability and operational validity of the measures. Customarily, the only reliability evidence researchers report are the findings from mathematical tests of reliability.

The discussion of the sample identifies the target population, sampling frame, sampling design, response rate, and when and how the data were collected. There are different ways to compute the response rate. To avoid ambiguity, the investigator should report the sample size, how many members of the sample were contacted, how many of those contacted belonged to the target population, how many refused to provide data, and how many supplied incomplete data. Statistics comparing respondents and nonrespondents should be reported. Any other sources of nonsampling error should be mentioned. For example, if researchers suspect that their sampling frame was inadequate, they should explicitly note their suspicion.

Minimal discussion is needed to describe cross-sectional or time-series designs. For a cross-sectional design, the measurement and sampling discussions are usually enough. For a time-series design, the researcher notes the beginning and ending points of the time series and the frequency of intervals. Apparent sources of non-random fluctuations and problems with data comparability should be mentioned.

Laboratory or field experiments require more extensive discussion, distinct from the measurement and sampling sections. The narrative should imply or state how the design and its implementation controlled for various threats to internal validity. Researchers should describe the experimental environment so that subsequent investigators can determine what, if any, features of the research conditions constituted a threat to external validity. The final project report should contain enough detail so that another researcher could repeat the experiment.

An audience should remember that quantitative investigations are not flawless. A study's purpose and limited resources require researchers to settle for imperfect measures, samples, or research designs. Similarly, researchers should not hesitate to report the flaws and limitations in their methodology. They should be sure to note shortcomings that may lead audience members to misinterpret the findings.

The Findings

The findings section reports the research results. The authors include an explicit statement of what was found and the statistical or qualitative evidence to support it. This section may include interpretation of the findings and tentative explanations for unexpected findings. To communicate the findings effectively, researchers must (1) organize the findings into a coherent presentation, (2) focus on the important findings and avoid overwhelming the audience with unnecessary detail, and (3) decide on how to present the findings, including the use of tables or graphs.

Traditionally, a study's background, model, and methodology are presented before the research results. The audience is told what questions were asked, why they were asked, and how they were asked. This prepares the audience to listen to and remember the findings. The findings are organized around related themes, variables, or questions.

The logical structure of the presentation may help focus the audience's attention. For example, when we discussed how to present the literature review we cited a study of citizen satisfaction with the police. The authors discussed how each variable was measured using the same order presented in the review of the literature, e.g., (1) demographic variables, (2) political variables, and (3) objective indicators of police performance. They continued this strategy in presenting their findings; they first looked at the effects of the demographic variables, then the political variables, and finally the objective indicators.

Just as the executive summary acknowledges that administrators may only give a report a passing glance, a report presentation should facilitate a review by hurried and distracted audience members. Presented with an uninteresting analysis or an overwhelming amount of detail, audience members may stop listening or reading. Graphs and tables, which may complement the verbal presentation, underscore important points and exhibit data efficiently. The location and the amount of space devoted to words or graphics should signal the importance of the findings. Unimportant and trivial findings do not deserve major emphasis, and researchers should not waste space on graphics that illustrate unimportant points.

A detailed discussion of a large amount of data or many numbers is not very effective. An audience may find the presentation difficult to follow and not take advantage of the opportunity to question the findings and explore their implications. Attractive graphics and clear explanations allow readers to access the richness of the data. Tables show exact numerical values and work well when the data presentation requires many specific comparisons. Examples of conventional types of tables include data arrays (Table 14.1), summary tables of regression statistics (Table 14.2 through Table 14.5), and contingency tables. Graphs are conventional for presenting time-series data and scatterplots. Graphs permit an audience to pick out movements over time including long-term trends, cycles, and seasonal fluctuations; and differences before and after an intervention.

Careful labeling of tables and graphs is important. Spell words out, avoid abbreviations, and use clear variable names. Try to place labels on the graphic rather than in a legend. Words on and around graphics are effective in telling viewers how to focus attention on the various parts of the display.[5]

The following summarizes several points and offers additional advice on presenting data:

1. Tables or graphs should have a precise, descriptive title. A title may list the dependent variable by independent variable by control variable (if any). Alternatively, a title may summarize a major finding supported by the graphic, for example, "City homicide rates have dropped over the past twenty years."

2. A good table supplements, not duplicates, the text. Each table and its data should be referred to in the text, but only the highlights should be discussed.

3. All variables and reported values or categories should be clearly labeled, and appropriate units (e.g., years) should be indicated.

4. The independent variable should be listed along the column, or top, of the chart, and the dependent variable should be listed along the row.

5. If percents are used, a percent sign (%) should be entered at the top of the columns. Also, avoid unnecessary decimals—they are easily overlooked.

6. The number of cases on which the 100 percent is based should be indicated. The total number of cases used in analysis also should be indicated.

7. Statistical measures, if any, should be listed at the bottom of the table.

8. All terms open to interpretation should be defined in the footnote section below the chart.

9. The source of the data should be indicated in the footnote section.

Recommendations

Program evaluations, policy analyses, and other studies done for a legislative or administrative client may include recommendations. Analysts may be reluctant to make recommendations. Analysts are trained to accurately describe a program or policy and what it is accomplishing. Recommendations are normative statements about changes that should be made in the program or policy. An analyst may be ill-equipped or uncomfortable in making normative statements or telling clients what they should do.

Research clients on the other hand may expect recommendations. Investigators may find that making recommendations improves the probability that their studies will be used. Recommendations should be carefully formulated; they may be developed and evaluated throughout the course of a study. They should naturally follow from the research findings, e.g., a reader should be able to figure out why the recommendations were made. In making recommendations the researcher should address changes that the client agency can make, for example, recommending a change in federal program requirements will not be of any value to a local social service agency. In some cases the costs and benefits of adopting a recommendation may be identified and included. Alternatively, the researcher may suggest several options for agencies to consider.[6]

Oral Presentations of Research Findings

Researchers who do studies for administrators need oral presentation skills. Administrators, depending on their learning styles and time demands, may prefer to listen to an oral presentation and ask questions rather than read a report. They may find that an oral presentation alerts them to what to look for in the report or, conversely, the oral presentation gives them an opportunity to ask follow-up questions. Oral presentations also have distinct advantages for researchers. They can better anticipate their audience and tailor their presentation to meet its needs and interests. Audience members may feel compelled to pay attention; analogous pressure to concentrate on a written report is virtually nonexistent. The social interactions among audience members may increase understanding of the results and may motivate the group or individuals to discuss and follow up on the findings.

The training of researchers stresses careful attention to detail and a willingness to examine findings from various perspectives. These skills can translate into tedious, unfocused presentations. In contrast, good oral presenters avoid covering too much; they concentrate on a few important points. A presenter may fill in the details or elaborate on alternative interpretations only if an opportunity opens up in a conversation or during a question-and-answer session.

Researchers should not discount the importance of one-on-one informal discussions of findings. Their informality can be deceptive. They offer an important opportunity to develop an administrator's interest in a project. A researcher should think about what she expects from informal communication. Does she want to alert an administrator to a problem? Does she want his insights about an unexpected finding? Does she want him to think about the value of the study and how its findings can be implemented? Her ability to communicate information clearly and to understand why she wants to communicate it to a particular administrator may improve her effectiveness.

Whether you are speaking to one person, a small group, or a large, formal audience, your ability to explain your work clearly will serve you well. Professionals feel continually pressed for time. Many people are "oral learners." Others value the chance to debate information and discuss it with researchers and other administrators. As teachers we have observed that many talented students avoid making oral presentations. These students lose opportunities to present their ideas clearly, to understand listeners' questions, and to provide effective answers (as well as to hone an important skill). If you are still in school as you read this chapter, consider the value of getting practice and feedback on your speaking skills. For additional materials on oral communications, see a technical communications text.

An effective presentation requires planning and practice. To plan a presentation, researchers select the points they want to emphasize, the evidence they will use to support these points, the order in which material will be presented, and visual aids. The researchers should have determined what the audience knows about their topic, what the audience wants to get from the presentation, and how long members will listen attentively.

The traditional order for a research presentation (background, methodology, and findings) usually works well. It develops the material logically. People with training in the sciences, including the social and behavioral sciences, have come to expect it. If audience members are informed about the program or policy, identifying the study's purpose and summarizing the methodology may be sufficient. Otherwise, a description of the program or policy is necessary to put the information in context and to help audience members to follow the presentation. Except for specialized audiences, technical details are not presented in the discussion of methodology. Presenters should encourage audience members to ask for the details which interest them, especially those details that affect their willingness to accept the findings.

Visual aids may be used throughout a presentation. PowerPoint slides, tables or graphs focus the presenter and the audience. To select a visual aid, consider whether it distracts attention, slows down the presentation, requires special equipment, or communicates information effectively and clearly. Too many visuals can bore an audience. Technically sophisticated presentations can be fun to put together, but they are often distracting and draw attention away from the content of the presentation. Fumbling around with unfamiliar equipment creates a serious distraction. Poor lighting can also cause problems. Detailed images leave people in the back rows squinting or feeling left out; however, the problem can be solved if a handout contains the same information. One must also be prepared to work without planned visual aids. Equipment failures happen and you should make sure that they don't undermine a presentation.

Selecting a visual aid without thinking about the audience can result in ludicrous situations. Employees of an agency for the blind were astonished that professionals, including ophthalmologists, consistently supplemented their presentations to agency staff with slides. Most of the staff had severe visual impairments and derived no benefit from the slide shows.

Inexperienced presenters may overlook the importance of practice. A researcher who has pored over a study may feel confident in her ability to ad lib the report. Unfortunately, this person may end up bogging down on the study's minutiae or moving erratically from point to point. One should practice with an audience of colleagues, team members, or friends. Practice session observers should make sure that the major points are clearly presented, the reiteration of key points does not become repetitious or condescending, the transitions are smooth, and the equipment operates correctly. The presenter should ask the observers to ask questions about the methodology or the interpretation of the findings. Preparing answers to "hard" questions avoids the embarrassment of stumbling around. If questions challenging the quality of the research go unanswered, the effectiveness of the entire report may be undermined.

ETHICAL ISSUES

In the 1980s the issue of professional research ethics began to receive systematic attention. Respected scientists were charged with scientific misconduct, including plagiarism and making up data.[7] To see what could be done to maintain the integrity of scientific research, a joint study committee of the National Academy of Sciences, the National Academy of Engineering, and the Institute of Medicine was convened in 1989. The committee was drawn from the biological and physical sciences, and its report focuses on practices of these sciences. The social sciences and administrative researchers have not received a similar degree of scrutiny. They still operate on an honor system, which assumes that researchers behave properly. Social scientists are probably no more ethical than biological and physical scientists. The stiff competition for basic research monies and the potential financial windfalls associated with patents may make the latter professions more susceptible to misconduct and to having their misconduct discovered and disclosed.

Our discussion relies heavily on the committee's final report. The report categorized inappropriate scientific research behavior into three categories: research misconduct, questionable research practices, and other misconduct. Research misconduct consists of acts of fabrication, falsification, or plagiarism. Questionable practices concern data retention and sharing, record quality, authorship, supervision of research assistants, statistical analysis, and release of information. Other misconduct refers to acts that are unacceptable but not unique to researchers—for example, misuse of funds, vandalism, violations of government research regulations, and conflicts of interest.[8] Our discussion focuses on research misconduct, handling research errors, and record-keeping issues—issues that affect all researchers. For a more complete picture of the issues, a reader should consult the committee's report and background papers.[9]

Research Misconduct

The study committee defined *fabrication* as making up data or results, and *falsification* as changing data or results. We assume that every reader knows that fabrication is wrong and recognizes if he or she has made up data or findings. Falsification can be a bit more ambiguous.

An easy way to falsify results is to drop cases from a dataset. Dropping selected cases can rescue a weak statistical model. The researcher may rationalize his decision. For example, he may argue that the dropped cases were tainted by measurement error and therefore do not belong in the dataset. If he thinks that measurement error occurred, he should try to confirm the measurement error. If he does not have time to track down the source of error or he cannot confirm the error, he can remove the cases. If he removes cases, he must indicate in his reports what he did, why, and its effect on the results. The more marked the effect, the more diligent he must be in alerting an audience of his decision. A decision that markedly affects the finding should not get buried in the small print.

Plagiarism is falsely presenting another's ideas or words as one's own. Quoted material should be placed in quotation marks and references cited. Closely following another author's diction or paraphrasing his words is wrong. The writer should either use her own words and sentence structure or quote directly from her sources.

Relying on the works of others is inevitable in research. No one knows this better than a textbook writer. We have referenced sources that we relied on to write segments of this manuscript or that provided a unique or valuable perspective on the material. We have not referenced sources for ideas and perspectives that we know are part of the common knowledge of social science researchers.

Younger researchers seem to cite sources for their ideas more frequently than experienced researchers. This probably does not occur because of different ethical standards. Younger researchers more often work on cutting-edge topics, and they read more original research. In our experience younger researchers are more likely to listen to panels at professional meetings and to read a wider range of journals. The experienced researcher is more familiar with the subject area. He can better distinguish between unique contributions to his thinking and ideas from the general body of knowledge about the subject.

Sometimes newer researchers may feel overwhelmed by the need to avoid charges of falsification or plagiarism. This need not be the case. To avoid charges of falsifying, a researcher documents her decisions and her reasons for them. The documentation makes her decisions accessible for peer review.

Avoiding charges of plagiarism should not be difficult. Diligent referencing and avoiding using another's wording should be adequate. If a report is to be published, the writer needs to pay attention to copyright laws. Researchers must get permission from the copyright holder to reproduce graphs, tables, long quotes, and other materials, including song lyrics, poetry, and cartoons. Government documents are not covered by copyright, and their contents can be reproduced without obtaining permission. Nevertheless, the researcher should use standard referencing procedures to cite a government document.

Handling Research Errors

Error is inevitable in research. Errors arise from constraints that require investigators to compromise the quality of their efforts. Errors also arise from any one person's or group's point of view, type of knowledge, and degree of ability. The potential for error occurs throughout the research process. The study committee identified four potential sources of error: the accuracy and precision of measurements, the generalizability of experiments, the quality of the experimental design, and the interpretation of the practical significance of the findings.[10] Researchers must ascertain that data entry and analysis procedures were conducted correctly. Errors that appear to be innocuous, such as miscoding data, can seriously distort the findings. If research findings differ from what is expected, researchers pore over the data to discover what happened. They check the raw data and computer programs. Expected results rarely receive similar attention. Richard Feynman, a winner of the Nobel Prize for physics, reminded researchers that "the easiest person to fool is yourself." He suggests that researchers analyze the data to see if other typical relationships between variables exist. If possible, researchers should also analyze the data to test alternative explanations.[11] In publishing a final report, the researchers indicate what alternative explanations they examined, what they found, and what explanations they were unable to examine and their possible effects.

To provide opportunities to identify and correct errors, researchers fully disclose their research procedures and subject their work to peer review. Researchers are expected to acknowledge and correct errors that are discovered after research is reported and disseminated. Full disclosure allows others to scrutinize the research. Errors may be found by examining the research documents or attempting to replicate the research. Concealing limitations is deceptive. Research reports should clearly identify and evaluate the limitations. The more troublesome a limitation, the more emphasis it should receive.

Complete information on research procedures can overwhelm readers with details and seriously diminish a report's effectiveness. The professional standards for program evaluation recognize the competing demands of providing useful information and full disclosure. To provide useful information, the standards advise evaluators to write clearly, present information that their audiences can understand, and indicate the relative importance of their findings and recommendations. To achieve full disclosure, the standards advise evaluators to state their assumptions, their constraints, and how readers may obtain full information on research procedures, including data analysis.[12] The standards relieve evaluators of the burden of providing complete research information in every report, but they must take reasonable actions to ensure the accessibility of the database and documentation.

Peer review helps detect errors prior to a report's publication. Peer reviewers are specialists who read and evaluate manuscripts and proposals submitted to academic journals or conferences. The specialists should be conversant with the research topic. The reviewers may recommend the research for publication or presentation. They may identify weaknesses that need to be addressed—for example, additional sources for the researcher to consult, sections of the papers requiring amplification, or alternative analytical procedures. A *blind review* means the reviewer does not know who conducted the research. Blind reviews diminish personal factors that may color a reviewer's judgment.

The peer-review process primarily interests academic researchers. Nevertheless, the public relies on peer review to "protect" it from flawed research. Whether we eat red meat, drink wine, or exercise regularly may be influenced by reports of research findings. Researchers may be tempted to go directly to the mass media with interesting results, but such behavior is viewed as inappropriate. Rather, researchers are expected to release their study first to their professional colleagues, who are in a better position to detect its flaws.

In 1993, an error in a study on a treatment for the human immunodeficiency virus (HIV) made headlines. An American research team reported an apparently successful drug therapy for treating HIV. The article appeared in the prestigious scientific journal *Nature.* Six months later the researchers announced their research was in error.[13] They had, in fact, fooled themselves. They had misread lab results. At the 10th cycle of two experiments the virus was undetectable, but by the 30th cycle it was flourishing. A columnist in the *New York Times* cited the error as a failure of the peer-review system. He suggested that the original research was flawed.

After the paper was published, researchers in the United Kingdom tried to replicate the experiment; their findings were contrary to the original findings. The Americans repeated their experiment and identified an error. The researchers sent a letter to *Nature,* correcting their findings. The researchers also publicly announced the flaw in the original research; their announcement was reported widely in national news media.

The example implies the dynamics of research on "hot" topics. The potential rewards for finding a successful drug therapy to treat HIV and AIDS are tantalizing. They may lead researchers to be less careful in their work and to push for acceptance of their theories. On the other hand, the research is more likely to receive scrutiny and criticism. Ultimately, researchers must be willing to listen and respond to challengers. Researchers are expected to acknowledge and take responsibility for significant errors they subsequently detect. Such errors change the interpretation of the findings.[14] The *New York Times* columnist noted, "Many other scientists, who have made mistakes in far less visible and less important research, have not been as quick to publish corrections or retractions, if they reported them at all."[15]

Saving the Data

Data must be saved and be accessible to allow research audits, replication of results, refinement of the analysis, additional analyses, or incorporation of data into contemporary research designs. Research data include completed data collection instruments, procedures for collecting and entering data, experimental procedures, data files, computer printouts, field notes, videotapes, or audiotapes.[16] With this information an investigator can reconstruct or replicate the research. Audits may be a component of ensuring scientific integrity; they can substantiate or repudiate charges of falsification or fabrication. Replication may be a part of a formal audit, or it may arise from an investigator's desire to confirm the findings. Researchers may work with "old" data to see if including different variables or changing the statistical analysis affects the original results. Existing data may be incorporated into a time-series design or a cross-sectional design.

Funders may have specific policies covering data ownership and data retention.[17] In other cases an investigator may have to make her own decisions. Misunderstandings can be avoided if investigators and administrators agree on who will retain data, how long they will be kept, and the conditions governing data sharing. If such agreements are not made explicit, administrators may find that they cannot access the data later for further analysis. The investigators may have discarded or misplaced data, information to retrieve data may not exist, or research documents may be scattered.

A review of professional scientific societies found that six had guidelines covering data retention.[18] The guidelines commonly held the principal investigator responsible for retaining the data. The American Psychological Association recommended that data be kept for at least five years after publication. This was the most specific recommendation on length of time.

Implicit in the question of storing data is deciding who can have access to the data. As mentioned in Chapter 8, issues affecting the confidentiality of respondents must be resolved prior to sharing data. Chapter 9 reviews the costs that primary researchers may incur in data sharing. These costs include competing interests, the openness of research versus proprietary rights of the researchers, promises of confidentiality, the competence of the secondary analyst, and costs of retrieving, duplicating, and transmitting the data.[19]

Administrative research ranges from exploratory studies to studies designed to answer specific one-time questions, to longitudinal studies conducted to evaluate programs and to guide policy making. A set of specific guidelines on storage may not adequately cover all types of studies. During any study, researchers should describe research processes and decisions and label all research documents. At the end of the study, researchers should organize and store the data and documents for a reasonable amount of time.

The exact amount of time may depend on the assumed "shelf life" of the data, agency custom, research agreements, or contracts. Completed questionnaires and records, needed primarily for research audits or to correct data-entry errors, may be kept the shortest time. Data files, data dictionaries, data collection instruments, and other research protocols may be saved indefinitely. Materials relating to a published work may be kept longer than those relating to an unpublished or in-house study. Alternatively, if an agency centralizes data collected on its behalf, it should develop a mechanism to exert quality control so that it does not get overwhelmed with useless data.

SUMMARY

Before presenting their findings, researchers identify the audiences for their information. The researchers identify each audience's characteristics, how to get its attention, and how to motivate its members to follow through on the report's findings and recommendations. Perusal of agency reports or listening to oral presentations may suggest how to organize information effectively for an agency.

Presentations tend to include the same material, although the amount of time or detail will vary according to agency needs. These sections are an executive summary, a statement of the study's purpose, background information, the description of the methodology, and results, along with supporting analyses. The methodology section describes the measures, sample, and research design. It explicitly identifies any limitations that may change the findings. The results section includes as appropriate the supporting statistical models, tables, or graphs. Researchers may include their own observations in a report; however, they should clearly separate observations based on data and observations based on judgment. Recommendations should be based on findings.

Reports are tailored for different audiences and different needs. Reports are organized so that important information is clearly distinguishable and receives major emphasis. Nevertheless, a researcher should remember that written reports may be passed around. He should not assume that every reader will know about a study's background or design. Consequently, he needs to include necessary elaboration and documentation in the report. The methodology and findings sections in particular should be sufficiently documented so that the careful reader can make her own judgment on the adequacy of the report.

Oral presentations involve a captive audience. Still, the presenters are not guaranteed its attention. They should practice the presentation so that it flows logically and listeners can easily follow it. Visual aids should be easily seen and interpreted. If visual aids require special equipment, the presenters should know how to operate the equipment with minimal effort and be prepared in case it fails.

Written reports include research proposals, final project reports, and academic papers. A research proposal's sections on the problem, related background information, the literature review, and the proposed methodology are later incorporated in the final project report. Final project reports and academic papers include similar material, but the project report may be organized to facilitate the needs of administrators, who vary in their degree of interest. Final project reports rely on clear chapter headings, subheadings, and highlighting to direct a reader's attention. Technical details are placed in an appendix.

Empirical researchers are expected to adhere to ethical practice. Plagiarism, fabrication, and falsification clearly violate research ethics. Although human error is inevitable, researchers should take reasonable steps to minimize errors in their work. They should check entered data, computer programs, and data analyses to make sure that their findings are reported accurately. The descriptions of the study's methodology should disclose problems encountered, design limitations, and other information needed to facilitate critical review. Where possible, researchers should subject their work to peer review. After a research report has been reviewed by peers and published, researchers are expected to acknowledge any errors they subsequently discover.

When a study is initiated, investigators and administrators need to agree on who will retain data, how long data will be kept, and any conditions governing data sharing. During the study investigators should write up descriptions of research processes and decisions and label all research documents. At the end of the study, data and documents must be organized and saved. These steps ensure that data are available for audit, replication, or further analysis.

NOTES

1. L. A. Olsen and T. N. Huckin, *Technical Writing and Professional Communication*, 2d ed. (New York: McGraw-Hill, 1991), 66–69. For an alternative approach, see D. E. Zimmerman and D. G. Clark, *The Random House Guide to Technical and Scientific Communication* (New York: Random House, 1987), 90–100.

2. See Zimmerman and Clark, *Random House Guide*, 87–90.

3. K. Brown and P. B. Coulter, "Subjective and Objective Measures of Police Service Delivery," *Public Administration Review*, January–February 1963, 50–51.

4. A. H. Church, "Incentives in Mail Surveys: A Meta-Analysis," *Public Opinion Quarterly* 57 (1993): 62–63.

5. Edward R. Tufte, *The Visual Display of Quantitative Information* (Cheshire, CT: Graphics Press, 1983), 182.

6. For further discussions of recommendations see R. C. Sonnichsen, "Evaluators as Change Agents," *Handbook of Practical Program Evaluation*, ed. by J. S. Wholey, H. P. Hatry, and K. E. Newcomer (San Francisco: Jossey-Bass, 1994), 534–548, and M. Q. Patton, *Utilization-Focused Evaluation: The New Century Text* (Thousand Oaks, CA: Sage Publications, 1997), 324–329.

7. For statistical information on the history of scientific misconduct, see "Misconduct in Science—Incidence and Significance," *Responsible Science: Ensuring the Integrity of the Research Process*, Vol. 1, Report by U.S. Committee on Science, Engineering, and Public Policy, Panel on Scientific Responsibility and the Conduct of Research (Washington, DC: National Academy Press, 1992), 80–97. The chapter's bibliography identifies sources for information on specific cases.

8. *Responsible Science: Ensuring the Integrity of the Research Process*, Vol. 1, 5–7. The report referred to research misconduct as "misconduct in science." The same behaviors are labeled as "research misconduct" in the Massachusetts Institute of Technology's "Report of the Committee on Academic Responsibility," *Responsible Science: Ensuring the Integrity of the Research Process*, Vol. 2, 171.

9. *Responsible Science*, Vols. 1 and 2.

10. *Responsible Science*, Vol. 1, 56–57.

11. R. P. Feynman, "Cargo Cult Science," *Surely You're Joking Mr. Feynman!* (New York: Bantam Books, 1989), 308–317.

12. The Joint Committee on Standards for Educational Evaluation, *The Program Evaluation Standards: How to Assess Evaluations of Educational Programs*, 2d ed. (Thousand Oaks, CA: Sage Publications, 1994). Seventeen standards address reporting issues. The standards' application is not limited to educational studies.

13. Information on this case is drawn from D. Brown, "Scientists Acknowledge Flaw in 3-Drug Attack on AIDS Virus," *Washington Post*, July 23, 1993, A–3m, and L. K. Altman, "The Doctor's World: Faith in Multiple-Drug AIDS Trial Shaken by Report of Error In Lab," *New York Times*, July 27, 1993, B6. The research paper and the follow-up letter were published in *Nature* by M. S. Hirsch and his colleagues, researchers at Massachusetts General Hospital.

14. Reporting of significant errors is part of American Psychological Association's Ethical Principles and Code of Conduct (2002), Section 8.10(b). M. McGue in "Authorship and Intellectual Property", in B. D. Sales and S. Folkman, eds., *Ethics in Research with Human Participants* (Washington, DC: American Psychological Association, 2000) discusses the author's responsibility in reporting errors.

15. Altman, "The Doctor's World," B6.

16. *Responsible Science*, Vol. 1, 47.

17. F. L. Macrina, *Scientific Integrity*, 3d ed. (Washington, DC: American Society for Microbiology Press, 2005). Chapters 9 and 11 cover data ownership and data records.

18. M. S. Frankel, "Professional Societies and Responsible Research Conduct," *Responsible Science: Ensuring the Integrity of the Research Process*, Vol. 2, 33–34. None of the societies included represented professional management associations or public administration; information was collected from societies representing historians, political scientists, sociologists, and psychologists.

19. *Responsible Science*, Vol. 2, 34.

TERMS FOR REVIEW

executive summary
literature review
fabrication

falsification
plagiarism
peer review

blind review

QUESTIONS FOR REVIEW

The following questions should indicate whether you have a basic competency in this chapter's material.

1. A study of citizen satisfaction with an urban police force found that residents living in the downtown area are markedly less satisfied with police performance than other residents. Based on the data, the researchers' recommend that the city increase police visibility in downtown neighborhoods.
   a. Identify possible audiences for the report.
   b. How might an oral briefing to police administrators differ from an oral briefing to the city council?
   c. Contrast the information the researcher would include in the following three presentations: (1) an oral briefing to the city council, (2) the information in the final project report, and (3) the information in an article submitted to *Public Administration Review.*
2. Create a checklist for researchers to use to make sure that they have covered the necessary topics in a presentation.

3. Examine three different quantitative research articles. Compare and contrast (1) their content and organization and (2) the literature review as presented.
4. To study the benefits of educational programs in prisons, researchers surveyed inmates at five institutions. The surveys were administered by prison staff. The surveys from one institution show little variation, and the researchers feel certain that the data were fabricated. Should the researchers include the data in their analysis? What should they say about the data in their report?
5. Write a paragraph on plagiarism. Plagiarize this text without using a direct quotation.
6. A state agency plans to contract with a victims' advocacy group to collect and analyze data on victims' experiences with criminal-justice agencies. Make recommendations on who should keep the data, where, and for how long.

PROBLEMS FOR HOMEWORK AND DISCUSSION

1. Find an article of interest in a public administration journal such as the *Public Administration Review.*
   a. Write an executive summary for the article.
   b. Prepare a 10-minute oral briefing describing the research.
   c. Participate in a debriefing session in which one person or a team presents the research and others ask questions. The questioners should take on appropriate roles—for example, policy analysts, political representatives, community activists.

2. Read an assigned article and see if and how the authors included the information on your checklist (see Review Question 20 in the previous section).
3. Write two memos, "Guidelines for Effective Oral Presentations of Research Results" and "Guidelines for Effective Written Presentations of Research Results." Work with your classmates to develop a class guide.
4. If you have worked on a quantitative study this semester, prepare an oral presentation which includes visual aids.

5. Find out what the practices are in your academic department or agency for data storage and retention.

6. Some organizations seem to keep data and data collection instruments for a long time, much longer than would be reasonably useful. Other organizations seem to discard data and records at the earliest possible moment. Why? In what ways are these organizations likely to differ? How and why are their goals and motives likely to differ?

RECOMMENDED FOR FURTHER READING

For information on effective oral and written research presentations, refer to technical communications texts. Most university libraries have a large number of suitable texts.

W. Strunk, Jr., and E. B. White, *The Elements of Style,* 3d ed. (New York: Macmillan, 1979) is often recommended to writers. Chapters 2 and 5 are especially valuable. Strunk and White's book also is available at http://www.bartleby.com/141/

R. T. Torres, H. S. Preskill, and M. E. Piontek, *Evaluation Strategies for Communicating and Reporting: Enhancing Learning in Organizations* 2nd ed. (Thousand Oaks, CA: Sage, 2005) covers strategies for effectively communicating findings and common reporting formats.

Students interested in ethical practices in research should consult *Responsible Science: Ensuring the Integrity of the Research Process,* Vols. 1 and 2, Report by U.S. Committee on Science, Engineering, and Public Policy, Panel on Scientific Responsibility and the Conduct of Research (Washington, DC: National Academy Press, 1992).

Deni Elliott and Judy E. Stern, eds., *Research Ethics: A Reader* (Hanover, NH: University Press of New England, 1997) was designed for use by engineers and scientists in a graduate course on research ethics. It includes articles on scientific misconduct and reporting research issues. A similar text, Francis L. Macrina, *Scientific Integrity: An Introductory Text with Cases,* 3d ed (Washington, DC: American Society for Microbiology, 2005) has interesting, readable chapters on record keeping, data ownership, peer review and relationships with mentors.

Paul Oliver, *The Student's Guide to Resarch Ethics* (Philadelphia: Open University Press, 2003), Chapter 8 has an accessible discussion of academic publishing and issues associated with plagiarism.

Glossary

Accuracy. A measure of the size of the sampling error, indicating how close a sample's finding is to the parameter.

Aggregate data. Data on groups or jurisdictions such as cities, counties, or organizations that are the result of a measure of smaller units within the larger group.

Alpha level. The probability that the investigator will reject as false a true null hypothesis. The probability of committing a Type I error.

American Community Survey. An annual survey initiated in January 2005 by the U.S. Census Bureau to collect social, economic, housing, and demographic data.

Analytic mapping. Plotting the values of one or more variables on a map to analyze the relationships between variables and geographic location.

Anonymity. Collecting information so that researchers cannot link any piece of data to a specific, named individual.

ANOVA (analysis of variance). The primary statistical tool for analyzing experimental data and the differences between group means. Provides information on the statistical significance of a relationship.

Applications program. Software designed for a specific activity or set of activities other than operating the computer. Statistical packages, spreadsheets, and database managers are examples of application programs.

Arithmetic mean. A measure of central tendency determined by adding together the values of a variable for all cases in the distribution and dividing this sum by the total number of cases. The use of the arithmetic mean requires that data be measured at the interval or ratio level.

Array. A listing of the values for each variable for all cases.

Associated probability. The probability that a specific value of a test statistic will occur if the null hypothesis is true; usually combined with other evidence to make inferences about hypotheses.

Asymmetric measure. A measure of association between two variables which may have different values depending on the variable designated as the independent variable.

Autocorrelation. A nonrandom relationship among the values of a variable at different time periods violating the assumption that residuals are independent of one another; may be eliminated if the researcher can identify and include an appropriate independent variable.

Average deviation. Calculation obtained by adding the absolute value of the deviation of each case from the mean of the distribution and dividing by the number of cases.

Bar graph. A graph showing the variable and its values or categories along one side and a scale for the frequency or percentage of cases along the other. The length or height of a bar indicates the number or percentage of cases with each value of the variable. The width of a bar does not have meaning.

Beta weights. Standardized regression coefficients, calculated by first standardizing the measure of all variables so that they are in standard units. Beta weights indicate the relative influence of each of the independent variables on the dependent variable.

Between-group variances. Indications of how the mean and variances of each group differ from the other groups.

Bias. A systematic difference between a sample statistic and the population parameter it is to estimate. Because of a flaw in the sampling design, its implementation, or the data collection procedure, the sample either systematically under- or overestimates the population parameter. In survey research, it includes inaccurate information resulting from unreliable or invalid questions.

Biased question. A survey question that elicits inaccurate information, because it is worded in such a way that respondents are encouraged to give one answer rather than another. (See Loaded question)

Bivariate distribution. The joint distribution of the values of two variables.

Bivariate statistics. Statistics that summarize the association between two variables.

Blind review. Review of a report or study when the reviewer does not know who conducted the research.

Block numbering area. Smallest statistical area defined by the U.S. Census Bureau; a well-defined piece of land bounded by a street, railroad, or similar physical feature.

Box plot. A graphic technique that illustrates the median of a variable, its minimum and maximum values, quartile locations, inter-quartile range, and in some cases, outliers. It gives a quick view of both central tendency and spread.

Case. One unit of analysis.

Case study. A type of study in which a single person, program, agency, or some other unit of analysis is examined in detail.

Categorical variables. Nominal and ordinal variables.

Census block. The smallest geographic unit for which the Census Bureau tabulates 100-percent data. Many blocks correspond to individual city blocks bounded by streets.

Census of Population and Housing. The census conducted every 10 years by the U.S. Census Bureau to count the population. Required by the Constitution of the United States.

Census tract. Statistical area encompassing a large neighborhood, averaging 4,000 in population and generally with a population between 1,500 and 6,000 within county lines; every metropolitan area is mapped with census tracts.

Census undercount. The underestimating of the total size of the U.S. population. Certain groups, particularly urban minorities, are more likely to be undercounted.

Chi-square. A test of statistical significance intended for use with nominal measures. Often applied to data in contingency tables.

Circle graph. A graph or pie chart showing the proportion of a total made up by each component. The size of each wedge of the circle indicates what proportion of the whole it encompasses.

Class interval. The grouping of values of a variable.

Classical experimental design. A design with at least one experimental group and one control group, with subjects randomly assigned to each by the investigator, with the independent variable under the control of the experimenter, and with a pretest and a posttest.

Closed-ended question. A type of survey question in which the respondent is given a list of possible answers and is requested to select an answer or answers from that list.

Cluster sampling. Probability sampling in which groups or jurisdictions comprising groups of units are randomly selected for a sample.

Coding. The process of converting information collected by surveys or other means into symbols, usually numbers, for storage, management, and analysis.

Coefficient of determination. The proportion of variation in the dependent variable that is accounted for, statistically, by one or more independent variables. Symbolized by r^2 or R^2.

Cohort. Cases experiencing the same significant event in a specific time period.

Comparison group design. A quasi-experimental design similar to the classical experimental design. However, the subjects in each group are not randomly assigned by the researcher, and the occurrence of the independent variable may not be controlled by the researcher.

Computer-assisted telephone interviewing (CATI). Administration of surveys in which the interviewer reads items from a computer terminal and keys in the responses. The computer paces the interview by branching for contingency questions and keeping track of the number of calls made and which numbers were called.

Concept. An abstract or general characteristic.

Conceptual definition. A definition of a concept or variable in terms of other concepts. Essentially a dictionary definition of a concept or variable.

Confidence interval. An interval placed around the value of a sample statistic. The investigator expects the value of the corresponding parameter to be located within the confidence interval.

Confidence level. The confidence that an investigator has that a sample estimate is within a specified range of the parameter.

Confidentiality. Protection of information, so that researchers cannot or will not disclose records with individual identifiers.

Constants. Elements in a research model that do not vary.

Content-based evidence of validity. Evidence that the items included in the operational definition are relevant to the concept being measured and adequately represent it.

Contingency table. A table showing how the distribution of one variable is related to the values of one or more other variables.

Control group. The group that is not exposed to the independent variable, but which is similar to the experimental group in all other respects.

Control variable. A variable included in an analysis to determine whether it affects the relationship between two other variables. The values of the control variable are "held constant," while the relationship between the other two variables is analyzed.

Convenience sampling. Nonprobability sampling in which units are chosen primarily on the basis of their availability.

Correlation coefficient. Usually meant to refer to the Pearson product-moment correlation coefficient, r, it is a measure of the strength and direction of association between quantitative variables. The correlation coefficient is also a test of the goodness of fit for a regression equation.

Covariation. The patterned relationship between an independent and dependent variable.

Cramer's V. A measure of the strength of association between two nominal variables. Typically used for contingency tables, it is based on the chi-square statistic.

Criterion-based evidence of validity. Statistical evidence that compares the data produced by a measure with the data produced by an alternate measure.

Cross-sectional design. A type of research design with all relevant variables measured at the same time.

Current Population Survey. An extensive survey conducted monthly in person or by telephone by the U.S. Census Bureau to gather current population labor-force data.

Cyclical variations. Changes in a variable recurring over time at regular intervals, usually of one to five years.

Database. A set of related data records storing information shared by several users for multiple purposes.

Database management system. An application program to enter, store, organize, and retrieve data. Some database programs can relate data from separate files.

Data control log. A record listing users' names and when they entered, used, or accessed data.

Data dictionary. A component of a database manager that names and describes each element and its location in the database, how it can be obtained, and the code for each value.

Data snooping. Using a computer program to relate many variables in a set of data to every other one with no model or hypothesis to guide the effort.

Decennial Census of Population and Housing. The U.S. Census Bureau's major effort of counting the population every 10 years.

Deductive disclosure. When information in a research project can be used to sort through the data to identify a specific person, or otherwise compromise the privacy of the subjects.

Degrees of freedom. A value needed for many statistical tests. This is the number of parameters that can vary independently of others.

Demographic questions. Survey questions that ask about a respondent's age, race, education, occupation, religion, and so forth.

Dependent variable. One of the variables in a hypothesis that represents or measures the characteristic or event being explained. It is sometimes referred to as an "outcome" or an "effect."

Descriptive statistics. Statistics used to describe and summarize a dataset.

Dichotomous variable. A variable that has only two possible values.

Direct relationship. A relationship between variables in which an increase in the value of one variable is associated with an increase in the value of the other variable.

Discriminant analysis. Also known as discriminant function analysis, this is a type of statistical analysis similar to regression in which the dependent variable is a dichotomous variable.

Disproportionate stratified sampling. A probability sampling procedure in which the sample comprises a larger percentage of the units in some strata than of others.

Dummy variable. A dichotomous variable, usually called a dummy variable when included in a regression equation.

Effects of a control variable. The addition of a control variable may show that the relationship between two variables (1) stays the same, (2) is stronger for some values of the control variable than for others, (3) changes direction, or (4) disappears.

Elements. The variables that are identified for inclusion in a model.

Empirical validity. Empirical demonstration that an instrument measures what it has been designed to measure. Predictive validity is a type of empirical validity.

Enumeration. The process of ordering data by variable value and grouping and counting the number of cases with similar values.

Equivalence (of a measure). Different investigators using the same measurement procedure would produce the same results. Different versions of the same measuring procedure should produce the same results.

Eta. A measure of association between a nominal or ordinal and interval variable; used with analysis of variance.

Executive summary. A section located at the beginning of a report that highlights its content and may include recommendations. The intended audience is the executive who has little time to read reports; thus, this section is designed to be understood independently of the report.

Expected frequency. The number of cases expected to have a particular value or set of values if the null hypothesis is true.

Experiment. A type of study in which randomly assigned subjects are exposed to a deliberately manipulated treatment and compared to other subjects, also randomly assigned, who are not exposed to the same treatment.

Experimental design. A type of design in which the researcher can assign subjects to different research groups, control who is exposed to the independent variable, when they are exposed to it, and the conditions under which the experiment takes place.

Experimental group. The group that is exposed to the independent variable.

External validity. The extent to which a study produces evidence that the findings of a study apply to cases not in the study.

F-test. A statistical test of significance that evaluates the ratio between the total amount of variance in a variable and that explained by an independent variable or set of independent variables. Commonly used for analysis of variance (AVOVA) procedures.

Fabrication. Making up, or inventing, the data or results of a research effort.

Factor analysis. A statistical procedure for identifying a small number of concepts underlying a large number of related measures and for reducing the larger number of measures to a few indices. Useful in identifying measures to include in indices and in creating indices.

Factor loading. A component of factor analysis that indicates how closely each individual item is associated with the underlying concept or factor.

Factor score. The value of a case or unit of analysis for an index developed by factor analysis.

Factor score coefficient. Weights for each item in factor analysis that are multiplied by a case's value on that item to arrive at a value on the index for each case.

Falsification. Changing the data or results of a report or research by a researcher; may be more ambiguous than fabrication because altering information may involve dropping a case or group to tailor the report to the researcher's needs.

Federal Register. A publication of the federal government listing regulations and proposed regulations of federal agencies. Used in this text in referring to regulations of the Department of Health and Human Services regarding research on human subjects.

Field. The columns occupied by the data for a variable.

File. A set of records.

Filter question. A type of survey question used to identify respondents who should answer specific follow-up questions.

Fixed format. Data entered in such a way that the values for each variable are in the same location in the data record for each case.

Focus group. A research tool utilizing small-group interviews to obtain qualitative data as well as items for questionnaires or surveys. Group interaction is an important component of a focus group.

Forced-choice question. A closed-ended question that requires the respondent to choose among available options with no provision for an "other" or "none of the above" response.

Forms manager. A computer program that takes data entered from a terminal and sets it up in a preset format in a record.

Frequency distribution. A table listing the variable values along with the number of cases with each value.

Frequency polygon. A line graph showing the frequency distribution of quantitative variables. A horizontal axis shows the values of the variable, and the vertical axis is a scale showing the frequency. The height of the polygon at any specific place indicates the number of cases with a particular value.

Gamma. A measure of the strength and direction of association between two ordinal variables.

Geographic Information System (GIS). A system of hardware and software that integrates computer graphics with a relational database to manage data about geographic locations. A GIS can display information on maps it generates to show the relationship between variable values and location.

Geometric mean. A measure used to calculate an average for rates of change measured over several successive time periods.

Goodness of fit. Evidence of how well the statistical model describes a dataset. Evidence of goodness of fit for linear regression includes a linear scatterplot, the size of the correlation coefficient, and the standard error of the regression coefficient.

Hardware. Computer hardware is the computer itself and peripheral equipment such as disk drives, printers, and other storage and input devices.

Histogram. A graph similar to a bar chart except that both the length and width of the bar have meaning. The widths represent the range of values included in a category; histograms can be used for quantitative (interval and ratio) variables.

Human subject. A living individual about whom an investigator obtains data through intervention or interaction with the individual or by obtaining identifiable private information.

Hypothesis. A tentative explanation for an observation, phenomenon, or problem that can be tested empirically. Typically a hypothesis specifies the relationship between two variables.

Hypothesis testing. Also called significance testing, it is a procedure used to determine the probability that a statement, called a null hypothesis, about variables in a population is false given data from a sample of cases selected from that population.

In-person interviewing. Also known as face-to-face interviewing. A form of survey research in which the interviewer meets personally with the respondent and records the answers as the respondent provides them.

Incidence. Common rate measure referring to the number of people who get a disease over a specified period of time, usually a year. Also applicable to other situations, for example, being a victim of a crime or having an accident.

Independent variable. One of the variables in a hypothesis that is used to explain the variation in the characteristics or event of interest. It is sometimes referred to as an "input" or "cause."

Index. A set of variables combined to measure a more abstract concept.

Index number. A number expressing the relationship between two figures, one of which is the base, that is used to describe changes over time in such things as prices, production, wages, and unemployment. The Consumer Price Index (CPI) is a well-known index number.

Inferential statistics. Statistics used to estimate the value of population characteristics from data obtained from a probability sample.

Informed consent. The principle that (1) prospective subjects of research must be informed of the purpose of the research and of any risks and benefits that may be incurred by participating, and (2) the subjects must give their explicit consent prior to participating in a study.

Institutional Review Board (IRB). An internal body created by an institution that receives federal money for research involving human subjects; the IRB reviews all institutional research involving human subjects to determine whether it conforms to ethical practices.

Intensive interviewing. An in-depth, lengthy, and extensive interview of respondents. It usually requires a skilled interviewer using an unstructured format. Typically a study using this technique involves relatively few respondents.

Internal consistency. The extent to which all items in a measuring procedure relate to the concept measured.

Internal validity. The extent to which a design provides evidence that a specific independent variable caused a change in a dependent variable.

Internet surveys. A type of research design where surveys are posted on the Web or sent as part of an e-mail message.

Inter-quartile range. The range of values encompassing the middle one-half of the observations in an ordered distribution.

Inter-rater reliability. The extent to which two different observers using the same instrument to measure a concept obtain the same results.

Interrupted time-series design. A quasi-experimental design incorporating an independent variable other than time into the time-series design. Several measures of the dependent variable are taken before and after the occurrence of the independent variable.

Interrupted time-series design with comparison group. An interrupted time series is compared to another time series that is not interrupted or is interrupted at a different time.

Interval scales. A measurement scale that measures quantitative differences between values of a variable. Each unit of the variable has the same quantitative value as every other unit. Equal-distance intervals are measured between values of the variable.

Inverse relationship. A linear relationship between variables in which an increase in the value of one variable is associated with a decrease in the value of the other variable.

Irregular fluctuations. Changes over time in a variable that cannot be attributed to long-term trends, or cyclical or seasonal variations.

Lagging. A process in which the value of the independent variable is measured at an earlier time than the value of the dependent variable.

Lambda. A measure of association between two nominal-level variables.

Level of analysis. Either individual, in which case the data are from individuals, or aggregate, in which case the measures are of group characteristics.

Likert scaling. A method of index construction, also known as summated rating. A numerical value is given to the response to each of a number of items, and the values are added or averaged to obtain a value for each case.

Linear model. A model that assumes that the relationship between the variables can be appropriately described by a straight line; if the linear model is appropriate, then a linear regression equation may be calculated.

Linear regression model. The relationship between variables when the regression equation defines a straight line; $y = a + bx_i \ldots bx_n$.

Literature review. The process of reviewing studies relevant to the research question. The literature review section of a report establishes the value of a research project and how it fits in with other research. The review may document that the research addresses a question not investigated in previous studies, fills a gap in previous research, tests a model under different conditions, corrects for errors in previous research, or resolves conflicting research findings.

Loaded question. A biased question worded in such a way that the respondent perceives that only one way of answering is acceptable. (See Biased question)

Logistic regression. Regression model in which the dependent variable is dichotomous. The regression equation calculates the probability that the dependent variable will have one of two values for given values of the independent variable or variables.

Logistic regression coefficient. Measures the predictive capability of the independent variables in a logistic regression.

Longitudinal design. A type of study utilized to collect information on each variable for two or more distinct time periods.

Long-term trend. General upward or downward movement in the values of a variable over a number of years.

Mailed questionnaires. A type of survey in which respondents are contacted by mail and are asked to fill out a questionnaire and return it by mail.

Mainframe computer. A very large computer capable of handling large amounts of data and performing extensive analysis. Most large agencies and universities have at least one mainframe computer.

Matrix. A listing of data in columns and rows. The rows constitute cases and the columns are fields containing the information for variables. The vertical dimension is related to the number of cases and the horizontal dimension to the number of fields.

Measurement. The process of assigning numerals to the values of variables according to a set of rules.

Measurement scales. Categorizes the relationships among a variable's values; nominal scales categorize variables; ordinal scales rank them along a continuum; in interval scales, values can be added and subtracted; ratio scales have an absolute zero and ratios comparing different cases can be computed.

Measures of association. Statistics that measure the strength of the relationship between variables. Common ones include lambda, gamma, and the Pearson product-moment correlation coefficient (Pearson's r).

Measures of central tendency. Measures indicating the value of a distribution that is representative, most typical, or central. These measures include the mode, median, and arithmetic mean.

Measures of dispersion. Measures that indicate the extent to which values in a distribution are different from each other. These include the range, inter-quartile range, percentiles, variance, and standard deviation.

Median. A measure of central tendency; the value of the middle case of an ordered distribution of values. The median requires ordinal or quantitative-level measurement.

Median absolute deviation. A measure of dispersion calculated by determining the average deviation of a set of cases from the median of the distribution.

Meta-analysis. A systematic technique utilized by researchers to analyze a set of existing studies. It is conducted to draw general conclusions from several empirical studies and to identify hypotheses that merit further testing.

Microdata. With reference to U.S. Census data, a sample of individual records with all identifying information removed.

MIS. Management Information System.

Mode. A measure of central tendency; the value of a variable that occurs most frequently.

Model. A representation of reality, it delineates certain aspects of the real world as being relevant to the problem under investigation and makes explicit the relationships among these aspects; it enables the formulation of empirically testable propositions regarding the nature of these relationships.

Model building. The process of constructing a research model to answer a research question, including selecting elements and postulating the nature of their relationship.

Multicollinearity. A condition existing when independent variables in a regression equation are closely related to each other and their independent effects on the dependent variable cannot be estimated.

Multiple regression. Regression analysis in which more than one independent variable is included in the regression equation and analyzed.

Multistage sampling. Probability sampling that proceeds in at least two stages. In each stage a grouping of units is selected as a sample, and then a smaller grouping of units is selected as a sample, from the first group.

Multivariate statistics. Statistics that apply to relationships among more than two variables.

New error. Used in the calculation of Lambda, a measure of association. Equal to the non-modal responses for each category of the independent variable.

Nominal scales. Scales that categorize and label the values of a variable. The investigator can group cases by the variable categories but cannot order them.

Nonexperimental design. Designs that do not control for the threats to internal validity.

Nonlinear relationship. A distinct pattern, other than a straight line, describing the relationship between variables.

Nonprobability sampling. Sampling done in such a way that the probability that any unit or set of units will be selected for the sample is unknown.

Nonrandom variations. Variations in a time series which are not associated with long-term trends, cyclical variations, or seasonal variations, but which can be explained by an event or a specific set of conditions.

Non-response rate. The proportion of people who do not respond to a survey.

Nonsampling error (bias). Error resulting from a flaw in the sampling design, from unreliable or invalid measures, or faulty data collection.

Normal curve. A theoretical distribution with the following characteristics: It is bell-shaped and symmetrical; the mode, mean, and median have the same value; and a fixed proportion of the observations lies between the mean and any other value.

Null hypothesis. A hypothesis stating that two variables are not related in the population. It is the null hypothesis that is actually tested by tests of statistical significance.

Null relationship. Relationship that occurs if a change in the independent variable is as likely to coincide with an increase as with a decrease or no change in the dependent variable.

Numerical variables. Variables measured on an interval or ratio scale.

Open-ended question. A type of survey question in which respondents are required to provide their own answers without a listing of possibilities from the researcher.

Operational definition. Detail of the procedures for measuring a concept or variable and for assigning values to a variable for each case.

Operational validity. The extent to which measuring procedures or instruments actually measure what they have been devised to measure.

Ordinal scale. A measuring scale that orders the values of a variable and allows an investigator to order cases based on their variable value. Ordinal scales do not, however, measure the quantitative difference between cases.

Original error. Indicates how much error there is in predicting the distribution of the dependent variable without knowing the values of an independent variable.

Outliers. In regression analysis these are data points well outside the range of the remainder of the data.

Panel design. A type of longitudinal design examining the same cases individually at each successive period; may reveal which individual cases change.

Parameter. The value of a characteristic of a population. Analysts draw samples in order to estimate parameters.

Partial regression coefficient. Indicates the effect of the independent variable on the dependent variable while controlling for all other variables in the equation.

Pearson's r. A measure of the strength and direction of the association between two interval-level variables.

Peer review. A process in which individuals well versed in a particular topic read and evaluate manuscripts and proposals submitted to academic journals, conferences, or funding agencies to detect errors or weaknesses prior to funding research or publication.

Percentage. A relative frequency calculated by dividing the frequency of cases with a value of a variable by the total number of cases and then multiplying this result by 100.

Percentage change. A relative frequency that converts to a percentage the amount of change in the value of a variable from one time to another for the same case.

Percentage difference. The difference between the columns in the percent of cases in a row (category of the dependent variable). Calculated by subtracting across the columns of a contingency table; can be used to analyze a relationship between two variables.

Percentage distribution. A table showing the values of a variable and the percentage of all cases having each value.

Percentile. A value below which a certain percent of the ordered observations in a distribution are located.

Perfect relationship between two variables. Relationship in which a change in the independent variable is always associated with the same change in the dependent variable.

Pie chart. A visual chart represented by a complete circle, indicating a quantity that is sliced into a number of wedges. The graph conveys what proportion of the whole is accounted for by each component and facilitates visual comparisons among parts of the whole.

Pilot study. A small study designed to test the adequacy of a proposed data collection strategy. A pilot study should test planned measures and analysis on a sample that represents the target population.

Plagiarism. The presentation of another's ideas as one's own.

Population. A total set of units sharing at least one characteristic of interest. It is from this set that the sample is selected.

Population variability. The extent to which members of a population differ from each other on the variables in which an investigator is interested.

Power. Refers to the probability that a test of significance results in the rejection of a false null hypothesis; it is related to the sample size and the strength of a relationship.

Practical significance. The extent to which a statistical finding is important or can be applied to solve a problem.

PRE (Proportional Reduction in Error). A measure that indicates how much knowing the distribution of the independent variable reduces the error in predicting the distribution of the dependent variable.

Predicted value. In regression analysis it is the value of the dependent variable for a case computed by using the regression equation.

Pretest. An initial test of a proposed questionnaire given to a small group of subjects who represent common variations found in the target population.

Prevalence. Common rate measure referring to the total number of people who have a disease at a given time. Also applicable to other situations, for example, total number of people who have been a victim of a crime or have had an accident.

Privacy. An individual's ability to control the access of other people to information about himself.

Probability sampling. A type of sampling in which each unit of the population has a known, nonzero chance of being in the sample.

Program file. A computer file containing instructions to the computer for running a program.

Proportion. A relative frequency determined by dividing the number of cases with a value of a variable by the total number of cases. A proportion is a decimal figure that is less than 1.

Proportionate stratified sampling. Probability sampling in which the same percentage of the units in each strata is selected for the sample.

Purposive sampling. Nonprobability sampling in which units are selected because the investigator judges that the units somehow are representative of the population. Also known as judgmental or expert-choice sampling.

Qualitative research. Refers to research involving detailed, verbal descriptions of characteristics, cases, and settings. Qualitative research usually involves relatively few cases investigated in depth.

Quality control. A set of procedures used by organizations to monitor the quality of goods produced or services delivered and to take corrective action if quality drops below a set standard. Probability sampling is important in quality-control programs.

Quantitative research. Refers to research in which values of variables are characterized by numbers. Data are summarized and analyzed with statistical techniques.

Quantitative scales.   A more inclusive term referring to both interval and ratio scales.

Quartile.   Specification of a range of values in four parts; the first quartile is that value below which 25 percent of the cases are found. The second quartile is the median, the third quartile is the value below which 75 percent of the cases are found, and the fourth quartile is the maximum value in the distribution.

Quasi-experimental design.   A design having some but not all of the characteristics of the experimental design. Often used in applied-research situations when the control necessary for a true experiment is not possible or practical.

Question sequencing.   Arranging the questions in a survey in such a way as to obtain the most information and to encourage the maximum number of respondents to answer.

Questionnaire design.   Question wording, sequencing, placement, and length of the physical layout of the questionnaire or survey.

Quota sampling.   Nonprobability sampling in which the units are chosen for the sample in the same proportion as selected characteristics are believed to exist in the population.

Random assignment.   Subjects are assigned in such a way that there is no systematic difference between the groups. Each subject has the same chance as any other subject of being in either an experimental group or control group.

Random digit dialing.   A method of selecting a sample of respondents for telephone interviewing. A set of telephone numbers is selected in such a way as to result in a representative sample.

Random relationship.   Two variables are independent of each other, i.e., a change in one variable is not associated with a change in the other variable.

Random variations.   Unexplained variations which are not associated with long-term trends, cyclical variations, or seasonal variations.

Randomized posttest design.   An experimental design with at least two groups and a posttest but no pretest.

Range.   A measure of dispersion giving the quantitative distance between the lowest and the highest values in an ordered distribution.

Rate.   A relative frequency used to standardize the occurrence of some event. Rates are calculated by dividing the frequency of occurrence of an event by a total frequency count, such as the population of a jurisdiction in which the event takes place. The result is multiplied by a base number which is a power of 10 for example, 10, 100, or 1000.

Ratio.   A relative frequency found by comparing the number of cases with one value of a variable with the number of cases with another value of the variable.

Ratio scale.   A measurement scale that allows researchers to rank objects on a scale and determine the exact difference between them, and also to use ratios to describe relationships between the values of the scaled objects. Ratio scales have an absolute zero point. In administrative work almost all scales that are interval are also ratio.

Reactive effects of experimental arrangements.   The fact that study situations often are necessarily artificial, and the study setting itself may affect the outcome.

Record.   The data from a case or unit of analysis. A line of data in a computer file.

Rectangular array.   A method of organizing data in which each case or unit of observation is represented by a row, each variable by one or more columns, and each row is the same length.

Regression coefficient.   The value in the regression equation (b or slope) that indicates how much the dependent variable changes with a unit increase in the independent variable.

Regression constant.   Often symbolized by the letter a. It is a component of the regression equation and is added to the value of the slope times the value of the independent variable to obtain a predicted value for the dependent variable. It is also the Y intercept and is the value produced by the regression equation when the value of X is zero.

Regression equation.   An equation computed from the data in a specific dataset to find the line that best describes the set of data points. The equation relates the values of the independent to a dependent variable.

Relational database.   A set of files in which two or more files have some variables in common, allowing information from separate files to be linked for analysis and reports.

Relationships in model.   The links between elements in a research model.

Relative frequency.   The number of times that a value of a variable occurs divided by another frequency count such as the total number of cases, the frequency of another value of the same variable, or the frequency of a second variable. Percents, ratios, and rates are all relative frequencies.

Reliability.   The degree of random error associated with a measurement. Reliable measures produce consistent or dependable data.

Research design.   Two meanings: (1) general plans that guide decisions as to what data to gather, from whom, when and how to collect the data, and how to analyze the information; (2) specific plans for when to collect data on dependent, independent, and control variables.

Research methodology.   The steps needed to test a research model, including plans for selecting study subjects, measuring each variable, collecting the data, and analyzing the data.

Research records.   Individual or aggregated data for the observations in a research project.

Residual. The difference between a value of the dependent variable for a case predicted by the regression equation and the actual value of the variable for that case.

Respondent. Someone from whom we collect information, usually through survey research procedures.

Response rate. The percentage of survey respondents from a sample who respond to a questionnaire or who are interviewed.

Response set. The tendency of respondents to a questionnaire or those interviewed to answer all items in the same way.

Sample. A subset of units selected from a larger set of the same units. The subset is used to infer something about the larger set, the population.

Sampling bias. A systematic misrepresentation of the population by the sample. It usually comes about because of a flaw in the sample design or its implementation.

Sampling design. The set of procedures for selecting the units from the population to be in the sample.

Sampling error. Refers to the difference between a sample estimate and the parameter, which is attributed to the fact that any one probability sample cannot precisely estimate a parameter.

Sampling fraction. The percentage of the population units selected for the sample.

Sampling frame. A list of the members of the population from which the sample is actually drawn.

Sampling unit. A unit or set of units considered for the sample.

Scale. A measurement procedure that assigns a value to a case based on how that case fits into a pattern of indicators.

Scatterplot. A graph of plotted points where the dependent variable (Y) is placed on the vertical axis and the independent variable (X) is placed along the horizontal axis. Examining the scatterplot is useful in deciding whether a linear model should be used to summarize the relationship between the two variables.

Schematic model. A model that illustrates the important links and relationships between elements with lines and arrows or similar graphical representations.

Seasonal variations. Changes in a variable over time that occur regularly during certain times of the year.

Secondary data. Existing data that were collected for a purpose other than the given study.

Selection bias. The introduction of error due to systematic differences in the characteristics between those selected and those not selected for a given study.

Sensitivity. The ability of a measure to detect meaningful differences among cases.

Sensitivity (of measure of association). A criterion for selecting a measure of association. The ability of a statistic to detect small differences in the strength of a relationship by assigning different numerical values to relationships that may have slight, even subtle, differences in strength.

Simple random sampling. Probability sampling done in such a way that the following are true: (a) each unit of the population has the same, nonzero probability of being selected for the sample as every other unit; (b) the selection of one unit of the population does not affect the probability that some other unit will be selected.

Skew. A characteristic of a frequency distribution. If the mode or median have values different from the arithmetic mean, the distribution is skewed. A negatively skewed distribution is one in which the median is larger than the mean; in a positively skewed distribution the median is smaller than the mean.

Skewed distribution. Occurs when a distribution has a few extreme values, either high or low, affecting the arithmetic mean. A distribution will be skewed to the left, negatively, if the extreme values are low, and to the right, or positively, if the extreme values are high.

Skip interval. The number of units in a list to be skipped when drawing a systematic sample.

Snowball sampling (referral sampling). A type of nonprobability sampling where members of a population know or are aware of each other and recommend subjects for the sample; snowball sampling is used when members of the population cannot be easily accessed by other methods.

Software. Computer programs and instructions necessary for computers to operate and carry out various tasks.

Somers' d (dyx). An asymmetric measure of association for ordinal variables.

Sponsored research. Research financially supported by government agencies, foundations, or other organizations.

Spreadsheet. A rectangular matrix of rows and columns.

Spreadsheet program. An application program that displays a matrix on the computer screen and allows the user to enter labels, data, and mathematical formulas into the cells of the matrix. The user can manipulate data in the matrix and perform statistical and mathematical analysis.

Spurious relationship. An apparent, but untrue, relationship between two variables that occurs because of the association of a third variable to each of the original two.

Stability. The ability of a measure to yield the same results time after time, if and only if what is being measured has not changed.

Standard deviation. A measure of dispersion. It is calculated by squaring the difference between the arithmetic mean of a distribution and the value of each case, summing these values, dividing by the number of cases, and taking the square root of the result. It is used in a number of statistical measures and tests.

Standard error. A statistical measure of the size of the sampling error based on theoretical distribution of a variable for a large number of probability samples of the same size. The standard error is normally distributed.

Standard error of the slope. An estimate of how much the regression coefficient, b, is likely to vary from sample to sample.

Standard score. Also called a z-score, this expresses the values of a distribution in terms of units of the standard deviation of the distribution. It is calculated by subtracting the arithmetic mean from the value of a particular case and dividing the result by the standard deviation.

Statistic. The value of a characteristic of a sample. Investigators use statistics to estimate parameters.

Statistical significance. The probability that the value of a statistic could have been found from a population in which the value of the corresponding parameter was much different.

Statistical software packages. Application programs to perform statistical analysis of data.

Statistically significant relationship. A relationship between variables in a sample that a statistical test suggests would also be found if the entire population from which the sample was selected could be studied; the relationship in the population may differ in strength from that in the sample.

Strata. Subgroups within a larger population.

Stratified random sampling. Probability sampling in which the population is divided into subgroups (strata). A probability sample is selected from each strata. Stratified sampling can be either proportionate or disproportionate.

Structured interviewing. Surveys in which respondents are asked the same questions, in the same order, and in the same way.

Subjects at risk. A research design in which participants could experience negative consequences. Such consequences could range from permanently harmful effects to less significant reactions such as anger or humiliation.

Survey research. A type of data collection procedure in which investigators question individual subjects in face-to-face interviews, over the telephone, by sending a questionnaire to them through the mail or by posting it on the Internet.

Symbolic model. A model using words, mathematical equations, or computer programs to illustrate the links and relationships among elements.

Symmetric measure. A measure of association between two variables that has the same value no matter which variable is designated as the independent variable.

Systematic sampling. Probability sampling which has an investigator select units from a list of members of the populations using a skip interval (population size divided by the sample size) and randomly determining a starting place in the list.

_t_-test. A test of statistical significance requiring an interval-dependent variable. It has wide application but is often used to test whether the difference between the arithmetic averages of two groups is significant.

Target population. The set of units to which investigators wish to apply their results.

Test-retest. A technique that requires that an instrument or test be administered to a subject at two points in time. This establishes the stability of a measure.

Text editor. A computer program allowing the user to enter information, store, edit, and retrieve it for use.

Threats to external validity. Factors that limit the ability to apply the findings of a study to cases not involved in the study.

Threats to internal validity. Factors that could be the cause of a change in a dependent variable and represent alternatives to the tested independent variable.

Time series. A set of data obtained at regular intervals for a single case; a type of line graph with the units of time displayed along the horizontal axis and the values of a variable or frequency of an occurrence on the vertical axis.

Time-series design. A design that collects data on a quantitative variable at regular intervals.

True experiment. A study in which the experimenter can assign subjects to either an experimental or control group and can manipulate the value and occurrence of the independent variable.

Type I error. Rejecting a null hypothesis as false when, in fact, it is true.

Type II error. Accepting a null hypothesis as true when, in fact, it is false.

Unit of analysis. The object whose characteristics are measured and in which the analyst is interested.

Univariate analysis. The statistical analysis of one variable at a time.

Univariate distribution. The distribution of the values of a single variable.

Variable. A measurable characteristic that has more than one value.

Variance. A measure of dispersion and variation. It is calculated by squaring the difference between the arithmetic mean of distribution and the value of each case, summing these values, and dividing the result by the number of cases. The variance is the square of the standard deviation. It is used in other statistical measures and tests.

Vital records. Records that include primarily vital statistics.

Vital statistics. Information collected by federal, state, and local governments on births, deaths, marriages, divorces, abortions, communicable diseases, and hospitalizations.

Voluntary research participation. When potential research subjects have clear and realistic information on the benefits and risks of participation, and have the ability to withdraw from a study at any time.

Weighting. A process by which different items are weighted to reflect their importance in an index.

Index

Accuracy, 150–156, 159, 162
Administrative issues, 248–249, 262–264
Alpha levels, 373–375, 381, 387
Alternative forms technique, 116
Analytic mapping, 327
Anonymity, 257–260
ANOVA, 414–416
Applications programs, 324–327
Archival information, 40
Arithmetic mean, 345–346, 356–357
Associated probability, 377, 381, 387
Association, measures of, 401–413, 418,
    427–429. *See also* Relationships
  bivariate, 397–413, 418–419, 431
  logic of, 404–406
  for multiple regression, 441–443
  multivariate, 397–401
  nominal and ordinal, 418
  statistics and, 413
  symmetric and asymmetric, 407, 419
Asymmetric measure, 407, 419
Attitude questions, 215
Attitude scales, 300
Autocorrelation, 452–454
Average deviation, 351–352
Averages, 345–348

Bar graphs, 332–333, 356
Behavior questions, 215
Beta weights, 443–445, 455
Between-groups variance, 414–417
Biased questions, 229–230, 242
Bivariate analysis, 431
Bivariate distribution, 324
Blind review, 481
Block numbering area, 289–290
Box plot, 354–356, 357

Case studies, 26, 40–43, 49
Categorical variables, 107
Causality, 91–93
  obtaining evidence for, 57
  Regression and, 454–455
CD-ROM, 276, 277
Census Bureau, 271, 280–282, 295
Census data, 280–292
  comparability among, 289–292
  in current population survey, 288–289
  of population and housing, 284–288
  uses of, 289–292

Census tract, 289–290
Census undercount, 285
Central tendency measures, 342–348,
  356–357
  guidelines for selection of, 347–348
Chi-square, 368, 376–378, 387, 407
  distribution, 394. Table 12.12
Class intervals, 329
Closed-ended questions, 220–222, 242
Cluster sampling, 137, 143–146, 162
  application of, 145
Coding, 324, 366–367
Coefficient of determination, 441
Cohort, 38
Common Rule, 260–262
Comparison group design, 78–81
Computer-aided Telephone Interviewing
  (CATI), 185, 204
Computer data files, 324–327
Computer models, 13
Computer programs, 324–327
Computers, 324, 356
  in data management, 324–327, 356
  software for, 324–327, 356
Concept, 101, 127, 301
Conceptual definition, 101, 126, 301
Confidence, 152–158, 161
  interval, 152
  level, 152, 155
Confidentiality, 257–260
Constants, 14–15
Consumer Price Index (CPI), 33, 299, 317
Content based validity, 120–121, 125,
  127, 301–302
Contingency tables, 368, 383, 397–401,
  418–419
  comparison of, 407
  strength of association in, 403
Control group, 69–71, 78–79
Control variables, 17, 400–401, 408–413,
  454–455
  effects of, 413, 419
Convenience sampling, 147
Correlation coefficient, 435–436
Covariation, 16
Cramer's V, 377, 404, 407, 411–412
Criterion based validity, 121–124, 125, 127
Cross-sectional design, 27–32, 48, 171,
  271–273, 482
  application of, 31

Current Population Reports, 281, 288
Current Population Survey (CPS),
  288–289
Curvilinear relationships, 406–407
Cyclical variations, 34–35

Data. *See also* Census data; Information;
  Statistics; Vital statistics
  collection of, 204–206
  computers and, 324–327
  definition of, 1
  displaying of, 327–337
  management of, 324–327, 356
  organization of, 356, 366–367
  preparation of, 356, 366–367
  secondary, 270. *See also* Census data;
    Vital statistics
  access to, 274–276
  evaluation of, 277–280
  storage of, 276–277
Data arrays, 327–328
Data dictionary, 366–367
Data fields, 325
Data files, 325
Database
  access to, 271, 273–276
  evaluation of, 277–280
  management of, 325–326
  quality of, 279
Database management system (DBMS),
  325–326
Datasets, 8
Decennial Census of Population &
  Housing, 281, 284–288, 292
DECIDE technique, 217, 234, 238–240
Deductive disclosure, 260
Degrees of freedom (df), 383, 417
Demographic questions, 235
Descriptive designs, 25–49, 65
  causality in, 56–57
  external validity of, 58–59
Descriptive statistics, 331
Designs. *See also specific types of*
  contamination of, 60, 63, 64
  definition of, 26
  for description, 25–49
  for explanation, 56–94
  to fill in details, 38–45
  non-experimental, 25
  for relationships and trends, 27–38

Direct observation, 40
Direct relationship, 16–17
Dispersion measures, 348–354, 357
Disproportionate stratified sampling, 141–142
    application of, 143
Distributions, 328–330
    describing characteristics of, 342
    skewed, 348–349
Documents, 40
Dummy variables, 440

Elements, 3, 21
    identification of, 7–11
Enumeration, 328
Equivalence, 110
Errors
    in measurement scale, 110–113
    new, 405–406
    nonsampling, 150, 159–160, 162
    original, 404–405
    proportional reduction in, 404, 407
    sampling, 150, 159, 162
    standard, 152
    Types I and II, 368, 372–373, 377–378, 381, 387
Eta, 396, 416, 417, 419
Ethical issues, 248–266
Executive summary, 469–472, 483
Experimental design, 58, 68–77, 93–94, 172–173
    classical, 68–77
Experimental group, 69–71
Experimental mortality, 38, 60, 62, 64
Expert Sampling, 148
Explanation, designs for, 56–94
Exploratory Data Analysis (EDA), 354–355
External validity, 59, 64–68

Fabrication, 478–479, 483
Factor analysis, 312–315, 316–317
Factor loading, 313
Factor score coefficient, 314
Factual questions, 215
Falsification, 478–479, 483
Filter questions, 222–223
Fluctuations, irregular, 34, 35–36
Focus group, 43–45, 49, 197–200, 205–206
Forced choice questions, 220
Fractions, 338–339
Frequency distributions, 328–330, 338, 356, 357
    line graphs, 335–337
Frequency polygon, 335
F-test, 398, 415–418, 419

Gallup Poll, 134
Gamma, 406, 407–408
Geographic Information System (GIS), 324, 326–327, 356
Geometric mean, 346–347
Goodness of fit test, 435
Graphical displays, 332–337, 356

Graphs, 323, 332–337, 356. *See also specific types of*

Histogram, 332–333, 356
History effects, 59, 60, 64, 66
Human subject, 261, 265
Humphreys study, 251
Hypothesis, 15–16, 20, 370–373, 378, 387

Incidence, 340–342
Index, 299–300, 303, 315
Index number, 315
Indicators, 299–317. *See also specific indicators*
Indices, 299–300. *See also types of*
    construction of, 300–305, 316–317
    content validity of, 301–302
    examples of, 308–312
    factor analysis and, 312–315, 316–317
    selection of items for, 301–302
    standardized indicators for, 305–308, 317
    types of, 303–305
    validity of, 301–302
    weighting of items in, 303–305, 316–317
Inferential statistics, 323–324, 369
Information. *See also* Data
    interpreting and filling in of, 41–42
    sources of, 39
Informed consent, 248–249, 252–255, 265
Institutional Review Board (IRB), 260–262
Instrumentation, 60, 62–63, 64
Intensive interviewing, 193–197, 205
Internal consistency, 110–114
Internal validity, 58–59
Internet, 273, 276, 295
Internet surveys, 182–184, 204
Interquartile range (IQR), 349–350, 357
Interrater reliability, 113, 115
Interrupted time series design, 81–86
    application of, 86–87
    with comparison group, 86–88
Interval scales, 106–107, 127, 317
Interval statistics, 378
Interview,
    in-person, 172, 191–200, 205
    intensive (unstructured), 193–197, 205
    practices of, 194–197
    structured, 192–193, 205
    telephone, 184–191
Interviewer training, 194–197
Inverse relationship, 15, 401–402
IQ scores, 107
Irregular fluctuations, 34–36

Job satisfaction index, 303–304
Judgement sampling, 147

Knowledge questions, 215

Lagging a variable, 438
Lambda, 405, 406
Library information, 8–11, 20
Library research, objective of, 8
Likert scaling index, 308–312, 316–317

Line graphs, 335–337, 356
Linear model, 432–435, 452–454, 455
Linear regression equation, 431–438
    statistical significance and, 446
Literature review, 472–473, 483
Loaded questions, 229
Logistic regression, 449–451, 456
Longitudinal design, 37–38, 48
Long-term trends, 33–35
Lottery method, 137

Macrodata, 290
Maps, 6, 12
Market research, 206
Matching, 70
Mathematical models, 12–13, 20
Maturation effects, 60, 61, 64
Means, 345–347, 356–357
Measurement, 105
    operational validity of, 118–125
    reliability of, 109–118, 127–128
    scales for, 105–109, 127
    sensitivity of, 126–127
    transforming of, 303
    variables in, 107–108
Measures of association, 368–369, 396–397, 401–405, 406–412, 417, 427–429, 441–443
Measures of dispersion, 348–354, 357
Median, 343–345, 356
Meta analysis, 45–48, 49
Microdata, 290
Milgram studies, 251–252
Mode, 342–343, 356
Models, 3–6, 19–20. *See also* Designs
    application of, 5
    building of, 7–11
    components of, 14–18
    elements in, 3
    limits, 13–14
    pretesting of, 11
    relationship in, 3
    sample, 5
    types of, 11–13
    use of, 3–6
Monotonically increasing or decreasing, 406
Motive questions, 215
Multicollinearity, 446–449
Multiple regression, 439
    equation, 439–441
    measure of association for, 441–443
    statistical significance and, 446
Multistage sampling, 143–146
    application of, 145
Multivariate analysis, 29, 324, 357, 418
Multivariate relationships, 430
Multivariate statistics, 324

Nominal association measures, 401, 403, 407–408, 418
Nominal scales, 105–106, 127, 376
Nonlinear relationship, 15, 406–407
Nonprobability sampling, 137, 146–150, 162

Nonrandom variation, 35–36
Nonsampling error, 150–151, 159–160, 163
Normal curve, 352–354
Null hypothesis, 16, 370–373, 378, 379, 381, 387–388, 437, 446
   rejection of, 371–373, 387
Null relationship, 401–402, 403–404, 409–410, 419
Numerical variables, 107–108
Nuremburg Code, 250

Open-ended questions, 175, 204, 216–220, 242
Operational definitions, 105, 126, 301
   formulation and evaluation of, 101–104
   importance of, 102
Operational validity, 59, 118–125, 127, 279
Opinion questions, 215
Ordered categorical variables, 108
Ordinal association measures, 401, 403, 406–413, 418
Ordinal scales, 106, 127, 349
Original error, 404–405
Outliers, 437–438, 455

Panel design, 37–38, 48
Parameters, 135, 137, 346, 369, 375
Partial regression coefficient, 439
Participant observation, 40
Pearson's r, 436
Peer interaction, 7–8
Peer review, 480–481, 483
Percentage change, 338–339, 337
Percentage difference, 398
Percentage distribution, 329, 338, 398–401
Percentages, 330, 338, 356
Percentile, 349–350
Perfect relationship, 401–402, 403–404, 406, 413
Periodicity, 139
Physical artifacts, 40
Physical models, 12
Pie charts, 333–335
Pilot study, 238–242, 243
Pilot test, 11, 19
Plagiarism, 478–479, 483
Planning, 1–2
Population, 134, 136, 162
   estimates of, 289, 290
   size of, 154–155, 162
   survey of, 284–288
   variability within, 150, 155
Potential experience, 440
Power, 159, 373
Practical significance, 370, 377–378
Pretest, 60, 62, 64, 66, 73, 78–81
Pretest, sensitizing effect of, 73
Prevalence rate, 340–342
Privacy, 248, 257–260
Probability levels, 377
Probability sampling, 137–146, 162–163
Proportion, 338, 356
Proportional reduction in error (PRE) measure, 404, 407
Proportional sampling, 154–156

Proportionate stratified sampling, 141
   application of, 142
Purpose, statement of, 2
Purposive sampling, 147–148, 162
   application of, 148

Qualitative information, 2
Qualitative research, 39–40
Quality assurance, 161–162
Quality control, 161–162
Quantification. *See* Measurement
Quantitative information, 2
   in decision making, 127
Quantitative research, requirement of, 14–15, 38
Quasi-experimental designs, 58, 77–88, 93–94, 172–173
   definition of, 77
   validity of, 79
Quasi-random sampling, 140
Questionnaires, 212–216 *See also* Questions
   advantages of, 176
   content of, 213–216, 242
   design of, 232–236
   disadvantages of, 176–178
   factors affecting response rate of, 174–181
   introduction of, 212–213
   mailed, 176–182
   postcards as follow-up reminders, 181, 182
   postcards to monitor, 177
   pretesting of, 238–242
   question sequencing in, 232–236
   structure of, 216–223
Questions, 212–216. *See also* Questionnaires; specific types of
   biased, 229
   content of, 232–233
   contingency, 222
   filter, 222–223
   in-person interviewing, 173, 191–192
   open- and closed-ended. *See* Closed-ended questions; Open-ended questions
   pretesting of, 238–242
   racial and ethnic, 285–288
   sequencing of, 232–236
   in telephone interviews, 185–186
   wording of, 223–232, 242
Quota sampling, 149–150

R values, 441–443, 455
Random assignment, 68–70, 94
   in quasi-experimental designs, 78–79
Random digit dialing techniques, 173, 185–187, 204
Random error, 109–110, 110–111
   degree of, 109
Random number table, 137–138
Random sampling, 137–138, 161
   application of, 138
   principles of, 137
   stratified, 137, 140–141

Random variations, 35–36
Randomized posttest design, 73–77
   application of, 75–76
   efficiency of, 91
Randomly related, 369–370
Range, 349–350, 357
Rate, 339–342, 356
   selection denominator for, 340–341
Ratio, 339, 356
Ratio scales, 104–106, 127
Reactive effects of experimental arrangements, 65, 66–67
Reference librarians, 8, 274
Regression, 431, 449
   causality and, 454–455
   logistic, 449–451, 456
   ordinal data and, 449
Regression analysis, 431–435
   multivariate case, 439–446
Regression coefficient, 436–437
   partial, 439
   standardized, 443
Regression equation, 431–435, 439–441, 455
   to quantify admissions criteria, 444–445
Reinterviews, 288
Relationships, 3. *See also* Association, measure of
   causal, 56
   criterion for strength of, 402–404
   nature of, 14, 16–18
   null, 401–402, 403, 404, 413, 419
   perfect, 401–402, 403, 404, 406, 413, 418
   specifying of, 410–411
   spurious, 16, 409–410, 419
   statistical, 68–69
   strength of, 401–402
   study designs to find, 27–37
Relational database, 325
Relative frequency measures, 338–339
Reliability, 109–118, 127
   criterion for, 109
   dimensions of, 109–110
   establishing of, 110–117
   interrater, 113, 115
Research. *See also specific types of*
   administrator concerns about, 262–264
   deceptive, 251–252
   definition of, 1–2
   designs, 26
   ethical issues of, 248–260, 478–482
   preliminary steps in, 1–20
   purpose of, 1–2
   records, 7–8, 19
   release of results of, 476–478
Research literature, 20. *See also* Data, secondary
   locating of, 8–11
Research methodology, 25
Research question, 2–3
Residual, 435
Response rate, 157, 174–175
   factors affecting, 176–180
Response set, 228

Sample(s), 133–163. *See also* Sampling
  accuracy of, 152–153, 161
  assessing quality of, 161–162
  bias, 136, 150, 160–161
  design, 136, 137–150. *See also specific*
    study designs
  means, 345–347
  probability, 137–143
  size of, 150–160
Sampling, 133–163. *See also* Sample(s)
  bias, 136, 150, 160–161
  designs for, 137–150. *See also specific*
    sampling designs
  nonprobability designs for, 136,
    146–150
  parameters of, 135
  probability designs for, 137–143
  purposes for, 133–134
  sample size in, 150–160
  standard error in, 153
  terminology for, 134–137
  unit, 135, 144
  units of analysis of, 135
Sampling error, 137, 150–151, 163
Sampling fraction, 136
Sampling frame, 135, 136
Sampling unit, 135
  assumptions about, 140
SAS program, 324–325
Scale, 300
Scatterplot, 432–435, 437–438
  patterns in, 437–438
Schematic models, 12, 19–20, 90
Screening questions, 223
Seasonal variations, 34–35
Secondary data, 270–271, 278, 294
Security issues, 276, 294
Selection effects, 59, 61, 64, 66, 148–149
Sensitivity, 108–109, 125–126, 127
  of measure of association, 403–404,
    406
Significance levels, 377–388, 383–384
Simple random sampling, 137, 162
  application of, 139
Skip interval, 138
Snowball sampling, 149, 162
Somer's d, 407–408
Spreadsheet, 325
SPSS program, 324, 381–383
Spurious relationship, 16, 409–410, 419
Stability, 109–110
Standard deviation, 155, 350–351, 357
  calculation of, 351
Standard error, 136, 152
  of b, 437
  calculation of, 168–169
  of slope, 437
Standardized indicators, 305–307
Statistic, 135
Statistical regression, 60, 61–62, 64
Statistical relationship, 68–69
Statistical significance, 369–370, 373,
    376–380, 383–387
  testing of, 383–387, 409–410

Statistical software package, 324–325
Statistics. *See also* Data
  accuracy of, 430–431
  bivariate case, 399–404, 418
  multivariate case, 404–407, 439
  univariate, 324
Stratified random sampling, 137,
    140–143, 162
  proportionate, 141–142, 162
  disproportionate, 141–143, 162
Structured interviewing, 192–193, 205
Studies. *See also* Research
  designing, 7–11. *See also* Designs
  types of, 25, 56–57
Subjects at risk, 248
Subjects. *See also* Informed consent
  initial contact with, 173–175
  payment of, 255
  protection of, 257–260
  risk to, 253, 255–256
    versus benefits to, 255–256
  of, 66–74
    by matching, 67–68
  voluntary, 253–254
Survey research, 172, 212–213
Surveys, 27. *See also* Questionnaires
  appropriateness of, 202–203
  Internet, 182–183
  multiple participation, 198
  participation rates of, 202–203
  telephone, 172, 184–191
Symbolic models, 12, 20
Symmetric measure, 407, 419
Systematic random sampling, 138
Systematic sampling, 138–140, 162
  application of, 140

t-Distribution, 395. Table 12.13
Tables, 327–330, 331. *See also* Contin-
    gency tables
  labeling of, 328–330, 331
  proportion and scale of, 328
  showing data relationships,
    397–401
  size and dimensions of, 401
Target population, 134–135
Tau, 407–408
Telephone directory, 186
Telephone surveys, 172, 184–191
Test statistic, 376
Testing effects, 60, 62, 64
Test-retest technique, 116
Threats to external validity, 64–68
Threats to internal validity, 59–64
Time series graphs, 337
Time series studies, 26, 32–37, 48
  applications of, 34
Transforming measures, 303
Trends, 27–38
  long-term, 37–38
Trimmed means, 354
t-Test, 368, 376, 378–380, 387
Tukey five-number summary, 354–355
Tuskegee Syphilis Study, 249–250

Undercount problem, 285
Unimodal distributions, 348
Units of analysis, 135, 137
Univariate analysis, 323–357
Univariate distribution, 328
Univariate statistics, 323–324
Unordered categorical variables, 108

Validity
  content-based, 120–121, 125, 127,
    301–302
  criterion-based, 121–124, 125, 127
    applications of, 122–124
  of experimental and quasi-experi-
    mental designs, 57–58, 91
  external, 57–58, 62–63
    threats to, 63–66
  internal, 57
    threats to, 58–62
  in interrupted time-series design, 79,
    80–81, 83
  of measurement scales, 118–125, 127
  operational, 118, 125
Variables, 14–18, 20
  causally related, 55–57
  continuous, 106
  control, 17, 400–401, 408–413,
    454–455
  dependent, 15, 20, 370
    causally related, 55–57
  dichotomous, 440
  discrete, 106
  distributions of, 328–330
  dummy, 440
  examples of, 14–15, 18
  independent, 15, 20, 25, 370
    casually related, 55–57
    importance of, 443–446
  interval, 430–438
  joint occurrence of, 397
  labeling of, 125
  measurement of, 98–128
  in measurement scales, 102–107
  nominal, 103
  number of, 30
  numerical, 104–105
  randomly related, 369
  relationships among, 357. *See also*
    Association, measures of;
    Relationships
    statistical relationship between, 67
  in time series studies, 33
Variance, 350–351, 357
Variation measures, 348–351
Verbal models, 11, 20
Vital statistics, 292–294, 295
Voluntary research participation,
    253–254, 265

Weighting, 303–305, 317
Within-groups variance, 416–418, 419

Zero order correlation coefficient, 436
z-Scores, 307, 321, 353–354